COMPUTER CHESS

COMPUTER CHESS

David E. Welsh
Chairman
U.S.C.F. Computer Chess Committee

wcb
Wm. C. Brown Publishers
Dubuque, Iowa

DEDICATION

To the hard-working members of the 1981-1982 Computer Chess Committee:

Southern California Working Group: International Arbiter Harold M. Bogner, Lina Grumette, David Kittinger, International Master John Peters, Ralph Slottow, Kathe Spracklen;

National Members: Hans Berliner, International Master Julio Kaplan, Evan Katz, Edgar T. McCormick, David Slate, Ken Thompson;

With sincere thanks for all they have done for the Committee, for the USCF, and for computer chess.

Library of Congress Catalog Card Number: 83–72899

ISBN 0–697–09900–8

2–09900–01

Printed in the United States of America

CONTENTS

PREFACE

It seems hard to believe that only five years have passed since the first chess microcomputers appeared, and the average player became aware that computers could be programmed to play chess. During this period, computer chess has evolved from a rather arcane specialty pursued by a few computer scientists interested in artificial intelligence to a subject of real interest to thousands of competitive chess players and millions of others who have purchased chess computers.

It is possible that within the lifetime of many readers, a computer program will be the chess champion of the world, provided that the rules of play permit this. At present, the best programs are far distant from this goal, and a conceptual breakthrough is needed. As to the date and even the possibility of such an event, the author is less optimistic than many computer chess experts, but the prospect is real: Grandmasters, get ready — the computers are coming!

For the rest of us chess players, what does the future of computer chess hold? Stronger programs — interesting opponents for speed and skittles games — challenges for developing players who need practice to speed their development. For the competitive player, there may also be an opportunity to play one of the strongest mainframe programs in a USCF tournament, and it is a particular goal of this book to give the player paired with a computer program some insights on which strategies and game plans offer the best prospects.

The reader will see that there is a great deal of progress yet to be made in computer chess, and that in several critical areas the surface has barely been scratched. In some ways, we are only now beginning to understand the problems. The programs of the future will not only be stronger than those of today, but more interesting as concepts advance. Their development is going to be an interesting story, and it will be fascinating to watch it unfold.

Los Angeles, California
March 1983

David E. Welsh

INTRODUCTION

This book has been written for the chess player who would like to have a better understanding of computer chess, especially the microcomputer chessplaying machines which are now so widespread. In particular, this book is designed for competitive chess players who participate in the tournaments sanctioned by the United States Chess Federation, in which computer programs are once again playing. However, the more casual player, and the computer programmer with an interest in computer chess, will each find much in here to interest them.

With the explosive proliferation of chess microcomputers in the last five years, millions of players who had previously never given a thought to computer chess are now the owners of chess computers — which, in principle, are no different from the giant mainframe computers which compete for the computer championships and which may not even be all that much lower in playing strength. Many of these machines now play considerably better than the average tournament player, and yet to most microcomputer owners — and to many of their opponents in tournament games — computer chess programs are something of a mystery. Yes, they play chess — but how? What goes on inside a chess program when it plays? Why do they play so well — always protecting their pieces, and instantly snatching anything left en prise?

To the expert and the master, on the other hand, chess programs are also mysterious, but for different reasons. Until recently, they were not good enough to take seriously. Now, however, the best mainframe programs are defeating experts and challenging masters, while the best microcomputers are a tough battle for an expert. To these players with a wide knowledge of the theoretical aspects of the game, computer chess games are a puzzling mixture of good and bad — strong tactics, sharp play, and frequent positional blunders. In a way, the chess program seems to have a sort of "coffeehouse" style. Why is this? What are the reasons for the computer program's inadequacies in endgame play? How should one play, if paired with a computer program in a tournament game?

This book attempts to answer these questions, and to give the reader — at any level of chess or computer expertise — some insights into how computer chess programs work, and their strengths and weaknesses. It is structured into two parts, each of several chapters. The first is an introduction to computer chess; the second, a detailed discussion of computer chess games.

The book begins with a short history of computer chess, and then moves to an overview of how computers work, in the form of a detailed look inside a modern chess microcomputer — along with a brief introduction to how chess programs are structured. Next the reader is introduced to the programs themselves, both the historic programs which are now retired from competition, and those which are still active and which will be discussed later in the book.

A detailed discussion follows of the ways in which chess programs deal with the problems computers have in playing chess, which are vastly different from those encountered by humans. Finally, the computer style of play and the reasons for its peculiarities are examined, plus the strategies that are most likely to be successful in playing a chess program.

All this is background for the second part — eighty-nine carefully annotated computer chess games from the three major events of 1982. In these games, the reader can see for himself how the programs played, and will get insights into their characteristics which no amount of generalized commentary could possibly provide. Another brief chapter presents some unannotated computer speed games from the 1982 U.S. Speed Championship, illustrating the exceptional strength of chess programs at this interesting pastime.

Appendices include a glossary of computer chess terminology, discussions of the USCF rating system and computer chess regulations, and the ACM tournament games (unannotated) from 1970 to 1981.

The reader who is not a tournament chess player may not be familiar with the style of notation used in this book, so a brief explanation is given below. The experienced reader may skip to the succeeding section on annotations.

CHESS NOTATION

Although chess has been played since about the sixth century A.D., the practice of recording games for later reference did not begin until the fifteenth century. Before that time, only fragments such as interesting openings and problems were preserved. The standard of play in those days was low, and the rules much different, so that the loss is not a great one except to the historian.

The first games recorded were written down in plain language, and this system was still used at the time that Francois Andre Danican Philidor wrote his famous *Analyze du Jeu des Echecs* in 1749. The first two moves of a game in the English edition (1750) are given as follows:

1

WHITE The King's Pawn two steps
BLACK The same

2

WHITE The King's Knight at his Bishop's third square
BLACK The Queen's Pawn one move

While there is a certain stately majesty to this, befitting the "game of Kings", it was not a very compact way of recording a game. When more chess books began to be published, it became necessary to find abbreviations. In 1889, the above opening was given in *Chess Openings Ancient and Modern* by Freeborough and Rankin:

1 P-K4, P-K4; 2 Kt-KB3, P-Q3

This is the Descriptive Notation still used today by many players. It has the virtue of describing the moves played from the viewpoint of each player, so that in symmetrical openings each player is shown as making the same moves: 1 N-KB3 N-

KB3 2P-KN3 P-KN3 3 B-N2 B-N2 and so on. As can be seen, today "N" is used as the abbreviation for Knight.

There are several significant problems with this system. First, the names used for the pieces are different in each language—a Bishop, for example, is abbreviated "B" in English, "L" in German, "F" in French, and "A" in Spanish (not to mention the complications encountered in Russian texts!). Second, each square has two names—one from the White point of view, and one from the Black point of view. Third, it is still not as compact as could be desired. As a result, there is a general trend today toward the system used in this book, which is based on the old Algebraic system of notation (1 e2-e4 e7-e5 2 Ng1-f3 d7-d6) originally used in European countries. This is the most compact way of recording chess games, allowing the publisher to give the reader more chess for the money.

Figurine Algebraic Notation

It did not take long for chess players writing down their games in Algebraic notation to realize that it was usually unimportant to record the square moved from, since the context of the game would generally make that obvious. Thus the opening moves of Philidor's Defense can be compactly recorded: **1 e4 e5 2 Nf3 d6.** A further refinement of this scorekeeping notation is to use the diagram symbol representing a piece, instead of a letter. This makes the score intelligible to anyone, whatever language they may speak. Naturally a player can't readily keep score this way, but it is an ideal system for publishing games.

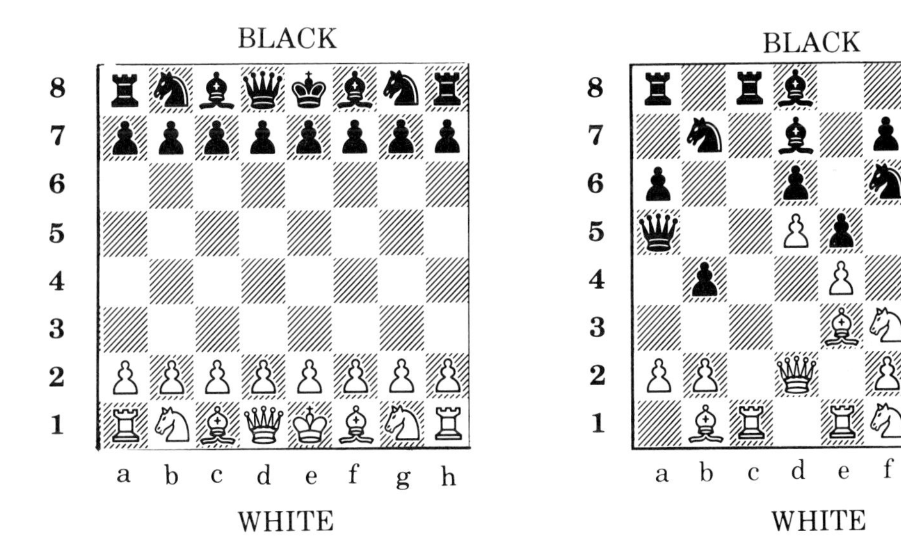

The two diagrams above show the chessboard in the initial position, and after 20 moves in a well-known variation of the Ruy Lopez:
1 e4 e5 2 ♞f3 ♞c6 3 ♝b5 a6 4 ♝a4 ♞f6 5 0-0 ♝e7 6 ♜e1 b5 7 ♝b3 d6 8 c3 0-0 9 h3 ♞a5 10 ♝c2 c5 11 d4 ♛c7 12 ♞bd2 cxd4 13 cxd4 ♝b7 14 d5 ♝c8 15 ♜b1 b4 16 ♞f1 ♞b7 17 ♝e3 ♝d7 18 ♜c1 ♜fc8 19 ♛d2 ♛a5 20 ♝b1 ♝d8.

The rules for Figurine Algebraic Notation are as follows:

1. Pawn moves are indicated by the absence of any symbol. Piece moves are indicated by the diagram symbol for the piece involved.
2. The move is indicated by naming the square moved to, with a letter and number indicating the rank and file on which it is located. Thus a1 is the initial square for White's Queen Rook, and is located on the a-file, at the first rank.
3. Only if two pieces of the same type can move to the same square, is any indication of the square moved from given. In this case, the file letter for the "from" square is given as first choice, and the rank number is substituted only if both pieces involved stand on the same file. Thus **12 ♞bd2** in the above score.
4. Captures are designated by inserting the symbol "x" between the piece symbol and the square moved to. If a Pawn makes the capture, the letter for the file on which it stood is used instead of a piece symbol, Thus **13 cxd4** in the above score.
5. Castling on the **King's Side** is indicated by **0-0**; on the **Queen's side**, by **0-0-0**.
6. Checks are indicated by the symbol "+". Promotions of Pawns to pieces are indicated by enclosing the piece symbol in parentheses—e.g. **53 a8(♛).**

As can be seen from the score given, this is an extremely compact system. In this book (as elsewhere), diagrams will be shown without any file letters or rank numbers, and White will always move from the lower side of the diagram.

ANNOTATIONS

Although the scores of games are often given without any comments, it is usually more interesting to play over a game that has been annotated for the reader.

Annotations are comments made by a strong player, frequently a master of high reputation, who has analyzed the game and noted its critical features. These consist both of positional considerations and tactical points. For the latter, supporting variations may be given.

In annotating a game, the analyst will employ both verbal and symbolic comments. The latter save space and are easier to read without losing the thread of the game. The symbolic comments used in this book are the following:

!? = an interesting move; clever but perhaps double-edged.
! = a particularly strong or unusually clever move.
!! = a very fine or brilliant move.
?! = a dubious or weak move.
? = a bad move; a mistake.
?? = a very bad move; a blunder.

The usual objectives of annotations in master games, which are almost the only ones ordinarily considered worth publishing, are to convey the quality of the game, the difficulty and originality of the decisions made by the players, the reasons for the eventual outcome, and frequently the chess lessons the game contains for the non-master reader.

The objectives of the annotations in this book are entirely different. Their purpose is to convey the style of play of computer programs, and the strengths and weaknesses of these programs as players. For these objectives, many games that would ordinarily be considered unworthy of publication are valuable. Computer programs make positionally weak moves and even more disastrous mistakes in their games rather often, and the reasons for these errors are frequently incomprehensible to the reader who is unfamiliar with the characteristics of computer chess programs. The actual causes, when they can be deciphered at all, are often rather amusing. And when a program really goes wrong, as happens in several games in this book, the result can be entertaining.

The reader will find a number of stylistic differences in these annotations. One important difference is the frequent use of the symbol "?!" to indicate a move which is definitely weak or irrelevant to the position, but which does not directly lead to disaster and is not a serious enough mistake to be labelled "?". This symbol must not be confused with its counterpart "!?", which indicates a move that is interesting and probably good, but not clear enough to deserve the comment "!".

The frequent occurrence of such weak, often senseless, moves in games by computer programs is due to their lack of positional understanding and inability to make plans. Masters rarely make such moves.

In order to economize on space, the game scores have been given in paragraph form rather than being organized in columns. To enable the reader to easily distinguish between the game score and variations in the annotations, the moves in the game score are in **bold face type**.

After the name of the opening system for each game, its Rabar classification number is given in parentheses. This is the system used in the Encyclopedia of Chess Openings (ECO), the principal chess reference work consulted.

Although the style is somewhat different, the annotations have been done very carefully. For most of the non-trivial games, the author spent much more time in analyzing the game than the players did in playing it. Fortunately, it was possible to secure the services of FIDE Master Boris Baczynskyj to review this part of the manuscript and check the annotations — which he did very thoroughly, making a number of corrections and adding many interesting insights, which have been incorporated where possible. However, no effort of this sort can be altogether free from errors in analysis or positional misjudgments, and the responsibility for these rests entirely with the author.

THE UNITED STATES CHESS FEDERATION

The United States Chess Federation is the official U.S. affiliate of the International Chess Federation (FIDE), linking its members with chessplayers around the world.

The USCF is a registered non-profit corporation whose objectives are to educate and instruct its members and the public about chess, to broaden and develop chess as an art and recreation; and to promote chess as a significant element of culture in America.

The USCF's most prominent activities are sanctioning and rating chess tournaments, and publishing *Chess Life* magazine — one of the best chess publications in the world. Less visible, though equally important, are activities such as supporting U.S. Chess Masters in international competition, chess education, and representing the U.S. in the International Chess Federation (FIDE).

Membership in the USCF is open to all, and the rates are very reasonable — the magazine alone is easily worth the membership fee. Benefits of membership include *Chess Life*, the right to play in USCF sanctioned tournaments and to acquire an official USCF rating, information on local chess clubs and publications, and the right to buy chess books and supplies at a significant discount through the USCF.

To inquire about joining the USCF, write to:

United States Chess Federation
186 Route 9W
New Windsor, NY 12550
Attn: Membership Services Director

1
A BRIEF HISTORY OF COMPUTER CHESS

AUTOMATONS

In the latter part of the eighteenth century, ingenious mechanical contrivances of all sorts became a popular diversion for the jaded aristocracy. One of the most sensational "automatons", as these devices were called, was exhibited to the Viennese court in 1770 by Baron von Kempelen, a famous inventor. The "Turk", as the machine was called, consisted of a cabinet with a chessboard on top (inside which a human of small stature could cleverly be concealed), and a manikin dressed as a Turk sitting behind it. By the same sort of trickery used by magicians today, the exhibitor opened various doors and drawers, convincing the audience that the cabinet contained nothing but clockwork. Then the exhibitor would wind up the manikin, and it would begin to play a strong game, defeating most if not all comers. Frederick the Great of Prussia was so fascinated by this automaton that he purchased it for a large sum. Upon discovering that it was a fraud, however, the King lost interest, and the machine lay idle in storage for twenty years. When Napoleon occupied Berlin in 1806, he saw the machine, and in 1809 played a game against it which the master Allgaier (concealed inside the cabinet) won easily, since Napoleon was a rather weak player. The "Turk" was a considerable commercial success, and was exhibited until 1837. It was then placed in a museum, where it was destroyed by fire in 1854.

Inspired by the commercial possibilities of this celebrated fraud, other so-called "automatons" were constructed — one in Germany in 1789, one in London in 1868 (named "Ajeeb"), and another in London in 1878 (named "Mephisto"). "Ajeeb" lasted until 1929, when it too perished in a fire; "Mephisto" was retired and broken up after a brief career.

In 1890 the Spanish scientist Torres y Quevedo constructed an automaton that really did play chess of a sort — it conducted the ending of King and Rook against King, and could always force mate, though not in the least possible number of moves.

After the invention of the electronic digital computer in the 1940s, interest in chess-playing machines revived, and by 1948 Wiener (1) had speculated on the possibilities for constructing machines capable of playing chess by using the minimax procedure discovered by Von Neumann and Morgenstern in 1944. In their pioneering work on game theory (2), these authors demonstrated for the first time that there exists a rigorous mathematical solution to all "finite 2-person zero-sum games of perfect information" such as chess. Having established that point (and not being at all concerned with the impossibility of ever calculating the nature of the solution), game theorists went on to consider more difficult and interesting games! A more practically important contribution was the minimax procedure, which is just a mathematical formulation of the proposition that in any position each player may be expected to choose the move that is best for the player's side.

CLAUDE SHANNON

On March 9, 1949, a research worker at Bell Telephone Laboratories in New Jersey presented a seminal paper (3) of astonishing foresight. This brilliant contribution marks the beginning of computer chess as a science, although Shannon himself never completed a chess program (the state of computer programming in those days was extremely primitive — all programs had to be written in binary machine language).

Shannon's "Programming a Digital Computer for Playing Chess" set forth the ideas on which every chess program of any significance today is based — the game tree, position scoring, and move selection by the minimax procedure. (The uninitiated reader will find these terms, and other technical language without which computer chess simply cannot be discussed, defined in the Glossary; they will be explained in detail later in the book.) Shannon then went on to describe two possible strategies for move selection: A) examine every possible move to a fixed depth of search, with the disadvantage that the program cannot look very far ahead in a reasonable time; B) examine only the "best" moves by eliminating those which are "obviously bad", which allows the program to look ahead farther but runs a considerable risk of overlooking important moves. As a feature of this latter strategy, Shannon introduced the concept of "stable" or quiescent positions — forcing variations were to be examined until the position had stabilized, and only such quiescent positions would be scored. This approach avoids the worst problem with the type A strategy — scoring positions in the middle of a combination, which frequently leads to wildly inaccurate results.

Shannon also identified computer chess as an important application of "artificial intelligence" — the process of automatic problem solving. He pointed out that the principles learned in the development of computer chess could be applied in other areas, such as design of electronic circuits, switching telephone circuits, language translation, military operations, and logical inference. Computer chess is a particularly valuable method of testing ideas in this field, because it is relatively easy to accurately determine whether the approach being evaluated works at all, and if so, whether it is better than the alternatives.

THE FIRST PROGRAMS

While Shannon was formulating the basic concepts of computer chess, the great British mathematician Alan Turing had also taken an interest in the subject. In 1951 he published the results of some experiments in which the operation of the proposed program was simulated by hand calculations (Turing apparently was a whiz at this sort of arithmetic). The "program" being simulated turned out to be a rather poor player (4,5). Turing later attempted to implement his "Turochamp" program on the Ferranti Mark 1 computer at Manchester University — among the biggest machines of its day, costing millions of dollars, but far less powerful than a modern personal computer. Not having the extreme patience required to develop working machine-language programs, Turing never completed the task.

In 1951, Turing's colleague Dietrich G. Prinz (4) brought up a program capable of solving simple chess problems, and Christopher Strachey (4,5) wrote a checkers program, in the course of which the "horizon effect" was discovered.

Meanwhile, some American scientists at the Los Alamos Scientific Laboratory were experimenting with chess programs (6) on the MANIAC I computer (yes, that was really its name — rather appropriate for a machine developed to design hydrogen bombs). For its day, MANIAC I was an extremely powerful machine, but since it ran about 100 times slower than a modern minicomputer, the moves in a full-scale chess game would have taken several hours each. Consequently the program was written to play on a 6x6 board, without Bishops, and with six Pawns per side that could only make single-step moves. The program was successfully given Queen odds by a good human player. Later, a full-scale program was implemented on the MANIAC II computer, but did not play much better.

The first real chess program was developed to run on the IBM 704, last of the vacuum-tube computers (7). This machine was about four times as fast as MANIAC I, and the program developed by Alex Bernstein and his colleagues was more sophisticated, using a type B (selective search) strategy. The program played a weak game, but was quite a bit better than its predecessors — the well-known chess author and International Master, Edward Lasker, commented after defeating the program that it played a "passable amateur game".

A problem common to all these early programs was the necessity of examining every possible position within the program's search depth. Since each move by one side multiplies the number of possible positions by a factor of about 36, these early programs were limited to a fixed search depth of not more than two moves, which of course is quite inadequate against even a fair human player.

THE ALPHA-BETA SEARCH METHOD

In 1955, Alan Newell, John Shaw, and Herbert Simon at Carnegie-Mellon University in Pittsburgh began work on the chess program CP-1, the first to be written in a high-level language (8). The added power of the language permitted the development of a much more sophisticated and complex program than any of its predecessors; but the associated speed penalty resulted in a very slow running program, which could take as much as an hour per move. Only one complete game by CP-1 was ever published (9); the program performed relatively well during the opening and early middlegame, but then started to make serious errors. Nonetheless, CP-1 was quite an advance over its predecessors, and Simon was sufficiently impressed by its performance to issue his famous 1957 dictum: "Within ten years, a digital computer will be the world's chess champion, unless the rules bar it from competition." Unfortunately for this prediction, the rate of progress has slowed down considerably since. 25 years later, no program had yet demonstrated play at a genuine Master level, although several had come quite close.

The program CP-1 used goal-setting functions to guide its search, and together with a complex position scoring function, these concepts represented a major advance in the art. The most significant achievement of CP-1, however, was the introduction of the alpha-beta search technique (10,11). This ingenious method is based on the observation that previous programs using von Neumann's minimax procedure have to look at every possible position within their search depth, but most of these positions are really meaningless, because the program has already found a better move than the one that leads to the position being examined. In chess terms, once one refutation for a move is found, it is unnecessary to examine its consequences further. The alpha-beta technique can result in a tremendous reduction in the number of positions to be examined — ideally, only twice the square root of the total number of positions that would be looked at by the minimax procedure (12).

The alpha-beta procedure has been used in every program of significance since, and has taken its place with Shannon's precepts as one of the fundamental principles of computer chess.

THE FIRST COMPUTER CHESS MATCH

In 1961 a student at M.I.T., Alan Kotok, wrote a chess program for his B.Sc. thesis. This was later improved by his advisor, John McCarthy, at Stanford. At the end of 1966, a four-game match was arranged between this program (running on an IBM 7090) and the ITEP program developed by a team of Soviet scientists (running on a Soviet M-20). The Russian program decisively won the match, a principal reason being that the Stanford program used a selective search method that frequently overlooked important moves (14). The quality of the games was not very impressive by human standards, but marked a considerable improvement over previous computer games — the programs had reached the point of being able to play the opening reasonably well, although middlegames were completely planless, and endgames abysmally bad (two games were agreed drawn in winning positions because neither program could win an endgame).

The match between the American and Russian programs generated a great deal of interest in computer chess, which until then had been a subject unknown to almost everyone except the scientists involved in it. Much more publicity was to come, for even as the match was being played, a new program was being developed at the Massachusetts Institute of Technology, which became a landmark in the history of chess programming — the first program to compete on even terms with average human players in tournament play. The emergence of the first really effective chess program marked the end of an era of tentative experimentation.

THE MODERN ERA IN COMPUTER CHESS

MAC HACK VI

The first of the modern programs was written by MIT undergraduate Richard Greenblatt, with the assistance of Donald Eastlake. Work on Mac Hack VI began in November 1966, and by the end of January 1967 it had competed in the Massachusetts Amateur Championship (scoring +0 -4 =1 for a provisional USCF rating of about 1240) (15).

It seems incredible that this historic program could have been developed and debugged so quickly, but there was a reason for this. Greenblatt, a highly capable programmer, had a powerful interactive computer at his disposal (the PDP-6), with excellent utilities, so that the environment in which the program was developed was more favorable than for any previous program. Also, Greenblatt prepared a number of utility functions in his program which made it possible to examine its internal workings in detail — the first time such "software tools" had been utilized in a chess program. The result was an impressive success (16).

Mac Hack VI featured a selective (Shannon type B) search strategy, and because the program was written in a high-level language, it was possible to give it a highly sophisticated "plausible-move" generator, using about fifty different criteria for selecting moves. Although not infallible, this worked rather well in practice. The program also employed such advanced concepts as storing the evaluations of positions in a "transposition table", so that if the same position came up again in its search, the evaluation would not have to be recomputed. Another novel feature was the introduction of a library of opening variations.

Mac Hack VI played in a number of tournaments during 1967, and by the end of the year, had a USCF rating of 1493. By December 1968 this had increased to 1529, a higher rating than that of the average USCF member. This rating was somewhat misleading because the program's opponents would resign in a lost position as if they were playing a human opponent, not realizing that Mac Hack VI's endgame play was very weak and that it would draw or even lose many easily won endings. Nonetheless, the program was tremendously strong for its day, and good even if compared to the programs of fifteen years later — its rating being better than a third of the contestants in the 1982 ACM tournament.

A version of Mac Hack VI was made available on many time-sharing computer services using DEC PDP series computers. This facility, and the interest which Mac Hack VI sparked, led to a rapid proliferation of chess programs — most of which competed informally against Mac Hack VI (17) on time-sharing networks. Within the three years following Mac Hack VI's debut, at least eight new programs appeared, and a great deal of interest developed in finding out which was the best. This led to the first tournament for computer programs.

THE FIRST UNITED STATES COMPUTER CHESS CHAMPIONSHIP

In planning the special events program for the 1970 annual conference of the Association for Computing Machinery, Kenneth King and Monroe Newborn conceived the idea of a computer chess tournament, an idea quickly and enthusiastically responded to by all the programmers contacted except Richard Greenblatt. The latter regarded Mac Hack VI as an experiment in modelling human thought processes, and had little interest in competition against other computer programs. It was unfortunate that the program then generally considered to be the unofficial champion could not be induced to enter this event (or any of the later ACM tournaments). One consequence of this lack of interest by Greenblatt was that the pace of development for Mac Hack VI was rather slow during a period when other programs made rapid improvements, so that the MIT program was soon equalled and then surpassed by several programs.

In 1968, Northwestern University undergraduates Larry Atkin and Keith Gorlen developed a weak chess program. David Slate, a graduate student in Physics and a strong chess player, heard of this and decided to write his own program. Around the beginning of 1969 it became clear to all concerned that the fastest way to make progress was to combine Slate's chess skills with the programming talents of Atkin and Gorlen (18). In October 1969, the product of this joint effort emerged — CHESS 2.0. By the time of the first ACM United States Computer Chess Championship in 1970, an improved version — CHESS 3.0 — had been developed. The program ran on a CDC 6400 and was written in assembly language.

The tournament was directed by Jacques Dutka, a chess master and mathematician (best known for his computation of the square root of two to 1,000,000 digits), and was a huge success, with hundreds of spectators and considerable press coverage. CHESS 3.0 played solidly, winning all three games and the first United States Computer Chess Championship. The tournament favorite, Hans Berliner's J.Biit (Just Because It Is There) finished in third place, losing to CHESS 3.0, and drawing with fourth place finisher COKO III in a game that became a famous example of endgame ineptitude. Second place was taken by the Daly CP, a "bare-bones" implementation of the Shannon type A strategy running on a minicomputer at the tournament site. SCHACH finished fifth, and last place went to the Marsland CP, which fell victim in its first game to a program "bug" in its position-scoring function, which led the program to choose between the best move and the worst move more or less at random. This game was published in the *New York Times* (19) under the headline "Chess Computer Loses Game in King-Size Blunder". This disaster was not the last of its kind; another program had the same problem during the 1982 ACM tournament.

THE SECOND UNITED STATES COMPUTER CHESS CHAMPIONSHIP

The 1971 ACM conference was held in Chicago, and was the first of a series of ACM tournaments to be directed by International Master David Levy. The tournament was organized by Professor Ben Mittman, director of Northwestern University's Vogelback Computing Center (where CHESS 3.0 was developed), who also chaired the first of the ACM seminars on computer chess. This year eight programs competed, and again CHESS 3.5 (an improved version of CHESS 3.0) won all its games and first prize. Second place went to TECH, an extremely primitive but fast "brute force" program with little chess knowledge, designed to serve as a technological benchmark for other programs. Third place was taken by GENIE, written by Marine Corps Captain Herbert Raymond, running on a Navy computer in San Diego. GENIE was rather lucky; its second-round game with sixth-place finisher COKO III was another all-time classic of computer ineptitude, in which COKO III had mate on the move for eight consecutive moves, refused to play it, and eventually lost.

THE THIRD UNITED STATES COMPUTER CHESS CHAMPIONSHIP

In 1973, the ACM conference was held in Boston, and David Levy directed the tournament. Once more, eight programs participated in a highly successful event with hundreds of spectators and considerable media coverage. Again CHESS 3.6 won all its games, though not so easily this year. The most significant new entry was OSTRICH, written by George Arnold and Monty Newborn, which ran on a Data General Nova 800 minicomputer at the tournament site. OSTRICH took second place after a playoff with an improved version of TECH, and with COKO III. By this time, the lessons learned in competition had developed the top programs considerably, and these four at least were probably better than or equal to Mac Hack VI. Another interesting newcomer was the USC Chess Program, written by Albert Zobrist and Fredrick Carlson, with assistance from Senior Master Charles Kalme. This program was structured so that a strong player (Kalme) could "teach" it chess without having to alter the program (20), and also employed pattern-recognition techniques. The USC CP finished in fifth place, losing to TECH and COKO III.

THE FOURTH NORTH AMERICAN COMPUTER CHESS CHAMPIONSHIP

The 1974 ACM conference was held in Atlanta, and again David Levy directed the tournament. Twelve programs participated in the Fourth United States Computer Chess Championship, and the interest was so great that another dozen entries had to be refused. The reigning champion had been completely rewritten (21), and CHESS 4.0 retained the title with a score of 3½—½. The Northwestern University program's perfect record was spoiled by a draw against the Dartmouth CP, which finished fifth. Another three-way tie for second developed, and after the playoff second place went to TECH II, an improved version of TECH running on the MIT PDP-10. Third place was taken by CHAOS, a strong selective-search program developed by Victor Berman, Ira Ruben, Fred Swartz, and Joe Winograd at Sperry-Univac. OSTRICH finished fourth.

A significant newcomer in this event was T.Belle, the ancestor of the future computer World Champion, written by Ken Thompson of Bell Telephone Laboratories. T.Belle ran on a PDP 11/45 minicomputer, and finished seventh with an even score. The USC chess program also entered, but won only one game, against the last-place program.

THE FIRST WORLD COMPUTER CHESS CHAMPIONSHIP

By this time, interest in computer chess had developed in nations other than the United States, and the idea of holding a World Computer Chess Championship was developed by Ben Mittman, Monty Newborn, and David Levy. This event was organized as a feature of the 1974 IFIP Congress in Stockholm, and again David Levy served as director and commentator. Thirteen programs from eight nations competed, and once more interest was so great that several entries had to be refused due to lack of space. The pre-tournament favorite was CHESS 4.0, but the first prize went to a Soviet program.

In 1971, a group of programmers at the Institute of Control Science in Moscow began to rewrite the ITEP program that had won the USA-USSR match in 1967. The resulting program was named KAISSA, after the mythological goddess of Chess, and ran on a British ICL 4/70 computer (the Russians would have preferred to use an IBM machine, but were not allowed to buy one). In 1972 the program played two correspondence games with the readers of the newspaper *Pravda*, scoring ½ — 1½ (the year before, World Champion Boris Spassky scored 1½ — ½ against the same readers).

KAISSA won all four of its games, and the tournament, but did not play either the second-place (CHESS 4.0) or third-place (RIBBIT) programs. The most interesting and decisive game in the event was a spectacular victory by CHAOS over CHESS 4.0, in which the Univac program sacrificed a Knight on positional grounds for a winning attack. This probably cost CHESS 4.0 the championship. CHAOS finished fourth, TECH II fifth, and OSTRICH sixth. OSTRICH missed several opportunities to win its game against KAISSA, including two forced mates. After the tournament, an exhibition game was arranged between KAISSA and CHESS 4.0, which ended in a draw.

Other than KAISSA, the most significant newcomer was the Canadian program RIBBIT, running on a Honeywell 6060 at the University of Waterloo. RIBBIT lost only to CHESS 4.0, but did so twice (once during the regular pairings, and again in a playoff for second place). The last seven places were occupied by three programs from Great Britain, and one each from Austria, Hungary, Norway, and Switzerland. Of these, the best was probably the British program MASTER, which suffered from an inadequate allocation of computer time (5).

The interested reader who would like more detail on these early tournaments, and the programs which played in them, will find it in Monty Newborn's excellent book (12).

THE FIFTH UNITED STATES COMPUTER CHESS CHAMPIONSHIP

In 1974, the ACM conference was held in San Diego, and for the first time the Northwestern program was dethroned. CHESS 4.0 gained sweet revenge for its defeat by CHAOS in the World Championship, with a decisive victory, but then lost to RIBBIT in the final round, and the championship went to the Canadian program. RIBBIT was lucky in that OSTRICH had a winning position against it but failed to push a passed Pawn, and TECH II forfeited on time when it could have mated RIBBIT in two moves. RIBBIT's victory over CHESS 4.0, however, was crushing.

A significant consequence of this event was that Ken Thompson became convinced that T.Belle (which finished "out of the money") wasn't going anywhere because "computer chess belonged to the fastest computer" (22). This led directly to an interest in specialized chess hardware, and the development of the future computer World Champion, BELLE.

THE SIXTH NORTH AMERICAN COMPUTER CHESS CHAMPIONSHIP

The 1975 ACM convention was held in Minneapolis. Since a Canadian program was the current champion, and two other Canadian programs were entered in the field of twelve, the tournament was renamed as the North American Computer Chess Championship.

RIBBIT had now metamorphosed into TREE FROG, and lost decisively in the last round to CHESS 4.4, which thereby regained the championship title. In the third round, CHESS 4.4 defeated perennial rival CHAOS in a fine game which Tournament Director David Levy described as "the best game ever played between two computer programs", and which impressed him so much that he annotated it in detail in two of his books (24,26). The Duke University program, DUCHESS, finished in seventh place after unluckily forfeiting to a weak newcomer, BLACK KNIGHT, because its computer was not available. OSTRICH finished eighth, losing to the strong newcomer ETAOIN SHRDLU (named after the Linotype keyboard), which finished third, in the first round. CHAOS took fourth place. Ken Thompson did not enter a program in 1975 or 1976, while BELLE was being developed.

THE SEVENTH NORTH AMERICAN COMPUTER CHESS CHAMPIONSHIP

The 1976 ACM convention was held in Houston, and as in every event since 1971, David Levy directed the tournament. TREEFROG did not enter, and CHESS 4.5 nearly didn't (Slate and Atkin wanted to work on their program to get ready for the 1977 World Championship, but Control Data agreed to enter CHESS 4.5 themselves). For the sixth time in seven years, the Northwestern program emerged victorious, this time with a perfect score. CHAOS finished fourth, DUCHESS sixth. Notable performances were turned in by BLACK KNIGHT, which finished second and was vastly improved over the previous year, and BLITZ IV which took third place. OSTRICH did not enter, since Monty Newborn had joined the team of another program, L'EXCENTRIQUE, which finished seventh.

THE FIRST EUROPEAN COMPUTER CHESS CHAMPIONSHIP

To determine the European qualifiers for the 1977 World Championship, a Zonal tournament was held in Amsterdam during 1976. The British program MASTER won the event easily, followed by ORWELL, TELL, and BS 66/76. The standard of play was not up to that of the ACM events and boded ill for the chances of the qualifiers in the World Championship. The game between ORWELL and TELL featured a most curious event which gave Tournament Director David Levy some anxious moments. ORWELL knew how to push passed Pawns, but not what to do with them when they arrived, and advanced one of its Pawns to the eighth rank without asking that it be promoted. Rather than forfeit the program for not following the rules, or give it a Queen that it hadn't asked for, Levy let the game continue on the grounds that it was up to the opposing program to take exception to the situation. TELL didn't object, even when ORWELL pushed another Pawn to the eighth rank and left it there. Having run out of Pawns to push, the program then mated poor TELL.

THE SECOND WORLD COMPUTER CHESS CHAMPIONSHIP

The Second World Computer Chess Championship was held in Toronto in 1977. Sixteen programs entered, overburdening the four-round tournament format, so that the second through fifteenth place programs were all involved in a series of ties which had to be broken.

Five of the first six places went to U.S. programs. CHESS 4.6 won the World Championship with a perfect 4—0 score. DUCHESS finished second, defeating the reigning champion and third place finisher, KAISSA, in the first round. Fourth place went to BELLE, an early version (22) of the program-chess processor combination that became so famous a few years later. CHAOS and BLACK KNIGHT finished fifth and sixth. Only BLITZ V of the U.S. programs failed to finish in the top half.

DUCHESS demonstrated in this event that it had "arrived" as a contender for the highest honors, losing only to CHESS 4.6. The British program MASTER finished ninth.

THE EIGHTH NORTH AMERICAN COMPUTER CHESS CHAMPIONSHIP

The 1977 ACM conference was held in Seattle. Twelve programs entered the tournament, which was again directed by David Levy. CHESS 4.6 and DUCHESS tied for first when Levy adjudicated their last-round game a draw. CHAOS finished third, and a new program, XENARBOR, took fourth place. BLACK KNIGHT was fifth and BLITZ V sixth. OSTRICH finished seventh. Of the other programs, the most notable was the first microcomputer program to enter an ACM tournament — 8080 CHESS. This program finished last, but scored a point when OSTRICH crashed due to a program "bug" in the process of announcing a forced mate!

THE LEVY BET AND CHALLENGE MATCHES

In August 1968, Professors John McCarthy of Stanford and Donald Michie of Edinburgh University had an argument with David Levy at a cocktail party, and each wound up betting him £250 that a computer program would be able to beat him within ten years. The next year, Professor Seymour Papert of MIT wagered another £250, and in 1971 Professor Ed Kozdrowicki of UC Davis added a further £250. Finally, in 1975 Michie increased his bet to £500. Thus Levy had wagered a total of £1,250 that no computer program could win a match from him by the end of August 1978.

In the early 1970's, when progress was rather rapid, this may have seemed a reasonable bet. When Levy told Mikhail Botvinnik about the bet, the latter commented "I feel very sorry for your money" (23), but by 1977 it became clear that the improvement of the best programs had slowed down considerably, and that Levy — who in the meantime had become a stronger player, winning the title of International Master — was probably safe. Then CHESS 4.5 won the Class B section at the 1976 Paul Masson tournament, winning five straight games against opposition with an average rating of 1735, and an exhibition game against an opponent rated 1886, and soon thereafter the program won the 1977 Minnesota Open. This gave the programmers some confidence that their program was performing at a level around 2000 on the Elo scale, and although Levy's rating was several hundred points above that, the apparent odds against the program had gone down to about 10 to 1 (27) and a challenge match seemed a reasonable proposition.

A two-game match was accordingly arranged between Levy and CHESS 4.5 at Carnegie-Mellon University in Pittsburgh, in April 1977. The conditions of the match favored Levy: if he won the first game, the match was over, since the program could at best tie. Levy had relatively little difficulty in winning the game, and the first match was over.

Meanwhile a challenge by the Russian program, KAISSA, was in the works. Finally arrangements were made for the progam to run on an Amdahl computer that was much more powerful than the Russian program's native machine. Another two-game match was scheduled for December 1977. The computer operators did not optimize the performance of KAISSA, and again Levy easily won the first game, ending the match.

A highly unexpected challenge was then received from Richard Greenblatt of MIT, who had integrated a chess processor named CHEOPS into the latest version of MAC HACK. Another two-game match was played at Cambridge, Massachusetts in August 1978, and once again Levy outplayed the program to win the first game and end the match.

Finally, the main event, a six-game match with CHESS 4.7, took place in Toronto later in August 1978. David Slate's new program was not yet ready, so Levy played the latest version of the old program. The match turned out to be interesting: in the first game Levy got a horrible shock when the program found a very nice Knight sacrifice which led to a winning position for CHESS 4.7. Levy fought back resourcefully and drew, but realized that he had to take his opponent seriously. Adopting a strategy of "doing nothing but doing it well", Levy let the program weaken its own position decisively before taking the initiative in the next two games, winning both. This satisfied Levy that he could beat the program at will using this method; so in the fourth game he tried to win tactically, playing a gambit opening. After Levy made several tactical errors, the program won. Then Levy reverted to his proven strategy, winning the fifth game and the match.

This marked the end of another era in the history of computer chess; Levy had proven his point, but on the other hand his last opponent put up a respectable battle and proved to be much stronger than Levy expected. The famous bet ended on a sour note when Prof. Kozdrowicki decided not to pay his wager. The reader who is interested in more detail about the Levy challenge matches and other events since the first World Championship, will find an account of the 1974 ACM tournament in Frey (21), and of later events in Levy's books (23-26).

The events of 1977—78 indicated that the development of computer chess had reached a plateau of sorts in the evolution of classical programs implementing Shannon's strategies on large general—purpose computers. Improvements could still be made, but the rate of progress was slow. The performance of the best programs had stabilized near the 2000 Elo level, and the "state of the art" had apparently stagnated—as often happens just before a revolutionary breakthrough.

BELLE AND THE MICROCOMPUTER REVOLUTION

The 1978 ACM tournament was a landmark in the history of computer chess. Not one, but two revolutionary developments were unveiled, and each achieved outstanding success.

The tournament was won by the first effective dedicated chess processor, BELLE. This had been under development for several years, and a prototype had competed in the 1977 World Championship, finishing fourth. The 1978 version of BELLE was much more sophisticated; the dedicated processor generated moves, evaluated positions, and stored position scores while the program ran on a minicomputer and called the processor when it needed information. Although the processor used only 325 integrated circuits, and the program ran on a PDP 11/70 minicomputer, the combination at least equalled the chess capacity of the largest mainframe computers. BELLE was seeded fourth going into the event and was credited with a USCF rating of 1475.

THE NINTH NORTH AMERICAN COMPUTER CHESS CHAMPIONSHIP

The 1978 ACM conference was held in Washington, D.C. Twelve programs entered, including the microcomputer progams SARGON II and MIKE. The tournament was again directed by David Levy. In the second round, BELLE and CHESS 4.7 played an exciting game which could have gone either way. CHESS 4.7 made a brilliant move that should have won, then followed it with a blunder which lost material, because its search ended in a "quiescent" position that was anything but! In the third round, BELLE outplayed CHAOS in the endgame, and in the fourth round, BELLE crushed BLITZ 6.5 tactically in a brilliant miniature which featured the most spectacular combination yet played by a computer program — a beautiful Rook sacrifice, five moves deep—winning the tournament in grand style with a 4—0 score and a performance rating of 2244.

Second place went to CHESS 4.7, and there was a three-way tie for third, between CHAOS, BLITZ 6.5 and — amazingly — SARGON II! The "mighty micro" program scored 2½ — 1½ for a performance rating of 1448, losing to CHAOS, but defeating the mainframe program AWIT. The latter was running on a huge Amdahl 470 computer costing millions of dollars, and much was made of the David vs. Goliath aspect of SARGON II's victory.

MICROCOMPUTERS

The first microprocessor, the 4-bit 4004, was developed by Intel in 1973 as the "brains" of a Japanese calculator. This was quickly succeeded by the 8008 — with an 8-bit data path — and then the 8080. To support software development for its highly successful new product, Intel developed a complete microcomputer development system around it, including the first micro operating system. The success of this led others to do likewise. In December 1974, the first microcomputer for hobbyists appeared, in *Popular Electronics* magazine — the Altair 8800 — using the Intel 8080 microprocessor.

Interest in programming microcomputers to play chess began in 1976, and in 1977 Ronald C. Nelson of Forest Park, Illinois invented the first microcomputer chess-playing machine, the CHESS CHALLENGER. This machine, marketed by Fidelity Electronics, was a box about the size of an encyclopedia volume opened flat, with a chessboard, keyboard and display on top. CHESS CHALLENGER was not much of a challenge, however, since it both accepted and played illegal moves. It was soon replaced by the CHESS CHALLENGER 3, which at least played legally but was very weak.

By the time of the 1978 ACM tournament, thousands of these devices had been sold, and chess players everywhere in the U.S. (and abroad) were learning what the word "microcomputer" meant. A later version, CHESS CHALLENGER 10, played much better, about equal to a human rated 1200. Some extremely misleading advertising claims were made for these early chess computers — CHESS CHALLENGER 3's different levels of play were claimed as "approximately 1200, 1400, 1650, as rated by the USCF" — quite a claim for a machine that did not even know whether it had checkmated its opponent if it stumbled into a mating position! An illustration of one of these early CHESS CHALLENGERS appears in Bell (5).

Shortly after the introduction of CHESS CHALLENGER, the Chafitz company brought out another chess microcomputer, BORIS. Although better than CHESS CHALLENGER 3, this was perhaps not quite up to the level of the CHESS CHALLENGER 10, but also became a big commercial success.

Meanwhile, a number of hobbyists had developed chess programs of their own, and in February 1978 the first tournament for microcomputer programs was held at the West Coast Computer Faire. The tournament attracted large numbers of spectators, and when the last game had ended the winner was SARGON, a program developed by Dan and Kathe Spracklen, with a perfect 5-0 score (three programs tied for second with a 3-2 score). After some improvements, this program entered the ACM tournament as SARGON II. The other microcomputer entry was MIKE, which won the first European Microcomputer Chess Championship ahead of BORIS and CHESS CHALLENGER 10. MIKE's performance in the ACM tournament (1½ — 2½, for a performance rating of 1268) was creditable, but helps to put the advertising claims for the commercial machines into perspective.

At this point, the development of microcomputer chess programs began what eventually became a vast proliferation. A year later, there were at least six different manufacturers of dedicated chess-playing microcomputers, as well as half a dozen programs marketed to run on personal computers.

THE TENTH NORTH AMERICAN COMPUTER CHESS CHAMPIONSHIP

The 1979 ACM conference was held in Detroit, and again 12 programs entered the tournament, which was directed by David Levy. The winner was CHESS 4.9, which drew its last-round game with BELLE — which had itself earlier missed a win in the endgame against CHAOS and had to settle for a draw. DUCHESS tied for second with BELLE; CHAOS tied for fourth with L'EXCENTRIQUE and microcomputer program MYCHESS, which achieved an event performance rating of 1552. SARGON 3.0 scored only 1½ — 2½, but was seeded high and played tough opposition, defeating MYCHESS, losing to DUCHESS and BELLE (in the latter game, SARGON 3.0 played very well and might have drawn), and then drawing with BLITZ 6.9, to earn a performance rating of 1614.

SARGON 3.0 then swept the Second Annual European Microcomputer Chess Championship with a 5—0 score, defeating second-place finisher VEGA, third-place MYCHESS, and fourth-place TINYCHESS.. MIKE II finished fifth, and VOICE

CHESS CHALLENGER was sixth. Three British programs filled out the field of nine contestants.

THE 1980 U.S. AMATEUR TEAM CHAMPIONSHIP

A team of four computer programs participated in this event — CHESS 4.9, BELLE, DUCHESS, and CHAOS. The computer team won four of its six matches, scoring 62.5%. Notable game results: CHESS 4.9 drew with 2393 rated Larry D. Evans; BELLE lost to a 1243 rated player; DUCHESS declined a draw offer from a 1582 rated player and lost on time; CHAOS could only draw with a player rated 1076. Event scores and performance ratings were: CHESS 4.9, 4—2, 2168; DUCHESS, 3—3, 1762; BELLE, 3—3, 1644; CHAOS, 5—1, 1946.

THE THIRD WORLD COMPUTER CHESS CHAMPIONSHIP

The 1980 World Championship was held in Linz, Austria, and was again directed by David Levy. Eighteen programs participated, including microcomputer programs MYCHESS and CHAMPION SENSORY CHALLENGER. At the end of the four rounds that had been scheduled, BELLE and CHAOS were tied for first place with 3½ points. A playoff game was arranged, which BELLE won to become computer World Champion. By this time, BELLE had again been upgraded, and its special chess processor ran more than thirty times as fast as the previous version. CHAOS was second, DUCHESS third with a 3—1 score; then came L'EXCENTRIQUE and CHESS 4.9, tied for fourth with 2½. David Slate's new program NUCHESS and the Soviet program KAISSA were among the six programs tied for sixth place. The British programs MASTER and ADVANCE 1.0, together with OSTRICH, MYCHESS, and the German entry PARWELL, tied for twelfth place.

1980 MICROCOMPUTER TOURNAMENTS

Like the programs themselves, microcomputer tournaments began to proliferate in 1980. It would be both outside the scope of this history, and distracting to the reader, to try to give a complete accounting of all the competitions; so only the most notable will be discussed.

The 1980 West Coast Computer Faire Microcomputer Chess Tournament was won by MYCHESS, with a score of 3½—½. An Atari program finished second with 2½; SARGON 2.5 tied for third with 1½. George Koltanowski directed.

The Stockholm tournament was won by a German entry, MEPHISTO (after the automaton). MYCHESS, SARGON 2.5 and the Auto-Response Board tied for second.

The First World Microcomputer Chess Championship was held in London in September 1980. Fourteen programs were entered. CHAMPION SENSORY CHALLENGER won the title with a 5—0 score; the BORIS EXPERIMENTAL program (ancestor of MORPHY) was second with 4—1. MIKE 3.0, SARGON II, the Swedish program ROOK 4.0, and the Dutch entry GAMBIET tied for third with 3—2.

The First U.S. Microcomputer Chess Championship was held in San Jose, California in September 1980. Eight programs were entered. Again, the CHAMPION SENSORY CHALLENGER finished first, with a 4—0 score. MYCHESS B, BORIS X, SARGON 2.5 and CHESS CHAMPION SUPER SYSTEM 3 tied for second with 2 ½ — 1½. George Koltanowski directed.

THE ELEVENTH NORTH AMERICAN COMPUTER CHESS CHAMPIONSHIP

The 1980 ACM conference was held in Nashville. Ten programs entered the tournament; David Levy directed his tenth and last event. BELLE finished first, with a 4—0 score and a performance rating of 2294. CHAOS was second at 3—1; CHESS CHALLENGER EXPERIMENTAL tied for third with BEBE at 2½—1½, and the micro program achieved a performance rating of 1807 — losing to BELLE, drawing with BEBE, and defeating OSTRICH and AWIT. CRAY BLITZ (the old BLITZ program implemented on the world's most powerful computer) tied for fifth at 2 — 2 with MYCHESS. A speed tournament was held, which was won by CRAY BLITZ, with BELLE second.

THE FREDKIN INCENTIVE MATCH 1981

In August 1981, the Fredkin Prize Fund sponsored a two-game match in Vancouver between the computer World Champion, BELLE, and a Canadian master, Carl Storey, whose rating at the time was 2206. Storey won both games, and a prize of $2,500.00.

FIDE - ICCA AGREEMENT

The 1981 General Assembly of the Federation International d'Echecs (FIDE — the International Chess Federation, which sponsors the official World Championship and sanctions other international events) approved an agreement with the ICCA (International Computer Chess Association). This agreement was ratified by the ICCA in June 1982.

The terms of the agreement provided that the ICCA recognized FIDE as the supreme organization of world chess, and as its representative to other world institutions (i.e., the U.N.). The agreement also provided that FIDE recognized the ICCA as the only official international organization for sanctioning computer chess tournaments and championships, and for associated organizational work.

The ICCA and FIDE established a joint commission for purposes of discussing mutual policy problems, such as qualifications for computer chess titles. It was agreed that such titles would be awarded by the ICCA, and ratified by FIDE.

1981 MICROCOMPUTER TOURNAMENTS

The proliferation of microcomputer tournaments continued in 1981. A few of the most prominent will be reported on.

The Second European Microcomputer Chess Championship was held in London in September. British programs took the top two places, and five of the first six. CYRUS won with a 5—0 score, ADVANCE 2.0 was second, and PHILIDOR EXPERIMENTAL tied for third with PHILIDOR and the Danish program LOGICHESS.

A nine-round Swiss system tournament for Dutch programs (not necessarily micros) was held in Utrecht in September. The tournament was won by micro YNCT 1.0 with a 7½ — 1½ score. Another micro, GAMBIET '81, was second with 7 — 2; PION was third with 6 — 3.

A microcomputer tournament held in Paris in May was won by MEPHISTO X, with 6 points. MORPHY tied for second with CHESS CHAMPION MARK V, each with 5 points. Eighteen programs competed.

A microcomputer tournament was held in Stockholm in November. CHAMPION SENSORY CHALLENGER won, with a 5 — 2 score. A three-way tie for second occurred between PRINCHESS B, CHESS CHAMPION MARK V, and PHILIDOR with 4½ — 2½; MEPHISTO ESB was fifth with a 4 — 3 score.

THE SECOND WORLD MICROCOMPUTER CHESS CHAMPIONSHIP

In September 1981 a unique event was held at the Baltic seaside resort of Travemünde. Eight programs competed in an open section, and five manufacturers entered chess microcomputers in a commercial section which was supposed to decide the question of which machine was the best that was commercially available.

The idea behind this was to avoid the problems of misleading advertising claims which had followed previous microcomputer tournaments. After the 1980 London tournament, for example, one distributor sold a weaker product and represented it as being the same as the winning program. Typically, the microcomputer products entered by manufacturers in such events had been "souped-up" by using microprocessors with abnormally high speed, extra memory, and other features not available in production units.

The ICCA and FIDE sanctioned the Travemünde event as an official World Championship. Unfortunately, there was not a sufficiently precise definition of what constituted a "commercially available" unit. With literally millions of dollars in sales at stake, the commercial section of the tournament was conducted more along the lines of a war than a sporting event. Considerations of fair play, courtesy, and even ethical conduct were overshadowed by the pressures of survival in the fiercely competitive chess microcomputer market. The result was that almost every decision by the tournament officials was made in an atmosphere of exteme tension and controversy, with various protests being made and even the possibility of legal actions. The whole experience soured the participants, the organizers, and the ICCA observers, and made it unlikely that such an event would soon be repeated.

The first problem faced by the organizers was the lone German entry, MEPHISTO II. Although commercial production of this unit was scheduled to begin in November, the machine did not technically meet the standard of immediate commercial availability. The organizers were unable to secure unanimous approval from the other four participants for MEPHISTO II to play in its prototype configuration. The sponsors of the German machine (as well as the German press) were angered by this, and chose not to enter their program in the open section either. A protest was also made against the participation of the CHESS CHAMPION MARK V, on the grounds that it was not yet commercially available either. This was only resolved by arranging for one of the consulates in Hong Kong to inspect the production line, and select samples to be sent to Travemünde. It was ultimately decided that the machine met the requirements, and it was allowed to participate, although under protest.

Another problem encountered was repetition of games. The tournament was a quadruple round-robin in the commercial section, and such computers tended to continually play the same openings and fall into the same traps over and over. The opening "books" of some programs have been adjusted to exploit this weakness in certain opposing programs. The decision that the loser was responsible for varying its opening in the next game was controversial, as were other decisions on tie breaks, draws by repetition, etc. It was in such an atmosphere of pressure and controversy, with the marketing representatives and even the company principals of the different manufacturers hovering over the harried officials, that Applied Concepts decided to withdraw its entry (the MASTER CHESS TRIO - consisting of the Gruenfeld, Morphy, and Capablanca programs) after playing eight games out of the twelve scheduled. The reason given was that a serious program "bug" had been detected in the Capablanca program module used, which apparently did not exist in the master program. The remaining four games were scored as forfeits.

The SciSys CHESS CHAMPION MARK V won the commercial section, with a score of 8½ — 3½, including two forfeit points. Fidelity's CHAMPION SENSORY CHALLENGER was second with 6½ — 5½, winning its individual match with CHESS CHAMPION MARK V by a 2½ — 1½ score, and scoring the same number of points in games actually played. Novag's SAVANT was third with 6 — 6, and the MASTER CHESS TRIO finished last with 3 — 9, including 4 points lost by forfeit.

In contrast to the difficulties in the commercial section, the open section of the tournament went smoothly, with the usual banter among the programmers. FIDELITY X finished first with a 6—1 score; PRINCESS 2.9 was second with 5—2. NOVAG X and PHILIDOR X tied for third with 4½ — 2½.

The final event of the tournament was a three-game match between the winners of the two sections. FIDELITY X won all three games and the overall championship.

The experience of Travemünde had a dampening effect on the previously high interest in organizing microcomputer tournaments.

THE TWELFTH NORTH AMERICAN COMPUTER CHESS CHAMPIONSHIP

The 1981 ACM conference was held in Los Angeles. Sixteen programs competed, including three micros. Again BELLE was the winner, with a score of 3½ — ½ and a performance rating of 2306. NUCHESS, CRAY BLITZ, and BEBE tied for second with 3 — 1. DUCHESS and PHILIDOR tied for fifth with 2½ — 1½. The latter's performance rating was a creditable 1923. OSTRICH, L'EXCENTRIQUE, CHESS CHALLENGER and SAVANT tied for seventh with 2 — 2.

During this event, a conference was held between the participants and representatives of the United States Chess Federation, to determine whether the USCF should rate the ACM tournament. It was decided that the lack of USCF ratings among the participants would make the calculation of the ratings unreliable, and that the matter should be reexamined at the next ACM conference.

COMPUTER VERSUS HUMAN

Until the events of 1982, relatively few recent tournament games had been played by computers against human opponents. This was not the desire of the computer chess programmers, who had always sought to pit their creations against humans; but a reflection of the attitude of human tournament players.

In the beginning (era of MAC HACK VI), a computer chess program was a curiosity and was welcomed by jaded tournament players. Also, at that time, prizes were much lower in chess tournaments, and the later vogue for large class prizes for the low-rated players, approaching the top prizes which masters competed for, had not developed. Entry fees were also much lower, and as a competitor of that era, the author remembers rather more interest in chess for art's sake, and less concentration on money.

The first appearance of MAC HACK VI in a 1967 tournament was front-page news in *Chess Life*, the USCF magazine (15). The program remained active in competition through 1972. By that time, other programs were entering tournaments, and by the end of 1978 there were ten chess programs on the USCF rating list headed by CHESS 4.6 with a 2040 rating. The April 1979 issue of *Chess Life* featured a two-page spread about BELLE's victory in the 1978 North American Computer Chess Championship.

All this computer chess publicity attracted the attention of a group of USCF members who resented the fact that computer programs were allowed to participate in USCF tournaments. In the September 1979 issue of *Chess Life*, Harold B. Dondis charged that computer programs were not legitimate tournament participants since they violated a strict interpretation of the laws of chess. This point of view has since been thoroughly discredited, but has never been abandoned by some of those most violently opposed to computers.

More cogent objections were raised to the effect that computer programs were a distraction to other players (keyboard and printer noise, etc), and that for many players the human nature of the opponent is an essential part of the enjoyment of playing in a chess tournament. Finally, there was a good deal of apprehension that computer programs would "take over" chess tournaments, winning an unfair share of prizes and distorting pairings — obviously groundless to anyone familiar with the very high costs involved in running a chess program on a large computer.

Thus a faction developed within the USCF, whose objective was to keep computer programs out of USCF tournaments. The fact that the then USCF President shared this viewpoint did their cause no harm. An effective lobbying effort led first to a special registration requirement for computer programs, and then to the 1980 USCF regulations on computer participation. These prohibited computers from entering any event not specifically designated as being for computers, and from winning prizes. These regulations had the effect of barring programs from almost all tournaments, since most organizers did not bother to indicate whether computers would be allowed, and the default was "No".

The author was appointed Chairman of the USCF Computer Chess Committee at the USCF Convention in August 1981. An ad hoc meeting revealed strong sentiment, among delegates interested in computer chess, for relaxing the restrictions on computer programs, but when these proposals were brought before the Board of Delegates they were defeated.

The Computer Chess Committee gave the matter much study during the next year, and in 1982 the USCF Board of Delegates adopted a more balanced set of rules (see Appendix A), which relieved the worst inequities. Computer programs were made eligible for a special limited class of USCF membership, and were allowed to enter all tournaments whose organizers did not specifically indicate that the programs were unwelcome.

Debate on this issue has tended to be less rational, and more acrimonious, than one would like. There is a genuine philosophical point involved in opposition to man-machine chess contests, which have (amusingly, and with some justice) been compared to entering a forklift in a weight-lifting contest. Such man-machine competitions have been held before, however, when machines were less capable (e.g. John Henry, the rock driller who beat the steam engine), and if forklifts were perceived as weaker than humans, there would probably be a good deal of interest in whether one could win a weight-lifting contest.

Another way to look at the matter is that the contest is not really between man and machine, but between man and an abstract intellectual creation termed a program. The program is distinct from the machine on which it runs, although its performance is affected by the machine's capabilities. This may seem an abstruse philosophical argument, but if one imagines a chess teacher trying to instill chess ability into an idiot savant, whose only talent is the ability to quickly and unerringly follow instructions (provided that they are sufficiently detailed that he never has to think), the idea becomes easier to deal with. If the effort is successful, to whom should the credit go — the idiot or the teacher?

Conceptually, there has been very little progress in computer chess during the last ten years. In technique it has been a different story, but technique will only carry so far — and it appears that this boundary has been approached, in view of practical limits on search depth. The best programs seem to have reached a definite barrier at an Elo rating of about 2200, the level that distinguishes the genuine master from the strong player—the expert or Candidate Master.

The answer to breaking the 2200 barrier may be to find a way of giving programs a capacity to formulate strategic goals and plans, the lack of which has proven to be a serious weakness in their play. For significant progress to be made, some such conceptual breakthrough is needed. When this happens (as eventually it must), new ideas and concepts of a variety and richness almost terrifying to contemplate (for a programmer who may have to carry them out) will emerge; and the true test of a program will then become the worth of its conceptual approach, rather than the efficiency of its implementation — although the latter will remain important.

Such a development would rekindle interest in computer chess among artificial-intelligence specialists, who in the early days followed events attentively, but whose interest waned once it became clear that progress had been reduced to improvements in programming mechanics and hardware. The development of these new concepts will be a long, difficult process, and the first efforts may be expected to have many defects, probably playing below the level of existing programs. In the evolution of computer capacity for strategic planning, it is of the greatest importance for programs to compete with humans, rather than other programs. Humans are so vastly superior to any kind of program in formulating concepts and plans, that it is hard to see how any real progress could be made otherwise.

2
INSIDE A CHESS COMPUTER

Many readers may not be very familiar with the details of how computers operate. It is not necessary to become a computer programmer to understand the basic principles by which computer chess programs play, but it is important to have some understanding of what a computer is, how it is organized, how it operates, and how a chess program is structured.

The easiest, and probably the most interesting, way to get some of the basics which will be helpful later on in this book is to take a detailed look inside a modern chess microcomputer. This will focus on the concepts involved, without a great deal of emphasis on technical details. The reader who is already knowledgable in this field may want to go on to the next chapter.

The microcomputer discussed in this chapter is the Great Game Machine, manufactured by Applied Concepts.

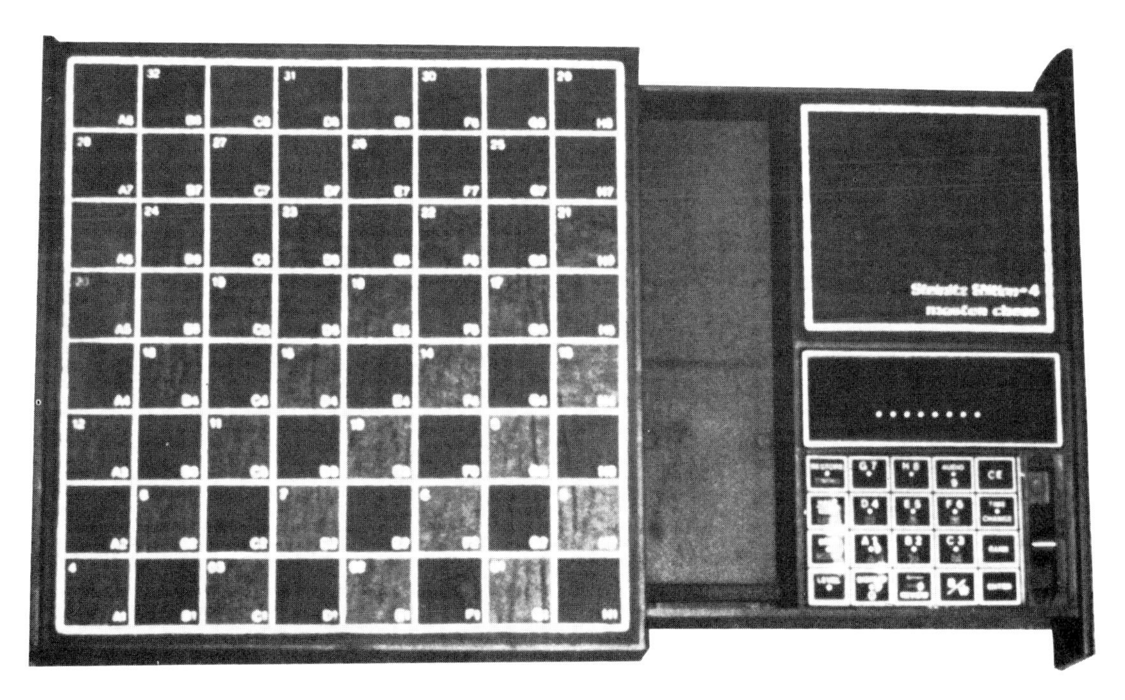

Fig. 2.1 The Great Game Machine, with program module installed.
(Courtesy of Applied Concepts.)

It is particularly well suited for this type of discussion, because of its modular construction — the program itself is in a plug-in module, so that the machine can run different types of programs, such as Checkers and Backgammon, and can also be upgraded to a stronger program by installing a new module.

Fig. 2.2 Programs for the Great Game Machine are stored in a plug-in module, the cover of which has been removed. *(Courtesy of Applied Concepts.)*

The chess program that will be discussed is called the Master Chess Trio, and consists of three modules, each of which plays a different part of the game.

This microcomputer has been selected as an example solely because of its unusual suitability for the purpose. The author, and more particularly the United States Chess Federation, have not endorsed this product in any way. The author considers it a good machine, but has no desire to get involved in the question of which chess microcomputer is best. Most of the higher-priced microcomputers are significantly stronger than the average tournament player, and nearly all of them are good value for the average purchaser.

HOW COMPUTERS WORK

Before getting into the details of the Great Game Machine, it is appropriate to take a brief look at what a computer is, and how it works. A chess microcomputer is just a specialized type of computer, which can be produced inexpensively. Its capabilities are more limited than a general-purpose computer, but it works in basically the same way.

INSTRUCTIONS

The simplest, and in many ways the most accurate, way to think of a computer is as a glorified adding machine. The instruction set (the basic operations that the computer can perform) of many computers—and almost all of the early ones—contains lots of instructions for moving data around, comparing it to other data and so forth; but when it comes to what the computer will do with the data, the machine's arithmetic capability is limited to the operations of addition and subtraction. These, the computer can do very quickly—perhaps millions of times per second.

In order to multiply two numbers on a machine of this type, a short sequence of instructions is called upon. This "subroutine" is likely to follow exactly the same steps that a human does when multiplying two numbers longhand with pencil and paper. Of course, to do this, one must know the multiplication tables. For a computer this is quite simple, since it is using binary numbers.

BINARY NUMBERS

A binary number is a number expressed in a system to the base of 2. The "new math" that was so controversial when introduced into our schools was intended to teach students that numbers could be expressed in other ways than to the base 10 (decimal numbers). Those who took "new math" already know what binary numbers are. For the benefit of those who don't, here's how they work.

When a number is expressed in the decimal (base 10) system, each digit represents a multiplier of a particular power of the number 10 (the base of the system). Thus

1,234,567 = 7 x 10 to the zeroth power. (7)
+ 6 x 10 to the first power (60)
+ 5 x 10 to the second power (500)
+ 4 x 10 to the third power (4,000)
+ 3 x 10 to the fourth power (30,000)
+ 2 x 10 to the fifth power (200,000)
+ 1 x 10 to the sixth power (1,000,000)

In binary numbers, a grouping of eight digits is particularly important to the organization of many computers. These eight-digit numbers are called "Bytes". For a binary example, here is the largest value that a byte can have:

11111111 = 1 x 2 to the zeroth power (1)
+ 1 x 2 to the first power (2)
+ 1 x 2 to the second power (4)
+ 1 x 2 to the third power (8)
+ 1 x 2 to the fourth power (16)
+ 1 x 2 to the fifth power (32)
+ 1 x 2 to the sixth power (64)
+ 1 x 2 to the seventh power (128) = 255 decimal.

The digits of binary numbers are referred to as "bits". Binary numbers quickly get very long compared to decimal numbers, but they have one highly important characteristic: there are only two values which a binary digit (bit) can have — 1 or 0.

This is extremely useful in designing computers, since it is easy to find electronic devices (such as transistors) that can be either "on" or "off". It is not easy at all to imagine devices which could have ten different states, so as to represent the decimal digits.

OPERATIONS

Returning to the subject of how a computer multiplies two numbers, the table of multiplication for binary numbers is very simple:

0 x 0 = 0;
0 x 1 = 0;
1 x 0 = 0;
1 x 1 = 1

This process can actually be carried out by the computer as a logical operation. Logical operations are based on the concept that the two values of binary numbers can be interpreted as representing the states "True" and "False". The **logical union** of two digits is 1 (true) if they are both 1; 0 (false) otherwise.

Instructions for logical operations are also part of the computer's instruction set. There are three important logical operations which all computers can perform, either on one digit (bit) at a time, or on larger units such as bytes. These are:

Logical negation (inversion) — NOT Example: NOT 1 = 0.
NOT 0 = 1.

Logical union (conjunction) — AND Example: 1 AND 1 = 1.
1 AND 0 = 0.
0 AND 0 = 0.

Logical separation (disjunction) — OR Example: 1 OR 1 = 1.
1 OR 0 = 1.
0 OR 0 = 0.

Using these few simple operations, and a variety of other instructions for moving data around, programmers can develop subroutines which enable the computer not only to multiply and divide, but to do more complicated functions such as taking logarithms, raising numbers to powers, and the like. It is also possible for the computer to manipulate letters or characters. These are coded as numbers. The most popular such code (except for some IBM computers) is the American Standard Code for Information Interchange (ASCII). The ASCII code consists of 128 binary numbers, each of which represents a character such as the letters of the alphabet, control signals to a terminal, punctuation, numerals, and so on. The capital letters of the alphabet in ASCII are:

A = 01000001;	H = 01001000;	O = 01001111;	V = 01010110;
B = 01000010;	I = 01001001;	P = 01010000;	W = 01010111;
C = 01000011;	J = 01001010;	Q = 01010001;	X = 01011000;
D = 01000100;	K = 01001011;	R = 01010010;	Y = 01011001;
E = 01000101;	L = 01001100;	S = 01010011;	Z = 01011010.
F = 01000110;	M = 01001101;	T = 01010100;	
G = 01000111;	N = 01001110;	U = 01010101;	

These codes, and the other codes for lower-case letters, numbers, and other symbols, allow the computer to communicate with humans using words and decimal numbers instead of binary numbers.

ORGANIZATION

Almost all computers are organized into five different functional units. Each unit has its own tasks to perform, and the computer cannot operate if any one of the five is not functioning. These units are organized as follows:

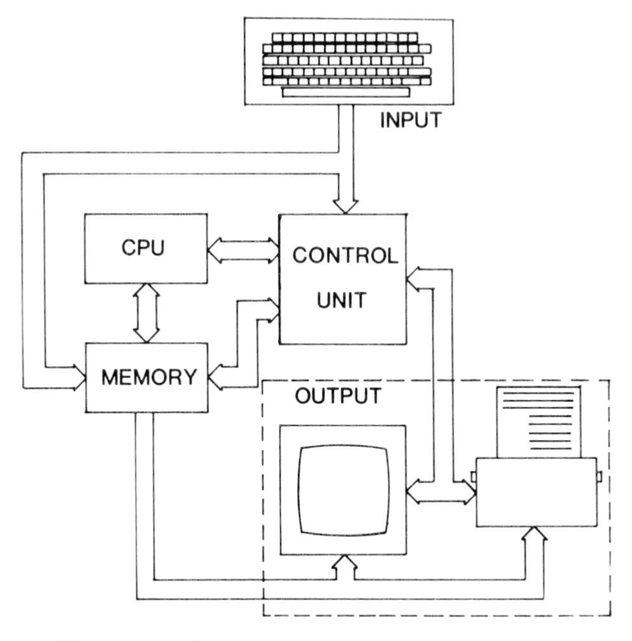

Fig. 2.3 The components of a computer.

The part of the computer that does the computing is the processor, usually referred to as the Central Processing Unit (CPU). The CPU performs various operations on data, such as addition, subtraction, logical operations, and so on. It also instructs other parts of the computer to do certain things which the CPU itself cannot do.

The memory is a storage unit. It holds data and instructions. The CPU itself has a very limited capacity to store data, usually only enough to carry out one operation at a time. The CPU reads its instructions from specified areas in the memory, gets data from other areas which the instructions specify, performs operations on the data, and then places the results into other locations in the memory which the instructions specify. These locations in the memory are called **addresses.**

The input and output units allow the computer to communicate with the outside world. The control unit handles the interface between the CPU and these units, and also has the ability to get data from memory and put data into memory. When the person using the computer communicates with it, such as by typing something on a keyboard (input unit), the control unit places the message into memory, where the CPU can read it. When the CPU is ready to transmit some results, it tells the control unit to send the contents of certain addresses in memory to the output unit.

PROGRAMS

What makes the computer much more valuable than an adding machine is not just the speed with which it can perform its operations — the time that it takes to key in the data is far greater than the time that most adding machines take to compute a result. The value of the computer lies in the fact that it is programmable.

A program for a computer is a list of instructions which the machine is to follow. These are placed beginning in a certain specified area of the memory, which is reserved for such programs. When the computer is turned on, it immediately goes to a specified area in memory and starts executing the instructions there. Usually, that part of memory contains a relatively small program, and is permanent—it does not "erase" when the power is turned off. This program sets up the computer to run other programs, and then sends the CPU to the address in memory where the program that the computer is to run begins. That program tells the computer where to look for and to place data, in the areas of memory which are not used to store the program instructions.

The ability to automatically execute a very long and detailed list of instructions without having to ask for any kind of human intervention, storing the results of each operation in memory for future reference, and doing so very rapidly — at the rate of thousands or millions of instructions per second — is what gives the computer so much power and makes it so useful.

The list of instructions which makes up the program is a list of binary numbers. Each of these binary numbers is called a "**word**". The length of a word depends on the computer. Longer words allow the machine to process more information in one operation, but also require more expensive hardware. The shortest words used in computers are eight bits, or one byte, long.

The program itself has to tell the computer what to do in the most minute detail imaginable. The computer can do almost nothing without a program to tell it how. In order to read a character typed on the keyboard, the computer has to execute a small program segment (subroutine). And in order to send a character to the terminal screen, it has to run another subroutine. Just to read from the keyboard, and store in memory, one paragraph of this book (which was written on a computer using a word processing program) required the execution of several million instructions. Of course, these were not all different — the same program segments were executed over and over.

These instructions all have to be absolutely correct and in the right sequence, or the computer is likely to do something totally unexpected — such as turning itself off and erasing all its memory. This can be disconcerting, to say the least, when one has just spent many hours typing a program into the machine. There are few if any programmers who have not had this experience, or one similar to it.

Fortunately—for if all programs had to be typed in as binary numbers, which was how the earliest computers were programmed, there wouldn't be very many programs written—there are a lot of utility programs to make the programmer's life a little easier. The most important are gathered together collectively in the form of the computer's operating system. This contains routines for operating the input and output devices, so that the programmer doesn't have to rewrite these instructions all the time. Also contained in the operating system is a program called an assembler, which lets the programmer write his instructions in something easier to deal with than binary numbers. For example, here is the assembler code for a short subroutine written for the Intel 8080 microprocessor, and the corresponding binary instructions:

```
assembler code                     binary code

TEST  XRA   A                      10101111
      OUT   1DH                    11010011 00011101
      IN    1DH                    11011011 00011101
      ANI   1                      11100110 00000001
      RZ                           11001000
      MVI   A,0FFH                 00111110 11111111
      RET                          11001001
```

The instructions in the assembler code are **mnemonics,** which help the programmer visualize the operation to be performed. For example, the mnemonic "XRA A" means to perform an exclusive OR operation between the register A and the accumulator (the accumulator is the CPU's working "scratchpad" memory); "ANI 1" means to perform an AND operation between the accumulator and the contents of the next byte in memory; "RET" means to return to the program that called the subroutine. Assembler language is still not very easy to master, but is a vast improvement over binary code. Most chess programs for microcomputers, and many of those for larger machines, are written in assembler language for maximum speed.

Other programs to make programming even easier have been developed. These are called compilers, and let the progammer write his instructions in statements which combine the effects of many assembler instructions, and more closely correspond to human thought processes. Such statements are said to be written in **high-level languages,** which are very powerful but somewhat slower in speed of execution than assembler language. Some of the most powerful chess programs are written in high-level languages, such as FORTRAN and C, because they are too complex for reasonable coding in assembler language.

THE GREAT GAME MACHINE

The Applied Concepts Great Game Machine uses the 6502 microprocessor as its CPU. This processor uses a word 8 bits long, and the standard version runs at a clock speed of 2 Mhz (2 million cycles per second). A high-speed version of the GGM uses a 4 Mhz 6502 as its CPU. The 6502 microprocessor was developed by MOS Technology, Inc. It is extremely popular with chess programmers, because of its simplicity, its speed, and its instruction set, which is very well suited to the operations required in chess programs. A 4 Mhz 6502 can execute as many as 1,000,000 instructions per second. The block diagram for the 6502 indicates its simplicity:

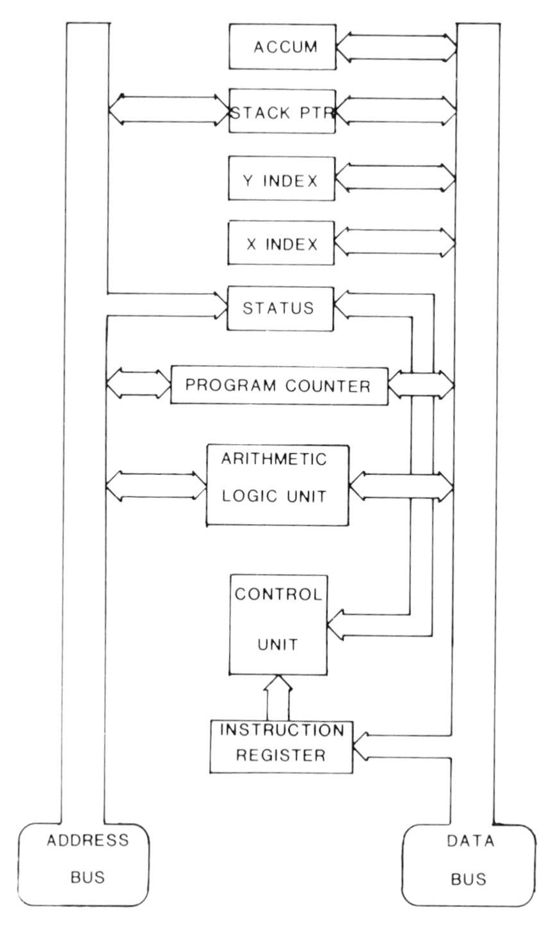

Fig. 2.4 Organization of the 6502 microprocessor.

The simplicity of the 6502 is shown by the fact that it contains only six registers — the instruction register, stack pointer register, status register, x and y index registers, and the accumulator. The instruction register receives the program instructions and tells the CPU what to do. The accumulator is used as the working memory, or "scratchpad", for many arithmetic and other operations. The index registers are available for other data storage, and for holding memory addresses. The status register keeps track of various conditions within the CPU, such as whether an addition has "overflowed" the accumulator. Finally, the stack pointer keeps track of the data stored in an area of memory known as the "stack", which is used to supplement the accumulator as scratchpad memory. The Arithmetic Logic Unit (ALU) performs operations on the data in the registers.

By way of contrast to the simplicity of the 6502, another popular microprocessor, the Z-80 (developed by Zilog, Inc.) contains no less than 23 registers! The instruction set of the Z-80 is also much larger. Programmers consider the Z-80 to be more powerful than the 6502, but somewhat slower. Many of its additional capabilities are of little use for chess programs.

The organization of the Great Game Machine is quite simple:

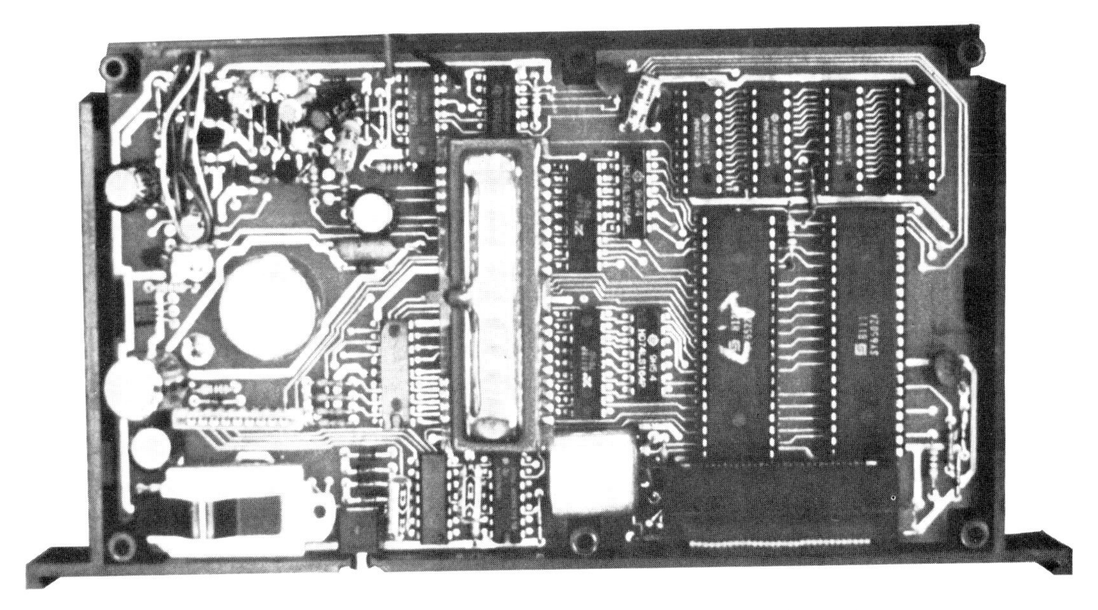

Fig. 2.5 Electronic circuitry within the Great Game Machine.
(Courtesy of Applied Concepts.)

The 6502 microprocessor communicates with the machine's keyboard, fluorescent display, and speaker through the 6522 Versatile Interface Adapter. This circuit performs many of the functions of the control unit in the generalized computer shown in fig. 2-3. The rest are handled by an address decode and gating circuit, which interfaces between the CPU and the machine's Random Access Memory. This is a small section of memory used for the "stack" and other data storage requirements that the CPU generates in executing the program.

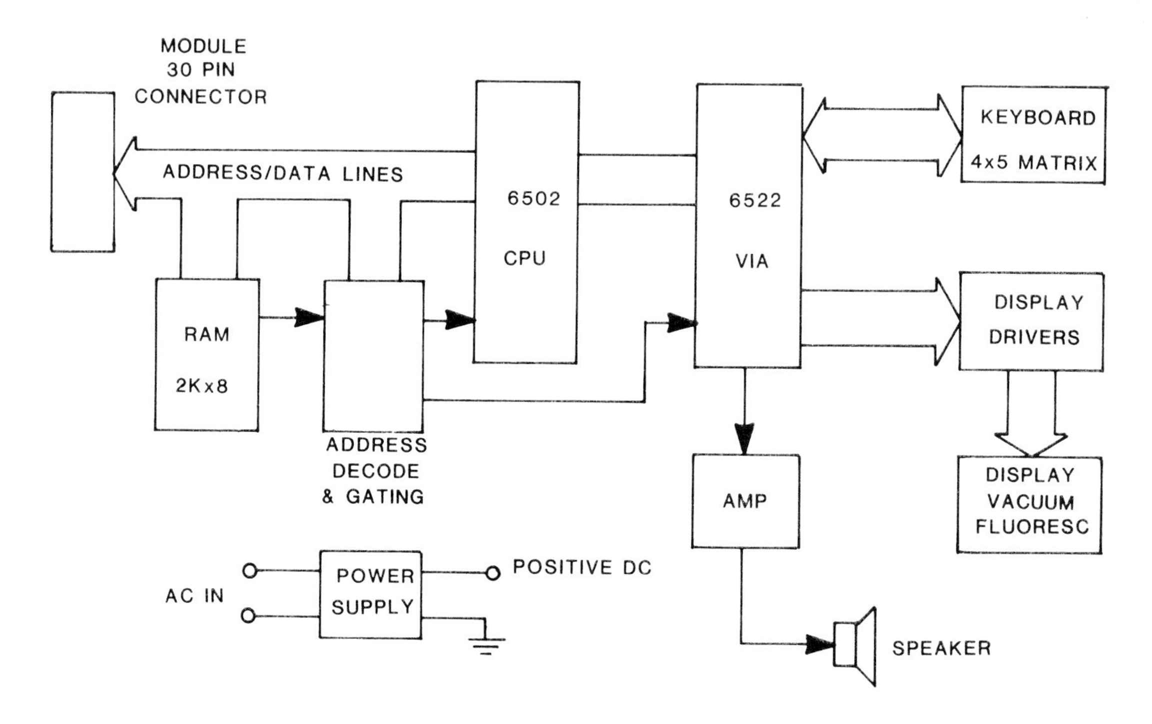

Fig. 2.6 Great Game Machine block diagram.

The program itself is stored on a separate module. This is a small cartridge which plugs into the Great Game Machine, communicating with the 6502 CPU through a 30-pin connector.

Fig. 2.7 Electronic circuitry within a program module.
(Courtesy of Applied Concepts.)

The address-decoding functions required are handled in the program module. This contains two kinds of memory: Read Only Memory, which the CPU can read but is not able to store data in; and Random Access Memory, which the CPU can use to store and retrieve data. The ROM is permanent, and keeps its data even when the power is turned off. The program itself is stored in this section of memory. The RAM is used to store such variable data as the board position, tables of various kinds, and the like, which are erased when the power is turned off.

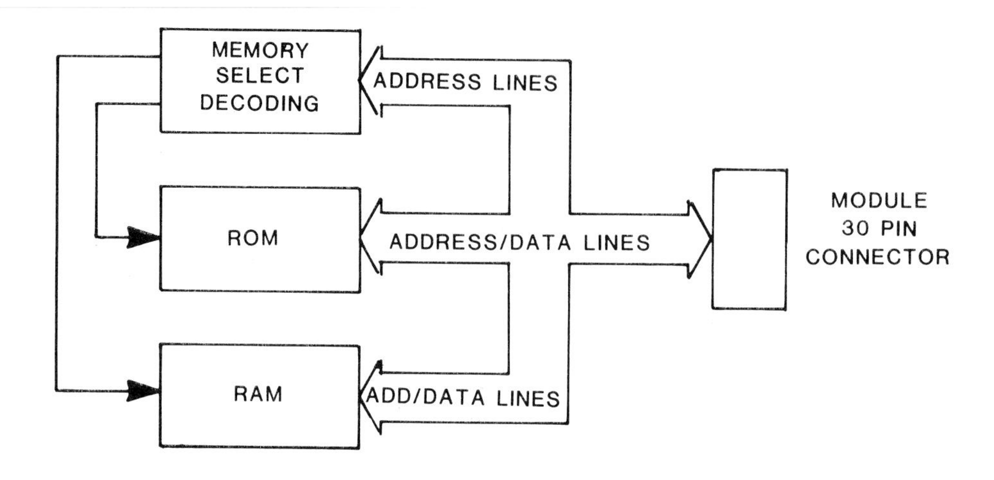

Fig. 2.8 Program module block diagram

The Great Game Machine is a special-purpose computer, and has no operating system or assembly language. Its programs are developed on other computers, which encode them in binary form into the ROM "chip" inside the program module.

USING THE GREAT GAME MACHINE

To play a game of chess with the Master Chess Trio on the Great Game Machine, the user first inserts the Gruenfeld Chess Openings cartridge in the machine, sets up the pieces on the board, and turns the machine on. At this point, the GGM displays the legend "MOVE?" and the numeral 1, indicating that it is the user's move. To accomplish this simple result, the GGM has already executed a large number of instructions — setting default values for parameters such as the initial positions of the pieces, time on the clock, level of play, random selection between moves, and so on. These parameters can, of course, be altered by the user through the keyboard.

The user then keys in his move, e.g., **"e2—e4"**, and the machine responds immediately with its reply, for example **"e7—e6".** The GGM does not have to spend any time calculating this reply, because it is stored in the Gruenfeld opening "book" — a table of variations selected from works on opening theory. Retrieving a move from this table, of course, involves executing a program routine involving many instructions, but the computer is so fast that it appears to do this instantly. The process continues until the game reaches a position not stored in the Gruenfeld module **— 2 d4 d5 3 ♞c3 dxe4 4 ♞xe4 ♞d7 5 ♞f3 ♞f6 6 ♞xf6 ♞xf6 7 ♝g5,** for example. At this point, the display on the GGM begins flashing "MIDGAME", alternating with the numeral 7. Gruenfeld defines the middlegame as beginning when its "book" ends, which may be more than twenty moves into the game in some variations — or the second or third move against an opponent who does not follow theory.

It is now time to change to the Morphy middlegame module. The power switch on the GGM has three positions — OFF, ON, and MEM. The latter is used when changing modules. The Gruenfeld module is removed and the Morphy module installed (a matter of a few seconds), after which the power switch is thrown back to ON. The GGM's display then begins to indicate that it is carrying out its move selection search by flashing the best move it has found so far. Finally the program decides on **7 ... ♝d7,**and play resumes. The Morphy program module carries out a move selection search routine after each move by its opponent. After its own moves, it assumes that the opponent will make the reply that it has already calculated to be best, and begins to analyze that while the opponent is thinking. The depth of search, and the time required to carry it out, may be varied from a few seconds to many hours by choosing the playing level accordingly.

Eventually the Morphy program decides that the amount of material on the board has been reduced far enough that the middlegame has become an endgame, and a period appears to the right of the numeral indicating the move number. This is a signal to repeat the process of changing modules, removing the Morphy module and inserting the Capablanca module. The latter then resumes play, using a similar search to select moves, but choosing them according to different reasons, and lets the user know it has a different personality by using higher-frequency "beeps" to signal its moves. Eventually, Capablanca wins or gets mated, and the game is over. The program does not know how to resign.

The Morphy module alone can play an entire game, but of course it is not as strong in the opening and endgame phases.

THE STRUCTURE OF A CHESS PROGRAM

The essential features of chess programs will be discussed in considerable detail in chapter 4. In describing how programs go about playing a game of chess, it is difficult to include much specific information about the methods programmers use to solve their problems, and still present the overall organization of the program clearly. For this reason, and to prepare the reader for an introduction to individual programs and their characteristics in chapter 3, this is an appropriate point to present a broad overview of how a typical chess program is organized.

The Master Chess Trio is an excellent example of the structure of a modern chess program, most of which recognize three phases in a game: the opening, the middlegame, and the endgame.

All chess programs contain certain features. These are likely to be implemented in different ways from program to program, but all perform essentially the same functions. The principal features of a chess program are:

1) A data base defining the current situation in the game—positions of the pieces, legality of castling, past positions that might be repeated to cause a draw, and so on. This is stored in the RAM in the program modules of the Master Chess Trio.

2) An opening "book" telling the program which moves to play in the opening. It is much easier to do this than to try to instruct the computer in the fine points of opening

play. Also, the program can save time on its clock by retrieving moves from the "book". This is stored in the Gruenfeld module's ROM.

3) A move generator, whose function is to determine which moves can legally be played in a given position. Most move generators do not discriminate between "good" moves and "bad" moves; they leave that up to the search routine. These are Shannon type A programs. Some programs, however, use selective or Shannon type B searches. In these programs, the move generation is handled by a plausible move generator, whose function is to select the "n" best moves (the factor n is called the **fanout**) in each position to be considered, and rank them in order of merit.

4) An evaluator function, whose purpose is to measure the value of a position numerically. This is not an easy thing to do accurately, and most of the problems that computer chess programs have are due to the limitations of their evaluator functions. The factors by which an evaluator measures positions are termed **heuristics**. It is essential that the evaluator be compact and fast to execute, at least for a Shannon type A program, since it will have to be called on many thousands, perhaps millions, of times during the course of selecting one move. The evaluation of positions uses most of the time consumed by a program looking for a move.

6) A forward search routine, which constructs a "game tree" of possible positions using the move generator, then searches it by means of the von Neumann minimax principle, the alpha-beta method, and other techniques. Such processes are termed **algorithms**. The use of these algorithms is critical to the speed of the search, and determines how deeply the program can "see". An efficient search does not have to evaluate as many positions for the same depth as an inefficient one, because it looks at the best moves first.

Move generation, forward search, and position evaluation are all performed both by the Morphy module and by the Capablanca module.

Most programs have some method of recognizing when the game has reached the endgame stage and modify the evaluator function, by using different heuristics, to encourage the King to take an active part, to allow Pawns to advance more freely, and to give the program some guidance when it is called upon to give mate. In the Master Chess Trio, this role is played by the Capablanca module.

The structure of a microcomputer chess program, the algorithms it employs, and the heuristics it uses to evaluate positions are all similar to those employed in programs running on large mainframe computers. When microcomputer programs first appeared in 1978, the computer chess world was startled by the defeat of some of the less potent mainframe programs by micros. The explanation for this is not difficult. Computer chess tends to be a sideline in many of the universities that sponsor chess programs. The programmers have other important things to do, and the amount of time they can spend on computer chess is strictly limited, however much they would prefer to be working on it. Their institutions receive little or no income from it. Traditionally, progress on a program is made in short spurts motivated by preparation for some big event, such as the ACM tournament.

Microcomputer programmers, on the other hand, can find their efforts rewarded by royalties from the manufacturers of chess microcomputers. Several such firms employ full-time programming staffs, and even chess masters as consultants. As a result, progress in microcomputer programs has been rapid. The best are playing within 200 Elo points of the top mainframe programs now, and the gap seems likely to narrow further.

3
THE PROGRAMS

This is an appropriate point to introduce the reader to some historic chess programs, and to those which will appear later in the book. The first group to be discussed will be the most notable programs of the past, which are no longer active in tournament competition. These will be reviewed in chronological order.

HISTORIC CHESS PROGRAMS

MAC HACK VI

Author: Richard Greenblatt, MIT

History: Work on MAC HACK VI began in November 1966, and its first tournament appearance was in January 1967. Thereafter, the program played hundreds of games against human competitors, many of them in tournaments, and attained a USCF rating of 1529 by December 1968. Mac Hack VI was awarded honorary memberships in the USCF and in the Massachusetts State Chess Association. It remained active in tournament play through 1972. Mac Hack VI was the first modern program and by far the strongest of its time, but did not compete in any of the ACM tournaments. It was resurrected to play a two-game challenge match against David Levy in 1978, using a specialized chess processor (CHEOPS), but lost the match by losing the first game.

Structure: Mac Hack VI was a Shannon type B program, using a plausible move generator to restrict the number of moves examined at each ply. The program employed the alpha-beta method, and at its tournament speed, searched to a fixed depth of four plies, examining 15 moves at ply 1, 15 at ply 2, 9 at ply 3, and 9 at ply 4. If the ply 4 position were not "quiescent", the program would examine one or two plies deeper using a 7-move fanout. Mac Hack VI used a transposition table to store position evaluations.

Heuristics: The plausible move generator used about fifty different heuristics, although many were only used in special situations. It ordered the moves to maximize the efficiency of the alpha-beta method. Scoring in terminal positions was based on material balance, piece ratio, Pawn structure, center control, and King safety. Moves were scored separately for material and for positional factors. Mac Hack VI also used a small library of opening variations.

Hardware: The program was developed on a DEC PDP-6, with a speed of about 225,000 instructions/second. It later ran on a DEC PDP-10, with a speed of about 400,000 instructions/second.

Programming language: MIDAS

Program size: 16K words

Playing Characteristics: Mac Hack VI was fairly impressive in the opening and middle game, but its endgame play was very weak, partly because its center control heuristic interfered with advancing passed Pawns. After Mac Hack VI "retired" from active tournament play, Greenblatt continued to work on it and by the time the program played David Levy improvements had been made. Its best known achievement was the discovery of a fine 9-ply combination that has eluded several masters (23).

CHESS

Authors: David Slate, Larry Atkin, Keith Gorlen (Northwestern University)

History: Work on CHESS began in the spring of 1968 when undergraduates Larry Atkin and Keith Gorlen began work on a chess program for Northwestern's new CDC 6400 computer. The first version of the program was completed by early summer, and was very weak. Graduate student David Slate saw it and started his own program, which wasn't very good either because it lacked the ability to search beyond the opponent's next move. Slate's program, however, had a relatively good evaluator function which the Atkin-Gorlen program lacked. After both programs proved unsuccessful in competition against humans, around the beginning of 1969, the two teams joined forces and Slate took charge of the project. By October 1969, CHESS 2.0 was ready. The new program combined the basic structure of the Atkin-Gorlen program with an improved version of Slate's evaluator, and proved to be vastly superior to either of its ancestors. In 1970 the program scored 2—3 in the Northwestern University Championship.

By the time of the First U.S. Computer Chess Championship in 1971, the program had been further improved and was now CHESS 3.0, which ran 65% faster than CHESS 2.0. CHESS 3.0 won all three games and first prize. Then Slate and Atkin began work on a complete rewrite, CHESS 4.0. This took a long time to complete. Meanwhile CHESS 3.0 was upgraded to CHESS 3.5, which made another clean sweep in the Second U.S. Computer Chess Championship in 1971. In the 1972 ACM tournament CHESS 4.0 still wasn't ready, and CHESS 3.6 again won all its games.

CHESS 4.0 finally made its debut in the Fourth U.S. Computer Chess Championship in 1973. The program finished first, but conceded a draw. In 1974 CHESS 4.0 finished second in the World Computer Chess Championship, and for the first time, a Northwestern program failed to win the U.S. Championship as CHESS 4.0 lost to RIBBIT. Next year CHESS 4.4 regained the title, and in 1976 CHESS 4.5 again swept through with a perfect score.

The Second World Computer Chess Championship was held in 1977, and this time CHESS 4.6 won the title. In the 1977 ACM tournament, CHESS 4.6 and DUCHESS tied for first. In 1978, CHESS 4.7 lost the ACM Championship to an early version of BELLE, but in 1979 CHESS 4.9 regained the title. In 1980, CHESS 4.9 was retired from competition, as David Slate had teamed up with William Blanchard to write a new program (NUCHESS). CHESS 4.9 still makes occasional appearances under the sponsorship of Control Data, such as in the 1982 U.S. Speed Championship.

Structure: The version described is CHESS 4.5, on which the most detail is available (21). CHESS 4.5 implemented a Shannon type A or full-width search strategy, using the alpha-beta technique. The program searched to a depth of four to six ply in the middlegame, with extensions for capture and checking sequences in positions that were not "quiescent". CHESS 4.5 employed a function similar to a plausible-move generator to order the moves so as to maximize the efficiency of the alpha-beta method, which was further improved by setting a "window" within which position scores were expected to fall. The program also employed a transposition table for storing position evaluations.

Heuristics: The dominant term in the program's evaluation function was material balance. If this fell outside the alpha-beta window, the positional factors did not have to be scored. The positional heuristics were extensive, including penalties for pieces subject to capture, factors for Pawn structure, mobility, square control, piece development, King safety, and the like. CHESS 4.5 employed the "killer" heuristic in its alpha-beta search ordering, storing a list of moves which had been particularly effective in producing refutations, and trying these first, if legal, The program used an opening "book" of several thousand positions.

Hardware: CHESS 4.5 was developed on the CDC 6400 computer used for all previous versions of the CHESS program, with a speed of about 1,600,000 instructions per second, on which the program achieved speeds of from 270 to 600 positions scored/second. CHESS 4.5 later ran on the more powerful CYBER 176, scoring more than 1500 positions/second.

Programming language: COMPASS

Playing characteristics: The CHESS program always displayed a more positional style than most of the other programs it competed against, being particularly careful about Pawn structure. It also had better endgame capabilities than most programs. On the whole, its play was well-balanced, although the program lacked any capacity for formulating strategic plans. Later versions of the program played a strong game of speed Chess (2300 Elo level). The rating of the later versions at tournament speed was in the low Candidate Master (2000—2050) range.

J.Biit

Author: Hans Berliner, Carnegie-Mellon University

History: J.Biit competed in the first U.S. Computer Chess Championship in 1970, finishing third with an even score. It did not compete in later tournaments. The program's influence on the development of computer chess was more significant than its competitive record, because of the papers and articles Berliner published about it.

Structure: J.Biit was a Shannon type B program with considerable emphasis placed on "chess knowledge" and restricting the number of positions to be examined. It searched to a variable depth, terminating in quiescent positions with an absolute limit of fourteen ply, a minimum of two ply in middlegames and four ply in endgames. J.Biit used the alpha-beta technique and incremental updating of board positions.

Heuristics: J.Biit employed very extensive chess heuristics and analyzed each position in its search in great detail. The program scored only about 30—100 positions during its search. J.Biit used an opening library with about 200 selected lines of play.

Hardware: J.Biit was developed on an IBM 360/91 with a speed of about 5,500,000 instructions per second.

Programming language: PL/1, version IV

Program size: 3500 statements; 200K bytes

Playing characteristics: J.Biit was rated as "somewhat weaker" than the 1968 version of Mac Hack VI by Berliner. Against CHESS 3.0, it proved to be the weaker program positionally and tactically, spoiling its Pawn structure early. Against COKO III, J.Biit showed that it could not play a simple King and Pawn ending. Its performance rating in the 1970 ACM tournament was 1197.

COKO

Authors: Dennis Cooper, Ed Kozdrowicki, UC Davis

History: COKO III competed in the first U.S. Computer Chess Championship in 1970, finishing fourth. In the 1971 Championship the program finished fifth, and in 1972 it finished fourth. In 1973 COKO IV finished eighth.

Structure: COKO III used a sophisticated tree-searching technique and incorporated a mate-finding subprogram called MATER. It searched until its time allowance for a move was used up, which meant that frequently only four to eight moves in the initial position were considered (the program did not use an iterative search).

Heuristics: COKO III incorporated a set of subroutines with specific tactical objectives such as pins, forks, checks, and so on. Its emphasis on tactical play was such that positional considerations were overridden if there were tactical possibilities.

Hardware: COKO III ran on many machines, the most powerful of which was the IBM 360/91, with a speed of about 5,500,000 operations/second.

Programming language: FORTRAN IV

Playing Characteristics; COKO III was very tactically oriented and made many positionally bad moves for transient tactical purposes. Its endgame play was very weak. COKO III's performance ratings in the 1970, 1971, and 1972 ACM tournaments were 1287, 1173, and 1319. In 1973, COKO IV achieved a performance rating of 1285.

TECH

Author: James Gillogly, Carnegie-Mellon University

History: TECH was inspired by the second-place finish of Daly's simple program in the 1970 ACM tournament. The philosophy behind TECH was to produce a fast "brute-force" program against which other programs could be benchmarked. TECH finished second in the 1971 U.S. Computer Chess Championship, and third in the 1972 event. In 1973, Alan Baisley of MIT entered an improved version of TECH called TECH II, which featured more positional heuristics and faster move generation. TECH II finished second, and TECH itself finished sixth in a 12-program field. TECH II finished fifth of 13 programs in the first World Computer Chess Championship in 1974. In the U.S. Computer Chess Championship of 1974, TECH II revealed a serious "bug" in its time control mechanism, running out of time after endless computation against RIBBIT, when it could have played a simple mate in two. TECH also played a number of games against human opponents, achieving a USCF rating of 1243.

Structure: TECH was a straightforward Shannon type A program with the addition of the alpha-beta technique. It searched to a full-width depth of five ply, adding capture sequences to indefinite depth. The program's search was very fast, and it would score up to 500,000 positions in the course of deciding on a move. TECH also introduced the feature of predicting the opponent's move and analyzing a reply to it on the opponent's time.

Heuristics: TECH employed a positional analysis routine to evaluate moves in the initial ply only. The principal reason was to maximize the efficiency of the alpha-beta method. Thereafter, only the material balance was used in scoring positions. TECH's evaluator was accordingly very simple; thus the program could search a ply or two deeper than most of its competitors.

Hardware: TECH ran on the DEC PDP-10, with a speed of about 400,000 instructions/second.

Playing Characteristics: TECH's limited heuristics were most effective in the opening (the program had no opening "book" but usually got reasonable positions). TECH's tactical orientation made it a formidable opponent for the weaker programs, but the program's positional ignorance would get it in trouble against a strong opponent. Its endgame play was weak, one reason being a heuristic to centralize the King regardless of other positional factors. In the 1971, 1972, and 1973 ACM tournaments, TECH achieved performance ratings of 1386, 1301, and 1267. In 1973 and 1974, TECH II's performance ratings were 1417 and 1110.

KAISSA

Authors: Mikhail Domskoy, Vladimir Arlazarov, et al., Institute of Control Science, Moscow

History: KAISSA was developed from the ITEP program which had won the 1966—67 match against the Stanford program. In 1971 work began on the new program, and in 1972 it performed creditably in a correspondence match with the readers of *Pravda*. In 1974 KAISSA won the World Computer Chess Championship, and drew an exhibition game against CHESS 4.0. In 1977, KAISSA tied for second place in the second World Computer Chess Championship, losing to DUCHESS. Again KAISSA was not paired with CHESS 4.6, and another exhibition game was arranged, which CHESS 4.6 won. In 1978 the program challenged David Levy, losing one game and the match.

Structure: KAISSA was basically a Shannon type A program, searching 5 to 7 ply full-width, with extensions for captures, checks, and forcing moves. The program employed the alpha-beta technique with a "window". Its search speed was about 200 positions scored/second. The program introduced a feature known as "best move service", storing a table of ten "best moves" used to improve move ordering for the alpha-beta method. Another feature was a "dummy move", i.e. one side does nothing at its turn, used to discover threats.

Heuristics: KAISSA used a complicated evaluation function, about which little is known.

Hardware: KAISSA ran on a British-made ICL 4/70, with a speed of about 900,000 instructions/second.

Playing Characteristics: KAISSA normally played very well for a computer program, but had an unfortunate tendency to make occasional blunders which significantly reduced its playing strength. The program's performance rating for the 1980 World Championship was 1637.

MASTER

Authors: Alex Bell, John Birmingham, Peter Kent, John Waldron; Atlas Computer Laboratory, Oxfordshire, England

History: MASTER evolved from a primitive program named ATLAS which was written in Algol by Bell in 1967. The program was not very good, but was improved by Kent, who added a few heuristics. In 1973 the program was demonstrated at the first Computer Chess Conference at Atlas Laboratories, and Birmingham became interested, rewriting the program into PL/1 and improving the search depth. MASTER competed in the first World Computer Chess Championship in 1974, finishing eighth of thirteen contestants. In this event, the program was seriously handicapped by an inadequate allocation of only two hours of computer time for four games. After this event it was very difficult to get computer time to work on the program, but by March 1975 further improvements had been made, and MASTER was playing at a level of approximately 1750. At the 1975 Computer Chess Conference in

Balliol MASTER played an exhibition game against Dr. Hans Berliner, performing creditably though (of course) losing. In 1977, MASTER competed in the Second World Computer Chess Championship, tying for sixth place out of 16. In the 1980 World Championship, MASTER finished twelfth out of 18 contestants.

Structure: MASTER was a Shannon type A program, employing the alpha-beta method. It employed a technique called "feedover" whereby the most important parts of the game tree are saved for use in speeding up the search on the next move. With this advance MASTER was able to reach a 9-ply search depth.

Heuristics: MASTER somewhat resembled TECH in that the chess-specific knowledge was minimized. The program used positional heuristics and material was the dominant term in its evaluator.

Hardware: MASTER ran on an IBM 360/195, with a speed of about 1,000 positions scored/second. In the 1980 World Championship, it ran on an IBM 3033.

Programming language: PL/1

Playing Characteristics: MASTER was handicapped by always being on "short rations" of machine time. As might be expected from its concentration on tactics, it played best in the early middle game, and was comparable in strength to a 1750 rated human until the endgame was reached, at which point the program's play fell off badly (5). In the 1980 World Championship, the program achieved a performance rating of 1654.

SARGON

Authors: Dan and Kathe Spracklen

History: SARGON was the first microcomputer program to play respectable chess. Work on the program began in September 1977, when Dan Spracklen began writing a chess program in pseudocode (at that point, the Spracklens didn't have a computer). In November, Kathe joined the effort, and in December they took delivery on a Wave Mate Jupiter III microcomputer, with a Z-80 microprocessor as the CPU. Like most programs, SARGON needed lots of debugging, and by the end of January 1978 it would make legal moves, but little more. Programmers will realize the effort needed to finish the program in just one month, in time for the first microcomputer chess tournament at the West Coast Computer Faire early in March 1978. SARGON easily won the tournament with a 5—0 score; a listing of the program at this stage was published in 1978 (28).

The Spracklens did not rest on their laurels, but continued to improve their program, concentrating on efficiency and move selection logic. In December 1978, SARGON II participated in the ninth annual North American Computer Chess Championship, where it made computer and chess history by tying for third place—defeating Tony Marsland's program AWIT (which ran on a powerful mainframe computer) in the final round. By this time SARGON II was considered the unofficial microcomputer World Champion and in February 1979 a special tournament—the Penrod Memorial—

was organized to select a challenger. In the championship match, SARGON II defeated the challenger (CHESS CHALLENGER 10) handily.

The Spracklens continued to work on their program, and in the tenth North American Computer Chess Championship in October 1979, SARGON 3.0 finished seventh, losing to the second and fourth place mainframe programs. In its game with BELLE, SARGON 3.0 could have drawn at the 38th move, but played for a win and lost. SARGON 3.0 defeated microcomputer program MYCHESS, and drew with mainframe program BLITZ 6.9. The program then swept the second annual European Microcomputer Chess Championships in November 1979.

Descendants: The reader is requested to forgive the author for his accounting of the offspring of SARGON; the tale is so long and convoluted, and some of the happenings so strange, that the language of the genealogies of Genesis was simply irresistible....

This is the enumeration of the generations of SARGON, which was blessed with descendants beyond all other programs. SARGON, the victorious, increased mightily in wisdom and strength; and SARGON begat SARGON II.

And SARGON II gained great renown; and waxed mightily, and lo, the fame of SARGON II was known everywhere; and the Chafitz company heard of its renown, and covenanted that SARGON II should serve with them. And it came to pass that SARGON II was brought to run on the 6502 microprocessor of the Modular Game System in 1979; and so it was that SARGON II begat SARGON 2.5.

And SARGON 2.5 begat the Auto-Response Board, first chess computer with a sensory playing surface; and this program did mighty battle in the 1979 Paul Masson tournament, and in other tournaments, and it came to pass that the USCF gave unto the program a rating of 1474.

And lo, there came a famine into the computer chess business, and it came to pass that the Chafitz company departed thence; and SARGON 2.5 was taken in ward by the maker of the Modular Game System, who had brought forth the BORIS chess computer, Applied Concepts; and Applied Concepts called SARGON 2.5's name BORIS 2.5; and lawsuits plagued the land. And the Auto-Response Board went in ward unto its manufacturer, AVE Electronics.

And it came to pass that Applied Concepts wrought changes upon BORIS 2.5, and BORIS 2.5 begat MORPHY, strongest of the descendants of SARGON 2.5; and MORPHY begat no descendants, but was succeeded by STEINITZ; and these were the generations of SARGON 2.5.

Now after begetting SARGON 2.5, SARGON II waxed mightier still, and begat SARGON 3.0; and SARGON 3.0 battled mightily in the 1979 North American Computer Chess Championship, and the ICCA awarded unto the program a rating of 1614.

And behold, after the departure of Chafitz, the Spracklens went unto the greatest of the manufacturers of chess computers, Fidelity Electronics, and covenanted with them; and they took with them SARGON 3.0. And SARGON 3.0 begat the CHAMPION SENSORY CHALLENGER; and that program was exceedingly mighty and strong, and battled victoriously in two great microcomputer tournaments.

And CHAMPION SENSORY CHALLENGER begat the ELITE, and the ELITE was mightier yet; and it came to pass that the ELITE begat SENSORY CHESS CHALLENGER 9.

Now SENSORY CHESS CHALLENGER 9 was not so mighty in battle as the ELITE, for its clock speed was less, but was blessed with more wisdom in its algorithm; and prospered exceedingly, and begat the PRESTIGE.

And in the PRESTIGE was gathered the wisdom of SENSORY CHESS CHALLENGER 9 and the brawn of the ELITE, so that the program gained renown as the strongest micro program of its day; and these were the generations of SARGON 3.0.

And these are all the generations of SARGON unto this day, but it is given to no man to know who their descendants may be, and what mighty deeds may yet be wrought.

Structure: SARGON was a Shannon type A program, using a depth-first search with the alpha-beta technique.

Heuristics: The original SARGON used a static evaluator and an exchange resolver. The original program's heuristics were not very elaborate, but later versions had much more "chess knowledge". SARGON had an opening book of only one move; SARGON 2.5's was three moves deep.

Hardware: SARGON ran on the Wave Mate Jupiter III with a Z-80 CPU. SARGON 2.5 and later versions ran on a custom chess computer, using a 6502 microprocessor at speeds of 2—5 megahertz.

Programming language: assembler

Program size: SARGON, 8K; SARGON II, 16 K.

Playing characteristics: SARGON 2.5 played best in classical positions involving control of the center. It conducted the Black side of the Sicilian defense particularly well, playing an early e5 and obtaining positions characteristic of the Lowenthal and Boleslavsky variations. Open games such as the Ruy Lopez, Giuoco Piano, Scotch Game, and Two Knights' defense suited the program's style better than slow closed openings. Against the King's Indian or the Pirc-Robatsch, SARGON 2.5 played well, building a classical big center.

In the middle game, SARGON 2.5 played aggressively and was dangerous when on the attack in an open position. In slow maneuvering games, the program did not know what to do, but generally marked time rather than spoiling its position. On defense, SARGON 2.5 counterattacked and always accepted gambits. Endgames were not the program's strongest point, though it was much better at endgames than most other microcomputers of its day. It could manage the basic mates, but misplayed King and Pawn endings. Significant weaknesses in the program were inability to detect trapped pieces, and a blind spot regarding the effects of pins and discoveries.

Availability: SARGON II is still available for many different types of personal computers. Its offspring are available in various models of chess computers manufactured by Applied Concepts and Fidelity Electronics.

MYCHESS

Author: David Kittinger

History: In 1978, Kittinger was living in Alaska (he has since moved to Southern California) and was a Category I player under the USCF rating system. This made him one of the top ten players in the state, and he had few opportunities to play opponents in his class, so when Dave acquired a personal computer, a chess program was high on his list of priorities. Originally, MYCHESS was designed as a speed chess opponent. Work on the program began in May 1978. Kittinger was pleasantly surprised to discover that his creation played ten times faster than the original version of SARGON (28), and decided to enter MYCHESS in competition. The program scored 3½—2½ in the 1979 Alaska Open, then went on to tie for fourth place in the 1979 North American Computer Chess Championship, with a performance rating of 1552. MYCHESS then traveled to London, finishing third in the second annual European Microcomputer Chess Championships.

MYCHESS' greatest success was its victory in the 1980 West Coast Computer Faire microcomputer chess tournament, in which the program defeated SARGON 2.5 and finished first with a 3½—½ score. The program then competed in the Third World Computer Chess Championship, tying for twelfth place out of 18, losing to KAISSA and drawing three games with other mainframe programs. In the 1980 North American Computer Chess Championship, MYCHESS finished in a tie for fifth place (with CRAY BLITZ), achieving a performance rating of 1545. By this time MYCHESS had acquired an official USCF rating of 1615, based on more than seventy games.

Kittinger meanwhile had become associated with the Novag company, a European manufacturer of chess computers, and reworked MYCHESS to run in the Novag SAVANT chess computer, with a 6 Mhz Z-80. A number of program changes were made; the most obvious to the user is that SAVANT allows multiple Queens, or for that matter, any other piece, correcting a well-known defect in the original program.

Structure: MYCHESS used an iterative Shannon type A search technique, with alpha-beta pruning. At tournment speed the program searched four to five plies deep, using static evaluations at most terminal positions. Search extensions were initiated for a few very limited criteria, which were relaxed somewhat for selected static terminal positions whose evaluations would otherwise be decisive in selecting the program's "best" move. This was not by any means equivalent to a full "quiescence" search, but helped the program to avoid playing into unfavorable tactical situations which would be misjudged by a static evaluator.

Heuristics: MYCHESS used extensive heuristics for move ordering to increase the efficiency of alpha-beta pruning, employing the killer move heuristic and capture heuristics. The program examined moves in the following order:

1) Best move from the previous ply
2) Winning or even captures
3) Castling
4) En Passant captures
5) Killer moves
6) Two best other moves from ply 1
7) Captures losing material
8) Other moves

Captures in terminal positions were evaluated by a static exchange evaluator routine, which resolved the material balance effects of exchanging sequences on a given square. This routine was very sophisticated, including the effects of pins, double attacks, skewers, and trapped pieces. The attack/defense table involved alone took about one millisecond to reset for each new position, seriously affecting the program's search depth in endgames. MYCHESS used an extensive positional evaluation function, with scoring for pawn formation, endgame evaluations, and a fianchetto-forcing function. The evaluator included no King safety factor.

MYCHESS employed a large opening "book", which treated King Pawn openings in more detail than others because Kittinger wanted his program to play the kind of openings that novice chess players would prefer.

Hardware: MYCHESS ran on the Z-80 microprocessor, under the CP/M operating system, at speeds of 1.77 (TRS-80) to 4.0 Mhz.

Programming language: assembler

Program Size: 28K

Playing Characteristics: MYCHESS shared an interesting characteristic with many good human players: it used a lot of time early in the game and had a mild tendency to get into "time trouble" at faster tournament speeds, such as 40 moves in 90 minutes. MYCHESS had a more positional style than SARGON 2.5, and a much larger opening "book". In some ways it was a very "human" opponent (for a computer program), and tended to be more interesting to play than other micro programs. Like all programs, MYCHESS was not at its best in the endgame, but seemed to be about equal to SARGON 2.5 there. Due to its lack of a quiescence search, MYCHESS occasionally made serious tactical errors. Because the program's evaluator did not consider King safety, MYCHESS would at times "walk into" an opponent's attack.

Availability: MYCHESS is still available for most personal computers that support the CP/M operating system.

1982 PROGRAMS

The programs which are currently active are, of course, not always as well documented as those which are now history. This is partly due to the fact that they are still being worked on—so that information would be likely to become obsolete as soon as it was given out—and partly due to the pressures of competition.

Nevertheless, a good deal of information has been gathered on most of the programs, which is presented below. These programs are listed in alphabetical order.

ADVANCE 2.4

Authors: Mike Johnson, Dave Wilson

History: Johnson and Wilson first met in 1973, when they both worked for the British Post Office, but until 1980 they had developed their own chess programs independently. Work on ADVANCE 1.0 began in January 1980, when the two decided to join forces to produce a new program for the 1980 World Computer Chess Championship. Johnson had already designed a novel search algorithm, which could not be implemented efficiently on standard hardware; Wilson had designed special-purpose hardware but was seeking a better algorithm.

The first version of the hardware was ready by August 1980, and the initial version of the program was brought up in September 1980. The program played in the First World Microcomputer Chess Championship in London that month, scoring 3—2 to finish third and win the prize for best amateur entry. After some modifications, ADVANCE 1.0 then played in the Third World Computer Chess Championship in Linz, tying for twelfth place with a score of 1.5—2.5.

In January 1981, work on ADVANCE 2.0 began. Wilson re-engineered the hardware to reduce its size and to enable it to run more than twice as fast; Johnson retailored the program to the new hardware, making additional improvements in the search and evaluation routines. In September 1981, ADVANCE 2.0 played in the second European Microcomputer Chess Championship in London, finishing second with a score of 4—1. The program was hampered by having to run at half-speed due to a puzzling hardware problem which defied all efforts at discovery for a further ten months.

In 1982, the authors worked on further program improvements, test facilities, and finding the hardware "bug". Versions ADVANCE 2.1 and ADVANCE 2.3 entered several tournaments for human players, with mediocre results due in part to the "bug", although the experience helped to significantly improve the evaluator function. In July the "bug" was found—a missing resistor! Then the program was further modified to think on the opponent's time and became ADVANCE 2.4.

This version won first prize in the third European Microcomputer Chess Championship in London, scoring 6—1 (two draws, no losses). After eliminating a minor "bug" in the King-safety term of the evaluator, the program played in the 1982 North American Computer Chess Championship in Dallas, tying for fifth with 2.5—1.5, and playing a very fine game against a German program.

Structure: ADVANCE 2.4 uses an iterative staged search strategy employing the alpha-beta technique. Each iteration always includes several plies of full-width search, followed by several plies of "3-ply" search extensions, followed by four plies of capture search extension. The "3-ply" search extension considers only moves that could have a material effect within 3 ply; a special 3-ply evaluator selects the moves that meet this criterion (2/3 of the moves) and orders them, pruning off those whose score is less than the full-width evaluator's optimum score at the time. The capture search includes moves that evade checks, which can extend it a ply. At each point in the search, moves are ordered using simple heuristics to speed the alpha-beta function. The latter uses a "window" of plus and minus half a pawn.

ADVANCE 2.4 typically searches 2—3 full width plies, with 5 plies of "3-ply" extension and 4 plies of capture extension. As the game approaches an ending, the program achieves a 4 ply full-width search with the same extensions.

Heuristics: ADVANCE 2.4 uses an evaluator function whose dominant term is material balance; if this falls outside the "window", the positional terms are not scored, so the maximum positional value is plus or minus half a Pawn.

The positional part of the evaluator includes many terms: trade-down bonuses, penalties for pieces that are pinned or "en prise," and factors for Pawn structure, piece position, mobility, King tropism, development, bad Bishops, Rooks cooperating, and King safety. There are also a few heuristics specially designed for endgames. Move ordering heuristics include: principal variation from the last iteration; killer moves; capture moves; and the "3-ply" algorithm.

The program uses an opening "book" of about 5,000 positions.

Hardware: ADVANCE 2.4 runs on special-purpose hardware. This comprises a high-speed sequencer with up to 4,096 microcoded instructions (each 96 bits in length), which controls a 16 bit "bit—slice" microprocessor of the AMD 2900 family, with up to 64K bytes of RAM; and a 64-bit TTL processor handling up to 1024 64-bit data maps ("bit boards") organized 8 bits × 8 bits.

The 16-bit and 64-bit processors are synchronized, and execute instructions concurrently. The 16-bit processor handles the arithmetic and logical instructions, and calculates addresses for the 64-bit processor to use in the same cycle. The 64-bit processor handles arithmetic and logical operations on the bit boards, and can also perform attack propagation functions in the 8 directions corresponding to chess moves, as well as locating and counting bits set in a bit board.

250 of the microcode instructions are used to emulate a 6502 microprocessor, so that parts of the program that are not time-critical can be written in 6502 assembler rather than (laboriously) being microcoded. The processor handles about 2.5 million instructions/second when running the chess program, scoring about 1500 positions/second.

Programming language: Special-purpose microcode for the tree search, move generation, evaluation function, and 6502 emulator. 6502 assembler for user interface, search iteration control, time control, and opening book.

Program size: 2K of 96-bit microcoded instructions; 16K of 6502 assembler code. Data storage: 1K of 64-bit data maps; 16K bytes of RAM.

Playing characteristics: ADVANCE 2.4 plays with a positional style during the opening and middle game, often getting advantages before entering the endgame. The program tends to go astray in the endgame, due to inadequate endgame heuristics.

Although ADVANCE 2.4 uses a selective search, it rarely makes tactical blunders, even against full-width search programs. The extra search depth used by the "3-ply" technique allows the program to find some winning tactical combinations that would be missed by a comparable full-width search.

ADVANCE 2.4's performance rating in the 1982 ACM tournament was 1649.

BELLE

Authors: Joe Condon, Ken Thompson (Bell Telephone Laboratories)

History: BELLE was originally a program written for the PDP 11/45 minicomputer by Ken Thompson, the author of the UNIX operating system. This program competed in the 1973 and 1974 ACM tournaments, finishing fourth in 1974, and played 13 USCF-rated games against opponents with an average rating of 1550, scoring 5.5—7.5 for a provisional USCF rating of 1464.

The first hardware version contained only 25 "chips", performing some of the program functions, with the program itself running on a PDP 11/70 minicomputer, and was basically an experiment. In the 1977 Computer World Championship in Toronto, this scored 2.5—1.5, providing valuable experience and an incentive to build a more powerful version.

The next hardware version was quite a bit larger—325 "chips"—and was again controlled by a PDP 11/70. This machine finished first in the 1978 ACM tournament, and second in the 1979 event. This combination of hardware and software turned out to be at least equal to the largest mainframe computers. The second hardware version of BELLE played 29 USCF-rated games against opponents with an average rating of 1717, scoring 19—10 for a USCF rating of 1884.

The current hardware version of BELLE was constructed in the summer of 1980, and contains about 1700 "chips". The structure is the same as the 1978 version, but the tree-search function is now done by the special chess processor. The machine is controlled by a LSI 11/23 running UNIX. This version won the third World Computer Chess Championship in 1980 with a 4.5—0.5 score, and then won the 1980, 1981, and 1982 ACM tournaments, allowing a total of three draws in the three events. The current version of BELLE has (as of March 1983) played a total of 80 USCF-rated games against opponents with an average rating of 2038, scoring 47—33 for a USCF rating of 2119.

Structure: BELLE is a "brute force" Shannon-A type program, which uses a modification of the alpha-beta technique and relies extensively on transposition tables in its search. The program usually achieves search depths of 8 ply in the middle game, and from 10 to 30 ply in the endgame (depending on material remaining and the position). The search is extended for captures and checking sequences.

Heuristics: BELLE includes heuristics for detecting and scoring passed Pawns, isolated Pawns, backward Pawns, and doubled Pawns. The program's evaluation for pieces is quite a bit different from the usual chess program heuristics—BELLE uses its special purpose hardware to detect the influence that a piece on any one square has on all the other squares (ray evaluation). This takes eight slow evaluator cycles. The result is a score that combines mobility, square control, King tropism, and all the other piece scoring heuristics in the result of one function.

BELLE uses the world's largest opening "book"—375,000 positions.

Hardware: LSI 11/23 combined with special chess processor. BELLE scores about 110,000 positions/second.

Programming language: Chess program in the LSI-11/23: C. Chess processor: special-purpose microcode.

Program size: 90 Kbytes; 5 Kbytes data; 128 Kbytes transposition table.

Playing characteristics: BELLE is tactically oriented, and in a purely tactical sense performs probably at a human Grandmaster level (or at least close to it). The program is very strong at speed Chess, which tends to be tactical, achieving a combined performance rating of 2457 for 18 games in the 1982 U.S. Open Speed Championship, and finishing in a tie for second place. BELLE's weakest point (like most programs) is positional play. The program is unable to plan, and tends to make antipositional moves that severely damage its position on occasion. Nevertheless, it has a tendency to make moves that are very active, even if sometimes inferior. The great depth of search that BELLE achieves helps it to find sequences of active moves. A game against BELLE is a demanding experience for a human player. Although superior positional skill should and often does defeat the program, the slightest inattention to tactics can be disastrous. The program tends to play endgames rather well, at least by computer standards, because its search expands to sometimes incredible depth as pieces disappear. BELLE's USCF rating in December 1982 was 2119; its overall play is slightly below human Master strength (2200 Elo).

CHATURANGA 2.0

Author: John Poduska

History: Work on CHATURANGA began in the fall of 1980. The program was running by mid-winter and participated in the 1981 North American Computer Chess Championship, scoring 1—3. Its victory over SCHACH 2.5 was by forfeit, after the German program's computer "crashed" several times and it ran out of time.

The program was then completely rewritten during the winter of 1981-82, and again participated in the 1982 North American Computer Chess Championship. In this event, the program and its talented but perhaps inexperienced author suffered through just about every kind of problem imaginable, losing all four games.

Structure: Like most programs, CHATURANGA 2.0 uses a Shannon type A search strategy, employing the alpha-beta method and using iterative search deepening and an alpha-beta "window." The program reaches depths of 3 to 5 ply during the middlegame, and does not have "quiescence" extensions, but does incorporate a static exchange resolver. Moves are ordered by looking at captures and "killer moves" first. CHATURANGA 2.0 employs a transposition table to store position scores, and uses an opening "book" of 2500 moves.

Heuristics: The major term in the program's evaluator is material balance. If this falls outside the "window," the positional evaluator is not called. This considers Pawn structure, mobility, and development among other heuristics.

Hardware: CHATURANGA 2.0 runs on an Apollo computer, which utilizes a 68000 microprocessor. A performance enhancement board is utilized.

Programming language: FORTRAN, 68000 assembler, and microcode for the performance enhancement board.

Program size: 20K; 60 K data.

Playing Characteritics: To quote Poduska, "BAD—I'm hoping this will change." The program clearly has potential far beyond its present level of play, but appears to need a lot of "debugging" before it will achieve it.

CRAY BLITZ

Authors: Robert Hyatt, Albert Gower, Harry Nelson.

History: The BLITZ program first competed in the ACM tournament in 1976, when BLITZ IV tied for second place and finished fourth on tiebreak. In 1977, BLITZ V tied for fourth place with a performance rating of 1535; in 1978, BLITZ 6.5 tied for third, with a performance rating of 1724. In 1979, BLITZ 6.9 finished in a tie for seventh with a performance rating of 1516. At this point the program had a USCF rating of 1690 and was running on a Xerox Sigma 9 computer. Next year BLITZ moved to the world's most powerful computer and became CRAY BLITZ, finishing fifth with a performance rating of 1791, but winning the ACM Speed Championship with a perfect score. In 1981, CRAY BLITZ finished first in the Mississippi State Championship Tournament, and tied for second place in the ACM tournament, losing to BELLE, with a performance rating of 2174. In 1982, CRAY BLITZ achieved a performance rating of 2108 in the U.S. Open Speed Championship, and finished in a tie for first place (second on tiebreak) with BELLE in the North American Computer Chess Championship, with a performance rating of 2053.

Structure: CRAY BLITZ is a Shannon type A program, using the normal methods of accelerating its search—the alpha-beta technique, move-ordering heuristics, iterative search deepening, and an alpha-beta window. CRAY BLITZ uses a huge transposition table, which allows it to search to 7 ply deep in the middlegame, and as far as 33 ply in some endgame positions. Search extensions are generated in many situations. The program uses an opening "book" of 30,000 positions.

Heuristics: CRAY BLITZ has a very detailed evaluation function, with several thousand statements. This includes the ability to evaluate certain endgame positions, such as whether a King is "in the square" of a passed Pawn.

Hardware: CRAY BLITZ runs on a CRAY-1 supercomputer, achieving as many as 20,000 positions scored/second.

Programming language: FORTRAN IV

Program size: 200K; 12 Megabytes(!) data

Playing Characteristics: CRAY BLITZ is very strong, and perhaps better than BELLE against human opponents. In December 1982, its USCF rating of 2123 was the highest of any computer program. The program suffered from the usual "computer" faults of being unable to plan and lacking positional judgment. Compared to BELLE, CRAY BLITZ is better positionally and not as strong tactically. CRAY BLITZ has a score of ½—2½ against BELLE in its ACM games.

NUCHESS

Authors: David Slate, William Blanchard (Northwestern University)

History: NUCHESS is the successor to CHESS 4.0 (and its later marks). Work on the program began in 1977, prior to the Levy Challenge Match. David Slate concluded that the CHESS program had reached its limits, and wanted to try a "brute force" tree-searching program with more chess knowledge, principally as the result of an improved evaluator function.

In order to achieve this, it was essential to use a high-level language rather than assembly language. After evaluating the available compilers for the Cyber 176, Slate selected FORTRAN—not because it was an ideal language for a chess program (it has serious defects, principally in typing variables and program structure), but because there was nothing better—the implementations of languages with theoretical advantages were too inefficient. Despite its antiquity and archaic structure, FORTRAN does offer highly efficient compilers. This is critical for a speed-intensive application such as chess programming.

Slate wanted to use data types representing chess concepts such as squares, bit boards, files, ranks, and moves; and chess operations such as adding squares to bit boards, Knight moves, and the like. This would allow separation of the chess content of the program from the mechanical problems of database management and the idiosyncrasies of a particular machine and compiler. Implicit data types for squares, bit boards, moves, and the like were accordingly defined and mapped as integers. Chess operations were defined as arithmetic function statements.

Some clever coding tricks, such as defining a bit board as a complex (2 word) variable, and the use of an optimizing compiler allow NUCHESS to run about half as fast as an assembly language program.

NUCHESS made its debut in the 1980 Computer World Championship in Linz, Austria, tying for sixth place with 2—2. The program was suffering from the usual ailments which afflict a brand-new program, and so was not entered in the 1980 ACM tournament. In 1981, NUCHESS competed in the 12th North American Computer Chess Championship tournament, drawing its game with BELLE and finishing with a 3—1 score, for second place. In 1982 the program competed in the Fredkin Incentive Match (with a 2—2 score, best of the computer programs) and in the 13th North American Computer Chess Championship tournament, tying for first place with BELLE with a 3—1 score, and being placed third on tiebreak.

Structure: Similar to CHESS 4.5, but somewhat simpler and without some of the refinements. NUCHESS was conceived as a test vehicle for special chess-related heuristics which partly take the place of full-width tree searching. The program does a full-width search (about 5-6 ply in middlegames) and then adds extensions to the terminal positions for the special situations defined in its heuristics.

Heuristics: In addition to the standard heuristics of the type used in CHESS 4.5, NUCHESS employs about six special heuristics for such obviously key middlegame situations as "Queen touching" checks—a Queen next to the enemy King, supported and not liable to capture—and also for the endgame of King, Pawn and other pieces vs. King and Pawn (which frequently occurs as a possibility in analyzing endings). The object of these heuristics is to enable the program to evaluate such situations as favorable, and if necessary to sacrifice material at the right time to achieve them. Each such heuristic added about one page of code to the program.

Hardware: NUCHESS runs on the Control Data Cyber 176 computer. The program scores about 1800 positions/second.

Program size: 30,000 lines of FORTRAN.

Playing Characteristics: The program performs at about the same level as CHESS 4.9—in December 1982, its USCF rating was 2052. Its style is more positional than most other programs. Its greatest weakness is probably in the opening book.

OSTRICH

Author: Monroe Newborn (with assistance in the past from George Arnold and Ilan Vardi)

History: Work on OSTRICH began in the summer of 1971 at Columbia University, when George Arnold and Monroe Newborn teamed together. The program was written in the style of Richard Greenblatt's MAC HACK VI Although a novice chess player, Arnold was an accomplished programmer who eventually became valedictorian of his class. Newborn was at one time a Category I player.

In 1972, OSTRICH made its first tournament appearance and finished second in the Third U.S. Computer Chess Championship in Boston. The following year it finished fourth, reflecting improvements made to other programs.

In 1974, OSTRICH nearly upset KAISSA in the first World Championship for Computers, held in Stockholm, Sweden. At one point the program had an easy forced mate in six moves, which unfortunately involved a sacrifice which the program was unable to make.

Since 1972, OSTRICH has participated in every ACM tournament except the 1976 event, and has always scored at least 1½ points.

Structure: OSTRICH is a unique program, which originally began with a selective-search structure, and has evolved into a Shannon type A program which in 1982 ran in parallel on eight NOVA 4 minicomputers. OSTRICH carries out an iterative alpha-beta search to the maximum depth that time allows; quiescence searching is also performed to a depth of 2-3 ply beyond the full-width search. OSTRICH does not use transposition tables.

OSTRICH's parallel-processing structure allows it to run on any number of computers linked together, which makes the program potentially very strong if enough machines could be assembled. In 1981, an earler version running on five machines searched 2.4 times as fast as a single-machine implementation; the search rate for the eight machine version is 4.6 times that of the single-machine version, and efforts are being made to bring this number closer to eight.

Heuristics: OSTRICH uses move-ordering heuristics to improve its alpha-beta search, and stores the principal variation (up to a maximum depth of 16 plies) from each search iteration. This then becomes the first branch of the game tree to be examined in the next iteration. OSTRICH uses a small opening "book" of about 1000 lines of play. This is loaded into the master computer to play the opening, and after the program determines that it is "out of book," the area of memory used is made available to the search function to store data.

Hardware: OSTRICH runs on a network of NOVA 4 minicomputers. Each NOVA 4 executes about 1,000,000 instructions/second, and the eight-machine network searches at a rate of approximately 800 positions/second.

Programming Language: Assembler

Program Size: 10 K; 12K per machine data

Playing Characteristics: OSTRICH achieved a performance rating of 1595 in the 1982 North American Computer Chess Championship, and is assessed by its author as playing at "somewhere around 1600 level." The program is better tactically than positionally, and tends to be particularly weak at Pawn play.

PION

Authors: Jan Derksen, John Huisman, Jaap van den Herik, Gerlach van Beinum, Harry Nefkens, Sito Dekker, Roger Hünen (Delft University of Technology)

History: The first version of PION was the result of an undergraduate project completed in December 1980 by Derksen, Huisman, and another student. It used a Shannon-A strategy with simple heuristics and could solve mate-in-two problems in a few minutes. Work on the program continued, and in the 1981 Dutch Championship PION finished third with a 6—9 score.

Meanwhile, research in the area of endgame programs and opening "book" construction was also underway, and PION was extended to incorporate the results of this research. The program played a number of test games against grandmasters, and was very successful in its test games against other Dutch programs.

In the summer of 1982, it was decided to replace the chess module which had undergone an excessive number of modifications, but initially the new version has been less successful, scoring 6—9 in the second Dutch Championship for fifth place, and 1—4 in the 1982 North American Computer Chess Championship for a performance rating of 1126. Research continues on a new version which will have more positional and tactical knowledge.

Structure: PION is a "Shannon-A" program, using the alpha-beta technique and iterative searching with capture and check extensions. In middlegame positions the program searches to a depth of four to six ply, with extensions to eight or ten ply. PION does not generate all possible moves at each position in its search, but rather incrementally updates its data base, which is much faster than generating all the moves each time.

Heuristics: PION has a positional analyzer that emphasizes strong and weak square recognition, particularly with respect to Pawn formations. This involves scoring a large number of positional heuristics. Positional patterns are stored and examined for several subsequent moves. The program uses an opening "book" of about 3500 positions.

Hardware: PION runs on a PDP 11/70, which executes about 500,000 instructions/second. The program's search rate is about 200 to 400 positions/second.

Programming language: Originally Pascal; now C.

Program size: 1982 version — 30 to 50 K bytes per module (middlegame and several endgame modules), 5 K data per module.

Playing Characteristics: PION has a positional style, and when the position is such that its pattern recognition heuristics are relevant, is capable of making some very good moves. The program is not so strong tactically. Its authors consider it an equal opponent for a Category II player; in the 1982 ACM tournament PION's performance rating was a disappointing 1126.

SAVANT X

Author: David Kittinger

History: SAVANT X was a "stock" SAVANT ROYALE, marketed by Novag. There is no provison for commercial programs in the ACM tournaments, so all such are classified as experimental.

SAVANT ROYALE is an embodiment of the modified MYCHESS program in a dedicated chess microcomputer. In 1981, the earlier SAVANT finished in a tie for seventh place (out of 16) in the twelfth North American Computer Chess Championship, with an ICCA performance rating of 1497. In the thirteenth North American Computer Chess Championship in 1982, SAVANT X scored 2—2, for an ICCA performance rating of 1579.

It should be noted that, at least for microcomputers, ICCA ratings tend to be more conservative than USCF ratings.

Structure: Similar to MYCHESS.

Heuristics: Similar to MYCHESS.

Hardware: Dedicated Chess microcomputer using a 7.5 Mhz Z-80 microprocessor.

Programming language: assembler

Program size: 32K (program); 4K (data)

Playing characteristics: Similar to MYCHESS, but somewhat stronger due to the faster hardware. A few improvements to the original MYCHESS program were added, the most obvious being that multiple Queens were allowed.

SCHACH

Author: Matthias Engelbach (Bundeswehrhochschule, Neubiburg)

History: Engelbach began working on a chess program shortly after beginning his studies at the Bundeswehrhochschule, in the spring of 1978, for the school's Burroughs B7700 computer. The first version used a selective search and was not particularly successful. Beginning in 1979, Engelbach wrote a completely new program using a "brute-force" or Shannon-A strategy, SCHACH 2.0. This was much more successful and convinced Engelbach that the full-width search was the right approach.

Successive improvements to SCHACH 2.0 proved successful in competition; version 2.2 placed third in the second European Computer Chess Championship in London in 1979; version 2.3, now running on the faster Burroughs B7800, surprisingly finished sixth in the third World Computer Chess Championship in Linz in 1980; in 1981 SCHACH 2.5 finished 11th, and in 1982 SCHACH 2.6 finished ninth, in the North

American Computer Chess Championship.

Structure: SCHACH is a classical Shannon-A program using the alpha-beta method to speed its tree search, and extensions for checks and captures.

Heuristics: SCHACH uses move-ordering heuristics to improve the effectiveness of its alpha-beta search, including "killer" moves. Its positional heuristics consider Pawn structure, and include special instructions for playing endgames, and piece position scoring factors that are different for openings, middlegames, and endgames. The program's opening "book" contains about 8000 positions.

Hardware: Burroughs B7800. The program scores between 700 and 1300 positions/second, which allows searching to a depth of 6 to 8 ply in the middlegame, and as much as 20 ply in the endgame.

Programming language: Algol

Program Size: 60K; 1.8 Megabytes data

Playing Characteristics: SCHACH 2.6 achieved a performance rating of 1356 in the 1982 ACM tournament. Its play in the ACM tournaments has been handicapped by computer problems. Its play is balanced, and particularly strong in the endgame.

SFINKS X

Author: William Fink

History: SFINKS 1.0 made its original appearance at the First North American Microcomputer Chess Championship in 1980. SFINKS scored 1½—2½, winning the prize for best noncommercial program. Later in 1980, SFINKS was expanded to play two variations on the game of chess, Pre-Chess and Transcendental Chess. The program was then marketed as SFINKS 1.81, for the TRS-80 microcomputer, early in 1981.

SFINKS 2.0 participated in the 1981 microcomputer tournament held in Paris. The program scored 4 — 3, tying for sixth place out of 18 entries, and again winning the prize for the best non-commercial program. Some modifications were then made to the program (to remove "bugs" and to add improvements), and SFINKS 3.0 was marketed for the TRS-80 in January 1982.

In the spring and summer of 1982, SFINKS X was prepared for the ACM tournament. This experimental version consisted of SFINKS 3.0 with a number of modifications. The program scored 1½—2½, for an ICCA performance rating of 1364. As noted above, the ICCA ratings tend to be lower than USCF ratings.

Structure: SFINKS X is a Shannon type A program, with an iterative full-width search using the alpha-beta method. The program uses a "window", transposition tables, and forward "pruning" to enhance its search speed. The program evaluates up to 200 positions per second on the hardware used in the 1982 ACM tournament.

Heuristics: Material balance dominates the evaluator function. "Killer" moves are used to enhance the alpha-beta method efficiency. In positional scoring, the heuristics depend on the phase of the game. Pawn structure, King safety, and mobility are the dominant components.

Hardware: TRS-80 Model III microcomputer (Z-80 microprocessor), specially modified for higher clock speed.

Programming language: assembler

Program size: 30K; 14K data

Playing Characteristics: SFINKS X does not have a USCF rating. The program's author claims that the latest version of the program plays "close to the 1800 level" at tournament speed. Although SFINKS X is an impressive program, more tournament results are required before this claim can be accepted. SFINKS' author notes that the program's play is stronger positionally than tactically, but that it makes sharp moves frequently, and that the program's endgame play, while good for a computer program, is weak by human standards. SFINKS X has an interesting style, often playing quite well positionally for a considerable part of the game. The program, however, is also capable of very serious positional errors at times. Tactically, it is not equal to other microcomputer programs running on specialized hardware.

Availability: Versions of SFINKS are available for the TRS-80 microcomputer, Model I or Model III.

SUMMARY DATA ON 1982 PROGRAMS

For those programs for which detailed information could not be obtained, the available facts are presented in summary form:

BEBE

Author: Tony Scherzer
Hardware: Dedicated Chess Engine
Language: Assembler
Program Size: 12K; 16K data
Opening Book: 400 moves
Positions scored/second: 20,000
USCF Rating 12/82: 1869

CHAOS

Authors: Mike Alexander, Fred Swartz, Jack O'Keefe, Mark Hersey
Structure: Selective-search
Hardware: Amdahl 470 v/8
Language: FORTRAN
Program Size: 700 K; 3 Megabytes data
Opening Book: 10,000 positions
Positions scored/second: 850
USCF Rating 12/82: 1714

DUCHESS

Authors: Tom Truscott, Bruce Wright, Eric Jensen
Hardware: IBM 370
Language: Assembler
Program size: 150 K; 1.5 Megabytes data
Opening Book: 3000 positions
Positions scored/second: 2500
USCF Rating 12/82: 1855

PRESTIGE X

Authors: Dan and Kathe Spracklen
Structure: Shannon type A
Hardware: Dedicated autoresponse machine
Language: Assembler
Program Size: 20K; 8K data
Opening Book: 16,000 positions
Positions scored/second: 1000
USCF rating 12/82: 1870

PHILIDOR

Authors: David Levy, Kevin O'Connell et al.
Hardware: Osborne-1 portable microcomputer
Language: Assembler
Program size: 32K; 16K data
Opening Book: 4,000 moves
Positions scored/second: 400

SENSORY CHESS CHALLENGER

Authors: Dan and Kathe Spracklen
Structure: Shannon type A
Hardware: Dedicated autoresponse machine
Language: Assembler
USCF Rating 12/82: 1765

4
HOW COMPUTERS PLAY CHESS

It is, regrettably, impossible to discuss the methods used in chess programs intelligently without going into a certain amount of technical detail. This has been kept to a practical minimum, but this chapter is still likely to be somewhat difficult for the non-technical reader, who is encouraged to stick with it and get as many insights as possible. It is hard to understand computer chess at all without some knowledge of the peculiar difficulties that chess programmers face.

In this chapter, the problem of representing a chess position in a way that a computer program can deal with will be discussed. Next, there will be a section on the techniques involved in finding legal moves, and then one on how a chess program evaluates positions. The concept of the "game tree" will be introduced next, and finally the methods used by programs to "search" the game tree, to find the move that the program considers to be best.

WHERE ARE THE PIECES?

Once, after an exhibition of computer chess, a couple of programmers decided to tease a chess master who had been pontificating about the games and making sarcastic comments about the play of the machines. They asked whether he would give his opinion of a certain position.

"Certainly—what is the position you would like me to analyze?" answered the master.

"We won't show it to you," replied the programmers, "but you can ask any question you like—as long as the answer is yes or no." The master assumed they were trying to test his memory and, being an expert blindfold player, accepted the challenge. "Is there a piece on a1?" he asked. "Yes." "Is it a Rook?" "No." And so on.

Eventually the master discovered that to visualize the position in his mind, he would have to ask an average of four questions for each piece on the board — three to discover the type of piece, and one to ascertain color — plus one question for each square on the board ("Is there a piece on this square?"). If no pieces have been captured, this would involve 192 questions to define the position. Even the master's powerful memory was not equal to this, and he became confused, losing track of the position.

"This is ridiculous!" exclaimed the master, and he strode away bewildered, angry—and just possibly, a little wiser. He had been subjected to some of the same tasks that a computer must perform to "visualize" a chess position.

THE BOARD

Once the computer finds out where the pieces are, it has to store the position in its memory. The representation of a chess board that the computer uses is a section of its memory in which an array (or arrays) of numbers will be stored. In microcomputer programs, especially in commercially available machines, memory is at a premium, and the board is represented by a simple table. Dan and Kathe Spracklen's original version of SARGON represented the board thus:

```
FF FF FF FF FF FF FF FF FF FF FF FF
FF FF FF FF FF FF FF FF FF FF FF FF
FF FF 04 02 03 05 06 03 02 04 FF FF
FF FF 01 01 01 01 01 01 01 01 FF FF
FF FF 00 00 00 00 00 00 00 00 FF FF
FF FF 00 00 00 00 00 00 00 00 FF FF
FF FF 00 00 00 00 00 00 00 00 FF FF
FF FF 00 00 00 00 00 00 00 00 FF FF
FF FF 81 81 81 81 81 81 81 81 FF FF
FF FF 84 82 83 85 86 83 82 84 FF FF
FF FF FF FF FF FF FF FF FF FF FF FF
FF FF FF FF FF FF FF FF FF FF FF FF
```

The array of memory addresses, of course, is not organized like this inside the computer.
To the programmer, it is simply a consecutive string of addresses. It is easier to visualize how all this relates to a chessboard if the string is broken up into the groups that represent individual ranks on the board, as above.

Each pair of characters represents a byte (eight bits or binary digits), the contents of one address in the computer's memory. The characters are hexadecimal numbers (0—9 as in the decimal system, plus A through F for 10 to 15 decimal) — a type of number much used in assembly language programs.

The piece types — Pawn, Knight, Bishop, Rook, Queen, King — are represented by the second number on each square, one through six. 00 represents an empty square. White pieces have the piece type prefixed by 0; Black pieces, by 8. In the initial position, the White pieces are at the "top" of the "board"—just the reverse of a printed diagram. This is what a chessboard would look like, viewed from below the board, if it were transparent. The addresses filled with "FF" define the edges of the "board" for the program. This array uses 144 bytes of memory.

Another pioneering microcomputer program, Dave Kittinger's MYCHESS, used a different technique:

(WR)	(WN)	(WB)	(WQ)	(WK)	(WB)	(WN)	(WR)
0B	16	21	2B	36	41	4B	56
(WP)	(WP)	(WP)	(WP)	(WP)	(WP)	(WP)	(WP)
0C	17	22	2C	37	42	4C	57
(BP)	(BP)	(BP)	(BP)	(BP)	(BP)	(BP)	(BP)
12	16	27	32	3C	47	52	5C
(BR)	(BN)	(BB)	(BQ)	(BK)	(BB)	(BN)	(BR)
13	1D	28	33	3D	48	53	5D

In this table, each memory address represents a specific piece (indicated by the characters in parentheses), and the value represents the square on the chessboard occupied by that piece, as a hexadecimal number. The same table converted to decimal numbers looks like this:

11	21	31	41	51	61	71	81
12	22	32	42	52	62	72	82
17	27	37	47	57	67	77	87
18	28	38	48	58	68	78	88

By substituting the corresponding letter of the alphabet for the first digit of each of these numbers, a square address in algebraic notation is obtained. Again, note that the "board" is reversed from the conventional "diagram" position.

Kittinger's ingenious approach demands only 32 bytes of memory to store the chessboard, a fourfold improvement over the SARGON board. It is difficult to imagine how a position can be stored in less memory on an 8-bit word-length machine. It has an amusing drawback: the original MYCHESS would not allow a Pawn to be promoted to a piece that had not already been captured! Dave has since modified his program to allow for more than one Queen at a time (or any other legal piece promotion). MYCHESS handles the problem of off-board moves in its move generator, rather than by storing "illegal" FF squares.

"Mainframe" programs running on large computers usually represent positions quite a bit differently. They have relatively huge amounts of memory available, and are aiming at speed of execution rather than compact programs. Monroe Newborn's OSTRICH program stores a position in the form of two lists, a Board Position List of 64 words and a Piece Location List of 64 words. This duplication is trivial in terms of memory consumed, and offers efficiencies in accessing other tables. OSTRICH runs on the Data General Supernova, a minicomputer with a 16 bit word length, and is thus unable to take advantage of "bit boards", which are most useful when implemented on a machine with a 64-bit word length.

A program such as CHESS 4.5 (and, presumably, its successor NUCHESS) represents the chessboard as a list of 12 64-bit words, each of which represents a subset of the board ("bit board") as follows:

White Rooks	White Knights	White Bishops	White Queens
1 0 0 0 0 0 0 1	0 1 0 0 0 0 1 0	0 0 1 0 0 1 0 0	0 0 0 1 0 0 0 0
0 0 0 0 0 0 0 0	0 0 0 0 0 0 0 0	0 0 0 0 0 0 0 0	0 0 0 0 0 0 0 0
0 0 0 0 0 0 0 0	0 0 0 0 0 0 0 0	0 0 0 0 0 0 0 0	0 0 0 0 0 0 0 0
0 0 0 0 0 0 0 0	0 0 0 0 0 0 0 0	0 0 0 0 0 0 0 0	0 0 0 0 0 0 0 0
0 0 0 0 0 0 0 0	0 0 0 0 0 0 0 0	0 0 0 0 0 0 0 0	0 0 0 0 0 0 0 0
0 0 0 0 0 0 0 0	0 0 0 0 0 0 0 0	0 0 0 0 0 0 0 0	0 0 0 0 0 0 0 0
0 0 0 0 0 0 0 0	0 0 0 0 0 0 0 0	0 0 0 0 0 0 0 0	0 0 0 0 0 0 0 0
0 0 0 0 0 0 0 0	0 0 0 0 0 0 0 0	0 0 0 0 0 0 0 0	0 0 0 0 0 0 0 0

White King	White Pawns	Black Rooks	Black Knights
0 0 0 0 1 0 0 0	0 0 0 0 0 0 0 0	0 0 0 0 0 0 0 0	0 0 0 0 0 0 0 0
0 0 0 0 0 0 0 0	1 1 1 1 1 1 1 1	0 0 0 0 0 0 0 0	0 0 0 0 0 0 0 0
0 0 0 0 0 0 0 0	0 0 0 0 0 0 0 0	0 0 0 0 0 0 0 0	0 0 0 0 0 0 0 0
0 0 0 0 0 0 0 0	0 0 0 0 0 0 0 0	0 0 0 0 0 0 0 0	0 0 0 0 0 0 0 0
0 0 0 0 0 0 0 0	0 0 0 0 0 0 0 0	0 0 0 0 0 0 0 0	0 0 0 0 0 0 0 0
0 0 0 0 0 0 0 0	0 0 0 0 0 0 0 0	0 0 0 0 0 0 0 0	0 0 0 0 0 0 0 0
0 0 0 0 0 0 0 0	0 0 0 0 0 0 0 0	0 0 0 0 0 0 0 0	0 0 0 0 0 0 0 0
0 0 0 0 0 0 0 0	0 0 0 0 0 0 0 0	1 0 0 0 0 0 0 1	0 1 0 0 0 0 1 0

Black Bishops	Black Queens	Black King	Black Pawns
0 0 0 0 0 0 0 0	0 0 0 0 0 0 0 0	0 0 0 0 0 0 0 0	0 0 0 0 0 0 0 0
0 0 0 0 0 0 0 0	0 0 0 0 0 0 0 0	0 0 0 0 0 0 0 0	0 0 0 0 0 0 0 0
0 0 0 0 0 0 0 0	0 0 0 0 0 0 0 0	0 0 0 0 0 0 0 0	0 0 0 0 0 0 0 0
0 0 0 0 0 0 0 0	0 0 0 0 0 0 0 0	0 0 0 0 0 0 0 0	0 0 0 0 0 0 0 0
0 0 0 0 0 0 0 0	0 0 0 0 0 0 0 0	0 0 0 0 0 0 0 0	0 0 0 0 0 0 0 0
0 0 0 0 0 0 0 0	0 0 0 0 0 0 0 0	0 0 0 0 0 0 0 0	0 0 0 0 0 0 0 0
0 0 0 0 0 0 0 0	0 0 0 0 0 0 0 0	0 0 0 0 0 0 0 0	1 1 1 1 1 1 1 1
0 0 1 0 0 1 0 0	0 0 0 1 0 0 0 0	0 0 0 0 1 0 0 0	0 0 0 0 0 0 0 0

In this tabulation, each 64-bit word has been divided into 8 bytes of 8 bits each, arranged in vertical sequence. Each byte represents one rank on the chessboard; each bit, one square. The binary (0 or 1) value of each bit simply defines whether the piece in question is located on the square represented by that bit. Here again, the board is reversed compared to a normal printed diagram — a1 being the top left corner in each board.

Bit boards are extraordinarily useful tools for the programmer whose machine has a 64-bit word, since the computer can perform logical operations—AND, OR, NOT—on all 64 bits at once. For example, the program will create a bit board representing squares occupied by White pieces, and another representing the squares that a White Knight could move to on an empty board. A NOT operation on the board of White pieces gives the squares that are not occupied by White pieces. An AND operation with this and the board of White Knight moves gives the squares to which the Knight may legally move (those squares to which the Knight could move on an empty board, AND which are not occupied by White pieces) if the King is not thereby exposed to check. These two operations may take less than a millionth of a second for a large computer to perform.

FINDING LEGAL MOVES

Computers have no capability at all for perceiving spatial relationships, and the apparently simple task of generating the moves that a piece may legally make takes up a large portion of any chess program's computing time.

There are eight directions of movement on the board. Three pieces — Rook, Bishop and Queen—are "sweep" pieces, i.e. capable of moving several squares along their lines of action; King, Knight, and Pawn are more restricted in their movements and easier to deal with.

Generating moves basically involves generating the possible squares to which a piece could move on an empty board, then comparing this list with other lists to determine which moves are legal. Here is SARGON's board with square addresses by rank and file (often referred to as the "mailbox" addressing system):

```
FF FF FF FF FF FF FF FF FF FF FF FF
FF FF FF FF FF FF FF FF FF FF FF FF
FF FF 11 21 31 41 51 61 71 81 FF FF
FF FF 12 22 32 42 52 62 72 82 FF FF
FF FF 13 23 33 43 53 63 73 83 FF FF
FF FF 14 24 34 44 54 64 74 84 FF FF
FF FF 15 25 35 45 55 65 75 85 FF FF
FF FF 16 26 36 46 56 66 76 86 FF FF
FF FF 17 27 37 47 57 67 77 87 FF FF
FF FF 18 28 38 48 58 68 78 88 FF FF
FF FF FF FF FF FF FF FF FF FF FF FF
FF FF FF FF FF FF FF FF FF FF FF FF
```

Now imagine that there is a Rook located at square 55 (e5 in algebraic notation). Its directions of movement look like this:

If a Bishop were located on the same square, its directions of movement would look like this:

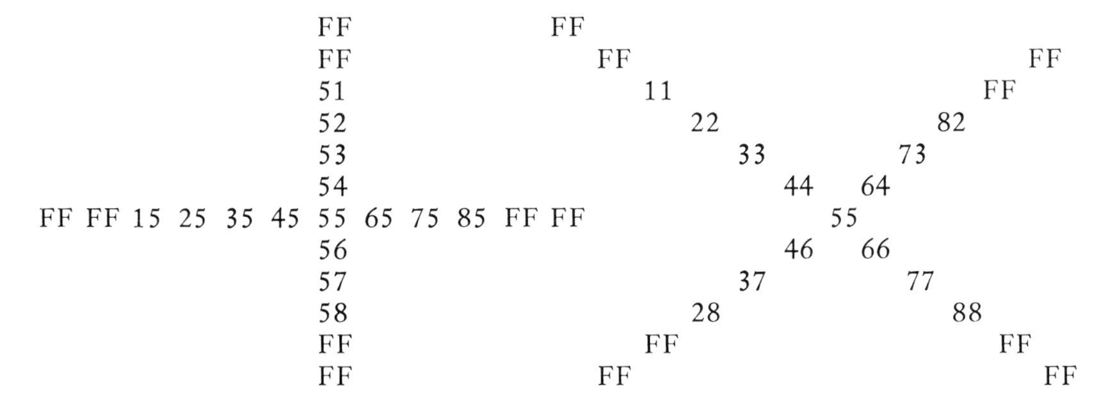

From these diagrams, methods (algorithms) for generating moves can be inferred. Clearly, the Rook moves along a rank consisting of numbers that differ by 10, and a file consisting of numbers that differ by 1. The Bishop moves along diagonals consisting of numbers that differ by 9 and 11 respectively. These rules apply for any square the piece is placed on.

Moves for the Queen and King follow from combining these directions, with the restriction that the King may move only one square. The Knight's move is an interesting problem:

```
    Knight at e5                    Knight at a1

     43      63                      FF      FF
  34             74               FF             FF
        (55)                              (11)
  36             76               FF             32
     47      67                      FF      23
```

Evidently the Knight may jump to squares whose addresses differ by 21, 19, 12, or 8. It is also not hard to see why the FF border of the "board" is two squares wide (otherwise the Knight could jump beyond it).

The Pawn presents several special problems, and is the most difficult piece to generate moves for. To start with, White Pawns and Black Pawns move in opposite directions.

The basic move is to a square that differs by +1 for White and by -1 for Black, but if the origin square number ends in 2 or 7 (if this is the Pawn's first move), the destination square may differ by + or - 2 (a two-square move). Then captures must be considered: capture moves differ from regular moves; possible capture squares differ by -9 and +11 for White, and by -11 and +9 for Black. Finally, there is the enpassant capture rule, which usually requires maintaining a table of "enpassant squares" and comparing it to a list of "capture squares". Naturally, Pawn promotion is a unique move which requires special treatment to handle all the bookkeeping involved.

The last move to be considered is castling, and this also presents special problems. Flags must be set and checked for prior King or Rook moves, and the squares occupied or passed by the King must be examined for attack by enemy pieces.

Programming for these special moves is rather involved, and the first chess-playing microcomputers were put on the market before all these techniques had been worked out. As a result, they could not make or accept such moves as castling, enpassant captures, or Pawn promotion. The frequently seen advertising claims that a given microcomputer "plays by official rules", "makes all legal moves", "promotes to all legal pieces", and so forth, recall the days (not so long ago!) when this was a major selling point for the manufacturer.

Once the program has calculated a POSSIBLE destination square for a given piece to move to, it must then determine if the move is LEGAL. A move is illegal if:
a) it takes the piece off the board (into the FF squares);
b) the destination square is occupied by a piece of the same color;
c) the destination square is beyond a square occupied by another piece, in the direction of movement (Knights excepted);
d) it exposes the King to check.

Microcomputer programs such as SARGON generate all possible moves in a given direction, until a blocking piece is encountered, and then test each for legality. Eventually, after a very considerable amount of computation, the program has a list of legal moves for all the pieces of the side to move.

Mainframe programs handle the problem in a less direct but more efficient manner. CHESS 4.5 generates a data base indicating which squares are attacked by which piece—a "bit board" for each piece depicting the squares that it could possibly move to, less those that are "masked" by intervening pieces (masking is determined by testing at each square to see whether it is occupied. If not, the attack is propagated to the next square beyond and the test is repeated). These attack bit boards are used in many ways—computing who controls a square, for instance. The legal moves for a piece are then found by an AND operation between this attack bit board and the bit board representing squares not occupied by pieces of the same color. If this reads a bit heavily, it is not difficult to visualize in practice. Here are the bit boards for White's King's Knight in the initial position:

Attack squares	White pieces	NOT White pieces	Legal moves
0 0 0 0 0 0 1 0	1 1 1 1 1 1 1 1	0 0 0 0 0 0 0 0	0 0 0 0 0 0 0 0
0 0 0 0 1 0 0 0	1 1 1 1 1 1 1 1	0 0 0 0 0 0 0 0	0 0 0 0 0 0 0 0
0 0 0 0 0 1 0 1	0 0 0 0 0 0 0 0	1 1 1 1 1 1 1 1	0 0 0 0 0 1 0 1
0 0 0 0 0 0 0 0	0 0 0 0 0 0 0 0	1 1 1 1 1 1 1 1	0 0 0 0 0 0 0 0
0 0 0 0 0 0 0 0	0 0 0 0 0 0 0 0	1 1 1 1 1 1 1 1	0 0 0 0 0 0 0 0
0 0 0 0 0 0 0 0	0 0 0 0 0 0 0 0	1 1 1 1 1 1 1 1	0 0 0 0 0 0 0 0
0 0 0 0 0 0 0 0	0 0 0 0 0 0 0 0	1 1 1 1 1 1 1 1	0 0 0 0 0 0 0 0
0 0 0 0 0 0 0 0	0 0 0 0 0 0 0 0	1 1 1 1 1 1 1 1	0 0 0 0 0 0 0 0

The computer loads the word representing the White pieces into one of its registers and inverts it (NOT operation)—generating the third bit board above. Then it loads the word representing attack squares into another register, and performs a logical union (AND operation) between the two. The result — after only four operations and less than a microsecond — is the fourth bit board, in which bits that are 1 in each of the boards being compared remain 1, and all others are set to 0. This represents the squares that the Knight can legally move to—f3 and h3 (again, remember a1 is at top left in the bit boards.)

This technique generates piece moves very rapidly, since large computers perform millions of logical operations per second. Pawn moves are more involved, but again the use of bit boards is advantageous, because the moves of all the pawns on one side can be generated at once. To generate the legal 1—square Pawn advances, the Pawn bit board is shifted a rank (another fast operation for the computer), and a logical union or AND operation is performed with the bit board of empty squares:

White Pawns	WPs shifted 1 rank	Empty Squares	1 square moves
0 0 0 0 0 0 0 0	0 0 0 0 0 0 0 0	0 0 0 0 0 0 0 0	0 0 0 0 0 0 0 0
1 1 1 1 1 1 1 1	0 0 0 0 0 0 0 0	0 0 0 0 0 0 0 0	0 0 0 0 0 0 0 0
0 0 0 0 0 0 0 0	1 1 1 1 1 1 1 1	1 1 1 1 1 1 1 1	1 1 1 1 1 1 1 1
0 0 0 0 0 0 0 0	0 0 0 0 0 0 0 0	1 1 1 1 1 1 1 1	0 0 0 0 0 0 0 0
0 0 0 0 0 0 0 0	0 0 0 0 0 0 0 0	1 1 1 1 1 1 1 1	0 0 0 0 0 0 0 0
0 0 0 0 0 0 0 0	0 0 0 0 0 0 0 0	1 1 1 1 1 1 1 1	0 0 0 0 0 0 0 0
0 0 0 0 0 0 0 0	0 0 0 0 0 0 0 0	0 0 0 0 0 0 0 0	0 0 0 0 0 0 0 0
0 0 0 0 0 0 0 0	0 0 0 0 0 0 0 0	0 0 0 0 0 0 0 0	0 0 0 0 0 0 0 0

Similarly, two-square advances may be generated by another AND operation between this result and the bit board representing squares on the third rank (here the same), shifting forward another rank, and performing a logical union with the bit board of empty squares:

1 square moves on third rank	shifted 1 rank	Empty Squares	2 square moves
0 0 0 0 0 0 0 0	0 0 0 0 0 0 0 0	0 0 0 0 0 0 0 0	0 0 0 0 0 0 0 0
0 0 0 0 0 0 0 0	0 0 0 0 0 0 0 0	0 0 0 0 0 0 0 0	0 0 0 0 0 0 0 0
1 1 1 1 1 1 1 1	0 0 0 0 0 0 0 0	1 1 1 1 1 1 1 1	0 0 0 0 0 0 0 0
0 0 0 0 0 0 0 0	1 1 1 1 1 1 1 1	1 1 1 1 1 1 1 1	1 1 1 1 1 1 1 1
0 0 0 0 0 0 0 0	0 0 0 0 0 0 0 0	1 1 1 1 1 1 1 1	0 0 0 0 0 0 0 0
0 0 0 0 0 0 0 0	0 0 0 0 0 0 0 0	1 1 1 1 1 1 1 1	0 0 0 0 0 0 0 0
0 0 0 0 0 0 0 0	0 0 0 0 0 0 0 0	0 0 0 0 0 0 0 0	0 0 0 0 0 0 0 0
0 0 0 0 0 0 0 0	0 0 0 0 0 0 0 0	0 0 0 0 0 0 0 0	0 0 0 0 0 0 0 0

Captures to the left and captures to the right may each be generated by shifting the Pawn bit board forward one rank and left or right respectively one bit, then ANDing it with the bit board of squares occupied by the enemy. Here's the result after the first move in the Center Counter Defense (1 e4 d5):

White Pawns	WPs shifted	Enemy Pieces	Left Captures
0 0 0 0 0 0 0 0	0 0 0 0 0 0 0 0	0 0 0 0 0 0 0 0	0 0 0 0 0 0 0 0
1 1 1 1 0 1 1 1	0 0 0 0 0 0 0 0	0 0 0 0 0 0 0 0	0 0 0 0 0 0 0 0
0 0 0 0 0 0 0 0	1 1 1 0 1 1 1 0	0 0 0 0 0 0 0 0	0 0 0 0 0 0 0 0
0 0 0 0 1 0 0 0	0 0 0 0 0 0 0 0	0 0 0 0 0 0 0 0	0 0 0 0 0 0 0 0
0 0 0 0 0 0 0 0	0 0 0 1 0 0 0 0	0 0 0 1 0 0 0 0	0 0 0 1 0 0 0 0
0 0 0 0 0 0 0 0	0 0 0 0 0 0 0 0	0 0 0 0 0 0 0 0	0 0 0 0 0 0 0 0
0 0 0 0 0 0 0 0	0 0 0 0 0 0 0 0	1 1 1 0 1 1 1 1	0 0 0 0 0 0 0 0
0 0 0 0 0 0 0 0	0 0 0 0 0 0 0 0	1 1 1 1 1 1 1 1	0 0 0 0 0 0 0 0

The uses for bit boards in mainframe chess programs are almost endless.

EVALUATING POSITIONS

Another process that occupies a large fraction of computation time is the evaluation of positions. A computer has no sense of what is right or wrong, appropriate or inappropriate. It must look at each position according to a specific set of rules, as though it had never seen the position before (unless it is in the program's opening book), or anything like it. Using these rules, the program generates a "score" which represents the value of the position according to its evaluation rules.

An example of the problems that programmers encounter is shown by the following position, which occurred in the game that decided the championship of the 1980 West Coast Computer Faire microcomputer tournament:

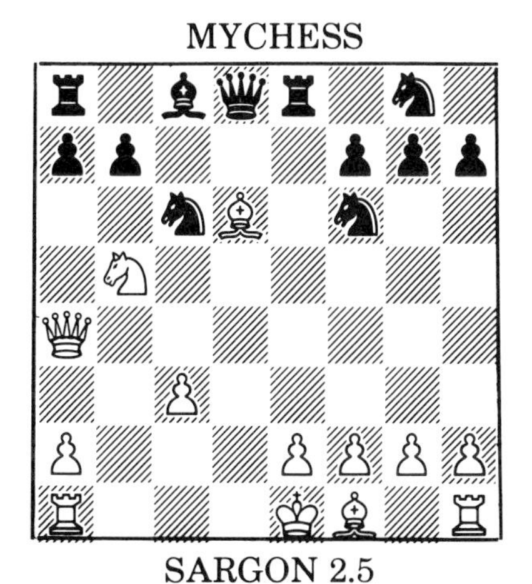

SARGON 2.5 has won a Pawn by aggressive opening play, and after 13 ♖d1 it could have had a winning positional advantage. Instead, it "thought" that it had an opportunity to win the exchange: **13 ♘c7? ♕xd6 14♘xa8 ♕b8** This is the position SARGON 2.5 evaluated at the end of its search at move 13. The Knight is obviously trapped — obvious to humans, perhaps, but not to SARGON 2.5. MYCHESS went on to win the game and the championship. After the game the author asked Dan Spracklen about this flaw in SARGON's search, and learned that it would simply have taken too much code to test for pieces that are liable to capture and have no defenders or escape moves. Under the set of rules it was "playing" by, SARGON 2.5 scored this position as a gain of material.

Evaluating positions is the key to chess ability, and the most difficult part of a program to write. The problem centers around giving the program enough guidance to have some "chess sense" without taking an unreasonable amount of time in the computation. This process involves conflicting goals, and no chess programmer ever feels that his latest creation has a satisfactory evaluation function—there is always a further improvement to be made, usually by trial and error.

The original SARGON considers the following factors in evaluating a position:
Material — Total value of points for White minus total value of points for Black,

scoring a Pawn as 1, Knight or Bishop as 3, Rook as 5, Queen as 9, and King as 10;

Mobility — Total number of squares White can legally move to minus total number of squares Black can legally move to;

Exchanges — The "value" of a piece on a given square is adjusted by examining all the attackers and defenders of the piece. If it is attacked by a piece of lower value, or "en prise" without defense, the number of points lost is stored in a table and a half-Pawn penalty is assessed;

Castling — a 6-point bonus is given for castling if the move is legal. This forces the program to castle whenever it is possible unless it can win material;

Development — A two-point penalty is assessed for moving a piece twice before the seventh move;

Limiter — A limiting value is placed on material score (30 points) and on mobility score (6 points). Bonus and penalty points are computed into the mobility score;

Scoring — The difference in material from the original position for which the computer is making a move, and for the position being evaluated, is computed and passed through the limiter; likewise the mobility difference. Then the material score is multiplied by 4 and added to the mobility score. The result is added to 128 to generate a position score, which is always a positive integer (White would like to get position scores greater than 128, Black less than 128).

This is an extremely primitive evaluator by later standards. The program has no positional knowledge at all beyond maximizing mobility, castling early, and developing its pieces. Nevertheless, this simple evaluator required more than 160 assembly-language program instructions, and calls a subroutine with another 10 instructions; it is the largest routine in the whole program. For its time, SARGON was a highly successful program, winning the 1978 West Coast Computer Faire microcomputer tournament with a 5—0 score.

Later versions of the SARGON family have much more sophisticated evaluation functions and still run much faster—an example of what clever programming and hard work can achieve. Still, there are strict limits to what can be put into the evaluator function of a microcomputer program without degrading the speed of computation to a degree that affects the playing strength more than the value of the knowledge added. The processes of setting up board and piece representations, move generation, searching for the "best" move (according to the evaluator), and other functions which a chess program must perform take time and effort, even some ingenuity to do well, but today these functions are sufficiently well understood to be more or less routine programming tasks. The real art is in the evaluator function.

Mainframe programs have more computing power available and can use more complicated evaluator functions. This does not automatically guarantee that they will find better moves. There is virtue in simplicity, and a well-designed microcomputer evaluator can be tested and "balanced" to produce reasonable moves much more easily than an evaluator with many more terms whose interdependence is less clearly defined. The Spracklens have made a virtue of necessity in this respect, and their microcomputer programs regularly defeat the weaker mainframe programs despite an enormous disparity in computing power.

CHESS 4.5 has a much more sophisticated evaluator function than SARGON, and one that works rather well. Its material scoring system is quite a bit different. Pawns are valued at 100 points, Knights at 325, Bishops at 350, Rooks at 500, and Queens at 900. The King is considered invaluable. The material balance score is generated by this formula:

$$S = D + ((DxNP)x(8000\text{-}T))/(6400x(NP+1))$$

in which:

D is the difference in material, in points;
NP is the number of Pawns for the side with the advantage;
T is the total value of material on the board.

The value of D is limited to 2400, and the value of S (the score) to 3100. Most players would agree that an advantage of several Queens suffices to win, and this prevents the program from calculating ridiculous scores.

In this formula, several concepts which human players use all the time in evaluating moves are combined by the art of the programmer into a mathematical statement which the program can evaluate rapidly. The ability to state chess concepts in a form that the computer can calculate quickly is the key to a good evaluator.

Using this formula, it is always good to win material (increasing D). Once a material advantage is obtained, the program can win evaluation points by exchanges (reducing the value of T). On the other hand, trading Pawns is unfavorable because the ratio NP/(NP+1) decreases. The side with the advantage therefore is encouraged to exchange pieces but to keep as many Pawns on the board as possible, which is generally good strategy for endgames.

CHESS 4.5's positional scoring system is somewhat complicated. First, the program looks to see whether any pieces are attacked by men of lesser value, or are "en prise". A penalty is assessed for each such situation, on the theory that time must be lost to deal with it (a tempo generally being valued at about 1/6 of a Pawn). The situation gets more complicated when more than one piece is so threatened, and CHESS 4.5 assesses additional penalties on the theory that double attacks are more than twice as bad as a single attack.

Pawn structure is another key part of the positional evaluation. Doubled Pawns are penalized 8 points, isolated Pawns 20 points. A doubled, isolated Pawn is thus penalized about a quarter of a Pawn. Pawn backwardness is also penalized, depending on whether the Pawn can be supported by other Pawns if advanced.

Passed Pawns get a bonus from a complicated formula whose basic term is the square of the Pawn's rank number, and which is multiplied by a term dependent on the status of the square in front of the Pawn — less if controlled or occupied by an enemy piece, more if controlled by a friendly piece, still more if connected to other Pawns. A passed Pawn on the 7th rank, supported by a Pawn on the 6th rank, with the Queening square controlled by friendly pieces, would get a large bonus, hinting that a piece such as a Knight might have to be sacrificed to stop it. These bonuses guarantee that Nimzovich's dictum "Passed Pawns must be pushed" will be obeyed.

Pieces are positionally scored differently for each piece type. Knights are evaluated for proximity to the central four squares, and proximity to the enemy King. Knights on the back rank are penalized. Bishops are evaluated for the number of squares controlled and penalized for being on the back rank. Rooks are evaluated for the number of squares controlled, proximity to the enemy King, being doubled, being on open or half-open files, and being on the 7th rank. .Queens are evaluated for square control and for proximity to the enemy King. In general, the proximity and square control terms are scored differently for each type of piece, and do not depend on other specific features of the position.

Finally, the King is evaluated for safety from attack (a term that depends in value on the number of enemy pieces remaining), for freedom from back-rank mates (encourages "making luft"), and for proximity to the center of the board and to Pawns during an endgame.

A different evaluation function is used when the winning side has a material advantage of at least four Pawns, a Queen or a Rook on the board, and the opponent less than 700 points worth of material; or when the winning side has no Pawns but mating material in minor pieces. CHESS 4.5 uses these criteria to decide that the game has reached the stage where it is time to play for checkmate, and calls on its mop-up evaluator.

This evaluator checks to see whether the defending King is stalemated, and awards increasing bonuses as it is driven to the edge and then to a corner of the board. King and Knights are given bonuses for proximity to the enemy King. Such a simple evaluation function will not suffice to mate with King, Bishop and Knight, but since there are fewer pieces to consider, the program can look farther ahead in searching for its moves. This factor, plus avoidance of draws by repetition, may eventually force the program to drive the enemy King from the wrong corner to the right one. This ending rarely occurs in practice (although the author once defended it in a tournament game—which ended in a draw by the 50-move rule). Certainly, these simple criteria will force a Queen or mate in other situations, though generally not by the most efficient path.

These positional evaluation criteria are all termed "heuristics" in artificial intelligence parlance. A heuristic is a rule or strategy used to improve the efficiency of a problem-solving method. Generally, problems with any degree of complexity (such as how to play chess) cannot be solved exactly — one tries to find approximate solutions or to create a more favorable situation in which an exact solution might be found, and is at least nearer. In chess, the exact solution would be a mate or draw.

It has been calculated that if the entire known universe were a giant computer processing an optimally efficient chess program at the speed of light, the first move in the ideal game of chess would not yet be made when the universe came to its end. So, although mathematically chess can in theory be solved exactly from the initial position, in practice we are compelled to rely on heuristics to play it at all. When a human player visualizes a position and thinks, "This is not good because my Pawns are doubled" or "That square is very weak", he is applying his own heuristics; even the notion that — all else being equal — it is good to have a material advantage, is a heuristic.

A skilled human player will immediately recognize that CHESS 4.5, even though its evaluator is much more complex than SARGON's and contains many more heuristics, is really rather ignorant about chess. For example: it has hardly any idea of what the actual value of controlling a given square in a particular position is; it usually cannot tell when a positional advantage is worth material sacrifice (positional terms are small compared to material terms); it has difficulty in retreating pieces to eventually locate them on more favorable squares; and most important of all, it does not make plans.

Like almost all programs, CHESS 4.5 is totally opportunistic. It simply looks around to see what the opponent has "left hanging"—a Pawn? A chance to develop a piece? Can evaluation points be won by doubling a Pawn, by exchanging Knight for Bishop, by driving an enemy Knight from the center? All these "judgments" are made according to a fixed set of rules which (with a few exceptions) is invariant, at least until the endgame. Frequently these rules are more or less inappropriate to the position, and the individual position assessments reached are inaccurate by human master standards — Knights are sometimes more valuable than Bishops; doubled Pawns are not always weak. The fact that, with all these defects, CHESS 4.5 achieved a rating of over 2000 Elo (Candidate Master level) is a tribute to the skill and patience of the programmers who gradually developed and refined its heuristics, and to the power inherent in the ability to search many moves ahead. In doing this search, the program must generate and consider all the moves that it or its opponent might play.

THE GAME TREE

Consider for a moment the position shown here, which is an elementary draw with accurate play. As long as the Black King goes into the corner, White cannot win. This is about as simple as a position can get and still offer the possibility of a win.

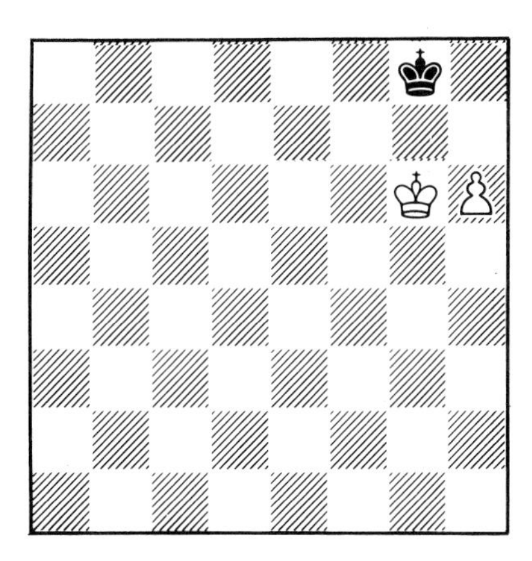

Now consider the possible moves for Black: ♔f8 and ♔h8. To each of these, White has six possible replies: ♔h5, ♔g5, ♔f5, h7, ♔f6, and either ♔f7 or ♔h7. To each of these replies, Black has one or more second moves — unless he is stalemated. Combining these possibilities leads to a GAME TREE:

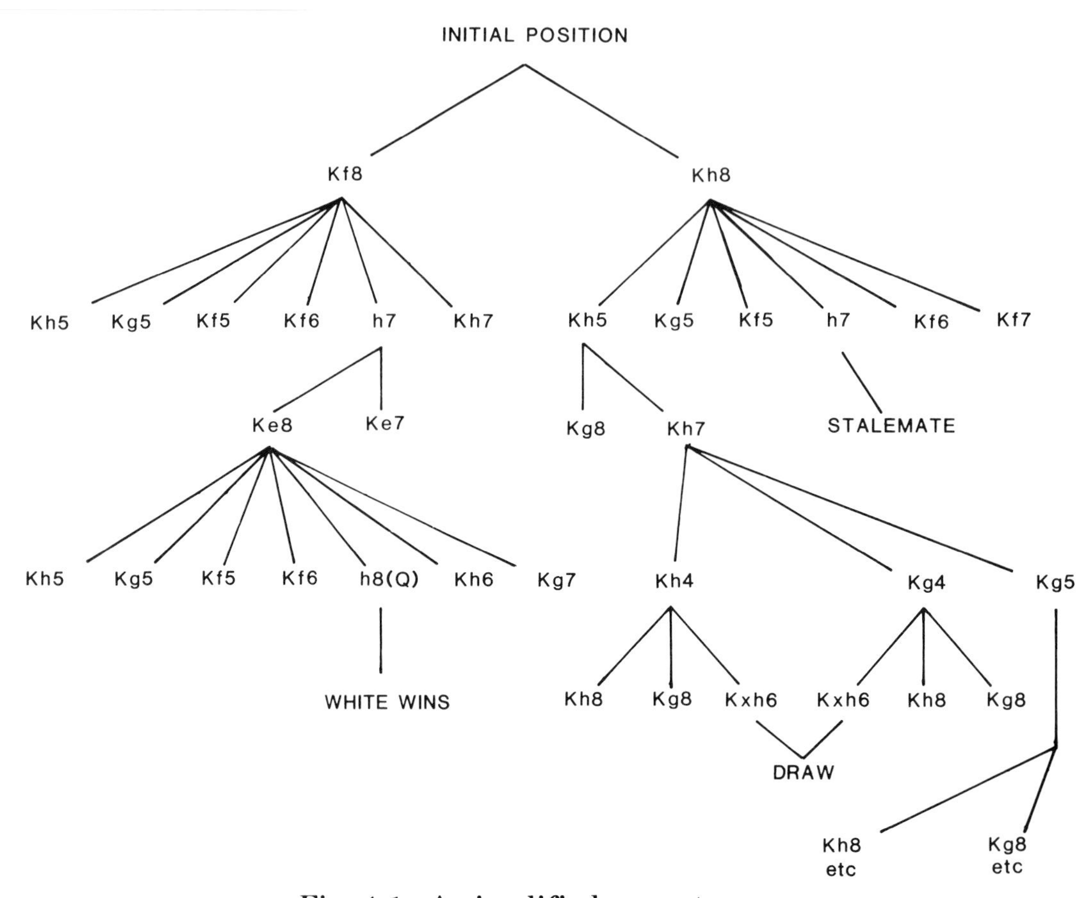

Fig. 4.1 A simplified game tree.

Here only a few of the lines are traced out, and it is quite clear that even in such a simple position, a complete tree several moves deep would be an impossible task to represent pictorially. An exhaustive game tree with an average of six moves per ply for White and two for Black would have more than 20,000 branches in it after only four moves for each side!

The average chess middlegame position contains about 35 legal moves for each side. If we constructed an exhaustive game tree for such a position, it would contain 2,251,875,391,000 branches after only four moves for each side — and that depth would by no means suffice to ensure that the "right" move could always be found from the information contained in the tree. It is frequently necessary for good human players to calculate six or eight moves ahead.

Almost all of a game tree is "garbage" by human standards. It is full of ridiculous moves and impossible positions, but a computer program has no a priori knowledge that a move is ridiculous or a position impossible. Within the game tree that its move generator creates, all moves are plausible. The best that one can do for the program is to tell it that certain moves are more likely to be important than others (and this is very important), but still — how can a program deal with such an enormous range of possibilities? Even the current world computer chess champion, BELLE, whose evaluation is so fast that it can look at more than 100,000 positions per second, would require thousands of hours to look at every branch of the four-move tree. The exponential growth of game trees is the key problem in computer chess programming. In checkers, for example, the possible number of moves at each turn is much smaller — forced captures are particularly convenient for the programmer — and game trees of quite respectable depth can be dealt with in a few minutes.

It should be noted that, in performing its lookahead, a computer program does not generate a game tree all at once. Clearly this would require a huge amount of memory being occupied, and great deal of time expended, before the program learned anything at all. Instead the program constructs the part of the tree that it needs at the moment, evaluates the positions, and stores the results.

SEARCHING THE TREE

When a skilled human player looks at a chess position, he first evaluates it according to his own individual chess heuristics and his intuition ("I don't like the look of that Bishop"), and comes to some conclusions about his game: White is a little better; the position calls for a minority Pawn attack on the Queenside; the Knight at e2 would be better located at b3; and so on. In the process, he acquires a set of goals. The process of selecting a move then becomes a question of how to achieve one's own goals while frustrating those attributed to the opponent. In making his selection, the player will rarely look at more than three or four possibilities at each turn — the others are simply irrelevant to the position. This process is known as a **selective search**.

Originally, it was thought that computer programs would have to adopt an equivalent approach, and indeed the first program to play acceptable chess (1500 Elo), MAC HACK VI, employed a plausible-move generator to determine which moves were worth looking at. The plausible-move generator generated the fifteen most plausible initial moves, ranking them in order of merit. For each of these, the fifteen most plausible replies were considered and ranked, then for each such reply, the nine most plausible second moves were generated and then the nine most plausible replies to each of those. Finally, the seven most plausible third moves for each second-move reply were generated. In order to search to a depth of five plies (still respectable by microcomputer standards), the program had to deal with a "game tree" of 127,575 moves. MAC HACK VI was an outstanding success in its day, and most experts consider that the art of selective-search programming has advanced relatively little since that time.

The reason for this is that a plausible move generator has to be very good indeed to be just barely acceptable. If we let **p** be the probability that the move generator will overlook a move that will lead to the program's losing the game at any given turn, and if the average game contains 40 turns, then the probability that the program will not **make such a blunder is (1—p) to the 40th power. If p is a mere 1%, the program has a 1/3** chance of making a fatal error at some time during the game! For the blunder probability to be less than 10% during a game, the move generator has to be 99.75% accurate.

Even this standard of accuracy would significantly affect the program's playing strength — if it loses 10% of its games on blunders against a player of comparable strength, its Elo rating is depressed by about 40 points. Worse yet, suppose it is playing an opponent rated one class (200 points) lower — the effect of losing 10% on blunders increases to about 65 points. The commercial chess computer VOICE CHESS CHALLENGER uses a selective search of this type, and such blunders are quite common in its play — the author's impression is that its **p** is at least 1%. This flaw in its play tends to create dissatisfaction in those owners who are good enough players to recognize the blunders when they happen — they wonder "How could a computer (supposedly infallible) make such an elementary blunder"? It's easy — ask any chess programmer!

The selective search process is often referred to as "forward pruning" of the game tree—the least plausible branches are simply "pruned off" without any further proceedings. This can have unfortunate effects if a key move resides in a branch that is pruned. This problem has no clear solution, and as programs have improved and their more obvious defects have been corrected, it has become harder and harder for the selective-search programs to make progress. It can take a tremendous amount of effort and a noticeable slowing of the program to make a very small reduction in the blunder probability **p** — the law of diminishing returns applies here with a vengeance.

The best-known selective search program today is CHAOS. CHAOS has a relatively slow search, looking at a few hundred positions per second — but in much greater detail than the programs that do not employ a selective search.

The other approach to searching game trees is the **full-width search**. In this procedure, the program deals with every branch of the tree and, if its evaluator function is accurate, will always find the "best" move according to the information contained in the tree. This does not necessarily correspond to finding the best move, as the following example will illustrate.

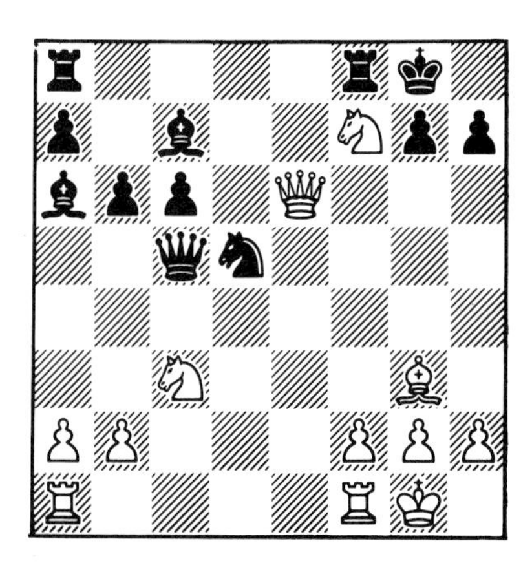

Chess players will recognize this position instantly as the famous "smothered mate". White continues: 1 ♘h6+ ♔h8 2 ♕g8+! ♖xg8 3 ♘f7 mate. This combination is five plies deep. Now suppose that the game tree is only generated to a depth of four plies. The terminal position in the branch that leads to the mate is not very attractive, since White simply appears to have lost a Queen! So a program depending on a fixed-depth tree would probably choose a move such as ♘g5+.

Another peculiarity of fixed-depth trees is the famous "horizon effect". Something unpleasant is going to happen, usually loss of material. The computer has no way of knowing that the loss is inevitable, and finds branches in the game tree in which the disaster does not appear, since it has been pushed "over the horizon" by some intermediate move.

CHAOS

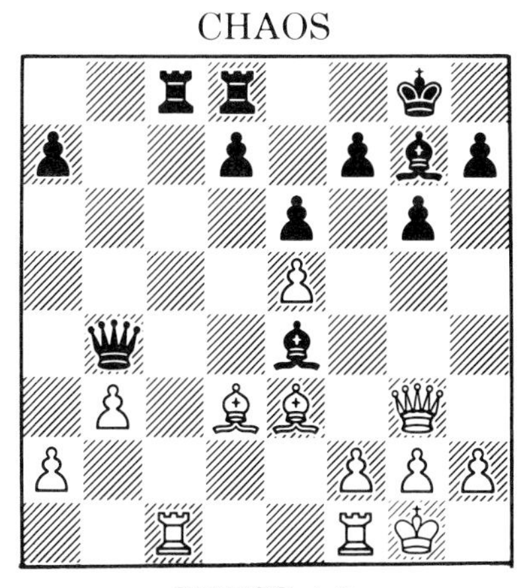

CHESS 4.0

The diagram illustrates a case of the "horizon effect" which occurred in the game CHESS 4.0 - CHAOS, from the Fifth United States Computer Chess Championship (San Diego, 1974). CHAOS has just blundered by **19 ... ♝e4?**, setting up a fatal pin which CHESS 4.0 created by **20 ♛h4!** Now CHAOS began to play very strangely by human standards — **20 ... d5 21 exd6 f5 22 ♜xc8 ♜f8 23 d7 ♛b7.**

At first glance, this sequence of moves appears incredible, but really it was all very logical according to the "rules" by which CHAOS was playing: **20 ... d5** (expecting 21 exd6 ♖xc1 22 ♗xc1 ♕xd6, and material loss is beyond the horizon) **21 exd6 f5** (Oops! ... ♖xc1 22 ♗xc1 ♕xd6 and now 23 ♗xe4 becomes visible. Now CHAOS expects 22♖xc8 ♖xc8 23 d7 ♖f8, and although the d-Pawn is getting a large bonus for advancement, this is relatively better than the loss of the Bishop which occurs in other branches.) **22 ♜xc8 ♜f8** (Oh no! ...♖xc8 23 d7 ♖f8 24 d8(♕) is a disaster! Now CHAOS intends 23 d7 ♕b7 24 ♖xf8+ ♗xf8, and the axe hasn't fallen yet) **23 d7 ♛b7 24 ♜xf8+ ♝xf8 25 d8(♛)** and CHAOS has indeed saved its Bishop, but at the cost of a Rook plus a Queen!

The "horizon effect" can be observed in most commercial chess computers. Simply set up a position in which a two-move mate is threatened, and the computer will throw all its pieces at you until it finally runs out of moves that push the mate over its horizon. It is not obeying some instruction to delay the mate as long as possible — it thinks that each piece sacrifice is PREVENTING the mate, since there is no mate in that branch of the game tree. One ply beyond the computer's search depth is total invisibility.

In order to deal with this effect, the most successful programs today use a variable-depth game tree. These programs generate a fixed-depth tree of from four to twelve plies, depending on the computing power available and the number of legal moves to be dealt with. All move sequences generated by the program's move generator (selective or full-width) are examined to this fixed depth. If the final position in a branch is a **quiescent** position (no captures are possible and neither King is in check), it is scored by the evaluator as a terminal position. Otherwise, a new branch, which includes only captures and checking moves, is grown from the position in question.

This technique allows the program to resolve exchanging sequences and to find checking sequences that lead to mate or gain of material, sometimes twelve or fifteen plies ahead—combinations that would tax good human players. However, it leaves the program vulnerable to sequences in which a move other than a check or capture is interposed—but these so-called "quiet moves" are hard for humans to foresee, too. The quiescence and capture search features have added tremendously to the strength of these programs, but are hard to manage. Unless very carefully controlled, they tend to "explode" and use huge amounts of time.

SEARCH METHODS

All chess programs employ some form of the "minimax" procedure in searching game trees. This algorithm, initially published by von Neumann and Morgenstern in their pioneering book on game theory, is very simple in concept. At each turn, the player who has the move will select the move that is "best" for him. The value of a position is expressed as a positive number, with high values being good for White. Thus Black will always select a move that MINImizes the ultimate position score, and White will always select a move that MAXimizes the ultimate position score. Naturally, we human opponents (and other computer programs too) don't always cooperate by picking the move that the program expects, but that's how the theory goes.

Here is an example of a (simplified) game tree showing the application of the minimax algorithm to the initial position. White to move must make a decision at ply 1; Black to reply will select a move at ply 2, and so on. Moves are numbered according to the ply involved. The program is assumed to have an evaluator that generates a score of 2000 for a level position.

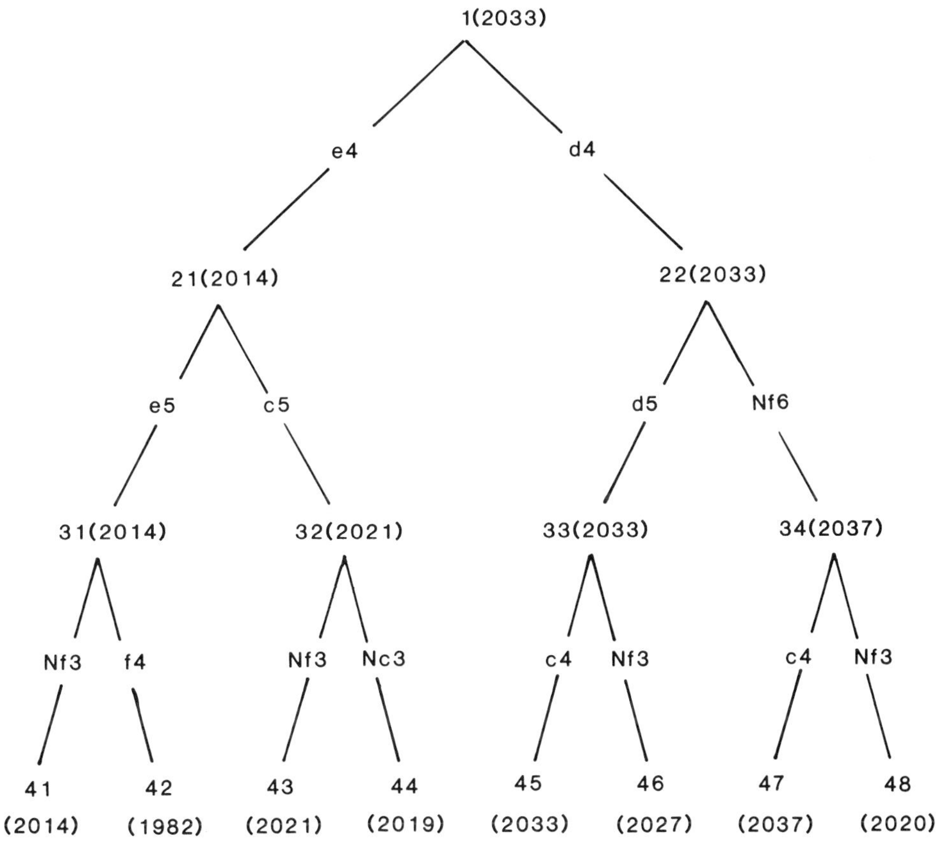

Fig. 4.2 The minimax algorithm.

The evaluator assigns scores to each terminal position (41, 42, and so on) according to the program's heuristics. These values are then BACKED UP through the game tree according to the minimax algorithm, to find the "correct" move. Here position 31 has the value 2014, since White will choose the better of 41 and 42; similarly, 32 is worth 2021, 33 is worth 2033, and 34 is worth 2037. Backing up one more ply, Black will always choose the lower score, so that position 21 is worth 2014 and position 22 is worth 2033. White therefore chooses to maximize his score at position 1 and opens the game with 1 d4. Although this is a highly simplified example, the principle is exactly the same as is used to search the huge game trees generated by chess programs.

In his 1949 paper "Programming a Digital Computer for Playing Chess", Claude Shannon dealt with two search strategies: the simplest (type A) being to generate a tree of fixed depth and search it with the minimax algorithm. Shannon recognized the problems of exponential tree growth and the horizon effect, and proposed a selective (type B) search based on a plausible move generator and quiescence search techniques. Accordingly, today selective search programs are often referred to as using a "Shannon B" strategy, whereas programs that generate a full-width tree are described as using a "Shannon A" strategy, even though the quiescence feature of strategy B may have been included.

The problem of how to search gigantic game trees was greatly simplified by the publication of the "alpha-beta" algorithm in 1958 by Newell, Shaw, and Simon. The basic principle behind this method is that most of the search time used by a classical minimax method is wasted, because tree branches are investigated that have no chance of being selected, since a better alternative has already been discovered. In chess terms, once one refutation to a move has been found, it is unnecessary to investigate it further.

The way in which this algorithm is applied in a program is to order all the moves at each ply in accordance with some simple rules or heuristics. The ordering does not have to be infallible, since failure to put a key move near the top of the list merely makes the program take longer — the move will eventually be considered. This ordering algorithm can accordingly be much simpler and faster than a plausible-move generator. Next, the program establishes two test values during its search of the first branch. Alpha is the **maximum** backed-up value which the program has achieved. Beta is the **minimum** backed-up value which the opponent can force. Each succeeding branch examined is tested, alternately, against alpha and beta.

If the program finds that the backed-up value for a given move will be less than alpha, it can immediately cease exploring the possible descendants of that move, and try another move. This is referred to as an alpha-cutoff. Similarly, if it finds that the backed-up value will be greater than beta when considering the opponent's reply, a beta-cutoff occurs and the program looks for another move for its opponent.

The savings achieved by the alpha-beta algorithm are enormous if the ordering of the moves is good. Theoretically, with perfect ordering, the number of positions scored in a tree having N descendants from each intermediate position is just twice the number scored by the minimax procedure for a tree of half the depth, less one. For the eight-ply tree mentioned earlier with an average of 35 descendants, the number of positions to be scored declines from 2,251,875,391,000 to 3,001,249 — a .00000133 ratio! BELLE can deal with this number of positions in about 30 seconds. Of course, in practice moves are not perfectly ordered, but the methods used usually provide a fair approximation.

The heuristics used in move ordering look odd until one recalls that the game tree is almost entirely composed of ridiculous positions with multiple pieces en prise and so on. The ordering of moves that produce legitimate game type positions is unimportant, compared to forcing cutoffs which get rid of the garbage quickly. This is most efficiently done through a combination of two techniques: iterative search deepening and lists of refutation moves.

The principle behind iterative deepening is simple. The program begins by evaluating the positions after all its legal moves, that is, after one ply; and ranks its legal moves in order, according to the scores. Next a two-ply (the program's moves plus the opponent's possible replies) alpha-beta search is performed and the program's legal moves in the original position are ranked accordingly, in order of their apparent merit. Now a three-ply search is performed, and the program's moves are reranked in accordance with its results; then a four-ply search, and so on. An obvious advantage of this approach is that the program always has a tentative move selected in case it has to abandon its search due to time constraints before completing a ply.

Why go through the process of evaluating all the intermediate positions over and over by repeating the search at progressively deeper levels? It is actually more efficient to do so, given the large number of legal moves in typical positions. In a five-ply search (with perfect move ordering at each level), the program looks at 35 positions at ply 1, 69 positions at ply 2, 413 positions at ply 3, 2449 positions at ply 4, and 14,493 positions at ply 5. The sum of all the intermediate positions is only 2966 — about 20% of the number of terminal positions examined at ply 5. In practice, the benefits of improved move ordering vastly outweigh the additional time required for iterative searching. It is noteworthy that the number of positions to be examined in succeeding plies increases as the square root of the average number of legal moves per position — a factor of about 5.5 during typical middlegames.

Another advantage of the iterative approach is that positions do not have to be re-evaluated if transposition tables are used. Each position evaluated may be stored in a table, together with its score. This table can be consulted prior to evaluating each subsequent position. If a position is already in the table, its score is retrieved. If not, the position and its score are added. Such table accesses are usually very much faster than the evaluator function, and the time required for the iterative approach becomes nearly the same as a search to the full depth, with perfect move ordering.

The heuristics used to order moves for plies 2 and upward are usually very simple. First, capture moves are ranked at the top. In the crazy positions that result after White (for example) puts his Queen en prise, Black does not have to look very far to find a good capture which refutes the move. Captures are important also because the number of legal moves after a capture is less, and this reduces the size of the tree for subsequent plies. Next, a list of "killer" moves is retained from the previous ply and constantly updated as the program progresses through the current ply. These are moves that cause refutations repeatedly. In chess terms, if White is confronted with the threat of 1 ... ♕e1+ 2 ♖xe1 ♖xe1 mate (a typical back-rank mate), then ... ♕e1+ is a killer move which will immediately refute most of White's options. If the 3-ply search reveals that 1 h3 is the way to avoid this threat, then 1 ... ♕e1+ will probably refute every other move in the 4-ply search also. Looking at 1 ... ♕e1+ first then saves a great deal of time.

A further refinement to the alpha-beta algorithm is the alpha-beta window. This heuristic (also known as aspirative searching) is based on the expectation that the score of the final optimum position in the last ply probably won't be very much different from the position score that exists before the program makes its move. A "window" is set around this score so that alpha becomes (S+w) and beta becomes (S-w), where S is the initial position score and w the window size. If carefully chosen, this results in a significant reduction of computation time in most positions, at the expense of having to redo the search for a few positions in which there is indeed a major change in the score.

5
THE COMPUTER STYLE OF PLAY

Although each computer chess program is very much an individual, and the differences in their approaches can be startling, the similarities among chess programs are much greater than the differences. Each shares a group of characteristics in greater or lesser degree, some of which (from the perspective of a human opponent) are definite strengths; others distinct weaknesses. The general course of a game between computers has an alien quality which is usually immediately recognized by the experienced observer, though occasionally computers do play a game in a relatively "human" style—such as the celebrated game CHESS 4.4 - CHAOS, Sixth U.S. Computer Chess Championship, Minneapolis 1975. Humans make much of this and think that perhaps computers are learning to play REAL chess. Actually, the computers involved have no ability to comprehend that they have even played a game, still less whether it was chess. They may build a file and store the score, perhaps even some variations from their lookahead, but to the computer this is just another file with no special significance. Any learning that occurred was done by the programmer.

SIMULATION

The first thing that must be understood is that the computer does not really play a game of chess with the same consciousness that a human does. It does not form plans, get anxious when it thinks it is in trouble (or even really know whether it is in trouble), or gloat when it has the advantage. It never gets nervous or tired. It just sits there following the programmer's instructions, and the situation the board and even the outcome of the game are only numbers that have no intrinsic meaning to the machine. It has no comprehension of what it is doing in anything like a human sense. There is limited satisfaction in crushing a computer chess program, because the opponent doesn't care in the least — it doesn't even really know that it is playing a game at all, much less whether it is winning or losing. It can be argued (in a theoretical sense) that what the program is really doing is simulating a human player.

There is a computer program named ELIZA (29), developed in 1966 at M.I.T., which simulates a nondirective psychiatrist—well enough to deceive many an unsuspecting human "guinea pig" coaxed into communicating with it over a teletype. Indeed, there is a dictum known as the Turing Test, which states that if a human communicates with a machine over a teletype or computer terminal, and cannot tell from the responses whether it is a machine or another human, then the machine may be considered to be "thinking". The weakness in this test is that the level of expertise of the human investigator is undefined. ELIZA can and does fool the layman, much to the glee of its operators, but it would be asking too much to pit it against an expert psychiatrist. Similarly, computer programs can easily convince the casual player that they are really playing chess as he knows it, but the degree of conviction falls off with increasing expertise, until the Grandmaster denies that the output of the machine has any resemblance to chess as he knows the game. On the other hand, his reaction to games by amateurs is likely to be much the same — so where does one draw the line?

PLAYING CHESS AS HUMANS DO

The author's personal (and debatable) opinion is that the real criterion for judging whether a program may be said to be playing chess in the same manner as humans do, is whether it follows processes equivalent to those used by human players. This is an opinion more likely to be shared by chess players than by computer scientists.

From this viewpoint, it is unimportant whether the program uses different techniques to "remember" positions and to "visualize" moves, or to store positions and "imagine" that a move has been made, if it has a method of "seeing" the resulting position in a manner equivalent to the visualization of a human player. It is similarly unimportant whether the computer uses different methods of analyzing which would be the best move, or even different approaches to evaluating the characteristics of a position, provided that it has some way of analyzing and of evaluating positions.

The essential characteristics of human chess play involve comprehending the game as a continuous sequence of real and possible positions interrelated by real and possible moves. Human chess players continually examine positions to try to ascertain the essential characteristics, which are used to set goals for their play, and in trying to achieve these goals, formulate plans. Human players also learn from their mistakes (at least some of the time).

No program has yet demonstrated much more than rudimentary capabilities in these areas, and it is fair to say that, according to this viewpoint, none of them is yet playing chess in quite the same manner as a human does. This situation is largely due to the peculiar limitations of the computer. In general, computers are unable to do anything other than manipulate numbers, and it is not always possible or reasonable to try to reduce everything to numbers.

DIFFERENCES BETWEEN CHESS PROGRAMS AND HUMANS

The infallible memory of the computer is counterbalanced by its total lack of spatial perception — trying to comprehend a pin is a very difficult task for chess programs. It has been argued that in a legal sense, computer programs cheat when they play chess because their internal move selection processes involve moving pieces around on a board that is indistinguishable from the computer's perception of the playing board. This is really an unjust and ignorant comparison. Much fairer would be an analogy to a blindfold player who has to have the moves relayed to him because he cannot see the board — no one accuses HIM of cheating because he visualizes moves with the same mental image that he uses to remember the board position!

The great difference between computers and human chess players lies in the area of selecting moves and evaluating positions. Most human chess decisions are in large **part intuitive and are based on associative memory. A human player KNOWS certain** things without being consciously aware of the process: — that square will be weak — this Bishop will be bad — positions of this type are disagreeable to him, even if objectively satisfactory — White must have a winning attack in this position — and so on. These value judgments are based on past experience, and represent things which the player has LEARNED.

In deciding what to do in a given position, a human player first looks to see whether he has a plan previously decided on and whether it is still valid. If not, or if he intuitively "feels" that there may be something else important in this position, he will evaluate it. This process consists of comparing the position with learned mental images and patterns, rather than arithmetical calculation. As a result of this evaluation, the player draws certain conclusions and forms a set of goals. He then examines the available moves, seeking to achieve his own goals while frustrating those attributed to the opponent. This process is variously known as planning, finding a move, or analyzing; different players do it differently, some more by inspiration and others more by logic — but all go through an equivalent process. Experience tells us that some players do it better than others.

In deciding what to do in a given position, computer chess programs now go through a vastly different process, which is not at all equivalent to the human move selection process. To begin with, the computer program has no learning capacity — it is somewhat like an insect which is totally driven by its instincts (i.e. heuristics), and will fall into the same traps over and over until its programmer makes a change (evolution?).

An excellent example of this occurred in the game Martinak-NUCHESS, played in the 1982 Fredkin Incentive Match. In the first round, NUCHESS lost decisively with Black (annotated in detail in chapter 6). Between rounds, the programmers rushed off to get something to eat, not realizing that in a team match colors are not necessarily alternated each round. In round 2, NUCHESS had Black again, against an opponent who had meanwhile been studying NUCHESS' first-round defeat. The result: an encore.

Martinak - NUCHESS Queen's Gambit Accepted

1 d4 ♞f6 2 ♞f3 d5 3 c4 dxc4 4 a4 ♝e6? 5 ♞c3 ♞c6?! 6 ♝g5 ♝f5 7 a5 h6? 8 ♝xf6 exf6 9 d5! ♞b4 10 e4 ♛e7? 11 ♝xc4 ♝xe4 12 0-0 f5 13 a6 bxa6 14 ♝xa6 ♞xa6 15 ♜xa6 ♛b4 16 ♜a4 ♛xb2 17 ♞xe4 fxe4 18 ♜xe4+ ♚d8 19 ♛a4 ♝c5 20 ♛c6 and White won a piece. The game followed the score of NUCHESS' round 1 game for a further four moves before White varied.

Computers also have no natural capability for associative memory. A computer can compare two positions and tell whether they are exactly alike rather easily, but it is extremely difficult to program a computer to recognize that two positions are SIMILAR. As a result, today's programs make no attempt to recognize positional patterns or to form positional strategies.

Moreover, a computer program cannot SEE anything. It has absolutely no grasp of the spatial relationships on a chessboard (or elsewhere), and no ability to deal with abstract concepts — everything has to be concrete, preferably in the form of a positive integer. Simply programming a computer to "recognize" uncomplicated objects from the image formed by a TV camera has turned out to be an enormously complicated task, on which highly talented and learned scientists have labored for many years without finding a solution — or indeed even defining the problem completely.

If a computer program has such difficulty in grasping such concepts as "square", "circle", "round", "sharp" and the like, how will programs deal with chess patterns and the abstractions that relate them? The whole problem of pattern recognition and forming and recognizing abstractions appears to be crucial to giving programs any real "chess knowledge" in a human sense. Thus far, very little progress has been made at it, although such researchers as Zobrist and Carlson (20) have achieved relatively weak programs using pattern recognition techniques.

So what the computer does is to blindly and accurately apply an elaborate set of "rules of thumb" or heuristics. Humans do that too, but can recognize (sometimes) that an exception must be made. Not so the computer, unless it has another heuristic to tell it exactly when to make an exception and just how to go about it. Moreover, computer chess programs—at least those yet developed—know little about why they decided on their last move; nor do they (with few and minor exceptions) form plans, set goals, or credit the opponent with forming plans and setting goals. Every position is in effect a new game, and the requirement is to maximize a number representing a position score, not to achieve an objective dictated by the position.

The program may not know what an objective is, let alone how to achieve one. It evaluates positions by the heuristics that it has been "taught" to use, which are heavily weighted in favor of material as compared to positional considerations. Computer programs continually start sequences of moves that seem favorable, only to abandon them on the next move because some other sequence seems better. As a result, computer play is opportunistic, inconsistent, planless, and usually materialistic to the nth degree.

A fine example of the planlessness of computer play is the following game from the 1982 U.S. Open, annotated in detail in chapter 7:

CHAOS - Hawes Nimzo-Indian
1 d4 ♞f6 2 c4 e6 3 ♞c3 ♝b4 4 ♛c2 0-0 5 a3 ♝e7 6 e3 b6 7 ♞f3 ♝b7 8 ♝d3 h6 9 ♝d2 CHAOS mechanically completes its development, ignoring better moves. **9...d6 10 0-0?!** Undervaluing the threat to its Kingside, the program continues its mechanical development. **10 ... ♞bd7 11 ♜ae1?** CHAOS ignores the threat again. **11 ... ♝xf3 12 gxf3 ♚h8 13 ♜e2?** This move reveals that CHAOS' heuristics have become irrelevant to the position. The program gets evaluator points for doubling Rooks on a central file, and cannot think of anything better to do. CHAOS' opponent (rated 1485) was able to form a plan of his own (attacking the King), and inflicted a crushing defeat on the much higher-rated program.

WEAKNESSES OF CHESS PROGRAM HEURISTICS

In his excellent book (30), Julio Kaplan quotes a hilarious little gamelet which reveals the weaknesses of the heuristics used to score positions: Computer - Kaplan: **1 e4 e5 2 ♞f3 ♝c5?! 3 ♞xe5 ♝xf2+??! 4 ♚xf2 ♛h4+ 5 ♚e3?** (5 ♔g1 ♕xe4 6 d4 wins easily, of course, but the computer has no idea that "enough is enough" and wants the e-Pawn just as badly as if material were still equal) **... ♛g5+ 6 ♚d4??** (Suicide, but after ♔f2 White has nothing to show for his exposed King.)**...c5+ 7 ♚d5 d6** and Black wins! Curious to see whether this could REALLY happen, the author tried it against two of the better microcomputers: Novag's SAVANT and the Applied Concepts MORPHY EDITION. Both programs obligingly marched their Kings to d4, and while SAVANT balked at putting its head in the trap (7 ♔c4!), MORPHY walked right in: **7 ♚d5 d6 8 ♝b5+ ♚f8 9 ♚c4(!)** (This move took 9 minutes 16 seconds to compute—the alpha-beta search wasn't working very efficiently, since all roads led to disaster) **9 ... ♝e6+ 10 ♚d3 ♛xe5 11 c3 ♞f6 12 ♛f3 a6 13 ♝c4 d5 14 ♝xd5 ♞xd5 15 exd5 ♝f5+ 16 ♚c4 ♝e4** and White had to give up its Queen to stop mate.

The reason for this emphasis on material is that computer programs cannot be trusted with determining whether a positional consideration (e.g. an attack) is worth a material sacrifice. A famous exception to this rule is the very fine piece sacrifice in the game between CHAOS and CHESS 4.0, First World Computer Chess Championship, Stockholm 1974:

CHESS 4.0

CHAOS

16 ♞xe6! fxe6 17 ♛xe6+ ♝e7 18 ♜e1 ♛d8 19 ♝f4 ♚f8 20 ♜ad1 ♜a7 and White had a tremendous bind, soon forcing a win.

In general, however, chess programs cannot judge whether positional factors compensate for material disadvantage, and so material factors and positional factors are scored separately, with material deliberately made dominant to prevent sacrifices played at random. If material gain is not possible, the program will play according to its positional lights—otherwise it may be expected to go after the material, like Korchnoi—a Pawn is a Pawn, and it's up to you to prove otherwise. Even the computer champion, BELLE, is notoriously materialistic. When "out of book" BELLE will always accept sacrifices unless it can "see" a clear loss on the transaction. This characteristic of computer programs makes them interesting opponents for the gambit player. A good example of this is the following game in romantic style, played as part of the author's evaluation of SARGON 2.5:

Welsh - SARGON 2.5 (1980) Evans Gambit
1 e4 e5 2 ♞f3 ♞c6 3 ♝c4 ♝c5 4 b4 ♝xb4 5 c3 ♝e7 6 d4 exd4?! 7 cxd4 ♞f6 8 0-0! ♞xe4 9 d5! ♝f6? 10 ♜e1 ♝xa1 11 ♜xe4+ ♞e7 12 d6! cxd6 13 ♞g5 ... Despite Black's material advantage, the program is helpless. **13 ... 0-0? 14 ♛h5 h6 15 ♞xf7 ♛b6 16 ♞xh6+ ♚h8 17 ♞g8 mate.**

LIMITS TO "BRUTE FORCE" TREE SEARCHING

Although it can be argued that computer chess programs are not yet able to play chess in quite the same manner as a human, the advocate of this viewpoint must admit that the quality of the computer play is starting to become difficult to tell from that of humans. The whole question—whether programs driven entirely by predetermined heuristics, without strategic goal setting abilities, can be considered as playing chess in the way humans do—is really a moot point if one has a sufficiently powerful computer. But what is a "sufficiently powerful" computer?

If a machine capable of a full-width 100 ply search is imagined, with a reasonable evaluator function, it would be impossible to tell how the machine found its moves in almost every imaginable position, since it would find the best moves purely by maximizing the terminal-position score. Such a machine would be unimaginably strong. Can one ever be built? It is interesting to speculate on the dimensions of such a computer.

Suppose that by some miracle of microelectronics technology, a chess processor 1,000,000 times as fast as BELLE were developed, and that it could be placed in a cube only one centimeter on a side (about 1/4 the size of the package for the Motorola 68000, an advanced microprocessor), and that each of these little marvels weighed only one gram. To eliminate extraneous factors, suppose that these processors could be organized into a supercomputer, like so many building blocks, with no loss of efficiency and no delays due to physical limits such as the speed of light.

BELLE searches 8 plies deep in about 3 minutes, or 180 seconds. The imaginary "super-BELLE" would achieve the same depth of search in .00018 second. The number of positions to be scored increases by a factor of about 5.5 with each additional ply beyond eight, which leads to the conclusion that the number of processors required for a computer capable of searching 100 ply in 3 minutes would form a sphere with a diameter of nearly 12 light-years. This would be many times as massive as the entire known universe.

If, as it seems, a 100 ply search is too much to ask for, then suppose for sake of argument that 50 ply were enough to play perfect chess — the dimensions of a 50-ply supercomputer are much more modest, but still hardly practical at 4/5 the size of the Moon!

It begins to look as though the "brute-force" approach has its limitations, and that there is not, and never will be, a computer "sufficiently powerful" to play apparently perfect chess without setting goals and forming plans.

THE FUTURE

Nevertheless there are real grounds for believing that in the foreseeable future a "brute force" machine without these qualities can be programmed, which will still be strong enough to play at the Grandmaster level and perhaps even to become World Champion. This argument rests on an experiment by Ken Thompson, in which BELLE was pitted against itself at varying search depths (22). The resulting data formed a rating curve that was nearly linear at an increase of about 250 Elo points per additional ply. If BELLE now plays at about a 2150 level, then an increase of four plies would raise its performance to 3150, more than 300 points above Bobby Fischer's highest rating — providing the apparent linearity holds at higher ratings.

Unfortunately for this thesis, there are many curves (such as parabolas) that are so nearly linear in a given range that they cannot be differentiated from straight lines, but behave quite differently outside that range. Ken Thompson himself suspects that the real curve is nonlinear, and that a law of diminishing returns applies. However, BELLE searching 12 to 13 plies deep in the middlegame would be a formidable opponent indeed. Since this would require a speedup factor of "only" 1000 over today's BELLE, and since the circuitry used in BELLE's dedicated chess processor is from 10 to 100 times slower than later developments, there are reasonable grounds for expecting that we will eventually get to see for ourselves what a 12 ply BELLE can do.

It is very unlikely that any program that attempts to follow the human approach to chess-playing will be able to cope with the best programs of the present type for quite some time after its introduction, if ever. Even the expert who knows what is really going on inside these programs finds himself emotionally deceived at times and reacts to the program as if it were a human opponent. Moreover, computer programs have now been officially recognized as chess players and have the right to participate in many tournaments with humans (although not to win prizes) — a situation for which the author must accept a good deal of the responsibility. So perhaps the reader will condone further references to the characteristics of these programs as if they were human players. Let us now consider some of the salient features of their play.

OPENINGS

Computer chess programs all utilize opening "books" of various sizes. The original version of SARGON has an opening "book" of one move — either e4 or d4 at random with White; ... e5 if White opens e4 or with the a, b, or c-Pawns; otherwise ... d5. Most programs today have a book of at least 1,000 positions or moves, several have tabulations of more than 10,000 and BELLE has an opening "book" of 375,000 positions — most if not all of the contents of the Encyclopedia of Chess Openings! This incredible inventory vastly exceeds that of any human player, and one would think that BELLE's knowledge of openings must be so decisive that the best a human player could hope for would be to leave the opening with a slight disadvantage.

But that is by no means the case. If in one sense BELLE is more learned than the greatest masters in opening theory, in another sense the program is more ignorant than most beginners — for BELLE looks these positions up in its tabulation and plays the recommended moves without the slightest understanding of the reasons behind them. When BELLE's list of moves ends, or when the opponent deviates from "theory" — and it is not hard to find reasonable, even good moves that are not in ECO or any other book — the program has no idea why it has arrived at the position before it, what its objectives should be, the principles of the opening system, or anything at all beyond what its heuristics and tree search can tell it about this position. This characteristic is common to all chess programs. In a sense, BELLE is like a correspondence player with a fantastic library, perfectly indexed, who does a magnificent job of finding the most obscure continuation known to theory, but whose capabilities for playing openings when "theory" gives out are at best mediocre. Examples of the good and bad side of BELLE as an openings connoisseur may be found in BELLE - NUCHESS (chapter 9) and BELLE - Kevin Toon (chapter 7).

Another problem faced by chess programs in playing openings is recognizing transpositions. Programs whose openings tabulations are organized by position are theoretically able to recognize transpositions, since the path by which a position is reached is not important. Many programs, however, have opening "books" organized as move lists, and cannot recover the sequence when a transposition occurs. Also, since it would obviously be a loss of time to consult the openings table in a middlegame or endgame position, most if not all programs either use a separate module to play the opening or set some kind of flag so that they will stop consulting the openings table after finding that the position being looked at is not in the program's "book". A later return to a book line will thus not be recognized (One way around this problem is to stop the table lookup only after several successive failures). At any rate, identifying transpositions is very problematic, and a wily human with a good knowledge of a particular opening system can usually exploit this to advantage.

Once a chess program has succeeded in finding its way through the perils of the opening without disadvantage, it faces perhaps the most dangerous moment in the whole game, for now it must make its initial evaluation of the position it is confronted with—without any guidance at all beyond its normal heuristics. Often this goes relatively well, and the computer finds a reasonable continuation. Distressingly often (to the programmer, not the opponent), however, the program is horrified to find itself in a position in which all its pieces are misplaced, and spends precious time shuffling them around to suit its idiosyncrasies rather than continuing with a move relevant to the position.

Variations in which the computer has sacrificed material present special problems, and the programmer is well advised to avoid them when possible. The natural tendency of a program that finds itself a Pawn down with the initiative as compensation is to take the first opportunity to force a draw. This can be suppressed by introducing a large "contempt factor" (a parameter defining how far negative the evaluation of the program's position can become before it should play for a draw), so that the program will play for a win even when a Pawn down; but that might not be wise later on, in the endgame.

THE MIDDLEGAME

During the middlegame, computers play opportunistically and without any plan other than to maximize the material and positional score at each turn. Often this involves shifting from one expected sequence of moves to something completely different at the next turn, without any reason discernible to the human mind. The total planlessness and lack of any aim or goal in computer play means that even the best machines are surprisingly vulnerable to long-range strategy. An excellent example of this is Smith - BELLE, played in the 1982 U.S. Open (chapter 7); BELLE got sidetracked with a host of short-range tactical threats which ultimately led to nothing, while its Category I rated opponent calmly built up a winning attack against BELLE's lonesome King. Most programs have very little ability to conduct a positional attack when no obvious weak point exists — simply sitting on a sound position and letting the computer take the initiative can have surprising results, as David Levy has shown in his challenge match games (26).

As compensation for their lack of long-range planning and positional judgement, chess programs—even the commercial microcomputers—are sharp tactically. When the author was writing a review of SARGON 2.5 (*Personal Computing*, Oct.-Nov. 1980), a number of games were played between the machine and the denizens of a well known chess club in Los Angeles. This apparently balanced position occurred in a game between SARGON 2.5 (at level 4) and a wily veteran who was one of the club's best players (Elo rating in the high 1900's) — and here the computer unleashed a terrific attack:

SARGON 2.5

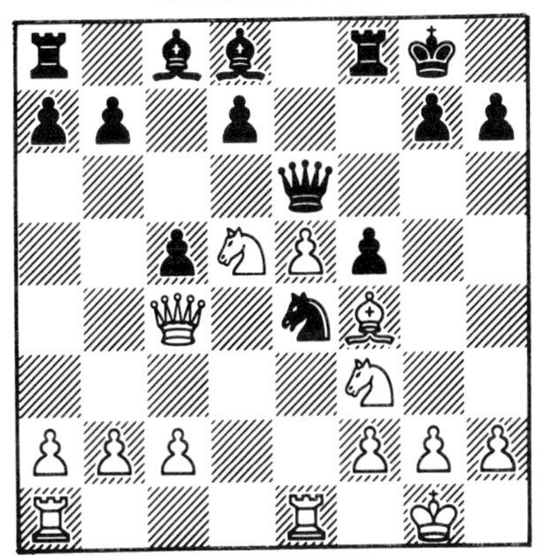

CATEGORY I PLAYER

1 ... b5! 2 ♕d3 ♝b7 3 ♞e3 (♖ad1 was better)**... c4 4 ♕e2 g5! 5 ♞d4** (White must lose a piece, but expects to get attacking chances)**... ♛b6 6 ♞exf5 gxf4 7 ♕h5.** Here White seems to have some vague threats, and the author was expecting the program to find ... ♕g6 consolidating its position. But SARGON 2.5 floored its opponent with **7 ... ♜xf5! 8 ♞xf5 ♛xf2+ 9 ♚h1 ♞g3+! 10 hxg3 ♛xg2 mate,** creating a sensation among the onlookers.

A much stronger player also came to grief tactically against a computer program, when International Master David Levy (26) found himself with a lost game against CHESS 4.7 in the first game of his famous challenge match, although his resourceful play and some positional mistakes by the program allowed Levy to escape with a draw. Here CHESS 4.7 taught the master a lesson about weakening the King's sanctuary:

CHESS 4.7

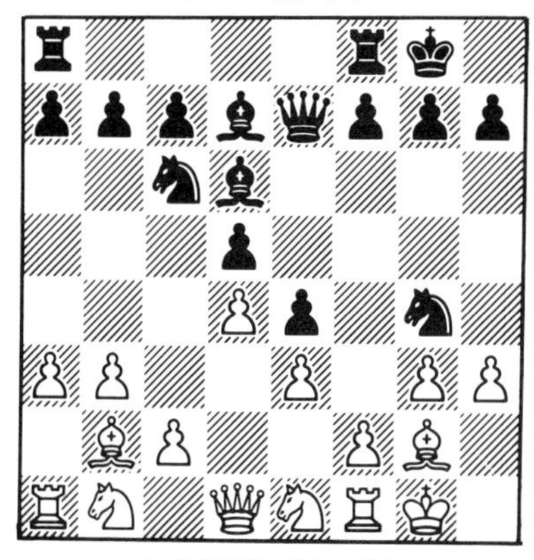

DAVID LEVY

12 ... ♞xe3!! 13 fxe3 ♛g5 14 g4 (Levy: "Realizing that I was completely busted, I thought my only hope was to sacrifice the Exchange to get the Queens off.")**... ♛xe3+ 15 ♜f2 ♝g3 16 ♛e2 ♛xf2+** ("Of course it would be crushing to take with the Bishop and keep the Queens on so that my King would die of exposure, but the program knows that it should trade down when materially ahead.") **17 ♛xf2 ♝xf2+ 18 ♚xf2 f5! 19 gxf5 ♞e7 20 c4 ♜xf5+ 21 ♚g1 c6 22 ♞c3 ♜h5 23 ♚h2 ♜f8 24 ♞d1 ♞g6 25 ♜c1 ♝xh3!** ("I had seen this coming but was powerless to prevent it.") **26 ♝xh3 ♜f1 27 ♞g2 ♜f3 28 cxd5 ♜hxh3+ 29 ♚g1 cxd5**

CHESS 4.7

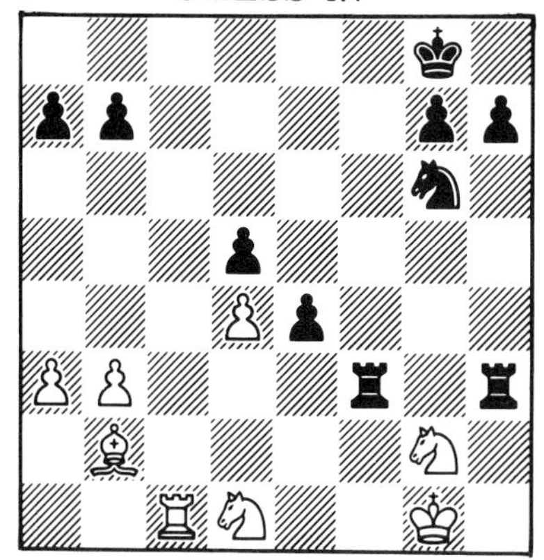

DAVID LEVY

30 ♜c8+ ♞f8? Here the program begins to find inferior moves, because it cannot understand their long-range implications. **31 ♝c3 ♜d3 32 ♞1e3 ♜hxe3 33 ♞xe3 ♜xe3 34 ♝b4** ("My first threat of the game, but I was not too happy about being three Pawns down.") **34 ... ♜f3 35 ♜d8 h6** ("The program no doubt saw that 35 ... ♖f5 36 ♗xf8 ♖xf8 37 ♖xd5 would be followed by the win of the e-pawn or the b-pawn and probably did not analyze beyond that point.") **36 ♜xd5 ♜xb3 37 ♜d8 ♜f3 38 ♜a8 g5 39 d5 h5 40 d6 ♚g7 41 ♜xa7 ♜f7 42 ♜a5** ("Suddenly the position is no longer TOTALLY hopeless—it is merely hopeless.") Hopeless or not, Levy found enough play to even get winning chances, but a further fine tactical shot by CHESS 4.7 enabled it to draw the game on its 64th turn. (Levy: "A remarkable game, and the first time a computer program has ever drawn with an International Master under tournament conditions.")

Within the limitations of its search depth (which can reach as far as nine or ten ply in the capture search, even in commercial microcomputer programs), the computer program is tactically perfect. It will not leave pieces hanging, and will always notice anything its opponent leaves en prise. This tactical consistency makes the program an opponent not to be taken lightly — there is never any room for tactical error against it; the program can easily afford to make a number of minor positional miscues if the opponent gets careless and hangs a Pawn. The only real way to defeat a computer program tactically is either to find a very long combination which exceeds its search depth, one which includes a **zwischenzug** or quiet move which the program prunes out in its quiescence search, or a combination yielding a crushing attack whose consequences the program cannot evaluate properly within its search depth. These are precisely the sorts of moves that are awarded !! when masters annotate games. It takes a really GOOD move to beat a computer chess program of any quality tactically.

Positionally, if the program has a decent set of heuristics it may not be able to generate any sort of meaningful plan, and may make minor positional errors — of which it takes several to add up to an initiative—but will seldom make a really major blunder. The program will develop its pieces, fight for control of the center, and do all the obvious, mechanical things to get a "good position". It may not be a promising one in terms of the program's being able to do anything further, but it is likely to require some effort and ingenuity to attack. It is also likely to have some weird features about it which tend to make human opponents uncomfortable, because such positions do not occur in games between humans.

These characteristics of computer middlegame play lead to an interesting characteristic of the faster mainframe programs, their exceptional strength at speed chess. Speed games are played with each player having five minutes to make all the moves of the game. Whichever player's flag first falls, loses. A variant of this used with computers that do not have sensory boards is to set the computer at a fixed rate of five seconds per move. If the opponent lasts to the 60th move, he wins. It usually takes an average of 20 seconds per computer move, with keyboarding, so that the opponent gets more time to think.

It appears, from the limited data of the 1982 U.S. Speed Championships, that microcomputers more or less maintain their tournament level performance rating at speed chess, while fast mainframe programs play several hundred Elo points stronger than at tournament level. The reason for this relates to the search depth. Five seconds a move is just 1/36 of the normal 3-minute tournament pace, and corresponds to a reduction of two plies in the program's full-width search. BELLE generally searches 8 plies in tournament middlegames, so gets 6 plies during speed games. That is quite formidable when one considers that capture and check sequence searches out to 10 or more plies are still performed. No wonder BELLE's speed chess performance is Grandmaster level!

The consistency of computer play is a major asset in speed chess. Even masters make tactical errors fairly regularly in their speed chess games — there simply isn't time to look at all the variations. One plays by instinct rather than calculation. The computer program doesn't make any tactical errors, at least not obvious ones, and always notices its opponents' blunders. The strange positions and unexpected moves that humans have to deal with against computers are a major factor in these speed games. A human naturally thinks about logical continuations during the computer's turn, and when it does something unexpected, he must use precious time in reacting to it.

The author has played nine speed games against the best computer programs — four with BELLE, four with CRAY BLITZ, and one with CHESS 4.8, and has lost all but two. With the exception of the game with CHESS 4.8 (in which the computer was mated), the games took one of the following courses: a) Human gets a big advantage in the opening and by sharp early middlegame play turns it into a crushing bind, then gets stuck figuring out how to turn it into a win; b) Human makes a tactical error early and resigns; c) Human plays a risky opening and gets the better of it in a wild position, but there is so much going on tactically that he runs short on time.

In a) and c) there always seems to come a moment, usually around the 30th move, at which the human finds himself uncomfortably short of time, and at precisely this moment the computer does something totally unexpected. In the author's best game with CRAY BLITZ, its King was being driven from g8 all the way to c5 (with Bob Hyatt gleefully announcing all the mates that were missed) when—with no time to think—the computer foiled the planned mate with an unexpected check, and the game ended in a draw. The interested reader can find excellent examples of how to play speed chess against a strong computer program in Mark Diesen's games with BELLE in the U.S. Speed Championship (chapter 8), and a classic example of how computers run human opponents out of time in Shapiro-BELLE from the same event.

ENDGAMES

When computer chess programs first appeared, they generally did not make any distinction between opening, middlegame, and endgame. An opening played by middlegame heuristics may seem a little strange, but an endgame played by the same "rules" tends to leave onlookers howling with laughter, as did the audience during COKO III - J.Biit in the first U.S. Computer Chess Championship (New York 1970):

J. Biit

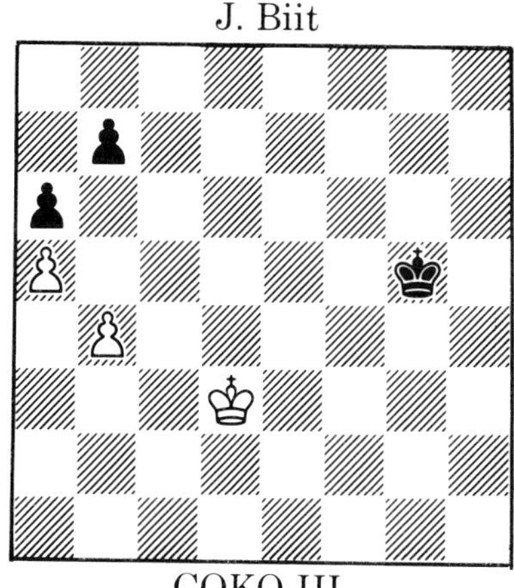

COKO III

82 ♚e3?? ... The opposition seems to be about the only endgame concept these programs understand. Of course ♔d4 wins easily. **... ♚f5 83 ♚f3?? ♚e5 84 ♚e3 ♚d5 85 ♚d3 ♚e5? 86 ♚e3?? ♚d5 87 ♚d3 ♚e5?** and the game ended in a draw by repetition. COKO III, a product of Bell Telephone Laboratories, was among the better early programs but had the misfortune to be involved in examples of computer endgame mismanagement which became classics. Here is an example from the Second U.S. Computer Chess Championship (Chicago, 1971). Even the COKO III programming team must have been satisfied with this position, for their program has two different mates in one to choose between and a multitude of variations leading to mate in two, three, four, or more moves — but this wealth of alternatives proved to be COKO III's undoing:

GENIE

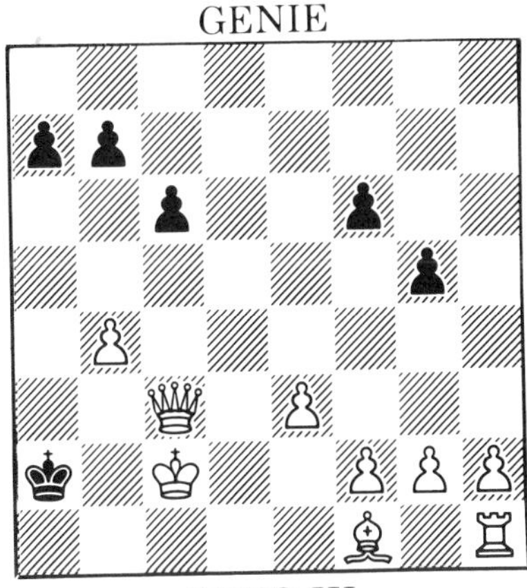

COKO III

38 ♚c1? f5 39 ♚c2? f4 40 ♚c1? g4 41 ♚c2?? f3 42 ♚c1?? fxg2 43 ♚c2?? gxh1(♛) ... COKO III sees mate in every variation, and of course one mate is as good as another, so it chooses between the mating continuations at random. Had there been only one mate available, COKO III would of course have played it. Now, however, comes the crowning indignity, for which no reasonable explanation has yet been made: **44 ♚c1???? ♛xf1+** and Black actually won the game! After this, programmers learned to give bonuses for mates that occur at earlier plies in the game tree.

DUCHESS

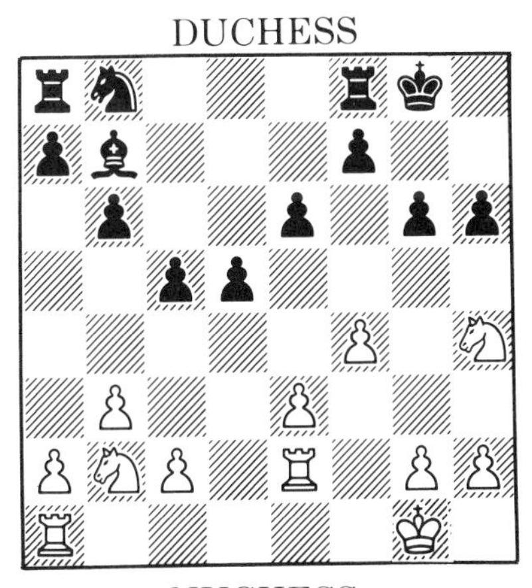

NUCHESS

It took a long time before computer programs began to merely play endings badly instead of laughably, Even in the Twelfth North American Computer Chess Championship (Los Angeles, 1981), major errors were made in games between strong programs, which betrayed a fundamental lack of comprehension of any end game principles. In this position from NUCHESS - DUCHESS, Black has a solid Pawn advantage, and White a serious weakness on e4 which DUCHESS could have exploited by ... ♘d7-f6. Instead, the program played the horrible **... d4? 19 exd4 g5 20 fxg5 hxg5 21 ♞f3 g4 22 ♞e5 cxd4 23 ♞xg4**, after which it had lost back the Pawn and all its winning chances. An even worse example occurred in the game between the sixth and eighth place finishers (out of a field of 16), PHILIDOR and L'EXCENTRIQUE.

L'EXCENTRIQUE

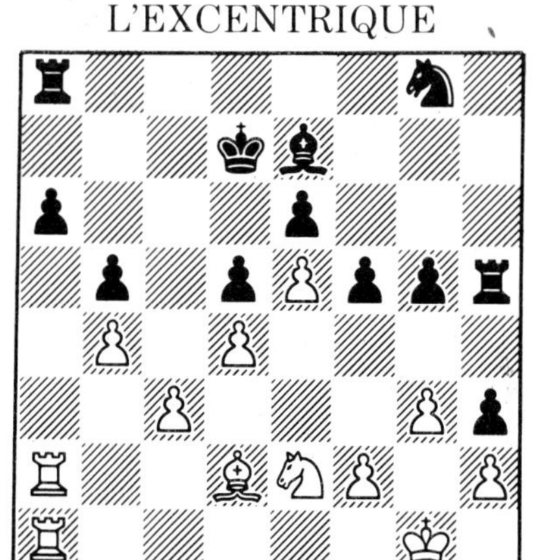

PHILIDOR

Here PHILIDOR played **29 f4??,** turning a "bad" Bishop into the most hopelessly imprisoned piece yet seen after **... g4**. One would think that this Bishop had absolutely no prospects for playing any further role in the outcome of the game, but after 50 moves had been played,

L'EXCENTRIQUE

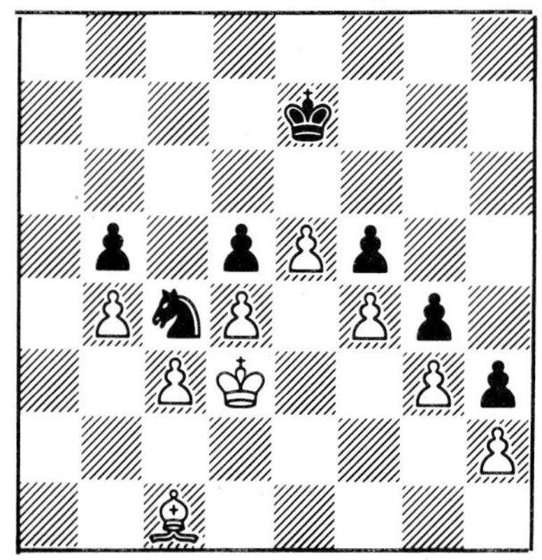

PHILIDOR

PHILIDOR (with absolutely no way to make progress) simply pushed its Bishop to d2 and L'EXCENTRIQUE captured it! Bishops are worth more than Knights, right? Well, perhaps not in this case—PHILIDOR was awarded the game by adjudication soon thereafter, even though all it had done was shuffle its King back and forth, without any indication whatsoever that it "saw" the key break c4, after which White lets Black get a Queen first but goes on to win by promoting his own e-Pawn.

While the mainframe programs were struggling to develop a rudimentary ability to handle endings, the first commercial microcomputer programs put on some exhibitions reminiscent of COKO III, as in the game VOICE CHESS CHALLENGER - ATARI 4K from the 1980 West Coast Computer Faire Microcomputer tournament. In this position, White obviously wins effortlessly by simply advancing his connected passed Pawns.

ATARI 4K

VOICE CHESS CHALLENGER

What actually happened was: **30 b3? ♞d2 31 ♔f2 ♞e4+ 32 ♔e3 ♞c3 33 a4? ♞d5+ 34 ♔e4 a6 35 ♞f4 ♞f6+ 36 ♔f5 ♞d7 37 ♞d3 ♞c5 38 ♞xc5 ♔xc5.** White has made absolutely no progress toward promoting a Pawn, while Black now has some possibilities of its own in the event of further dallying.

ATARI 4K

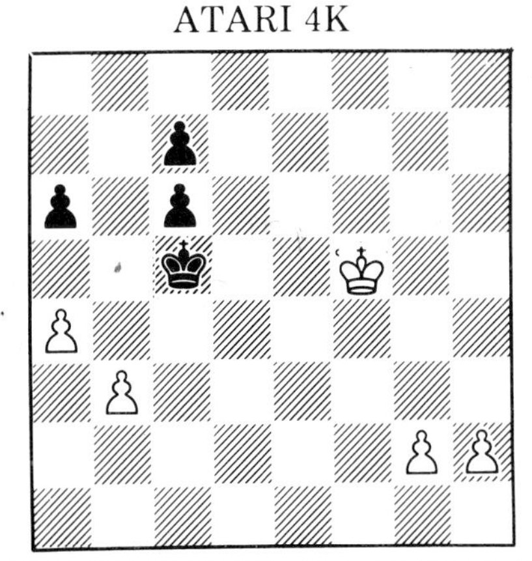

VOICE CHESS CHALLENGER

What followed showed that neither program had much idea of what was going on, VCC less than ATARI: **39 ♚e5? ♚b4 40 h4 ♚xb3 41 h5 ♚xa4? 42 ♚e4??** (Seizing the "distant opposition") **... c5 43 h6 c4 44 g4? c3 45 h7 c2 46 h8(♛) c1(♛) 47 ♛f6 ♛c2+ 48 ♚e5 c6? 49 g5 ♚b4? 50 ♛d6+ ♚b3 51 ♛e6+ ♚b4 52 g6 a5 53 ♛g4+ ♛c4?? 54 ♛d7??** (Obviously ♕xc4+ wins) **... a4 55 ♛a7??** (♕d4 still wins) **... a3 56 ♛e3??**(♕b6+ ♔c3 57 ♕e3+ seems to offer good drawing chances) **... a2 57 ♛a7 ♛c5+! 58 ♛xc5+ ♚xc5 59 ♚f6 a1(♛)+** and ATARI 4K won the game after another 18 moves.

The heuristics necessary for limited-depth programs to play endgames reasonably well are quite different from those that are needed during the middlegame, and one major manufacturer of chess computers has even come out with a special program module (Applied Concepts' CAPABLANCA EDITION) for playing endgames. The author has evaluated it, and finds that it handles simple endings such as K + P vs. K quite accurately, and more difficult endings rather well (for a computer program). Such simple concepts as "Rooks belong behind passed Pawns" are quite difficult for programs to deal with, since there are times when Rooks do NOT belong behind passed Pawns (for example, when lateral checks of an advancing King are indicated).

A classic example of misapplying this is the game SFINKS X - SAVANT X presented in chapter 9. On the other hand, the faster programs sometimes play quite respectable endings because of the tremendous search depth they achieve when most of the pieces are off the board. BELLE has achieved search depths as great as 30 plies in some situations and often reaches 12 or more plies during endgames. Although such programs tend to play endgames with a tactical flavor, the results can be fairly accurate play and often interesting variations, as in the cliffhanger between CRAY BLITZ and BELLE (also presented in chapter 9).

ADVANCE 2.4

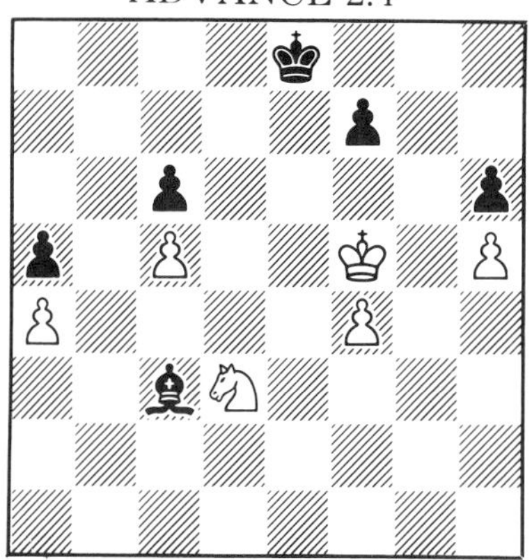

BEBE

A classic example of the focussing effects of a great depth of search occurred in the game BEBE - ADVANCE 2.4 (full score presented in chapter 9), when after 55 moves BEBE found a 7-move forced win: **56 ♞e5! ♝xe5 57 ♚xe5 ♚e7 58 ♚f5 ♚e8 59 ♚f6 ♚f8 60 f5! ♚e8 61 ♚g7 ♚e7 62 ♚xh6** (BEBE "saw" this capture at move 56) **... ♚f8** (On ... ♔f6, 63 ♔h7 forces a promotion) **63 ♚h7 f6 64 ♚g6 ♚g8 65 ♚xf6 ♚h7 66 ♚e6** and BEBE promoted its f-pawn in a few more moves.

To summarize computer endgame play, it shares the strengths and defects inherent in computer middlegames—sharp tactical play and an almost total lack of strategic insight. In blocked positions, most computer programs do not do well. There is a tendency to misplace pieces and tie them down defensively instead of going after counterplay. Endgame play is still the weakest part of the computer program's game, but vast strides have been made and it is perhaps also the most improved part as well.

HOW TO PLAY AGAINST A CHESS PROGRAM

What is the best strategy for playing against a strong computer in a tournament game? After observing many human-computer contests, the author has formulated these ten maxims:

1) Play a quiet strategic opening, and get the game "out of book" at the first GOOD opportunity.

2) Alternatively, the attacking player may be able to get good results with a gambit opening, IF the game is taken "out of book" early, so that the program has to play in a positional environment in which materialism is suicidal. This can be risky if the program is thereby given tactical opportunities.

3) Try to get a middlegame demanding long-range planning. Examples are: minority Pawn attacks, play against hanging and isolated Pawns, slow Kingside Pawn attacks (as in the King's Indian Defense), and just about any kind of strategic Pawn play. Blockaded positions are particularly hard for computer programs to play well.

4) Another approach which offers promise for success and can be more fun is to play for an overpowering attack whose outcome is beyond the program's horizon (12 ply at most). A Pawn or piece sacrifice yielding such an attack will almost always be accepted even if an objectively superior alternative exists. However, once the program understands what is happening to it, it will begin to defend accurately. Few programs (despite the effort devoted to this heuristic) have a "sense of danger" or an adequate appreciation of King safety.

5) Do not play "classically" (a la Tarrasch) unless you are a good enough player to beat the program at its own game. Its heuristics are probably optimized for classical open center-control games such as the Giuoco Piano or the Two Knights' Defense.

6) If you have a chance to play for a variation in which you MIGHT be able to get a strategically better ending if the program doesn't react properly, and which doesn't risk loss if it does, take it. The odds are good that unless the program can find some obvious material or positional factor, it won't know the difference.

7) In endgames against a computer program, expect it to play tactically, and with great accuracy in doing so. The way to win is to outmaneuver the program strategically. A Pawn sacrifice at the right moment can be a devastating weapon because unless a forced loss appears within the program's horizon, it is almost always obligated to accept.

8) Computer programs have difficulty in playing all types of endings, but probably have the most trouble in Rook endings and in King and Pawn endings. Try for this kind of ending, with lots of Pawns left and several breaks available. Minor piece endings seem to be easier for chess programs. Queen endings can be simple for a program, or very difficult depending on the situation (i.e.if strategy is required).

9) Expect the program to be able to play all the basic mates, including that with King, Bishop, and Knight. It was once possible to escape from a program with a stalemate — but the better programs now avoid this.

10) It is sometimes possible to take advantage of a program's heuristics in a drawish ending. The program is required to avoid draws by repetition unless it thinks it is definitely losing otherwise. It will do so even if it has to make an inferior move, and if the program can thus be forced into making enough inferior moves, it can lose the game.

SHOULD COMPUTERS PLAY IN USCF TOURNAMENTS?

Aside from all the interest in computer chess by the programmers and their artificial-intelligence colleagues, what reasons are there for competitive chess players to welcome (or at least tolerate) a computer invasion of their tournaments?

First, there really are not all that many computer programs. It is also very costly in terms of computer time for a big mainframe computer to run a chess program for a tournament game. Moreover, the cost of a long-distance telephone hookup for the duration of a tournament game is substantial. The cost factor alone is a sufficient guarantee that chess programs will participate in tournaments for purposes of scientific research rather than to win prizes. The probability that any individual human will ever be paired with a computer program is not great.

Second, the computer programs are really not very dangerous if one knows how to play them. As human-computer contests become frequent, the computer programmers will be unpleasantly surprised to discover how quickly their human opponents fasten upon the many weaknesses which exist in today's programs. Masters need not fear any of the present-generation programs, provided that they keep cool and do not get careless tactically. The strategic weaknesses are so severe that a strong player who recognizes and exploits them will be almost assured of an easy point. The resulting degradation of computer ratings will be a strong incentive to make the kind of conceptual breakthroughs that are needed. Excellent examples of how to exploit computer weaknesses are provided in Goodside's games in the Fredkin Incentive Match 1982 (chapter 6).

It is going to take a long, long time for computers to become good enough to seriously compete for major prizes in tournaments — if they are allowed to win prizes at all. In the process, humans will learn something from the computers just as the computers learn from the humans. The author does not think that there is any real probability of a computer Grandmaster, let alone a computer World Champion, developing for at least ten years—perhaps not until the end of the century. As mentioned above, early efforts with the new concepts that are needed will probably involve a significant decline in playing strength from present fixed-heuristic levels.

Third, the development of strong mainframe programs which can compete successfully against humans (after years of effort) will have an extremely beneficial effect on chess in the United States and in the rest of the Western world as well. Developments in microcomputer programs follow closely upon their larger cousins, and in fact, the differential between the best microcomputer programs and the best mainframe programs is only about 250 Elo points. When a 2500 rated mainframe program is developed, microcomputers playing at a 2200 level may be expected. Imagine being able to buy a microcomputer that will play a really strong game at skittles speed or even at rapid-transit!

The effects of really strong microcomputers will be to generate an interest for the casual player who buys one to improve his game so that he can compete on a more equal level with the machine. Here are excellent prospects for new members for the USCF, more chess book sales, and more tournament entrants. Making computers eligible to win prizes could and should actually result in a major increase in the prizes won by professional players, due to the increased interest on the part of the public. The "human interest" content of this kind of man-machine contest will be enormous, particularly if the human is perceived as the underdog. Players who resent the fact that chess has never become a "major-league" spectator sport should give this serious thought. An audience equipped with powerful microcomputers could find much more interest in following tournament games between masters than is now the case.

Fourth, computer chess devices can be extremely useful to the serious tournament player. The reason that Socialist countries develop so many more International Masters and Grandmasters than Western nations is not that their people are inherently more talented. It is the support and training facilities made available by the state. Imagine the effect on our developing juniors of having a master opponent available at all times! And when a player reaches a level at which invitations to international events are received, there is a new problem: adjournment analysis. How many players can afford to bring a "second" to such events? The capacity of the USCF and other organizations to pay for this sort of thing is highly limited, and such grants are made only to the most promising players—leaving the rest at a serious disadvantage when it comes to obtaining international titles. Imagine being able to bring a "second" in a briefcase!

Finally, the lessons learned in chess programming will find applications in many other areas which will improve the quality of living. Direct applications may be expected in the development of "robots" which will do our chores and perform unpleasant but necessary jobs, in controllers which can pack many more communications circuits onto a single channel, in exploration vehicles which will search the depths of the seas and the furthest reaches of the solar system—perhaps beyond. Every application for electronic decision-making will be a potential beneficiary of the efforts of tomorrow's chess programmers.

Yes, there are compelling reasons for not only allowing, but encouraging, computer programs to play in our tournaments. Now let us see what happens when they do.

6
THE FREDKIN INCENTIVE MATCH

As an incentive for the development of computer chess programs (which can be an expensive process - the value of the computer time consumed by CRAY BLITZ during a tournament game, for example, is many thousands of dollars at prime-time rates), a prize fund was established in 1980 by Edward Fredkin. $10,000.00 is offered to the first program with an established rating above 2450, and a grand prize of $100,000.00 will be awarded to the first program to win the World Championship. The Chairman of the Fredkin Prize Committee is Dr. Hans Berliner of Carnegie-Mellon University, former World Correspondence Chess Champion. Dr. Berliner organizes a match each year for the purpose of evaluating the progress of the strongest programs, with prizes financed by the interest earned by the fund. In 1980 BELLE won its match with a candidate master, 1½—½; and CHESS 4.9 drew its match with another candidate master, 1—1. In 1981, BELLE lost to Vancouver master Carl Storey, 0—2.

On August 15 through 17, 1982, the Fredkin Prize Fund in conjunction with the national meeting of the American Association for Artificial Intelligence, sponsored a team-style round robin between the four best computer programs in the world and four Pittsburgh candidate masters. Each program played each candidate master once. The result was a convincing victory for the human team. Among the computers, only NUCHESS managed to achieve an even score.

CROSSTABLE

		rtg	perf	1	2	3	4	total
1	Tom Martinak	2097	2351	B5 1	W4 2	B6 3	W8 3½	3½
2	Mike Goodside	2050	2239	W6 1	B8 2	W5 3	B4 3	3
3	Ron Zaffuto	1998	2060	W4 1	B6 1	W8 2	B5 2	2
4	NUCHESS	U/R	2034	B3 0	B1 0	W7 1	W2 2	2
5	CRAY BLITZ	2258	2001	W1 0	B7 ½	B2 ½	W3 1½	1½
6	BELLE	2161	1986	B2 0	W3 1	W1 1	B7 1½	1½
7	Paul Resnick	1995	1978	B8 ½	W5 1	B4 1	W6 1½	1½
8	DUCHESS	1855	1844	W7 ½	W2 ½	B3 ½	B1 1	1

ROUND 1

CRAY BLITZ - Martinak
Two Knights' Defense(C57)

Martinak came out swinging with a wild opening, and when CRAY BLITZ lost time due to its computer being "down", the program was unable to cope with the resulting complications. **1 e4 e5 2 ♞f3 ♞c6 3 ♝c4 ♞f6 4 ♞g5 d5 5 exd5 b5 6 ♝f1 ♞d4 7 c3 ♞xd5 8 ♞e4 ♛h4 9 ♞g3 ♝g4 10 f3 e4 11 cxd4 ♝d6 12 ♝xb5+ ♚d8 13 ♚f2?! ...** Thus far the game has followed "book", but here White ought to play 13 0-0, according to Estrin. The point is that then after 13 ... exf3, White has 14 ♕b3! fxg2 15 ♖f2 and Black is thrown on the defensive. Now White gets in trouble. Unfortunately for CRAY BLITZ, a power failure at the computer site in Minnesota cost it 1½ hours on its clock, and it simply didn't have time to compute all the variations. Martinak exploits his opponent's time trouble cleverly **... exf3 14 gxf3 ♝e6 15 ♞c3 ♛xd4+**

MARTINAK

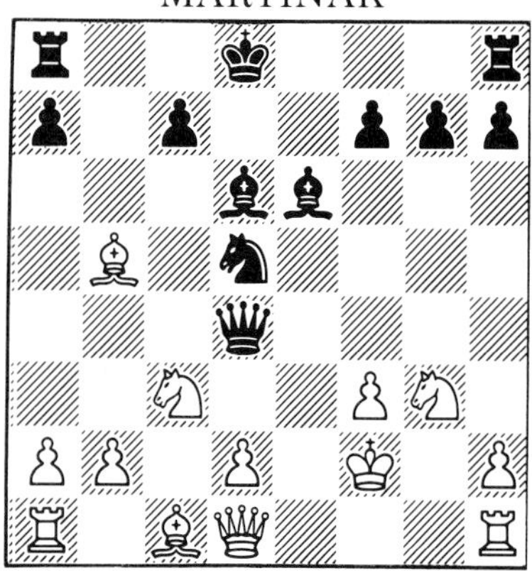

CRAY BLITZ

16 ♚f1? ... CRAY BLITZ inexplicably lets Martinak bring the Bishop back to harass its King, with check! Unappetizing as it looks, White should play 16 ♔e1! after which it is not easy to find a good continuation for Black, who after all is a piece down here. Then ... ♗h3 can be answered by 17 ♕e2 ♘f4 18 ♕e4; or ... ♘f4 may be parried by 17 ♕a4 and it is not clear that Black has compensation. The move played falls right in with Martinak's plans. **... ♝h3+ 17 ♚e1 ♝g2 18 ♝c6 ♞f4 19 ♛a4 ♞d3+ 20 ♚e2 ♞b4 21 ♝xa8? ...** After 21 ♖e1, Black can simply play ... ♕c4+ recovering the piece with a better game. **... ♜e8+ 22 ♚d1 ♝xh1 23 ♞ge2 ...** No better for White is 23 ♘ce2. Now Martinak strikes: **... ♛f2! 24 ♛xe8+ ...** Unfortunately 24 d4 ♕f1+ 25 ♔d2 ♗f4+ 26 ♘xf4 ♕e1+ is mate **... ♚xe8 25 d4 ♝xf3 26 ♝xf3 ♛xf3 27 ♝d2 ♝xh2 28 a3 ♞c6 29 ♚c2 ♛f5+** 0-1

DUCHESS - Resnick
Petroff (C43)

Resnick was making progress after some weak moves by the program, when he missed a tactical point and lost a piece for two Pawns. But DUCHESS' King was somewhat exposed, and when the program didn't find the best continuation, Resnick got the initiative and, with further assistance from DUCHESS, managed to draw the game. **1 e4 e5 2 ♞f3 ♞f6 3 d4 ♞xe4 4 ♝d3 d5 5 ♞xe5 ♝e7 6 0-0 0-0 7 c4 ♞f6 8 c5?! ...** All "book" up to here, but now DUCHESS makes an antipositional move relieving the pressure on d5. More in the spirit of the opening would be 8 ♗g5 or 8 ♘c3. **... c6 9 ♜e1 ♞bd7 10 ♝g5 ...** DUCHESS might as well play 10 f4. **... ♞xe5 11 ♜xe5 ♝e6 12 ♛c2 h6 13 ♝d2 ♞g4 14 ♜e1 ♛c7 15 g3 ♜ae8 16 f3?! ...** DUCHESS ought to continue 16 ♘c3 with the idea b4-b5. **... ♞f6 17 ♞c3 ♞h5** Now the weakening of the Kingside is obvious. **18 ♞e2 ♝h3?** Resnick lets his Bishop get trapped! Although computer programs tend to have difficulty in detecting trapped pieces, here there are no intermediate moves to push the win of the piece over the program's horizon. DUCHESS does not miss its opportunity. **19 g4 ♞f6 20 ♞f4 ♞xg4 21 fxg4 ♝xg4 22 ♝f5 ♝xf5 23 ♛xf5 ♝f6 24 ♝c3 ♝h4 25 ♜xe8** Here 25 ♖e5 seems preferable; as played, Black gets the initiative **... ♜xe8 26 ♚h1?! ...** The idea behind this odd move is to put the Rook on the half-open g-file. Unfortunately, Black doesn't stand still! 26 ♘d3 looks like a reasonable idea; ... ♖e2 can be answered by 27 ♕f4, and the Rook can't do anything on the 2nd rank.

... ♜e4 27 ♜f1 ♝g5 28 ♞h3? ... ♘d3 was still best, but the program wants to trade down since it is ahead material. Unfortunately its opponent doesn't cooperate, and DUCHESS gets all tangled up **... g6 29 ♛f3 ♝e3 30 ♞f2 ♜h4 31 ♞g4 h5 32 ♞e5** This is not bad, but a human player might have simplified White's task by 32 ♕xe3, e.g. ... hxg4 33 ♕f4, or ... ♖xg4 33 ♕e8+ ♔g7 34 ♕e5+. Despite the use of "trade-down" bonuses, programs frequently overlook opportunities for favorable simplification. **... ♜f4.**

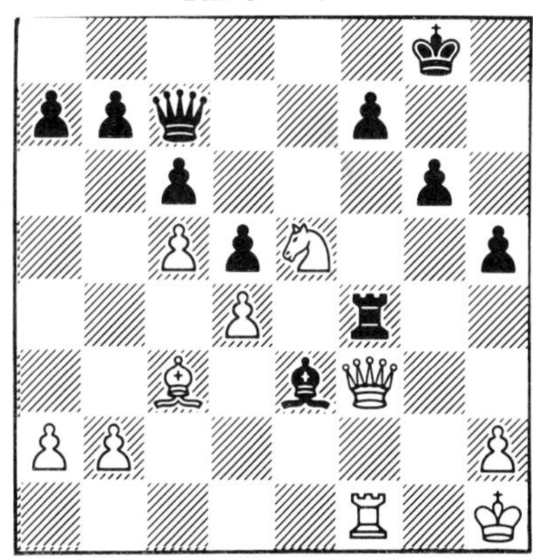

DUCHESS

Resnick is playing with the courage of desperation, finding one move after another to keep the position complicated. And now his efforts are handsomely rewarded: **33 ♛xf4? ...** Was DUCHESS getting tired of this nonsense? If so, this is not the way to stop it! In this sort of position the Queen can become very dangerous. After 33 ♕g2! an exchange of Rooks is forced and White should win rather easily. Probably DUCHESS calculated that it gets Rook, Bishop and Pawn for the Queen, and its trade-down bonus made the transaction seem favorable. **... ♝xf4 34 ♜xf4 ♛e7 37 ♜xf7 ♛g5 36 ♜xb7 ...** So far it looks if giving up the Queen might not have been a bad idea. This Pawn-snatch, however, is inaccurate; better is 36 ♖f1 and White should win with careful play. In playing with several pieces vs. a Queen, it is of paramount importance to keep them coordinated, — a concept which computer programs have little capacity to deal with. Now we see what a Queen can do on an open board — one of the long-range considerations that computer programs can't judge yet. **36 ... ♛c1+ 37 ♚g2 ♛g5+ 38 ♚f1 ...** Better chances may have been offered by 38 ♔f3. **... ♛f4+ 39 ♚e1 ♛xh2 40 ♞xc6 h4 41 ♞e7+ ♚f8 42 ♞xg6+?!** Better, of course, is 42 c6, taking the lead in the race for a new Queen. The program, however, does not understand the value of a tempo in this kind of situation. **... ♚e8 43 ♞e5 ♛g1+ 44 ♚d2 h3 45 ♜xa7?** More loss of time; 45 c6 is still best. **... h2 46 ♜a8+ ♚e7 47 ♜h8 h1(♛) 48 ♜xh1 ♛xh1 49 ♚c2 ♛f1 50 b4? ...** A final blunder; after 50 a4! White retains winning chances. Now the game ends in a draw. **... ♛e2+ 51 ♚b3 ♛d1+ 52 ♚b2 ♛e2+ 53 ♚a3 ♛c2 54 ♝b2 ♛d2 55 b5** Giving up a Pawn needlessly, but the position is drawn anyway. **... ♛a5+ 56 ♚b3 ♛xb5+** ½ - ½

Zaffuto - NUCHESS
Queen's Gambit Accepted(D23)

In this game Zaffuto found some weak points in NUCHESS' heuristics, and sent his a-Pawn on a bayonet charge which the program didn't know how to handle. Then NUCHESS misplaced its Queen and could not develop, after which the program was crushed.
1 d4 ♞f6 2 ♞f3 d5 3 c4 dxc4 4 a4 ... Considered objectively, this move is a loss of time for White since Black does not have to allow a continuation in which a4 is useful. However, this move had the distinct virtue of taking NUCHESS out of its book. The program responded with an elementary mistake: **... ♝e6?** It might be well to give chess programs a heuristic which penalizes the blocking of a center Pawn on the 2nd rank. **5 ♞c3 ♞c6?!** This is not wise either. The c-Pawn should not be blocked, and the Knight is exposed to attack. **6 ♝g5 ...** The apparently strong move 6 e4 would actually be a major mistake—after ... ♗g4! 7 ♗e3 ♗xf3 8 gxf3 ♘a5, White is in trouble positionally. **6 ... ♝f5** NUCHESS admits that its 4th move was an error. **7 a5 ...** To prevent ... ♘a5. **7 ... h6?** At the U.S. Open, Grandmaster Arthur Bisguier advised players paired with a computer to push their Rook Pawns, because the program would not recognize the threat; ... a6 was necessary here. **8 ♝xf6 exf6 9 d5! ...** Of course not 9 e3? ♘b4! 19 ♖c1 ♘d3+. **9 ... ♞b4 10 e4 ♛e7?** This seemingly active move leads to a disaster for NUCHESS. The Queen is misplaced on e7, and prevents the development of the Kingside. The program ought to have moved its Bishop, developed the other one, and castled, with a somewhat inferior position. This is an excellent example of the handicap that its inability to form plans places on a program — here a human player would be thinking about where his pieces "belong", and one need not be a master to realize that the King does not belong stuck in the center, with the Queen in front of it. **11 ♝xc4!?** Safer was 11 ♘d2 ♘d3+ 12 ♗xd3 cxd3 13 0-0 ♗d7 14 ♘c4 with an excellent position, but this turns out to be effective. **11 ... ♝xe4 12 0-0 f5** Virtually forced, due to the threat 13 ♘xe4 ♕xe4 14 ♖e1 winning the Queen. NUCHESS is now in serious difficulties. **13 a6 bxa6 14 ♝xa6 ♞xa6 15 ♜xa6 ...**

NUCHESS

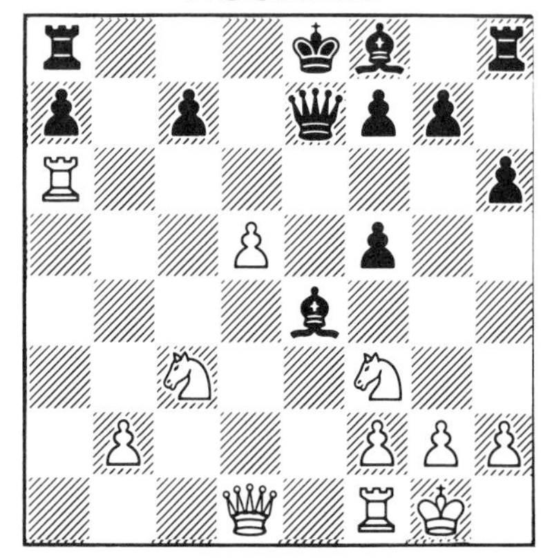

ZAFFUTO

The Rook now comes powerfully into action, and NUCHESS has a lost position, with its King horribly exposed to attack. **15 ... ♛b4** Not ... ♗xf3? 16 ♕xf3 ♕e5 17 d6 ♗xd6 18 ♕xa8+ ♔e7, when of course 19 ♕xh8?? allows mate — but after 19 ♘d5+! ♔e6 20 ♖xd6+! White wins. No better is ... ♕c5 16 ♕a4+! ♔e7 17 ♘e5. The program is lost whatever it does, but NUCHESS apparently has no idea of the threats accumulating, and simply wants to grab a Pawn. **16 ♜a4 ♛xb2 17 ♞xe4 fxe4 18 ♜xe4+ ♚d8 19 ♛a4 ♝c5** NUCHESS offers a piece to stave off disaster — if ... ♗d6, then after 20 ♖fe1 the only uncertainty is whether Black will resign or be mated. **20 ♛c6 ♜b8 21 ♛xc5 ♛f6 22 ♛xa7 ♛b6 23 ♛a4 ♛b5 24 ♛d4 f6 25 ♜fe1 ♛d7 26 h3 ♜b7 27 ♛a1 ♚c8 28 ♛a8+ ♜b8 29 ♛a6+ ♜b7 30 ♜b4 ♛xd5 31 ♛a8+** 1-0

Goodside - BELLE
Reverse Gruenfeld(D02)

In this game Goodside cleverly chooses an ideal opening system to play against a computer program, in which critical strategic decisions arise very early in the game. BELLE finds itself taken "out of book" in a critical position.

1 ♞f3 d5 2 g3 c5 3 ♝g2 ♞c6 4 d4 ... "An excellent system for White. The extra move means Black must proceed with the utmost caution." - R. D. Keene, *Flank Openings*. **... ♞f6 5 0-0 cxd4 6 ♞xd4 e5** BELLE would do better to play ... e6. **7 ♞xc6 bxc6 8 c4 ♝e7 9 ♞c3 e4** Here the apparently safe move ... ♗e6 gets Black into difficulties after 10 cxd5 cxd5 11 ♕a4+. White's pressure on the Black center is acute - the corresponding variation of the Gruenfeld Defense is difficult for White to play since his center hangs by a thread. The whole system is, at best, dubious for Black. BELLE, however, is simply retrieving moves from ECO and of course has no idea what is happening. **10 ♝g5! ...**

BELLE

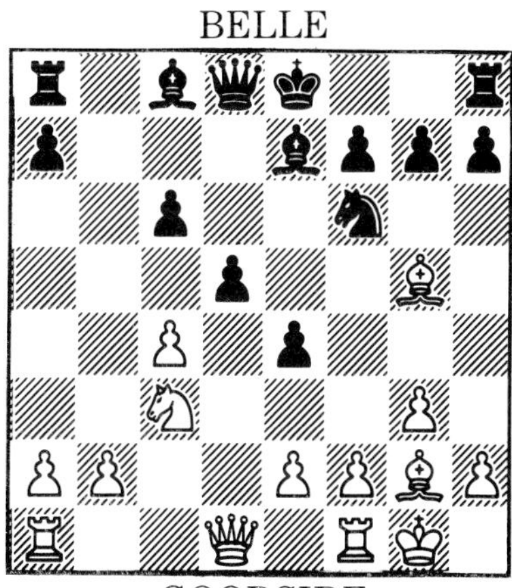

GOODSIDE

Goodside varies with a strong move which may well be an improvement on the line 10 ♕a4 ♗d7 11 ♕a6 0-0 (Kavalek - Radulov, Montilla 1975) in ECO. White simply threatens to capture the d-Pawn, and the threat is by no means easy to defend against, e.g. ... h6 11 ♗xf6 ♗xf6 12 cxd5 ♗xc3 13 bxc3 cxd5 14 c4! and Black is obviously in difficulties; if 12 ... cxd5 13 ♕xd5 simply wins a Pawn, or 10 ... ♗e6 11 cxd5 cxd5 12 ♕a4+ again. BELLE either did not comprehend the threat or could not find a defense, and simply conceded the Pawn: **10 ... 0-0 11 cxd5 ♞xd5 12 ♝xe7 ♛xe7 13 ♞xe4! ...** Here BELLE may have been expecting 13 ♘xd5 cxd5 14 ♕xd5 ♗b7, after which Black at least has some compensation for the Pawn. Goodside prefers to leave the program with a weak isolated c-Pawn. **... ♝a6 14 ♜e1 ♜fd8 15 ♛c2 ♜ab8 16 a3**

BELLE

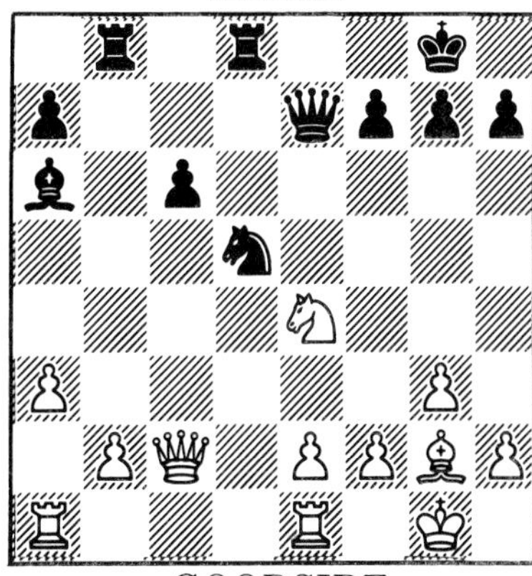

GOODSIDE

Goodside is in no hurry at all to capture the weak c-Pawn, and instead calmly strengthens his position. Now BELLE commits another strategic error: **... f5? 17 ♞c5 ♝b5 18 e4! fxe4 19 ♝xe4 ♛f7 20 ♝xh7+ ...** Finally the Pawn is ripe for taking. **... ♚h8 21 ♝g6 ♛f6 22 ♜e4! ...** BELLE is being crushed; a rare sight! **... ♚g8 23 ♝h7+ ♚h8 24 ♜ae1 ♞c7 25 ♜h4 ...** This is the end. **... ♜d4 26 ♝e4+ ♛xh4** Unfortunately for BELLE, if ... ♔g8 then 27 ♕b3+ wins material, e.g. ... ♖c4 28 ♘d7, or ... ♕f7 28 ♖h8+. **27 gxh4 ♜c4 28 ♛d1 ♜xc5 29 ♛d6 ♞a6 30 ♛g6 ♚g8 31 ♝f5 ♝e2** 1-0 A most impressive victory for the human player.

ROUND 2

Martinak - NUCHESS
Queen's Gambit Accepted(D23)

Between rounds the programmers rushed off to get something to eat, not realizing that in a team round-robin it is impossible for all players to alternate colors each round. In the second round David Slate was unpleasantly surprised to discover that his program had Black again, against a player who had meanwhile been studying NUCHESS' first-round game. Here we see a classic case of the inability of a program to learn from its mistakes, and the ability of a human expert to exploit this.

1 d4 ♞f6 2 ♞f3 d5 3 c4 dxc4 4 a4 ♝e6 5 ♞c3 ♞c6 6 ♝g5 ♝f5 7 a5 h6 8 ♝xf6 exf6 9 d5 ♞b4 10 e4 ♛e7 11 ♝xc4 ♝xe4 12 0-0 f5 13 a6 bxa6 14 ♝xa6 ♞xa6 15 ♜xa6 ♛b4 16 ♜a4 ♛xb2 17 ♞xe4 fxe4 18 ♜xe4+ ♚d8 19 ♛a4 ♝c5 20 ♛c6 ♜b8 21 ♛xc5 ♛f6 22 ♛xa7 ♛b6 23 ♛a4 ♛b5 24 ♛d4 f6

NUCHESS

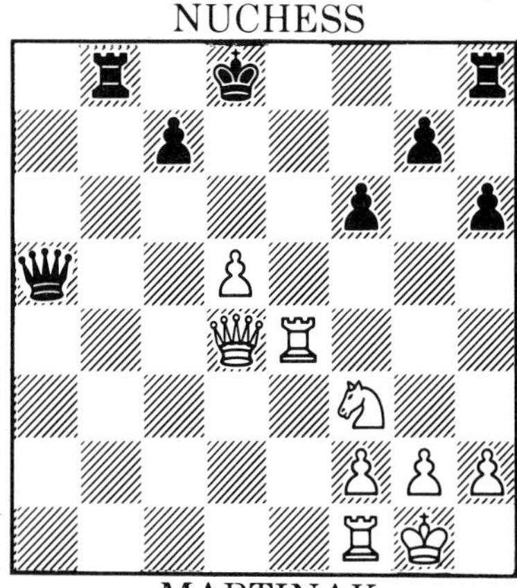

MARTINAK

Here Martinak, who of course has a won game already, finds an "improvement" over Zaffuto's continuation (25 ♖fe1), which turns out to be a slower win. **25 d6 c5 26 ♛d5 c4 27 ♛xb5 ♜xb5 28 ♜xc4 ♜e8 29 ♜c7 ♜d5 30 ♜a1 ♜xd6 31 ♜xg7 ♜c6 32 ♞d4 ♜a6 33 ♜d1 ♚c8 34 g3 ♜b6 35 ♞f5 h5 36 ♜dd7 h4** 1-0

Resnick - CRAY BLITZ
Closed Sicilian(B23)

In this game, Resnick obtained no advantage in the opening, and after an exchanging combination failed to win a Pawn, he forced a draw.

1 e4 c5 2 ♞c3 e6 3 g3 d5 An effective system against the Closed Sicilian, and one particularly well suited to a computer program. Black gets an open game without any problems. **4 exd5 exd5 5 d4 cxd4 6 ♛xd4 ♝e6 7 ♝g2 ♞c6 8 ♛d1 ♞f6 9 ♞ge2 ♝c5 10 0-0 0-0**

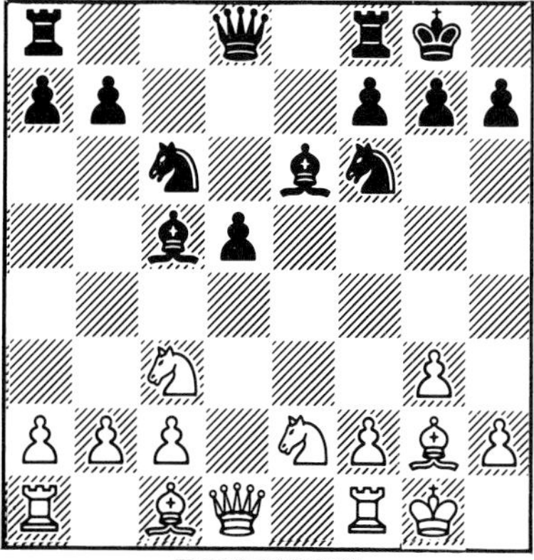

RESNICK

CRAY BLITZ' free development and spatial advantage compensate for the isolated Pawn. Now Resnick, who has gotten no advantage from the opening, plays a combination which he mistakenly expects to win a Pawn: **11 ♝g5 ♝e7 12 ♝xf6 ♝xf6 13 ♞xd5 ♝xd5 14 ♛xd5 ♛b6 15 ♛b3 ♝xb2** Recovering the Pawn with equality. **16 ♜ad1 ♜fd8 17 ♛xb6 axb6** Now both sides have equally weak Pawns, and White's are more subject to attack. **18 ♝d5 ♞d4 19 ♞xd4 ♜xd5 20 ♞b3 ♜xd1?!** Here ...♖ad8 was clearly better, leaving Black with whatever small winning chances might exist in such a position. **21 ♜xd1 g6 22 ♜d7 ♜xa2 23 ♜xb7 ♝c3 24 ♜xb6 ♜xc2 25 ♜c6...** Resnick catches CRAY BLITZ in a pin, but cannot find a way to exploit it. So he forces a draw. **... ♚g7 26 ♚g2 ♚f8 27 ♞d4 ♜d2 28 ♞b3 ♜c2 29 ♜c7 ♚e8 30 ♞d4** Here Resnick could have tried 30 ♔f3 with the idea ♔e4-d3. If then 30 ... f5, 31 ♘d4 ♖d2 (... ♖c1? 32 ♘e2) 32 ♘xf5 winning a Pawn. **... ♜d2 31 ♞b3 ♜c2 32 ♞d4 ♜d2 33 ♞b3 ♜c2 34 ♞d4** 1/2 - 1/2

DUCHESS - Goodside
Sicilian (B41)

Another impressive victory for Goodside, who gives a virtuoso performance in putting strategic pressure on DUCHESS, which (like most programs) is severly handicapped in defending because it has no idea of what is happening to it.

1 e4 c5 2 ♞c3 e6 3 ♞f3 a6 4 ♝e2 ♞c6 5 d4 cxd4 6 ♞xd4 ♛c7 Goodside has cleverly transposed several times to get to a position in which the program is out of its book, and is rewarded when DUCHESS plays a dubious move: **7 ♞xc6?! ...** There is a neat little trap here for the unwary: 7 f4? ♘f6 8 0-0?? ♘xd4 9 ♕xd4 ♗c5 winning the Queen. But there was no need to strengthen Black's center thus; 7 0-0 maintains White's options. **... bxc6 8 0-0 ♞f6 9 ♝e3 ♜b8** Goodside now gets pressure along the half-open b-file which looks at least as effective as the play Black expects on the c-file in a normal Sicilian. **10 b3?! ...** This weakening of the vital c3 square was unnecessary. DUCHESS should have played 10 ♖b1, and if then ... ♗b4, 11 ♕d3. **... ♝b4 11 ♛d3 0-0 12 ♞a4 d5 13 ♝c5?! ...** A typical computer move, all tactics and no strategy whatsoever. Clearly DUCHESS anticipated something like ... ♗xc5 14 ♘xc5 ♘xe4 15 ♘xe4 dxe4 16 ♕xe4, but of course its opponent doesn't oblige. A reasonable continuation for White is 13 exd5 cxd5 14 c4! with at least an equal game. **... ♜d8 14 ♛e3 ♞d7 15 ♝xb4 ♜xb4**

GOODSIDE

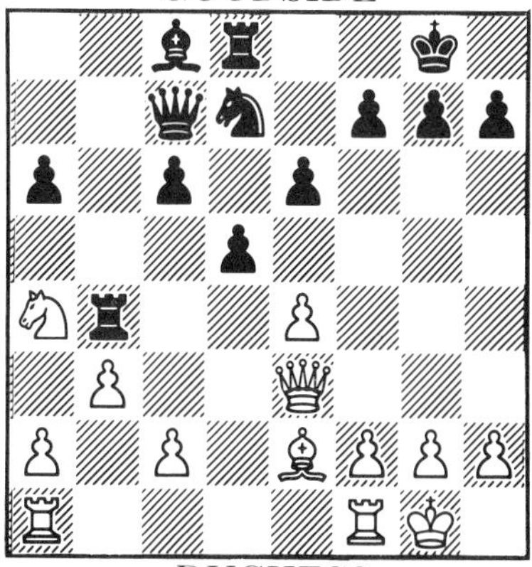

DUCHESS

16 ♝d3?! ... Again, 16 c4! was about the only move worth considering here. This failure to fight for the center lets Goodside get a bind on DUCHESS' position, which it does not react to properly and which eventually leads to disaster. **... d4 17 ♛d2 c5 18 ♜fd1 ...** A move completely irrelevant to the position. 18 ♘b2-c4 was a plan worth considering. **... e5 19 ♜ac1 ♛d6 20 c3 ♜b8** Of course! Goodside is quite willing to let the program give him a passed d-Pawn. **21 ♞b2 ♞f8 22 ♛e2 ♞e6 23 ♞c4?! ...** Here it would probably have been better to play 23 g3, since Black gets nothing from ... dxc3? 24 ♖xc3 ♘d4 25 ♕e3. The program would then have at least one well-placed piece after eventually playing ♘c4. As the game went, its pieces became misplaced. **23 ... ♞f4**

(See diagram next page)

24 ♞xd6?! ... After 24 ♕f3! ♕e7, DUCHESS would have its last reasonable prospects for holding the position, e.g. 25 cxd5 cxd5 26 ♖d2-c2 with counterplay on the c-file. The program's inability to formulate this kind of plan proves fatal, since it leaves the initiative in Goodside's hands and lets him choose the moment to open the d-file for a breakthrough. **.. ♞xe2+ 25 ♝xe2 ♜xd6 26 ♜d2 ♝b7 27 f3 ♜bd8 28 ♝c4 ♚f8 29 g3? ...** This weakening of the h1-a8 diagonal immediately leads to trouble. **... g5!**

Position after 23 moves.
GOODSIDE

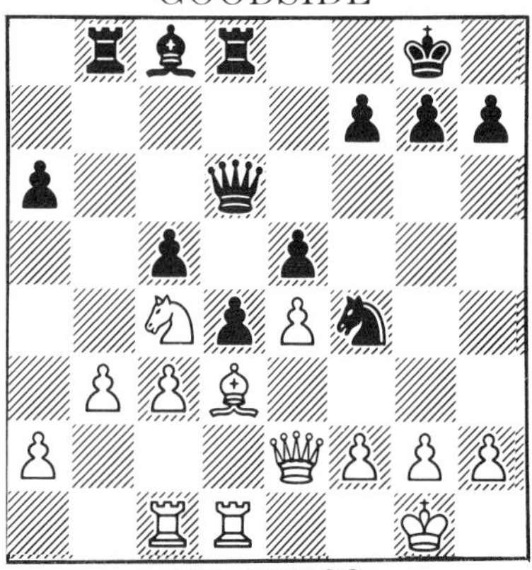

DUCHESS

30 ♜d3 g4 31 ♜e1 dxc3 32 ♜xc3 ♜d1 A decisive penetration. **33 ♚f2 ♜1d2+ 34 ♜e2 h5 35 a3 ♜8d4 36 ♚e3 ♜d1** With the simple and compelling threat ... ♖f1, winning the e-Pawn. **37 ♚f2 ♜h1 38 ♚g2 ♜dd1** And now the program is faced with mating threats. **39 fxg4 hxg4 40 ♜ee3 f5! 41 ♝e2 ...** The loss of the e-Pawn is now so inevitable that even DUCHESS understands it, but Goodside correctly wants more! **... ♜dg1+ 42 ♚f2 ♜a1 43 ♚g2 f4!** Not ... ♗xe4+? 44 ♖xe4 fxe4 45 ♗xg4 and White gets out of the bind. After this White could well have resigned. **44 ♝xg4 fxe3 45 ♜xe3 ♜hg1+ 46 ♚h3 ♜xa3 47 ♜f3+ ♚e7 48 ♜f5 ♜xb3 49 ♜xe5+ ♚d6 50 ♜e6+ ♚c7** 0-1

BELLE - Zaffuto
Sicilian(B22)

BELLE managed to get itself in serious trouble in this game, and at one time Zaffuto had a very strong continuation which might have given him a winning position. He missed it, perhaps in time pressure, and soon his game fell apart — illustrating one of the strengths of computer programs compared to human players: they don't get in time pressure, and they don't get rattled.

1 e4 c5 2 c3 d5 3 exd5 ♛xd5 4 d4 e5(?) ... This is not the way to play against BELLE — giving it an open game with a slightly better position. The road to equality here is ... e6!, e.g. 5 ♘f3 ♘c6 6 ♗e2 ♘f6 7 0-0 cxd4 and Black has play against the isolated Pawn. **5 dxe5 ♛xe5+ 6 ♝e3 ♞f6 7 ♞f3 ♛c7 8 ♞a3 ...** So far according to theory, but now Zaffuto varies with an inferior move: **8 ... ♝d7?!** Correct is ... a6; this Bishop belongs at f5 or g4. **9 ♝c4 ♝d6?!** More prudent would have been ... ♗e7. Zaffuto dares BELLE to double his f-Pawns, which the program accepts: **10 ♝g5! 0-0 11 ♝xf6 ♜e8+ 12 ♝e2 gxf6 13 ♛d3 ♝f4** Zaffuto wants to keep BELLE from castling Queenside. **14 g3? ...** This weakening of the Kingside was unnecessary, and allowed Zaffuto to get a great deal of counterplay. Simply 0-0 followed by something such as ♗d1-c2 would have been strong. **... ♝h6 15 0-0 ♝h3 16 ♞b5?! ...** BELLE is too optimistic here. The way to play this position was 16 ♖e1 followed by ♗f1. BELLE walks into a combination by which Zaffuto undoubles his Pawns: **... ♛c6 17 ♜fe1 ♞d7 18 c4**

ZAFFUTO

BELLE

♜xe2! 19 ♜xe2 Or 19 ♕xe2 ♗g4 20 ♘fd4 ♗xe2 21 ♘xc6 bxc6, and Black winds up with a material advantage. **... ♞e5 20 ♜xe5** Clearly forced. **... fxe5 21 ♛a3? ...** BELLE defends poorly — in fact, does not even recognize that defense is necessary, in a strategic sense. As long as the immediate tactical threats are covered, that's good enough for the program! 21 ♘c3 was much more appropriate. **... a6 22 ♞h4 ♝g5! 23 ♞f3 ...**

ZAFFUTO

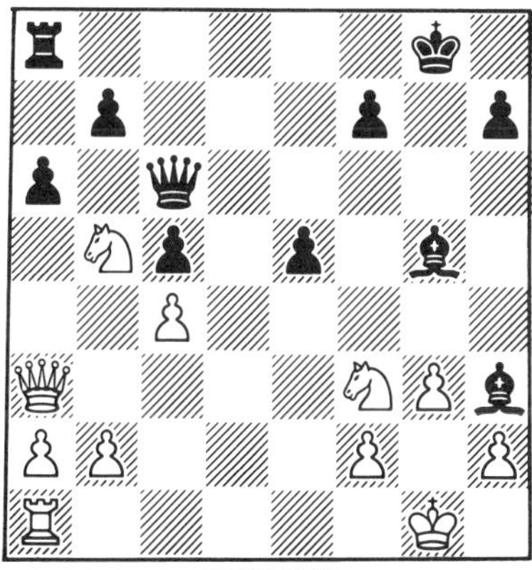

BELLE

A critical moment. After ... ♗f6! it is hard to see how BELLE could have survived. Black threatens ... ♖d8 winning the Knight at b5, and there doesn't seem to be a good answer; if 24 ♖d1? ♖d8! wins; or on 24 ♖e1? e4! wins. So it seems White would have to play 24 ♘e1, after which 24 ... ♖d8 25 ♘c3 ♖d4! 26 b3 (not ♕a4? ♕xa4 27 ♘xa4 ♖xc4 28 b3 ♖e4 29 ♘xc5 ♖e2 and the Rook on the seventh rank and the Bishops are too much; or 26 ♕b3 ♗e6 winning the c-Pawn) ... b5! 27 cxb5 (or 27 ♘d5 b4 28 ♘xf6+ ♕xf6 and: 29 ♕a5 ♕d6!; 29 ♕b2 e4! 29 ♕c1 ♗g4 and White has a miserable position in each case) ...axb5 and now: 28 ♘e2? ♖d2 winning; 29 ♕b2 ♗g5 and Black's attack looks unstoppable; 29 ♕c1 ♔g7 threatening ... h6 followed by ... ♗g5, among other things. From the course of the game, however, it appears Zaffuto was pressed for time here. **23... ♝h6 24 ♞h4 ♜d8?!** If so, he should have taken the draw by ... ♗g5 etc. **25 ♞c3 ♝g5** Here ... ♗e6 was better. **26 ♞d5 ♚h8** Threatening to win by ... ♗xh4 followed by ... ♖g8+, but BELLE parries this easily; **27 ♞f3 ♝f6 28 ♞xf6 ♛xf6 29 ♛c3! ♚g8** Here sacrificing the Exchange by ... ♖d4 was worth considering. It would not then be easy for BELLE to deal with the mating threats and the passed d-Pawn. **30 ♜e1 ♛c6 31 ♛xe5 ♛g6 32 ♛xc5 ♜c8 33 ♛d5 ♝e6 34 ♛xb7 ♜xc4 35 ♞e5** 1-0

ROUND 3

Goodside - CRAY BLITZ
English(A30)

Three consecutive masterful performances by Goodside! In this game, CRAY BLITZ is continually faced with decisions whose consequences are purely strategic, and blindly commits positional hara-kiri. This game is an excellent example of how to defeat a computer program — keep the game tactically quiet, but strategically complicated. At no time does CRAY BLITZ get an opportunity to unleash its tactical ability.

1 ♞f3 ♞f6 2 g3 b6 3 ♝g2 ♝b7 4 0-0 c5 5 c4 g6 6 ♞c3 ♝g7 7 d4 cxd4 8 ♞xd4 ♝xg2 9 ♚xg2 0-0 10 e4 ♛c7 Evidently CRAY BLITZ out of its book here, for this is a weak move — the Queen is exposed to attacks by ♘b5 or ♗f4. A better continuation is ... ♘a6. **11♛e2 ♞c6** ... ♘a6 was still the best move. CRAY BLITZ "thinks" that White will not exchange on c6, because then... dxc6 gives Black control of d5 and eliminates a potential weakness on d7, but there is another consideration which the computer cannot evaluate. **12 ♞xc6 dxc6?!** Now it would have been better to play 12 ... ♕xc6, maintaining pressure on the c-file, with possibilities for a good game after ... d6 and ... ♘d7. This allows Goodside to develop his Bishop to a strong square with tempo. **13 ♝f4 ...**
(See diagram next page)

13 ... e5 A critical decision, which the program makes with no understanding of the tradeoffs involved. CRAY BLITZ is unable to consider the long-range

Position after White's 13th move.
CRAY BLITZ

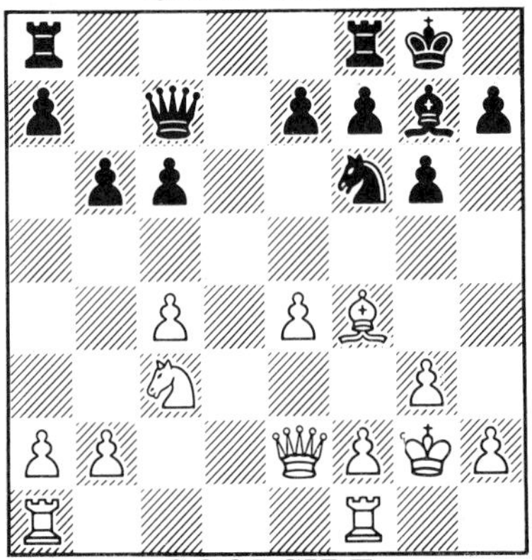

GOODSIDE

implications of blocking its Bishop's diagonal, as against the advantages of controlling and perhaps occupying d4. Computer programs as yet still do not deal well with problems involving weak and strong squares. After the alternative ... ♕b7, Black would have a slightly inferior but defensible position. **14 ♝e3 ♜ad8 15 ♜ad1 ♜fe8 16 ♜xd8 ♜xd8 17 ♜d1 ♛b8** An unnatural move. Either ... ♖d7 or ... ♘h5 (intending ... ♗f8, ♘g7-e6) would be better. **18 f3 ♜xd1?** This is a mistake often made by computer programs — surrendering control of an open file, CRAY BLITZ might have tried the maneuver ... ♘e8-c7-e6, threatening to post the Knight on d4. **19 ♛xd1 h6** The program is drifting now; this simply creates a target. After ... ♘e8 CRAY BLITZ could have contested the d-file. **20 ♛d2 ♚h7 21 g4 b5?** Another unwise move, creating more weaknesses which Goodside cleverly exploits. **22 cxb5 cxb5 23 ♝c5 b4?** And here ... ♘e8 would have been a useful defensive move; CRAY BLITZ drives the Knight where it wants to go anyway, in the process placing its a and b Pawns on squares where they are indefensible. From the evidence of this game, it seems clear that CRAY BLITZ does not have any understanding of what a "bad Bishop" is. **24 ♞d5 a5 25 ♞xf6+ ...** Goodside sees an easy win in the ending and steers for it **... ♝xf6 26 ♛d6 ♛xd6 27 ♝xd6 h5 28 h3 hxg4 29 hxg4 g5 30 b3 ♝g7** CRAY BLITZ is lost in any case, but it may have been better to abandon the e-Pawn and activate its Bishop by 30 ... ♗d8 31 ♗xe5 ♗b6. Now both the a- and b-Pawns are lost, and Black's game collapses. **31 ♝c7 ♝f6 32 ♝xa5 ♝e7 33 ♚f2 ♚g6 34 ♚e2 f6 35 ♚d3 ♚f7 36 ♚c4 ♝f8 37 ♝xb4 ♝h6 38 ♚d5 ♝g7 39 ♚c6 ♚e8 40 a4 f5** 1-0

NUCHESS - Resnick
Sicilian(B23)

NUCHESS played by far the best chess of the four programs participating. In this game, it held its own strategically in a semi-closed position, until its human opponent made a tactical error, which the program exploited flawlessly.

1 f4 ... NUCHESS often plays Bird's opening, which may not be a bad idea for a program confronting human opponents. **... g6 2 ♞c3 ♝g7 3 e4 c5 4 ♞f3 ♞c6 5 ♝c4 a6 6 0-0 e6** White was threatening to play f5. **7 a4 ...** Played to restrain b5. If immediately d3, then ... b5 8 ♗b3 ♘d4 is embarrassing **... ♞ge7 8 e5! ...**NUCHESS displays some strategic "insight", although this move is tactically justified. After 8 d3?! d5!, Black has a fine game with control of the center. **... d5** After anything else, 9 ♘e4 is crushing. **9 exd6 ♛xd6 10 ♞e4! ...** A nice point: the Pawn on f4 is poisoned (... ♕xf4?? 11 ♘fg5 ♕e5 12 ♘xf7! and if ... ♕xe4?? 13 ♘d6+ wins the Queen.) **... ♛c7 11 d3** Of course not 11 ♘xc5?, after which ... ♘a5 wins a piece. **... b6**
(See diagram next page)

12 c3 ?! ... A typical computer solution to a positional problem: direct attack. The program wishes to develop its Bishop on c1, and does not consider the long-range implications of weakening the d-Pawn, which allows Black unnecessary play. A better approach was 12

Position after 11 moves.

RESNICK

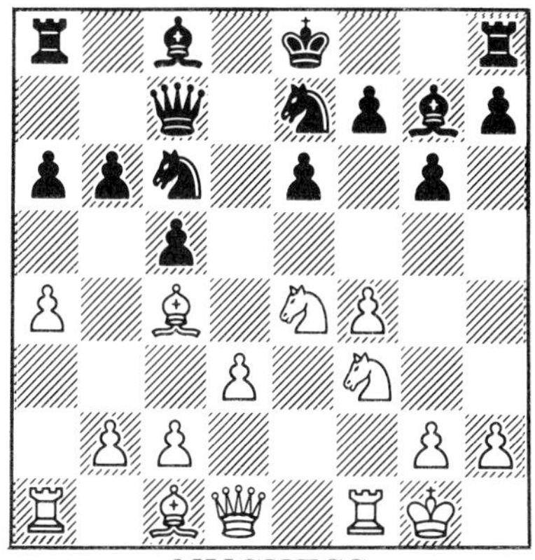

NUCHESS

♖b1. **... 0-0 13 ♝d2 ♝b7 14 ♛c2** This is probably not the best square for the Queen; 14 ♕e2 or 14 ♕e1 (with the idea g4 and ♕h4) would be more active. **... ♞a5 15 ♝a2 ♜fd8 16 ♜ae1 ♛d7?!** Creating a dangerous Knight fork possibility on f6, which NUCHESS promptly exploits. Better play for Black was ... ♗d5! more or less forcing an exchange on d5 (17 ♗b1? ♗b3 18 ♕c1 ♗xa4; 17 b3?! b5), and after 17 ♗xd5 exd5 18 ♘g3 ♘ac6 Black has a reasonable game. **17 ♝b1**

RESNICK

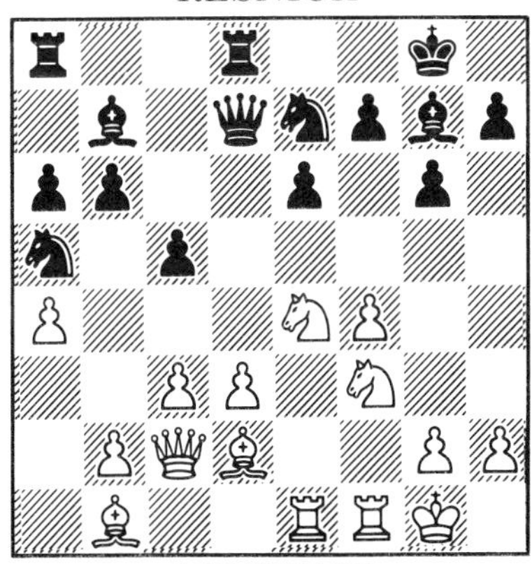

NUCHESS

... ♝c6? A mistaken plan which ultimately loses the Exchange. Better was ... ♘ac6, preventing the following Knight incursion, with a slight positional advantage for Black. **18 ♞e5! ♝xe5?** Here Resnick could have played the surprising ... ♗xa4!, after which: a) 19 ♕c1 ♕c7 with a Pawn plus; b) 19 ♘xd7 ♗xc2 20 ♘xb6 ♗xb1 21 ♖xb1 ♖ab8 22 ♘a4 c4 with a roughly even game. The move played creates a dark-square weakness which ultimately proves fatal. Another superior alternative was ... ♕c7. **19 fxe5 ♝xa4?** Resnick should have played ... ♗xe4! 20 ♖xe4 c4! 21 d4 ♘d5, after which White is better but Black seems to have a defensible position. **20 ♞f6+ ♚g7 21 ♝h6+ ♚h8** ... ♔xh6 would lose to 22 ♕d2+, of course. **22 ♞xd7** of course this is good enough, but a human master might play 22 ♕f2 with the idea ♕h4, ♗g7+, ♕xh7 mate, which appears unstoppable. **... ♝xc2 23 ♞xb6 ♝xb1** An unpleasant concession, but ... ♖b8 24 ♗xc2 ♖xb6 25 ♗g5! ♘ac6 26 ♖xf7 ♖e8 27 ♗a4 is worse. **24 ♞xa8 ♞f5 25 ♝g5 ♜xa8 26 ♜xb1 h6 27 ♝f6+ ♚g8 28 b4 cxb4 29 ♜xb4 ♞e3?** Black's position is of course quite hopeless, but ... ♘c6 would have offered more resistance. **30 ♜fb1 ♞d5??** Apparently Resnick overlooked the ensuing back-rank mate, probably in severe time pressure. **31 ♜b8+ ♜xb8 32 ♜xb8+** 1-0

Zaffuto - DUCHESS
Queen's Gambit Declined(D35)

In this game, Zaffuto plays an ideal game plan against a computer program — a minority attack in the Exchange Variation of the Queen's Gambit Declined. This is easy for White to play and rather hard for Black to defend, a strong weapon against human opponents. Poor DUCHESS never had a chance.

1 d4 d5 2 c4 e6 3 ♞c3 ♞f6 4 ♝g5 ♝e7 5 e3 0-0 6 cxd5 exd5 7 ♝d3 c6 After only seven moves, all reasonable, the opening is in uncharted waters. The "book" moves are ... ♘bd7, ... c5, and ♗e6. **8 ♛c2 ♞bd7 9 ♞ge2 ♜e8 10 0-0 ♞f8 11 ♜ab1 ...** Zaffuto now employs one of the stock game plans familiar to most tournament players, the minority Pawn attack. The objective is to leave Black with a backward Pawn on a half-open file. The effectiveness of this strategy is such that theory now prefers to avoid playing c6 in this opening. **11 ... ♝g4** For this plan of action, it might be slightly more accurate to play ... h6 first, the point being that after 12 ♗h4 ♗d6 13 b4 ♗g4 14 h3, Black could play ... ♗h5 and if White then continued with ♘f4, capture the Knight which would spoil White's Pawn structure. Another, and probably better, approach is 11 ... ♘e4, countering the minority attack by generating threats to the safety of the White King, but this is the sort of strategic judgment which Chess programs cannot yet make. **12 b4 ♝d6 13 h3**

DUCHESS

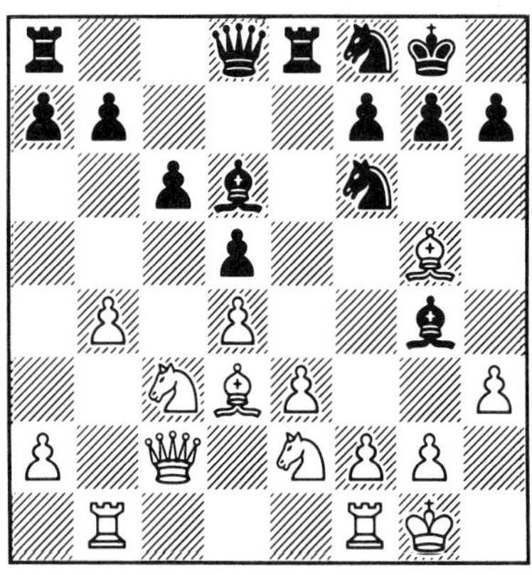

ZAFFUTO

♝xe2?! This Bishop is important to Black, and should not lightheartedly be exchanged. The right continuation here was to oppose the strong White Bishop, e.g. ... ♗h5 14 ♘f4 ♗xf4 15 ♗xf4 ♘e6 16 ♗g3 ♗g6, and although Black has had to allow the exchange of its "good" Bishop, all the Black pieces are well placed. **14 ♞xe2 ♜e6?** DUCHESS wants to play ... ♕c7, which is simply a positional mistake ... h6 15 ♗h4 ♖c8 is the right way to defend here; e6 should be reserved for the Knight at f8. **15 b5**

DUCHESS

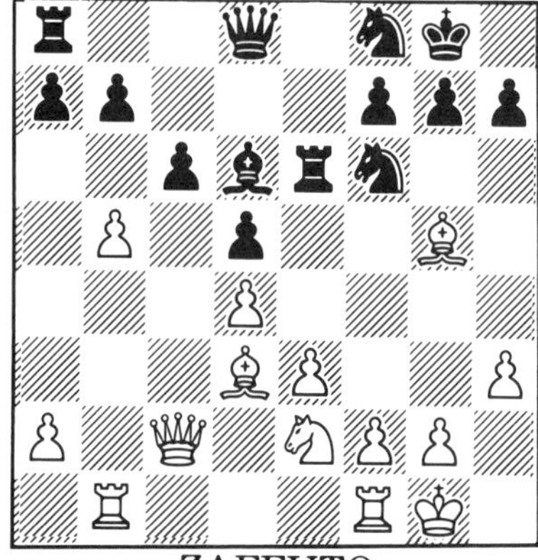

ZAFFUTO

15 ... ♛c7? DUCHESS continues with its "plan", which leads to positional disaster. **16 ♞f4 ♜ee8 17 bxc6 ♝xf4** After ... bxc6 18 ♗xf6 gxf6 19 ♘h5 it is not at all clear how Black can survive. But now an exchange of Queens is forced, and DUCHESS has no play at all since White holds all the cards — the Bishops, a Pawn weakness to attack, and control of an open file. These add up to a winning advantage. **18 ♝xf4 ♛xc6 19 ♛xc6 bxc6 20 ♜fc1 ♞e6 21 ♝e5 ♞d7 22 ♝d6** Zaffuto does not fall into 22 ♖xc6 ♘xe5 23 dxe5 ♘d8 and Black exchanges its weak c-Pawn for the solid White d-Pawn — a typical short-range tactical computer approach to defense. **... ♞d8** The Knights are clumsy in this defensive role, and wind up miserably posted as DUCHESS is driven back all along the line. **23 a4** Slightly more accurate was 23 ♗f5. **23 ... ♜e6 24 ♝g3 ♞b6 25 a5 ♞c8 26 ♝f5 ♜e7 27 a6** This turns out well, but a more reliable way to win was 27 ♖b2 followed by doubling on the b-file. **... ♞b6?** Here DUCHESS should have played 27 ... g6 followed, if necessary, by ... f5 driving away one of the Bishops. The program would then have prospects for untangling its pieces by ... ♖d7, ... ♘e7 etc. **28 ♝d6 ♜e8 29 ♝c7** With the exchange of the defender of c6 and b7, DUCHESS' doom is sealed. **29 ... ♞c4**

30 ♗xd8 ♖axd8 31 ♗d3 ... Now DUCHESS must lose at least a Pawn; the program chooses to sacrifice its Knight in "desperation". **... ♞xe3?! 32 fxe3 ♖xe3 33 ♗f1 ♖ee6 34 ♖b7** As usual, this invasion of the 7th rank is immediately decisive **... ♖a8 35 ♖c7 ♖e4 36 ♖1xc6 ♔f8 37 ♖c8+ ♖xc8 38 ♜xc8+ ♚e7 39 ♜c7+ ♚f6 40 ♜xa7 ♖xd4 41 ♖c7 ♖e4 42 a7 ♖e8 43 ♗b5 ♖d8 44 ♗c6** 1-0

BELLE - Martinak
Ruy Lopez(C88)

In competition with other computer programs, which do not formulate positional plans and which tend to play relatively open games because of their heuristics, BELLE has proven to be virtually unbeatable because of its superior opening "book" and search depth. Even when BELLE gets into difficulties, it usually finds some tactical shot that rescues the game. Against human opponents, however, the computer World Champion does not do so well, particularly in situations requiring positional judgment and long-range planning. This game is an excellent example of the effects of BELLE's positional weaknesses in closed positions. Martinak, known as a tactical player, plays a closed game and simply waits for BELLE to commit positional suicide.

1 e4 e5 2 ♞f3 ♞c6 3 ♝b5 a6 4 ♝a4 ♞f6 5 0-0 ♝e7 6 ♜e1 b5 7 ♝b3 0-0 8 a4 ♝b7 9 ♞c3 b4 10 ♞d5 ♞a5 11 ♝a2 ... Here BELLE varies from ECO (11 ♘xf6+); it is unclear why the program chose a line which keeps the position closed and gives White no prospects for an advantage. One would think that its chances would be much better in the wild positions resulting from the Marshall Attack (8 c3 d5), where its encyclopedic opening knowledge and tactical strength might be decisive **... d6 12 ♞xe7+?!** The first, although slight, positional concession; no doubt Martinak was delighted to have his "bad" Bishop exchanged. Few computer chess programs have any understanding at all of what makes Bishops "good" or "bad", as BELLE's play in this game demonstrates. **... ♛xe7 13 d3 h6 14 c3 bxc3 15 bxc3 ♝c8 16 ♞d2? ...** The Knight is badly posted on d2, blocking the diagonal of the Bishop. This error deserves the more criticism because BELLE had an excellent move available in 16 ♘h4! with the neat threat ♘g6. This would naturally lead to a strong Kingside attack after moves such as ♕f3, ♘f5, g4-g5 etc., with good prospects for winning. **... ♝e6**

MARTINAK

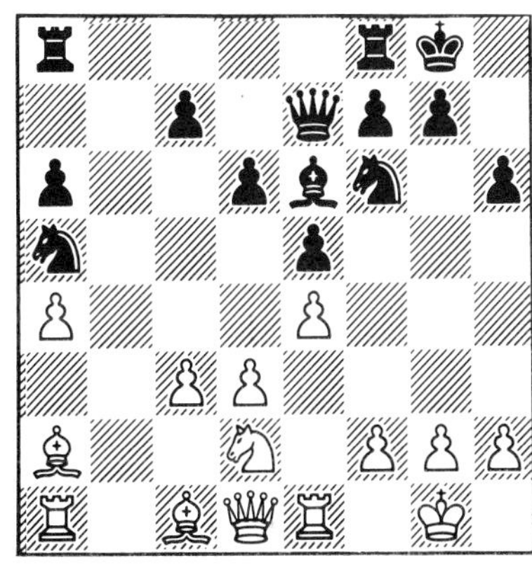

BELLE

17 c4?? A terrible positional blunder! The program "thinks" that it has to prevent ... d5, which was not really a threat at all, and locks in its Bishop for the rest of the game. This move allows Black to transform a semi-open position, which could be opened up at an opportune moment to give the two Bishops full play, into a closed one — much to the detriment of the side that has the advantage of the two Bishops. **17 ... c5 18 ♝a3** Now both of BELLE's Bishops are hemmed in — one by its own Pawns, the other by Black's. This position is a good example of how it is possible for a Knight to sometimes be much more valuable than a Bishop. **... ♞c6 19 ♜f1 g5!**

Preventing the only possible break for BELLE, which now has no way of avoiding slow strangulation. **20 ♜b1 ♜ab8 21 ♜xb8? ...** Like other programs, BELLE seems to have little understanding of the value of controlling an open file, and unnecessarily surrenders the b-file. Here White is already under considerable pressure because of the threatened Knight invasions at d4, b4, and f4. A reasonable plan would be 21 ♖e1 followed by ♘f1-e3-d5, and if Black exchangs on b1 and then plays ... ♖b8, BELLE would have the resource ♕a1 (21 ♖e1 ♖xb1 22 ♕xb1 ♖b8 23 ♕a1! ♘d4 24 ♖b1)**.... ♜xb8 22 f3?...** It was still possible to play ♖e1 followed ♘f1, etc. This blocks the last possible line of action for the Bishop at a2, and allows Martinak to plant a Knight at f4 as well. **... ♞h5 23 ♜f2 ♞f4 24 ♞f1**

MARTINAK

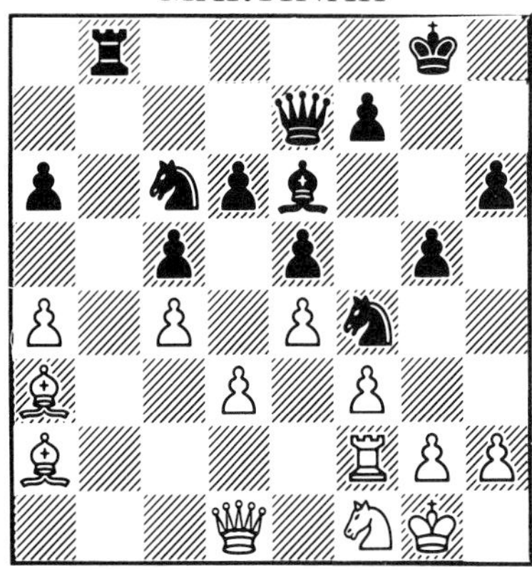

BELLE

Finally BELLE finds a meaningful move, but this is purely by accident and the program is not expecting to play the effective continuation ♘e3-d5, after which White might have some slender prospects for holding the game, and could at least put up much more resistance. **... ♛c7 25 ♝c1 ♚h7** Martinak, of course, welcomes the exchange of the Knight on f4, which will give him another open file to play on and will leave BELLE with a terminal case of dark-square weakness. **26 ♝xf4?** Again ♘e3 was the only move worth considering. **... gxf4 27 ♞d2?!** Another move played with no thought to the future. BELLE should immediately play ... g3, hoping either to get some freedom along the f or g files, or to eliminate the cramping f-Pawn. **... ♝d7 28 g3 ♜g8 29 g4?! ...** It was relatively better to play ♘f1, but BELLE's position is so riddled with weaknesses that nothing can save it now. **29 ... ♛b6 30 ♚h1??** The last opportunity for a prolonged resistance was 30 ♘b1 ♕b4 31 ♕c1!, sacrificing the a-Pawn (which will fall soon anyway) to activate the Knight. BELLE allows a decisive Queen penetration instead. **... ♛b2 31 ♝b1 ♞d4 32 a5 ♛c3 33 h3 ♛xa5 34 ♝c2 ♛b4 35 ♜g2 ...** BELLE has absolutely no play at all, and can only mark time while Martinak gets another Queen. **... a5 36 ♜f2 a4 37 ♝b1 a3 38 ♞f1 ♝a4 39 ♛c1 ♜b8 40 ♝a2 ♜b7 41 ♚g2 ♝c2 42 ♜xc2 ♞xc2 43 ♛xc2 ♛b2 44 ♛d2** 0-1

ROUND 4

Martinak - DUCHESS
Queen's Gambit Accepted(D24)

In the last round Martinak, with three successive victories against the strongest programs, perhaps became slightly overconfident. Playing White against the weakest program, he essayed a dubious variation which should have resulted in a positional disaster; but DUCHESS missed the strongest continuation and Martinak recovered the initiative, developing it into a dangerous attack which should have won the game. At a crucial moment, Martinak missed the winning move and DUCHESS found a clever resource to defuse the attack. Martinak then missed other chances to win, could do no more than recover material equality, and eventually the game ended in a draw.

1 d4 d5 2 c4 dxc4 3 ♞f3 ♞f6 4 ♞c3 a6 5 a4 ♞c6 6 d5 ... White's best try for an advantage is 6 e4. **... ♞a5** Black gets easy equality after ... ♘b4 7 e4 e6. **7 e4 ♝g4 8 ♝e2 ♝xf3**

DUCHESS

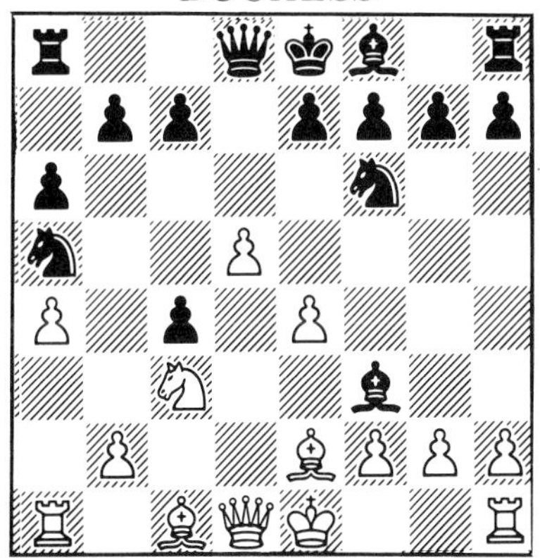

MARTINAK

9 gxf3?! ... This is certainly unnecessary. After 9 ♗xf3 White has a strong position, with possibilities for embarrassing Black by an eventual e5. **... g6 10 ♝g5** Here 10 e5, followed by f4 would have been more consistent with White's previous play. **... ♝g7 11 ♛c2 ♞h5 12 ♜d1 ♛d6** The weakening effect of Martinak's ninth move is now clear; DUCHESS cannot be prevented from planting its Knight on f4. **13 ♝e3 ♞f4 14 ♝d4 ♝xd4 15 ♜xd4 c6?** Very strong was ... e5!, seizing control of d4 and reinforcing the Knight on f4; e.g. 16 ♖d1 ♕b4! and White, faced with the threat of Black playing ... ♘b3-d4, is really in a mess. Now Martinak has a chance to get untracked. **16 ♜d1 cxd5?!** And here ... c5! would have been partly redeemed DUCHESS' error on the previous move. **17 ♞xd5** The strongly posted Knight, and control of the d-file, compensate Martinak for his other positional problems and Pawn minus. The first dividend is the elimination of the bothersome Knight on f4. **... ♞xe2?!** Here it is quite obvious that the Knight on d5 is a better piece than the Bishop on e2 — except to a computer program; DUCHESS captures the wrong minor piece. After ... ♘xd5 17 ♖xd5 ♕b4+, Black can retain its extra Pawn. **18 ♚xe2 0-0 19 ♛c3 b6** Not 19 ... ♕c5? 20 ♘xe7+ and White recovers the Pawn. **20 ♞e3 ♛e6 21 h4** Now Martinak is starting to take control of the game, and his attacking chances are greatly enhanced by DUCHESS' feeble reply. **21 ... ♜fe8?** Here ... h5 would have saved DUCHESS from a great deal of trouble to come, and kept the advantage for the program, but this is the sort of prophylactic defensive move that computer programs don't yet know should be played on general principles. **22 ♞d5 ♛d6 23 h5 ♜ec8 24 f4 ♞b3** DUCHESS begins to exploit White's Queenside weaknesses; as will be seen, just in time to ultimately save the game. **25 hxg6 fxg6**

DUCHESS

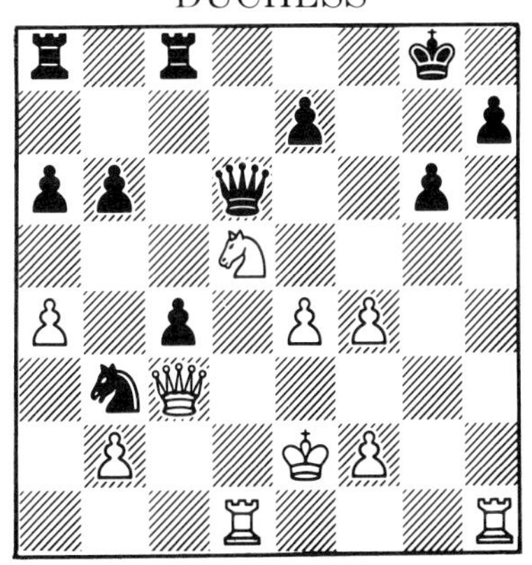

MARTINAK

26 f5 Martinak keeps a strong grip on the game, threatening to win brilliantly by a Rook sacrifice. But there was more in the position: 26 ♖xh7!! is immediately decisive: 26 ... ♔xh7 27 ♖h1+ ♔g8 28 ♘xe7+! and: a) ... ♕xe7 29 ♕h8+ ♔f7 30 ♖h7+ ♔e6 31 ♕e5+ ♔d7 32 ♖xe7+ with mate next move; b) ... ♔f8 29 ♖h8+ ♔xe7 30 ♕g7+ ♔e6 31 f5+ gxf5 32 ♖h6 mate; c) ... ♔f7 29 ♖h7+ and now: c1) ... ♔e6 30 ♕h3+ ♔f6 31 e5+ etc; c2) ... ♔e8 30 ♕h8+ ♔d7 31 ♘xc8+ and: c21) ... ♔e6 32 ♕g8+ ♔f6 33 ♕f7 mate; c22) ... ♔c6 32 ♕e8+ ♔c5 33 ♘xd6, and White comes out a Rook ahead. The variations resulting from 26 ♖xh7!! are clear-cut, but deep — 16 plies in variation c22. Probably no program with the possible exception of BELLE could have "seen" all this — DUCHESS certainly didn't. As for Martinak, he probably didn't look for it because he thought he was winning anyway — and he was. **26... e5** Faced with a concrete variation within its search depth (augmented by capture and check extensions), DUCHESS "sees" the threat: 27 ♖xh7 ♔xh7 28 ♖h1+ ♔g8 29 ♕h8+ ♔f7 30 ♖h7 mate, and makes the only possible move to avert immediate disaster, by blocking the a1-h8 diagonal. **27 ♜dg1?!...** Now Martinak could have driven his attack home by simply playing 27 fxe6! with the same threat, as well as that of winning the Queen by ♘f6+. The only possible reply is ... ♕xe6, after which 28 ♘f6+ tears open the Black King's sanctuary with brutal consequences, e.g. ... ♔f8 29 ♖xh7 ♘c5 30 ♘d7+! ♘xd7 31 ♕g7+ ♔e8 32 ♖h8+ forcing mate. Possibly Martinak was feeling the effects of time-pressure here; the move played seems and is strong, but DUCHESS has a clever, if desperate, resource: **... ♞d4+ 28 ♚e1 ♞xf5!? 29 ♞xb6?** Here Martinak misses another opportunity to win by 29 ♕h3, with the double threat of 30 ♕xf5 and 30 ♕xh7+. **... ♛xb6 30 exf5 ♛c6 31 ♛c2** Of course, White cannot take the Pawn at e5, and his whole attack is dislocated.**... ♚g7 32 ♜h4 ♜ab8 33 fxg6 hxg6 34 ♜hg4 e4 35 ♜xg6+?** This exchanging sequence recovers material equality in an ending whose natural outcome is a draw, but Martinak still could have won by 35 ♕c3+ ♔f7 36 ♖f4+ and the White heavy pieces converge on Black's King. **35 ... ♛xg6 36 ♜xg6+ ♚xg6 37 ♛xe4+ ♚f6 38 ♛f4+ ♚e6 39 ♛h6+ ♚d5 40 ♛d2+ ♚c6 41 ♛d4 ♜e8+ 42 ♚f1 ♜b4 43 ♛f6+** A better try for winning chances is 43 b3,but the ending is still drawish.**... ♚c5 44 ♛g5+ ♚d6 45 ♛d2+ ♚c5 46 ♛g5+** 1/2 - 1/2

CRAY BLITZ — Zaffuto
Sicilian (B43)

Computer programs seem to do rather well in the semi-open positions characteristic of the Sicilian Defense, which apparently suit their heuristics — the SARGON family, for example, is notorious for this. Here Zaffuto employs the Kan variation, and in unwisely taking his time developing his Kingside, gives CRAY BLITZ an opportunity to get the kind of positional advantage that a computer program can understand.

1 e4 c5 2 ♞f3 e6 3 d4 cxd4 4 ♞xd4 a6 5 ♞c3 ♛c7 6 ♝d3 b5 7 0-0 ♝b7 8 ♜e1 ♞c6 9 ♞xc6 ♝xc6 ECO gives only ... ♕xc6; however this move is also quite reasonable; in fact Black won with it in Fernandez — Zapata, Malta Olympiad 1980. **10 ♝d2** Fernandez tried to exploit Black's lack of development by 10 ♘d5, which ultimately led to nothing; this would probably have been more effective had 11 a4 b4 first been interpolated.

ZAFFUTO

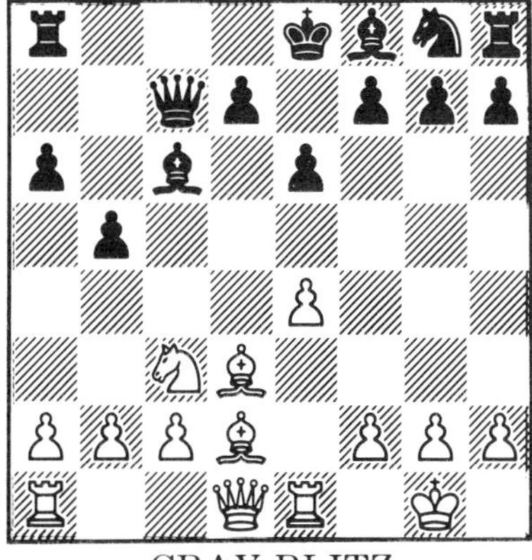

CRAY BLITZ

... ♞e7? This soon leads to trouble; Black cannot afford to delay developing his Kingside. ... ♘f6 followed by ... ♗e7 appears to be necessary here. **11 a4 b4 12 ♞a2 a5 13 c3 bxc3 14 ♞xc3 g6 15 ♞b5!** White's last five moves form a coordinated plan which harmonizes with the character of the position — someting of a rarity in computer games. **... ♝xb5** This involves giving CRAY BLITZ a large advantage, but there doesn't seem to be any alternative; e.g. ... ♕b8? 16 ♗c3 e5 17 ♗c4 and Black's position is ruined. After 10 ... ♘f6 11 a4 b4 12 ♘a2 a5 13 c3 bxc3 14 ♘xc3 ♗e7 15 ♘b5, however, Black would not have had to exchange and could have considered moves such as 15 ... ♕b7 or ... ♕b8. **16 axb5!! ...** A very fine move, opening lines. Many programs would be unable to make this move because of positional scoring penalties for doubled Pawns. But doubled Pawns are not always weak! This Pawn is a tower of strength on b5, controlling c6 and constantly threatening to advance; also, the Black a-Pawn now becomes fatally weak. **... ♝g7 17 ♛b3** Here a grandmaster such as Tal would no doubt play 17 b4! ♗xa1 18 ♕xa1 e5 (... 0-0 19 ♗h6 f6 20 ♗xf8 ♖xf8 21 bxa5 and wins) 19 bxa5, and then rip apart the Black position with the irrestible interaction of the two passed Pawns and two Bishops. The program's move is also strong, but more prosaic. **... ♛b6 18 ♛a3! ...** This is exactly the kind of position that a computer program can play almost infallibly; going after a weak Pawn in an open position. **... ♝d4 19 ♜e2 a4** Zaffuto may have intended ... ♗c5 here, which would lose quickly after 20 b4! ♗d4 21 bxa5 ♗xa1?? 22 ♕xa1 ♖g8 (... 0-0 23 ♝h6 f6 24 ♝xf8 and wins) 23 ♝c3! and Black's position collapses. **20 ♝b4 ♞c8 21 ♜a2 d6 22 ♜d2** Here CRAY BLITZ did not play 22 b3, because of the variation 22 b3 axb3 23 ♕xa8 bxa2 and: 24 ♕xc8+ ♔e7 and wins; 24 ♕xa2 0-0 and Black has exchanged the doomed a-Pawn and has a blockade at b6 which will not be so easy to overcome. **... 0-0 23 ♝c2 ...**

ZAFFUTO

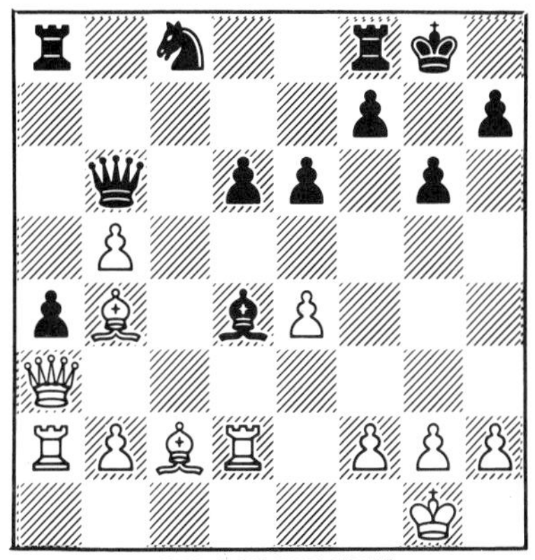

CRAY BLITZ

23 ... ♞a7!? Zaffuto's situation is desperate; the a-Pawn is doomed and all his pieces are tied down. He cannot even make a waiting move, e.g. 23 ... ♔h8?? 24 ♖xd4! So he seeks counterplay by giving up both Rooks for the Queen to get rid of the Pawn on b5. Although this turns out badly, it is really unclear what else Black can do in this situation, other than waiting to be positionally crushed — which CRAY BLITZ was undoubtedly capable of in such a position. **24 ♛xa4 ♞xb5 25 ♛xa8 ♜xa8 26 ♜xa8+ ♚g7 27 ♝d3 ♞c7 28 ♜a4 ♛c6 29 ♜a1 e5 30 ♜c2 ♛b6?** This loses a piece ... ♕d7 was forced, after which White certainly has much the better game, but Black seems to have considerable defensive resources. **31 ♝a5 ♛b3 32 ♜a3 ♛e6 33 ♝xc7 ♜c5 34 ♜a1 h5** There was really not much point in playing here; a program of CRAY BLITZ' tactical ability is not going to fall for a "cheapo". **35 ♝d8 ♛g4 36 h3 ♛f4 37 ♜a6 g5 38 ♝e7 g4 39 ♝xd6 ♝d4 40 hxg4 hxg4** Now Zaffuto threatens ... g3, and of course 41 g3?? is no solution. But CRAY BLITZ has a good answer prepared: **41 ♜a4!**

♗xb2 42 ♗f1 ♗c1 43 ♗xe5+! ♕xe5 44 ♖xc1 g3 45 ♖c2 ♔g6 46 ♗e2 gxf2+ 47 ♔xf2 ♕f6+ 48 ♔g3 ♕d6+ 49 ♔f3 ♕f6+ 50 ♔e3 ♕b6+ 1-0

NUCHESS - Goodside
King's Indian(E91)

Goodside's string of crushing victories comes to an end in this game, the first part of which was very well played by NUCHESS, which made some positionally excellent moves. The program, however, went in for the "win" of a poisoned Pawn, and found itself on the receiving end of a winning attack — which Goodside misplayed, ultimately overlooking the impending loss of a piece.

1 c4 ♘f6 2 ♘f3 g6 3 d4 ♗g7 4 ♘c3 0-0 5 e4 d6 6 ♗f4 ... This is not a particularly effective variation for White; the Bishop is misplaced on f4. On the other hand, it may not be a bad idea for the program to bypass the highly positional Pawn-chain battles characteristic of many variations of the King's Indian. **... ♘bd7** This natural move, so characteristic of the King's Indian Defense, is a missed opportunity: ECO gives ... ♘c6! 7 d5 e5 8 ♗g5 ♘d4 with easy equality (e.g. 9 ♘xd4 exd4 10 ♕xd4 ♘xe4!). **7 ♗e2 ♘h5 8 ♗e3 e5 9 dxe5 dxe5** Thus far Benko-Pilnik, Buenos Aires, 1955. White has no advantage to speak of. **10 0-0 ...** NUCHESS varies from Benko's continuation (10 ♕d2). This is a natural enough move, and given the heuristics of a computer program, almost impossible to avoid at this point; but ♕d2 seems slightly better, preparing to dominate the d-file and attacking the dark-square complex around Black's King. **... c6 11 g3!? ...** A double-edged move, somewhat surprising from a computer program; the Black Knight at h5 now looks rather silly, but the Bishop at c8 may eventually become very strong. **... ♕c7?!** This mechanical move overlooks a surprising and strong reply. Better would have been ... ♕e7, keeping c5 under observation.

GOODSIDE

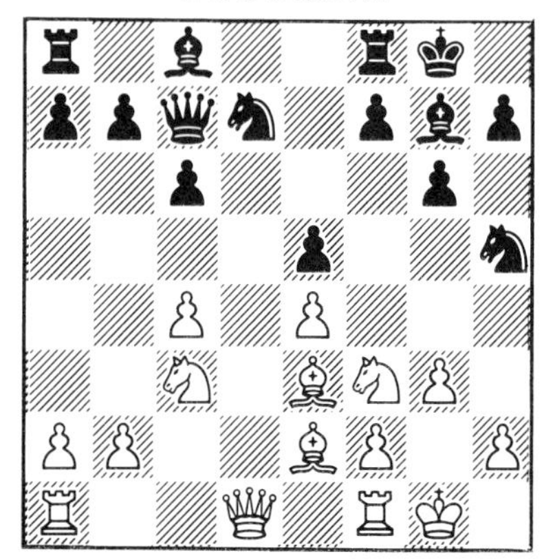

NUCHESS

12 c5! ... Very well played, whatever the reason for NUCHESS' selecting this move. The point is that Black cannot effectively challenge the advanced Pawn - e.g. ... b6 13 ♘a4 and NUCHESS maintains control of c5. Meanwhile, the Pawn cramps Black's position, and the positional threat ♘d2-c4-d6 must constantly be taken into consideration. **... ♖d8 13 ♕b3 ♘f8 14 ♖fd1 ♗e6 15 ♕a3 a6?!** Creating an unnecessary weakness. After 15 ... b6! 16 ♘a4 ♘d7, Goodside would have counterplay. **16 ♖d6!** NUCHESS dares Goodside to create a monster passed Pawn. This would not have been possible after 15 ... b6, e.g. 16 ♖d6? ♘d7 with the threat ... ♗f8. **... ♗g4?** It was now essential to play ... ♘d7, after which Goodside could have answered White's next by ... ♘hf6. **17 ♗g5! ♖e8** ... f6? loses dramatically: 18 ♘xe5! and now: a) ... ♗xe2 19 ♕b3+ ♘e6 (... ♔h8? 20 ♘f7+ etc.) 20 ♕xe6+ ♔f8 21 ♘d7+ and wins; b) ... fxe5 19 ♗xd8 ♖xd8 20 ♗xg4 and wins. **18 ♖ad1** NUCHESS now has a huge positional advantage, and Goodside is under unbearable pressure. He immediately acts to drive away that paralyzing

Bishop: **... h6 19 ♝e3 ♞f6!**

GOODSIDE

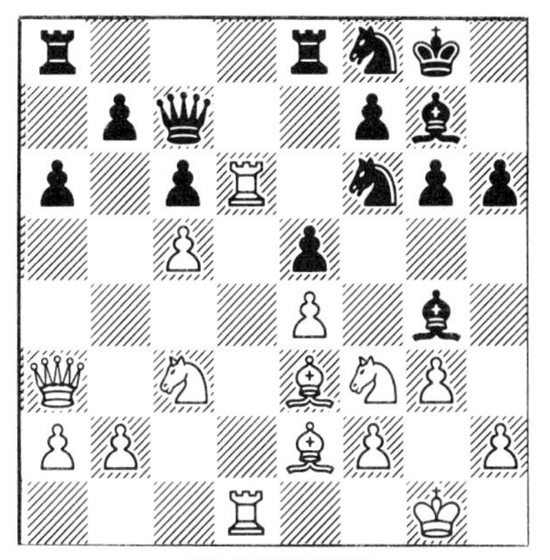

NUCHESS

This gambits and ultimately loses a Pawn. The only other way to reorganize is ... ♗e6 followed by ... ♘d7 and THEN ... ♘f6, providing Black is given time to carry out such a maneuver, which is not likely. **20 ♝xh6? ...** It is certainly questionable whether the positional advantage surrendered by taking the Pawn (assuming that it weren't poisoned) is not worth more than the Pawn. Positional advantages tend to be ephemeral and, after all, a Pawn is a Pawn, but most human players would be very hesitant to place a Rook in a position where it could so easily be trapped. NUCHESS incorrectly calculates that it can "get away" with snatching the Pawn, and swallows the cyanide. **... ♝xh6 21 ♜xf6 ...** Goodside probably found this continuation astonishing, since he had thought this tactically impossible, and if so he was correct. **... ♝e6!?** This definitely gambits the Pawn for an initiative. The right way to trap the Rook and recover the material is 21 ... ♘e6, e.g. 22 ♘d2 ♗g7 23 ♖xg6 fxg6 24 ♗xg4 with an even game. **22 ♞d2 ♜ed8 23 ♞f1 ♜xd1 24 ♝xd1 ♜d8 25 ♝c2 ♞h7** In the process of extricating its Rook NUCHESS has allowed Black to develop a dangerous initiative, which has now become at least compensation for the Pawn. The remainder of the game suggests that Goodside may have been in time pressure, since he is unable to make the most of it. **26 ♜f3 ♞g5 27 ♜d3 ♜xd3 28 ♝xd3 ♛d7 29 ♞e2** Goodside's pieces are all poised to strike at NUCHESS' King, and the program's pieces have become misplaced, which should have led to the usual result after 29 ... ♘f3+ 30 ♔h1 (not ♔g2? ♕xd3) ♘e1! 31 ♗b1 ♕d1 and wins. Instead of taking advantage of this opportunity, Goodside goes in for a simple trap, which the program has no trouble in coping with: **... ♝g4? 30 ♛c3 ♝f3** With the subtle threat of ... ♘h3 mate. **31 ♞e3 ♞h3+ 32 ♚f1 ♝xe3 33 fxe3 f6?!** The best try for maintaining an initiative is 33 ... ♘g5! 34 ♘g1 ♗xe4 35 ♗xe4 ♘xe4 36 ♕xe5 ♕d1+ 37 ♔g2 ♕d5! **34 ♞g1 ♞g5?** But this loses a piece and the game. ... ♘xg1 was forced. **35 ♛c4+ ♚g7 36 h4 ♝xe4 37 ♝xe4 ♛d1+ 38 ♚f2 ♛d2+ 39 ♞e2** 1-0

Resnick - BELLE
Ruy Lopez(C69)

In this game, Resnick played the opening accurately and got a winning advantage when BELLE made several serious positional errors, but — perhaps short on time — he could not drive his advantage home in the endgame.

1 e4 e5 2 ♞f3 ♞c6 3 ♝b5 a6 4 ♝xc6 ... A good choice of opening against a computer program, since important strategic decisions must be made early. **... dxc6 5 0-0 f6 6 d4 ♝g4** Possibly not the best variation for a stellar tactician like BELLE to choose, since the Queens come off right away. **7 dxe5 ♛xd1 8 ♜xd1 fxe5 9 ♜d3 ♝xf3 10 gxf3 ♝d6 11 ♝e3 ♞e7 12 ♞d2 ...** All "book" so far, but now BELLE makes a rather strange and quite risky move:

BELLE

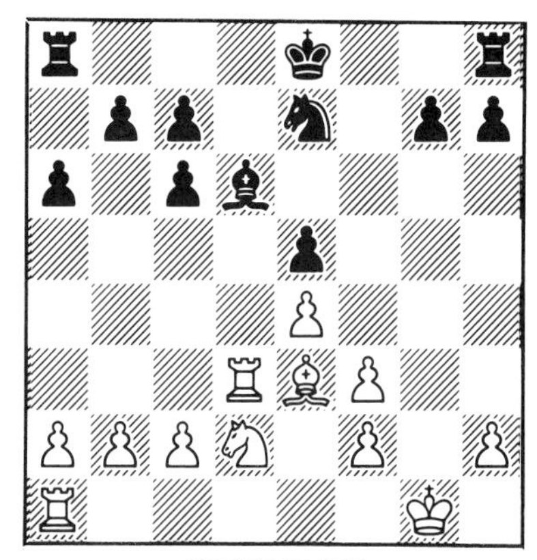

RESNICK

... ♞c8? Certainly the "book" move 12 ... 0-0-0 is more natural. This leads to a serious loosening of BELLE's Queenside Pawns. **13 ♞c4 b5** When Black, as here, is forced to make this move, something has gone badly wrong in the opening. **14 ♞a5 c5 15 ♞b7** Stronger is 15 c4! followed by ♖c1, and the weak Pawn on c5 won't last long. **... c4 16 ♞xd6+ cxd6** This gains evaluator points for undoubling the c-Pawns and supporting the isolated e-Pawn, which might otherwise become indefensible, but creates an obvious target which Resnick proceeds to pile up on. Everything considered, it would be better to play ... ♘xd6 and if 17 ♖d5, ♘f7. **17 ♜d5 0-0 18 ♚g2 ♜f6** Here BELLE should get the Rooks connected by ... ♖b8-b7-f7, piling up on White's only weakness. **19 ♜ad1 ♜g6+** BELLE's only counterplay pivots around the doubled White f-Pawn, which however is not so easy to get at. **20 ♚f1 ♜e6 21 h4** This move is unnecessary, and this Pawn becomes a liability later. **... ♜f6 22 ♚g2 ...** It would appear that 22 ♔e2 was possible, which would certainly be preferable **... b4?!** A further, and unnecessary, weakness. BELLE should march its King to e6 and try to maneuver its other Rook to f7, e.g. by ... ♖b8-b7-f7, for counter-play against the weak White f-Pawn. **23 b3 c3 24 ♜1d3**

BELLE

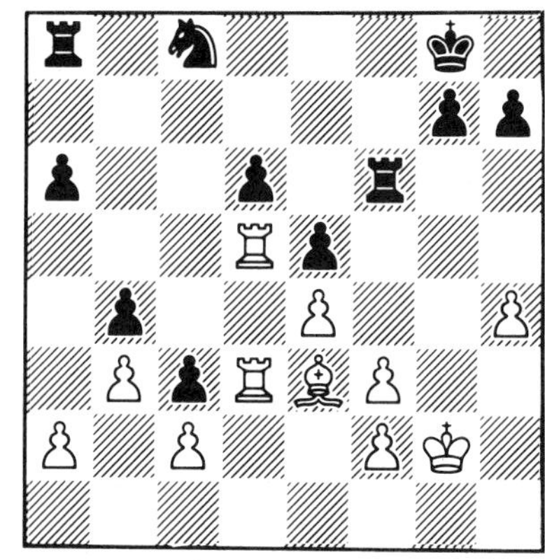

RESNICK

24 ... a5? This lets Resnick penetrate with a Rook, which should have been fatal. ... ♔f7-e6 was still a reasonable continuation. **25 ♜b5 ♞e7 26 ♜b6 ♜g6+ 27 ♚f1 ♞c8 28 ♜b7 ♜e6 29 ♜d5 ...** 29 ♗c5 is answered by .... ♖f6 (Not ... dxc5?? 30 ♖d8 mate). **29 ... ♞e7 30 ♜db5 ♞g6 31 ♜b8+ ...** After 31 h5 ♘f4 32 ♗xf4 exf4 the White h-Pawn would ultimately be lost. **... ♜e8 32 ♜xe8+ ♜xe8**

BELLE

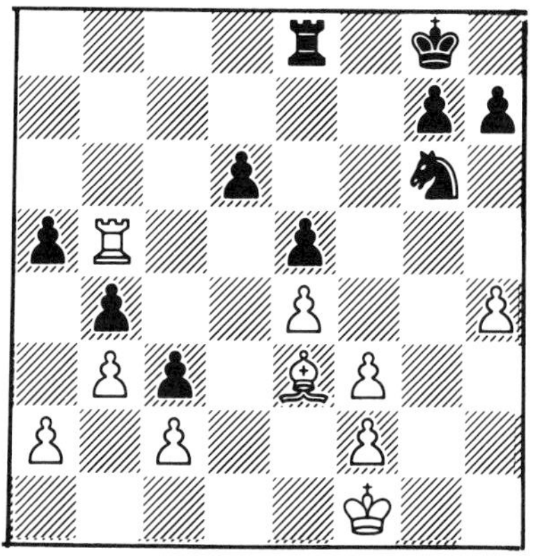

RESNICK

33 ♜xa5? ... 33 h5 ♘f4 (... ♘h4 34 ♔e2

♖a8 35 ♖b6; ... ♘e7 34 ♖xa5) 34 ♗xf4 exf4 35 ♖xa5 looks like an ending easily won for White. This should also win, but with much more difficulty. **... ♞xh4 34 ♚e2 ♞g2 35 a4 bxa3 36 ♜xa3 h6** BELLE is waiting for Resnick to tip his hand. Of course, this is a dangerous loss of time. **37 b4 ...** This is ineffective. Far better was 37 ♖a6 ♖e6 38 ♖c6 - BELLE's Pawn weaknesses are too difficult to defend. **... ♜b8 38 ♜b3** And now it is no longer easy to win - with White's Rook tied down to supporting the Pawn. **... h5** Finally BELLE can see that the advance of this Pawn is essential. **39 b5 h4 40 ♝a7** Locking the Bishop up thus hardly seems wise. Better would be 40 b6, e.g. ... ♖b7 41 ♔f1! ♘xe3 (... h3? 42 ♔g1 and wins) 42 fxe3 g5 (else 43 f4 wins) and now White simply brings his King into play, e.g. 43 ♔g2 ♔g7 44 ♔h3 ♔h6 45 ♔g4 ♔g6 46 f4 exf4 47 exf4 and White should win: If ... h3 48 f5+; or else 47 ... gxf4 48 ♔xh4 ♔f6 49 ♔g4 ♔e5 50 ♔f3. **... ♜b7 41 b6 h3 42 ♚f1 ♞e1!** A clever resource which Resnick may not have expected, ensuring the draw. **43 ♚g1 ♞xf3+ 44 ♞h1 ♞d4** The Knight gets back just in time to rescue the Rook. **♜xc3 ♞b5 46 ♜c8+ ♚f7 47 ♜b8 ♜d7 48 b7** There is clearly no future in either 48 ♖a8 or 48 ♔h2, but this also leads to a dead draw. **... ♞xa7 49 ♜f8+ ♚xf8 50 b8(♛)+ ♚e7** 1/2 - 1/2

7
U.S. OPEN

St. Paul, Minn. AUGUST 8-21, 1982
CROSSTABLE OF COMPUTER GAMES

NOTE: BELLE did not play in rounds 7-9 due to a schedule conflict with the Fredkin Incentive Match 1982. Its 11th round opponent became ill and had to resign after a few moves. So BELLE played a 9th round make-up game against David Levin (Assistant TD).

Ratings are taken from the official USCF crosstable. Opponents' ratings are those computed after the event was rated. Ratings in parentheses are the programs' ratings before the event. Performance ratings have been calculated from the opponents' ratings.

	ROUND	1	2	3	4	5
BELLE	opp rtg	1845	1918	2106	1936	2052
(2161)	clr-res	B-1	W-1	B-0	W-1	B-1
CHAOS	opp rtg	1485	1609	1701	1861	1765
(1820)	clr-res	W-0	B-0(F)	W-1	B-0(F)	B-1
CC 9	opp rtg	1873	2210	1875	1929	1714
(U/R)	clr-res	W-1	W-0	B-0	B-0	W-0
PRESTIGE	opp rtg	2028	1843	2017	2142	2049
(U/R)	clr-res	B-½	W-1	W-1	B-0	W-0

	ROUND	6	7	8	9	10
BELLE	opp rtg	2088	--	--	1527	1835
	clr-res	W-0	0F*	0F*	W-1*	B-1
CHAOS	opp rtg	1622	1648	1715	1582	1380
	clr-res	W-1	W-0(F)	W-0	B-0(F)	W-1
CC 9	opp rtg	1553	1630	1781	1921	1726
	clr-res	B-1	W-1	W-½	B-0	B-0
PRESTIGE	opp rtg	1899	1773	1883	1801	1548
	clr-res	B-0	B-1	W-0	B-0	W-1

	ROUND	11	12	SCORE	PERF RTG	POST RTG
BELLE	opp rtg	1815	1883	7-3	2050	2146
	clr-res	W-1*	B-0			
CHAOS	opp rtg	1598	1701	6-6	1639	1714
	clr-res	B-1	W-1			
CC 9	opp rtg	1513	1617	5½-6½	1765	1765
	clr-res	W-1	W-1			
PRESTIGE	opp rtg	1755	1755	6-6	1868	1868
	clr-res	B-½	B-1			

The 1982 U. S. Open was declared a computer-eligible tournament by the USCF Office on the suggestion of the USCF Computer Chess Committee. Despite the relatively short notice given, four programs were entered — the famous mainframe programs BELLE and CHAOS, plus two microcomputer programs sponsored by Fidelity Electronics.

BELLE had to miss three rounds due to a conflict already noted. CHAOS was plagued throughout the tournament by a program bug which affected its time control system, losing four games on time forfeits and more than 100 rating points. Microcomputer PRESTIGE CHESS CHALLENGER entered the event with expectations of a 2000 level performance, largely based on a high provisional rating obtained by its predecessor ELITE CHESS CHALLENGER, and although its performance was impressive, the resulting rating (1868) came as a disappointment. Of all the programs entered, only SENSORY CHESS CHALLENGER 9 performed to the satisfaction of its programmers, achieving a rating of 1765.

Fig. 7.1 Jim Marfia plays a speed game against Belle.

ROUND 1

Dave Parker (1845) - BELLE
Ruy Lopez(C82)

BELLE played a wide-open line of the Open Defense, and in a complicated position its opponent went badly astray, losing quickly.

1 e4 e5 2 ♞f3 ♞c6 3 ♝b5 a6 4 ♝a4 ♞f6 5 0-0 ♞xe4 The Open Defense to the Ruy Lopez is better suited to the heuristics of a computer program than the Closed Defense. **6 d4 b5 7 ♝b3 d5 8 dxe5 ♝e6 9 c3 ♝c5** A move recommended by Larsen, as good for the club level player. **10 ♞bd2 0-0 11 ♝c2 ♞xf2** The most aggressive continuation, but not the soundest - ... ♗f5 or ... f5 offer prospects for equality. This, however, suits BELLE's style. **12 ♜xf2 f6 13 exf6 ♝xf2+ 14 ♚xf2 ♛xf6** Parker now has a slight material advantage and excellent long-term prospects, but must play carefully for a few moves in this complicated position.

BELLE

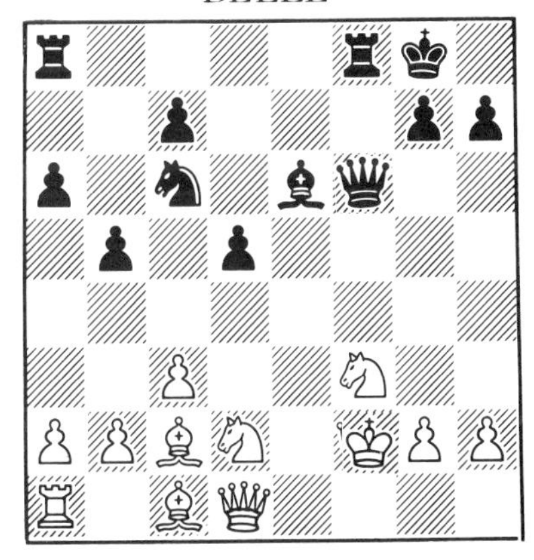

PARKER

15 ♞b3?! ... This plan loses valuable time. ECO gives the safe move 15 ♔g1, and also ♘f1. The right idea for White is play ♘f1 to get his Bishop out to e3, where it will control d4 and c5, then unpin by ♔g1 and be able to reinforce f3 by ♘1d2 if necessary. **... ♞e5 16 ♞d4?** Necessary here is ♗e3 followed by ♘d2, for reasons that will soon be clear. **... ♝g4** In the battle being waged over the pinned Knight, Parker has achieved exactly nothing (the Knight on d4 is of course exposed to being driven away by ... c5 at any time). Meanwhile BELLE has added two pieces to the attack, and threatens ... c5. White is obviously in great difficulties here; if 17 b4 to secure the Knight's position, then ... a5! **17 ♝g5?? ...** A curious blunder, since the Knight is pinned twice, but the game was almost certainly lost anyway. **... ♛xg5** The rest of the game is a massacre. **18 ♚g1 ♞xf3+ 19 ♚h1 ♞xh2 20 ♛d3 ♛h5 21 ♚g1 c5 22 ♛g3 cxd4 23 ♛xh2 dxc3 24 ♝b3 cxb2 25 ♛xh5 bxa1(♛)+** 0-1

CHAOS - Chris Hawes(1485)
Nimzo-Indian(E32)

Here CHAOS unwisely lets its King sanctuary be opened up by an exchange on f3, and then fails to react to its opponent's attack — resulting, naturally, in disaster for the program.

1 d4 ♞f6 2 c4 e6 3 ♞c3 ♝b4 4 ♛c2 0-0 5 a3 ♝e7?! Loss of time. The exchange ... ♗xc3 is, as a rule, unwise unless White plays a3, and mandatory after a3. **6 e3** More thematic (and aggressive) is 6 e4, taking advantage of Black's last move. **... b6 7 ♞f3 ♝b7** Now the opening has transposed into a Queen's Indian in which White is a move ahead. **8 ♝d3 h6** More loss of time, though this is more or less forced in view of the threat e4-e5. **9 ♝d2 ...** Too slow. CHAOS has at least two good plans at its disposal; a) 9 b4 followed by ♗b2, 0-0-0, and a Pawnstorm; b) 9 e4 with play in the center. Instead the program mechanically completes its development, presenting its opponent with no particular problems to solve. **... d6**

HAWES

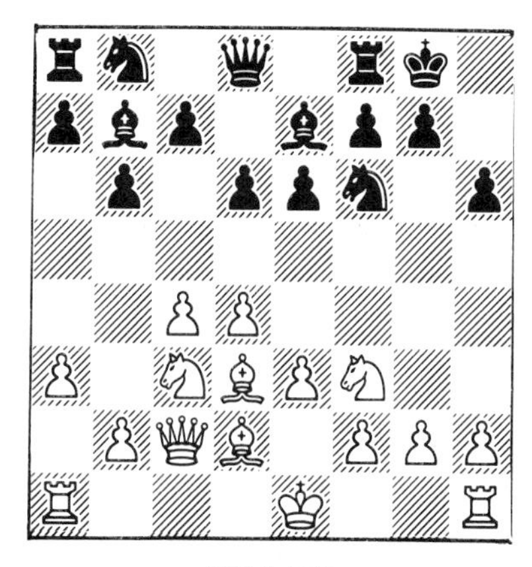

CHAOS

10 0-0?! CHAOS should not castle short without resolving the threat to double its f-Pawn. Still very good was 10 e4. **... ♞bd7?!** Of course Black should play ... ♗xf3. **11 ♜ae1?** Mechanical development again. CHAOS clearly undervalues the problems of defending its King after the exchange on f3. **... ♝xf3 12 gxf3 ♚h8 13 ♜e2?** This is a real "computer move", motivated by heuristics that have become irrelevant to the position. CHAOS obviously gets "bonus points" for doubling Rooks on a center file, and clearly does not think that the doubled f-Pawns are a serious weakness. The move might be considered good had the program played it with the plan e4 - f4 - f3 - ♖g2, making the most of its Pawn structure, but of course CHAOS has no capability to formulate this kind of plan. **... ♜g8** Meanwhile, Hawes, although not a high-rated player, **has** formed a plan - which, in the absence of any effective answer, turns out to be deadly. **14 ♜fe1 ♞f8 15** ♕a4?! CHAOS gets points in its evaluator for increasing the mobility of the Queen and for exploiting the weak square c6. Unfortunately, the problems on the Kingside take priority! **... g5 16 ♛c6 a6** Black obviously cannot allow ♘b5, but this is the last defensive move he has to make and now CHAOS' Queen is out of play. **17 b4 ♞g6**

HAWES

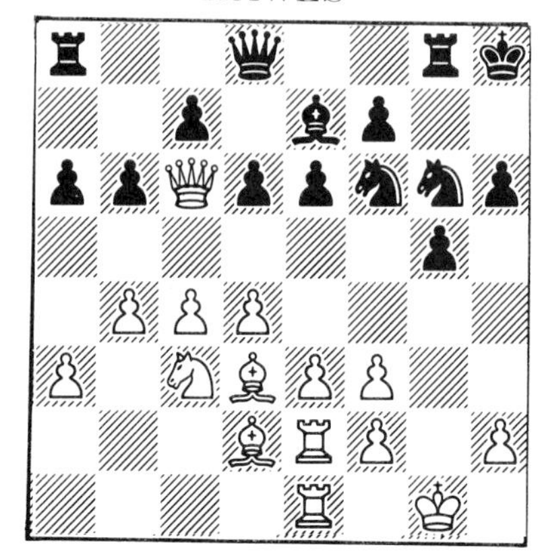

CHAOS

18 ♝c2? Another motiveless move. An immediate ♔h1 planning ♖g1 - ♖ee1 - ♗f1 might have given some chances if Black failed to find the best attacking continuation. CHAOS, however, still doesn't understand that it is in trouble. **... ♞h4 19 ♚h1** Finally the program realizes that there is a threat — too late. **... g4 20 fxg4?** This rapidly leads to disaster. After 20 f4, keeping the g-file closed, CHAOS would have a most unpleasant position after ... ♘f3, but could still put up prolonged resistance. **... ♜xg4 21 f3 ♜g7 22 f4 ♛g8 23 ♛xc7??** An incredibly ill-chosen moment to go Pawn-hunting. After 23 ♘e4 ♘f3, CHAOS would have to give up the Exchange by 24 ♘g3 ♘xe1! (... ♖xg3? 25 hxg3 ♕xg3 26 ♕xa8+ ♔h7 27 ♕xf3 gets White out of trouble), and after 25 ♗xe1 White is still lost but the end is not imminent. **... ♞f3 24 ♝g6 ♜xg6** 0-1

Fig. 7.2 The main playing hall at the 1982 U. S. Open.

SENSORY CC9-Somner Sorenson(1873)
Vienna Game(C28)

CC9 did not get any real advantage out of the opening, and the game was fairly even when its opponent (perhaps unwisely) opened the position up, and then made a tactical error which gave CC9 a won game.

1 e4 e5 2 ♞c3 ... The Vienna Game is one of the openings recommended for the "books" of the Fidelity microcomputers by Fidelity's chess adviser, Fide Master Boris Baczynskyj. The idea is that the positions arising from it are well suited to the program's heuristics. **... ♞c6 3 ♝c4 ♞f6 4 d3 ♝b4 5 ♝g5 h6 6 ♝d2** CC9 must have been out of its "book" here, for this move is a loss of time; ECO gives 6 ♗xf6. It is interesting to note that the earlier versions of the SARGON family would exchange Bishop for Knight at the drop of a hat; presumably the Spracklens have added some heuristics making their later programs reluctant to do this. **6 ... ♞a5** This seems premature. A solid continuation for Black is ... d6. **7 ♝b5 c6** It may be better to drive the Bishop away by 7... a6 instead. **8 ♝a4 b5** It is arguable whether this Pawn advance is an asset or a liability for Black, who now winds up playing ... d6 with a defensive Pawn chain rather than trying for an eventual break by ... d5. There was, however, little choice but to carry through with this in view of the threat 9 a3 ♗xc3 10 ♗xc3. **9 ♝b3 ♞xb3 10 axb3 0-0** Here Black could have played ... d5, taking the initiative. **11 ♞f3 ♜e8 12 0-0** The game is now more or less even. **... d6 13 ♝e3 ♛e7 14 ♛e1!?** A peculiar and rather subtle move, voluntarily pinning the Queen. **14 ... d5** Apparently strong, but CC9 has a good answer ready: **15 d4! ♞xe4 16 ♞xe5 ...**

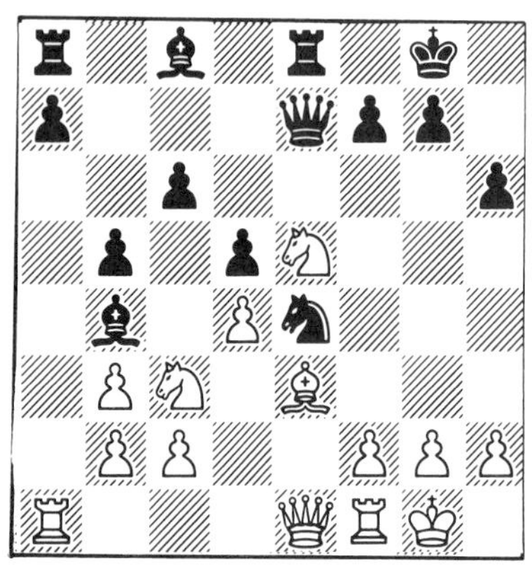

SENSORY CC9

16 ... ♛f6? Losing material to the following combination. A solid continuation was ... ♗d7 with a reasonable game. **17 ♞xe4! ...** There is no room for tactical errors when playing a computer program! **... ♝xe1 18 ♞xf6+ gxf6 19 ♞xc6 ...** The point: Black's Bishop is trapped, and CC9 wins at least two Pawns, e.g. ... ♗b7 20 ♘xa7 ♗b4 21 ♘xb5. Sorenson prefers to give up the Exchange: **... ♜xe3 20 fxe3 ♝h4 21 ♞e7+ ♚f8 22 ♞xd5 ...** CC9 gets the second Pawn anyway, and then a third, after which the remainder of the game is of little interest. **... ♝b7 23 ♞xf6 ♚g7 24 ♞h5+ ♚g6 25 ♞f4+ ♚g7 26 c4 ♝d8 27 cxb5 ♝e4 28 ♜a6 ♝b6 29 ♜6a1 ♜e8 30 ♞h5+ ♚g6 31 ♞f6 ♜e6 32 ♞xe4 ♜xe4 33 ♜f3** 1-0

Charles Fenner(2028) - PRESTIGE
Queen's Gambit Declined (E00)

Without any guidance from theory, PRESTIGE got the worse of the opening, but its opponent was unable to realize his advantage.

1 d4 d5 2 ♞f3 ♞f6 3 g3 e6 A special tournament opening "book" of 12,000 moves had been prepared by Boris Baczynskyj especially for the U. S. Open tournament. However, the opening module had not been properly plugged in before this game, and the program was "on its own" after the second move. The result was a rather strange opening. **4 ♝g2 ♝d6** The Bishop belongs on e7. On this square it is exposed to attack. **5 0-0 0-0 6 c4 c5** After ... c6, White could continue 7 c5, taking command on the Queenside. **7 ♞c3 dxc4 8 e4 ♞c6 9 ♝g5 e5** The explanation for this strange move centers on the Pawn on c4. A human player, knowing that this Pawn must fall eventually, would play ... cxd4 here to meet the threat 10 e5. But that brings the recovery of the Pawn by White within the program's horizon after 10 ♘xd4 ♘xd4 11 ♕xd4. So the program plays an alternative which it calculates will retain the Pawn. **10 dxe5 ♝xe5** Normally the program would try to hang onto its Bishop by ... ♘xe5, but then 11 ♘d5 is awkward to meet. **11 ♛xd8 ♜xd8 12 ♞xe5 ♞xe5 13 f4** Fenner does not want to give up his "good" Bishop by 13 ♗xf6, although that would not be bad after ... gxf6 14 ♘d5. **13 ... ♞g6** ... ♘d3 is much sharper.

PRESTIGE

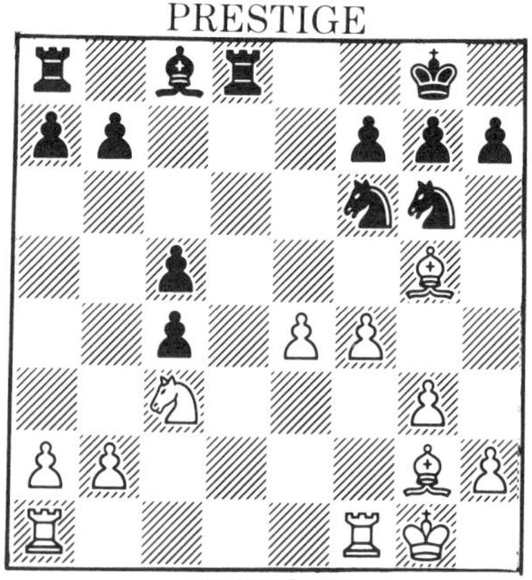

FENNER

Here it would seem that White had some attacking chances, but these were dissipated by inexact play. **14 ♞d5 ...** Stronger was 14 e5 h6 15 exf6 hxg5 17 fxg5 with several unpleasant threats. **... ♜d6 15 f5?!** This achieves absolutely nothing. Much better was 15 e5 ♖xd5 16 exf6 ♖d4 (not ... ♖d2?? 17 f5) 17 f5 ♘e5 18 ♖ae1. **... ♞xd5 16 exd5 ♞e5 17 ♝e7 ♜b6 18 ♝xc5 ♜xb2 19 ♝d4 ♜e2 20 ♜fe1 ♜xe1+ 21 ♜xe1 f6** Not ... ♘d7? 22 ♖e8+ ♘f8 23 ♗c5 and wins. **22 ♝xe5 fxe5 23 ♜xe5 c3 24 d6 ...** Better winning chances were offered by 24 ♗e4. **... c2 25 ♜c5 ♝xf5 26 ♝d5+ ♚h8** Not ... ♔f8? 27 ♗xb7 winning back the Pawn. **27 ♝b3 b6 28 ♜c7 ♜d8 29 ♝xc2 ♝h3** Of course the Pawn on d6 is immune because of mate. **30 ♜xa7 g6 31 d7 ♝xd7 32 ♜b7 b5 33 ♝e4 ...** Not 33 ♗d3? ♗c6 winning. **... ♝e6 34 ♜xb5 ♜d1+** At any point hereabouts, the game could have been abandoned as a hopeless draw. Fenner offered a draw, but PRESTIGE played on. **35 ♚f2 ♜d2+ 36 ♚e3 ♜xa2 37 h4 ♜a7 38 ♚f4 ♚g7 39 h5 ♜f7+ 40 ♚e3 ♝c4 41 ♜g5 ♜f6 42 hxg6 hxg6 43 ♜xg6+ ...** Forcing matters to a conclusion. **43 ... ♜xg6 44 ♝xg6** 1/2 - 1/2

ROUND 2

BELLE - Daniel Varichak (1918)
Caro-Kann(B18)

BELLE is at its best in this game — incisively exploiting a weak move in the opening to force an early win of material. For a moment it seemed that the program's Queen might be trapped, but BELLE had a nice tactical answer prepared.

1 e4 c6 2 d4 d5 3 ♞c3 dxe4 4 ♞xe4 ♝f5 5 ♞g3 ♝g6 6 ♞f3 ♛c7?! ECO gives ... ♘f6 or ♘d7 here. **7 h4 h6 8 ♞e5 ♝h7 9 ♝f4! ...** Winning a tempo and underscoring the inferiority of Black's sixth move. **... ♛a5+ 10 ♝d2 ♛c7 11 ♝c4 ...** BELLE now has a dangerous lead in development. **...e6 12 f4 ♝d6**

VARICHAK

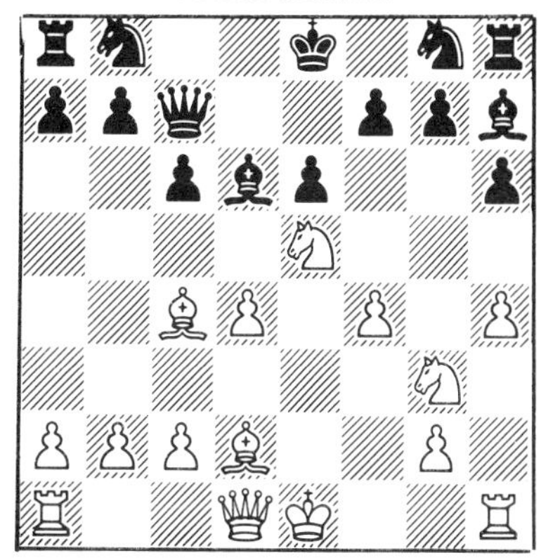

BELLE

13 ♛g4! f5 There is no good way to protect the g-Pawn; the lesser evil was probably ... ♔f8. This leaves Black with a fatal Pawn weakness. **14 ♛f3 ...** Here it is unclear why BELLE did not play 14 ♕h5+, winning at least a Pawn. **14 ... ♛e7 15 ♛b3! ...** BELLE is obviously a virtuoso at attacking Queen maneuvers. This double attack wins at least a Pawn. **15 ... ♝xe5 16 dxe5 ♚f7?** Overlooking BELLE's threat. Black is so completely tied up, however, that the position is already quite hopeless, but ... g6 17 ♗xe6+ ♔e8 would have prolonged the agony. **17 ♝xe6+ ♛xe6 18 ♛xb7+ ♛e7 19 ♛xa8 ♞f6** Now how is BELLE going to get its Queen out of the trap? **20 0-0-0 ♞d5 21 ♞f1 ...**
(See diagram next page)

The program does not seem to be at all concerned about the impending loss of its Queen. **... ♞b6** The point behind BELLE's last move is that unless this attack is tried immediately, the program will play 22 ♗e3. **22 e6+!...** BELLE gets its Queen out with this clever stroke. Every King move loses. **... ♛xe6 23**

Position after White's 21st move.

VARICHAK

BELLE

♕xa7+ ♘8d7 24 ♗b4 ♖a8? Black could well have resigned here, avoiding a rather brutal finish. **25 ♖xd7+ ♕xd7 26 ♕xb6 ♖xa2 27 ♔b1 ♖a7 28 ♘e3 ♖b7 29 ♕c5 ♕e6 30 ♕f8+** 1-0

Mike Purcell(1609) - CHAOS
Sicilian(B33)

CHAOS' opponent made an elementary blunder in the opening, losing a Pawn, after which the program had a won game but unwisely took no steps to prevent a desperation attack. CHAOS could still have held the game, but its quiescence search "blew up" and it lost on time.

1 e4 c5 2 ♘f3 ♘c6 3 d4 cxd4 4 ♘xd4 ♘f6 5 ♘c3 e6 6 ♗g5 ... An ineffective continuation. Usually considered best is 6 ♗e2 offering a Pawn: ... ♗b4 7 0-0 ♗xc3 8 bxc3 ♘xe4 9 ♗d3 with attacking chances (Euwe). **... h6** Inviting 7 ♗xf6 ♕xf6 8 ♘db5?! ♗c5! and Black takes the initiative (Boleslavski). **7 ♗e3 ♗b4 8 ♘4e2??** White should simply play ♗d3 with equality. **... ♘xe4 9 ♕d3 d5** Of course, CHAOS has a won game here. **10 0-0-0 ♘c5** This is not very wise. CHAOS ought to play 10 ... ♘xc3 11 ♘xc3 0-0 with an easily exploitable advantage. The program expected 11 ♕d2 0-0 12 a3 ♘e4, and clearly had no idea of what was coming. Chess programs have a tendency to unnecessarily complicate things at times. **11 ♗xc5 ♗xc5 12 f4 ...** Purcell's position is not ideal for launching this desperation attack, but there is no hope in a normal middlegame. **12 ... 0-0** It is unsafe to leave the King in the center because of the threat f5. **13 g4 ...**

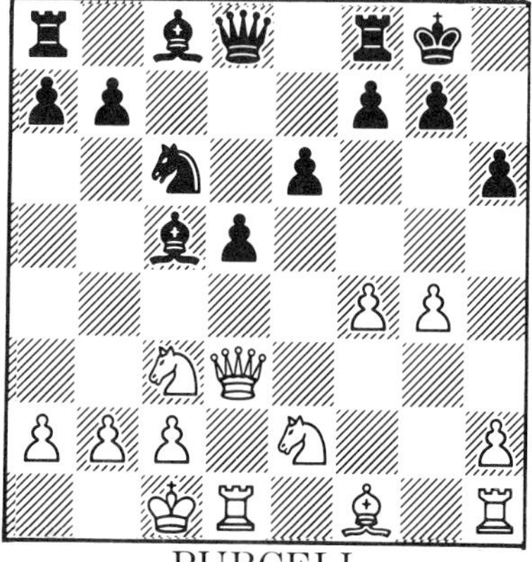

PURCELL

13 ... ♘b4?! A strong defensive move, which would have dislocated Purcell's attack, was ... ♕h4! Finding such a move, however, requires long-range thinking and CHAOS cannot do this. **14 ♕g3 ♗d7 15 h4 ♕c7 16 h5 ♗d6 17 g5 hxg5** This is virtually forced, but now CHAOS finds itself confronted with too many possibilities in its quiescence search, which starts to "blow up" — the program consumed more than 16 minutes on this move. **18 ♕xg5 f6?!** A good defensive move was ... ♕d8, and after 19 ♕g3, ... ♕f6 and the attack comes to nothing. **19 ♕h4 ♗a4** This also has its points, but demands accurate play and deep calculation — not at all wise in view of the program's time control problem (which was discovered in this game). **20 h6 ...** Here CHAOS had nearly 90 minutes left on its clock, but was unable to decide on a move and forfeited. After ... g6 Black could still hold on and win, e.g. 21 h7+ ♔h8 22 ♕h6 ♗e8. 1-0(time)

SENSORY CC9 - Pedro Marcal(2210)
Sicilian(B71)

CC9 played a sharp opening and had the edge when its "book" ran out. Then, several strategically weak moves by the program gave Marcal the initiative and, eventually, the game.

1 e4 c5 2 Nf3 d6 3 d4 cxd4 4 Nxd4 Nf6 5 Nc3 g6 6 f4 Nc6 7 Nxc6 bxc6 8 e5 Ng4 9 Qf3 Bd7 A reasonable alternative to the continuations given in ECO— ... Qb6 and ... d5. **10 h3 Nh6 11 exd6 exd6** So far CC9 has played an exemplary opening, but now it makes a questionable move.

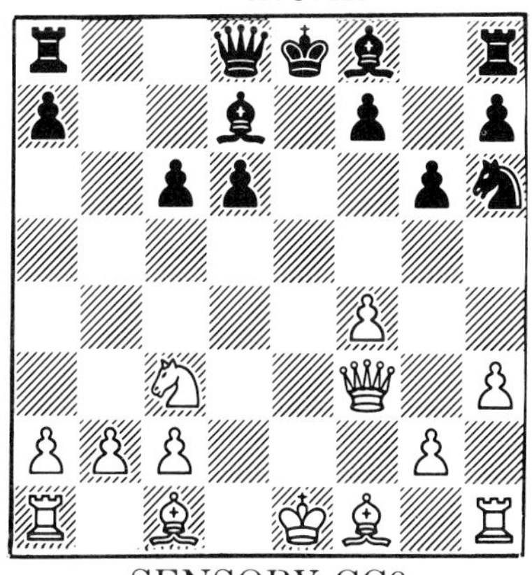

SENSORY CC9

12 Qe4+?! ... It is difficult for computer programs to resist the temptation to give check whenever possible; this misplaces the Queen. A stronger move was 12 Bd2 planning 13 0-0-0. **... Be7 13 Bd3 0-0 14 0-0?!** Again, a strategically questionable move. There was still time for 14 Bd2 Re8 15 0-0-0 Bf6 16 Qf3 with attacking chances. As in many variations of the Sicilian, White is more or less obligated to play for a Kingside attack, because Black's latent superiority in the center spells trouble in the long run — if the game lasts that long! These are good lines to play against a computer program, which has no way of forming such judgments and is not likely to conduct an efficient Pawnstorming attack. **... Nf5 15 Qf3 Bf6** Already Black has the initiative. **16 Be3?! ...** Misplacing the Bishop, which soon leads to trouble. 16 Bd2 was better — ... Nd4 does not accomplish anything in particular. **... Re8 17 Bxf5 ...** Now after 17 Bf2, Nd4 is quite unpleasant because the Queen does not have f2 to go to. **... Bxf5 18 Bf2 d5** CC9 is now in serious positional trouble — Black's Bishops are a potent force, and the program still hasn't gotten any kind of attack going. **19 Rac1 Qa5**

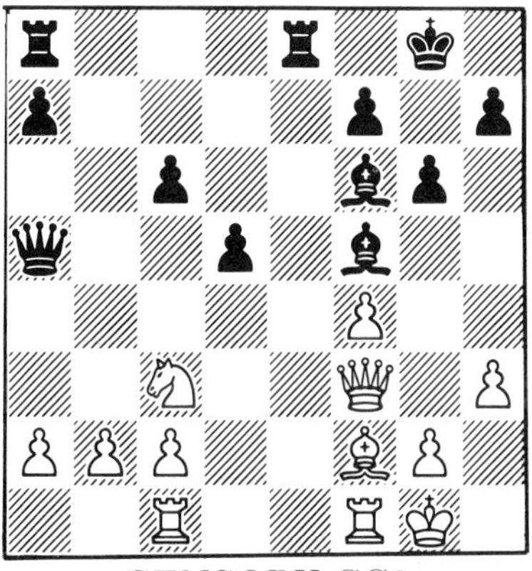

SENSORY CC9

20 g4? ... The last slender chance to save the game was 20 a3, keeping the Queen out of b4. White then has a bad game, but can still put up resistance. **20 ... Be4 21 Qg3 Qb4** Apparently winning a Pawn. **22 Nxe4 Rxe4 23 b3 Qa3 24 Rce1 ...** This ultimately avoids losing the Pawn, but at a fatal positional price. **... Qxa2 25 Rxe4 dxe4 26 Qe3 Re8 27 Qc5 Qa6 28 Qxa7 Qxa7 29 Bxa7 e3 30 Rb1 ...** It is too late for 30 Re1: ... e2 and then either 31 ... Bc3 or ... Bh4 decides matters. **... Bc3 31 b4 e2 32 Bf2 e1 (Q)+ 33 Bxe1 Rxe1+ 34 Rxe1 Bxe1 35 Kf1 Bxb4 36 Ke2 f5 37 Kd3 Kf7 38 gxf5 gxf5 39 c3 Bd6 40 Ke3 Ke6 41 c4 Bc7 42 h4 h5** 0-1

PRESTIGE - David Moody(1843)
Vienna Game(C26)

After some weak moves by its opponent, PRESTIGE won a Pawn but was under positional pressure. When it weakened its Pawn structure, Moody had drawing chances but blundered in time pressure. **1 e4 e5 2 ♞c3 ♞f6 3 g3 ♝c5 4 ♝g2 a6** This loss of time lets PRESTIGE take the initiative. There was no real need for Black to worry about the Bishop being exchanged by ♘a4. **5 ♞f3 d6 6 d4 exd4 7 ♞xd4 ♝g4 8 f3?! ...** An unnecessary loosening of the Kingside Pawn structure; 8 ♕d3 was better. **... ♝e6?!** More natural, and certainly better, is ... ♗d7 with ... ♘c6 to follow. **9 ♞xe6 fxe6 10 ♝h3** The weakening of Black's position caused by Moody's eighth move now clear, but 10 ♕e2 followed by ♗e3 was a stronger continuation. **... ♛e7 11 ♞a4 ...** A more appropriate continuation was 11 ♕e2, intending ♗e3 and 0-0 **... ♝a7 12 ♛d3 b5?!** Another weakness, which soon causes trouble. Black should play ... ♘c6! with no fear of 13 ♕b3? ♘d4! taking the initiative. **13 ♞c3 ♞c6 14 a4! ♞e5 15 ♛e2 c6?!** Better was ... b4 16 ♘a2 a5 17 c3 ♗c5. **16 axb5 axb5 17 ♝e3 0-0?**

MOODY

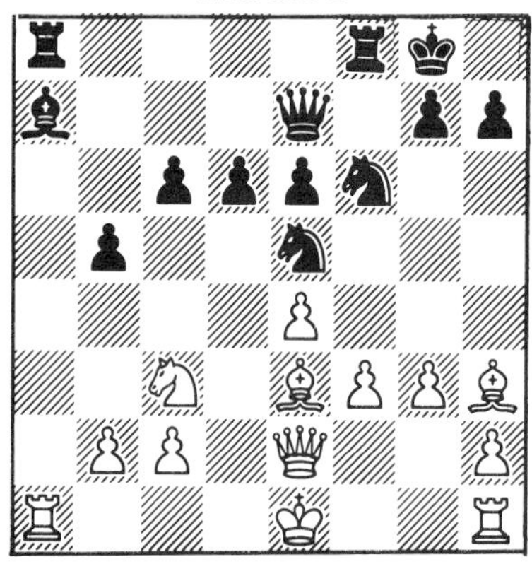

PRESTIGE

Giving PRESTIGE a chance to show its tactical strength. ... ♘c4 would have resolved the tactical situation; this allows the following combination (5 plies deep in the main line — The search depth in this case is increased by capture extensions). **18 ♝xa7 ♜xa7 19 ♝xe6+! ...** Winning a Pawn: ... ♕xe6 20 ♖xa7. **19 ... ♚h8 20 ♜xa7 ♛xa7 21 f4?! ...**Although it has won a Pawn, PRESTIGE's position is uncomfortable since it is unable to castle. The program reacts by starting a Kingside attack, which leads to a serious weakening of its Pawn structure. A better alternative was 21 ♗h3 keeping White's options open (♗g2-♕f2, for example). **...♞g6 22 h4 ♛a1+ 23 ♞d1 ♜e8 24 f5 ♞e5?** Here Moody missed ... ♘f8 recovering the Pawn with the better game, but he was already in time pressure. **25 0-0 ♞c4 26 c3! ...** Not 26 b3?! after which the Black Queen becomes active on the a1 - h8 diagonal. **... ♛a7+ 27 ♚h2 h5** Moody now sets up a blockade that is not easy to overcome. The program, however, is in no hurry, and calmly maneuvers while its opponent's time pressure increases. **28 ♞f2 ♞e3 29 ♜e1 ♞eg4+ 30 ♞xg4 ♞xg4+ 31 ♚g2 ♛e7?** After ... ♖a8, Black could continue ... ♕c5-e5 and White's extra Pawn is of questionable value. **32 ♜a1 ♜b8 33 ♛d2 ♞f6 34 ♛e3 c5** A playable alternative was ... ♘g4. **35 ♛f3 b4 36 c4 ♜e8 37 b3 ♜d8 38 ♛e3 ♜e8 39 ♛g5 ♚h7 40 ♜a2 ♚h8 41 ♛g6 ♛b7 42 ♝d5 ♛e7 43 ♜a1 ♛e5 44 ♜a7 ♛b2+??** Moody was now in extreme time pressure. After ... ♖e7 it is not clear how White can break through. **45 ♚h3 ♞xd5 46 ♛xe8+** 1-0

Fig. 7.3 Two human grandmasters: Arthur Bisguier plays white against Andrew Soltis.

ROUND 3

David Marshall(2106) - BELLE
Ruy Lopez(C82)

BELLE plays the same variation of the Open Defense, and again gets strong pressure. But Marshall defends well, and then outplays BELLE in the endgame.

1 e4 e5 2 ♞f3 ♞c6 3 ♝b5 a6 4 ♝a4 ♞f6 5 0-0 ♞xe4 6 d4 b5 7 ♝b3 d5 8 dxe5 ♝e6 9 c3 ♝c5 10 ♞bd2 0-0 11 ♝c2 ♞xf2 12 ♜xf2 f6 So far as in BELLE's first-round game. Now Marshall varies from theory with an inferior move: **13 ♞b3?! ...** As noted in Parker - BELLE, White should play 13 exf6 ♗xf2+ 14 ♔xf2 ♕xf6 15 ♔g1 followed by ♘f1.**... ♝xf2+ 14 ♚xf2 fxe5 15 ♚g1(!)** ... Unlike Parker, Marshall realizes that he is in trouble and starts to defend. **... ♝g4 16 h3! ...**

BELLE

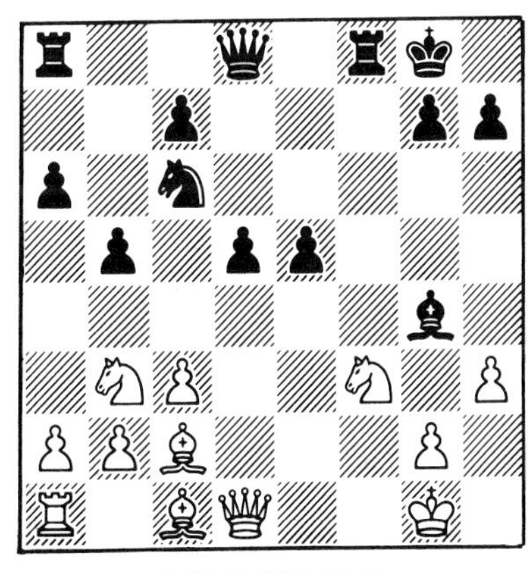

MARSHALL

16 ... ♝xf3?! The wisdom of this is open to question; White's Bishops are potentially very strong. Much better seems ... ♗h5! provoking a further weakness; play could then become quite interesting after 17 g4 e4! 18 ♘fd4 ♕f6! 19 ♘f5 ♗f7. **17 gxf3 ♚h8?!** Even though it gives up a Pawn with check, the logical continuation to Black's play is ... ♕h4!? immediately; e.g. 18 ♕xd5+ ♔h8 19 ♗e4 ♕e1+ with a draw by perpetual. Instead BELLE prepares this Queen sally with a defensive move, giving White time to bring another piece into action. Computer programs don't have the ability to correctly assess the value of a tempo. As played, BELLE's attack stalls — and when the immediate tactical situation has been resolved, the game settles down to a strategic contest. BELLE has a small material advantage, as well as threats against the White King. But the power of two unopposed Bishops on an open board is something to be reckoned with. **18 ♝e3 ♛h4 19 ♚h2 ...** Of course White has no time for 19 ♕xd5? ♕g3+ 20 ♔h1 ♖xf3 winning much material or mating. **... ♜ad8** Ineffective is 19 ... e4?! 20 ♘d2 ♘e5 21 ♗d4 ♖ae8 22 fxe4! **20 ♛e2 ♛h5 21 ♜f1 e4 22 ♞d4 ♞xd4 23 ♝xd4 ♜f7** BELLE calculates that if it grabs the f-Pawn, it won't be able to hold it after 23 ... ♖xf3 24 ♖xf3 ♕xf3 25 ♕xf3 exf3 26 ♔g3 ♖f8 27 ♗d1. **24 ♛e3 ...**

BELLE

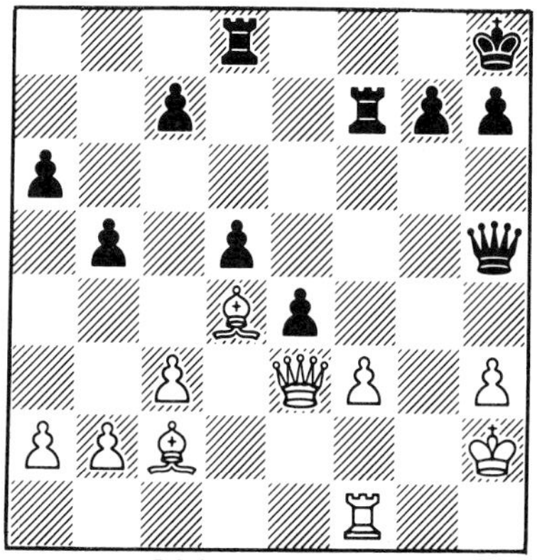

MARSHALL

24 ... ♜xf3? But now BELLE changes its mind. After this exchange, BELLE goes into an ending with Rook + two Pawns vs. two Bishops, which is unfavorable for the program because its Pawns are so weak and the Bishops are so strong. A prolonged initiative could have been maintained by ... ♖df8. **25 ♜xf3 ♛xf3 26 ♛xf3 exf3 27 ♚g3 ♜f8 28 ♝d1 f2 29 ♝xf2 ♚g8 30 b4 ...** Fixing the Queenside Pawns. Here lie White's winning chances; if BELLE can trade its four Pawns for the three White Pawns, the game would be a draw. But the Pawns are too weak. **... ♚f7 31 a4 g6** A further weakness, though White can force this eventually anyway. It might be accurate to say that White's biggest asset in this ending is BELLE's inability to "think" strategically. **32 ♝d4 ♚e8 33 a5 ♚d7 34 ♚h4 ♚e6** The weakening effects of BELLE's 31st move are clear, and soon cost it both the g- and h-Pawns. **35 ♝g4+ ♚f7 36 ♚g5 ♜d8 37 ♚h6 ♜e8 38 ♚xh7 ♜e4 39 ♚h6 ♜e8 40 ♝d7 ♜b8 41 ♚g5 ♚e7 42 ♝g4 ♜g8 43 ♝e5 c6 44 ♝d4 ...** Zugzwang! BELLE has to let the King penetrate now. **... ♚d6 45 ♚f6 ♜e8 46 ♚xg6** 1-0

CHAOS - Robert Morris(1701)
Queen's Gambit Declined(D57)

In this inaccurately played game, CHAOS is handed a Pawn when its opponent blunders in the opening, but returns it to reach a dead drawn ending — which Morris, by creative play, manages to lose.

1 d4 d5 2 c4 e6 3 ♞c3 ♞f6 4 ♝g5 ♝e7 5 e3 0-0 6 ♞f3 h6 7 ♝h4 ♞e4 8 ♝xe7 ♛xe7 9 cxd5 ♞xc3 10 bxc3 exd5 11 ♛b3 ♜d8 12 c4 dxc4 13 ♝xc4 ♞c6 14 ♝e2 ... So far the opening has followed theory, and an interesting game would have resulted from any of several moves by Black: ... ♖d6, ... ♖b8, ... ♕b4 among others. But Morris blunders: **... ♝g4? 15 ♛xb7 ♝xf3**

MORRIS

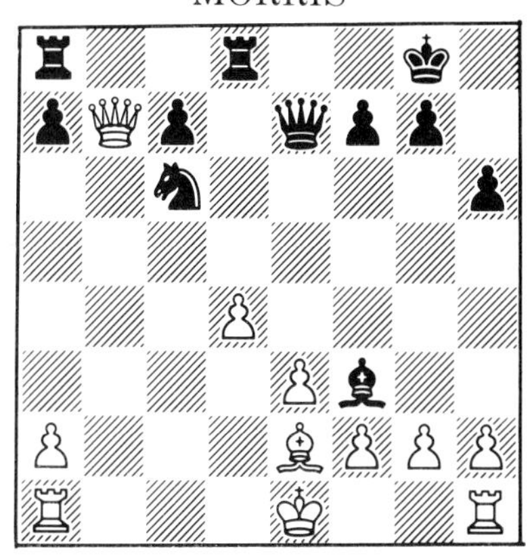

CHAOS

16 gxf3? ... As in its first-round game, CHAOS misevaluates the weakness created by the doubling of its f-Pawn. 16 ♗xf3 leaves Black with a lost game. **16 ... ♞a5?!** A good continuation is ... ♘b4. This ties Black up. **17 ♛b5 ♛a3 18 0-0 ♜ab8 19 ♛d3? ...** This ultimately loses back the Pawn, although that event is far over CHAOS' horizon. The program should play play 19 ♕f5, with attacking chances. **... ♛xd3!** CHAOS expected Black to play for a win by keeping the Queens on and going after the program's drafty King by ... ♕e7, but this was undoubtedly too slow — so it's best to simply go after the Pawn. The very least this will achieve is to exchange the weak c-Pawn, leaving CHAOS with an isolated d-Pawn. **20 ♝xd3 c5 21 ♜fb1 ...** An apparently clever trap is 21 ♖fd1 cxd4 22 exd4 and the Pawn is immune, but if Black plays 21 ... ♔f8, the d-Pawn is rather weak. **... ♜xb1+** Forced, e.g. ... ♖c8 22 ♝f5 ♖c7 23 ♖b5 ♘b7 24 ♖ab1 ♘d6 25 ♖b8 ♘c8 26 ♖c1. **22 ♜xb1 cxd4 23 exd4 ♞c6**

MORRIS

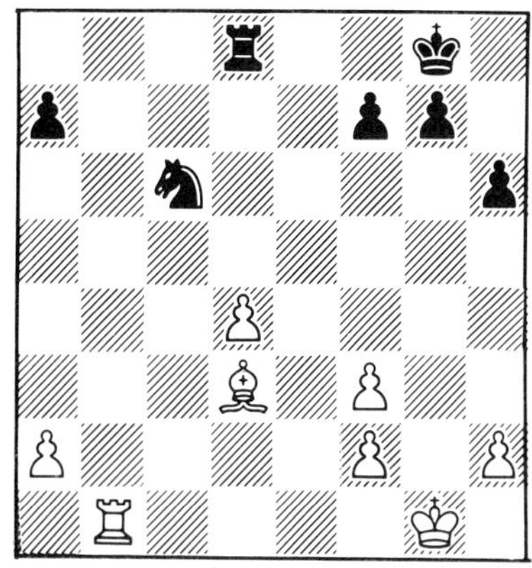

CHAOS

24 ♜e1?! ... This is definitely weak, and would dissipate the program's winning chances if it had any — but after 24 ♖b7 ♘xd4 25 ♔g2 ♘xf3, the ending turns out to be a draw anyway. **... ♞xd4 25 ♜e3 ♚f8 26 ♚g2 ♜e8** The draw is much easier if the Rooks are kept on: Black might even try for an edge by 26 ♘e6 27 ♔g3 g5, and the Knight takes up an ideal post at f4, while the White Bishop has no targets. **27 f4 ♞e6 28 ♚f3 ♞c5 29 ♝c4** CHAOS naturally values the Bishop higher than a Knight. **... ♜xe3+?!** One advantage held by computer programs: they don't get bored. This ending is a dead draw if Black is patient and plays with reasonable accuracy, but as usual it is unwise to try to force matters. This undoubling of White's Pawns and getting the Rooks off increases CHAOS' winning chances from zero to slight. The program, incidentally, understood this — it was expecting g6. **30 fxe3 f5** Now Morris is faced with the possibility of White's playing e4, which leads to further reductions in the flexibility of his position. Black still should not have difficulty drawing the game, but ... f6 with the idea g5 was better, one point being that White can hardly play f5 because the Black Knight would get a perfect post at e5. **31 h4! ...** CHAOS begins to display a level of technique which is not bad, and at least adequate to the occasion. **... ♚e7** Naturally Black does not want to put all his Pawns on white squares. Here CHAOS had been expecting Black to play ... g6 for the last six moves. Black really does not have to fear h5 however, because the h-Pawn would then become weak after ... ♘d7-f6. **32 h5 ♚f6?!** As explained above, ... ♘d7 was correct. **33 a3 a5** The Pawn must not stop on a white square. **34 ♝b5 ...** One of the points behind this move is that ... g6 can be answered by ♗e8. **... ♞b7 35 ♚e2 ♞d6?!** This markedly increases Black's peril by letting the White King into d3. CHAOS anticipated 35 ... ♘c5. **36 ♝c6! ♞e4 37 ♚d3 ...**

MORRIS

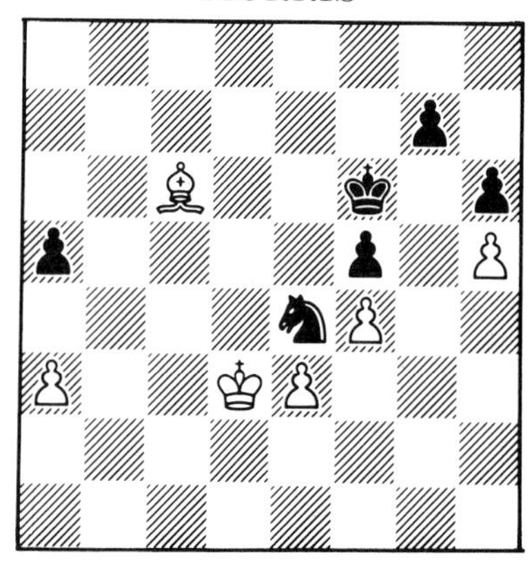

CHAOS

37 ... ♞g3? And now he's done it — the Knight is trapped out of play. CHAOS could win slowly after ... ♘d6 by going after the a-Pawn. **38 ♝f3 ♚e6 39 ♚d4 ♚d6 40 a4 ...** Zugzwang! **40 ... ♞f1** Now CHAOS (with a few false starts) "triangulates" with its Bishop to force Black into exchanging the h-Pawn for the f-Pawn: **41 ♝e2 ♞g3 42 ♝d1 ♞f1 43 ♝c2 ♞g3 44 ♚c4 ♚c6 45 ♚d4 ♚d6 46 ♚c4 ♚c6 47 ♝d3 ...** Finally CHAOS finds the winning line. **47 ... ♞xh5 48 ♝xf5 ♞g3 49 ♝g4 h5 50 ♝f3+ ♚d6 51 ♚b5 h4 52 ♝g4 ...** Now the win is clear. **... ♞f1 53 e4 ♞e3 54 ♝h3 ♞c2 55 ♚xa5 ♚c5 56 e5 ♞d4 57 ♚a6 ♚c6 58 f5** 1-0 An ending played rather well (for a computer program) by CHAOS, but weakly by its human opponent.

Michael Muff(1875) - SENSORY CC9
Sicilian(B34)

CC9's opponent slyly alters the move order in his opening, and the program — thrown out of its "book" — gives an all-time classic exposition of how NOT to play the opening.

1 e4 c5 2 ♞f3 ♞c6 3 d4 cxd4 4 ♞xd4 g6 5 ♝e3(!) ... This transposition throws CC9 out of its "book", and the program soon gets itself in trouble. This is excellent opening strategy against computer programs — a change in move order often baffles them. **... ♞f6 6 ♞c3 ♛a5?!** This premature development of the Queen leads to a comic-opera pursuit of the Black pieces, with sad results for CC9's position. **7 ♞b3 ♛e5?** The only good move is ... ♕c7, after which the loss of a tempo may not be too serious; if White continues 8 ♘b5, then ... ♕d8, after which White must defend the e-Pawn and Black can play ... a6 with tempo. CC9 now makes many bad moves, which at any rate lend the game a sort of macabre humor, and which need no individual comments. **8 f4 ♛c7?! 9 e5 ♞h5? 10 ♞b5 ♛b8 11 g4 ♞g7 12 ♞3d4 e6? 13 ♞f3 h5 14 ♞g5 ♝b4+ 15 c3 ♝e7 16 ♞e4 ♝h4+ 17 ♝f2 hxg4? 18 ♞bd6+ ♚f8 19 ♛xg4 ♞f5 20 ♝xh4 ♜xh4 21 ♛g5 ...**

SENSORY CC9

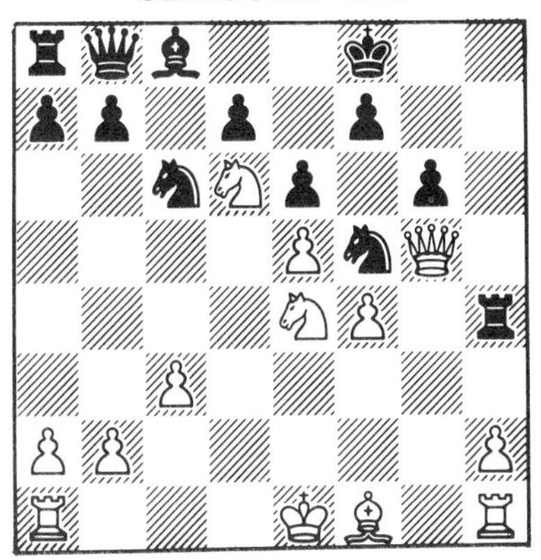

MUFF

An incredible positional disaster, on which further comment is hardly necessary. **... ♞xd6 22 ♞xd6 ♜h7 23 ♝d3 ♛c7 24 ♝xg6 fxg6 25 ♛xg6 ♛b6** CC9's way of resigning. The Spracklens are die-hards, however, and Kathe plays on to the bitter end. **26 ♛e8+ ♚g7 27 ♛f7+ ♚h6 28♛f6+ ♚h5 29 ♛g5 mate** 1-0

PRESTIGE - Tim Radermacher(2017)
Sicilian(B71)

Boris Baczynskyj's opening "book" gets PRESTIGE an advantage theoretically slight, but in practical play decisive. The program performs impressively in turning its edge into a win.

1 e4 c5 2 ♞f3 d6 3 d4 cxd4 4 ♞xd4 ♞f6 5 ♞c3 g6 6 f4 ♝g7 7 e5 dxe5 8 fxe5 ♞fd7 9 e6 ♞e5 10 ♝b5+ ♞bc6 11 exf7+ ♚xf7 12 0-0+ ♝f6 13 ♞xc6 bxc6 14 ♛xd8 ♜xd8 15 ♝a4 ♚g7 Why anyone would want to play this variation with Black is not obvious. ECO credits White with a slight advantage, but it will take accurate play to hold the Black position together in view of its Pawn weaknesses. **16 ♝f4 ♝f5?** This leads to the loss of the c-Pawn in complicated play, after which the ending is hopeless. An immediate ... ♗d7 or 16 ... ♖b8 seems to hold the position. **17 ♜ae1 ♞f7 18 ♝xc6 ♜ac8**

RADERMACHER

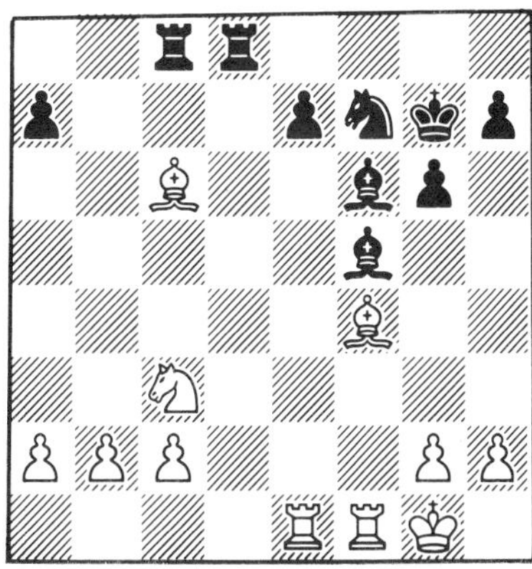

PRESTIGE

19 ♝e4! ... Ultimately securing the gain of the Pawn — and eventual connected passed Pawns. **... ♝xe4 20 ♜xe4 ♜d4** Here Black must have been shocked to realize that ... ♗xc3? 21 bxc3 ♖xc3 loses instantly to 22 ♖xe7. This threat colors the play for some time to come. **21 ♜e6 ...** Black threatened ... ♖xc3. **... ♜b4 22 ♝c1 ♜c5** Otherwise 23 ♘d5 is devastating. **23 ♚h1 ♞e5 24 a3 ♜b6** On ... ♖b7, 25 ♗e3 is very strong. **25 ♞a4! ...** Presumably Radermacher had counted only on 25 ♖xb6 axb6, after which the defense is easier. It is this kind of unexpected tactical shot which makes computer programs such difficult opponents in complicated open positions. **... ♜xe6 26 ♞xc5 ♜c6 27 b4 ♞c4 28 g4 ♝d4 29 ♞b3 ♝e3?!**

RADERMACHER

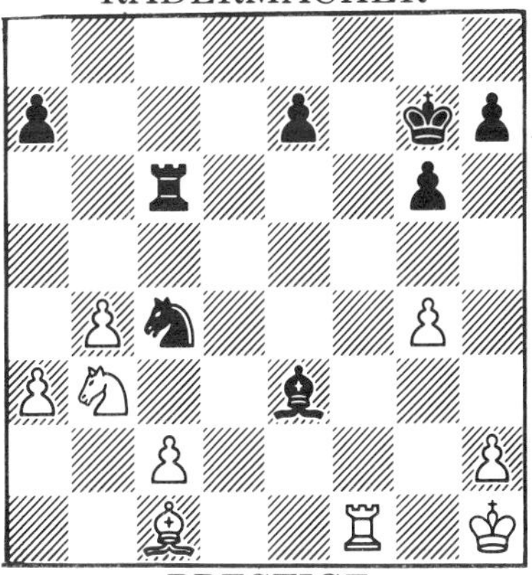

PRESTIGE

Expecting to win back the Pawn by this, Radermacher gets another tactical surprise:

30 ♞a5! ♜c7 Clearly bad is ... ♘xa5 31 ♗xe3 ♘c4 32 ♗xa7 ♘xa3 33 c3! e5 34 ♖c1 and the end is in sight. **31 ♞xc4 ♝xc1 32 ♜xc1 ♜xc4 33 g5 e5 34 ♜d1! ...** PRESTIGE is playing the ending rather well. Black cannot afford to let the Rook on the 7th rank. **... ♜c7 35 c4 ♚f7 36 c5 ...** Now the win is clear. The rest of the game was a time scramble. **... ♚e7 37 ♚g2 a5 38 ♜c1 axb4 39 axb4 ♚d7 40 b5 ♚c8 41 b6 ♜f7 42 c6 ♜f5 43 ♜a1 ♜xg5+ 44 ♚h1 ♚b8 45 ♜a7 ♜f5 46 c7+ ♚c8 47 ♜a8+ ♚d7 48 c8(♛)+ ♚e7 49 ♜a7+ ♚f6 50 ♛d8+ ♚e6 51 ♛d7+** 1-0

ROUND 4

BELLE - Andy McGowan(1936)
Pirc(B08)

BELLE plays rather impressively in this game, presenting its opponent with an unusual strategic plan which is not countered effectively and which affords the program considerable play in a difficult middlegame. McGowan makes several weak moves under pressure, and finally his position collapses.

1 e4 d6 2 d4 ♞f6 3 ♞c3 g6 4 ♝e2 ♝g7 5 ♞f3 ... BELLE plays a fairly conservative opening here. This development is well tuned to the program's heuristics. **... 0-0 6 0-0 ♞c6 7 d5 ♞b8 8 h3 c5** ECO gives ... c6. The disadvantage of this move lies in the absence of any tension in the center. In this Benoni-like position, White stands well because e4 has been achieved without the necessity of playing c4. By maneuvering its Knight on f3 to c4, the program could aim at a powerful position. **9 ♝g5 h6 10 ♝e3 ♞bd7** Here Black would do well to play ... e6, creating tension and the possibility of ... e5 at an opportune moment.

McGOWAN

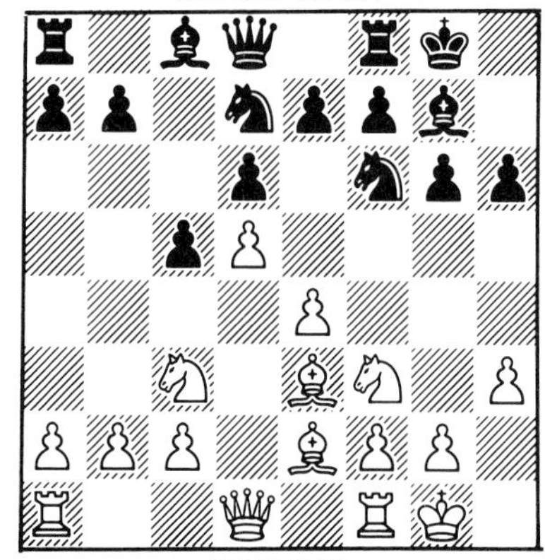

BELLE

11 ♜b1!? ... A very interesting, if rather strange, "plan". Most players would continue 11 a4 or ♘d2 with the idea a4, ♘d2-c4, perhaps followed by a5, and the Pawnstorm f4—e5. **... a6 12 b4 cxb4?!** It would seem better to play...b6, avoiding the pressure BELLE now gets. **13 ♜xb4 ...** BELLE now has the half-open b-file to play on with its Rook, and a weak Pawn to attack, but the program's c-Pawn is potentially weak. **... ♛a5** The course of the game suggests that Black should play ... b5 here or next move. **14 ♛b1 ♞c5 15 a4 ♞fd7** Black has some problems here. The b-Pawn ties down the Bishop and he can't finish developing his pieces. **16 ♝d2 g5 17 ♛b2 ♛c7 18 ♛a3 a5?!** This lets BELLE take control of b5. Black could try ... b6 here, with the idea ... ♗b7, then ... ♖fc8 and counterplay on the c-file. **19 ♜b5 b6 20 ♜e1 ♝a6 21 ♜bb1 ♝xe2** Exchanging an inactive piece for a strong one, but now b5 is even weaker. **22 ♜xe2 ♞e5 23 ♞xe5 ♝xe5 24 ♞b5 ♛d8?!** It would be better to play ... ♕d7, with possibilities for doubling Rooks and ... e6. **25 ♜f1 f5?** This creates a weakness on e6 which proves very unpleasant later. **26 exf5 ♜xf5 27 ♝e3 ♞d7** McGowan ought to be delighted by an exchange on c5, which would transform the weak backward b-Pawn into a protected c-Pawn; this also loses a tempo. **28 ♛b3 ♝g7** A nothing move at a critical moment. 28 ... ♖c8 seems appropriate; Black has to get some counterplay going. **29 c4 ♞c5** It seems better to play the Knight to e5. **30 ♝xc5 ...** It would have been better to play 30 ♕c2 with the idea ♗d4; the weaknesses on the b and e files would be fatal in an ending. **... bxc5 31 ♛c2 ...**

McGOWAN

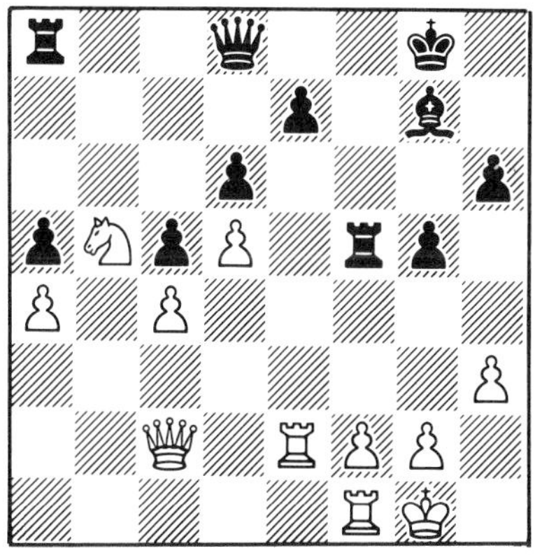

BELLE

31 ... ♜e5? McGowan should play ... ♕f8 or ... ♖f6, keeping pressure on the f-file. This lets the White Queen in with devastating results. **32 ♜xe5 ♝xe5 33 ♛g6+ ♝g7 34 f4 ...** Black is now in terrible difficulties. **... ♛e8** This creates a tactical opportunity for BELLE, but it is hard'to see what else Black can do. The problem with this move is the Knight fork it sets up. **35 ♛e6+ ♛f7** Losing a Pawn and the game, but King moves lose to ♘c7. **36 ♛xf7+ ♚xf7 37 fxg5+ ♚g6 38 gxh6+ ♝xh6 39 g4 ...** With two connected passed Pawns, and all its Pawns on white squares, BELLE has an easy win in the ending. **... ♝e3+ 40 ♚g2 ♜h8 41 ♞a7 e5?** And this makes it even easier. **42 dxe6 ♝g5 43 ♜d1 ♝f4 44 ♞c6 ♜e8 45 e7 ♝g5 46 ♜xd6+ ♚f7 47 ♜d5 ♝xe7 48 ♜f5+ ♚e6 49 ♞xe7 ♜xe7 50 ♜xc5** 1-0

Douglas Hanson(1861) - CHAOS
Nimzo-Indian(E48)

CHAOS played a dubious move in the opening, getting an inferior position, which Hanson exploited to start a Kingside attack. The program failed to recognize its danger, and lost a Pawn. Then, as CHAOS slipped into time pressure, Hanson slowly mobilized all his pieces for a decisive Pawnstorming attack. The program forfeited in a lost position.

1 d4 ♞f6 2 c4 e6 3 ♞c3 ♝b4 4 e3 c5 5 ♝d3 0-0 6 ♞e2 d5 7 0-0 ♞c6 8 cxd5 exd5 9 a3 ...

CHAOS

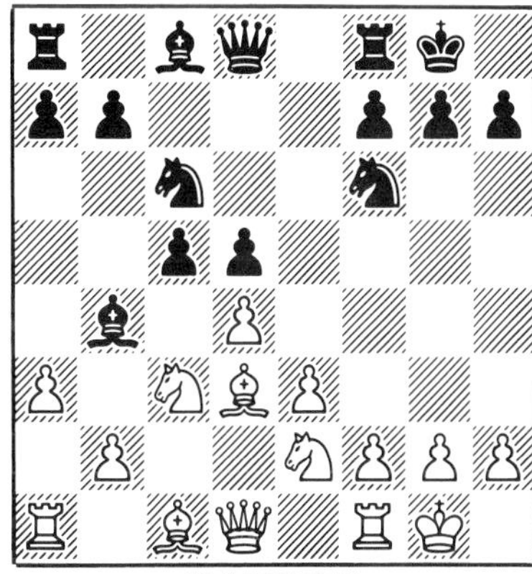

HANSON

9 ... c4?! ECO considers only ... cxd4. This release of tension frees White for active operations. CHAOS expected 10 axb4?! cxd3 11 ♕xd3 ♘xb4, which would have been bad judgment on White's part. **10 ♝b1 ♝e7** Now CHAOS thought that it had a slight advantage! **11 ♞f4** Here an immediate b3! would reveal the drawbacks of Black's 9th move. **... ♜e8 12 ♛f3!?** b3 was still possible and effective. This leads to complicated play. **12 ... ♝g4** Here the program assessed its advantage at .55 of a Pawn. **13 ♛g3 ♝d6?** Better would have been ... a6! with the idea of playing ... ♕d6. This uncovers f6 and also d5, a strategic error of a type often made by computer programs, which can (usually) "see" the immediate tactical consequences, but not the long-term liabilities of such moves. **14 f3** Here White could have won a Pawn by 14 ♘cxd5. **... ♝d7?!** The Knight at f4 is too strong, and should be exchanged: 14 ... ♗xf4 15 ♕xf4 ♗h5-g6, defusing the Kingside pressure. **15 ♛h4 ...**

CHAOS

HANSON

15 ... ♛a5? It was now essential to play either ... ♗xf4, after which 16 ♕xf4 ♘e7-g6 holds things together for the time being, or ... h6. This misplaces the Queen and immediately loses a Pawn. CHAOS expected 16 ♕g5 after which it would play ... h6 with tempo. **16 ♞h5! ♝e7** After ... ♘xh5, either the h-Pawn or the d-Pawn goes. At this point, CHAOS began to "see" that it is White who has the advantage! **17 ♞xf6+ ♝xf6 18 ♛xh7+ ♚f8** For the next 22 moves, the program assesses the positions fairly consistently, giving itself anywhere between .15 and .93 of a Pawn positional compensation for the Pawn minus. In reality, of course, White has the better game in addition to his material edge, but the program's heuristics can't assess the potential activity of a piece — they rate it based on the square it inhabits at the moment. **19 ♝d2 ♚e7 20 ♛c2 ♜h8 21 ♞e2 ...** Stronger was 21 ♘e4! ♕a6 22 ♘xf6 ♔xf6 23 e4! and Black is in trouble. **... ♛a6 22 ♝c3 ♝g5 23 ♛d2 ...** Strong here was 23 e4, activating the Bishops. **... ♛b5 24 ♝c2 ♚f8** Here CHAOS had used 81 minutes on its clock, and begins to drift into time pressure. **25 ♜ae1 ♜h6 26 ♞g3 ♜e8 27 ♛f2 ♝h4 28 e4 ...** Hanson has certainly been in no hurry to exploit his advantage, preferring to finish developing his pieces. His moves have been sound and now CHAOS is confronted with serious problems as White takes control of the center. **... ♞e7 29 ♝b4 a5 30 ♝c3 b6 31 e5 ♞f5** At this point CHAOS was rather happy, calculating that its positional "compensation" was worth almost a Pawn — while in reality it was just about to be crushed! Also, the program had now used nearly two hours and thus had only 1 minute 40 seconds for each of the next 19 moves before the time control, thus began to reduce its search depth to speed up its play. **32 f4 ♚g8 33 ♛f3 ♞e7 34 f5 ...**

CHAOS

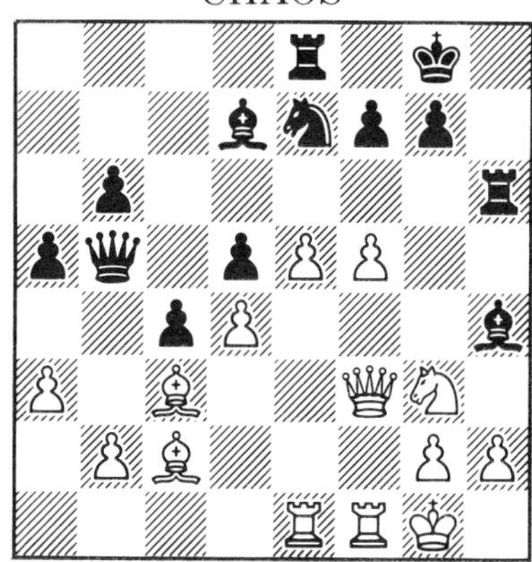

HANSON

Positionally decisive. CHAOS is completely tied up and can't undertake anything at all, while Hanson gets everything ready for the final push. **34 ... ♚h8 35 ♜e2 ♚g8 36 ♝b1 ♝g5 37 ♝d2 ...** First, CHAOS' only active piece is exchanged for the least valuable of

White's pieces. ... **♝xd2 38 ♜xd2 ♞c6 39 ♛f4 ♛b3 40 ♜f3 ♛b5** CHAOS' time-control system was coping with its time pressure; here the program had more than 20 minutes left. Unfortunately its position was now untenable. **41 f6 ...** This wins outright, e.g. ... ♗e6 42 fxg7 ♔xg7 43 ♕g5+ ♖g6 44 ♘h5+ and: a) ... ♔h7 44 ♗xg6+ fxg6 45 ♘f6+ winning the Rook; or b) ... ♔h8 42 ♗xg6 fxg6 43 ♕h6+ ♔g8 44 ♕g7 mate; or c) ... ♔g8 42 ♗xg6 fxg6 43 ♕xg6+ any 44 ♕g7 mate; or d) ... ♔f8 42 ♗xg6 fxg6 43 ♕f6+ ♔g8 44 ♕g7 mate. CHAOS "sees" the disaster in its game tree, and plays a "desperation" sacrifice (after some 9 minutes "thought") which pushes it "over the horizon": **... ♞xe5 42 dxe5 ...** There is still no answer; CHAOS ran out of time looking and forfeited. 1-0(time)

Ali Shahin(1929) - SENSORY CC9
Queen's Gambit Accepted(D20)

CC9 gets itself into a terrible mess in the opening, losing a piece early. Shahin became overconfident and gave it back, but the program was still lost. Shahin did not play the ending perfectly, but the program made things easy for him by missing drawing opportunities.

1 d4 d5 2 c4 dxc4 3 ♞c3 e5 4 ♞f3 exd4 5 ♛xd4 ♛xd4 6 ♞xd4 a6 The "end of the line" theoretically; ECO rates the position as equal. **7 a4 ♝c5 8 e3 ...** (See diagram)

Position after White's 8th move.

SENSORY CC9

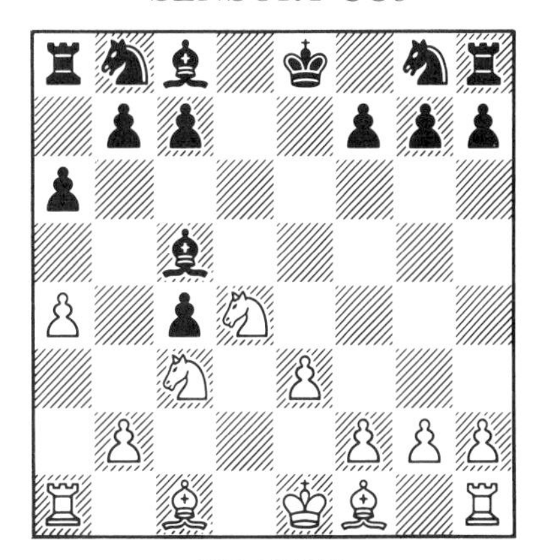

SHAHIN

8 ... ♝xd4? This is very unwise. The isolated d-Pawn becomes potentially strong; lines of action are opened for White; and CC9 finds itself confronted with tactical problems. Black should simply play ... ♘e7 and castle. **9 exd4 ♞c6?** This apparently simple position is very dangerous for Black, as the game certainly shows. White is ahead in development, and the program should be thinking in terms of King safety, not counterplay. Thus ... ♘e7 was the move to play. **10 ♞d5 ♚d7?!** Better is 10 ... ♔d8, not blocking the Bishop. CC9's position now becomes most uncomfortable, with its King stuck in the center. **11 ♝f4 ♞xd4??** Creating a dangerous lineup on the d-file, which soon costs CC9 its Knight. A certain inability to fully evaluate the consequences of pins and discovered attacks has always characterized the Spracklens' programs — this is an extremely difficult problem for the chess programmer. The only continuation, of course, was ... ♘f6, though after 12 ♘xc7 ♖a7 13 ♗xc4 ♖f8 Black has a horrible game. **12 ♜d1 ♞c2+ 13 ♚d2 ♞b4** Or 13 ... ♘d4 14 ♔c3. **14 ♞xb4 ♞e7 15 ♝xc4 a5 16 ♚c2+ ...** Here Shahin, misled by CC9's difficulties in a game whose character could hardly have been better chosen to reveal the weaknesses in the program's heuristics, began to take his opponent too lightly, behaving as if the game were a farce. **16 ... ♚e8**

SENSORY CC9

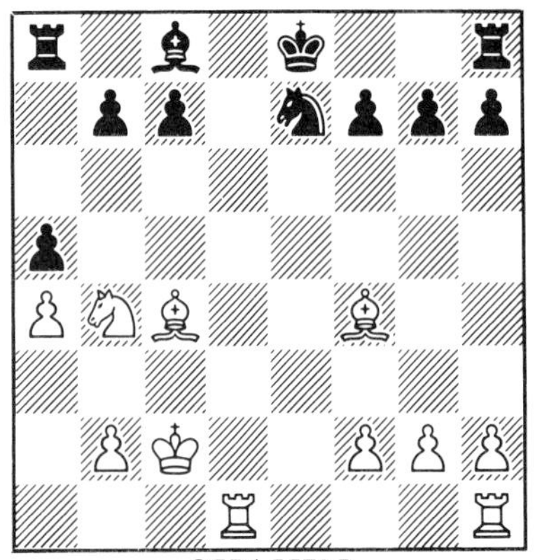

SHAHIN

17 ♝xc7? ... Pride goeth before a fall! Now the program gets the piece back (much to the satisfaction of Kathe Spracklen), although it still has a lost game. **... ♝f5+ 18 ♞d3 ♜c8 19 ♚b3 ♜xc7 20 ♞e5 ♞c6 21 ♜he1 ♞xe5** Now Shahin gets a material advantage again — not as large, but large enough. Black would certainly like to castle here, but unfortunately it is no longer legal to do so. There isn't any other way to avoid the loss of a Pawn, e.g. ... ♗e6 22 ♘xf7. **22 ♜xe5+ ♝e6 23 ♝xe6 fxe6 24 ♜xe6+ ♜e7 25 ♜ed6 ♜f8 26 ♜d8+ ♚f7 27 ♜xf8+ ♚xf8 28 ♜d2 ♜e4 29 f3 ♜h4?!** The ending is still not easy to win if the White King can be kept penned up. After ... ♖b4+ 30 ♔a3 ♔e7 31 ♖d3 with the threat ♖b3, White can still make progress, but it would be easy to go wrong. **30 g3 ♜b4+ 31 ♚a3 b5** This resolves the situation on the Queenside, after which Shahin's technique proves to be (if less than perfect) better than the program's. **32 b3 bxa4 33 bxa4 ♜c4** Otherwise 34 ♖d5 just wins the a-Pawn without compensation. Now Shahin gets an outside passed Pawn. **34 ♜d5 ♜c3+ 35 ♚b2 ♜xf3 36 ♜xa5 ♜f2+ 37 ♚b3 ♜xh2 38 ♜e5** Cutting the King off. **... ♜d2?!** The program begins to show its lack of strategic capacity and ignorance of endgame principles. After ... ♖h1!, threatening to get the Rook behind the passed Pawn, the ending is a draw: 39 ♖e2 (or 39 ♔b2 ♖h2+ etc) ♖a1 40 ♖a2 ♖xa2 41 ♔xa2 ♔e7 and Black gets a passed Pawn too. **39 a5 ♜d3+?** CC9 refuses to use its Rook to stop the a-Pawn! The program could still have drawn by 39 ... ♖d8, after which White can force the win of the Rook for the Pawn — but meanwhile the Black Pawns and King are advancing, and White will eventually have to give up the Rook to stop the h-Pawn, resulting in a draw. **40 ♚b4 ♜xg3?** The losing move; CC9 could still have drawn with ... ♖d8. It is impossible for the program to search far enough ahead to find the drawing strategy, and in the absence of any heuristics telling it how to play this ending, it goes after material. **41 a6 ♜g2** Finally the danger posed by the Pawn is recognized — far too late. **42 a7 ♜a2 43 ♜a5 ♜xa5 44 ♚xa5** 1-0

Peter Moscatelli(2142) - PRESTIGE
King's Indian Attack(A04)

PRESTIGE easily wins the opening of this game against a player of near master strength, and its position is so powerful that it proves to be amazingly durable when the program starts to go wrong. When Moscatelli (perhaps in desperation) formulates a plan for a Kingside attack, the program makes one inferior move after another, capped by a couple of outright blunders — all caused by its inability to recognize the threat.

1 ♞f3 c5 2 g3 ♞c6 3 ♝g2 g6 4 0-0 ♝g7 5 d3 e5 6 ♞c3 ♞ge7 7 a3 0-0 8 ♜b1 d5 9 ♝d2 a5 10 ♞a4 ... Varying from ECO, which gives 10 a4. Black has a fine game here, with at least equality. **10 ... b6 11 c4 dxc4** Here ... e4! would be strong: 12 dxe4 dxe4 13 ♘e1 f5 14 ♗c3 ♘d4 (for example) would leave Black with a fine game. **12 dxc4 ♝g4 13 h3 ♝f5 14 ♜c1 h6 15 ♝c3 ♛c7 16 ♞d2**

♜fd8 17 ♛b3 ♜ab8 18 ♛a2 ♞d4 19 ♜fe1 ♝d7 20 b3 ...

PRESTIGE

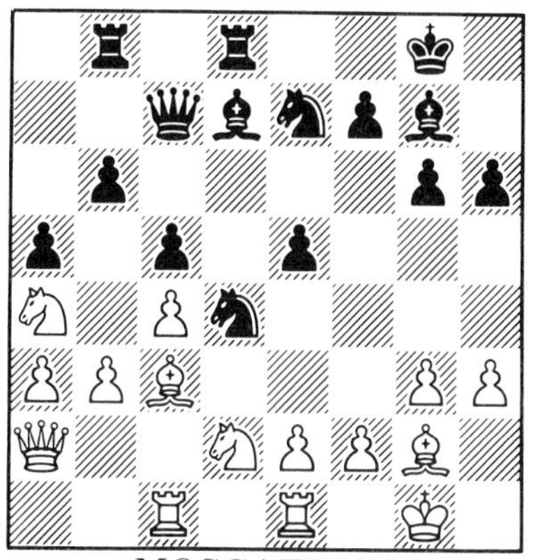

MOSCATELLI

20 ... ♝xa4?! PRESTIGE has much the better game here, and could increase its advantage by ... ♗c6, neutralizing White's only active piece. The doubled a-Pawns do not become weak — the program's b-Pawn does! This is exactly the kind of positional subtlety that completely escapes computer programs. **21 bxa4 ♞e6 22 ♛c2 ♚h7 23 ♜cd1 f5** This Pawn advance, that on the next move, are rather double-edged. The program is putting pressure on the White position, at the cost of exposing its King, which requires accurate play. **24 e3 e4 25 ♝xg7 ♞xg7** Black might as well take with the King. The Knight was well placed. **26 ♞b1 ♛e5?!** Now the program starts to dissipate its advantage by inexact play. ... ♘c6-e5, with strong pressure on d3 and f3, was correct. **27 ♞c3 ♞e6 28 ♛b3 ♞g5 29 ♞d5 ♞xd5 30 ♜xd5 ♜xd5 31 cxd5 ♞f7 32 ♝f1 ♛c7?!** The Queen is excellently posted on e5, and should stay there. PRESTIGE would then have excellent prospects after ... ♘d6. **33 ♜d1 ♞d6 34 h4 c4?!** This is premature. As noted earlier, Bisguier had "spread the word" that computer programs couldn't recognize the problems that an advancing Rook Pawn can cause. The right move was ... h5, blockading the Kingside. **35 ♛c3 ♜c8 36 h5 gxh5** This is not necessarily bad, but much safer is ... ♕g7 with good endgame prospects if White exchanges. **37 ♝e2 ...**

PRESTIGE

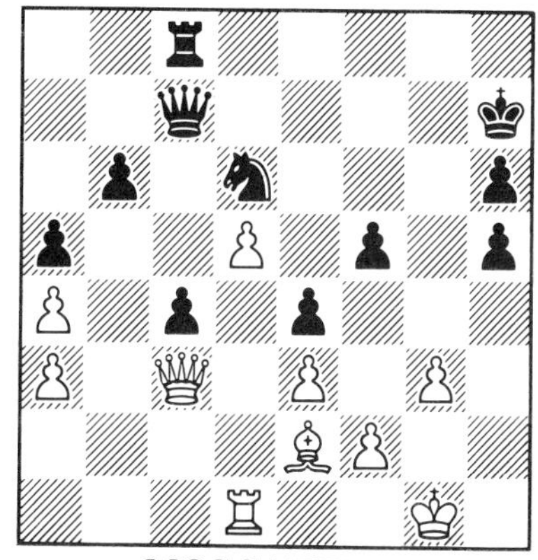

MOSCATELLI

37 ... ♚g6? Even now, the program could have held the edge—after ... h4! and it is White whose King is exposed. The program's excessive materialism drives it into suicidal behavior, which its opponent immediately exploits. **38 ♚g2 ♛d7?** It was not too late to play ... ♕g7 with a good game. The program, however, wants another Pawn. So Moscatelli decides to offer it a Bishop: **39 ♝xh5+! ♚g5?!** Obviously ... ♔xh5 40 ♕f6 forces mate. It would have been more prudent to play 39 ♔h7, however. The program did not want to let the White Queen into f6, but this can be countered by ... ♖g8. **40 ♜h1 ♛e7 41 ♜h4 ♛f6 42 ♛c1 ♛e5 43 ♛h1 ♛xd5?** PRESTIGE goes Pawn-hunting when its house is afire! After ... ♖h8, Black still has a tenable position and good endgame chances. **44 ♝e8! ♚f6** Part of the horrible truth has finally dawned on the program: mate is threatened if the Bishop is taken — 45 ♖xh6 and there's no defense. **45 ♜xh6+ ♚e7 46 ♝b5 ♞xb5 47 axb5 ♛xb5??** Even now, it might be possible to save the game by 47

... ♖f8. The program simply has no sense of danger, since its King safety heuristics deal mainly with castled positions and are not able to assess the dangers to an exposed King. **48 ♜h7+ ♚e6 49 ♛h6+ ♚d5 50 ♜f7 ♜f8** Tantamount to resignation, but as usual the game goes on to the bitter end. **51 ♛xf8 ♛a4 52 ♛d8+ ♚e5 53 ♜e7+ ♚f6 54 ♛f8+ ♚g5 55 ♜g7+ ♚h5 56 ♛h8 mate** 1-0

ROUND 5

Richard Sharpe(2052) - BELLE
Sokolsky(A00)

In this game, the reader can see how BELLE's rating (about 2150) may be calculated. Take a Grandmaster level of tactical play (2600), add a Category II level of strategic play (1700), and divide by two — very simple! In this game, Sharpe loses a Pawn to a nice combination in the opening. Then he outplays the program strategically and equalizes, only to fall victim to another tactical shot which wins for BELLE.
1 b4 e5 2 ♝b2 ♝xb4 From a strictly theoretical viewpoint, this line ought to be good for White because he exchanges a flank Pawn for a center Pawn. But Black gets an edge in development. **3 ♝xe5 ♞f6 4 ♞f3 d5 5 e3 0-0 6 ♝e2 c5 7 ♞c3 ♝e6** The end of the line theoretically; ECO rates the position as equal. **8 a3 ...** This does not accomplish anything, and actually reduces White's options. After 8 0-0 ♘c6 9 ♘a4 is not bad, as White can continue ... ♘xe5 10 ♘xe5 and if ... ♘e4, then c3 with tempo. **... ♝a5 9 0-0 ♞c6 10 ♞a4?! ...** Not a good square for the Knight, and one on which it later becomes vulnerable. After 10 ♗g3?! ♗xc3 would be strong, since the doubled Pawns would be very weak. It would be best to play 10 ♘b1, which admittedly doesn't say much for White's opening. **... ♞xe5 11 ♞xe5 ♞e4 12 c3 ♛e8**

BELLE

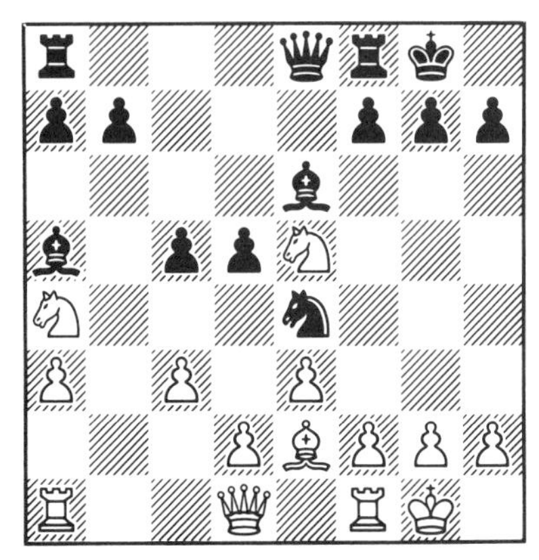

SHARPE

13 ♞b2? ... Giving BELLE a chance to show its tactical strength. It was necessary to play 13 ♘f3. **... ♞xc3!** Winning a Pawn, through a very fine five-move combination which many a human master might overlook. **14 dxc3 ♝xc3 15 ♞ed3 ...** Sharpe probably looked this far in evaluating his 13th move, and concluded that this move wins for White. **... c4!** Now something has to fall,the pretty point being that after a capture on d3 the Bishop is attacked. **16 ♛c2 cxd3 17 ♝xd3 ♝xb2 18 ♛xb2 ♛e7** BELLE now confronts some significant technical difficulties realizing its advantage, which are increased by the program's strategic shortcomings. **19 ♜ab1 b6 20 ♝a6 f5?!** An unnecessary weakness, which further restricts the Bishop. 21 **♛e5 ♜ae8 22 a4 ♛f7 23 ♛f4 ♝c8 24 ♝d3 ...** Of course Sharpe does not want to trade his strong, active Bishop for BELLE's bad Bishop. **... ♝d7?!**

BELLE

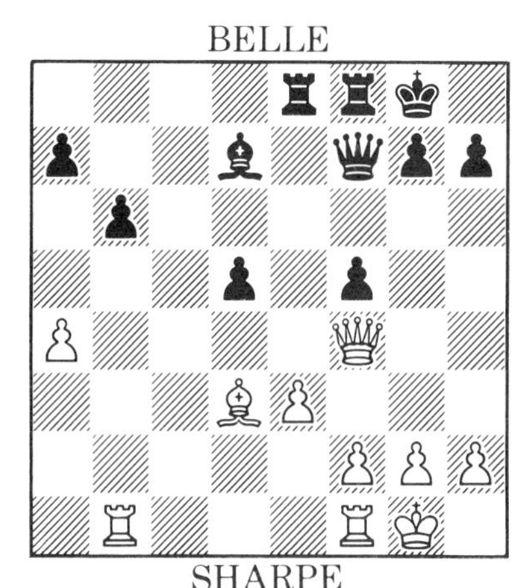

SHARPE

25 a5! bxa5 Now the Black a-Pawn becomes weak. This allows White to put up strong resistance. **26 ♛c7 ♜e7 27 ♛xa5 ♝c6 28 ♛c5 ♜c7 29 ♛d4 ♛g6 30 ♜fc1 ♛d6** BELLE wants to play ... f4. **31 g3 ♝a8 32 ♜xc7 ♛xc7 33 ♜a1 ♜f7** Here it would be fair to say that White has almost achieved full positional compensation for the Pawn minus. The problem is a little more complicated here because this compensation now consists of continual threats to recapture the Pawn, which are just as comprehensible to BELLE as to a human player, so that all the program's formidable tactical strength can be brought to bear. **34 ♝e2 ♝c6 35 ♝f3 ...** This is not particularly effective, and uncovering a6 eventually allows the Pawn to advance. **... ♛b7 36 h4 ♜d7 37 ♛e5 g6 38 ♛e8+ ♚g7 39 ♛e5+ ♚f7 40 ♜a5 ♝b5 41 h5 ♝c4 42 ♚g2 a6 43 h6 ♛c6 44 ♛g7+ ♚e6 45 ♛d4 ...** After 45 ♕g8+ it is not at all clear how Black can make any progress, with the White Queen roaming about on the eighth rank: e.g. ... ♖f7 46 ♕d8. **... ♝b5 46 ♜a1 ♜c7 47 ♛h8 ♛d7 48 ♛g8+ ♛f7 49 ♛a8 ♜c5** (See diagram)

Position after 49 moves.

BELLE

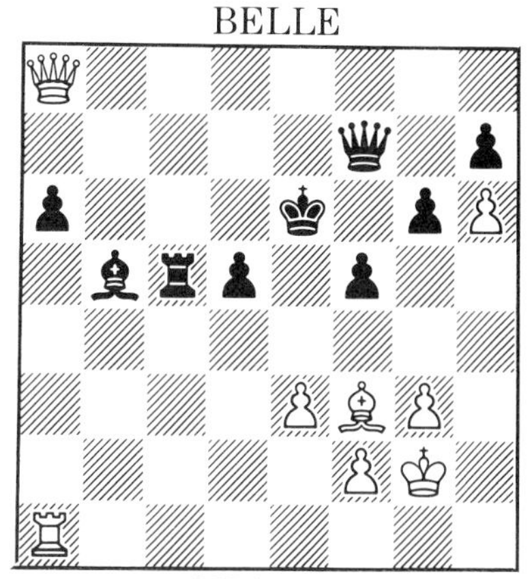

SHARPE

50 ♜c1? ... On the last move of the first time control, Sharpe walks into another tactical shot. Here there are many ways to draw, perhaps the clearest being 50 ♖xa6+ ♗xa6 51 ♕xa6+ ♔d7 52 ♕b7+ ♖c7 53 ♕xd5+. **... ♜xc1 51 ♝xd5+ ...** This certainly LOOKS decisive, and the crowd which had gathered around the game started to get excited. But those who knew something about BELLE realized that there had to be more to the combination than this; it is mathematically impossible for the program to overlook something this simple. **... ♚e5 52 f4+ ♚d6 53 ♝xf7 ♝c6+** The simple and crushing point. **54 ♛xc6+ ♜xc6 55 ♝g8 ...** White could resign here. The rest is easy. **... ♜c7 56 ♚f3 a5 57 e4 fxe4+ 58 ♚xe4 a4 59 g4 ♜c8 60 ♝f7 a3 61 g5 ♜c2 62 ♚d3 a2 63 ♝xa2 ♜xa2 64 f5 gxf5 65 ♚e3 ♚e5** 0-1

SENSORY CC9(1765) - CHAOS(1714)
Sicilian(B30)

In conformance with USCF rules, each player in the U.S. Open had the right to notify the Tournament Director that he, she (or it!) did not wish to be paired with a computer program, and about 70 players did so. The programmers, of course, did not wish to increase the "anti-computer" statistics and did not so notify the Director. In a 12 round tournament with 370 "eligible" humans and 4 computer programs, the probability of any one program being paired with another program at some point during the event works out to 24.2%, and the probability that any three programs can finish the tournament without facing another computer (which would automatically mean that the fourth did too) is only 43.5%. Thus this pairing was by no means surprising.

1 e4 c5 2 ♞f3 ♞c6 3 ♝b5 ♞f6 4 e5 ♞d5 5 ♞c3 e6 6 0-0 ♝e7 7 ♞xd5 exd5 8 d4 ♛b6 ECO gives ... a6, with a slight edge for White.

CHAOS

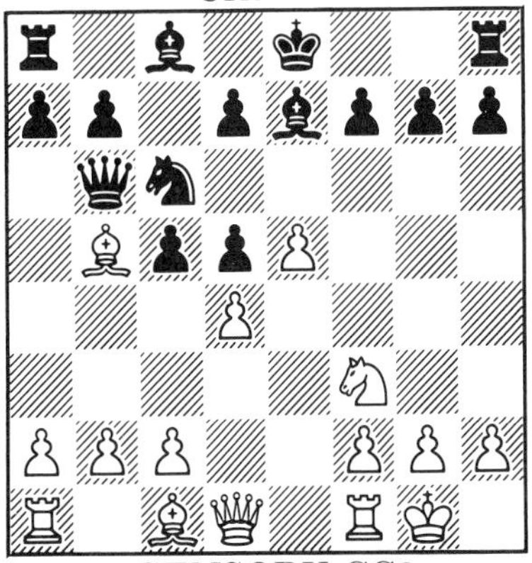

SENSORY CC9

9 ♝xc6?! ... To the computer program, this move is virtually forced, since CC9s' positional penalty for the tripled Pawn that results from 9 ♗e2 cxd4 is not very much greater than that charged for the doubled Pawn Black already has, and in any case is insignificant compared to the value of a Pawn, so that the net loss on the transaction seems to be almost an entire healthy Pawn! CHAOS, with more positional knowledge, anticipated 9 ♕e2 ♘xd4 10 ♘xd4 cxd4, and assessed the resulting position as about equal. **9 ... dxc6** But now CHAOS credits Black with a significant positional edge (.57 of a Pawn). **10 dxc5 ♝xc5 11 c3 ♝g4** CHAOS is right. White is under pressure, and Black's Bishop's are strong. **12 b4?! ...** CC9 now weakens its Pawn structure. A wiser continuation was 12 ♕d3, unpinning the Knight and threatening ♘d4. **... ♝e7 13 ♝e3 ♛a6?!** CHAOS might have increased its advantage by 13 ... ♕c7. This eases White's problems somewhat. **14 a4 ♛c4 15 ♛d4 ♛xd4 16 ♞xd4 h6 17 a5 ♝d7!** Much better than ... a6; CHAOS keeps its Pawns flexible. **18 ♜fe1?! ...** Wrong Rook! CC9 is going up a blind alley on the a-file, and should play f4-f5 at the earliest opportunity to mobilize its majority. **... 0-0 19 ♝d2 b6!** Fine Pawn play by CHAOS, which proves superior in this respect to CC9. The point behind this is not that there is any threat of ... bxa5?, which would seriously weaken Black's position, but that ... c5 evicting the Knight is now threatened. **20 e6 ...** CC9 reacts energetically; it is hard to see what else the program could do. **... fxe6**

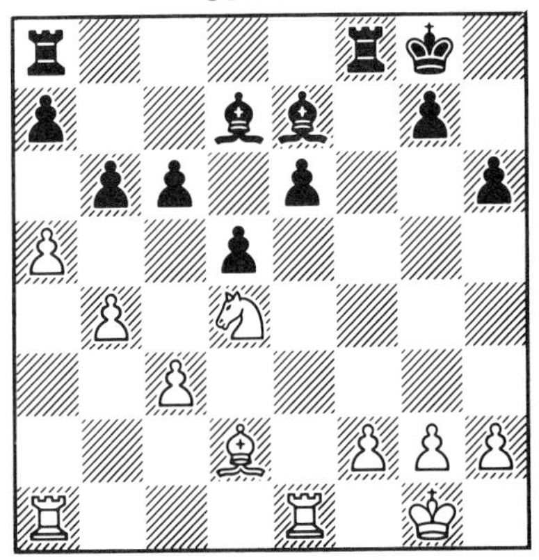

SENSORY CC9

21 axb6? ... CHAOS expected the better continuation 21 ♘xe6 ♖fc8, after which White could continue 22 ♘c7! This surrenders an open file. **21 ... axb6 22 ♜xa8 ...** Otherwise White can't recapture on e6. **... ♜xa8** CHAOS now expected 23 ♘xe6 ♖a2 24 ♗c1 ♖c2 25 ♘xg7 ♖xc1 and concluded that its advantage had increased by a full Pawn. **23 ♞xe6 ♜a2 24 ♝c1 ♜c2 25 ♞xg7 ♝f6** CHAOS thinks this is even better (it's not, but still wins). **26 ♝xh6 ♚f7 27 ♞h5 ...** Both the c-Pawn and the b-Pawn are doomed, leading to an unusual position. **27 ... ♝xc3 28 ♜c1?!** ... CC9 would have better drawing chances after 28 ♖d1, keeping the Rooks on. **... ♜xc1+ 29 ♝xc1 ♝xb4**

CHAOS

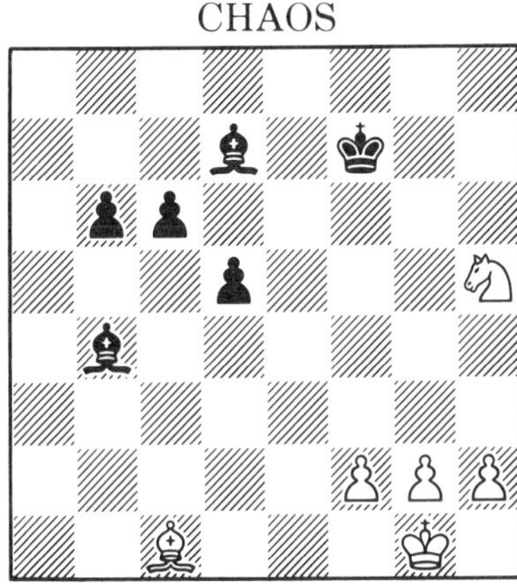

SENSORY CC9

Material is now equal, with three connected passed Pawns on each side, but CHAOS has a winning advantage because its Pawns are advanced and the Bishops are so strong. **30 h3?!** CC9 plays the ending inaccurately, although this just shortens its agony. It was better to play 30 f3, getting the King out. **... d4 31 ♞f4 ♝f5 32 g4 ♝h7 33 ♚f1 d3 34 ♞h5 d2 35 ♝xd2 ♝xd2 36 f4 ♝d3+** The win is easy now. As usual with the Spracklens, the game goes on to the bitter end. **37 ♚f2 b5 38 f5 b4 39 h4 b3 40 g5 b2 41 g6+ ♚g8 42 ♞f6+ ♚h8 43 ♞h5 b1(♛) 44 ♞g3 ♝xf5 45 ♚g2 ♝xg6 46 ♚h3 ♛g1** 0-1

PRESTIGE - Andy Unger(2049)
Vienna Game(C25)

Again PRESTIGE badly outplays a Candidate Master in the opening, and gets a significant advantage in the early middlegame. But, just as in the fourth round, the program (unable to formulate any kind of strategic plan) does not know what to do with its advantage and eventually loses it. Finally Unger mobilizes his Kingside majority while the program fails to do anything with its own Pawns, and drives it home for a win.

1 e4 e5 2 ♞c3 ♞c6 3 ♝c4 ♝c5 4 ♛g4 g6 5 ♛f3 ♛f6?! It has long been known that this gives White the better game. **6 ♞d5 ♛xf3 7 ♞xf3 ♝b6 8 c3 d6 9 d4 h6** Loss of time, but White threatens 10 ♗g5 taking control of f6, after which Black would really be in difficulties. **10 0-0 ...** Not bad, but here PRESTIGE could easily have afforded to lose a tempo in turn with 10 h3, keeping the Bishop out. But positional prophylaxis is a hard concept for computer programs. **... ♝g4 11 ♝e3 ♝xf3 12 gxf3 ♞ge7** Black finally gets to develop, since 13 ♘f6+ leads nowhere. **13 ♞xb6 axb6**

UNGER

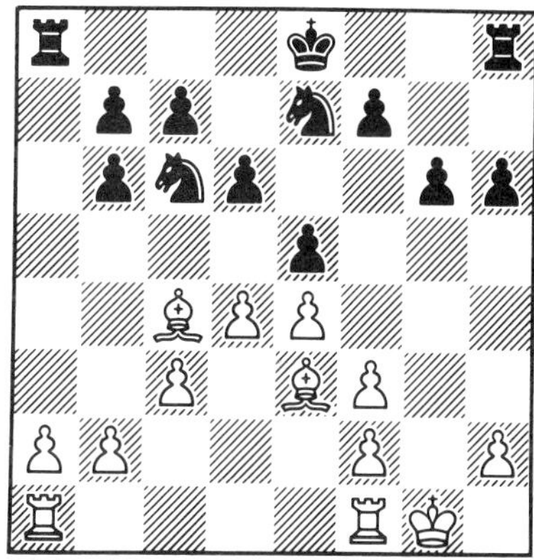

PRESTIGE

14 d5?! ... PRESTIGE is incapable of judging that the position should be opened up to increase the power of the Bishops. Attempts were made to include this feature in the program's evaluator, but this slowed the program down too much. Very good was 14 f4, with strong pressure on Black's center. **... ♞d8 15 f4 f6 16 fxe5 fxe5 17 f4 ♞f7 18 ♝b5+ ♚f8?!** It was clearly better to play ... ♔d8, as after 19 fxe5 ♘xe5 Black would at least have one well-posted piece. **19 fxe5 dxe5 20 ♝c4?! ...** Much more effective here is 20 d6! cxd6 21 ♗xb6 and the Bishops are overpowering. **... ♞c8 21 ♜f6 ♞d6 22 ♝d3 ♚g7 23 ♜ff1 ♜hf8 24 a4** A nothing move; the program should immediately push its Queenside Pawns, and drive the Knight away. **... ♞h8 25 ♜xf8 ♜xf8 26 ♜f1 ♜a8 27 b3 ♞hf7 28 ♚f2 ♜h8 29 ♚e2 ♞g5**

UNGER

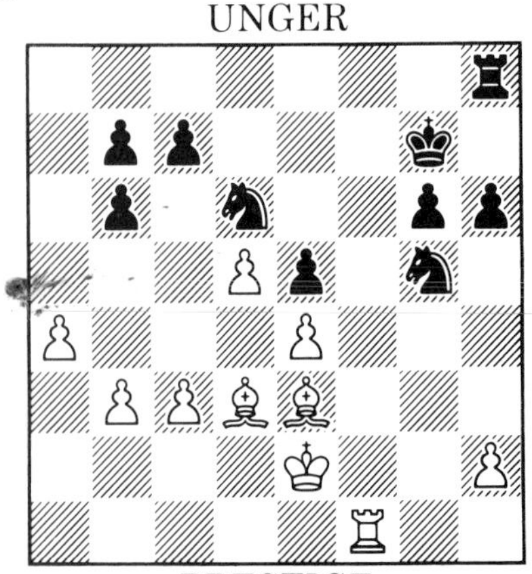

PRESTIGE

30 ♝xg5 ... This exchange is forced now, as a result of the opportunities PRESTIGE has missed, and suddenly the program is at a disadvantage, with a rather bad Bishop against a strong Knight, and with Black having a Pawn majority on the Kingside. **... hxg5 31 ♜f2 ♜h4 32 ♚e3 ♜f4 33 ♜a2?! ...** In spite of its problems PRESTIGE would not stand badly after 33 ♖g2, followed by a vigorous Pawn advance on the Queenside. Instead, unable to formulate any kind of plan, the program loses time with aimless moves while its opponent marches forward to get a new Queen. **...g4 34 ♜f2 g5** Here is a doubled Pawn formation that is not weak at all. **35 ♜f1 ♚g6 36 b4 ♚h5 37 ♜f2 ♚h4 38 c4 g3 39 ♜g2 gxh2 40 ♜xh2+ ♚g3 41 ♜h5 ♜f3+ 42 ♚d2 ♚g4 43 ♜h7 ♜f7 44 ♜h1 ♚f3 45 ♜e1 ♜f4 46 ♜e3+ ♚g2 47 c5 ...** Finally PRESTIGE plays a break that it should have gotten ten moves ago, probably because there aren't any playable Rook moves (47 ♖e2+? ♖f2 and wins). Now it comes too late. **... bxc5 48 bxc5 ♞f7 49 a5 g4 50 c6 bxc6 51 a6 ♞d6 52 ♜e2+ ...** PRESTIGE would like to trade Rooks now — but unfortunately Black doesn't oblige. **... ♚h3 53 dxc6 g3 54 ♜e1 g2 55 a7 ♜f8 56 ♚e3 ♜a8 57 ♚f3 ♜xa7 58 ♜d1 ♜a3 59 ♚f2 ♚h2 60 ♚e2 g1(♛)** 0-1

ROUND 6

BELLE - Kevin Toon(2088)
Irregular(B00)

BELLE is mystified by its opponent's unorthodox opening and slow development. After the program makes some questionable moves, Toon traps its King in the center and his attack forces a win.

1 e4 ♞a6?! The "word was out" by now — since the Tournament bulletins published all the computer games — that it was not a good idea to try to match opening "books" with BELLE. This certainly takes care of that problem! **2 ♞f3 d6 3 ♞c3 ...** BELLE plays a rather restrained opening, mechanically developing its pieces. Most players would form a broad Pawn center. **... g6 4 d4 ♝g7 5 ♜b1** Another mysterious Rook move — actually, BELLE is simply protecting its b-Pawn so that it can develop the Bishop. But this is slow and does not set Black any problems. **... e6**

TOON

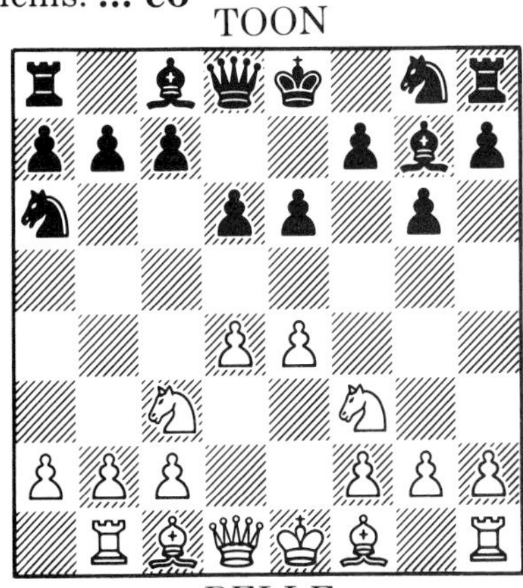

BELLE

6 ♗xa6 ... "I just can't stand it any longer, Boss..." - J. Marfia, in the Tournament Bulletin. **... bxa6 7 ♗g5 ♕d7 8 ♕e2 h6 9 ♗h4 ♘e7 10 ♗xe7?!** BELLE is clearly as puzzled as any of the onlookers (some of whom anticipated that Toon would be absolutely massacred for his temerity) by Toon's slow style. The program apparently feared ... f5, but that was not a serious threat yet. White should simply castle and see what Black does. **... ♕xe7 11 b4? ...** Again, BELLE tears open its Queenside—this time with less attractive results. White still ought to castle, and soon won't be able to. **... 0-0 12 ♘d1 ♖b8 13 ♖b3?!**

TOON

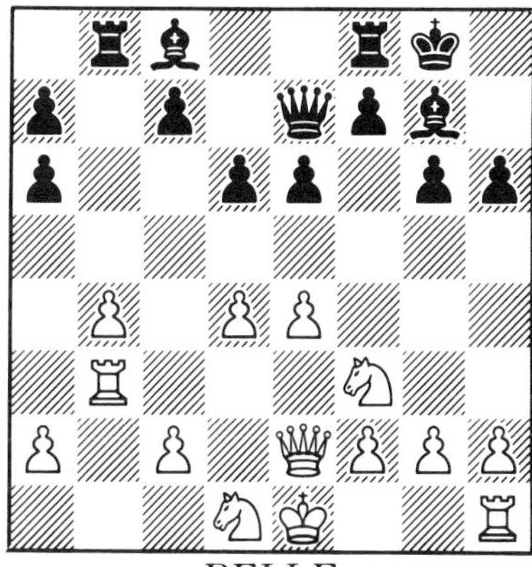

BELLE

BELLE's last chance to castle. Now Toon finds a move which is brilliant "psychology" against a computer program: **... ♗d7!** A very clever idea — the program is forced by its heuristics to grab the Pawn, but the heuristics are badly wrong here. Black trades a worthless doubled Pawn for several tempi and prevents BELLE from castling to boot. **4 ♕xa6 ♗b5 15 ♕a5 ...** Of course not 15 ♕xa7?? ♖a8 16 ♕b7 ♖fb8 and the Queen is trapped. **... f5** Toon now takes the initiative, and BELLE's King becomes most uncomfortable. **16 e5?! ...** As noted before, BELLE is not a good defensive player — "Best defense is a good offense" school. Here the program should play 16 ♖e3 and try to keep the position closed. **... dxe5 17 ♘xe5 ♗xe5 18 dxe5 ♕d7 19 f4 ...** With its Queen trapped out of play, and its King stuck in the center, BELLE's position is most unpleasant. A better try at holding the game is 19 a4!, hoping for ... ♗xa4 20 ♖d3, but computer programs aren't allowed to make that sort of Pawn sacrifice — so BELLE tries unsuccessfully to hold everything. **... ♖fd8 20 ♔f2 ♕d2+ 21 ♔g3 ...**

BELLE

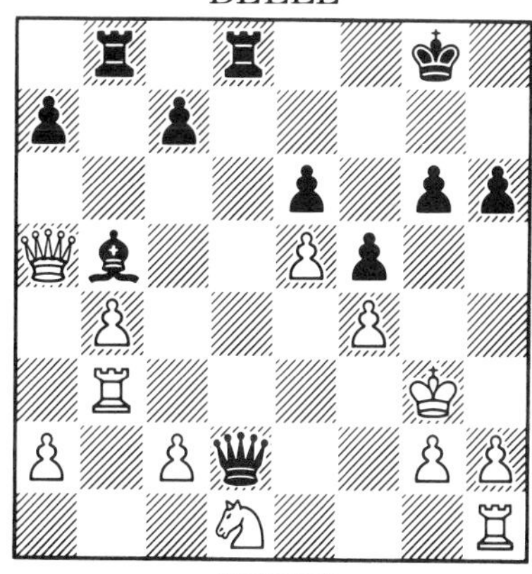

TOON

21 ...g5! Decisive. BELLE puts up a lot of resistance,but the position is lost. **22 ♖f3 gxf4+ 23 ♔h3 ...** Not 23 ♖xf4? ♔f7! **... ♗e2 24 ♕xc7! ...** Not 24 ♖f2 ♗g4+ 25 ♔h4 ♕d7 26 ♖xf4 ♕e7+ 27 ♔g3 ♗xd1 and wins. **24 ... ♕d7** BELLE doesn't mind ... ♗xf3 25 gxf3 and the mate threat lets White get untangled. **25 ♕xd7 ♖xd7 26 ♖xf4 ...** It is no better to give up the Exchange by 26 ♘f2 ♗xf3 27 gxf3 ♖xb4 28 ♘d3 ♖c4 and the Black Rooks are overpowering. This way, BELLE gets some play ... **... ♗xd1 27 ♖c4 ♗e2 28 ♖c6 ♔f7 29 ♖e1 ♗g4+ 30 ♔g3 ♖xb4 ...** But not very much. **31 h3 ♗h5 32 ♖c5 ♔e7 33 ♖c8 ♗e8 34 ♖e2 ♖bb7 35 c4 ♖dc7** Toon is quite willing to give up a Pawn temporarily to exchange a pair of Rooks, after which

Black has an easier task. **36 ♜b2 ♜xc8 37 ♜xb7+ ♝d7 38 ♜xa7 ♜xc4 39 a3 ♜a4** This puts an end to BELLE's play and the rest is just technique. **40 ♜xa4 ♝xa4 41 ♚f4 ♚f7 42 ♚e3 ...** There is no way to trade off the Pawns, e.g. 43 g4 fxg4 44 hxg4 ♔g6. **... ♚g6 43 ♚f4 ♝d1 44 g3 ♝c2 45 g4 fxg4 46 ♚xg4 h5+ 47 ♚f4 ♝d1 48 h4 ♝c2 49 ♚e3 ♚f5 50 ♚d2** 0-1

CHAOS - Kevin Ah Tou(1622)
King's Indian(E70)

CHAOS played the opening rather inexactly, and soon its temporary space advantage was reversed as Black mobilized his Pawn majority. Things were looking bad for the program, which was driven back all along the line as Black developed first a strong initiative and then a winning attack. Just at the crucial moment, however, Ah Tou missed a mate in four, then later failed to find the right continuation to force the win, and CHAOS got an undeserved point.

1 d4 ♞f6 2 c4 g6 3 ♞c3 ♝g7 4 e4 0-0 This is not very prudent and demands careful play by Black. More usual is ... d6. **5 e5 ♞e8 6 f4 d6 7 ♞f3 ♝f5** Sharper is ... dxe5 (ECO). **8 ♝d3 ...** CHAOS should place its Bishops on e2 and e3, after which the position of the Bishop at f5 might become an embarrassment to Black, e.g. by ♘h4. **... ♝xd3 9 ♛xd3 ♞d7** Black's continuation is very slow for such a critical variation. **10 ♝d2?! ...** It seems quite obvious that the Bishop would be much better placed on e3, where it also would not block the d-file. **... c5!** Now the program's center is demolished. CHAOS still assesses the position as better for White. **11 dxc5 dxe5 12 fxe5 ♞xe5 13 ♞xe5 ♝xe5 14 ♛e4 ♝xc3?!** There was absolutely no need to exchange this strong Bishop. After 14 ... ♕d4! White's position would be uncomfortable. **15 ♝xc3 ♛c7 16 b4 ♜d8 17 0-0 ♞g7 18 ♜ae1 ♜d7**

AH TOU

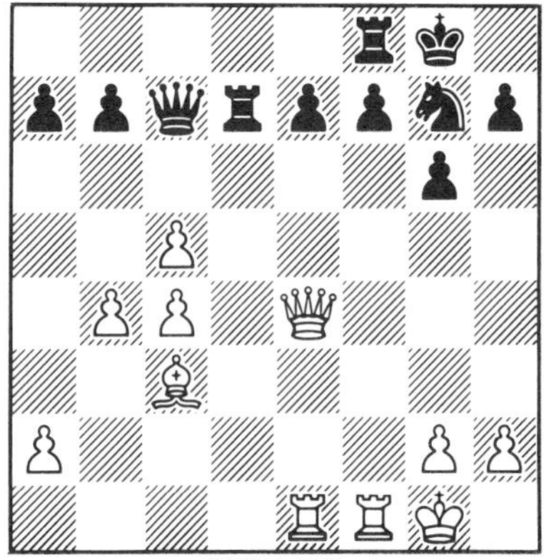

CHAOS

Now it looks like CHAOS really does have the better game, but the Black Kingside Pawn majority will become a factor soon, and CHAOS has no time to lose in getting its Pawn majority going. And this turns out to be far from easy to do. **19 ♝e5 ...** This LOOKS strong, but in fact the Bishop is misplaced on e5. From what follows, it seems that going into a double-Rook ending immediately by 19 ♗xg7 ♔xg7 20 ♕e5+ may have been best. **19 ... ♛c8 20 ♜e3? ...** This is too slow, and also leaves the Bishop on a bad square. Again ♗xg7 looks best, after which it is not so easy for Black to mobilize his Pawns. **... f6** But now Black expands with tempo, and the spatial advantage undergoes a sudden reversal. **21 ♝c3 e5 22 ♜ef3 ♜df7 23 a3?! ...** A nothing move at a critical moment. It would seem better to try 23 ♖d3, hoping to have time for ♖d6 and c6. **... ♞e6 24 ♝d2? ...** And this is just plain bad; CHAOS obviously can't afford to let the Knight in, and should restrain it by 24 g3. **... ♞d4 25 ♜3f2 ♛e6 26 ♝h6?!** This doesn't accomplish anything — driving the Rook to the open file. **26 ... ♜d8 27 ♛d3 e4** CHAOS now pays for its sins by being driven from pillar to post, as Black takes charge of the game. **28 ♛c3 ♛g4!** With the neat point: 29 ♖xf6?? ♘e2+. **29 ♚h1 ♞f5 30 ♝f4**

♜d3 Black's attack begins to assume frightening proportions. **31 ♛b2 e3 32 h3 ♛h4 33 ♜f3 ...** Better would be 33 ♖e2, slowing down the advance of the e-Pawn. **... ♜fd7 34 ♛a2 ...** Clearly CHAOS has no idea of how to defend in this position, although in truth it cannot successfully be defended at all. The program assessed Black's advantage at 1 Pawn here, which seems ridiculously low — but remember that material factors are emphasized. **... ♜d2 35 ♛b1 ♜7d3 36 a4 e2!** Forcing a win. **37 ♜xd3 exf1 (♛)+ 38 ♛xf1 ♜xd3 39 ♛xd3 ♛xf4 40 ♛d5+ ♚f8 41 ♛xb7**

AH TOU

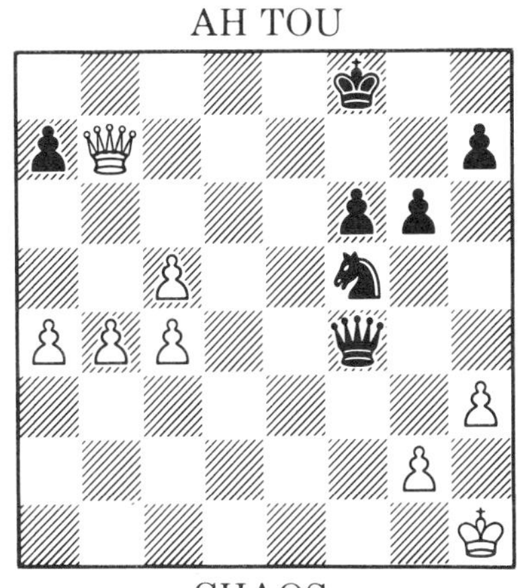

CHAOS

41 ... ♛xc4?? But now comes a stunning reversal: Black misplays the attack and loses! He may have been short of time here; at any rate, he could have won immediately by 41 ... ♘g3+ 42 ♔g1 ♘e2+ 43 ♔h1 ♕f1+ 44 ♔h2 ♕g1 mate. **42 ♛b8+ ♚g7 43 ♛xa7+ ♚h6 44 ♛b8 ♛f1+?** Black could keep winning chances by ... ♘e3 threatening mate: a) 45 ♕g3 ♕c1+ 46 ♔h2 ♘f1+ etc; b) 45 ♕f8+ ♔g5 46 h4+ (What else?) ... ♕xh4+ 47 ♔g1 ♕e1+ 48 ♔h2 ♘g5+ 49 ♔h3 ♕h4 mate; c) 45 ♕b7 ♕c1+ 46 ♔h2 ♘f1+ and: c1) 47 ♔h1 ♘g3+ 48 ♔h2 ♘e2 and mate cannot be prevented; c2) 47 ♔g1 ♘g3+ 48 ♔f2 ♘h1+ and: c21) 49 ♔f3 ♕c3+ 50 ♔f4 (50 ♔g4 or e4, ♘f2+) g5+ 51 ♔e4 ♕e5+ 52 ♔d3 ♘f2+ and the King has no shelter and eventually gets mated; c22) 49 ♔e2 ♕c2+ and if the King tries to stay near his Pawns he is driven away by ... ♕f2+, and eventually mated. **45 ♚h2 ♞h4 46 ♛g3 ♚h5?** Black can still put up a fight after ... ♘f5. **47 ♛g4+** 1-0

Jack Yoos(1553) - SENSORY CC9
Caro-Kann(B12)

After CC9's opponent blunders in the opening, the program has an easy win, but (like many human players) gets careless. Yoos, however, misses his chance to trap CC9's Rook, and loses.

1 e4 c6 2 d4 d5 3 f3 Yoos plays this rather questionable variation in an attempt to take CC9 out of its "book". **... e6** Which works — instead of this rather conservative reply, the program could continue 3 ... dxe4 4 fxe4 e5! threatening ... ♕h4+. **4 ♝e3 dxe4 5 fxe4? ...** White has to gambit the Pawn here by 5 ♘d2 exf3 6 ♘gxf3 with compensation. This leads to yet another variation of an ancient opening trap: **5 ... ♛h4+ 6 g3? ...** Guaranteeing that the disaster will be even more expensive. Relatively best is 6 ♗f2 ♕xe4+ 7 ♘e2, and at least White gets some development for his Pawn. **... ♛xe4 7 ♛f3 ♛xc2** CC9 has an advantage of two Pawns now, and the game should for all intents and purposes be over. **8 ♛e2 ♝b4+ 9 ♚f2 ♛xe2+ 10 ♞xe2 ♞f6 11 ♚f3 ...** White's game is so miserable that this move is almost forced. **... ♞d5 12 ♝f2 0-0 13 a3 ♝d6 14 ♞d2 ♞a6 15 ♞e4 ♝c7 16 ♞2c3 ♞xc3 17 bxc3 b6** CC9 is not playing especially accurately, but then it hardly has to. However, ... e5 would speed things up. **18 ♝d3 ♝b7 19 ♜he1 ♜ad8 20 ♚e2 ♜d5 21 c4 ...**

SENSORY CC9

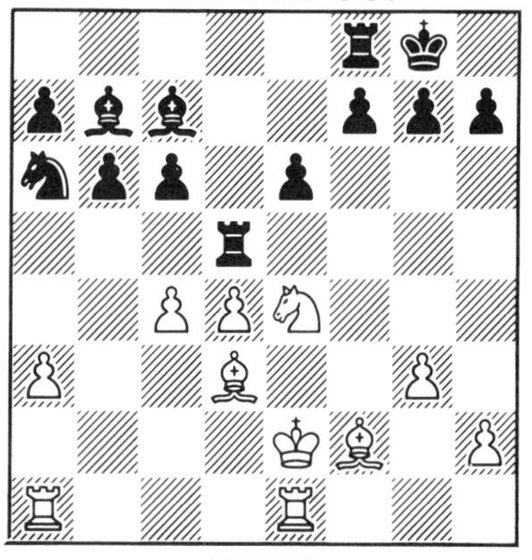

YOOS

21 ... ♜h5?! Now CC9 gets its Rook trapped, which with better play by White, might have been embarrassing. **22 h4 ♜d8 23 g4 ♜h6?** The program should play ... ♖a5, avoiding the difficulties that might have followed. **24 h5? ...** Here White could have saved the game by 24 g5! ♖h5 25 ♔e3! c5 26 dxc5 ♘xc5 27 ♘xc5 bxc5 28 ♗e2 g6 29 ♗xh5 gxh5 30 ♖ed1, although the draw is still not all that easy. **... f5 25 gxf5 exf5 26 ♞g5 ♜xh5 27 ♝e3?** 27 ♘f3 was mandatory. **... ♜e8!** CC9 could have played ... f4 28 ♘e6 fxe3 29 ♘xd8 ♗xd8, winning two pieces for Rook and Pawn, but this move wins a whole piece. **28 ♚d2** Or 28 ♔f3 h6. **... f4 29 ♝f2 ♜xe1 30 ♜xe1 ♜xg5 31 ♚c3 ♜a5 32 ♚b3 ♝d6 33 a4 ♞b4 34 ♝e4 ♜h5 35 c5 ♜h3+ 36 ♚xb4?** On 36 ♔c4, ... a5 forces mate anyway, but 36 ♔b2 keeps White alive a little longer. **... a5+** 0-1

William Howell(1899) - PRESTIGE
Sicilian(B34)

This game illustrates the limitations of a chess program's heuristics with particular clarity. PRESTIGE retrieves a gambit opening variation from its "book" (the game illustrates why such lines are unwise for computer programs), and in a position requiring play for the initiative, grabs a Pawn — missing a chance to win. Then the endgame should have been an easy draw, but again the program, unable to plan, made aimless moves while Howell simply pushed his passed Pawn.

1 e4 c5 2 ♞f3 ♞c6 3 d4 cxd4 4 ♞xd4 g6 5 ♞c3 ♝g7 6 ♝e3 ♞f6 7 ♞xc6 bxc6 8 e5 ♞d5 9 ♞xd5 cxd5 10 ♛xd5 ♜b8 11 0-0-0 ♝b7 12 ♛d4 0-0 13 ♛xd7? ... . ECO gives 13 f4. This opens the position up too much, and ought to have gotten White in trouble. **... ♛a5 14 ♛xe7 ♝xe5** Now the position is completely opened up, and a strong human player would know (without even having to calculate variations) that a mighty attack is about to descend on the White King. **15 ♝d4 ♝xd4 16 ♜xd4 ...**

PRESTIGE

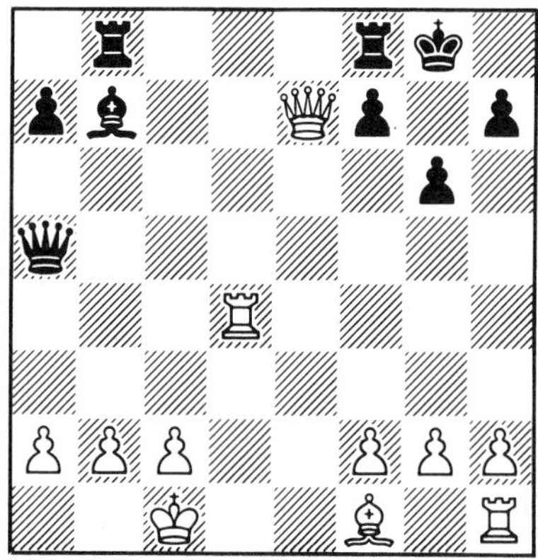

HOWELL

16 ... ♛xa2? The program has no guidelines at all for playing to maintain the intiative in an attack — and once out of its "book", sets out to grab material. 16 ... ♖fe8 would have left Black with an enduring and probably winning attack: a)17 ♕b4 ♕xa2 18 ♖d1 ... (18 ♕a3? ♖e1+ 19 ♖d1 ♖xd1+ 20 ♔xd1 ♕b1+ 21 ♔d2 ♖d8+ and wins) ... ♗f3! 19 ♕a3 ♕xa3 20 bxa3 ♗xd1 21 ♔xd1 ♖b1+ 22 ♔d2 ♖ee1 and wins; b) 17 ♕a3 ♖e1+ 18 ♖d1 ♕g5+ and wins; c) 17 ♕d6 ♖bd8 and wins; d) 17 ♕f6 ♖e1+ 18 ♖d1 ♖xd1+ 19 ♔xd1 ♕xa2 and Black seems to have a winning position since White can't develop. **17 ♛a3 ♛xa3 18 bxa3 ♜fe8**

19 ♔d2 ♗c6 20 ♗c4 ... This leads to an endgame which PRESTIGE should have been able to draw, but it is not clear how else White can develop his pieces.... **♗xg2 21 ♖e1 ♖xe1 22 ♔xe1 ♔g7?!** Here it is much better to play 22 ... ♖b7, keeping the Rook off the 7th rank. Unfortunately, the program knows hardly more than the most elementary endgame concepts. **23 ♖d7 ♖b1+?** Loss of time, driving the King where it wants to go. **24 ♔d2 ♖b7 25 ♖xb7 ♗xb7 26 ♔e3 ...** (See diagram)

26 ... ♔f6? This is planless play; Black must get its Kingside Pawns rolling without delay, and for this purpose ... f5 is essential. Now the King impedes his own Pawns, and PRESTIGE never does get a passed Pawn of its own. **27 ♔d4 g5**

Position after White's 26th move.

PRESTIGE

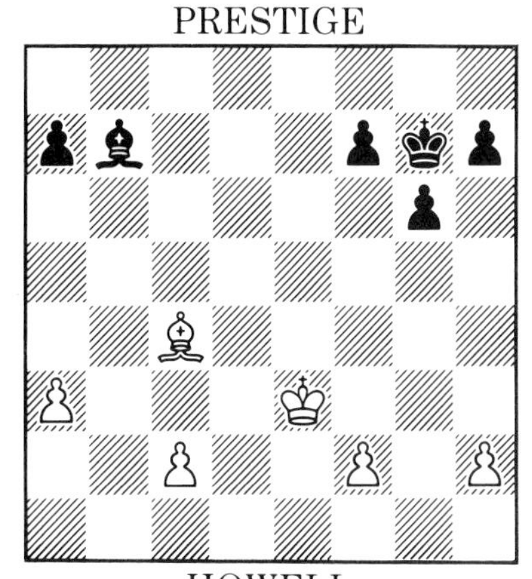

HOWELL

28 ♗d5 ♗c8 29 c4 ♔e7 30 ♔c5 f6 31 ♔c6 g4 PRESTIGE obviously has no concept of what is happening in this ending, and lest the typesetters run out

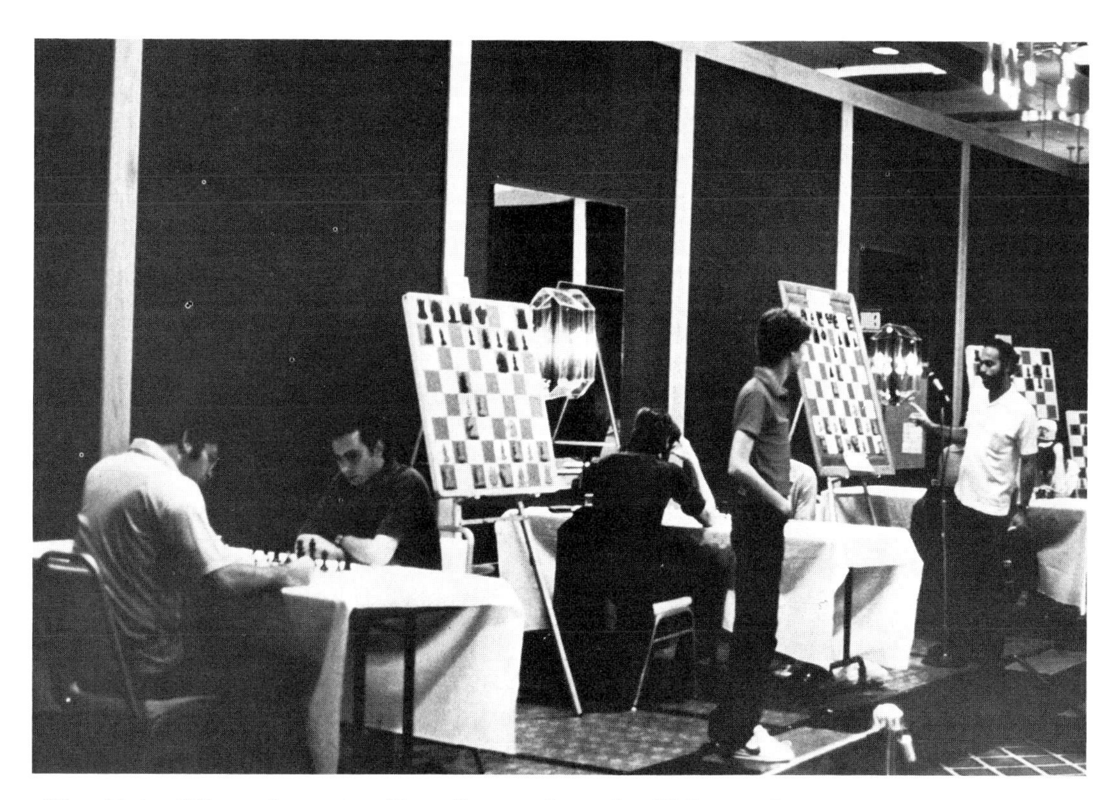

Fig. 7.4 "Grandmaster Row"—cordoned off from the spectators.

of question marks, the rest is given without comment. **32 ♚c7 ♝d7 33 c5 ♝f5 34 c6 h5 35 ♚b8 ♚d6 36 ♝g2 h4 37 c7 ♝e6 38 ♝b7 f5 39 ♝c8 g3 40 fxg3 hxg3 41 hxg3 ♝c4 42 ♝xf5 ♝a6 43 c8(♛)** 1-0

ROUND 7

Truc Dac Ho(1648) - CHAOS
English(A15)

CHAOS, baffled by its opponent's slow style, gets an inferior game. Then White plays a complicated combination, and in a position featuring five pieces en prise, the program's quiescence search explodes.

1 ♞f3 ♞f6 2 c4 e6 3 g3 b6 4 ♝g2 ♝b7 5 0-0 ♝e7 This is not a good opening for a computer program. Slow development without immediate operations in the center does not suit the program's style of play at all. **6 d3 ♞c6?!** More natural is ... c5; it is not a good idea to block the c-Pawn from advancing. **7 ♝f4 ♞h5?!** This is premature, and the Knight is exposed on this square. It was best to castle. **8 ♝d2 d5** Undertaking active operations in the center before castling, and with the Knight hanging at h5, is definitely unwise. The Knight belongs on f6 if such an advance is intended. **9 cxd5 ♛xd5** Consistent, but bad. Now White wins two tempi. **10 ♞c3 ♛c5?!** CHAOS compounds the felony by placing its Queen on another exposed square. **11 ♜c1 0-0 12 e4 ...** With the unpleasant threat ♘d5. **... ♛d6** In addition to its positional problems, CHAOS now begins to experience blowups in its quiescence search due to the many tactical possibilities involving discovered attacks. This move took 20.5 minutes. **13 ♝g5 f6** And this took 12.9 minutes. **14 e5!?** Objectively better was 14 ♗e3, leaving Black with an unpleasant position — there are threats of 5 ♘b5 or 15 d4, for instance. But the resulting complications turn out to be too much for the program. **14 ... ♞xe5** 32.9 minutes! **15 ♞xe5 ...**

CHAOS

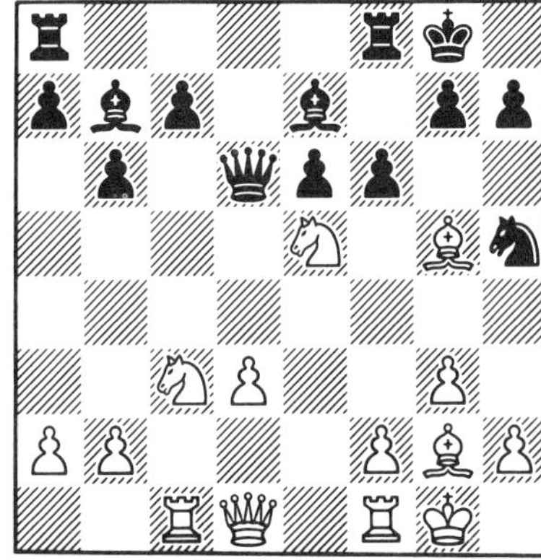

HO

In the middle of the combination, the blowup finally occurs — CHAOS' clock ticked off 61 minutes and its flag fell before the program could select another move. After ... ♗xg2 16 ♔xg2 ♛xe5 7 ♛xh5 ♛xg5 18 ♛xg5 fxg5 19 ♘e4, the program would be a Pawn ahead. 1-0

SENSORY CC9-Albrecht Hamann(1630)
French(C18)

CC9 plays the opening very well, and gets a solid edge when Hamann plays an inferior variation. The program then goes in for a highly dubious win of a Pawn, which might have trapped its Knight, and even after Hamann lets CC9 trade its Queen for two Rooks, the program is in trouble because the Queen threatens to penetrate its position. But after its opponent misses two opportunities to do so, CC9 gets in a tactical shot, picking up a Pawn with very good winning chances. Eventually Hamann loses his Queen, and CC9 avoids his desperation stalemate try.

1 e4 e6 2 d4 d5 3 ♞c3 ♝b4 4 e5 c5 5 a3 ♝xc3+ 6 bxc3 c4?! It is not good to remove tension in the center so early; this is known to be good for White, who gets a solid plus. **7 ♛g4 g6 8 ♝e2 ♛a5 9 ♝d2 ♞e7 10 ♞f3 ♞bc6 11 0-0 ♝d7 12 ♜fb1 ...** CC9's positional scoring rules have led the program to play a good opening, with its pieces well placed for this variation. **... ♛c7** Black, on the other hand, has not played very accurately. Here b5 is better. **13 ♝h6 ♞f5 14 ♛g5 ...** CC9 undervalues the potential strength of its dark-square Bishop, which could be extremely effective in exploiting Black's weak squares at f6 and h6. The program, however, has no instructions on recognizing or exploiting weak squares. **... ♞xh6 15 ♛xh6 0-0-0 16 ♞g5 ♜df8**

HAMANN

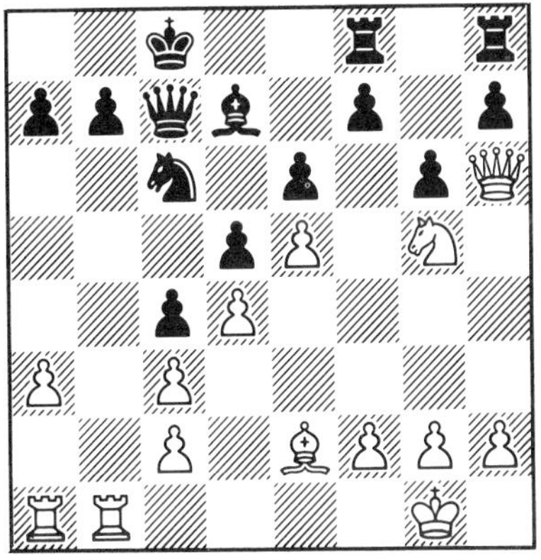

SENSORY CC9

17 ♞xh7? ... Computer programs have no fear at all! Most, if not all, human players would never play such a move, since even if the Knight gets out, the open h-file may become a problem. Even if the program gets to carry out its intentions, as in the game, the resulting position can hardly be favorable for White. **... ♝e8?!** Falling in with the program's intentions. After ... ♖fg8!, White has problems — Black threatens ... ♗e8 followed by the Pawn advance ... f5, and it is not clear how the Knight can be extracted. Now CC9 gets two Rooks for the Queen — temporarily. **18 ♛xf8 ♜xf8 9 ♞xf8** This exchange in theory wins material, but in reality is not very good for the program because its pieces are scattered and its position is extremely vunerable if the Black Queen can penetrate it. **... ♛a5 20 ♜b4! ...** The program recognizes that it can't afford to let the Queen into its position. It's almost worth an Exchange to straighten out White's Pawns, anyway. **... ♞xb4 ♝a4 25 g3 ♛g5 26 f4 ♛f5 27 ♜c1 21 cxb4 ♛b6?!** Here Hamann misses his first opportunity to get his Queen into the White position: 21 ... ♕a4! 22 ♗d1 c3! followed by ... ♕a6 and ... ♗b5, after which Black penetrates via c4. **22 c3 ♛d8 23 ♞h7 ♛h4 24 ♞f6 ♝a4 25 g3 ♛g5 26 f4 ♛f5 27 ♜c1 ...** Superficially, this looks like a very favorable position for CC9, since Black's Bishop is so bad. But the position is so blockaded that it is not clear how the program can make progress; meanwhile, Black's Queen continually threatens to penetrate the White position. CC9 however, plays quite well for the remainder of the game, which is more than can be said for its opponent.

HAMANN

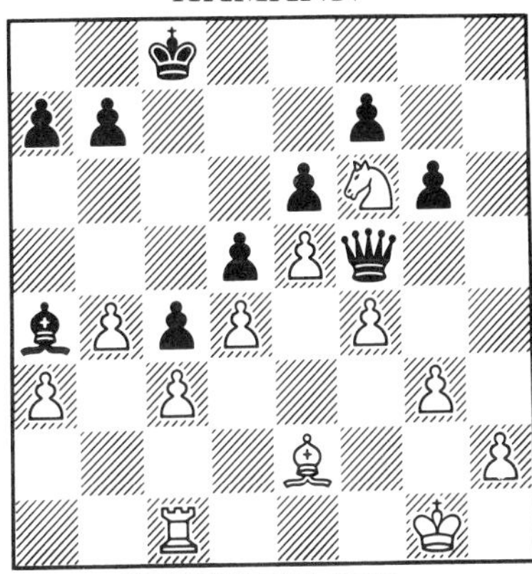

SENSORY CC9

27 ... ♛h3?? This not only doesn't accomplish anything positionally, it gives CC9 a chance to show its tactical strength. After ... g5!, the program would be in real trouble; 28 ♗g4 doesn't work: ... ♕d3 and now 29 ♘xd5? loses a piece after ... ♔d8. On any other 28th move for White, the Queen infiltrates with fatal consequences. **28 ♝g4 ♛h8 29 ♞xd5! ♝c6 30 ♞e3 b5 31 d5! ♝d7 32 d6 ...** Now the program has a protected passed Pawn, which ultimately proves decisive. **... ♛d8?!** Another weak move; Black should try ... f6 here. **33 h4 ♛b6 34 ♚f2**

a5 35 ♝f3 axb4?! This is probably unwise; the open file is most likely to benefit White's Rook. After ... a4 it is still difficult for White to make any headway. **36 axb4 ♛a7 37 ♝e4 ♛b6?** Now that the a-file is open, the Queen ought to keep control of it. 37 ... ♕a2+ 38 ♖c2 ♕a1 makes things much more difficult, although after 39 g4 ♔d8 40 h5 gxh5 41 gxh5 ♔e8 White can probably still win by maneuvering the Knight to f6. **38 ♜a1 ♝c6 39 ♝xc6 ♛xc6 40 ♜a7 f5??** After 40 ...♕e4, Black can still put up resistance, though the program could win by 41 ♖xf7 ♕d3 42 h5 gxh5 (or ... ♕d2+ 43 ♔f3 and there are no more checks) 43 f5 exf5 44 e6 etc. **41 ♜c7+ ♛xc7 42 dxc7 ♚xc7 43 ♞c2 ...** One would think that the rest would be routine; not quite.**... ♚c6 44 ♞d4+ ♚d5 45 ♚e2 ♚e4 46 ♞xe6 ♚d5 47 ♞d4 g5 48 hxg5 ♚e4 49 g6 ♚d5 50 g7 ♚e4 51 g8 (♞)!** Hamann has been playing for stalemate. But the program is able to recognize this, and underpromotes to force mate. **51 ... ♚d5 52 ♞f6 mate** 1-0

Larry Johansson(1773) - PRESTIGE
Modern(A45)

In this game, the tendencies of computer programs to steer the game into weird, inhuman positions clearly distracted Johansson.

1 d4 ♞f6 2 c3 g6 3 ♝g5 ♝g7 4 ♞d2 0-0 5 e4 h6 ECO gives ... d6. The loosening of the King's position resulting from driving away the Bishop favors White, but computer programs do not know what patience is and usually tend to deal with a problem (if it is perceived at all) by direct action. **6 ♝h4 g5 7 ♝g3 d5?!** Positionally dubious, to say the least. More normal would be ... d6 and play almed at ... e5. **8 e5 ♞e4 9 ♞gf3 f5 10 exf6 exf6 11 ♝d3 g4** This looks like a positional atrocity, but because of the constricted position of the White pieces, turns out to be rather effective. **12 ♞h4 f5 13 f3 ♞xg3 14 hxg3 ♛d6 15 f4 c5**

PRESTIGE

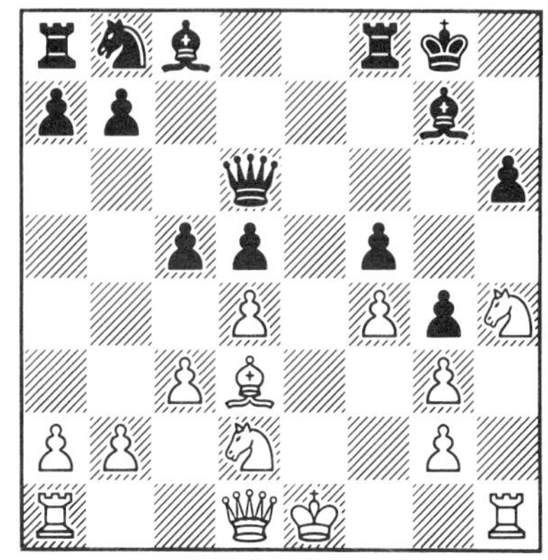

JOHANSSON

16 ♞b3?? The program's strange, inhuman play has clearly baffled Johansson. This of course loses a piece. White should play 16 dxc5 ♕xc5 17 ♕e2 with an unclear position.**... c4 17 ♞c5 cxd3 18 ♞xd3 ♜e8+ 19 ♞e5 ♞c6 20 ♞g6??** Another blunder by the rattled Johansson, and another piece goes. After this game is no longer worth commenting on **... ♛xg6 21 ♚d2 ♞xe5 22 dxe5 ♛b6 23 ♛c2 ♛f2+ 24 ♚c1 ♛xg3 25 ♛d2 ♝e6 26 b3 ♚h7 27 ♜b1 a5 28 b4 axb4 29 ♜xb4 ♜xa2!** 0-1

ROUND 8

CHAOS - Richard Peterson(1715)
Benko Gambit (A57)

Peterson picks a good opening to play against a computer program, for CHAOS has no way to evaluate the positional pressure Black gets. To realize Black's positional initiative requires careful play, however, which is not forthcoming in this game. After Black gives up his strong Bishop to "win" back the Pawn — which is soon lost again — CHAOS has some winning chances in the ending. Then the program overlooks a tactical shot and loses.

1 d4 ♞f6 2 c4 c5 3 d5 b5 4 cxb5 a6 5 e3 g6 6 ♞c3 ♝g7 7 ♝c4 0-0 ECO gives ... d6. In D. Blumin - Benko, Atlantic Open, NY 1969, the position of the Bishop on c4 became a liability for White, as Benko used it to gain time for development. **8 ♞f3 d6 9 ♝d2 axb5 10 ♝xb5 ♝a6 11 ♛b3 ♞e8 12 0-0 ♞c7 13 ♝c4 ...** There is no real reason not to exchange on a6 here. **... ♛d7 14 ♜fe1 ♝xc4 15 ♛xc4 ♞ba6 16 a3 ♜fb8 17 ♜a2 ♞b5 18 ♜ea1 ♞ac7 19 e4 ♞a7?!** This slow continuation gives White an opportunity to get out of the positional bind on the Queenside. More in keeping with Black's positional objectives would be ... ♘xc3 20 ♗xc3 ♖a4. **20 e5 ...** Here CHAOS should have liquidated the position on the Queenside by 20 b4!, after which the program gets a passed Pawn and eliminates Black's pressure on its position. But CHAOS does not know it is under pressure; the program thinks it is simply a Pawn ahead with the better game to boot. **... ♞c8 21 exd6 exd6 22 ♛e4 ♞b6 23 ♛d3** CHAOS finds its evaluator function mysteriously dropping, and now thinks Black has some compensation for the Pawn.

PETERSON

CHAOS

23 ... ♝xc3? This is unwise and unnecessary. Black can continue ... c4! and if now 24 ♕e4, ... ♖e8 and Black takes charge of the game. The Pawn at d5 is not going anywhere, must eventually fall, and it was a pity to give up such a powerful Bishop just to get the Pawn back. **24 bxc3 ♞bxd5** The capture of the Pawn should still be preceded by ... c4. **25 c4 ♞b6** Here ... ♘e7 is better. **26 ♝f4 ...** Now it is Black who has the weak Pawn, and CHAOS' evaluation of its advantage starts to increase again. **... ♜d8 27 ♝g5 ♜db8 28 ♝f4 ♞e6** It is certainly unclear why Black was unwilling to repeat moves here; he can hardly have imagined that he had the better game. **29 ♛xd6 ♜d8 30 ♛xb6 ♞xf4** No, ... ♕d1+ isn't mate (31 ♘e1). **31 ♜d2 ...** It is now clear that White has a big advantage. **... ♛e7 32 ♜xd8+ ♜xd8 33 ♜e1 ♞e6 34 a4 ♜a8 35 a5 ♛a7 36 ♛xa7 ♜xa7 37 ♜a1 ♜a6 38 ♞e5** White can make faster progress by bringing the King into the game by ♔f1, and leaving the Knight on f3 to keep Black's Knight out of d4. Although a passed a-Pawn often isn't enough to win in a Rook ending, the c-Pawns offer White winning chances — the King can attack the Pawn on c5 while the a-Pawn ties Black up. **... ♞d4 39 ♜a3 f6**

PETERSON

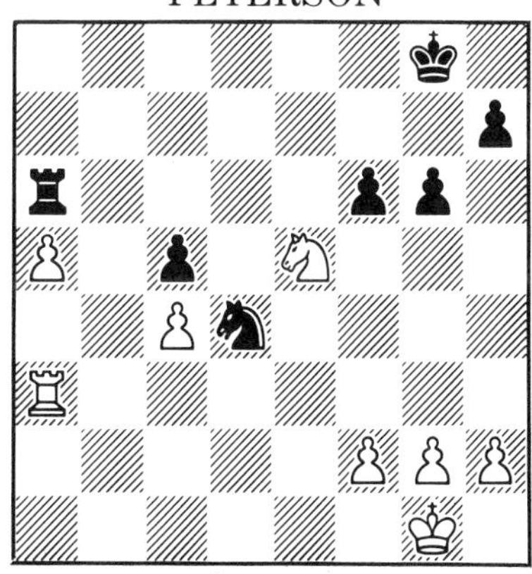

CHAOS

40 ♞d7? ... This loses, although it is not obvious why. CHAOS had to play 40 ♘d3, after which the ending should be a draw: ... ♘c6 41 ♘xc5 ♖xa5 42 ♖xa5 ♘xa5 43 ♘d7 ♘xc4 44 ♘xf6+ and White keeps a Pawn plus, but this is not enough to win since all the Pawns are on the same side. **... ♜d6 41 ♞xf6+** Suddenly CHAOS notices that 41 ♘xc5 is met by ... ♘b3! and Black wins. Back-rank mating threats are sometimes very difficult for computer programs to evaluate. **41 ... ♜xf6 42 a6 ♜f8 43 g3 ♜a8** White's a-Pawn is doomed, after which the win is not difficult for Black. **44 f4 ♚f7 45 ♚f2 ♜a7 46 ♜a2 ♞c6 47 ♚f3 ♚e6 48 ♜a1 ♞d4+ 49 ♚g4?!** Putting the King in front of the Pawns, a strategic misdirection frequently seen in computer endgame play. 49 ♔e4 was much better. **... ♞c2 50 ♜c1 ♞e3+** Black might as well go after the a-Pawn by 50 ... ♘b4; the King isn't going to do anything from g4. **51 ♚f3 ♞f5 52 ♜a1 ♞d6 53 ♜a4 ♞c8 54 ♜a1?! ...** The best chance (not much of one at that) was 54 ♖a5 ♔d6 55 g4 ♘b6 56 f5 ♘xc4 57 ♖a4 hoping that somehow Black will misplay it. **54 ... ♞b6 55 ♜e1+ ♚f6 56 ♜a1 ♞xc4 57 ♚e4 ♞b6 58 ♜a3 ...** Now CHAOS makes many aimless Rook moves, while the Black King penetrates its position. But of course White was lost, even with best play. **... ♜e7+ 59 ♚d3 ♜d7+ 60 ♚c3 ♜a7 61 ♜a1 ♚f5 62 ♜a5 ♚e4 63 ♜a2 ♚e3 64 ♜a1 ♚f2 65 ♜a2+ ♚f3 66 ♜a3 h5 67 ♚c2+ ♚g2 68 h4 ♞d5 69 ♚d2 ♞b4** Finally the a-Pawn goes, and it's all over. **70 ♜c3 ♞xa6 71 ♜a3 ♜d7+ 72 ♚c3 ♞b4 73 ♚c4 ♞d3** Black doesn't mind giving back the piece now, with such an obvious win in the King and Pawn ending. **74 ♜xd3 ♜xd3 75 ♚xd3 ♚xg3** 0-1

SENSORY CC9 - Danny Hoffa(1781)
Catalan(E01)

In this fairly quiet game, Hoffa equalized on schedule and after some inexact play by CC9, won a Pawn. The ensuing ending offered some winning chances for Black, but a tactical error enabled the program to force a draw.

1 c4 ♞f6 2 d4 e6 3 g3 An opening not very well suited for a computer program. **... d5 4 ♝g2 ♝b4+ 5 ♝d2 ...** White gets the better game after 5 ♘d2!, the point being that in some variations a3 forces an exchange. **... ♝xd2+ 6 ♞xd2 c6 7 ♞gf3 0-0 8 0-0 ♞bd7 9 ♛c2 ♜e8 10 ♞g5?! ...** A silly "computer move" made to increase the mobility points of the Knight and Bishop. Natural and best is 10 e4. **... h6 11 ♞gf3 e5 12 cxd5 ♞xd5** ... cxd5 leaves Black with an isolated d-Pawn. **13 e4 ♞5b6 14 ♜ac1** Not bad, but White has a stronger continuation in 14 ♘xe5 ♘xe5 15 dxe5 ♖xe5 16 f4!, mobilizing his Pawn majority. **... exd4 15 ♞xd4 ♞e5 16 ♞2f3 ♞xf3+ 17 ♞xf3 ♝g4** Black has equalized. **18 ♜fe1 ♛f6 19 ♛b3?!** This gives Black opportunities to harass the Queen. 19 ♕c3 would have avoided these difficulties. **... ♝e6 20 ♛a3 ♞c4 21 e5 ♛d8 22 ♛b4 ♞b6 23 ♜ed1 ♛c7 24 ♛a5 ♛e7 25 ♜d4 ♝d5 26 ♜e1 ♞c4 27 ♛c3 ♞b6 28 b3 ♛a3 29 ♛c2 ♛a5 30 ♛d2 ♛xd2 31 ♜xd2 ♜ad8**

HOFFA

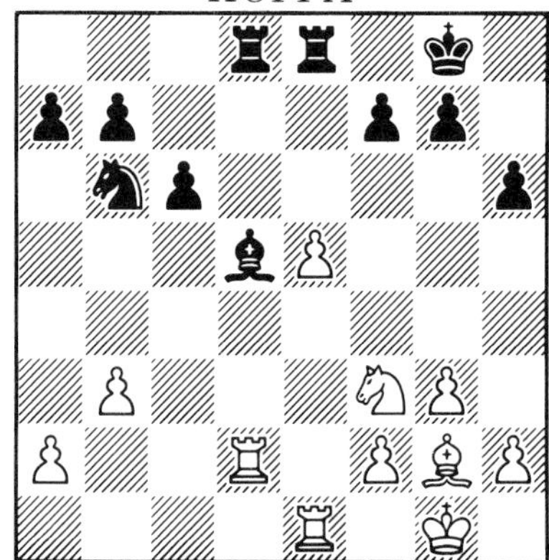

SENSORY CC9

32 ♜d4? ... The program is oblivious to the danger to its e-Pawn; it was necessary to play 32 ♖de2. **... ♜d7 33 ♜f4** Black threatened 33... ♗xf3 34 ♖xd7 ♘xd7 35 ♗xf3 ♖xe5, and the

Rook has to leave the d-file to avoid this. **... ♜de7 34 ♜f1?! ...** There is no way to avoid the loss of the e-Pawn now, but this is strangely passive. Why not 34 ♖d1? **... ♝xf3 35 ♝xf3 ♜xe5 36 ♜d1 ♜e1+ 37 ♜xe1 ♜xe1+ 38 ♚g2 ♚f8 39 h3 ♚e7 40 ♜g4 ...** The Rook is active on the fourth rank. **... g6 41 ♜d4 ♜e5 42 b4 ♞d5?!** This is premature, as White's next move shows. After ... a6, Black would have better winning chances. **43 b5 ♚d6 44 bxc6 bxc6 45 ♜h4 h5 46 ♜a4 ...** The activity of the Rook, and the power of the Bishop, offer some compensation for the Pawn minus, although the ending is still probably a win for Black. Computer programs have a tendency to use Rooks to good effect laterally — many human players tend to think of Rooks as pieces which act only along files, until they get to the 7th or 8th rank. **... a5 47 ♚h2 ♞b6 48 ♜a3 ♞c4 49 ♜c3 ♜c5 50 ♝g2 ♚e5?!** After this , the draw is forced . Black can play for a win by ... ♘b6 and eventually advancing the c-Pawn. **51 ♝f1 ♚d4 52 ♜d3+ ♚e5 53 ♜c3** 1/2-1/2

PRESTIGE - Keith Smith(1883)
Vienna Game(C28)

Another variation on what is by now a familiar theme - PRESTIGE gets an advantage in the opening, then fails to make the most of it, letting its opponent equalize, and then loses the endgame by very inaccurate play. Once more, the program fails to respond to an opportunity to take the initiative.

1 e4 e5 2 ♞c3 ♞c6 3 ♝c4 ♞f6 4 d3 ♝b4 5 ♝g5 h6 6 ♝xf6 ♛xf6 This is a an inaccuracy, and gives White the better game. ECO gives 6 ... ♗xc3+ 7 bxc3 ♕xf6 leading to equality. **7 ♞e2 ♞a5 8 0-0 c6 9 a3 ♝xc3 10 ♞xc3 0-0?!** Here, of course, Black should play 10 ... ♘xc4. Now PRESTIGE keeps the Bishop, and the stranded Knight has to be rescued at additional positional expense. **11 ♝a2 b5 12 ♛d2 ♞b7 13 f4 exf4**

SMITH

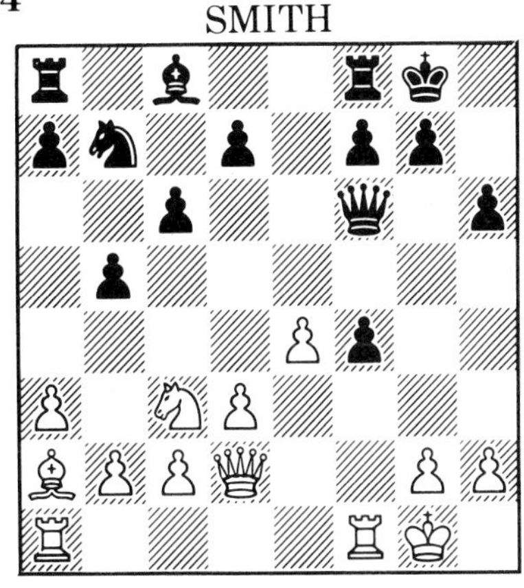

PRESTIGE

14 ♛xf4? ... Again, the program shows no understanding of the value of an initiative. Few human players would fail to play 14 ♖xf4 with a strong attack. **... ♛xf4 15 ♜xf4 d6 16 ♜af1 ♝e6 17 d4 ♝xa2 18 ♞xa2 ♜ae8 19 ♞c3 a6** The ending is about even, although PRESTIGE has a small space advantage. **20 d5?? ...** A horrible positional blunder, which ruins the program's game. This move weakens e5, weakens the e-Pawn, lets Black push his Queenside Pawns, and prevents the Knight from occupying d5 — quite an achievement for only one move! **... c5 21 ♚h1?! ...** It is not hard to see that the program really has very little idea of how to play an endgame demanding strategy. Unable to plan, it simply makes aimless moves while Black piles up on the e-Pawn and wins it. **... ♜e7 22 ♚g1 ♜fe8 23 ♜4f3 f6 24 ♜f4 b4 25 axb4 cxb4 26 ♞a2 a5 27 c3?!** White would do better to play 27 ♘c1; this further weakens the program's position. **... b3 28 ♞c1 ♞c5 29 c4?! ...** And this simply creates another target. **... ♜xe4 30 g3 ♜xf4 31 ♜xf4 ♜e1+ 32 ♜f1 ♜e4 33 ♜f4 a4** Here Black can win very simply and quickly by ... ♖xf4 34 gxf4 a4 (intending a3) 35 ♘e2 ♘d3 etc. **34 ♜xe4 ♞xe4 35 ♞d3**

SMITH

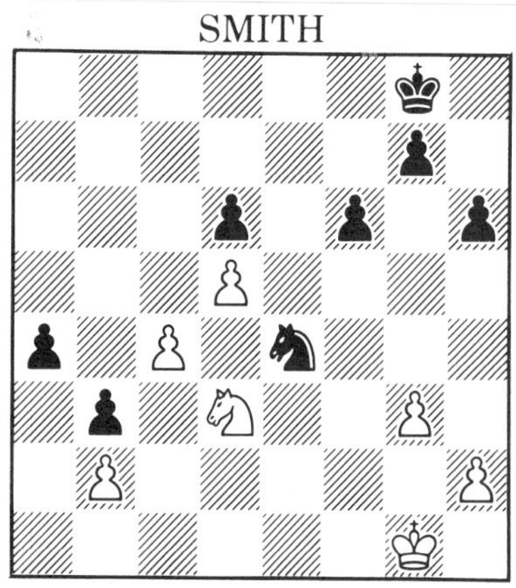

PRESTIGE

35 ... ♚f7(?) Now the game enters a new phase, in which Black purposefully marches his King to the Queenside, while the program, unable to bring its King into action by ♔f1 or ♔f3 due to the threat ... ♘d2+ winning a Pawn, marks time. Had Black been a computer program, however, the game might have continued 35 ... ♘c5! winning immediately: a) 36 ♘xc5 dxc5 37 ♔f2 a3!, etc.; b) 36 ♘c1 a3! and wins. **36 ♚g2 ♚e7 37 ♚g1 ♚d7 38 ♚g2 ♚c7 39 ♚g1 ♚b6 40 ♚g2 ♞d2** This, of course, is quite good enough. **41 c5+ dxc5 42 d6 c4 43 ♞c5 a3 44 bxa3 c3 45 ♞a4+ ♚c6 46 ♞xc3 b2 47 a4 b1 (♛) 48 ♞xb1 ♞xb1 49 ♚f3 ♚xd6 50 ♚f4 g6 51 h4 ♞c3 52 a5 ♞d5+ 53 ♚e4 f5+ 54 ♚d4 g5 55 hxg5 hxg5 56 ♚c4 f4 57 gxf4 gxf4 58 ♚d3 ♚c6 59 ♚e4 ♚b5** 0-1

ROUND 9

BELLE - David Levin(1527)
Ruy Lopez(C88)

This game was actually played after BELLE's Round 11 opponent resigned early due to illness. A player of Levin's rating is, of course, badly outclassed against BELLE, and after Levin blunders a Pawn early and then gets into further problems in the middlegame, it is not much of a contest. **1 e4 e5 2 ♞f3 ♞c6 3 ♝b5 a6 4 ♝a4 ♞f6 5 0-0 ♝e7 6 ♜e1 b5 7 ♝b3 ♞a5?** A Pawn sacrifice unknown to opening theory. The usual moves are ... 0-0 and ... d6. **8 ♞xe5 ♞xb3 9 axb3 ♝b7 10 ♛f3 0-0 11 ♞c3 ...** Otherwise Black might play ... d5. **... ♜e8 12 ♞g4 d6 13 ♞xf6+ ♝xf6 14 d3 ♛d7 15 ♝d2 c5?!** Positionally unwise, since this weakens d5 and the d-Pawn. **16 ♝f4 ♝d4 17 ♞d1 f5?!** Another weakening move, though it appears strong superficially. **18 c3 ♝f6?!** 1t would be wiser to play ... fxe4 first. **19 ♛g3 d5 20 e5 ♛c6** Black is relying on the following combination, which unfortunately has a "hole" in it. The top computer programs (of which BELLE is the best) don't make tactical errors at this level — the opponent who thinks the computer has overlooked a three-mover or even a four-mover (no matter how clever) would be well advised to look again! **21 ♞e3 ...**

LEVIN

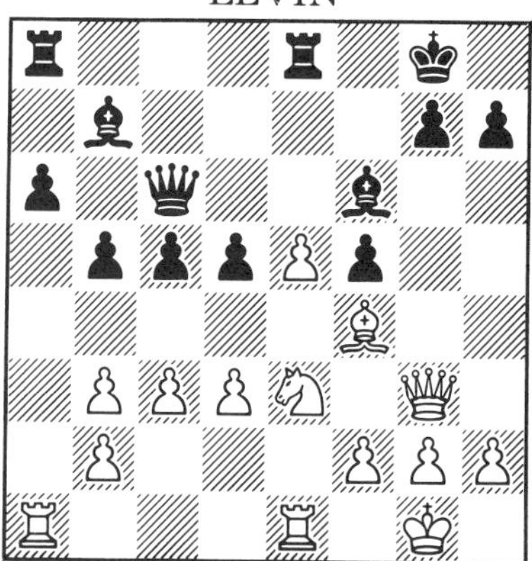

BELLE

21 ... ♝h4?? A hallucination. Even if the combination worked, it would lose material. Black is, however, about to be crushed after 21 ... ♗d8 22 ♘xf5. **22 ♛xh4 d4 23 cxd4 cxd4 24 ♜ac1 ♛g6 25 ♜c7! ...** The move Black had overlooked. As usual, BELLE plays the most active move in an open position; here it is also the best. **25 ... dxe3 26 ♜xb7 exf2+ 27 ♛xf2 ♛c6 28 ♛b6 ♛d5??** The exchange of Queens was forced. **29 ♛c7 ♛xb7** Very sad, but otherwise it's mate. **30 ♛xb7 ♜ad8 31 e6** 1-0

Matt Rhodes(1582) - CHAOS
King's Indian Attack(A08)

CHAOS never does figure out what's happening in this game. Baffled by White's tame opening, the program lets him get an advantage. Then Rhodes starts an attack and plays an unsound sacrifice, which the program grabs for a winning advantage. But that's not enough and CHAOS riskily grabs still another piece — meanwhile using up all its time calculating the variations.

1 ♞f3 ♞f6 2 g3 d5 3 ♝g2 c5 4 0-0 e6 5 d3 ♞c6 6 ♜e1 ... ECO gives 6 ♘bd2. **... ♝e7 7 ♞bd2 ♞g4?!** CHAOS hasn't a clue as to how this opening should develop — the program expects 8 ♘b3 b6. The purpose of this move is unclear. **8 e4 0-0 9 exd5 ...** In this variation, White usually chooses to play e5 and play for a Kingside attack, and this strategy could be implemented by 9 h3 ♘f6 10 e5 ♘e8 and White is two tempi ahead of the normal variation (Tringov-Lee, Hague 1966). This is very tame and not at all in the spirit of the opening. **... exd5 10 ♞b3 ...** The Knight would probably stand better at f1. **... c4?!** This weakening of d4 gets CHAOS nowhere, since White doesn't have to exchange on c4. **11 ♞bd4 ♝c5 12 c3 ...**

CHAOS

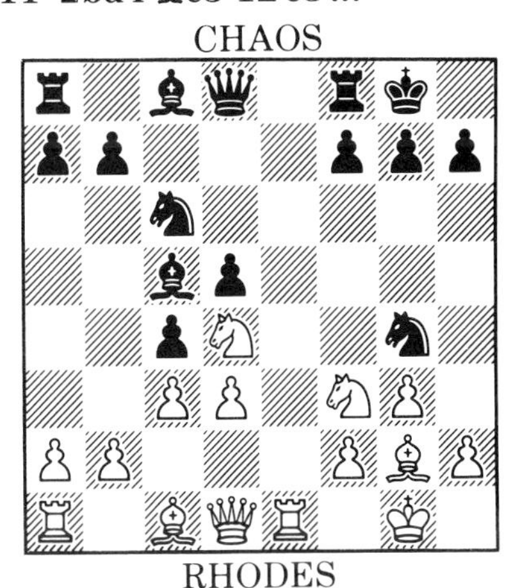

RHODES

12 ... ♝d7?! Black should exchange twice on d4, with equality. Now White gets to establish a favorable Pawn formation. **13 h3 ♞f6 14 ♞xc6 ♝xc6** Somewhat better is ... bxc6, with a Pawn that can attack d4. **15 d4 ♝e7?!** Allowing White to control a strong diagonal; ... ♗d6 was the move to play. **16 ♝f4 ♝d7** CHAOS still hasn't grasped the elements of the position at all. The program expects 16 ♖e5?! ♗d6. **17 ♛c2 ♜e8 18 ♜e2 ♞h5 19 ♝d2 ♞f6 20 ♜ae1 h6** Like many (if not all) programs, CHAOS can't find anything to do in slowly developing positions, and marks time waiting for something to happen. **21 ♝f4 ♞e4 22 ♞e5 ♝f5 23 ♛c1 ♛a5 24 a3 ♛b5 25 g4 ...** White obliges by starting a Kingside attack. **... ♝h7 26 f3?!** This move cuts off the retreat of the Knight at e5, which could be embarrassing after a later ... f6. **... ♞d6 27 ♝f1?** This should lose to ... f6, trapping the Knight. The best continuation was 27 ♘g6 ♗xg6 28 ♗xe7. **... ♝h4**

CHAOS

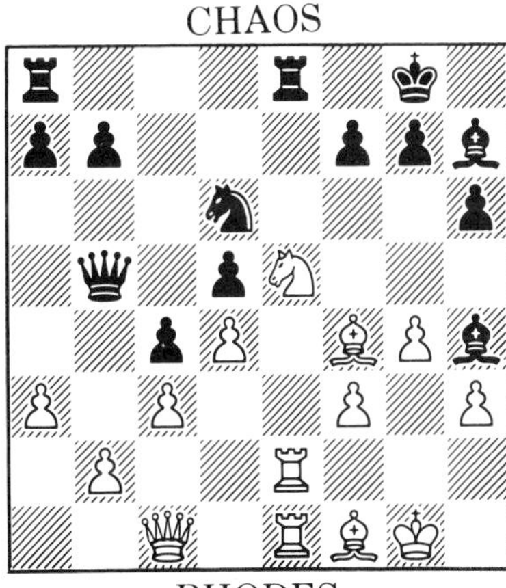

RHODES

28 g5?! ... This Exchange sacrifice is dubious, and unnecessary since after 28 ♖d1 f6 White still has 29 ♘g6. **... ♝xe1** Greedier and better is ... hxg5, but this still ought to win. **29 gxh6? ...** And this is definitely unsound. After 29 ♕xe1

White has some attack as compensation. **... ♝h4 30 ♝g5 ♞f5 31 ♝xh4 ♞xh4 32 ♛g5 ♞g6 33 ♜g2 f6** A totally materialistic move which weakens the King position. CHAOS is driven by its heuristics to grab all the material that it can — a Rook ahead isn't enough for the program, it wants the Knight too. A simple solution to White's pressure is ... ♕a6-f6. Nevertheless, although unnecessarily complicated, this move should still win. **34 ♛f5 fxe5 35 h4 ♛c6** This move took 25.6 minutes to calculate, and by now CHAOS has only 20 minutes left on its clock. **36 h5 ...** And once more, the minutes ticked away and the program's flag fell before it could compute a move. Black would have a winning position after ... ♖e6. 1-0(time)

Stephen Leary(1921) - SENSORY CC9
English(A19)

In this game, CC9 gives a convincing demonstration of its total ignorance of the principles of consolidation and simplification when exploiting a material advantage. The program won two Pawns, although its opponent got some pressure for them, but then failed either to develop or to simplify, leaving its King stranded.
1 c4 ♞f6 2 ♞c3 e6 3 e4 c5 4 e5 ♞g8 5 d4 cxd4 6 ♛xd4 ♞c6 7 ♛e4 ♝b4 8 ♞f3 ... An inaccuracy; ECO gives 8 ♗d2 leading to a slight advantage for White. **... ♝xc3+!?** The program finds a theoretical novelty; ECO gives ... d6 with equality. This doubled Pawn formation is quite unfavorable for White, as the program's next move shows. **9 bxc3 ♛a5 10 ♝d2 ♞ge7**

SENSORY CC9

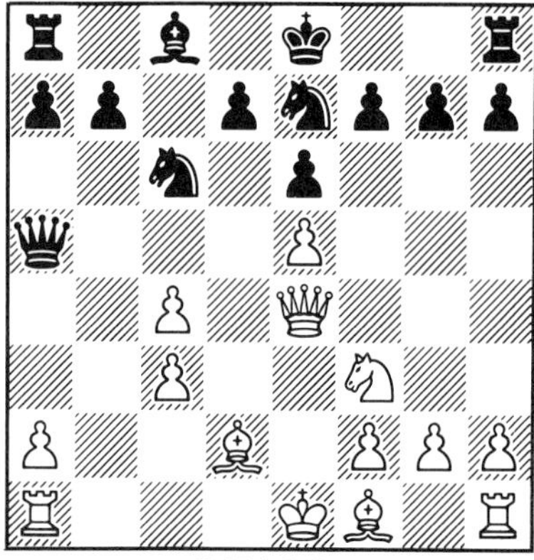

LEARY

11 ♜c1 ... White has to give up a Pawn here, and correctly chooses the a-Pawn. This gives him some play due to his lead in development. Still, it would probably be better to play 11 ♖b1 with a more active Rook. **... ♛xa2 12 ♝d3 ♞g6 13 ♚e2!? ...** White's play is rather eccentric, but ingenious. 13 0-0 is not possible because of ♘xe5, but 13 ♗f4 would have solved that problem. The text threatens 14 ♖a1 winning the Queen. **... ♛a5 14 ♜a1 ♛c7 15 ♝f4 f6!?** Black wins the e-Pawn. The program cannot just wait around, since after ♗g3 and h4-h5 White gets a strong attack. Nevertheless, this does involve a weakening of the Black position. **16 ♝g3 ♞gxe5** Here it looks better to capture with the Knight on c6, opening the c-file and giving the Queen more room to maneuver. **17 ♞d4 d6 18 ♞b5 ♛e7 19 ♜he1 ♚f8?** CC9 is under pressure. The program vaguely senses this and registers discomfort, but this move is senseless — there is no reason to give up Castling and leave the Rook out of play. After ... f5, White's compensation for the two Pawns minus is far from sufficient. **20 ♚f1 a6 21 f4 f5?!** No need for this; ... ♘xd3 breaks up the attack: 22 ♕xd3 axb5! 23 ♖xa8 bxc4 and: a) 24 ♖xc8+ ♔f7 25 ♖xh8 cxd3 and wins; b) 24 ♕xc4 ♔f7, and Black, with two Pawns for the Exchange, has no real problems. Now CC9 gets in trouble. **22 ♕e3 ♞g4 23 ♕b6 ...**

SENSORY CC9

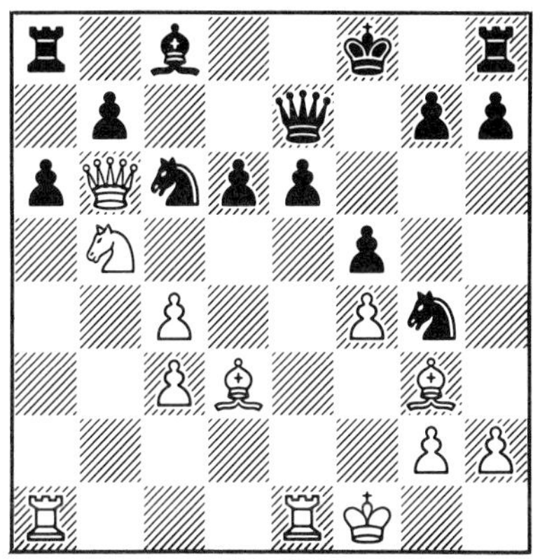

LEARY

23 ... ♛f6? A serious error of judgment, trading the vital d-Pawn for an insignificant doubled c-Pawn. Black's position leaves much to be desired, but ... g6 looks like a viable plan of defense. **24 ♘xd6 ♛xc3 25 ♗xf5!** Demolishing the program's position. CC9 had expected to win a tempo here. **... ♞e3+** Anything else lets White have a winning attack, but being a piece down with such a miserable position doesn't offer much hope, either. **26 ♕xe3 ♛xe3 27 ♖xe3 ♞d4 28 ♗e4 ♜b8 29 f5!** The rest is a total crush. **... exf5 30 ♘xf5 ♞xf5 31 ♗xf5 ♜a8 32 ♖a5 ♚f7 33 ♗e4 ♝e6 34 ♖f3+ ♚g8 35 ♖c5 b6 36 ♖c7 ♜e8 37 ♗e5 ♝xc4+ 38 ♔g1 ♝f7 39 ♖cxf7 ♜xe5 40 ♖f8 mate.** 1-0

Tom Tingblad(1801) - PRESTIGE
French(C19)

This gamelet is a bizarre exhibition of exploiting the heuristics of a computer program. Should White be praised for his ingenuity in finding the program's weaknesses, or censured for the bad Chess which he plays?

1 e4 e6 2 d4 d5 3 ♘c3 ♝b4 4 e5 c5 5 a3 ♝xc3+ 6 bxc3 ♞e7 7 ♘f3 ♞d7?! ECO gives the more normal alternatives ... ♕a5, ... ♕c7, and ... ♘bc6 and ♗d7. This impedes the development of Black's Queenside. The Winawer variation leads to positions which are not very suitable for computer programs. At this point the Spracklens were not using Boris Baczynskyj's tournament "book". The program is out of its regular "book" now, and plays an inferior move. **8 h4 ...** Tingblad adopts Bisguier's advice and pushes his Rook Pawn — a strategy that succeeds famously in this game. **... f6** This is very sharp, but without it Black's 7th doesn't make sense. **9 h5 0-0 10 ♘h4?** This is unsound. White cannot afford to give up the e-Pawn so lightly. **... fxe5 11 ♗d3 cxd4?!** After ... e4, the error of White's ways would be apparent even to him. **12 ♗xh7+?** Another, more weighty, unsound sacrifice, after which PRESTIGE has a won game. **... ♚xh7 13 h6**

PRESTIGE

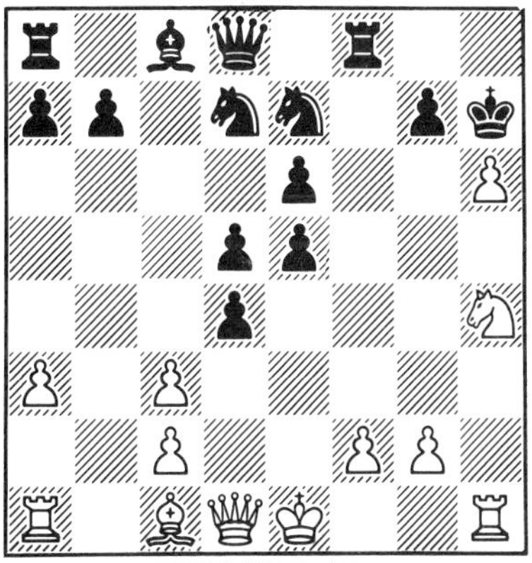

TINGBLAD

13 ... dxc3?? But the program's heuristics won't let it win! PRESTIGE is forced to go after more material, when almost any human player would start defending by ... g6, after which White has nothing. But now it is a different story! **14 hxg7 ♚xg7 15 ♕g4+ ♚f6 16 ♗g5+** Tingblad efficiently carries out the execution. **... ♚f7 17 ♕h5+ ♚g8 18 ♘g6 ♞f6 19 ♗xf6 ♚f7 20 ♘xf8+ ♚xf6 21 ♕h8+ ♚f7 22 ♖h7+ ♚e8 23 ♘xe6+** 1-0

ROUND 10

Raymond Safdie(1835) - BELLE
Colle System(D05)

In this game, one of the many antipositional moves made by BELLE in this tournament causes the program serious difficulty. Safdie exploits the weakness caused effectively, but the tactical method chosen gets him into time pressure — and eventually he loses first the initiative and then the game.
1 d4 d5 2 ♞f3 ♞f6 3 e3 e6 4 ♝d3 c5 5 c3 ♞bd7 6 ♞bd2 ♝d6 7 0-0 0-0 8 e4 cxd4 9 cxd4 dxe4 10 ♞xe4 ♞xe4 11 ♝xe4 ♛b6 12 ♜e1 ECO gives 12 ♗d3 as the move to play here, with equality.

BELLE

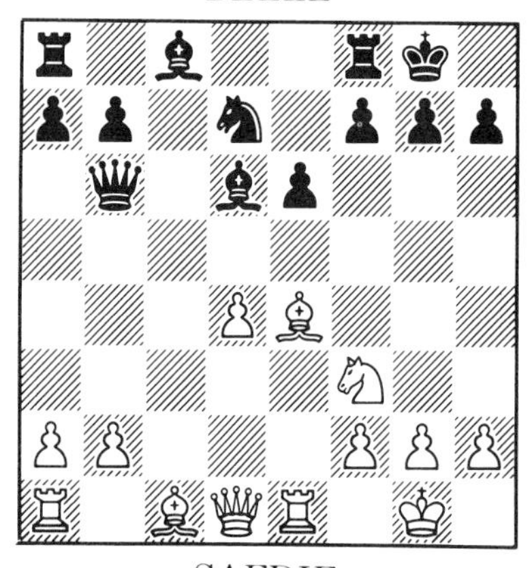

SAFDIE

12 ... f5? Antipositional, seriously weakening the e-Pawn. Black stands very well after ... ♘f6 13 ♗d3 ♗d7-c6. But now BELLE gets into serious difficulties, against a much lower-rated player. **13 ♝c2** This Bishop now threatens to take up a very strong post on b3. **13 ... ♞f6 14 ♞g5!?** A simpler and sounder way to show the drawbacks of BELLE's 12th move is 14 ♗b3, after which the defense of the e-Pawn becomes onerous. **... ♞g4 15 ♞xe6!?** And here h3 would put BELLE in an awkward situation. **... ♝xh2+ 16 ♚f1 ♝xe6 17 ♜xe6 ♛b5+** Of course 17 ♕xe6 loses the Queen. **18 ♝d3 ♛d7 19 ♛b3 ♚h8 20 d5** The d-Pawn now becomes strong. **... ♜ac8 21 ♝g5 ♝d6 22 ♜ae1 ♛c7**

BELLE

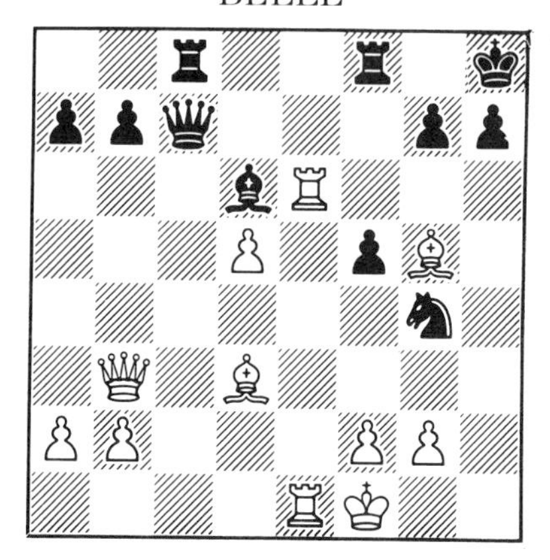

SAFDIE

23 ♛d1? There was not the least necessity to hand over the initiative in this fashion; White overlooks a double attack. **... ♛c5 24 ♛c2?** Unfortunately, 24 ♕f3 (apparently the move envisioned when White played his 23rd move) loses to ♘h2+. Safdie was already in time pressure. **... ♛xc2 25 ♝xc2 ♜xc2 26 ♜xd6 ♜xf2+ 27 ♚g1 ♜xb2 28 ♜d7** Here it would be better to play 28 ♖d8, after which the passed d-Pawn could become very dangerous. **... ♜xa2 29 ♜xb7 h6 30 ♝e7 ♜c8 31 ♝f8** Unfortunately, after 31 d6 ♖cc2 White gets mated. Safdie seems to be lost here. **... ♜xf8 32 d6 ♜d8 33 d7 ♜d2 34 ♜e8+ ♚h7 35 ♚f1** 35 ♖xd8?? allows mate — a point overlooked in time pressure on White's 31st move. **... ♜8xd7 36 ♜bb8 ♜d1+** At this point BELLE announced mate in five moves. **37 ♚e2 ♜7d2+ 38 ♚f3 ♜f1+ 39 ♚g3 ♜d3+ 40 ♚h4 ♜h1 mate** 0-1

CHAOS - Russell Lind(1380)
Queen's Gambit Declined(D06)

CHAOS crushes a newcomer to tournament play.

1 d4 d5 2 c4 ♞f6?! The Marshall variation, a dubious line of play for Black. **3 cxd5 ♞xd5 4 ♞f3!** After 4 e4 ♘f6 5 ♘c3, Black can play ... e5!, a specialty of Marshall's. **... h6?** After this loss of time, it becomes clear that Black is not much of an openings theorist. **5 e4 ♞f6 6 ♞c3 c6 7 ♝e2 ♝d7?!** First, Black should develop his Kingside and his Knight at b8, which this obstructs. **8 ♛b3** CHAOS develops its pieces effectively. Meanwhile, Black loses more time. **... ♛c8** The Queen would stand better on c7. **9 ♝f4 g5?!** An unujustified thrust, weakening the Kingside for a transitory purpose. **10 ♝e5 ♝g7 11 ♝c4 e6 12 h4!** CHAOS now begins to exploit the opportunities its opponent has so generously offered. **... g4 13 ♞d2 h5 14 0-0 ♜g8?!** After the violence he has done to his own position, Black is afraid to castle — which is understandable. Still, it would have been better to do so. **15 ♛b4** More pressure on the weakened dark squares. **15 ... ♞a6?** After this, Black's position goes from miserable to untenable. A better plan was ... a5, followed by ... ♘a6. **16 ♝xa6** Black's Queenside Pawn position is destroyed, and CHAOS' evaluator starts to generate increasing scores. Here the program assessed its positional advantage at 1.15 Pawns, which serves to illustrate the dominance of material factors in the evaluation function — Black is much worse off than that! Still, it is remarkable that CHAOS correctly evaluates its positional advantages as being worth more than a Pawn, when material is in fact even. In many other programs, the only positional factor capable of producing a positional score greater than a Pawn is a far-advanced passed Pawn, when combined with other advantages. **... bxa6 17 ♞c4 ♝f8 18 ♛a5 ♞h7 19 ♝d6**

LIND

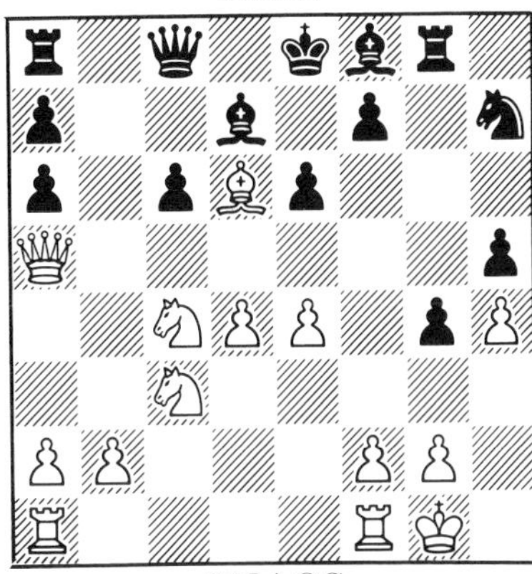

CHAOS

There is just no word to describe the magnitude of the dark-square "holes" in the Black position! **... ♛d8 20 ♛xh5 ♜h8?** An obvious tactical error. ... ♘f6 would have held out for a while. **21 ♝e5** 5.43 Pawns! Now CHAOS begins to compute scores which seem to increase almost exponentially. **... c5 22 ♝xh8 ♞f6 23 ♝xf6 ♛xf6 24 dxc5 ♜c8 25 e5** 9.72 Pawns! **... ♛f5 26 ♞d6+ ♝xd6 27 ♛xf5 exf5 28 cxd6 ♚f8 29 ♜fd1** 12.03 Pawns! At this point, it becomes more appropriate to measure the program's advantage in terms of Queens. CHAOS thinks it is 1.33 Queens ahead. This is still remarkable, because the program actually has a material advantage of 7 Pawns according to the standard "point-count" — thus values its positional edge at 5 Pawns. **... ♜c5 30 ♞d5 ♜c8 31 ♞f6 ♝e6 32 d7 ♜d8 33 ♜d6 ♚e7 34 ♜xa6 ♜a8** There's just no salvation; ... ♗xd7 35 ♖xa7 ♔e6(relieving the pin) 36 ♖d1 (creating another and winning the Bishop). **35 ♜c1** Now it's 1.75 Queens. One might wonder why Black plays on — Lind, a local player, was unrated before the event, and this may have been his first tournament. Some players don't know that it is possible to resign! So the game goes on to the bitter end, and possibly an all-time record in evaluator scores. **... ♝xd7** This winds up being forced anyway. **36 ♜c7 g3** A human example of the "horizon effect"? **37 fxg3 ♚f8 38 ♜axa7 ♜xa7 39 ♞xd7+ ♚g7 40 ♜xa7** 2.5 Queens! **... ♚h7 41 ♞f6+ ♚g6 42 ♞e8 f4 43 g4** 4.45 Queens! **... f3 44 gxf3** At this point, CHAOS' evaluation function peaked at the incredible level of 4.55 Queens. After this, the program decided that it had enough material. **... f6 45 f4** And CHAOS announced mate in 3 moves: **... f5 46 h5+ ♚h6 47 ♞f6 fxg4 48 ♜h7 mate** 1-0

Joseph Camero(1726) - SENSORY CC9
Gruenfeld(D80)

The program misplays the opening badly, and is crushed.

1 d4 ♞f6 2 c4 g6 3 ♞c3 d5 4 e3 A meek continuation, formerly much played, but now passe.

SENSORY CC9

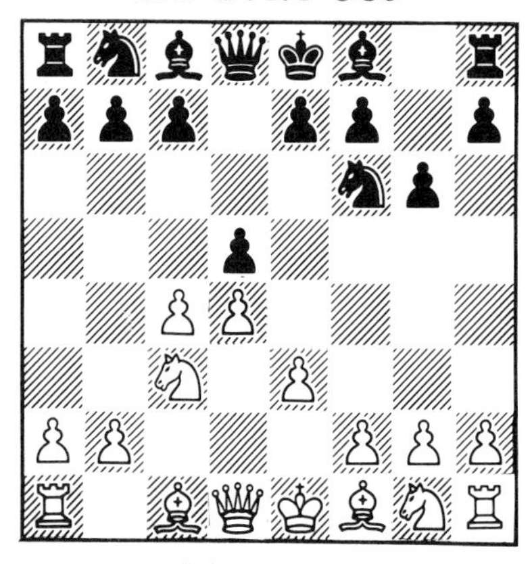

CAMERO

4 ... dxc4?! Obviously taken out of its "book", CC9 shows that it has no comprehension at all of the positional principles behind this opening, and plays a move very helpful to White — defusing the central tension and aiding in his development. After ... ♗g7 5 ♕b3 c6, a position with many features of a Queen's Gambit Declined would result. **5 ♝xc4 ♞c6?!** Obviously best was ... ♗g7, but CC9 (like its ancestors in the SARGON tribe) has no heuristic to tell it that a fianchetto, once begun, ought to be completed. Now White gets a chance to force a weakness. **6 ♛b3 e6 7 ♝e2 ♝b4?!** The Bishop still belongs on g7. Now it is exchanged, further weakening the program's dark squares. **8 ♝f3** More natural is the simple developing move 8 ♘f3. **... ♝xc3+ 9 ♛xc3 ♝d7 10 d5!?** White opens up the position, giving up his center Pawn to build a threat on the long diagonal. This is not really justified in view of his lack of development, but with less than optimum defense, turns out to be effective. **... exd5 11 ♝xd5 0-0 12 ♝f3 ♜e8 13 b3 ♞e4?** Here it would be better to play ... ♘e5, with pressure on the weak square d3; then if 14 ♗b2 ♗b5 and White has problems; or 14 ♗e2 and then ♘e4, with much more force than in the game. White should then be in difficulties, but the program misses its opportunity. **14 ♝xe4 ♜xe4 15 ♞f3 ♛e7 16 0-0 ♜f8 17 ♝b2 f6 18 ♜ac1** Now that White has caught up in development, he has a clear advantage. **... ♝e6 19 ♞d2 ♜g4 20 f3 ♜h4 21 ♞e4 ♚g7** White is slowly building up his positional attack, and Black is now under crippling pressure. **22 ♞c5 ♝c4!?** A strange variation for the materialistic program to play—CC9 offers the Exchange. Possibly the program did not see this due to limited search depth, and chose this instead of the more normal ... ♗c8. **23 bxc4 ♛xc5 24 ♝a3 ♛e5 25 ♝xf8+ ♚xf8 26 f4 ♛xc3 27 ♜xc3**

SENSORY CC9

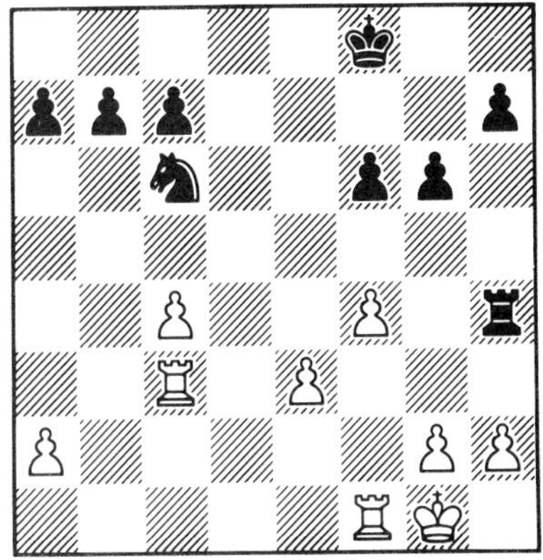

CAMERO

Black's position is now far from enviable, but after ... ♖h5, the program could still put up some resistance. Instead, CC9 allows its Rook to be trapped out of play. **... f5? 28 g3 ♜h5 29 ♜fd1 ♚e7 30 a3 ♚e6 31 ♜cd3 ♞a5 32 ♜1c1 b6 33 c5** Forcing an entry into Black's position. Since CC9 is in effect a Rook and an Exchange down, the rest is not much of a contest. **... a6 34 cxb6 cxb6 35 a4 h6 36 ♜c7 g5 37 ♜a7 ♞c4 38 ♜xa6 ♜h3 39 ♚g2 ♜h5 40 ♜a8 gxf4 41 exf4 ♞d6 42 ♜b8 ♞c4 43 ♜e8+ ♚f7 44 ♜c8 ♞b2 45 ♜d4 ♚e7 46 ♜c7+ ♚e6 47 ♜c6+** 1-0

PRESTIGE - Mike Hall(1548)
Irregular(A46)

Its opponent plays an eccentric opening, giving PRESTIGE the opportunity to show that computer programs can play the attack. The program responds brilliantly, handling the initiative with a precision not usually seen in computer games.

1 d4 ♞f6 2 ♞f3 ♞c6 Developing a piece — and yet, on the second move, the game is already in uncharted waters. Was this an attempt to take the program out of its "book"? **3 d5** If so, it was not a good idea, for PRESTIGE develops smoothly and builds a powerful center. **... ♞b4 4 ♞c3 b6** Here ... e6 is better. **5 e4 ♝b7 6 a3 ♞a6 7 e5 ♞g4 8 h3 ♞h6**

HALL

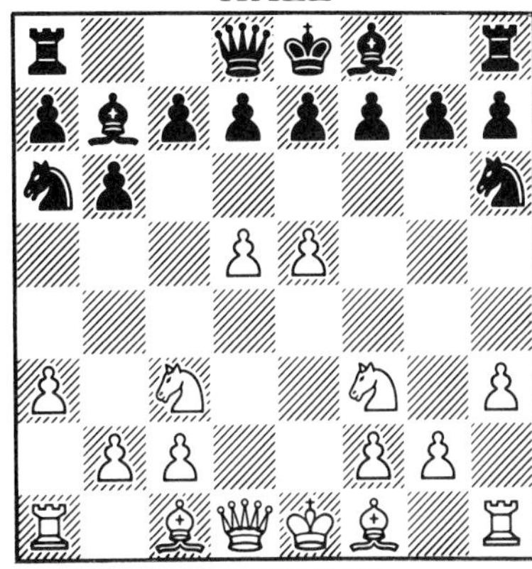

PRESTIGE

This position does not say much for Black's opening strategy. **9 ♝d3 e6** A weakening move, but the threat of 10 e6 must be dealt with. **10 0-0 d6?** A grave error. Now BlacK loses the right to castle, and his King is trapped in the center, exposed to many grievous threats. It was essential for Black to play ... ♗e7, after which his position is rather miserable, but a quick crush is at any rate avoided. **11 ♝b5+ ♚e7 12 dxe6 dxe5** Not ... fxe6??, after which 13 ♗g5+ is conclusive. **13 ♛e2!** PRESTIGE plays the attack very well, unusually so for a computer program. **13 ... ♞c5 14 ♜d1 ♛c8**

HALL

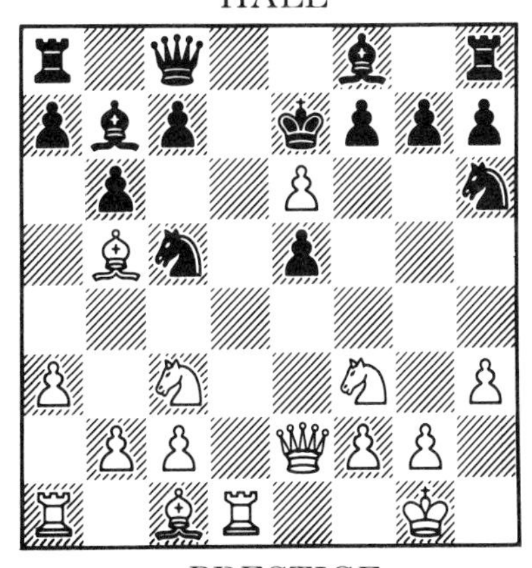

PRESTIGE

15 ♜d7+! ... A fine move, which must

have come as a horrible shock to Black. **... ♛xd7** Not ... ♘xd7 16 exd7 ♕d8 17 ♕xe5 mate. The rest is a massacre. **16 exd7 ♝xf3 17 ♛xe5+** No rest for the wicked! **... ♞e6 18 ♝xh6 f6 19 ♛f5 ♞d4** There is no way to defend against the threat of 20 ♖e1. **20 ♜e1+ ♚f7 21 ♝c4+** 1-0

ROUND 11

BELLE - Tom Barber(1815)
Irregular(B00)

In an attempt to baffle BELLE, Barber dared the program to refute his mockery of an opening. BELLE did its best, but before the program could finish its demonstration, Barber became ill and resigned.

1 e4 f6? It's all very well to take the program out of its "book", but this is going a bit far! **2 d4 ♚f7?** A sort of "joke" opening sometimes resorted to in five-minute games, by good defensive players who wish to goad their opponents into overplaying the attack. **3 ♞c3 e6 4 d5!** ... BELLE obliges. The threat of 5 dxe6+ is most unpleasant. **... ♛e8 5 ♝f4 e5** Now Black simply has a miserable position without any counterplay. **6 ♝e3 ♝b4 7 ♝c4 d6 8 ♞e2 ♞e7 9 0-0 a6** Here Barber became ill and had to withdraw from the tournament. In truth, his position

BARBER

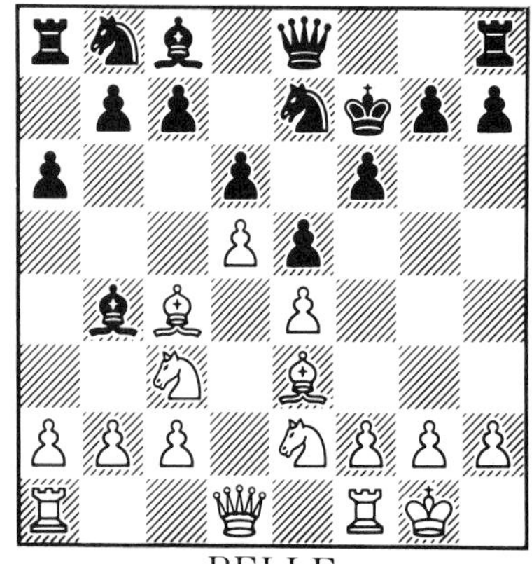

BELLE

was rather sickening; still, after ... ♖f8 and ... ♔g8, it is not all that easy for White to break through and exploit its spatial advantage. BELLE would have done well to open lines earlier, for example by 5 dxe6. 1-0

Gary Osgood(1598) - CHAOS
Queen's Indian(E43)

CHAOS equalizes easily in the opening, then loses the initiative. After Osgood hangs a Pawn, the program gets the advantage in a complicated endgame (with some fine tactical points which one wonders whether either player saw), and is in the process of driving it home, when Osgood blunders just at the time control.

1 d4 ♞f6 2 ♞f3 e6 3 c4 b6 4 ♞c3 ♝b7 5 e3 ♝b4 6 ♝e2 More active is 6 ♗d3. **... ♞e4 7 ♛c2 ♞a6** ECO gives ... f5 with equality, but this is also quite reasonable. **8 0-0 ♞xc3** While this is not exactly bad, it is certainly against the principles of the Queen's Indian for Black to give up control of e4. It was better to play ... ♗xc3 9 bxc3 c5, making a sort of Nimzoindian out of it. CHAOS does not understand that it has to fight for control of e4. **9 bxc3 ♝e7 10 ♞e5** Also not bad, but White would do better to play e4 here, with a powerful Kingside attack to follow. **10 ... f5 11 ♝h5+** This accomplishes nothing. **... g6 12 ♝f3 ♝xf3 13 ♞xf3 0-0** The game is even. **14 ♞e5 ♛c8 15 a4 d6?!** In this position, which has some of the characteristics of a Nimzoindian, Black should first play ... c5. **16 ♝a3 ♛e8 17 ♞f3 ♛c6 18 ♛d3 ♜f7 19 ♜fe1 ♜af8 20 ♝c1 ♛e4 21 ♛e2 c5 22 ♛b2 ♞c7?!** It seems better to retreat the Queen to b7 or c6. Now White takes the initiative. **23 a5 ♛b7 24 axb6 ♛xb6 25 ♛a2 a6 26 ♛a4 ♛b7** Instead of marking time, CHAOS ought to bring its inactive Rooks over to the Queenside and try to do something with the passed a-Pawn. **27 ♝d2 ♝f6 28 ♛a3** CHAOS was "threatening" to play ... d5, which White should allow as it dissolves the weak doubled Pawns. **... ♛c6 29 h4 ♝e7**

CHAOS

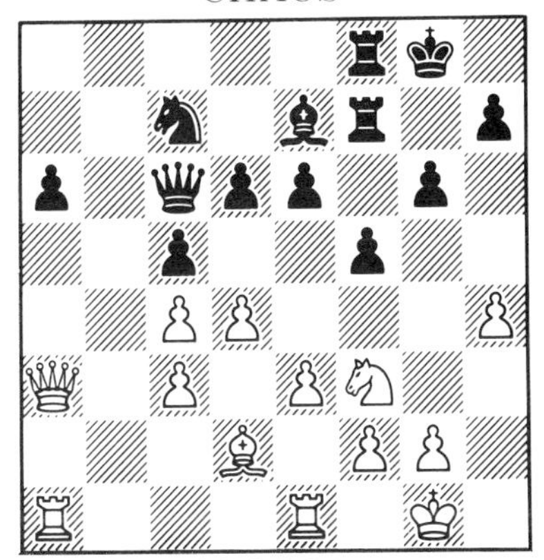

OSGOOD

30 ♜e2? ... White could maintain the initiative by 30 ♕a4!, offering to exchange Black's active Queen. This simply loses a Pawn. **... cxd4 31 cxd4 ♛xc4 32 ♜ee1 d5** And now Black has the initiative as well. **33 ♛a5 ♝d6 34 ♜ec1 ♛b5 35 ♛a2** White's best chance may have been 35 ♕xb5 axb5 36 ♖c6 ♖d7 37 ♖a7, with very active Rooks. **... ♛b7 36 ♜ab1 ♞b5 37 ♝b4 ♝xb4 38 ♜xb4 ♛b6** Instead of wasting time with unnecessary Queen moves, the program should get its Rooks into play. Here ... ♖c8 looks effective. **39 ♛b3 ♛d6** Another unnecessary Queen move; ... ♖c7 was indicated. **40 ♞e5** Now there is a crucial tempo's difference, which should have enabled White to draw. **... ♜c7 41 ♜xc7 ♛xc7** Here the program assessed its advantage at 1.2 Pawns, but in reality its edge is now insufficient to win, since the White Knight takes up an ideal post in the nick of time. **42 ♞d3 ♜a8** It is now too late to come to the support of the a-Pawn, which White is about to win by the combined action of the Knight at c5 and a heavy piece on the a-file. **43 ♞c5 ♛d6 44 ♛a4** Threatening 45 ♘xa6, with a clear draw. **... ♞c3 45 ♛a3?** Just at the moment when Osgood's efforts were about to be rewarded with half a point, he blunders, allowing CHAOS to start its Pawn advancing. After 45 ♕a5, it is unclear how Black can cope with the threat of 46 ♖b6 winning the a-Pawn. **... a5 46 ♜b7 ♞e4 47 ♜d7** This Rook on the seventh rank looks powerful, but the game is being decided on the a-file. **47 ... ♛f8!**

CHAOS

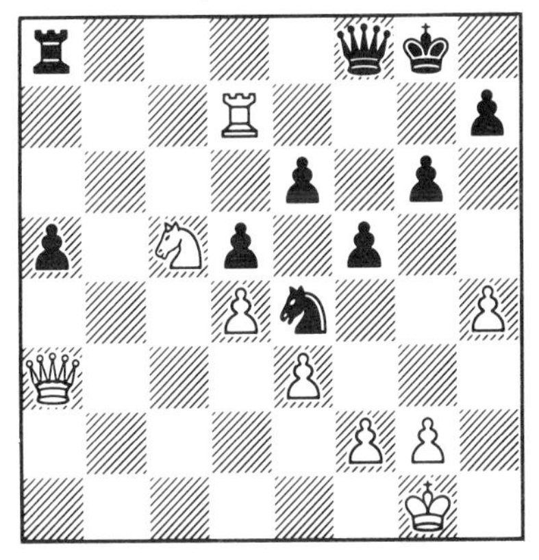

OSGOOD

CHAOS maintains its threats along the a3-f8 diagonal, which prevents the White Queen from blockading at a4. **48 ♜b7 ...** An elegant try for a draw is 48 ♘xe4!! and if ... ♕xa3, 49 ♘f6+ ♔f8 50 ♘xh7+ with perpetual check; if ... fxe4 49 ♕c3! and White has powerful activity on the 7th rank and threats against the e-Pawn, which should give excellent drawing chances. **48 ... a4 49 ♛b4?** White (in time pressure) could have made a stubborn resistance after 49 ♖b4, one point being that ... ♘xc5 50 dxc5 ♕xc5?? loses the Queen. **... a3 50 ♛b6 ♞xc5** This is forced by the threats of doubling along the 7th rank. **51 ♛c7??** After dxc5, Black would have to play brilliantly to win: ... ♕c8! (51 ... a2? 52 ♕xe6+ with perpetual) 52 ♖c7 ♕xc7!! 53 ♕xc7 a2 and wins. **... ♞xb7** 0-1

SENSORY CC9 - Tim Petermeier(1513)
From's Gambit(A02)

CC9's oponent in this game reacts violently to Bird's opening, with the risky From's Gambit — then loses his initiative after advancing the wrong Pawn.

1 f4 e5 2 fxe5 d6 3 exd6 ♝xd6 4 ♞f3 h5? Pure loss of time. One may imagine Petermeier thinking, "I know I'm supposed to charge forward with a Pawn now — but which one?". The right move is 4 g5. **5 e4 ♞c6 6 ♝b5** More natural is 6 d4. **... g5?!** Finally he gets the idea, but now that the initiative has been lost, it may have been better to play a developing move instead of this further weakening of the Kingside. **7 ♝xc6+ bxc6 8 d4 g4 9 ♞e5 ♝a6** Now CC9 can't castle, and it begins to look like Black might yet succeed in getting an attack started. **10 ♝f4 ♛f6 11 ♛d2 ♞e7?!** Here it was necessary to interrupt White's development by ... ♖b8, if Black were to maintain any chances. **12 ♞c3 ♜b8 13 0-0-0 ♜g8 14 ♜he1**

PETERMEIER

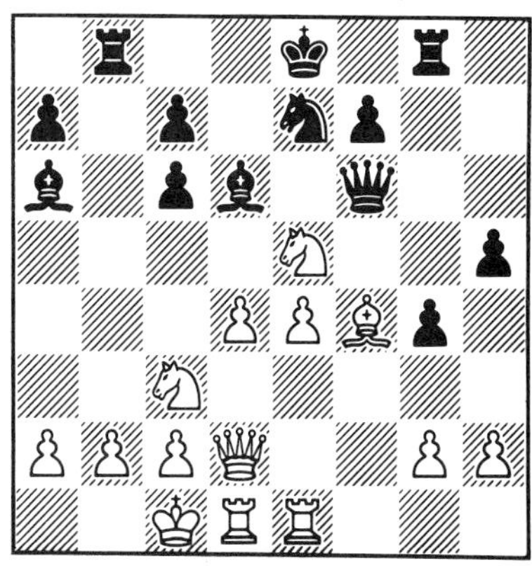

SENSORY CC9

Now CC9 has finished its development, in the most approved manner according to computer program heuristics. With the Black King stuck in the middle, this powerful centralization is most effective. **... h4** It is not easy to find a reasonable move for Black. **15 ♛e3 ♝b4 16 g3 ♛e6?! 17 gxh4 f6** Black thinks that the eviction of this Knight will be awkward for White, as indeed it would be after 18 ♘d3 ♗xc3 19 bxc3 ♕xa2. But CC9 has a surprise prepared.

PETERMEIER

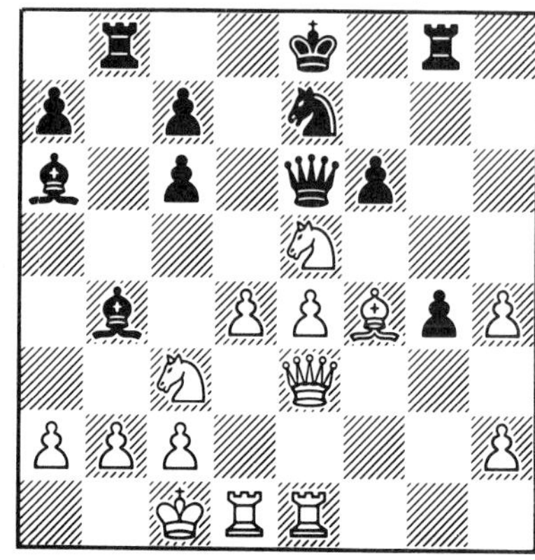

SENSORY CC9

18 d5! A decisive breakthrough. **18 ... cxd5 19 exd5 ♞xd5?** More resistance is offered by 19 ... ♕b6 20 ♘c6 and: a) ... ♗c5 21 ♕xe7+!! ♗xe7 22 ♖xe7+ ♔f8 23 ♘xb8 ♕xb8 24 ♖xc7 with a winning position for White; b) ... ♕xe3+ ♖xe3 and: b1) ... ♖b7 22 d6! cxd6 23 ♘d5 and wins; b2) ... ♖b6 22 ♘xb4 ♖xb4 23 d6 cxd6 24 ♖xe7+ ♔xe7 25 ♗xd6+. **20 ♞xd5 ♛c8 21 ♞xc7+! ♛xc7** Or a) ... ♔e7 22 ♘d7+ ♔f7 23 ♕e6+ any 24 ♕xf6+ any 25 ♕h6 mate: b) ... ♔f8 22 ♗h6+ ♖g7 23 ♘d7+ ♔g8 24 ♘xf6+ ♔f7 25 ♖d7+ etc. **22 ♞d7+** 1-0

Martha Petersen(1755) - PRESTIGE
English(A28)

Neither PRESTIGE nor its opponent show any signs of wanting to take the initiative in this game. The result is a placid draw.

1 c4 e5 2 ♞c3 ♞c6 3 d3 A very slow continuation. **... ♞f6 4 ♞f3 ♝b4 5 ♛c2** Another tame move. White is obviously not trying to create any particular problems for PRESTIGE in the opening. **... 0-0 6 a3**

PRESTIGE

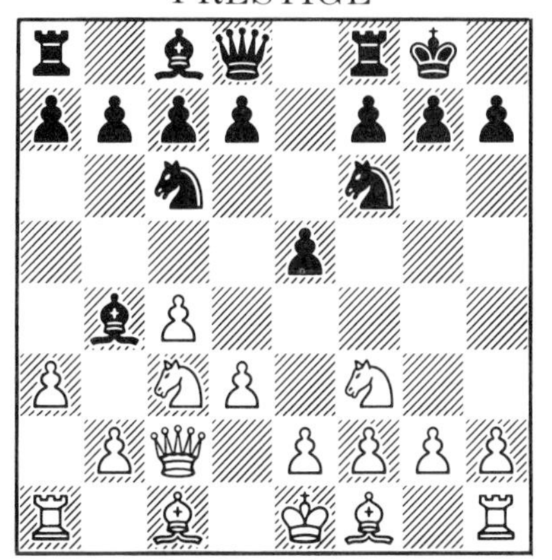

PETERSEN

6 ... ♗c5?! Loss of time; the program should have played ... ♗xc3 immediately, and then after 7 ♕xc3, PRESTIGE might have tried for the initiative by ... e4!?. The change in heuristics from its SARGON ancestors (which were too eager to trade Bishop for Knight) seems to have made the program a little too reluctant to give up its Bishops. It is not easy to find just the right balance, and the program also has no understanding of the value of a tempo or an initiative. **7 b4 ♘d4 8 ♘xd4 ♗xd4 9 e3 ♗xc3** So the program has had to make the exchange after all, and in the meantime White has gotten two tempi for development — offering chances for an initiative even in this closed position. **10 ♕xc3 ♖e8 11 ♗b2 d5 12 ♗e2 ♗f5 13 0-0 d4** PRESTIGE wisely blocks the long diagonal; otherwise the program would constantly have to deal with the threat of mate. **14 exd4?!** It would have been better to keep the e-file closed by 4 ♕c2, with some prospects for an advantage. **... exd4 15 ♕d2 ♕d6 16 ♗f3 ♘g4 17 ♗xg4** White could play for a win by 17 g3, but this weakens the Kingside. **17 ... ♗xg4 18 ♖fe1 ♔h8** PRESTIGE is constitutionally unable to form a plan, and since White isn't doing anything either, the program makes a waiting move. **19 f3 ♗f5 20 ♖ad1 ♖ad8** Monkey see, monkey do. **21 g4 ♗d7 22 ♕f2 ♗a4** Virtually forcing an exchange of both pairs of Rooks, after which the Bishops of opposite colors make the game very drawish. **23 ♖xe8+ ♖xe8 24 ♖e1 ♖xe1+ 25 ♕xe1**

PRESTIGE

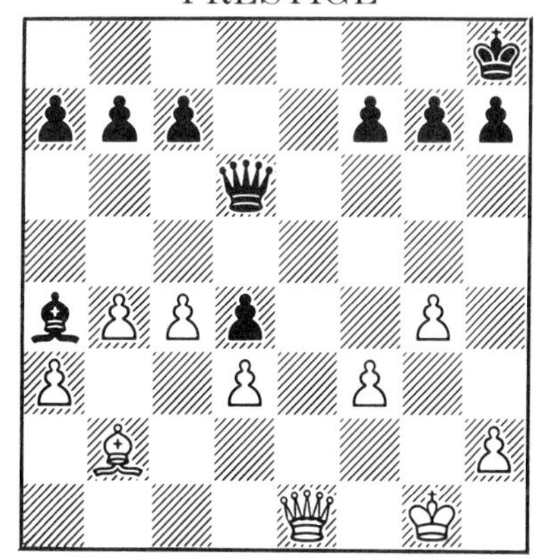

PETERSEN

25 ... ♔g8? PRESTIGE should play ... ♗d7 now. **26 c5?!** After 26 b5 trapping the Bishop, PRESTIGE would not be very happy! **... ♕f4 27 ♕e4** An invitation to a draw; after the exchange of Queens, neither side has any serious winning chances. **27 ... ♕e3+ 28 ♕xe3 dxe3 29 ♔f1 ♗d1 30 ♔g2 ♗c2 31 d4** Now everthing is locked up. **... c6 32 ♗c1 e2 33 ♔f2 ♗d3 34 ♗d2 ♔f8 35 f4 ♔e7 36 ♔e3 ♗c4 37 f5 g6** It looks as if PRESTIGE might have a heuristic encouraging it to put its Pawns on the opposite color squares from White's Bishop, but this is not the case — the program evidently has other reasons for doing so. **38 ♔f4 gxf5 39 ♔xf5 ♗d3+ 40 ♔f4 ♔e6 41 ♔e3 ♗b5 42 ♔e4 ♗c4 43 ♗e1 h6 44 ♗d2 f6** But a Bishop tied down by a Pawn about to Queen need not be feared at all. **45 h4 b6 46 ♗e1 ♗b5 47 ♗f2 ♗a6** 1/2 - 1/2

ROUND 12

Keith Smith(1883) - BELLE
Semi-Slav(D31)

Keith Smith had defeated PRESTIGE in Round 8, and used his experience to good advantage in this exciting and impressive victory over BELLE, which for the connoisseur of tactics is easily the game of the tournament. When the program weakens its King's position, Smith carefully starts to build up an attack — interrupting it for accurate defensive moves against BELLE's counterattacks, but slowly and steadily adding to the pressure. The program conjures up one threat after another in this extremely complicated game, but finally the threats run out and BELLE can no longer stave off the breakthrough.

1 d4 d5 2 c4 e6 3 ♞c3 c6 4 e4 dxe4 5 ♞xe4 ♝b4+ 6 ♞c3 ♞f6 ECO gives ... c5! with equality. It is strange to find BELLE deviating from a "book" line. **7 ♝e3 0-0 8 ♛c2 ♞g4!?** Typically aggressive play on the part of BELLE, which sees a chance to trade a Knight for a Bishop. The move is premature, and involves a loss of time; a more solid continuation is ... ♘bd7, playing for either ... e5 or ... c5. **9 ♞f3 ♞xe3 10 fxe3 c5** BELLE has freed its position, but White has the edge in development now and the program's Kingside nakedly invites attack. **11 0-0-0 ♛a5 12 ♝d3 ♝xc3**

Fig. 7.5 BELLE replies to Keith Smith's opening move.

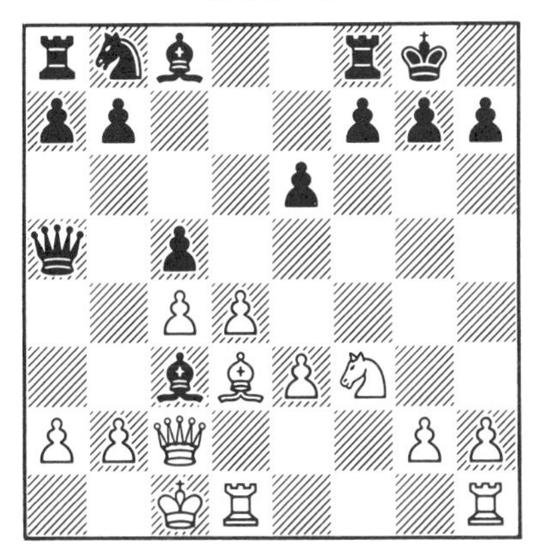

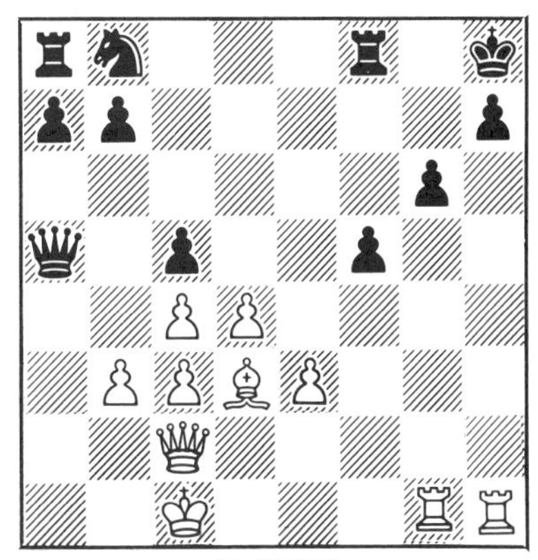

13 bxc3! Smith correctly values his attacking chances as good, and decides to keep the Queens on, although for the moment his own King is the more exposed. After 13 ♕xc3 ♕xa2? Black has grabbed a Pawn at the expense of time that can't be afforded; 14 ♗b1 ♕a6 15 g4! with an awe-inspiring attack. It might have been wise to go in for this after all, since BELLE would probably have grabbed the Pawn — such judgments are far beyond the capacity of present-day computer programs. **13 ... f5?** Creating a gaping hole at e5, and weakening the e-Pawn. BELLE has a distressing tendency to play this antipositional move, seen in several other games recorded earlier in this bok. It was better to play ... h6, although this invites a Pawnstorm. **14 g4! ♝d7** BELLE develops with tempo. **15 ♞d2** Not bad, but perhaps better was 15 ♖dg1 getting another piece into the attack and keeping the Knight on. **15 ... ♝a4 16 ♞b3 ♝xb3** It is desirable to exchange the Bishop on positional grounds, since it is obstructed by Black's Pawns, but this leaves BELLE with only its Queen developed. **17 axb3 g6** Virtually forced. **18 gxf5 exf5 19 ♜dg1 ♚h8 20 h4**

20 ... f4?! A purely tactical maneuver. BELLE does not realize that doom impends on the Kingside; this is too far away for any program (or human) to calculate the variations. Of course Black should play ... ♘c6, and hope that his King can hold the fort long enough for help to arrive. After 21 h5, though, Black's King position is likely to be ripped open even with accurate defense. **21 ♚b2!** BELLE's tactical threats are not to be taken lightly; 21 h5 fxe3 22 ♔b2 (22 hxg6 ♕a1+ 23 ♕b1 ♕xc3+ 24 ♗c2 cxd4 is unclear) ... ♖f2 23 ♗e2 cxd4 24 cxd4 ♘c6 and Black has taken the initiative. **... fxe3 22 ♜g2** Smith is in no hurry; the Black King is not going to run away, so first he takes some steps to secure his own position. **22 ... ♜f6?!** BELLE refuses to develop its Queenside. Here ... ♘c6 threatening 23 ... cxd4 was far better; if 23 d5, the Knight gleefully occupies e5. **23 h5 ♜a6** Threatening mate, and once more forcing White to delay his own attack to deal with the threat. But BELLE is getting its pieces further away from its King, not closer. **24 ♛b1 cxd4 25 cxd4 gxh5 26 d5** Finally White gets back on the attack.**... ♞d7 27 ♜xh5 ♞f6 28 ♜h3 ♛a3+ 29 ♚c2**

BELLE

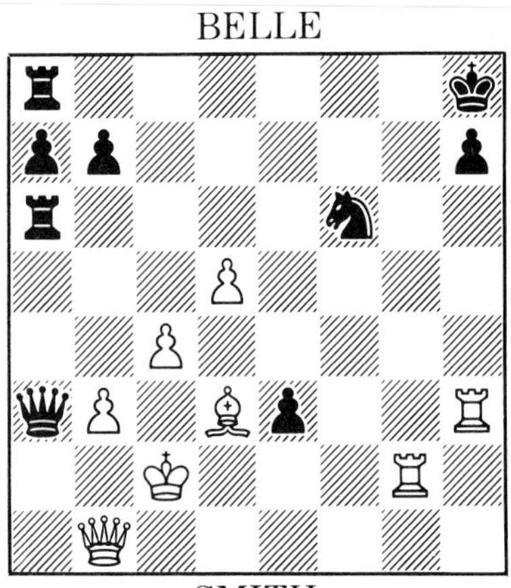

SMITH

29 ... b5? BELLE's last opportunity (more than the program deserved) to hold the position was ... ♕a2+ forcing an exchange of Queens. After 30 ♕b2 ♕xb2+ 31 ♔xb2 ♖g8 it is not clear how White can force an immediate decision, or even whether White has an advantage. **30 ♛h1!** Now Smith's attack can no longer be denied. **... ♛a2+ 31 ♚c3 ♛a5+ 32 ♚d4** A fearless King! **... ♛c7 33 ♝xh7!** The attack requires precise play, e.g. 33 ♖h2? ♕f4+ 34 ♔c3 b4+! 35 ♔c2 (35 ♔xb4? ♘xd5+ and a) 36 ♔c5 ♖c8+ 37 ♔xd5 ♖d6 mate; b) 36 ♔b5 ♖b8+ 37 ♔xa6 ♕d6+ 38 ♔a5 ♕a3 mate; 35 ♔b2 ♕d4+ 36 ♔c1 ♕c3+ 37 ♔d1 ♕xd3+ 38 any ♖a1 mate). Now the King has a necessary flight square, and can face BELLE's checks with confidence. **36 ... ♞xh7** Now, however, ... ♕f4+ does not work, because of 37 ♗e4 discovered check. **34 ♜xh7+ ♛xh7 35 ♜h2 ♛xh2 36 ♛xh2+ ♚g8** BELLE has gotten two Rooks for its Queen, and is technically even materially after White captures the e-Pawn. But White's passed Pawns are immediately decisive. **37 ♛g3+ ♚h8 38 ♛e5+ ♚g8 39 c5 ♜a1 40 ♛xe3 a6 41 d6 ♜f8 42 ♚d5 ♜af1** Now its Rooks are united, and BELLE seems capable of making some difficulties. At this point, the program's evaluation function still thought it was doing all right! **43 ♛g5+ ♚h7 44 ♚c6 ♜8f6 45 ♚c7 ♜1f5 46 ♛xf6!** Putting a stop to all this nonsense. **... ♜xf6 47 d7** 1-0

Fig. 7.6 Keith Smith played a very fine game against BELLE.

CHAOS - Edward Stackpole(1701)
Queen's Gambit Declined(D63)

In this game CHAOS gets a large but not immediately decisive positional advantage, and maintains the pressure on its opponent's position with the patience (if not the skill) of a Petrosian. Its unfortunate opponent, subjected to the exquisite torment of utter boredom, eventually cracks.

1 d4 ♞f6 2 c4 e6 3 ♞c3 d5 4 ♝g5 ♞bd7 5 e3 ♝e7 6 ♞f3 0-0 7 ♜c1 After some transpositions, the opening has developed as the main line of the Queen's Gambit Declined. **... b6** The "Old Orthodox" variation — today considered unpromising for Black. **8 cxd5!** The refutation, ensuring that Black's Queen's Bishop gets no open diagonal. **... exd5** Capturing with the Knight loses at least a Pawn. **9 ♝b5 ♝b7 10 0-0 c6?!** ECO gives ... a6; Black should aim at playing ... c5. **11 ♝d3 ♜e8 12 ♛c2 h6 13 ♝f4 ♞f8 14 h3** CHAOS has a more positional style than most programs. This move ensures that White's Queen's Bishop will only be exchanged for its Black counterpart, not for his Knight. **... ♝d6 15 ♝xd6 ♛xd6 16 ♜fe1 ♜ac8?! 17 ♝f5.** White's significant advantage is now clear; a strong Bishop vs. a bad one, and strong pressure on the c-file. **... ♜cd8 18 ♛a4 ♛b8 19 ♞e5** CHAOS is playing the positional attack very well, although it is not difficult to find these moves. **... ♜d6 20 ♜e2 ♞8d7 21 ♞xd7** This is better than 21 f4, after which White's e-Pawn is potentially weak and limits the Knight on e5. **... ♞xd7 22 ♜ec2 ♞f6 23 b4!** Both preventing ... c5 , and also threatening b5 in some variations. **23 ... g6?!** Another weakness; but the Bishop is so strong as to be almost intolerable, and cannot be countered by ... ♗c8, which loses a Pawn after the exchange on c8. **24 ♝d3 ♜c8 25 ♞e2**

STACKPOLE

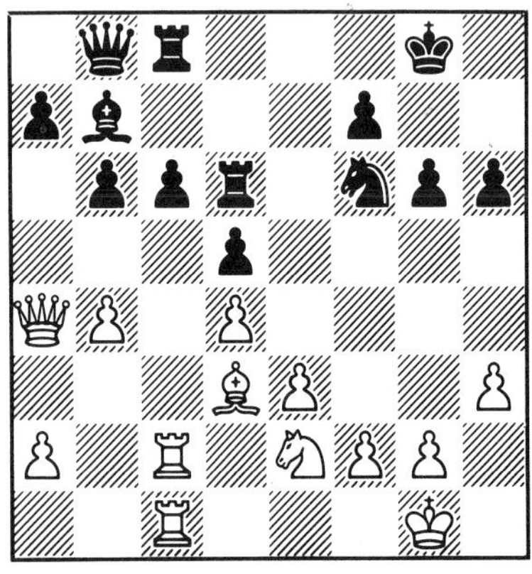

CHAOS

25 ... b5? Permanently fixing the weakness on c6. Positionally, Black's eventual doom is now almost assured. **26 ♛b3 ♜e6** Here Black should try to play the standard maneuver in such situations: ... ♘d7-b6-c4, and the Knight shields the Pawn weakness. CHAOS could counter that, however, by 27 a4!. **27 ♞f4 ♜ee8 28 ♝e2 ♚g7 29 a3 a6 30 ♚h1 h5?!** Apparently Stackpole thought all his pieces were optimally placed, and elected to make a waiting move. Black should have played ... ♘e4 here. **31 ♞d3** CHAOS is displaying an impressive (by computer standards) capacity for maneuvering its pieces,but Black will not let the Knight into c5 or e5. **... ♞d7 32 ♞f4 ♞f6?** Here and later, Black misses the opportunity to play ... ♘b6-c4, with prospects for eventually equalizing after ... ♗c8. **33 ♞d3 ♞d7 34 ♛b2 ♛d6 35 ♞f4 ♞f6? 36 ♚g1 ♛b8 37 ♞d3 ♞d7 38 ♞f4 ♞f6? 39 ♞d3 ♞d7 40 ♛b3 ♛d6 41 ♞f4 ♞f6? 42 ♝d3 ♛b8 43 ♝e2 ♛d6 44 ♝d3 ♛b8 45 ♛c3 ♛d6 46 ♝e2 ♝a8 47 ♛d3 ♝b7 48 ♛b3 ♝a8 49 ♛d3 ♝b7 50 ♛b3 ♝a8 51 ♝d3 ♝b7 52 ♛a2 ♝a8 53 ♜c3 ♝b7 54 ♛c2**

STACKPOLE

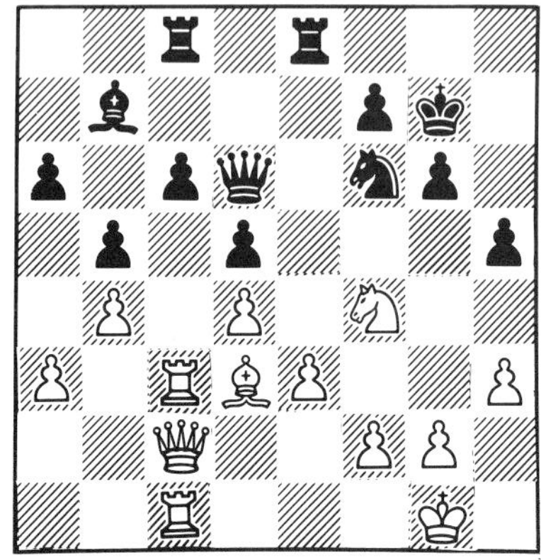

CHAOS

After some 20 moves of shuffling wood, during which the program several times flirted with a threefold repetition, CHAOS finally discerns a way to put some additional pressure on the Black position. This threatens 55 ♗xg6. **... ♞e4?** Playing right into the program's hands. After 54 ... ♘d7, White has to try another tack. **55 ♝xe4!** Now CHAOS can get its Knight to c5, after which something must fall. **... ♜xe4** If 55 ... dxe4 then 56 d5! wins (56 ... g5 57 ♘xh5+ and the d-Pawn is still immune). **56 ♞d3 ♜e7 57 ♞c5 ♝a8** Otherwise, White simply exchanges on b7 and then captures the c-Pawn, but this may have been relatively better for Black since the Knight is so much stronger than the Bishop. **58 ♞xa6 ♜a7 59 ♞c5 ♚f8 60 ♚h1** More waiting moves; CHAOS takes a painfully long time to find a plan, but then it's remarkable that the program can find one at all. **... ♚g7 61 ♚g1 ♚f8 62 ♚h1 ♚g7 63 f3 ♜e8 64**

♕d2 ♖d8?! A move accomplishing nothing. Black could at least double on the e-file. **65 ♕f2 ♔h6 6 ♕h4 ♕e7 67 ♕f2 ♕d6 68 ♕h4 ♕e7 69 ♕g3 ♕d6 70 ♕xd6** Correct; Black's Queen is a major obstacle to further progress. **... ♖xd6 71 h4 ♖d8 72 ♔g1 ♔g7 73 ♔f2 ♔f6 74 ♘d3 ♖a6 75 ♔g1** Again, CHAOS is unable to find any kind of plan, and plays a waiting move. At this kind of game, the program is unbeatable — its patience is infinite. **... ♔e7 76 ♘c5 ♖a7 77 ♔f2 ♔f6 78 ♘d3 ♖a6 79 ♔g1 ♔e7 80 ♖1c2 ♔f8 81 ♔f1 ♔e7 82 ♔f2 ♔f6 83 ♘e5 ♖d6 84 ♘d3 ♖d8 85 ♘e5 ♖d6 86 ♖c1 ♔g7 87 ♘d3**

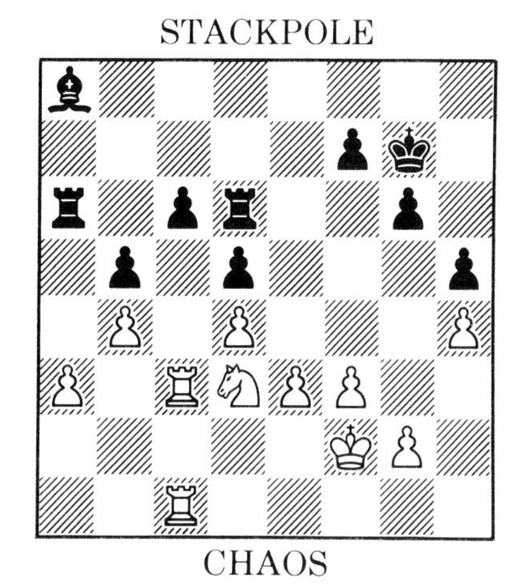

87 ... ♔f6? Bored into a stupor by this

Fig. 7.7 Fide Master Boris Baczynskyj (Chess Advisor to Fidelity Electronics) ponders his position.

woodpushing, Stackpole makes a fatal mistake. ... ♔f8 would have prolonged the piece-shuffling. **88 ♞c5 ♜a7 89 e4!** Finally the program has managed to maneuver its opponent into a position where this break is possible, and his position collapses. **... ♜d8 90 e5+ ♚e7 91 g3 f6 92 e6 ♜d6 93 g4 ♜d8 94 gxh5 gxh5 95 ♜g1** 1-0

SENSORY CC9 - Edward J. Conway (1617)
Sokolsky's Opening(A00)

In this inaccurately played game, CC9 got itself in trouble as early as the third move(!), and on the ninth move made an error that should have speedily cost it the game. Conway missed one opportunity after another to drive home a mating attack, and finally allowed an exchange of Queens, after which the advantage suddently shifted to the program, which went on to win the endgame.

1 b4 ♞f6 2 ♞f3 e6 3 ♝a3? The program is obviously out of its "book"; ECO gives 3 a3 and 3 b5. **... d5 4 e3 ♝d6 5 ♝e2 ♛e7 6 c3** The evil consequences of CC9's 3rd move are now apparent. **... e5 7 0-0 0-0 8 d4 e4 9 ♞g5?** Another obvious error; CC9 was not at its best in this game. Computer programs tend to make such pseudo-attacking Knight moves wth distressing regularity, driven by the bonuses from their King tropism and mobility heuristics. The Knight should, of course, go to d2, where it could support an eventual c4. Altering the mobility scoring heuristic to allow the program to play this move would have other and incalculable effects on its play and would probably do more harm than good — such are the problems faced by the programmer trying to improve the play of a program using fixed heuristics. **... h6 10 ♞h3 ♝h3 11 gxh3 ♞h7**

CONWAY

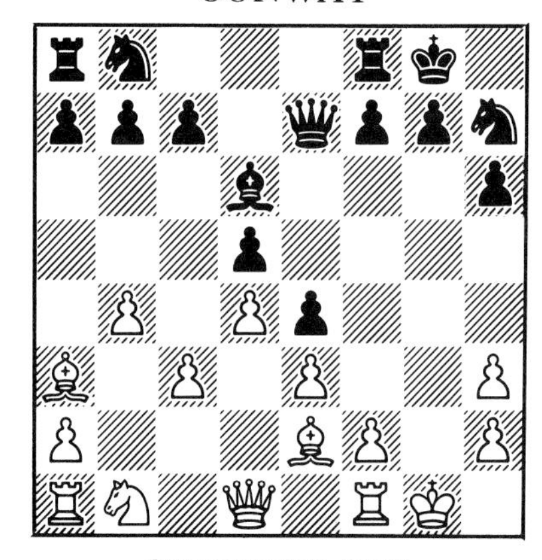

SENSORY CC9

Now White's King is exposed to the elements, and should by rights have died of exposure very swiftly. **12 ♞d2 ♞d7** It's difficult to criticize Black for developing his pieces, but ♕h4 demolishes White right away after 13 ♗g4 f5, or 13 ♔g2 ♘g5 14 ♗g4 f5. **13 ♛b3 c6 14 c4 ♛h4 15 ♝g4 ♞df6?** Too slow! After ... f5! White is again crushed: 16 cxd5 fxg4 17 dxc6+ ♔h8 18 cxd7 ♕xh3 and mate follows. **16 b5 ♝xa3** Black insists on being timid, and passes up a multitude of winning attacking continuations. One crushing line is ... ♗xh2+ 17 ♔xh2 (if 17 ♔h1 or ♔g2, 17 ... ♘xg4) ♘xg4+ 18 ♔g2 ♘g5 19 hxg4 (19 ♖h1 ♕xf2 mate) ♕h3+ 20 ♔g1 ♘f3+ 21 ♘xf3 exf3 22 any ♕g2 mate. **17 ♛xa3 dxc4?!** It is unclear whether Black took pity on CC9 at this point and thus refrained from ... h5 winning the h-Pawn and the game. **18 bxc6 bxc6 19 ♝e2 ♞g5 20 ♜ab1 ♞xh3+ 21 ♚g2 ♞g5?!** Still too slow although this should still win; quicker is ... ♘g4 22 ♗xg4 (22 ♘xe4 ♘f4+ 23 ♔f3 ♘xh2 mate) ♕xg4+ 23 ♔h1 ♕e2 and wins, although more laboriously than in earlier variations. **22 ♞xc4 ♞f3 23 ♛d6 ♜fd8** Black continues to miss opportunities; ... ♘h5 threatening ...

♖d8 keeps the attack alive, though the outcome is unclear after 24 ♗xf3 exf3+ 25 ♔xf3. **24 ♛g3 ♛xg3+ 25 hxg3 ♞g5 26 ♞e5**

CONWAY

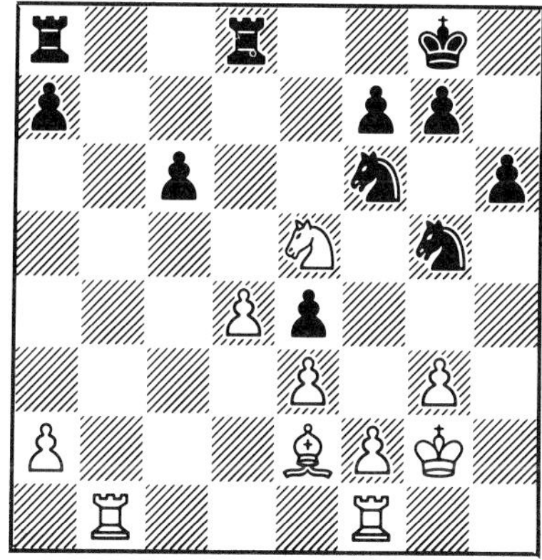

SENSORY CC9

But now it is a new game and CC9 holds all the advantages, with its superior Pawn structure, strong Bishop, and active Rook. **... ♜dc8 27 ♝a6 ♜c7 28 ♝b7 ♜b8 29 ♝xc6 ♜b6?** This creates another weak Pawn. **30 ♜xb6 axb6 31 ♜b1 ♜a7 32 a4 ♚f8 33 ♜xb6 ♞e6 34 ♚f1 ♚e7 35 a5!** CC9 thinks so highly of Rooks on the 7th rank that it is apparently willing to give up its passed a-Pawn to get one. **... ♞d8** Had Black accepted the offer, the result would have been painful after 35 ... ♖xa5 36 ♖b7+ and: a) ... ♔d6 37 ♘c4+ ♔xc6 38 ♘xa5+; b) ... ♔d8 37 ♘xf7+ ♔c8 38 d5 ♘xd5 39 ♘d6+ ♔d8 40 ♖d7 mate. **36 a6 ♚d6?** Black thinks that CC9 can't take the Pawn since it involves losing the Exchange. **37 ♝xe4+!** All this for a mere Exchange? CC9 grabs it instantly.

Fig. 7.8 Sensory CC9 considers its 14th move against a really dedicated tournament player, Edward J. Conway.

... ♚c7 38 ♜b7+ ♞xb7 39 ♝xb7 Now the Rook is a pathetic sight indeed, and the program can recover the Exchange at any time by ♘c6. **... ♞e8 40 ♞xf7 ♚b6 41 ♞d8 ♞d6 42 ♚g2** CC9 is playing with Black like a cat with a mouse. If now ... ♘xb7 (thinking to get out of the trap), 43 axb7 ♔c7 44 b8(♕)+ ♔xb8 45 ♘c6+ **... ♚c7 43 ♞c6 ♜xb7 44 axb7 ♞xb7 45 d5** The ending is now an easy win. **... ♚d6 46 e4 ♞c5 47 ♚f3 ♞d3 48 ♚e3 ♞c5 49 ♞d4 ♚e5 50 f4+ ♚f6 51 e5+ ♚e7 52 ♞f5+ ♚f7 53 e6+ ♞xe6** On ... ♔f6, 54 e7 ♔f7 55 d6 and there's no defense against the combined threats of ♘g7 and d7. **54 dxe6+ ♚xe6 55 ♞xg7+ ♚f6 56 ♞h5+ ♚g6 57 g4** 1-0

Michael Wangen(1755) - PRESTIGE
English(A28)

PRESTIGE achieved a fine game out of the opening, in spite of some inaccuracies, but allowed the middle game to drift into a locked position. Just at the point where a draw seemed inevitable, White made a crucial blunder, allowing PRESTIGE's Knight to hop all around his position, picking up a Pawn and an Exchange. The program should then have had an easy win, but did not know what to do with its

Fig. 7.9 "Computer Corner" — the two Fidelity entries and BELLE played in one corner of the main hall; CHAOS played its games in Fred Swartz's hotel room because its moves had to be telephoned in.

advantage, and allowed White's Bishops to dominate the position. After the game had drifted along for a while in this uneasy balance, PRESTIGE finally spotted a chance to sacrifice the Exchange and win several Pawns in the process, which quickly proved decisive.

1 c4 e5 2 ♞c3 ♞c6 3 ♞f3 ♞f6 4 d4 e4 5 ♞d2 ♝b4 5 ... ♘xd4 leads to equality, according to ECO. PRESTIGE is already out of its "book". **6 e3 d6 7 ♝e2 0-0 8 0-0 ♝f5** Now PRESTIGE once again shows that the balance of its Bishop vs. Knight heuristic has been tilted too far in favor of the Bishop. Here, and for several moves to come, the obvious continuation is ... ♗xc3, doubling White's Pawns and getting rid of a badly placed piece. It is difficult to balance the relative value of minor pieces satisfactorily, however; so long as the program is constrained to use fixed values without the ability to actually calculate the effectiveness of a piece in a given position, it is bound to go wrong at times. **9 ♛b3 ♜e8 10 h3 a5 11 a4 ♛d7 12 ♚h2 ♚h8** PRESTIGE shows that it does not know what to do. The machine is unable to form plans in the way a human player would, for example a Kingside Pawnstorming attack —which would be impossible because of its King safety heuristic, anyway. **13 f3 exf3 14 ♞xf3 ♞e4 15 ♞h4 ♝xc3** Now the exchange is virtually forced. **16 bxc3** 16 ♘xf5 seems more promising. **... ♞e7 17 g4** Of course the b-Pawn is not just innocently sitting there en prise, and were White to swallow it, he would expire instantly from a lethal dose of cyanide after ... ♖eb8. **... ♝g6 18 ♞xg6+ ♞xg6 19 ♝d3 c5** Although White has the two Bishops, Black is better because his Knights are active — while White's King position is weakened, and his center is none too mobile. **20 ♜a2 f6 21 d5?** A positional mistake. White's center is strong, if immobile with the Pawn on d4; when it's on d5 everything becomes weak, as Nimzovich showed long ago. **... ♜e5 22 ♜b2 ♜b8 23 ♛c2 ♜be8 24 ♜b5 ♛c7 25 ♜f5 ♜5e7 26 ♜f1 ♚g8** Unable to form a plan, the program makes a waiting move to see what White will do. **27 ♛b2 ♞g5 28 ♛b1 ♞e5** One has the feeling that a human player would have found a way to arrange his pieces during the last few moves so as to be able to play ... f5 or h5 to get at White's King, even if this involved giving up a Pawn on the Queenside; the program of course, is unable to formulate this kind of plan. **29 ♝e2 ♞g6**

PRESTIGE

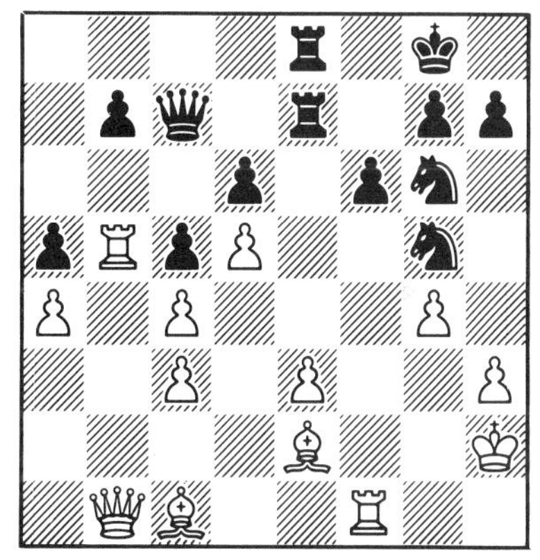

WANGEN

Although PRESTIGE holds some positional trumps, its position is rather restricted, and were White content to shuffle his Bishop between e2 and d3, it is not clear how the program could make progress. But now White blunders: **30 ♚g3?** Losing the Exchange and Pawn, as well as White's positional pressure. **... ♞e4+ 31 ♚h2 ♞xc3 32 ♛c2 ♞xb5 33 axb5 ♜e5** The simplest way to win is to sacrifice back the Exchange to win another Pawn, by ... ♖xe3. Then Black should have an easy win in the ending. Now the program allows White's Bishops to become strong. **34 ♝d3 ♛f7 35 ♜f3 ♚h8** Again PRESTIGE does not know what to do. **36 ♚g3 b6 37 h4 ♜5e7 38 ♝f5 ♞e5 39 ♝e6 ♛g6** Again, the sacrifice of the Exchange by ... ♖xe6 is simplest. **40 ♝f5 ♛h6 41 e4 g5 42 hxg5 fxg5 43 ♝b2** All this, of course, has been quite unfavorable for the program and quite unnecessary. **43... ♛h1 44 ♜f2 ♜a7 45 ♛d2 ♜g7 46 ♛e3 ♛g1+ 47 ♚h3 ♛b1** At this point, PRESTIGE could have made things unpleasant for White by ...h5!, e.g. 48 gxh5? g4+ 49 ♔h4 ♕h1+ 50 ♔g3 ♕h3+ 51 ♔f4 ♘d3+ etc. **48 ♛d2 ♜ee7 49 ♝e6 ♛h1+ 50 ♚g3 ♛h4+ 51 ♚g2**

PRESTIGE

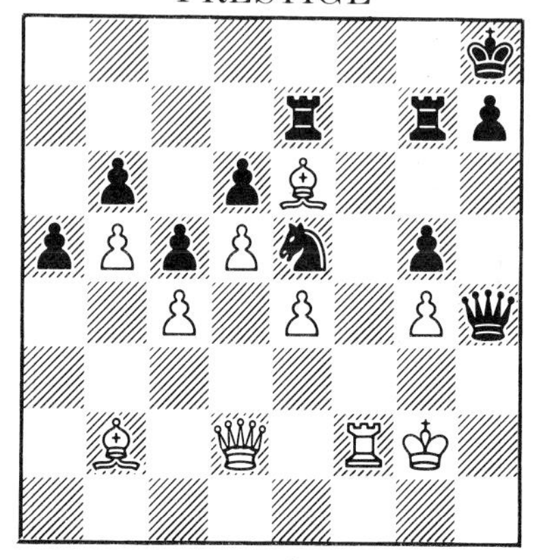

WANGEN

51 ... ♜xe6! Finally PRESTIGE sees that it can collect enough Pawns to make the Exchange sacrifice attractive, even to its materialist viewpoint. **52 dxe6 ♛xg4+ 53 ♚h2 ♛h4+ 54 ♚g2 ♛xe4+ 55 ♚g1 ♛g4+ 56 ♚h2 ♛h4+ 57 ♚g1 ♛g3+ 58 ♚f1 ♛h3+ 59 ♚g1 ♛xe6** White will not fall into any various Knight forks, so the program grabs yet another Pawn. **60 ♜f8+ ♜g8 61 ♜xg8+ ♚xg8 62 ♛xg5+ ♛g6** 0-1

8
U.S. SPEED CHAMPIONSHIP 1982

This event consisted of a number of preliminary qualifying round-robin sections, from each of which the top two finishers were seeded into the final Swiss-system tournament. In the finals two games (alternate colors) were played at each pairing, except for some players paired with BELLE (no sensory board) which took too long to play its games — so some of BELLE's games were worth 2 points.

PRELIMINARIES

	ROUND	1	2	3	4	5	6
	opponent	Andy Unger	David Marshall	Eugene Kerkay	BYE	Tom Ward	John Meyer
BELLE	rtg	1980	2033	2097		2238	2445
(2161)	clr-res	B-1	W-1	B-1		W-1	B-½
	opponent	Thomas Fineberg	Pat Long	John Greene	BYE	George Kraus	Philip Wong
CHESS 4.9	rtg	1667	1862	2202		2203	2072
(2060)	clr-res	W-0	B-1	W-1		W-1	W-1
	opponent	Kees Hoogendijk	Ali Shahin	James Davis	Fred Lindsay	Russell Miller	Peter Thompson
CRAY BLITZ	rtg	U/R	1773	U/R	2289	1722	2338
(U/R)	clr-res	W-0	B-1	W-1	B-0	W-1	W-0
	opponent	Gerry Mortimer	Don Griffith	Erik Olson	Curt Brasket	Hugh Myers	Jerry Hanken
PRESTIGE	rtg	2034	2109	1092	2396	2152	2255
(U/R)	clr-res	B-0	W-1	B-1	B-0	W-1	B-0

PRELIMINARIES

	ROUND	7	8	9	TOTAL	PLACE	PERF. RTG
BELLE	opponent	Alan Haas	Stu Robb	Roy Knuth			
(2161)	rtg	1469	1696	1787	7½	FINALIST	2412
	clr-res	W-1	B-1	W-1			
CHESS 4.9	opponent	Ron Finegold	Erwin Heisler	John Watson			
(2060)	rtg	2187	1917	2503	6	FINALIST	2202
	clr-res	B-1	W-1	B-0			
CRAY BLITZ	opponent	Ron Elmquist	Randall Hough	David Ratliff			
(U/R)	rtg	2135	2130	2022	5	--	2108
	clr-res	B-0	W-1	B-1			
PRESTIGE	opponent	Mark Zuilius	Chip Kraft	Tunc Alankus			
(U/R)	rtg	1994	1785	2025	3	--	1856
	clr-res	W-0	B-0	W-0			

FINALS

	opponent	Mark Diesen	Benjamin Finegold	John Meyer	Peter Thompson	Dan Shapiro
BELLE	rtg	2483	2088	2445	2338	2364
(2161)	result	0-2	2-0	1-1	2-0	2-0
	opponent	Peter Thompson	Paul Rejto	Fred Lindsay	Dan Shapiro	John Meyer
CHESS 4.9	rtg	2338	2133	2289	2364	2445
(2060)	result	0-2	1-1	2-0	2-0	0-2

	SCORE	PLACE	PERF RTG
BELLE	7-3	2-5	2494
CHESS 4.9	5-5	10-12	2314

Fig. 8.1 Crowd control for the computer games was a real problem during the 1982 U.S. Open Speed Championship.

The U.S. Open Speed Championship was played on Saturday, August 14 — no regular tournament games were played that day because of the USCF Delegates' Meeting.

The results of the 1982 U.S. Open Speed Championship indicate that mainframe Chess programs are very strong at speed chess, confirming the results of a number of previous man-machine speed chess games in which the programs defeated titled players. CRAY BLITZ was suffering from program "bugs" and did not play up to its usual standard. PRESTIGE appeared to maintain its rating at tournament speed.

Fig. 8.2 Sid Samole, President of Fidelity Electronics, observes one of PRESTIGE Chess Challenger's games in the U.S. Open Speed Championship.

Games by CHESS 4.9 and CRAY BLITZ were unfortunately not "saved" when the computers unloaded the programs. BELLE's games in this event illustrate the type of play characterizing all 3 programs.

Speed chess, which is normally played using a regular chess clock and with each player having five minutes to make all his moves—the first to run out of time loses—is an entertaining spectacle and fun for the players, but the games of course are not of the same quality as regular tournament games. Tactical blunders are common. Accordingly, these games are given without annotations.

Fig. 8.3 CRAY BLITZ vs. David Ratliff

BELLE'S GAMES IN THE U.S. OPEN SPEED CHAMPIONSHIP

PRELIMINARIES

Andy Unger(1980) - BELLE
Four Knights' Game

1 e4 e5 2 ♘f3 ♘c6 3 ♘c3 ♘f6 4 d4 exd4 5 ♘d5 ♗e7 6 ♗f4 d6 7 ♘xd4 ♘xd5 8 exd5 ♘xd4 9 ♕xd4 ♗f6 10 ♕e4+ ♗e7 11 0-0-0 ♗d7 12 ♗d3 f5 13 ♕e2 0-0 14 h4 ♗xh4 15 ♕h5 g5 16 g3 ♗e8 17 ♕e2 gxf4 18 ♖xh4 fxg3 19 ♕e6+ ♖f7 20 ♖dh1 g2 21 ♖xh7 ♕g5+ 22 ♔b1 g1(♕)+ 0-1

BELLE - David Marshall(2033)
Queen's Fianchetto Defence

1 e4 b6 2 d4 ♗b7 3 ♗d3 ♘c6 4 ♘f3 g6 5 ♘c3 ♗g7 6 d5 ♘b8 7 ♗g5 h6 8 ♗f4 ♘f6 9 ♖b1 0-0 10 ♕d2 ♔h7 11 e5 ♘h5 12 ♗e3 ♗h8 13 ♗xh6 ♘a6 14 ♗xf8 ♕xf8 15 ♕g5 ♘b4 16 ♕xh5+ ♔g8 17 ♕g4 ♘xd5 18 ♘xd5 ♗xd5 19 ♕xd7 c6 20 ♗e2 a5 21 c4 ♗xf3 22 ♗xf3 ♗xe5 23 ♕xc6 ♖b8 24 0-0 ♔g7 25 c5 b5 26 b4 a4 27 ♗e2 ♗xh2+ 28 ♔xh2 ♕h8+ 29 ♔g3 ♕d8 30 ♗xb5 ♕d2 31 ♗xa4 ♕g5+ 32 ♔f3 ♖d8 33 ♖fd1 ♕f5+ 34 ♔e3 ♕g5+ 35 f4 1-0

Eugene Kerkay(2097) - BELLE
Reti System

1 ♘f3 d5 2 c4 e6 3 b3 ♘f6 4 ♗b2 ♗e7 5 g3 0-0 6 ♗g2 a5 7 a3 a4 8 cxd5 axb3 9 dxe6 ♗xe6 10 0-0 ♘c6 11 ♘c3 ♖a5 12 d4 ♗c4 13 ♖e1 b5 14 e3 b4 15 axb4 ♖xa1 16 ♕xa1 ♘xb4 17 ♕a4 ♕e8 18 ♘d2 ♕xa4 19 ♘xa4 ♘d3 20 ♖b1 ♗e6 21 ♗f1 ♘xb2 22 ♖xb2 ♖b8 23 ♘c5 ♗xc5 24 dxc5 ♖a8 25 ♖b1 ♖b8 26 ♗c4 ♗xc4 27 ♘xc4 ♘e4 28 c6 ♘c3 29 ♖b2 ♘a4 30 ♖b1 b2 31 ♔g2 f6 32 ♔f3 ♖b4 33 ♘xb2 ♘xb2 34 ♔e2 ♔f7 35 ♖a1 ♖c4 36 ♖a2 ♖c2+ 37 ♔f3 ♔e6 38 g4 ♔d6 39 h4 ♔xc6 40 ♔g3 ♔d5 41 h5 h6 42 f4 ♔e4 43 g5 fxg5 44 fxg5 hxg5 45 ♖a5 ♘d1 46 ♖xg5 ♘xe3 0-1

BELLE - Tom Ward(2238)
Modern Defence

1 e4 g6 2 d4 d6 3 c4 ♗g7 4 ♘c3 ♘c6 5 ♗e3 e5 6 d5 ♘d4 7 ♘ge2 ♘xe2 8 ♗xe2 ♘e7 9 g4 0-0 10 g5 f5 11 gxf6 ♗xf6 12 h4 ♔h8 13 h5 g5 14 c5 ♘g8 15 ♖g1 ♘h6 16 f3 ♖g8 17 ♕b3 ♕e8 18 ♘b5 ♕xh5 19 ♘xc7 ♖b8 20 cxd6 ♕h2 21 ♘a6 ♖a8 22 ♘c5 ♖d8 23 d7 ♗xd7 24 ♕xb7 ♖ab8 25 ♕a6 ♘g8 26 ♘xd7 ♖xd7 27 0-0-0 ♖b6 28 ♗xb6 axb6 29 ♔b1 ♖c7 30 ♕xb6 ♖c8 31 ♕b7 ♖c5 32 ♖h1 1-0

Fig. 8.4 Control Data Corporation entered CHESS 4.9 in the U.S. Open Speed Championship.

John Meyer(2445) - BELLE
Queen's Gambit Declined

1 d4 d5 2 c4 e6 3 ♘c3 c6 4 e3 ♘f6 5 ♘f3 ♘bd7 6 ♗d3 dxc4 7 ♗xc4 b5 8 ♗e2 a6 9 0-0 ♗b7 10 a4 b4 11 ♘b1 c5 12 ♘bd2 ♗e7 13 ♘c4 ♖c8 14 b3 cxd4 15 ♘xd4 ♘e4 16 ♗b2 ♘c3 17 ♗xc3 bxc3 18 ♖c1 ♗b4 19 ♘c2 ♕g5 20 ♗f3 ♗xf3 21 ♕xf3 ♗e7 22 ♖fd1 ♘c5 23 ♘b6 0-0 24 ♘xc8 ♖xc8 25 b4 ♘xa4 26 ♕b7 ♖f8 27 ♕xa6 ♘b2 28 ♖d7 ♗f6 29 b5 ♕f5 30 b6 e5 31 ♖a7 ♘d3 32 ♖a8 ♗e7 33 b7 ♕xf2+ 34 ♔h1 ♘xc1 35 ♖xf8+ ♗xf8 36 b8(♕) e4 37 h3 ♘e2 38 ♕a1 ♘g3+ 39 ♔h2 ♘f1+ 1/2 - 1/2

BELLE - Alan Haas(1469)
Ruy Lopez

1 e4 e5 2 ♘f3 ♘c6 3 ♗b5 a6 4 ♗a4 b5 5 ♗b3 d6 6 ♘c3 ♘f6 7 ♘g5 ♗e6 8 ♘xe6 fxe6 9 ♗xe6 ♘d4 10 ♗b3 ♗e7 11 0-0 ♘xb3 12 axb3 0-0 13 d3 ♕d7 14 ♗g5 ♖f7 15 ♗xf6 ♗xf6 16 ♘d5 ♖af8 17 d4 c6 18 ♘xf6+ ♖xf6 19 dxe5 ♖g6 20 ♔h1 ♕e6 21 f4 dxe5 22 f5 ♕f6 23 fxg6 ♕xg6 24 ♖xf8+ ♔xf8 25 ♕d8+ ♔f7 26 ♖f1+ ♔e6 27 ♕g8+ ♔d6 28 ♖d1+ ♔c5 29 b4+ ♔xb4 30 c3+ ♔a5 31 b4+ ♔b6 32 ♕b8 mate 1-0

Fig. 8.5 Kathe Spracklen operated BELLE during the speed tournament, since its regular operator (Dave Cahlander of Control Data) was running CHESS 4.9.

Stu Robb(1696) - BELLE
Queen's Gambit Declined

1 d4 d5 2 c4 e6 3 ♘c3 c6 4 cxd5 exd5 5 ♘f3 ♗d6 6 e3 ♘f6 7 ♗d3 ♗g4 8 0-0 ♘bd7 9 h3 ♗xf3 10 ♕xf3 ♗b4 11 a3 ♗xc3 12 bxc3 0-0 13 ♖b1 b5 14 a4 bxa4 15 ♗a3 ♖e8 16 c4 ♘e4 17 ♕e2 ♘c3 18 ♕c2 ♘xb1 19 ♗xh7+ ♔h8 20 ♖xb1 g6 21 ♗xg6 fxg6 22 ♕xg6 ♕f6 23 ♕h5+ ♔g8 24 ♕g4+ ♕g7 25 ♕f4 ♖ab8 26 ♖xb8 ♖xb8 27 ♕c7 ♖b3 28 ♗d6 ♖b1+ 29 ♔h2 dxc4 30 ♕d8+ ♘f8 31 ♕e8 ♖b6 32 ♕d8 c3 33 ♗c5 c2 34 ♗a3 ♖b1 35 ♕c8 c1(♕) 36 ♗xc1 ♖xc1 37 d5 a3 38 d6 a2 39 d7 a1(♕) 40 d8(♕) ♖h1 mate 0-1

BELLE - Roy Knuth(1787)
Ruy Lopez

1 e4 e5 2 ♘f3 ♘c6 3 ♗b5 d6 4 d4 exd4 5 ♕xd4 ♗d7 6 ♗xc6 bxc6 7 ♘c3 ♘f6 8 b4 ♗e7 9 ♗g5 h6 10 ♗xf6 ♗xf6 11 ♕e3 0-0 12 0-0 ♖e8 13 ♘d4 d5 14 f3 ♕e7 15 a3 c5 16 bxc5 ♕xc5 17 ♖fd1 ♕c4 18 ♘de2 c6 19 ♖ab1 c5 20 ♖xd5 1-0

FINALS

Mark Diesen(2486) - BELLE
Queen's Gambit Declined

1 d4 d5 2 c4 e6 3 ♘c3 c6 4 cxd5 exd5 5 ♘f3 ♗d6 6 ♕c2 a6 7 g3 ♘f6 8 ♗g5 ♗e6 9 ♗g2 ♘bd7 10 0-0 0-0 11 ♖ad1 b5 12 ♗xf6 ♘xf6 13 ♘g5 ♗g4 14 h3 ♗h5 15 ♘f3 ♗g6 16 ♕c1 b4 17 ♘a4 ♕c7 18 ♘c5 ♗h5 19 e3 ♗xc5 20 ♕xc5 ♗xf3 21 ♗xf3 a5 22 ♖c1 ♖ac8 23 ♗g2 ♖fe8 24 ♕c2 ♕a7 25 ♕d3 c5 26 dxc5 ♖xc5 27 g4 ♕c7 28 ♖xc5 ♕xc5 29 ♖d1 ♖e5 30 ♕d4 ♕c2 31 ♖d2 ♕c7 32 ♕d3 ♕c1+ 33 ♔h2 ♕c5 34 ♖c2 ♕d6 35 ♔g1 ♕e6 36 ♕d4 h5 37 gxh5 ♖xh5 38 ♕c5 ♖g5 39 ♕c8+ ♔h7 40 ♕xe6 fxe6 41 ♖c5 a4 42 ♖b5 b3 43 axb3 axb3 44 ♖xb3 e5 45 ♔f1 ♔g6 46 ♖b5 d4 47 exd4 exd4 48 ♖xg5+ ♔xg5 49 ♔e2 ♘h5 50 ♗f1 ♘f4+ 51 ♔f3 ♔f5 52 b4 g5 53 b5 ♘d5 54 ♗c4 ♘b6 55 ♗d3+ ♔e5 56 ♔g4 ♘a4 57 ♔xg5 ♔d5 58 ♔f4 ♘b2 59 ♗b1 ♔c5 60 h4 ♔xb5 1-0(time)

BELLE - Mark Diesen(2486)
French Defence

1 e4 e6 2 d4 d5 3 ♘d2 dxe4 4 ♘xe4 ♘d7 5 g3 ♘gf6 6 ♘xf6+ ♘xf6 7 ♗g2 c5 8 ♘e2 ♗e7 9 ♖f1 0-0 10 ♗e3 ♘d5 11 ♗xd5 ♕xd5 12 dxc5 ♕c6 13 ♕d4 ♖d8 14 ♕c3 e5 15 f4 ♗g4 16 fxe5 ♖ac8 17 ♕c4 ♗e6 18 ♕f4 ♗xc5 19 ♗xc5 ♕xc5 20 ♘c3 ♖d4 21 ♕g5 ♕b4 22 ♕c1 ♖xc3 23 ♔f2 ♖c8 24 ♔g1 ♕c5 25 ♖f2 ♖cd8 26 ♕e1 ♖d2 27 a3 ♖xf2 28 ♕xf2 ♕xf2+ 29 ♔xf2 ♖d2+ 30 ♔e3 ♖xc2 31 ♖d1 g5 32 ♖d2 ♖xd2 33 ♔xd2 ♔g7 34 ♔e3 ♔g6 35 ♔e4 ♗d7 36 ♔d5 ♗c6+ 37 ♔d6 ♔f5 38 h4 g4 39 h5 ♔g5 40 ♔e7 ♗d5 41 ♔d6 ♗e6 42 ♔c7 ♔xh5 43 ♔xb7 a5 44 b4 axb4 45 axb4 ♔g5 46 b5 ♗d5+ 47 ♔a7 h5 48 b6 h4 49 gxh4+ ♔g6 50 b7 ♗xb7 51 ♔xb7 g3 52 h5+ ♔xh5 53 ♔c6 g2 54 e6 fxe6 55 ♔d6 g1(♕) 56 ♔xe6 ♕g5 57 ♔d6 ♕f5 58 ♔c6 ♔g6 59 ♔d6 ♔f6 60 ♔c6 0-1 (time)

BELLE - Benjamin Finegold(2088)
Center Counter

1 e4 d5 2 exd5 ♕xd5 3 ♘c3 ♕a5 4 d4 c6 5 ♘f3 ♘f6 6 ♗c4 ♗g4 7 h3 ♗h5 8 g4 ♗g6 9 ♘e5 e6 10 ♘xg6 hxg6 11 ♕d3 ♘bd7 12 ♗d2 ♕c7 13 g5 ♘d5 4 0-0-0 ♘7b6 15 ♗xd5 ♘xd5 16 ♘xd5 cxd5 17 ♕b5+ ♕c6 18 ♕b3 ♗e7 19 f4 a5 20 ♕e3 a4 21 a3 ♖c8 22 c3 ♕c4 23 ♕e5 ♕b3 24 ♕xg7 ♖f8 25 ♕e5 ♗xa3 26 bxa3 ♖xc3+ 27 ♗xc3 ♕xc3+ 28 ♔b1 ♕b3+ 29 ♔a1 ♕xa3+ 30 ♔b1 ♕b3+ 31 ♔c1 ♔d7 32 ♔d2 ♖c8 33 ♔e2 ♕g3 34 ♖c1 ♕g2+ 35 ♔d3 ♖xc1 36 ♖xc1 ♕xh3+ 37 ♔d2 ♕h2+ 38 ♔c3 ♕a2 39 ♕f6 ♕b3+ 40 ♔d2 ♕b2+ 41 ♖c2 ♕b4+ 42 ♔e2 ♕b5+ 43 ♔f2 ♔d6 44 ♕d8+ ♕d7 45 ♕f8+ ♕e7 46 ♕b8+ ♔d7 47 ♖c7+ ♔d6 48 ♖xb7+ ♔c6 49 ♕c8+ 1-0

Fig. 8.6 The crowd around CHESS 4.9 became so dense at times that it disturbed the program's opponent.

Benjamin Finegold(2088) - BELLE
King's Indian Attack

1 g3 e5 2 ♗g2 d5 3 d3 c6 4 ♘f3 ♗d6 5 0-0 ♘e7 6 e4 0-0 7 ♘bd2 ♘a6 8 c3 f5 9 ♗e1 ♘c5 10 ♕c2 dxe4 11 dxe4 fxe4 12 ♘xe4 ♗f5 13 ♘fd2 b5 14 b4 ♘xe4 5 ♗xe4 a5 16 bxa5 ♕xa5 17 ♘b3 ♗xe4 18 ♖xe4 ♕a7 19 ♗e3 ♕a3 20 ♖d1 ♘f5 21 ♖xd6 ♘xd6 22 ♗c5 ♕xa2 23 ♕xa2 ♖xa2 24 ♗xd6 ♖fxf2 25 ♖xe5 ♖g2+ 26 ♔f1 ♖xh2 27 ♗c5 ♖h1+ 28 ♗g1 ♖a3 29 ♔g2 ♖xg1+ 30 ♔xg1 ♖xb3 31 ♖c5 b4 32 cxb4 ♖xg3+ 33 ♔f2 ♖g6 34 ♔e3 ♖e6+ 35 ♔d4 h6 36 ♖f5 g5 37 ♔c5 g4 38 ♖f4 ♖g6 39 ♖f1 g3 40 ♔d4 g2 41 ♖g1 h5 42 ♔e4 h4 43 ♔f5 ♔f7 44 ♔f4 h3 45 ♔f3 h2 46 ♖a1 h1(♕) 47 ♖a7+ ♔e6 48 ♖a5 g1(♕)+ 49 ♔e2 ♕e4+ 0-1

John Meyer(2445) - BELLE
Queen's Gambit Declined

1 d4 d5 2 ♘f3 ♘f6 3 c4 e6 4 ♘c3 c6 5 e3 ♘bd7 6 cxd5 cxd5 7 ♗d3 ♖b8 8 0-0 ♕b6 9 ♗d2 ♕xb2 10 ♘b5 ♘e4 11 a4 ♘xd2 12 ♘xd2 ♗b4 13 ♘b3 a6 14 ♖b1 ♕a2 15 ♖a1 ♕b2 16 ♖b1 ♕a2 17 ♖a1 ♕b2 1/2-1/2

Fig. 8.7 Because BELLE was not equipped with an auto-response board, its games lasted twice as long as the others.

Peter Thompson(2338) - BELLE
Nimzovich-Larsen Attack

1 b3 e5 2 ♗b2 ♘c6 3 e3 d5 4 ♗b5 ♗d6 5 ♘f3 f6 6 d4 e4 7 ♘fd2 f5 8 ♘c3 ♘f6 9 ♕e2 0-0 10 ♗xc6 bxc6 11 0-0-0 a5 12 f3 ♗a6 13 ♕f2 c5 14 ♘a4 cxd4 15 exd4 ♕e7 16 ♔b1 e3 17 ♕e1 exd2 18 ♕xd2 ♖fe8 19 ♖he1 ♕f7 20 ♘c5 ♗xh2 21 ♕g5 f4 22 ♕f5 ♗b5 23 a4 ♖xe1 24 ♖xe1 ♗g3 25 ♖h1 ♗e8 26 ♘d3 ♘h5 27 ♕e5 c6 28 ♗a3 ♕g6 29 ♕e2 ♕f6 30 ♘e5 ♕f5 31 ♗c5 ♘f6 32 ♔b2 ♕c8 33 ♕d3 ♕b7 34 ♕f5 ♔h8 35 ♘g4 ♗d7 36 ♕d3 ♗xg4 37 fxg4 ♘e4 38 ♕f3 ♕d7 39 ♗a3 ♘f2 40 ♖f1 ♘xg4 41 ♕d3 ♖e8 42 ♖h1 ♖e4 43 ♖f1 ♘e3 44 ♖h1 ♘xg2 45 ♕f3 ♘h4 46 ♕d3 f3 47 ♖f1 ♕e8 48 ♗c5 ♖e1 49 ♖xf3 ♘xf3 50 ♕xf3 ♖e3 51 ♕f8+ ♕xf8 52 ♗xf8 ♗e1 53 ♔c1 ♗c3 54 ♗b4 ♖e1 mate 0-1

Dan Shapiro(2364) - BELLE
English

1 c4 e6 2 ♘c3 ♘f6 3 ♘f3 c5 4 g3 ♘c6 5 ♗g2 d5 6 cxd5 ♘xd5 7 0-0 ♗e7 8 d4 0-0 9 ♘xd5 exd5 10 dxc5 ♗xc5 11 a3 a5 12 ♗d2 ♗g4 13 ♖c1 b6 14 h3 ♗xf3 15 ♗xf3 ♕d7 16 ♗g2 ♖ac8 17 e3 f5 18 ♗c3 ♖cd8 19 ♕b3 ♕d6 20 ♖cd1 ♘e7 21 ♖d2 ♖d7 22 ♖fd1 ♖fd8 23 ♗d4 ♗xd4 24 ♖xd4 ♕c6 25 ♔h2 b5 26 e4 fxe4 27 ♗xe4 ♔h8 28 ♗g2 a4 29 ♕f3 ♕c8 30 ♕g4 ♖f8 31 ♖1d2 ♖f6 32 h4 ♖dd6 33 ♕h5 ♖f5 34 ♕e2 ♖e6 35 ♕d3 ♖ef6 36 f4 ♖d6 37 ♖c2 ♕b7 38 ♖c5 b4 39 ♖b5 ♕a8 40 ♖dxb4 ♖f8 41 ♖b6 ♖xb6 42 ♖xb6 ♕d8 43 ♖b4 ♕a8 44 ♕d1 ♕a5 45 ♖xa4 ♕c7 46 ♕d4 ♕c2 47 ♖a7 ♘f5 48 ♕e5 ♖g8 49 g4 ♘h6 50 ♔h3 ♕d3+ 51 ♔h2 ♘xg4+ 52 ♔g1 ♘xe5 53 fxe5 ♕e3+ 54 ♔h2 ♕xa7 55 ♗xd5 ♕f2+ 56 ♔h3 ♖f8 0-1

9

13th NORTH AMERICAN COMPUTER CHESS CHAMPIONSHIP

Dallas, Texas October 24-26, 1982

CROSSTABLE

Place	Program	Rtg	Perf	ROUND 1	2	3	4	total
1	BELLE	2150	2120	W9 =	B4+	W3+	B2 =	3
2	CRAY BLITZ	U/R	2053	B8+	W5 =	B7+	W1 =	3
3	NUCHESS	U/R	2040	B10+	W7+	B1-	W5+	3
4	CHAOS	1800	1888	B14+	W1-	B8+	W9+	3
5	BEBE	1850	1907	W11+	B2 =	W6+	B3-	2.5
6	ADVANCE 2.4	U/R	1649	W12 =	B9+	B5-	W10+	2.5
7	PRESTIGE X	U/R	1636	W13+	B3-	W2-	B11+	2
8	SAVANT X	U/R	1579	W2-	B12+	W4-	B13+	2
9	OSTRICH	U/R	1595	B1 =	W6-	W12+	B4-	1.5
10	SCHACH 2.6	U/R	1356	W3-	B13+	W11 =	B6-	1.5
11	PHILIDOR	U/R	1322	B5-	W14+	B10 =	W7-	1.5
12	SFINKS X	U/R	1364	B6 =	W8-	B9-	W14+	1.5
13	PION	U/R	1126	B7-	W10-	B14+	W8-	1
14	CHATURANGA 2.0	1000	814	W4-	B11-	W13-	B12-	0

CODE: W2= means: played White vs. 2, draw; B means played Black; + means win; - means loss.

RATINGS: Are official ICCA ratings calculated by Ken Thompson (roughly equivalent to USCF ratings).

TIES: Were broken to determine order of finish by using the sum of the opponent's scores at first tiebreak, and the sum of the opponent's tiebreaking points as second tiebreak.

The 1982 ACM tournament will probably be the last one played with a 4-round schedule. The 1981 event had 16 entrants, and the scores for the top 8 places were the same as in 1982, except that BELLE scored 3.5 rather than 3. The 4-round format has become overburdened, allowing too many ties. Theoretically, a Swiss-system tournament of N rounds can find a clear winner from 2 to the Nth power contestants. In practice, if the number of contestants exceeds ¾ of the theoretical maximum, an objectionable number of ties results.

In 1982 the inevitable happened, with a 4-way tie for first, which had to be broken in order to establish a winner. As might be expected, this turned out to be the top seed, BELLE. Future events are expected to use a 5-round format.

Fig. 9.1 The tournament hall at the 1982 North American Computer Chess Championship.

ROUND 1

BELLE - OSTRICH
Center Counter(B01)

In this game, Monty Newborne's OSTRICH nearly scored a stunning upset. BELLE got into deep trouble and had to fight for a draw.
1 e4 d5 2 exd5 ♞f6 3 d4 ♞xd5 4 ♞f3 ♝g4 5 ♝e2 ♞c6 It is more prudent to play ... e6, discouraging White from the following expansion. **6 c4 ♞f6 7 d5 ♝xf3 8 ♝xf3 ♞e5 9 ♝g5 e6 10 0-0 ♝c5?!** This is too optimistic, and lands OSTRICH in difficulties. After 10 ... ♗e7, breaking the pin of the e-Pawn, Black has a reasonable game. **11 ♜e1 ♞xf3+ 12 ♛xf3 ♝b4**

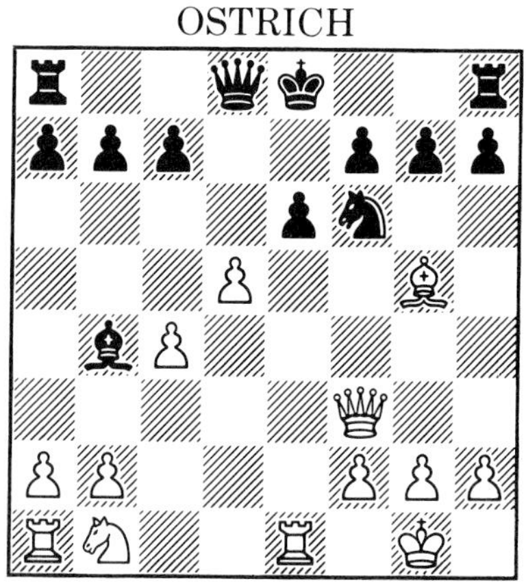

13 ♜e4? BELLE places too much reliance on the pin of the Knight. A human player might have recalled that pins can be broken, and played 13 ♘c3, after which Black must either lose a

Pawn or make terrible positional concessions, leading to a strong attack for White — in fact, BELLE would have a winning advantage. **... ♛e7 14 dxe6?!** BELLE should play 14 a3 driving away the Bishop, so that it can develop its Knight. By starting tactical operations before completing its development, the program violates a basic principle, for which it later pays a heavy price. **... 0-0-0 15 ♛e2?!** Consistent, but bad. The program should have played 15 ♘c3, accepting the doubling of its c-Pawn. **15 ... h6 16 ♝xf6** This is forced because of the misplacement of e4. As a result of BELLE's persistent refusal to take the time to develop its Queenside, OSTRICH has a deadly attack on b2. **... ♛xf6 17 g3?!** BELLE refuses to face reality. After 17 exf7? (which the program wants to play), Black wins by ... ♕xb2!; however after 17 ♘c3 ♗xc3 18 bxc3 ♕xc3 19 ♖e1, the program would only have conceded equality. Instead it loses the Exchange: **... ♜he8**

OSTRICH

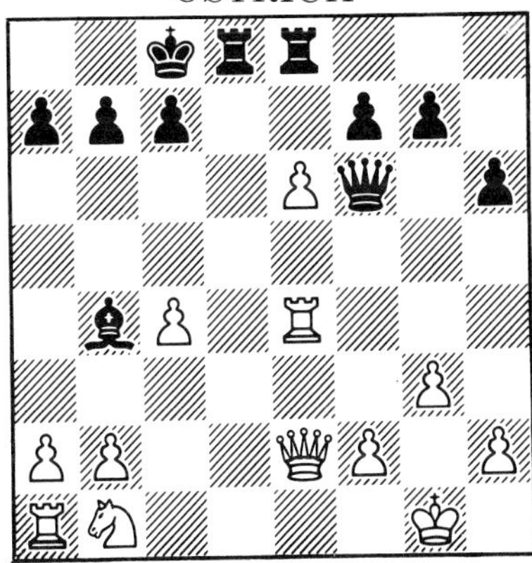

BELLE

18 exf7? Here ♘c3 was forced, but BELLE has miscalculated. **... ♜xe4 19 ♛xe4 ♛xb2 20 c5** BELLE thinks it is winning a piece, and in fact the program very nearly does. Human players know that consistent violations of basic principles such as development simply can't work, no matter how attractive they may appear. Thus BELLE is caught in a rare instance of tactical miscalculation. **18 ... ♝xc5 21 ♛f5+ ♜d7 22 ♛xc5 ♜xf7 23 ♛xa7** When BELLE went in for this line on move 18, it had apparently concluded that 23 ♕c3 held everything, but just beyond the horizon there lurked a mate in two. **... ♛xa1 24 ♛a8+ ♚d7 25 ♛xb7 ♛xa2** With the advantage of the Exchange plus an outside passed Pawn, OSTRICH has a won game, although the technical difficulties are significant. **26 ♛b5+ c6 27 ♛b7+ ♚d6 28 ♛b4+ ♚c7 29 ♞d2 ♛a7?!** This misplaces the Queen. The powerful centralization ... ♕d5 would make things much easier for Black, although in view of OSTRICH's exposed King and the ease with which Queen and Knight cooperate, the win is still difficult. This inaccuracy makes it more difficult, if not impossible. **30 ♞e4 ♛a1+ 31 ♚g2 ♛e5** Now the Queen takes up a strong central post, but not so good a one as d5, and after losing a tempo. 32 ♕a4 ♖e7 33 ♕a7+ ♔d8 Or 33 ... ♔e8 34 ♕xc6+ drawing. **34 ♛a8+ ♚d7 35 ♛b7+ ♛c7 36 ♛b3**

OSTRICH

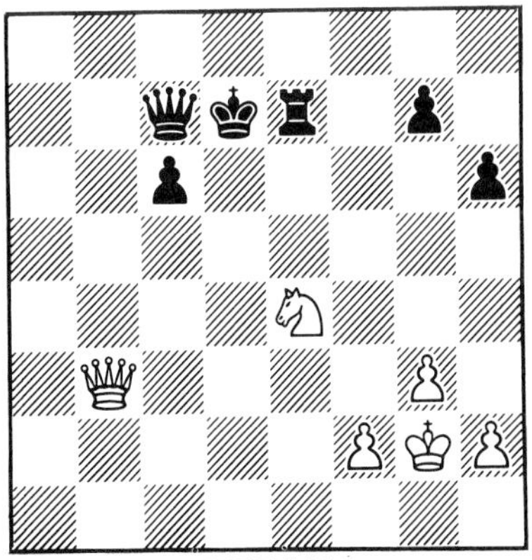

BELLE

Inviting ... ♖xe4, returning the Exchange, which however only leads to a draw after 37 ♕d3+ ♕d6 38 ♕xe4 ♕d5

39 ♕xd5 cxd5 40 ♔f3, with a drawn King and Pawn ending. BELLE could also try 36 ♘c5+, after which a perpetual is probable. **... ♛e5** OSTRICH sees the tactical trap, but still cannot find any way to make progress, and so concedes a half point. **37 ♛b7+ ♛c7 38 ♛b3 ♛e5 39 ♛b7+** 1/2 - 1/2

SCHACH 2.6 - NUCHESS
King's Indian(E91)

In this game, NUCHESS' ability to look ahead one or two plies farther than SCHACH 2.6 was decisive. The Northwestern University program got two connected passed Pawns, after which the outcome was no longer in doubt.

1 e4 g6 2 d4 ♝g7 3 c4 d6 4 ♞c3 ♞f6 5 ♝e2 0-0 6 ♞f3 ♞c6 7 0-0 This is rather tame; the only real try for an advantage is 7 d5. **... ♝g4 8 ♝e3 ♛d7 9 ♛b3** Again, 9 d5 is better; but chess programs tend to make moves which seem to place pieces on "active" squares, rather than those which actually accomplish something. **... b6?!** An unnecessary weakness. Black should simply play ♖ab8. **10 h3 ♝xf3 11 ♝xf3 e5 12 ♞e2?!** A very strong continuation is 12 d5! after which ... ♘d4 is unfavorable for Black: 12 ... ♘d4 13 ♗xd4 exd4 14 ♘e2 ♘e8 15 ♖ad1 and the weakness of the d-Pawn is clear. **... exd4 13 ♝xd4** Why not the more natural 13 ♘xd4, keeping the Bishop? **... ♜ae8 14 ♝xf6** This, unfortunately, is virtually forced. Now NUCHESS gets the upper hand. **... ♝xf6** (See diagram)

Position after 14 moves.
NUCHESS

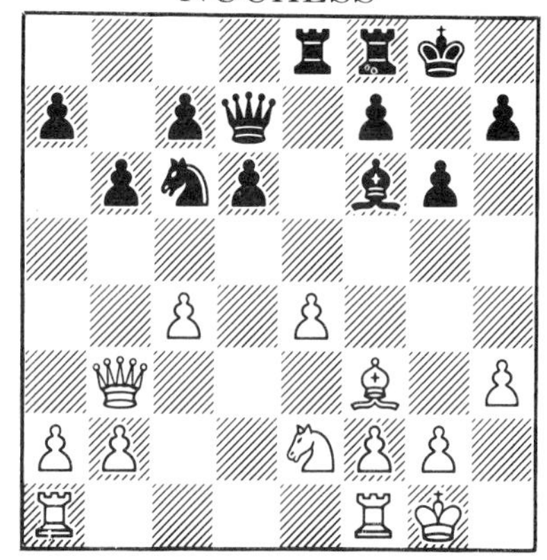

SCHACH 2.6

15 ♛b5? A miscalculation which costs a Pawn. A sound continuation was 15 ♖ad1. **... a6 16 ♛a4** It was still possible to play 16 ♕b3 with the loss of only a tempo, but SCHACH 2.6 still doesn't "see" what's coming. **... ♝xb2 17 ♜ab1 ♝g7 18 ♝g4 f5 19 exf5 gxf5 20 ♝h5 ♜d8 21 ♛xa6 ♜a8** As usual in games between computers, one program has "seen" a ply further than the other. **22 ♛b5 ♜xa2 23 c5!?** Again SCHACH 2.5 "thinks" it is winning back the Pawn, but NUCHESS has seen further ahead. It seems quite obvious that White should play 23 ♘f4. **... ♜a5 24 ♛b3+ ♚h8 25 cxb6 ♜b8!** The point. Now NUCHESS just wins the Pawn back. **26 b7 ♞d8 27 ♝f3 c6** The loss of the Pawn at b7 can no longer be prevented. **28 ♛b6 ♜c5 29 ♜fd1 ♜xb7 30 ♛a6 ♜xb1 31 ♜xb1 d5** The endgame is a clear win for NUCHESS, even though there are Bishops of opposite colors. The program's technique is good enough, though neither side's play is very accurate. **32 ♜b8 ♜c2 33 ♛a8 ♝f6 34 ♛a4 ♜d2 35 ♞f4 ♛d6 36 ♛b4 ♛xb4 37 ♜xb4 ♝e5** NUCHESS' task would be much easier after ... ♖d4, forcing the exchange of Rooks. 38 **♜a4 ♞f7 39 ♞e6 ♜b2 40 ♜a8+ ♝b8?!** Clearly better was ... ♖b8, after which the Rook can support the passed Pawns. But NUCHESS values the Rook on the seventh rank and its mating threats too highly, and allows an awkward pin, which eventually costs the program its Bishop. **41 g3 ♜b4 42 ♚g2 h6 43 ♝e2 ♞e5 44 f4?!** This loosening of the White King's Pawn sanctuary invites trouble. **... ♞d7 45 ♝d3 ♜b2+ 46 ♚h1?** SCHACH 2.6 voluntarily traps its King out of play. The program should have played ♔f3. **46 ... ♞f6 47 ♞d4?!** This looks effective, but 47 ♘c5 was more accurate, preventing the advance of the c-Pawn. **... c5 48 ♞c6 c4**

NUCHESS

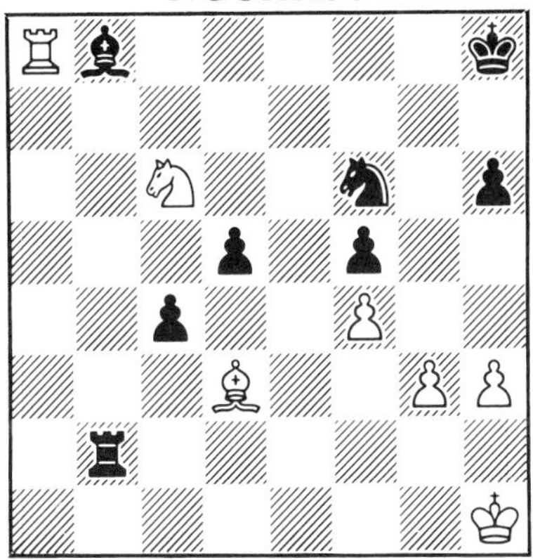

SCHACH 2.6

49 ♝xf5? White's only try for a draw was 49 ♘xb8! cxd3 50 ♘c6+ ♔g7 51 ♖a1 d2 52 ♘d4, which breaks up the terrible connected passed Pawns and at least makes things more difficult, e.g. 52 ... ♘e4 53 ♘xf5+ ♔f6 54 ♘e3. **49 ... ♞h5 50 ♚g1 ♞xg3 51 ♝g4 h5 52 ♝f3 c3 53 ♞xb8** Finally White wins the piece, but now the advance of the c-Pawn is decisive. **... c2 54 ♞a6+ ♚h7 55 ♜a7+ ♚g6 56 ♜c7 ♞e4 57 ♞b4 ♜b1+** Now NUCHESS wins the Rook for its two Pawns, after which the program has the material advantage of the Exchange for a Pawn, in a position that is very unfavorable for SCHACH 2.6. **58 ♚g2 c1(♛) 59 ♜xc1 ♜xc1 60 ♞xd5 ♜c2+ 61 ♚h1 ♞g3+ 62 ♚g1 ♜d2 63 ♞e7+ ♚f6 64 ♞d5+ ♚f5** Black's active King is the difference. **65 h4 ♜a2** Zugzwang! **66 ♝g2 ♞e2+ 67 ♚f1 ♞xf4 68 ♝e4+** After 68 ♗f3, ... ♘xd5 69 ♗xd5 ♖h2 wins easily. **... ♚g4 69 ♞c3 ♜b2 70 ♞d1 ♜d2 71 ♞c3 ♚xh4 72 ♞d5** 0-1

BEBE - PHILIDOR
Sicilian(B34)

PHILIDOR gets in trouble early, and is clearly outclassed in this one-sided game against the powerful BEBE, which displayed championship quality form in this event.

1 e4 c5 2 ♞f3 ♞c6 3 d4 cxd4 4 ♞xd4 g6 5 ♞xc6 dxc6? An obvious error; theory does not consider 5 ♘xc6 dangerous for Black, but the program recaptures with the wrong Pawn; ... bxc6 was necessary. **6 ♛xd8+ ♚xd8 7 ♞c3 ♝g7 8 ♝d2 b5 9 0-0-0 ♚c7 10 ♝e2**

PHILIDOR

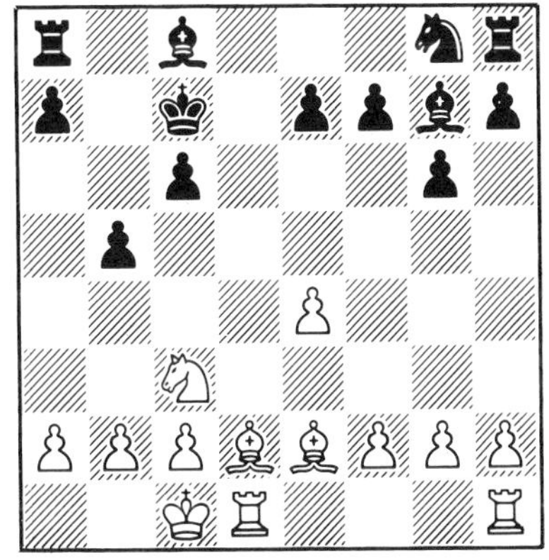

BEBE

10 ... b4? This, of course, is much too ambitious given the advantage in development held by BEBE, and unnecessarily weakens PHILIDOR's position, allowing the White pieces to take up strong posts. **11 ♞a4 ♜b8 12 ♝c4 ♞h6 13 h3 ♝d7 14 g4!** BEBE's last two Pawn moves — gaining space and at the same time threatening to win a Pawn — are rather unusual for a Chess program. **... ♜hf8 15 ♞c5 ♝c8** BEBE was already threatening a decisive win of material by 16 ♘xd7 ♔xd7 17 ♗f4+, not to mention the more obvious threat 16 ♘a6+. **16 ♞d3 ♜d8?** PHILIDOR falls victim to the horizon effect, overlooking the imminent attack along the h2-b8 diagonal. After ... ♖e8, the program would have a very bad game, but some chances for further resistance. **17 ♗f4+ e5 18 ♘xe5 ♖xd1+ 19 ♖xd1 g5 20 ♗g3 f5** Desperation; the rest is just a massacre, which ought to have been avoided by a timely resignation. But David Levy has seen too many games lost in winning positions due to program bugs or computer failures, and so it goes on to the bitter end. **21 gxf5 ♖a8 22 ♘xc6+** There's just no salvation for poor PHILIDOR. **... ♔b6 23 ♘b8 a5 24 ♖d5!** Threatening mate, and forcing the win of the Exchange after all. **24 ... ♖xb8 25 ♗xb8 g4 26 f6!** BEBE's superiority in search depth is all too obvious in this game. **... ♗xf6 27 ♖d6+ ♔c5 28 ♖xf6 ♔xc4 29 ♖xh6 ♔d4 30 e5 gxh3 31 e6 ♔c4 32 e7 ♗d7 33 ♖xh7 ♔b5 34 ♖xh3 ♗c6 35 ♖h5+ ♔c4 36 ♗a7 b3 37 axb3+ ♔b4 38 ♗e3 ♗d5 39 e8(♕) ♗xb3 40 ♕b5 mate** 1-0

SAVANT X - CRAY BLITZ
Petroff(C42)

In this game, SAVANT's limited search depth leads the program into tactical disaster, again illustrating that in games between computers (where planned play is absent and everything depends on taking advantage of tactical opportunities which appear more or less at random), victory usually goes to the program that can look ahead one ply further.

1 e4 e5 2 ♘f3 ♘f6 3 ♘xe5 d6 4 ♘f3 ♘xe4 5 d4 d5 6 ♗d3 ♗e7 7 0-0 ♘c6 8 c4 ♘f6 9 ♘c3 dxc4 ECO gives ... 0-0 leading to a slight edge for White. This exchange was recommended by Hooper in his 1966 book on the Petroff, as leading to equality. **10 ♗xc4 0-0 11 ♗g5?!** SAVANT is out of "book"; the sharpest contination here is 11 d5. The move played is a tactical liability. **... ♗g4 12 ♗e3?!** SAVANT ought to continue 12 ♗xf6 ♗xf6 13 d5 ♘a5 14 ♗d3, with such possibilities as ♗e4 and ♕d3. After this loss of tempo, CRAY BLITZ begins to take the initiative, in a typically strange, planless computer middlegame. **... ♖b8 13 d5 ♗xf3 14 ♕xf3 ♘e5 15 ♕e2 ♘xc4 16 ♕xc4 a6 17 a4 ♘e8 18 ♖fe1 ♘d6** An extremely effective square for the Knight. Has CRAY BLITZ been studying Nimzovich? **19 ♕f4 ♖e8 20 ♖ac1 b5** CRAY BLITZ weakens its position by unnecessary moves, but the program is unable to find effective piece play in this position. A human player would probably play ... ♗f6 or ... ♕d7, intending to double Rooks on the e-file. **21 ♖e2 f5**

CRAY BLITZ

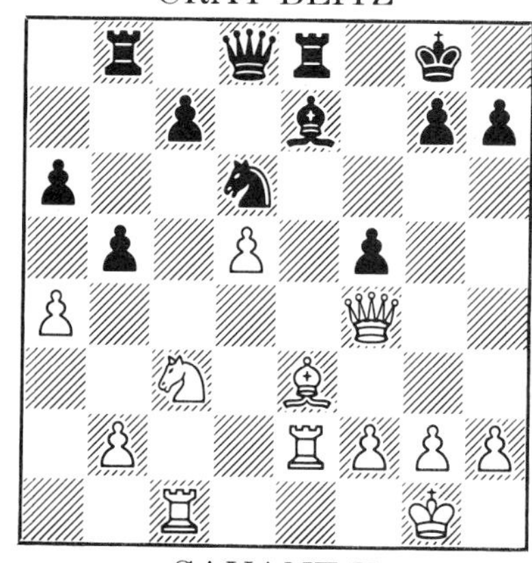

SAVANT X

22 ♗c5?? A decisive tactical blunder by SAVANT, which author Dave Kittinger attributed to the program's lack of a "quiescence" search feature. 22 ♖ce1 is the natural (and much better) continuation. **... b4 23 ♗xb4 ♗g5 24 ♗xd6** SAVANT prefers to give up its Queen for two pieces, rather than lose a Rook. **... ♗xf4 25 ♖xe8+ ♕xe8 26 ♗xf4 ♖xb2 27 ♗xc7?** Another tactical error by the outclassed SAVANT, after which the game becomes a rout. The program fails to see a back-rank mate threat six plies ahead. The only way to offer continued resistance (if such a position can be thought of as offering resistance at all) was to relieve the mate threat by a move such as 27 ♔f1.... **♜c2! 28 ♜a1** SAVANT had apparently calculated on 28 ♗f4 xc1 29 ♗xc1 at its 27th move, overlooking 29 ... ♕e1 mate—a classic illustration of the dangers of a fixed-depth search. **... ♜xc3 29 d6 ♛xa4!** Another variation on the same theme! **30 ♜b1 ♜d3 31 ♜b8+ ♚f7 32 g3 ♜d1+ 33 ♚g2 ♛c4 34 d7 ♛f1+ 35 ♚f3 ♛h1+ 36 ♚f4 ♛e4+ 37 ♚g5 ♛g4 mate** 0-1

PRESTIGE X - PION
Pirc(B08)

In the ACM tournaments, commercial entries are not allowed, and all programs entered by the programming teams of chess microcomputer manufacturers are coded "X" to prevent their results being exploited for commercial purposes. PRESTIGE X was simply a stock Fidelity PRESTIGE CHESS CHALLENGER, with Boris Baczynskyj's special tournament opening "book". This game develops along positional lines, and might have been mistaken for a game between human players until PION went in for an exchanging combination which subjected it to a dangerous attack, and then misplayed the defense.

1 e4 d6 2 d4 ♞f6 3 ♞c3 g6 4 ♞f3 ♝g7 5 ♝e2 0-0 6 0-0 c6 7 a4 ♛c7 8 h3 ♞bd7 9 ♝e3 e5 10 dxe5 dxe5 11 ♛d2 ♞h5 12 ♜fd1 ♞f4 13 ♝f1 ♜e8 14 a5 ♝f8 15 ♝c4 ♞e6 16 ♞h2 During this game, TD Mike Valvo commented that both programs were playing remarkably human-like moves and that each side was actually pursuing a strategic plan. This is hardly surprising, since both programs were simply retrieving the same "book" line from ECO. Here PRESTIGE's book ends, and the program finds a move which is quite interesting, but does not seem to be as effective as 16 ♘g5 (Geller - Szabo, Hilversum 1973). **... ♞f6 17 a6** It is probably best to bring the Knight back to f3, but one could hardly expect that of the program. As it plays, the Knight is out of play for many moves. **... b5?!** Creating unnecessary weaknesses; ... b6 was a sounder continuation. **18 ♝d3 ♝d7 19 ♝h6 b4 20 ♞e2 ♝e7** PION correctly concludes that without its dark-square Bishop, h6 and f6 will be very weak. **21 ♝c4 ♜ad8 22 ♛e3 ♞c5** Now PION takes over the initiative. **23 ♞g3 ♝c8 24 ♜xd8 ♜xd8 25 ♛e2 ♛d6 26 c3?!** This weakens d3, and lets PION liquidate its weak b-Pawn. The program should get its Knight back in play at f3. **... bxc3 27 bxc3 ♞e8 28 ♛f3 ♝e6 29 ♝e2 ♛c7 30 ♞g4 ♝xg4 31 hxg4 ♞d6 32 ♜a2?!** The motive for this is not clear. At this point, PION has a slight advantage since White's isolated Pawns are easier targets than Black's—but of course games between computer programs are rarely decided by such positional niceties. **32 ... ♛b6 33 ♜a1**

PION

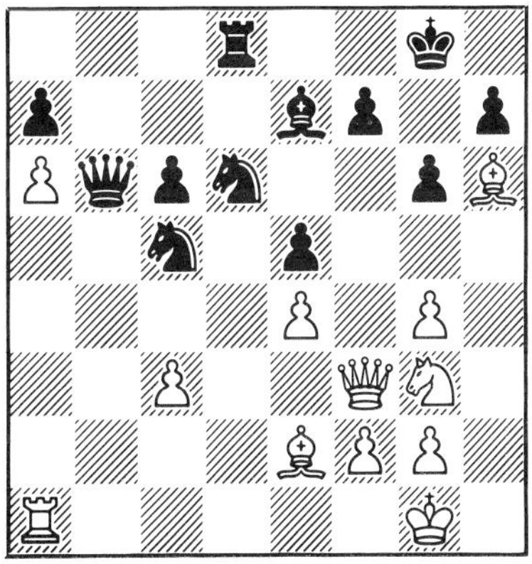

PRESTIGE X

33 ... ♛c7?! PION is too cautious; here ... ♕b2! would have presented White with some unpleasant problems, e.g. 34 ♖d1 ♘b5. **34 ♝f1 ♞b5 35 ♝c4 ♞d6 36 ♝e2 ♞e8** Up to this point, PION has played reasonably well, and

might have deceived a casual observer into thinking that it was following a positional plan, but now it becomes clear that the program really has no ideas and is merely shuffling its pieces around, waiting for a stimulus from the opponent. **37 ♞f1 ♞f6 38 ♞d2 ♜d7 39 ♝c4 ♜d8?** A fatal error! PION overlooks the threat to f7; ... ♗d8 was correct. **40 g5 ♝f8** About the only move, losing "only" a Pawn, but also allowing the Black King to become fatally exposed. Of course ... ♘e8 allows an immediate mate. Now the game explodes tactically in PION's face: **41 ♝xf8 ♚xf8 42 ♛xf6 ♜xd2** PION expects that it can keep material equality after 43 ♕h8+ ♔e7 44 ♕xh7 ♘xe4, and thinks it is doing quite well. **43 ♜b1!** Threatening mate by 44 ♖b8+ ♕xb8 45 ♕xf7, and tying the Knight down. **43 ... ♜d8 44 ♛h8+ ♚e7 45 ♛g7** This is more accurate than taking the h-Pawn, because it ties down the Black Queen. **... ♜f8** PION now has all its forces committed to vital defensive tasks. **46 f3 ♚e8 47 ♛xh7** 47 ♕f6 would put Black in Zugzwang, except for ... ♘d7.
(See diagram next page)
47 ... ♛a5?? Although Black already has a lost game, this leads to an immediate catastrophe. PION shows that (like many other programs, including its opponent) it has no sense of danger at all, and goes off Pawn-hunting while its King is under attack. **48 ♜b8+ ♚e7 49 ♜xf8 ♛a1+** PION is shocked to notice that the planned recapture ... ♔xf8 allows mate on the

Fig. 9.2 Mike Valvo directed the tournament, and as in 1981, did a brilliant job of entertaining the audience with his commentary.

Position after White's 47th move.

PION

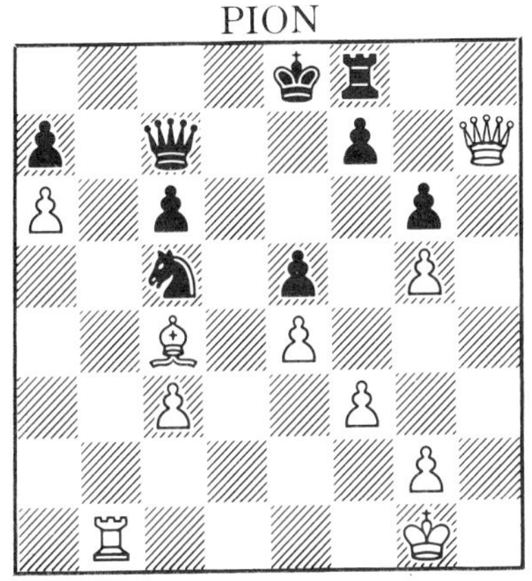

PRESTIGE X

move. **50 ♚h2 ♚d6 51 ♜xf7 ♞xa6 52 ♜xa7 ♚c5 53 ♝xa6 ♛xc3 54 ♛e7+ ♚d4 55 ♜d7+ ♚e3 56 ♜d3+ ♛xd3 57 ♝xd3** Now PION has seen enough, and resigns. 1-0

CHATURANGA 2.0 - CHAOS
Sicilian(B23)

In this game, teenager John Poduska's CHATURANGA 2.0 gave notice that it was going to be a long tournament for the boy wonder (whose father is president of the Apollo Computer Co.), showing many signs of not being ready for competition, including serious problems in its evaluator function. In 1981 CHATURANGA scored a point when SCHACH 2.5 had to forfeit; this year it was not to be so fortunate, and actually seemed to be considerably the worse for a complete rewrite into FORTRAN and 68000 assembler, from its original PASCAL version. It is no small task to write a computer chess program that can play the game at all, let alone well, and the reader who finds CHATURANGA 2.0's tribulations humorous should give it a try himself before forming a final judgment. With more experience and more time to work on his program, Poduska may yet produce a champion.

1 e4 c5 2 ♞f3 ♞c6 3 ♞c3 e6 4 ♞g1? A theoretical novelty, which does not turn out too well in this game; more usual is 4 g3. CHATURANGA is out of "book" already and thinks the Knight is misplaced on f3 ... **4 ... ♞f6 5 ♝b5 ♝e7 6 ♛f3? ...** Because it wants to play the Queen there. **6 ... ♞d4 7 ♛d3?** And now 7 ♕d1 was necessary; this gets the Bishop trapped. **... a6 8 ♝a4 b5 9 ♝xb5 axb5 10 e5?** CHATURANGA "sees" that 10 ♘xb5 ♘xb5 11 ♕xb5 does not really win a Pawn, because of 11 ... ♘xe4. But this is ineffective. **... ♞g4 11 h3**

CHAOS

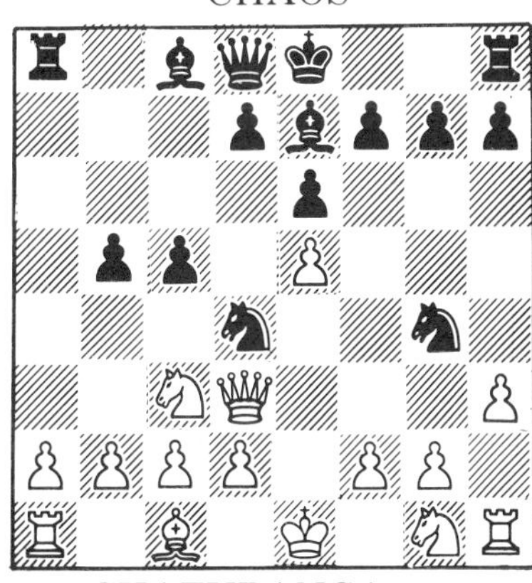

CHATURANGA 2.0

11 ... ♞xe5! 12 ♛e4 CHATURANGA thought that the Pawn was immune because of this move. **... d5** With a mighty attack which would easily be worth a piece, even if it didn't lead to immediate gain of material. **13 ♛xe5 ♝f6 14 ♛f4 ♞xc2+ 15 ♚d1 ♞xa1 16 d4?** The purpose of this Pawn sacrifice is unclear. **... cxd4 17 ♞xb5 ♜xa2 18 ♞d6+ ♚e7 19 ♞f3??** At this point it became evident that CHATURANGA was suffering from several "bugs", and was not playing a normal game. **... ♛xd6 20 ♛d2 ♞b3 21 ♛c2 ♛b8 22 ♚e1 ♜a1 23 ♚d1 ♛f4 24 ♞e5 ♜xc1+ 25 ♛xc1 ♛xc1+ 26 ♚e2 ♛c2+ 27 ♚f3 ♛e4+** 0-1

ADVANCE 2.4 - SFINKS X
Sicilian(B83)

In this inaccurately played game, SFINKS X acquired a significant positional advantage, and was in a position to make progress when the program completely misevaluated the situation and lost two Pawns. ADVANCE 2.4 then had a winning advantage, but missed several opportunities to drive it home, after which the game drifted into a draw.

1 e4 c5 2 ♞f3 e6 3 d4 cxd4 4 ♞xd4 ♞f6 5 ♞c3 ♞c6 6 ♝e2 ♝e7 More usual is ... ♗b4; this transposes into the Scheveningen variation. **7 0-0 d6 8 ♞xc6** This strengthening of the Black center is decidedly unwise, but quite typical of a computer program playing outside its opening "book" — most programs tend to resolve potential exchanges immediately, rather than play with continuing tension. Here White ought to try to get in f4, and so the usual moves are 8 ♗e3 and 8 ♔h1. **... bxc6 9 ♝e3 e5** An immediate ... d5 is also possible; after 10 e5 ♘d7 11 f4 c5 Black does not stand badly at all. **10 ♛d3?!** A weak move. White should play f4. **... 0-0 11 h3?** Pure loss of time. Given the placement of the Queen on d3, White ought to play f4 immediately and try to get some attack going, but this is a concept foreign to computer programs. **11 ... a5?!** Quite strong here was ... d5! and Black takes control of the center. **12 ♜ad1 ♜b8 13 ♝c1 ♝e6 14 ♛g3 ♚h8** SFINKS X recognizes the threat of 15 ♗h6. **15 ♛e3?!** Another weak move, but of course ADVANCE 2.4 has no comprehension of the value of the initiative, and so passes up the strong move 15 f4. **... ♛b6**

SFINKS X

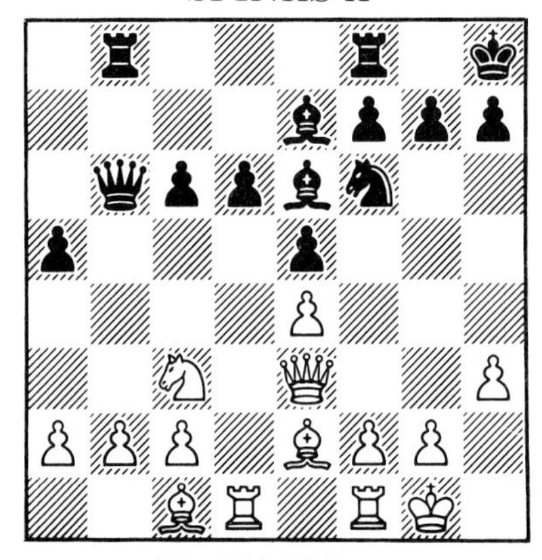

ADVANCE 2.4

16 ♛xb6?! As usual in a Sicilian, White ought to keep the Queens on and play for an attack — the ending favors Black. Such concepts are, however, far beyond the capability of either program. **... ♜xb6 17 ♝f3 ♝c4** This just drives the Rook to a better square. A meaningful plan for Black (which of course SFINKS X has no capacity to formulate) is ... ♖d8, followed by an eventual ... d5. **♜fe1 ♜b7 19 ♝e2 ♝e6** There was no good reason not to accept the exchange; certainly none worth the loss of a tempo. **20 ♝a6 ♜b6 21 ♝d3 ♜fb8** This piling-up on the half-open b-file looks impressive, but the Bishop at c1 is an adequate defender. Meanwhile, the positionally critical Pawn advance ... d5 is not being prepared. Black should continue ... ♖d8 as noted above. **22 a3 ♜6b7 23 ♞a4 ♞d7 24 ♝d2 ♜a8 25 ♝c3 f6** Finally SFINKS X plays this necessary move, protecting the e-Pawn to prepare ... d5. **26 ♜e3 d5 27 exd5 cxd5 28 ♜ee1 ♝b4?** This is unnecessarily "clever" and reduces Black's advantage; the simpler continuation ... ♘c5 29 ♘xc5 ♗xc5 leaves White with an awkward problem to cope with in the defense of the b-Pawn. **29 ♝d2 ♝xd2 30 ♜xd2 ♜ab8 31 c3 ♚g8 32 ♝c2**

SFINKS X

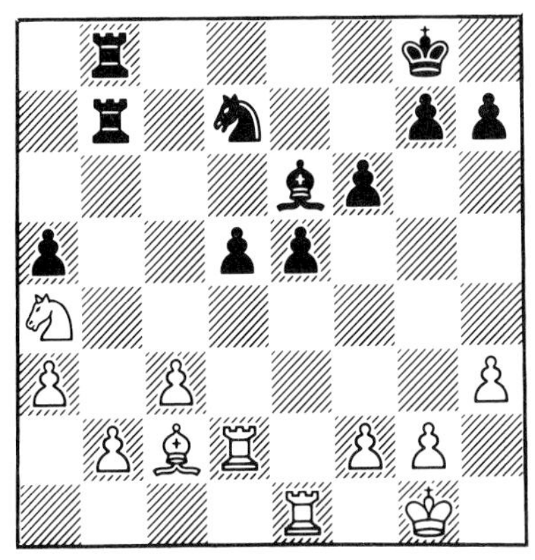

ADVANCE 2.4

... e4? Instead of this premature advance, SFINKS X should play 32 ♔f7, protecting the Bishop on e6 which may become vulnerable in some variations, and preparing to mobilize its center. In this variation White cannot play 33 ♗xh7 because then the Bishop is trapped after ... g6. This, however, is a concept neither program is equipped to deal with, and so SFINKS X compromises its position to prevent a nonexistent threat to the h-Pawn. **33 c4!** This wins at least one Pawn, and should have won the game. **33... ♞e5** The alternative is ... dxc4 34 ♗xe4 ♖c7 35 ♗xh7+ ♔xh7 36 ♖xe6. **34 cxd5 ♝f5 35 ♝xe4 ♞c4 36 ♜de2 ♝xe4 37 ♜xe4 ♞xb2 38 ♞xb2?** It is so difficult for computer programs to pass up exchanges! Here, obviously, it would be much better to play 38 ♘c5, and if Black ventures ... ♖b5?, 39 d6! seems decisive, e.g. ... ♖xc5? 40 d7 and Black must give up a Rook to stop the Pawn. Instead, ADVANCE 2.4 exchanges its potentially strong Knight for the misplaced Black Knight on b2, letting SFINKS X get its Rook behind the d-Pawn as well — after which the program is unable to win. **... ♜xb2 39 d6?** Correct is 39 ♖d4, with good winning chances. Computer programs lack knowledge of such basic endgame precepts as placing Rooks behind passed Pawns. Now White can no longer get his Rook behind the d-Pawn. **... ♜d2 40 ♜e8+ ♜xe8 41 ♜xe8+ ♚f7 42 ♜e7+ ♚f8 43 ♜a7 ♜xd6 44 ♜xa5 ♜d1+ 45 ♚h2 ♜d2 46 ♚g3 ♜d3+?!** SFINKS X in its turn also displays ignorance of the most fundamental principle of Rook endings — placing the Rook behind the passed Pawn. Black should simply play ... ♖a2, with a theoretical draw. **47 ♚f4 ♜d7 48 ♜a8+** At this point, ADVANCE 2.4 might have transformed the Rook ending into one offering some winning chances by 48 ♖b5 ♖a7 49 ♖b3, placing the Rook on the side rather than in front of the passed Pawn. Computer programs, however, simply don't have the knowledge to play Rook endings with any accuracy at all. **... ♚f7 49 a4 ♚e6 50 a5?** After this White loses the a-Pawn; 50 ♖b8 was essential, with the idea of placing the Rook alongside the Pawn at b5 or b6. This ending would be quite similar to a famous endgame in which Alekhine defeated Capablanca. Neither side is playing the ending at all well, but SFINKS X has the advantage that it can now formulate a "plan" — to capture the a-Pawn! **... ♚d5 51 a6 ♚c5 52 ♚g4 ♚b6 53 ♚h5? ♜d2** After this, White is even in danger of losing. **54 ♜g8 g5?!** After 54 ... g6+ 55 ♔h6 ♖xf2, SFINKS X would threaten to get a dangerous passed Pawn of its own. **55 f3 ♜xg2 56 ♜f8 ♚xa6 57 ♜xf6+ ♚b5 58 ♜f5+ ♚c4 59 ♜xg5 ♜f2 60 ♜f5 ♚d4 61 ♜f7 ♚e3 62 ♜xh7 ♜xf3** The position is now a theoretical draw. 1/2 - 1/2

ROUND 2

NUCHESS - PRESTIGE X
Benko System(A00)

In this interesting game, microcomputer

program PRESTIGE clearly wins the opening against the powerful NUCHESS (which runs on a huge mainframe computer) and achieves a far superior position with excellent attacking chances. But PRESTIGE does not know what to do with its strong position, and begins to play weak moves — losing first its advantage, then equality, and finally the game.

1 g3 e5 2 ♝g2 d5! 3 d4?! A weak continuation, after which the game is already in uncharted waters. Best for White is the thematic move 3 c4. **... exd4 4 ♛xd4 ♞f6 5 ♝g5 ♝e7 6 ♛a4+** When computing its third move, NUCHESS may have "thought" that it could win the d-Pawn in this position by 6 ♗xf6 ♗xf6 7 ♕xd5, but of course 7 ... ♕xd5 8 ♗xd5 ♗xb2 would be disastrous for White. The premature development of the White Queen is now a clear liability, which PRESTIGE exploits to gain the advantage. **6 ... ♞c6 7 ♞c3?!** More prudent would be 7 ♘f3 followed by Castling, but this clearly concedes equality. NUCHESS is still lured by the illusion that it has pressure on the d-Pawn. **... h6** Once again, the impossibility of exchanging on f6 upsets White's plans. **8 ♝e3?!** Clearly better is ♗d2. The program evidently felt compelled to prevent a potential ... d4, but as any human player could have informed NUCHESS, it is not a good idea to set up a potential Pawn fork. **8 ... ♝b4 9 ♛b3 0-0 10 0-0-0?!** This is very risky. Much more prudent is 10 ♘f3 followed by 0-0. **... ♝xc3 11 ♛xc3 ♝f5 12 ♛b3?** Again NUCHESS misevaluates the position, and now its situation starts to become serious. Developing the Knight by 12 ♘h3 was the only move worth considering. **... ♞a5 13 ♛b4 b6 14 ♝h3** Finally it becomes clear to NUCHESS that the Pawn at d5 is a tower of strength, rather than a weakness, and that its Bishop is not doing anything on the long diagonal. **... c5 15 ♛h4 ♛d7 16 ♝xf5 ♛xf5 17 ♛f4 ♛e6** With its Knight ready to hop to c4, PRESTIGE has excellent middlegame attacking chances, and correctly decides that it would be a mistake to ease White's game by exchanging Queens. **18 b3 d4!** After this, Black gets an unpleasant bind on the White position. **19 ♝d2 ♞c6 20 ♚b1 ♞d5 21 ♛f3**

PRESTIGE X

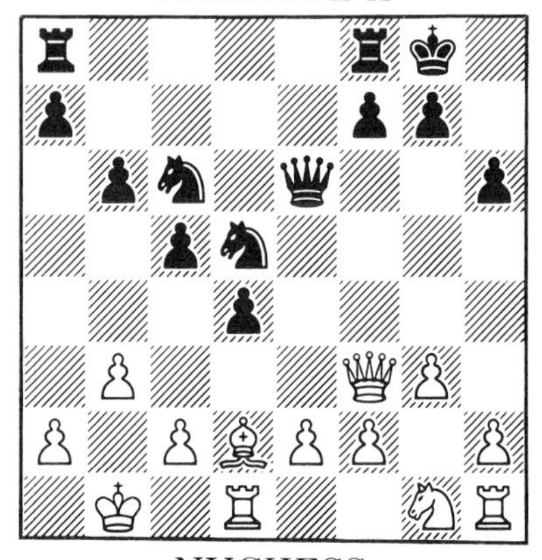

NUCHESS

NUCHESS is now in serious trouble. **21 ... ♞db4** This is not bad, but here PRESTIGE could really have driven its advantage home by ... ♘e5! 22 ♕e4 f5, and now if 23 ♕h4 to prevent c4, 23 ... ♘g4 is crushing, so NUCHESS would have to fianchetto its Queen — after which Black obviously has a strong attack. **22 ♜c1 a5 23 a3?!** The unfortunate NUCHESS is now practically in Zugzwang; but this looseening of the Queenside pawns does not ease the defense. A continuation with some promise is 23 h4 with the plan ♘h3-f4-d3, and if Black misplays the attack, White may have time to get organized. **... ♞d5 24 a4 ♞db4 25 h4 ♞e5 26 ♛b7? ♜ab8** Although PRESTIGE has not always chosen the very best continuation, on the whole its play has been purposeful and powerful, whereas NUCHESS has played its

Queen back and forth, neglecting its Kingside development, and weakening the position of its King. It seems clear that NUCHESS made a poor choice of opening in this game, since its opponent was able to obtain such an advantageous position by the kind of simple, classical center-oriented moves that are easy for computer programs to find. In the next few moves, however, PRESTIGE misses a number of clear wins — greatly disappointing the Fidelity team, which would have been delighted to take the scalp of this powerful opponent, several plies more powerful in its search — and which eventually tied for first place. 26 ... ♖ab8 is by no means a bad move, but infinitely stronger was ... ♘d5, cutting off the Queen's retreat and threatening to win it with ... ♖fb8, to which there appears to be no real defense. **27 ♛g2**

PRESTIGE X

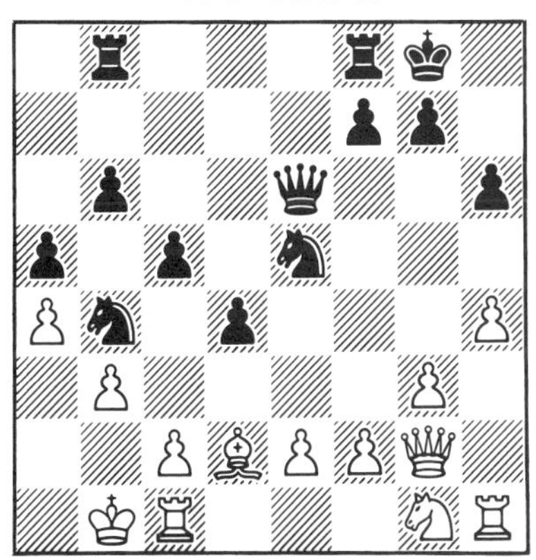

NUCHESS

27 ... d3!? This seems premature, and does not lead to anything. The program had a slower but very strong continuation available in either ... c4! or ... b5!, after which most human players would consider the White King's long-term survival prospects to be poor indeed. Here PRESTIGE again demonstrates that playing to increase an initiative into an all-out attack is a concept too advanced for today's programs, and seeks to force an immediate tactical decision. The program does not know how to open lines to get at White's King. **28 exd3 ♞bxd3 29 ♜d1** Obviously 29 cxd3?? ♕xb3+ 30 ♔a1 ♘xd3 is disastrous, but this capture is not forced and now the cramping d-Pawn is gone. **... ♞b4** Of course there is no necessity for this retreat; 29 ... b5! might even justify Black's 27th move, preparing a coffin for the White King. **30 ♞e2 ♜bd8?!** After this silly move, it becomes obvious that PRESTIGE really has no idea of what to do with its strong position, and does not understand how to drive home its advantage. Either ... b5 or ... c4 would have posed disagreeable problems for White. The Rook goes to the open file because of position scoring bonuses for doing so, while the powerful attacking Pawn moves don't pay off within the program's search depth — and get no bonuses on positional grounds. Now PRESTIGE's heuristics, which enabled it to play the early part of the game so well, start to lead it astray — as happened in a number of games in the U.S. Open. **31 ♝xb4 axb4 32 ♞f4 ♛g4** PRESTIGE still has the better position, but the game is no longer lopsided since NUCHESS has finally erased its deficit in development. **33 ♞d5 ♜fe8 34 f4 ♞g6?** A horrible misplacement of the Knight. 34 ... ♘c6 would have kept the advantage, since 35 ♘f6+ does not work: ... exf6 35 ♕xc6 ♖xd1+ winning the Rook, or 35 ♖xd8 ♘xd8 winning a piece. Here PRESTIGE anticipates 35 ♘xb6 ♘xf4, one more example of how badly wrong a program can go by making decisions based on tactical considerations. **35 ♛f2 ♜d7 36 ♜d2!** Now Black's tactical counter-threats are parried ... **36 ... ♞f8** ... and PRESTIGE discovers that there is no good way to defend the b-Pawn. **37 ♞xb6 ♜xd2 38 ♛xd2 ♛xg3** PRESTIGE has managed

to maintain temporary material equality, and still has somewhat the better position. **39 h5 ♞e6 40 ♞d5 ♜d8?!** Another tactical misjudgment. A strong continuation for Black was ... ♘d4. **41 f5 ♛f3** This double attack seems to hold everything. ... **42 ♞e7+ ...** Zwischenzug! **... ♚f8 43 ♛e1**
(See diagram)

Position after White's 43rd move.

PRESTIGE X

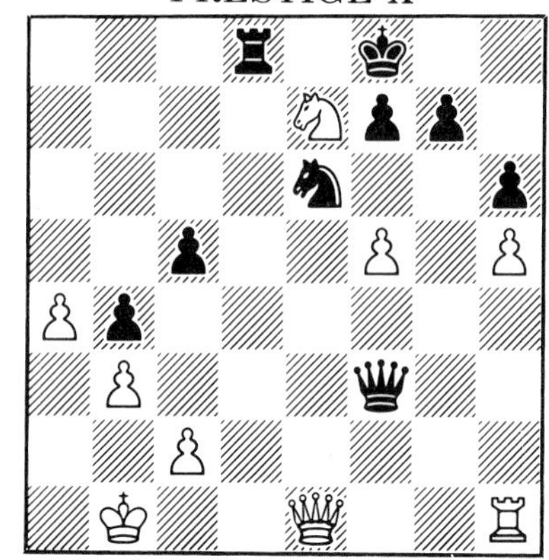

NUCHESS

43 ... ♚xe7? PRESTIGE X passes up the active move ... ♘d4! for the "win" of an untenable Pawn, after which NUCHESS springs to life and takes the initiative. Even were this greedy move tactically justified (as is far from the case) it would still be bad judgment by human standards, since now Black's King is dangerously exposed. **44 fxe6 fxe6 45 ♜g1** Suddenly, all of Black's Pawns are weak, and the Black King is exposed. **45 ... ♛f7 46 ♜g6 ♜d5 47 ♛g3! ♚f8 48 ♛b8+ ♛e8** It may be better to play ... ♔e7. **49 ♛f4+ ♜f5?** A decisive mistake. After ... ♕f7, it appears that White has no more than a

Fig. 9.3 Although Valvo put on his usual iron-man performance, he still had to take occasional breaks. Danny Kopec relieved Valvo at the microphone.

draw. In this position, however, some of NUCHESS' special heuristics are beginning to influence its play, which now becomes much more accurate than that of its opponent. **50 ♛e4 ♛f7** Here ... ♔f7 loses to 51 ♕b7+. Also bad, but requiring a more subtle refutation, is ... ♖f6 51 ♖xf6 gxf6 52 ♕g6!, and since after ... ♕xg6 53 hxg6 the King and Pawn ending would be lost for Black, the Pawn at h6 would fall and the Queen ending would be very unfavorable for PRESTIGE. **51 ♜xe6** Now NUCHESS has its Pawn back, and a decisive positional advantage. To begin with, the threat of 52 ♕a8+ forcing mate induces PRESTIGE to move its Queen so as to create a flight square for the King. Before this can be done, the Rook must be moved so as not to be left en prise. **51 ... ♜f1+** 51 ... ♔h7 loses outright after 52 ♖e8+ ♔h7 53 ♖e5 g6 54 ♖e7. **52 ♚a2 ♛d7 53 ♜e5!** A quiet, but extremely strong move. The c-Pawn must fall after which the b-Pawn will go as well. **... ♛d6??** The game is clearly lost anyway, but this leads to an immediate catastrophe by allowing a decisive penetration of the eighth rank; like many programs, PRESTIGE cannot adequately evaluate threats to the safety of its King — the crucial variations are too deep for its search to find, and it has inadequate information from its positional heuristics. NUCHESS, however, has a special search extension heuristic for examining back-rank mate possibilities, which could hardly have been better chosen to play this position. **54 ♜e8+ ♚f7 55 ♜a8 ♜c1** PRESTIGE prepares to threaten a mate of its own after ... ♕e1, but NUCHESS gets there first. **56 ♛e8+ ♚f6 57 ♛g6+ ♚e5 58 ♜e8+** 1-0

CRAY BLITZ - BEBE
Sicilian(B55)

In this game, tactically powerful CRAY BLITZ plays a dubious opening variation, and then really tempts fate by opening the e-file with its King stuck in the center. BEBE couldn't take advantage of this and the game ended in a quick draw, but one wonders whether a human master might not have found a way to make CRAY BLITZ regret its daring.

1 e4 c5 2 ♞f3 d6 3 d4 cxd4 4 ♞xd4 ♞f6 5 f3 This has long been considered too slow for White to get any advantage. **... e5 6 ♝b5+ ♝d7 7 ♝xd7+ ♞bxd7 8 ♞f5 d5 9 exd5 ♛a5+ 10 ♞c3 ♞b6 11 ♞e3?!** This invites a sham sacrifice which has long been known to favor Black. CRAY BLITZ ought to play 11 ♕e2! leading to an even game (Boleslavski). **... ♞bxd5 12 ♞exd5 0-0-0 13 ♛e2 ♜xd5** It seems stronger to play ... ♘xd5, after which 14 ♗d2 (14 ♕xe5?? ♗b4 with an overwhelming attack) ... ♗b4 15 ♘xd5 ♖xd5 16 c3 ♗e7 17 0-0 (c4?? ♖xd2! 18 ♕xd2 ♗b4) ... ♖fd8 is clearly favorable for Black. **14 ♝d2 ♜d7 15 ♞e4** Here 15 0-0-0 is stronger. **... ♛a4** Not 15 ... ♗b4?? 16 ♕c4 winning a piece. **16 ♝c3 ♞xe4 17 ♛xe4 ♛a6**

BEBE

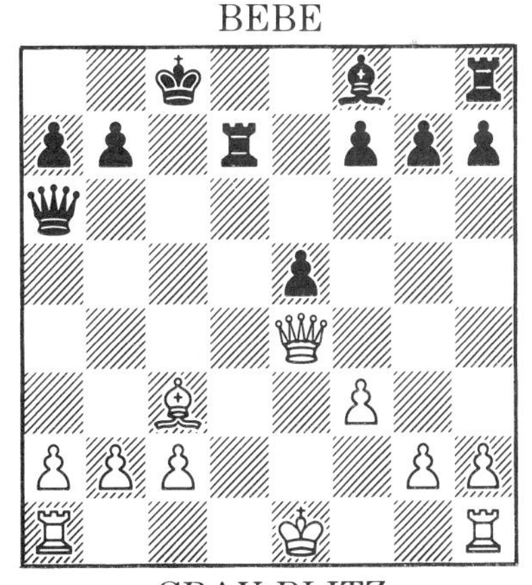

CRAY BLITZ

BEBE invites CRAY BLITZ to dine on the e-Pawn, which would obviously be suicidal. **18 f4?!!** An astonishing reply. Can CRAY BLITZ do this and live?

"Don't worry, Boss — I've got it all figured out." **... exf4 19 ♕e8+ ♖d8 20 ♕xf7 ♕b5** The position is not as simple as it seems — ... ♗c5?? of course loses to 21 ♕f5+, and ...♗d6 allows 21 0-0-0. So BEBE has to make a preparatory move before launching its attack, which allows CRAY BLITZ to escape by a hairsbreadth. **21 ♕e6+ ♔b8 22 ♕e5+ ♕xe5+ 23 ♗xe5+ ♗d6 24 ♗xd6+ ♖xd6 25 0-0 ♖f8?!** Better is ... g5, allowing the Rook to take up a more active position. **26 ♖ae1 g5 27 ♖e7 ♖d2 28 ♖f2** This allows BEBE to force an immediate draw, but there were no winning chances for White anyway. **... ♖d1+ 29 ♖f1 ♖d2 30 ♖f2 ♖d1+4 31 ♖f1 ♖d2** 1/2 -1/2

CHAOS - BELLE
Queen's Gambit Declined(D31)

CHAOS plays a Pawn sacrifice line, and as soon as the game leaves "book", the program displays a lamentable ignorance of the meaning of its positional compensation. Gradually BELLE achieves a clear advantage, and finally drives it home with an elegant display of tactical fireworks.
1 d4 d5 2 c4 e6 3 ♘c3 c6 4 ♘f3 dxc4 5 a4 ♗b4 6 e3 b5 7 ♗d2 a5 8 axb5 ♗xc3 9 bxc3!? So far the programs have been following the main line of the Semi-Slav (the Noteboom variation), but now CHAOS varies with an interesting move first tried in 1955 by Boleslavsky against Randvir. The main line continues 9 ♗xc3 cxb5 10 b3 ♗b7 11 bxc4 or 11 d5!? leading to an unclear position. The point of the move played is that White takes control of the center, with an attack as compensation for the Pawn sacrificed. **9 ... cxb5 10 ♕b1 ♗a6 11 ♗e2 ♘c6 12 0-0 a4?!** Now BELLE varies with a rather dubious move (it seems clear that Black should finish developing and then play for an eventual ... b4), which, however, throws CHAOS out of its "book".

BELLE

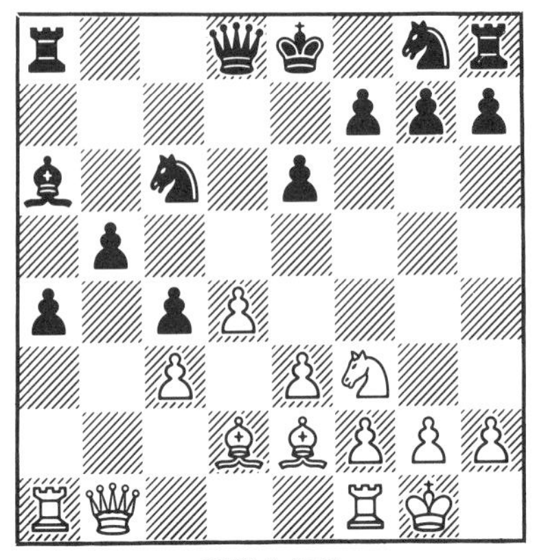

CHAOS

13 ♕e4? CHAOS now shows that it has no understanding of its positional compensation for the Pawn, and rapidly dissipates it in a series of premature attacking moves, after which BELLE is just a Pawn ahead. The program should have played e4 with control of the center, but it is not an easy task to program a computer to understand that the move e4, which results in a momentary decrease in the mobility of the White pieces, is more effective than the apparently ideal placement of the Queen on e4. If there is an answer to this problem at all, it is probably a matter of programming the computer to have a better understanding of the concept of controlling squares. **... ♘ge7 14 ♘g5 h6 15 ♘f3 0-0 16 ♖fb1 ♕d6 17 ♕g4 f5 18 ♕h5 e5!** After this, it is clear that the initiative belongs to BELLE. **19 dxe5?!** CHAOS cannot afford to give up its central Pawn in this fashion. The program should play 19 ♗c1 - a3 with drawing chances. **... ♘xe5 20 ♘d4 ♘5c6 21 ♗f3 ♕d7 22 ♖a2 ♖ab8** BELLE easily counters CHAOS' "threats" against the b-Pawn. **23 ♖ab2?!** It is a mystery why CHAOS does not find the obvious maneuver ♗c1-a3. There is no real threat that Black would answer 23 ♗c1 by ... b4 (23 ♗c1 b4? 24 ♘xc6 ♘xc6 25 ♗xc6 ♕xc6 26 cxb5). **... ♜f6 24 ♛h3 ♜c8 25 ♛h4** CHAOS has no idea of what to do in its position, which in truth is now rather poor. **... ♞xd4** BELLE correctly decides to exchange White's best piece, after which it can seize control of the open e-file. **26 exd4** Of course cxd4?? loses a piece, but now BELLE takes over the e-file. **... ♜e6 27 h3** CHAOS is unable to form a plan or to find a maneuver which would improve its position, so the program "makes luft" to prevent the possibility of a back-rank mate. **... ♞d5**

BELLE

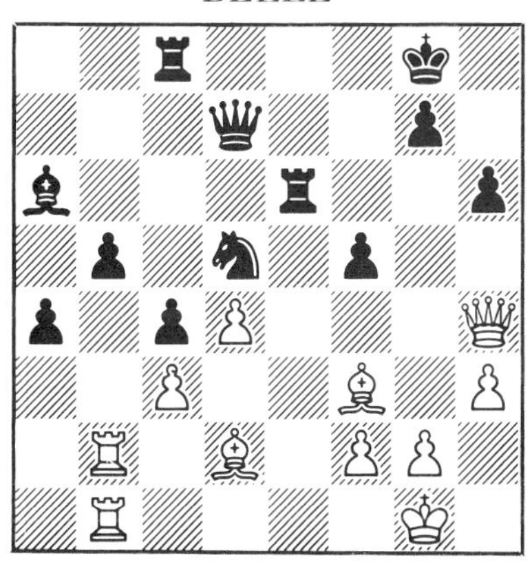

CHAOS

28 g4?! Again CHAOS can't find anything constructive to do. In such situations, computer programs have a distressing tendency to make weakening Pawn moves. **... ♜ce8!** BELLE invites its opponent to further weaken its position by capturing the f-Pawn. **29 gxf5?** CHAOS obliges. A sounder continuation was 29 ♔h1, preparing ♖g1, after which both g5 and gxf5 would be threatened. **... ♜f6 30 ♝e4** Somewhat better is ♗g4. **30 ... ♞e7 31 ♛g4 ♞xf5 32 f3 ♜e7 33 ♚h1 ♛c8 34 h4 ♚h8** (See diagram)

Position after 34 moves.

BELLE

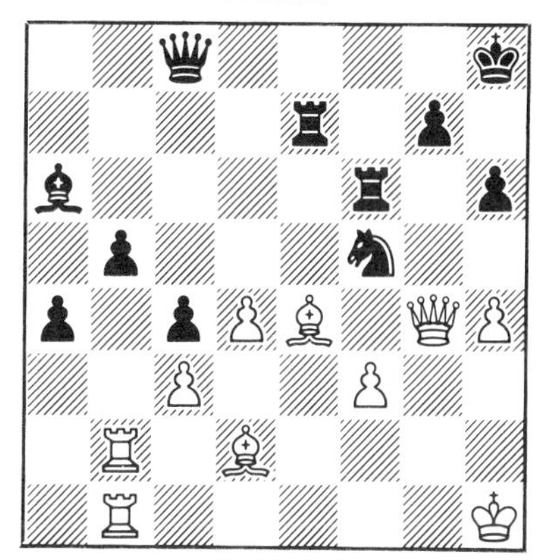

CHAOS

35 ♝f4? CHAOS could put up continued resistance by the Exchange sacrifice 35 ♖xb5 ♗xb5 36 ♖xb5, and if ... ♖f7 then 37 ♗c1-a3 and all of White's pieces are well posted and the Bishops may become very powerful. **... ♞xd4!** An elegant conclusion by the tactically supreme BELLE. The first point is that neither cxd4 or ♕xc8+ work, because after the exchange of Queens, one of the White Bishops is hanging. **36 ♛g3 ♞xf3!!** The fine point behind this is revealed in the continuation of the game. **37 ♝xf3** If 37 ♕xf3, CHAOS would be stung by ... ♖xe4! (38 ♕xe4? ♗b7 etc.) **... ♛f5! 38 ♜xh6** If 38 ♗d6, then ... ♖e3 is convincing. **... ♛xf3+ 39 ♛xf3 ♜xf3** Now the tactical fireworks are over, and BELLE has an easy win. **40 ♝g5 ♜ef7 41 ♜c1** CHAOS is helpless, and can only await developments. **... ♜h3+ 42 ♚g2 ♜ff3 43 ♝d2 a3! 44 ♜b4** ♖a2 is countered by ... ♗b7! and: 45 ♖xa3? ♖xc3+ picking up the Rook; 45 ♔g1 ♖g3+ 46 ♔f2 ♖g2+ 47 any ♖h1 mate. **... a2** But now BELLE goes on to get another Queen. **45 ♜a1 ♜fg3+ 46 ♚f1** Unfortunately, after 46 ♔f2, ... ♗b7 threatening mate in 2 forces ♔f1 anyway.... **♜h1+ 47 ♚f2 ♜xa1 48 ♚xg3 ♜g1+ 49 ♚f2 a1(♛) 0-1**

OSTRICH - ADVANCE 2.4
Sicilian(B95)

OSTRICH plays too tamely with the White pieces in this Sicilian, and then it allows ADVANCE 2.4 to disrupt its Queenside Pawns, which leads inexorably to a lost position. ADVANCE 2.4 is not as powerful in terms of tree-search as some of the other programs, but in this tournament the program played creditably — here it conducts a thematically unified game, taking advantage of its opponent's strategic errors.

1 e4 c5 2 ♞f3 d6 3 d4 cxd4 4 ♞xd4 ♞f6 5 ♞c3 a6 6 ♝g5 e6 7 ♝e2 This tame move is only good for equality, but considering the limitations of today's programs, this is undoubtedly a wiser continuation than the double-edged main line f4. **... ♝e7 8 ♝e3?!** But there is no real reason for this loss of tempo, after which the initiative passes to Black. OSTRICH should Castle here. The program may have been concerned about the reply ... ♘xe4?!, which is much too risky for Black, e.g. 9 ♘xe4 ♗xg5 10 f4 with a strong attack. The game has now transposed into a position from the Scheveningen variation, with Black a tempo ahead. **... ♞bd7 9 0-0 ♞c5 10 f3** This is rather passive. The program could establish a restricted but sound position by 10 ♗f3, though this blocks White from playing f4 (which the program apparently has no intention of doing anyway). **10 ... ♛c7**

(See diagram)

11 a4?! This ultimately allows the derangement of OSTRICH's Queenside Pawns. The program should play 11 ♘b3 and if ... ♘xb3, 12 axb3, after which Black still cannot play ... b5, and it is questionable whether that move would be strategically desirable anyway. **11 ... 0-0 12 ♛e1?!** Many years ago, a system was developed in the Scheveningen variation, where White would play ♕e1, ♖ad1, and ♕g3 looking for a Kingside attack. The whole line was eventually shown to be quite harmless, and it is not clear that OSTRICH actually intends such a plan. If so, its strategic capability has significantly advanced, although here the placement of the Queen on g3 would be less forceful because White has omitted the thematic f4. In this year's event, OSTRICH does show a rather substantial improvement over its previous level of play. Still, it was better to play 12 ♗d3 so as to give the Knight a square to go to. **... e5 13 ♞b3 ♞xb3 14 cxb3 ♝e6 15 b4 d5!** As usual in the Sicilian, when Black gets this in, White's space advantage is neutralized and Black starts to take control of the game. **16 exd5 ♞xd5 17 ♞xd5 ♝xd5 18 b5?!** Clearly, an immediate ♖ac1 was called for. Computer programs have difficulty understanding the concept of controlling an open file. **18 ... ♝c5 19 ♝xc5 ♛xc5+ 20 ♚h1 a5!**

Position after 10 moves.
ADVANCE 2.4

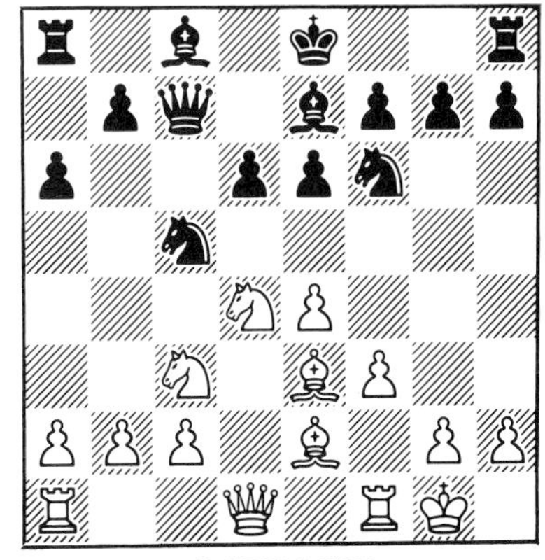

OSTRICH

ADVANCE 2.4

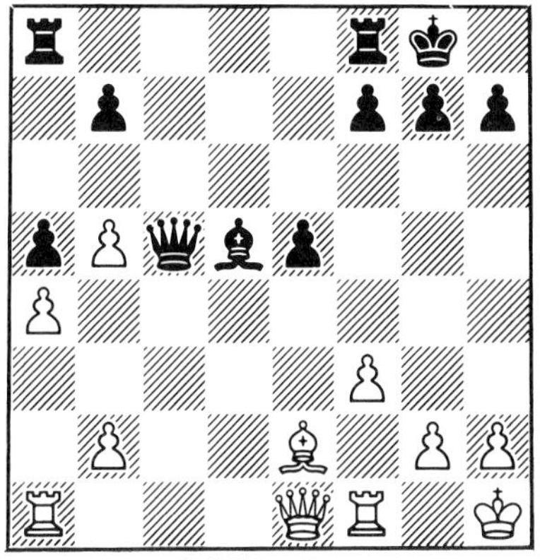

OSTRICH

Now the White Queenside is immobilized, and in the absence of any effective counterplay, OSTRICH's Pawns are tempting targets. **21 ♛g3?** This accomplishes nothing, and leaves the Queenside unprotected. A sound continuation would be 21 ♕c3. **... ♛d4 22 ♜ad1** There's no future at all in 22 ♖fb1 ♖ac8. OSTRICH is in fact lost. **... ♕xb2 23 ♕f2** OSTRICH can't get the Pawn back by 23 ♖xd5 ♕xe2 because the Rook is hanging, but 24 ♖e1 then leaves the White pieces actively placed. **... ♜ad8 24 ♜d3 ♝b3 25 ♛g1** The purpose of this is unclear. **... ♜xd3 26 ♝xd3 ♝xa4** Now ADVANCE 2.4 has a passed Pawn, and the contest is for all practical purposes over. **27 ♛c5 ♜d8 28 ♝c4 ♛b4 29 ♛xb4 axb4 30 h3 ♝c2 31 g3 b3 32 ♚g2 ♜d4 33 ♜a1 ♚f8 34 ♜a8+ ♚e7 35 ♝xb3** Sooner or later, the b-Pawn must cost a piece. OSTRICH tries to get some counterplay with its Rook, but it's too late. **... ♝xb3 36 ♜h8 h6 37 ♜c8 ♜d2+ 38 ♚f1 ♝d5 39 f4 ♜d3 40 fxe5 ♜xg3 41 h4 ♜g4 42 ♜g8 ♝c4+ 43 ♚e1 ♝xb5 44 ♜b8 ♝c6 45 ♜g8** 0-1

Fig. 9.4 Valvo takes on BELLE in a speed game.

SFINKS X - SAVANT X
Albin Countergambit(D08)

The longest game (of a tournament that saw many long games between programs with little knowledge of how to play endgames) turns out to be one of the most interesting. SAVANT X nursed a slight edge from the opening until SFINKS X blundered away a Pawn, and then won another Pawn, after which the ending should have been an elementary win; but SAVANT X trapped its own Rook, and allowed its opponent to get a bind which should have resulted in a draw. Then SFINKS X began to play creatively, forcing the Queening of its passed Pawn at the expense of letting SAVANT X run its own Pawn. The result was an ending with SAVANT X having the advantage of ♕ + g-Pawn vs. ♕, which should have been extremely interesting and difficult, but which turned out to be a relatively easy win since SFINKS X did not know how to defend properly.

1 d4 d5 2 c4 e5 This tricky gambit is a specialty of Dave Kittinger, author of the MYCHESS program which runs in the Novag Savant. **3 cxd5** A weak continuation, offering White no more than equality. Usual is 3 dxe5 d4 4 ♘f3 ♘c6 5 g3, and Black has trouble demonstrating any compensation for the sacrificed Pawn. **3 ... ♛xd5 4 e3 exd4 5 ♞c3?!** Showy, but ineffective. Usual is 5 ♕xd4 with an even game. **... ♝b4 6 ♛xd4 ♛xd4 7 exd4 ♞f6** Now SAVANT X has a slight advantage, and in a game between computer programs, White's isolated d-Pawn is a liability, although its spatial influence and the fact that the Queens have been exchanged might compensate in a game between human players. For computer programs, Pawn structure tends to assume more importance, since attacking weak Pawns is a process for which program heuristics are well suited. **8 ♝f4?** The Bishop is misplaced here, and should go to d2 or e3 immediately. Now SAVANT X is able to force exchanges, which are usually unfavorable to the player with the isolated Pawn. **... ♞d5 9 ♝d2** Here it is probably better to play 9 ♘e2 developing another piece, with the possibility of a later a3. **... ♝e6 10 ♞xd5?** Here it is necessary to play 10 ♘f3; now the d-Pawn is ultimately doomed. **♝xd2+ 11 ♚xd2 ♝xd5** SAVANT's advantage is now much clearer. **12 ♞e2 0-0 13 ♞f4 ♜d8!**

SAVANT X

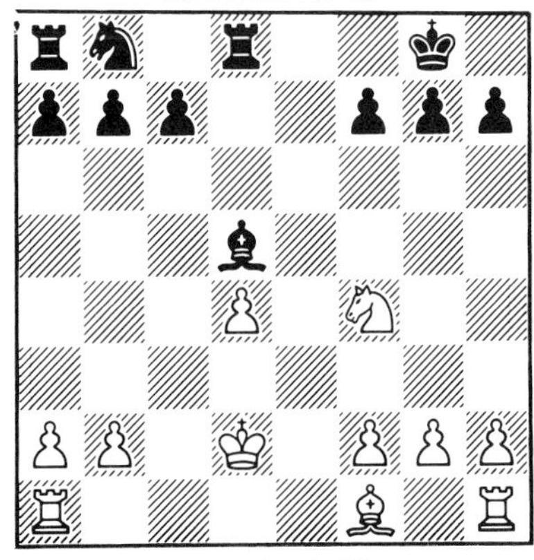

SFINKS X

A nice point; SFINKS X cannot afford to take the Bishop, because the d-Pawn would fall. **14 ♚c3 ♞c6 15 ♞xd5?** SFINKS X concedes the loss of the d-Pawn. The program should play f3, followed by developing its Bishop. **... ♜xd5 16 g3 ♜xd4 17 ♝d3** It would seem that the Bishop would stand better on g2. Computer programs have a tendency to start a fianchetto and then fail to finish it with a Bishop move, and several programs have special heuristlcs intended to force the completion of fianchettos if they are taken "out of book" in the opening. **... ♜ad8 18 ♜ad1 ♜4d6** SAVANT X intends ... ♘e5, which if played immediately would lose to 19 ♗xh7+. **19**

a3 a5 20 ♜he1 ♜h6? This allows SFINKS X too much play. SAVANT X should simply continue ... ♔f8 making "luft" — a factor whose lack soon becomes important — and also threatening ... ♘e5. **21 ♝a6!** A very interesting resource, which many strong human players might not find. **... ♜b8!?** One would expect ... ♔f8 immediately, but this also has its points... **22 ♝xb7 ♚f8 23 ♝a6 ...** one of which is that 23 ♗xc6 is now not possible. **... ♜xh2 24 ♜d2** Stronger than this defensive move would be 24 ♖d7. **... h5?!** Loss of time. Black should play ... f6. **25 b3 g6 26 ♚c4 ♜d8 27 ♜de2** With a Pawn advantage for Black, it is clearly not in White's interest to allow exchanges. **... ♜d4+ 28 ♚b5** SFINKS X has a fearless King, which now becomes a strong piece. **28 ... ♜d6 29 ♜e8+ ♚g7 30 ♜f1 ♞d4+ 31 ♚xa5 ♞xb3+ 32 ♚b4 ♞d2** SAVANT X now gains an advantage of two Pawns, after which one would expect the ending to be an easy win. But not many endings are really easy for a computer program to win! **33 ♜d1 ♜xf2 34 ♝e2 ♞e4 35 ♜xe4 ♜xe2 36 ♜xe2 ♜xd1** These exchanges have materially simplified Black's task. **37 ♜c2**

SAVANT X

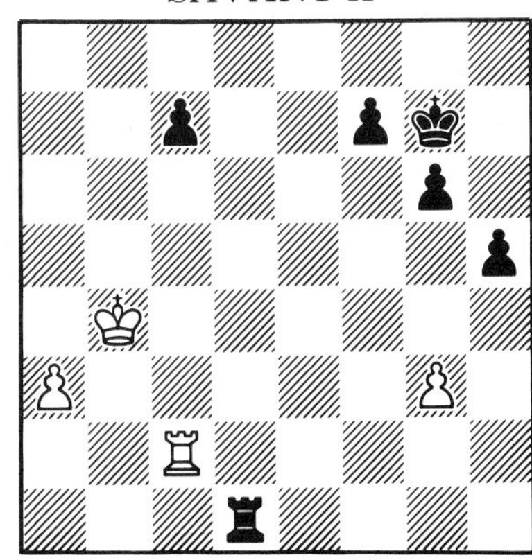

SFINKS X

37 ... ♜d4+?! SAVANT X starts to go wrong. ... ♖d3 wins rather easily, e.g. 38 ♖c3 ♖xc3 39 ♔xc3 ♔f8, and Black's King can stop the a-Pawn and protect his c-Pawn, while the Kingside Pawns advance; or 38 ♖g2 c5+ 39 ♔xc5 ♖xa3, and again the win is not difficult. **38 ♚b5 ♜d5+?! 39 ♚c6 ♜a5?** Here again, ... ♖d3 is the move, although the win is no longer so easy. **40 ♜c3 ♜a7?** SAVANT X has accomplished its goal of stopping the a-Pawn and protecting its own c-Pawn, but this is hardly an achievement to be proud of — the Rook is horribly misplaced on a7. The program should forget about defending its c-Pawn and get the Kingside Pawns moving. **41 ♚b5 f5?** After this, the win becomes problematic. The right continuation is 41 ... g5. Now the King gets cut off from supporting the advance of his Pawns. **42 a4 ♚f8?!** Another weak move, but it's really not clear that Black has any way to make progress. **43 a5 ♚f7 44 a6 ♚f6 45 ♜c6+ ♚f7** Or 45 ... ♔g5 46 ♖e6 f4 47 gxf4+ ♔xf4 48 ♖xg6 h4 49 ♖h6 ♔g3 50 ♖h8 with a clear draw. **46 ♚c5 ♚g7** Or ... g5 47 ♔d4 f4 48 gxf4 gxf4 (... g4 49 ♖h6) 49 ♖h6 h4 50 ♔e4 h3 51 ♔xf4 h2 52 ♖xh2 ♖xa6 53 ♔e4, with a theoretical draw. **47 ♚d4 ♚h6 48 ♚e5 ♚g5 49 ♚d5 ♚h6**

SAVANT X

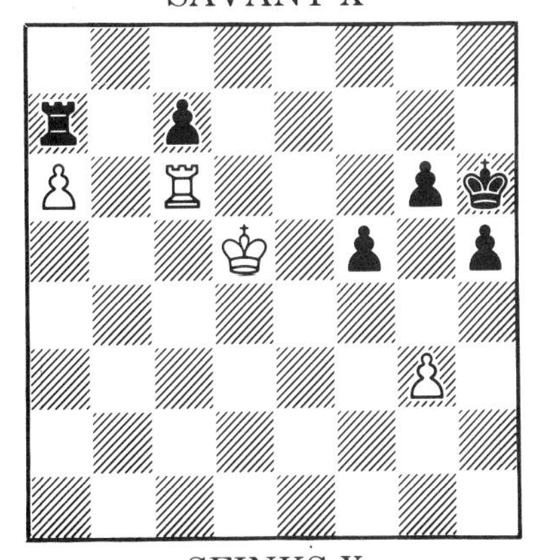

SFINKS X

50 ♔e6?! Perhaps inspired by its opponent's play, SFINKS X now embarks on a fatal misadventure. **... ♚g7 51 ♚d7?** ♔e5 holds the draw; this ultimately loses. **... h4!** Finally SAVANT X gets a chance to start its Pawns rolling. **52 gxh4 f4 53 ♚c8 f3 54 ♜xc7+ ♜xc7+ 55 ♚xc7 f2 56 a7 f1(♛) 57 a8(♛) ♛f4+ 58 ♚d7 ♛xh4** The game has now reached a classic endgame position, of notorious difficulty, in which Black has slight winning chances with the best play. With the inexactitudes to be expected of computer programs, however, the Pawn swiftly proves to be a decisive advantage. **59 ♛a7?** SFINKS X obviously has no idea as to how to play this ending. Once again, to conserve question marks, the rest shall pass without comment. **... g5 60 ♛a1+ ♚g6 61 ♛b1+ ♚h5 62 ♛h7+ ♚g4 63 ♛e4+ ♚g3 64 ♛e3+ ♚g2 65 ♛e2+ ♚h3 66 ♛f3+ ♛g3 67 ♛e4 g4 68 ♛h1+ ♛h2 69 ♛f1+ ♛g2 70 ♛c4 ♛d2+ 71 ♚e6 g3 72 ♛b3 ♛f4 73 ♛d3 ♛h6+ 74 ♚d5 ♚h2 75 ♛c2+ g2 76 ♛f2 ♛h5+ 77 ♚d4 ♚h1 78 ♛f8** 0-1

PION - SCHACH 2.6
King's Indian Attack(A08)

PION opened both its games with White with the King's Indian Attack, a slow system in which White tries to force the move e4-e5, and then play for a Kingside attack. With Black, the program played the Pirc or Modern defense, using a similar setup. This approach has one major advantage, in that a large opening book is not necessary since the program can generally play the same moves (whatever the opponent plays) each time. On the other hand, the positions resulting are not very well suited to computer heuristics. In this game, PION made a number of positional errors after leaving its opening "book", and soon was in a bad way. When the program failed to take advantage of the only real error by SCHACH 2.6 (which might have led to a draw), it lost a piece and the game.

1 ♞f3 d5 2 g3 e6 3 ♝g2 c5 4 0-0 ♞c6 5 d3 ♝d6 6 e4 ♞ge7 7 ♞bd2 0-0 8 ♜e1 ♛c7 9 c3 ♝d7 10 ♛e2 f6 The end of the line in ECO — theory considers this position unclear. It is certainly interesting; the struggle for control of e5 is intense. **11 d4?!** Typically, once out of "book", the program tries to accomplish its primitive positional goals by direct action rather than maneuvering. The consequent opening of the c-file favors Black. **11 cxd4 12 ♞xd4?!** PION now demonstrates a complete lack of understanding of the position. After 12 cxd4, the threat of e5 is renewed. **... ♞xd4!** SCHACH 2.6, on the other hand, is playing rather well. A tempting continuation, perhaps even a good one, was 12 ... a6 preparing for ... e5, taking control of the center, but the text is much simpler and leads to a clear advantage for SCHACH 2.6, which gets immediate control of the c-file. **13 cxd4 ♛c2** This turns out to be more effective than it deserves. A strong continuation for Black is ... ♕b6!, after which 14 e5?? is impossible: 14 ... fxe5 15 dxe5 ♗c5 and a catastrophe on f2 cannot be prevented. **14 exd5 ♞xd5**

SCHACH 2.6

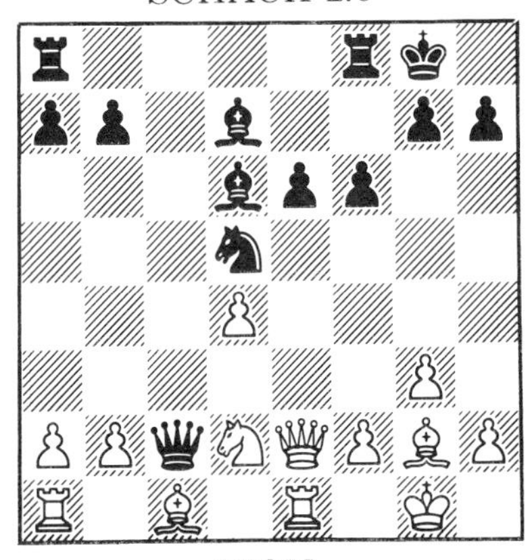

PION

15 ♛h5? With the subtle threat ♗e4, which SCHACH 2.6 easily parries. PION misses the better continuation 15 ♘c4!, e.g. ... ♕xe2 16 ♖xe2 ♗c7. After this loss of time, SCHACH 2.6 takes the initiative, and handles it well. **... f5 16 ♛e2 ♜ac8 17 ♞f3?!** And after this error, the initiative grows into an attack. It was necessary to play 17 a3 first. **... ♝b4 18 ♛xc2 ♜xc2 19 ♜d1 ♝b5 20 ♞e1!** PION's position is now critical, because of the powerful Black Bishops. The program has to do something about the cramping Rook on c2 before it can finish its development. This move sets a clever (and apparently unwitting) trap ... **20 ... ♜e2?!** Which SCHACH 2.6 falls into. Black should retreat its Rook here.

SCHACH 2.6

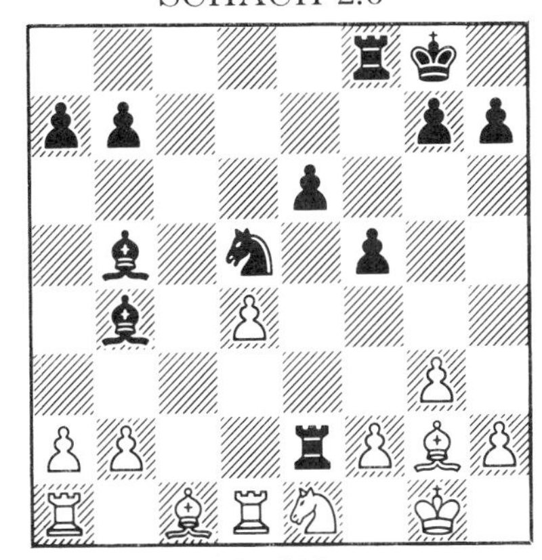

PION

21 ♞d3? 21 ♗f1! would have led to a drawish position after ... ♖xe1 22 ♖xe1 ♗xe1 23 ♗xb5; this loses. **... ♝xd3 22 ♝xd5** PION's horizon has now expanded to include 22 ♖xd3 ♖e1+ 23 ♗f1 ♖c8, winning the Bishop at c1. **22 ... ♝c2!** The point behind PION's last move is that now ... exd5 23 ♖xd3 ♖e1+ 24 ♔g2 ♖c8 wins nothing after 25 a3!. and PION will be able to either develop its Bishop at b2, or break the attack by ♖c3. **23 ♝xe6+ ♜xe6 24 ♝d2** This just speeds things up by forcing exchanges, but PION is hopelessly lost anyway. **... ♝xd1 25 ♝xb4 ♝h5 26 d5 ♜a6 27 ♝xf8 ♚xf8 28 b4 ♜d6** Now the d-Pawn falls, and the rest is easy. **29 ♜c1 ♜xd5 30 ♜c8+ ♚f7 31 ♜c7+ ♚f6 32 g4?** PION reacts strangely to the threat of 33 ... ♗f3; one would expect ♔g2 from a human player. Perhaps its evaluator is being confused by the material minus. **... ♝xg4 33 a4 ♝f3 34 ♜c1 ♜d4 35 b5 ♜xa4 36 h3 ♜a5 37 ♜b1 b6 38 ♚f1 ♝e4 39 ♜b3 ♜xb5!** The coup de grace. **40 ♜xb5 ♝d3+ 41 ♚e1 ♝xb5 42 f4 g5 43 fxg5+ ♚xg5 44 ♚f2 ♚f4 45 ♚e1** 0-1

Fig. 9.5 BELLE-NUCHESS: Left, David Slate; right, Ken Thompson.

PHILIDOR - CHATURANGA 2.0
Ruy Lopez(C68)

This game illustrates with particular clarity the perils which confront chess programmers. Dissatisfied with CHATURANGA's Round 1 fiasco, Poduska made some last-minute changes in his program — and then watched in horror as CHATURANGA computed the alternatives and proceeded to select the WORST possible move.

1 e4 e5 2 ♞f3 ♞c6 3 ♝b5 a6 4 ♝xc6 dxc6 5 0-0 Now CHATURANGA 2.0 is out of its "book", and an incredible exhibition begins, on which no further comment is necessary. **... ♛xd2 6 ♛xd2 a5 7 ♞xe5 a4 8 ♞c3 b6 9 ♞xc6 ♝d7 10 ♛d5 ♝xc6 11 ♛xc6+ ♔e7 12 ♞d5+ ♔d8 13 ♛xa8+ ♔d7 14 ♛xf8** 1-0

ROUND 3

BELLE - NUCHESS
Irregular (C20)

BELLE's incredible opening "book" (programmer Ken Thompson has typed in most if not all of the contents of ECO) catches top challenger NUCHESS in an ancient trap.

1 e4 e5 2 c3?! ♞f6?! Best for Black is the thematic ... d5, as in Ponziani's opening (1 e4 e5 2 ♘f3 ♘c6 3 c3 d5). NUCHESS proceeds to follow the skittles game Morphy-Bottien, played in the Cafe de la Regence in 1858! By the time the program realizes what's happening, it's too late. **3 d4 ♞xe4 4 dxe5 ♝c5?** NUCHESS marches straight into the jaws of the trap, which almost any of today's programs (including BELLE) would also do without prior knowledge — the payoff to White's attack is too far "over the horizon". Black should play ... d5 with equality.

NUCHESS

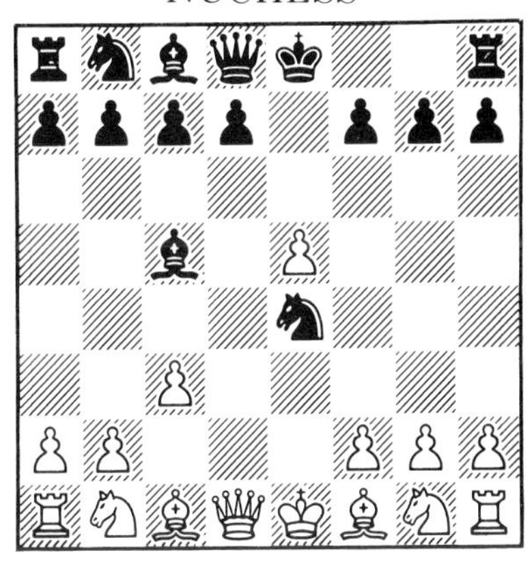

BELLE

5 ♛g4! ♞xf2 At this point Ken Thompson is said to have been concerned that Black might play ... ♗xf2+, after which BELLE would be out of its "book", but that move is no good either (6 ♔e2 ♕h4 7 ♕xg7 ♖f8 8 ♗h6). **6 ♛xg7 ♜f8 7 ♝g5 ♛xg5** Bottien played ... f6, which also loses after 8 exf6 d5 9 ♗e2 ♗g4 10 ♗xg4 ♘xg4 11 f7+ ♖xf7 12 ♕xf7+ ♔xf7 13 ♗xd8 ♘f2 14 ♗h4 ♘xh1 15 ♘f3, and White wins because the Knight at h1 is trapped (analysis by Morphy). **8 ♛xg5 ♞xh1 9 ♞f3 ♞c6 10 ♝d3 h6 11 ♛xh6 ♜g8 12 g3 ♞f2** NUCHESS has managed to extricate its Knight, but BELLE still has a decisive material advantage. **13 ♛h7 ♞xd3+ 14 ♛xd3 ♜h8 15 ♞bd2 ♜h5 16 0-0-0 ♞xe5?** This loses outright, but NUCHESS' chances for holding the game are nil anyway — the cramping e-Pawn prevents the program from developing and can't be removed without fatal exposure of the Black King, and even if that problem could be solved, the White h-Pawn will soon prove decisive. **17 ♜e1 d6** Here NUCHESS discovered that it loses a piece after 18 ♘xe5 ♖xe5 19 ♖xe5+ dxe5 20 ♕b5+, and resigned. 1-0

BEBE - ADVANCE 2.4
Sicilian(B92)

After a rather aimless opening and middlegame, the programs reach an endgame, in which BEBE has the advantage, and which turns out to be quite interesting. BEBE outplays ADVANCE 2.4 in the endgame, forcing a win with a deeply calculated exchanging combination.

1 e4 c5 2 ♞f3 d6 3 d4 cxd4 4 ♞xd4 ♞f6 5 ♞c3 a6 6 ♝e2 e5 7 ♞f3 Normal is 7 ♘b3; this blocks the f-Pawn. **... ♝e7?!** This has been known to be weak ever since Westerinen crushed Stean at Hastings 1972/73; Black should play ... h6, to prevent ♗g5. **8 0-0 0-0 9 ♝g5** A strong move aiming at control of d5. **... ♞bd7?** Black should play ... ♗e6 first. **10 ♛c1?** Loss of time; the motive for this is probably to overprotect g5, so that moves like ♘h4 become sound; but the Queen is passively placed. A strong continuation is 10 a4. **... h6 11 ♝xf6 ♞xf6 12 ♜d1 ♝d7 13 ♞d2 ♝c6?** A weak continuation, after which Black is saddled with an isolated d-Pawn. Black should play 13 ... b5. **14 ♞c4 ♞xe4** Or ... ♕c7 15 f3 followed by ♘e3. **15 ♞xe4 ♝xe4 16 ♞xe5 ♛c7 17 ♞d3 ♜ae8** Of course Black would have an almost certain draw after 17 ... ♗xd3, but the drawing tendencies of Bishops of opposite colors are one of the many things that chess programs don't know about. On the other hand, with the advantage of the Two Bishops, Black does not really stand worse — so why

Fig. 9.6 Famous Texas master Ken Smith discusses BELLE's crushing victory over NUCHESS with Ken Thompson, as Mike Valvo comments on the game for the spectators.

give up Bishop for Knight? **18 ♕d2?!** After this, BEBE is forced to weaken its Kingside. **... ♝g5 19 f4 ♛b6+ 20 ♞f2 ♝h4 21 g3 ♝f6 22 c3 ♝c6**

ADVANCE 2.4

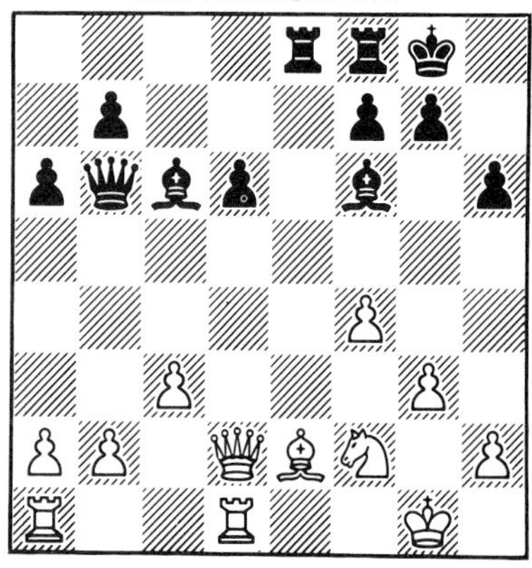

BEBE

Black's d-Pawn is weak, but its Bishops are very powerful. The White Kingside is porous, and BEBE's position can easily become critical. **23 ♜ac1 d5** This looks like it's blocking the Bishop's diagonal — but ADVANCE 2.4 is preparing the advance d4, opening up the position for its Bishops. **24 ♝h5 ♜e7** Better is an immediate ... d4 e.g. 25 cxd4 ♖d8 26 ♖c4 ♗b5 etc. **25 ♜c2 ♜fe8 26 ♝f3 d4** This has been "in the air" for some time, and Black now should get a considerable positional edge. **27 ♝xc6 dxc3 28 bxc3 bxc6?!** There was no need for ADVANCE 2.4 to mutilate its Pawn structure; 28 ... ♕xc6 was much better. **29 c4 ♛c5 30 ♚g2 ♛f5 31 g4 ♛c8 32 ♛a5 ♛b7** ADVANCE 2.4 has the better game, since the White King is very exposed. Much stronger, though, was ...

c5! preparing a strong post for the Bishop at d4, and opening the long diagonal for the Queen. **33 ♛c5 ♜e2 34 ♜dd2 ♜e1 35 ♞d3 ♜1e4 36 ♛f5 ♛c8?!** Exchanging Queens is not favorable for Black, with the white King so exposed. Correct and probably leading to a winning advantage is 36 ... ♗d4, e.g. 37 ♘e5 c5, or 37 ♘f2 g6 38 ♕xe4 (♕a5 ♖xf4) ♖xe4 39 ♘xe4 c5 40 ♖e2 f5 and wins. **37 ♛xc8 ♜xc8 38 ♚f3 ♜ce8 39 ♜e2 ♜xe2 40 ♜xe2 ♜xe2 41 ♚xe2**

ADVANCE 2.4

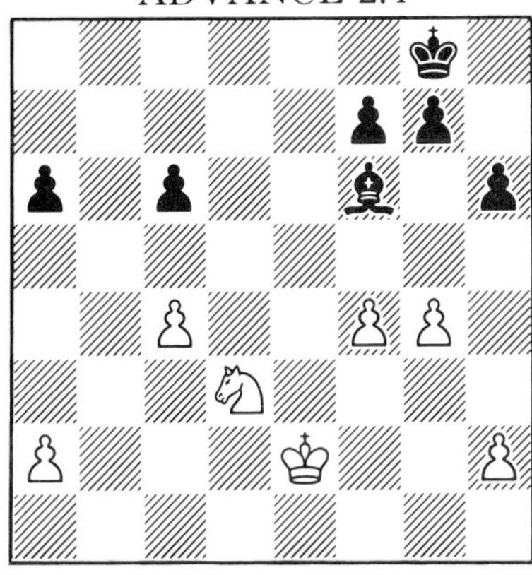

BEBE

After an aimless dozen moves, the middlegame has evolved into an endgame that superficially seems to be a certain draw. In reality, White has definite, perhaps decisive advantages — better King position, the absence of any target for the Black Bishop, the threat of ♘b4 winning a Pawn. **41 ... a5** If 41 ... ♗e7, then 42 ♔f3 and the King marches forward. **42 a4 ♚f8 43 ♚e3 ♚e8?!** ADVANCE 2.4 is strangely reluctant to advance with its King — possibly its King safety heuristic is affecting its endgame play. 43 ♔e7, taking up the distant opposition, was better, though White still keeps the edge after 44 ♘c5 ♗c3 45 f5. **44 ♞c5 ♝d8 45 ♚f3** BEBE cannot formulate any kind of plan, and is awaiting developments. Of course it's better to play ♔e4. **... ♝e7 46 ♞b3 ♝b4 47 h4 g6 48 ♚e4 ♚d7** Again, ... ♔e7 was the move to play. **49 c5?!** This Pawn will require constant watching now. Better and thematic was 49 h5, fixing the h6 Pawn. **... ♝e1?!** A waste of time. Black should play ... f6!, after which the classical breakthrough recipe g5 doesn't work: 50 g5 f5+ and there's no way to get in: 51 ♔e5 ♗c3+ 52 ♘d4 ♗xd4+ 53 ♔xd4 h5 54 ♔e5 ♔e7 with a draw. Alternatively, 50 h5 leads to interesting play after ... f5+! 51 ♔d3!. All this is of course far beyond ADVANCE 2.4, which has only the vaguest guidance from its heuristics in the ending, and is primarily driven by the desire not to lose material. **50 h5 gxh5?** The only (not very promising) try to hold the game is 50 ... f5+!? with complications, e.g. 51 ♔d3! **51 gxh5 ♝b4 52 ♚e5 ♚e7 53 ♚f5 ♝c3 54 ♞c1** BEBE finally finds a way to force a breakthrough. **... ♚e8 55 ♞d3 ♚f8** No better is ... ♔e7, after which White continues as in the game but plays 57 fxe5 instead.

ADVANCE 2.4

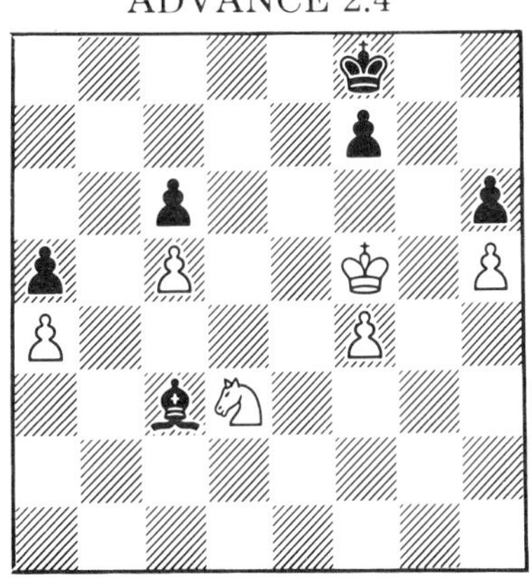

BEBE

56 ♞e5! BEBE now forces a winning King and Pawn endgame with this move, which required a particularly deep calculation to forsee that a win was forced. When the program made this move, it based its decision on the capture of the Pawn at h6 thirteen plies ahead — an impressive example of the search depth which chess programs can achieve in simplified positions. **... ♝xe5 57 ♚xe5 ♚e7 58 ♚f5 ♚e8 59 ♚f6 ♚f8 60 f5** Decisive; Black is in Zugzwang. The rest is easy. **... ♚e8 61 ♚g7 ♚e7 62 ♚xh6 ♚f8 63 ♚h7 f6 64 ♚g6 ♚g8 65 ♚xf6 ♚h7 66 ♚e6 ♚h6 67 f6 ♚h7 68 ♚d7 ♚g8 69 ♚e7 ♚h8 70 h6 ♚h7 71 f7 ♚xh6 72 ♚d8** BEBE is enjoying this so much that it can't bear to end the game. **... ♚g7 73 ♚e8 ♚f6 74 f8(♛)+ 1-0**

PRESTIGE X - CRAY BLITZ
Vienna Game(C25)

Again the Fidelity opening book proves effective, and PRESTIGE has a good game going against CRAY BLITZ until it makes a serious mistake by giving up the center. In support of the old adage that one bad move leads to another, the program quickly follows up with a real atrocity, after which it speedily loses three Pawns and the game.

1 e4 e5 2 ♞c3 ♞c6 3 ♝c4 ♝c5 4 ♛g4 g6 5 ♛f3 ♞f6 6 ♞ge2 d6 7 d3 ♝g4 8 ♛g3 ♝xe2 9 ♞xe2 ♞a5 The "book" continuation is ... ♘h5 10 ♕f3 ♕f6 with an even game. **10 ♝b3 0-0!?** This is rather risky. **11 ♝h6?!** More effective is 11 ♗g5 exploiting the dark-square weaknesses around Black's King. This move would set up a long-lasting and unpleasant pin (11 ... ♔g7 12 ♕h4), which could be strengthened by f4 and ♖f1; the Black Rook will not stay at f8, anyway. **... ♞xb3 12 axb3 ♜e8 13 0-0 d5** The natural consequence of White's inaccurate 11th move; CRAY BLITZ equalizes. **14 ♛f3 ♜e6 15 ♞c3 c6** (See diagram)

Position after 15 moves.
CRAY BLITZ

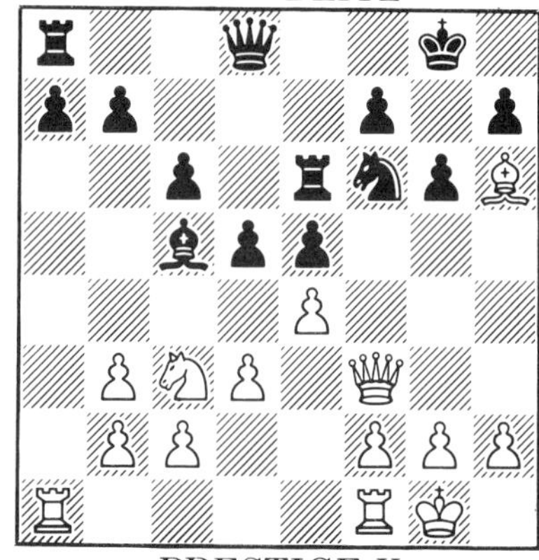

PRESTIGE X

16 exd5?! Giving up the center thus is wrong; PRESTIGE had an excellent continuation available in 16 ♗g5, forcing Black to do something about the threat to the d-Pawn. **... ♞xd5!** More accurate than ... cxd5, after which 17 ♗g5 is still effective. **17 ♞e4 ♝e7** CRAY BLITZ now stands better, since it has control of the center. Black also threatens 18 ... g5, trapping the Bishop at h6 (19 ♕h5 ♘f4). **18 c4??** PRESTIGE feels the lack of a central Pawn and the threat ... g5, but this is not the way to deal with the problem — in fact, the move loses the d-Pawn by force, as well as creating gaping weaknesses at d4 and b4. The best move is 8 ♗d2, after which Black maintains the advantage. **... ♞b4 19 ♜fd1 f5** Now if Black should play 19 ... g5, 20 ♕h3 successfully defends the Bishop. **20 ♛h3 ♛d7 21 ♞c3 ♜d6 22 ♝e3** There's no way to save the d-Pawn, and it might be wise to try to exchange Queens in its capture — not that it is good for White to get the Queens off, since the ending is probably lost, but because the Black Queen is too much of a threat to the weakened Pawns. PRESTIGE however, is still primarily concerned with the danger to its Bishop. **... ♜xd3 23 ♜xd3 ♛xd3 24 ♜d1 ♛c2 25 ♜d2** It may look as though White might still make a fight out of it by 25 ♖d7, but after ... ♖d8 the exchange of Rooks is forced. There's nothing PRESTIGE can do here but watch while the Pawns fall, after which the rest of the game should not have held much interest; PRESTIGE could well resign here, but the Spracklens have seen too many games lost in winning positions due to computer failure, so on it goes to the bitter end. And this tenacity is almost rewarded. **... ♛xb3 26 ♝h6 ♛xc4 27 ♜d7 ♛a6!?** It is still possible to play ... ♖d8, since 28 ♖xe7 is answered by ... ♕xc3!! **28 ♛e3 ♝f6 29 ♞d1 ♞d5 30 ♛b3 ♜b8 31 ♞e3 f4 32 ♞f1 ♚h8 33 ♛h3 ♜e8 34 ♝xf4** CRAY BLITZ has not played very accurately, and now PRESTIGE recovers one of its Pawns. **... h5 35 ♝d2 ♜e7 36 ♜xe7 ♞xe7 37 ♛e6 c5?!** Allowing an unnecessary mutilation of Black's Pawn structure; ... ♘d5 was much better. **38 ♛xa6 bxa6 39 ♝e3 c4 40 ♞d2 ♞d5 41 ♝xa7?** CRAY BLITZ has carelessly squandered its advantage, and if PRESTIGE would play 41 ♘xc4, it would be extremely difficult to find a win for Black. Here, however, PRESTIGE's desire to preserve its Bishop from being exchanged for the Knight winds up costing the program half a point. **... c3** Forcing a win, although the technical difficulties remain significant. **42 bxc3 ♞xc3 43 ♝b6 ♚g7 44 ♝a5 ♞d5 45 ♚f1 ♝e7 46 ♞c4 ♚f6 47 ♚e2 ♝c5 48 f3 ♞f4+ 49 ♚f1 ♚e6 50 g3 ♞d5 51 ♝d2 ♞e7 52 ♚e2 ♞c6 53 ♚d3 ♚d5 54 h3 ♞d4 55 ♞e3+ ♚e6 56 f4?!** More resistance is offered by 56 ♔e4; exchanging Pawns is a good idea for White, but this is the wrong way to go about it, and just offers Black another target. **... exf4 57 gxf4 ♞f3 58 ♝c3 ♞g1 59 h4 ♞f3 60 ♞g2** Now Black wins easily by ...♗f2, so PRESTIGE X resigns. 0-1

SCHACH 2.6 - PHILIDOR
Sicilian(B94)

PHILIDOR played this game very well, and impressively, up to a point. After some weak moves by SCHACH 2.6, PHILIDOR got a terrific bind on the German program's position and the game seemed to be headed toward a quick crush, but PHILIDOR missed a number of opportunities to decide matters in the middlegame, and even though two Pawns ahead, saw the endgame adjudicated a draw.

1 e4 c5 2 ♞f3 d6 3 d4 cxd4 4 ♞xd4 ♞f6 5 ♞c3 a6 6 ♝g5 ♞bd7 7 ♝e2 e5?! Too ambitious; Black cannot afford to let the Knight into f5. Usual and better is ... e6. **8 ♞f5 ♛b6** More natural is ... ♘b6. **♛c1** This is rather passive. White could gambit the b-Pawn by 9 ♕d2!?. **9 ... ♛c6 10 ♝f3 g6 11 ♞e3 ♝e7 12 0-0 0-0 13 ♞g4?!** This does not lead to anything, and uncovers the vital square d5. SCHACH 2.6 should continue 13 ♖d1 or 13 ♕d2, and pile up on d5. White would then have a significant advantage, because of the weaknesses in the Black position. **... ♜e8 14 ♞h6+ ♚f8 15 h3 b5 16 a4?!** This is not good either; 16 a3 was more appropriate. **... b4 17 ♞d5 ♞xd5 18 exd5** After this, all White's pressure is gone, and PHILIDOR takes charge of the game. **... ♛c4 19 ♝xe7+ ♚xe7 20 b3?!** A further weakness, which makes things easier for the British program **... ♛c3 21 ♜d1 ♞c5 22 ♞g4 e4 23 ♝e2 ♝xg4 24 ♝xg4 f5**

PHILIDOR

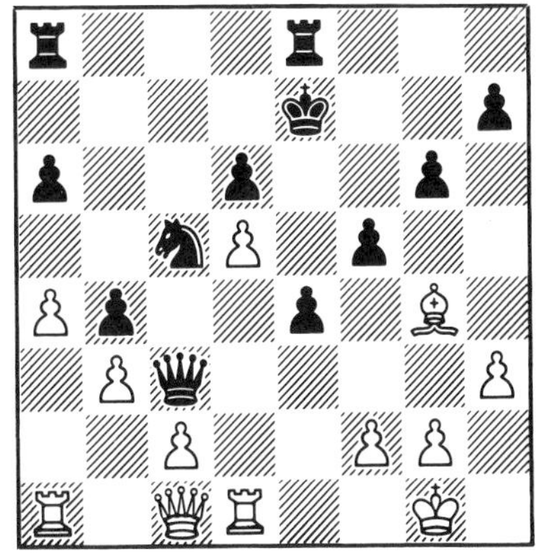

SCHACH 2.6

PHILIDOR now has a positional advantage which ought to be decisive. **25 ♝e2 ♚d7 26 ♜a2** Not a very impressive post for the Rook. **... e3!** Opening the e-file for Black's Rooks, giving the Knight e4 to go to, and blocking the White Queen's control of the c1-h6 diagonal — quite an accomplishment for one move. **27 fxe3 ♜xe3 28 ♝c4 ♜c8?!** Clearly better is ... ♖ae8, with the elegant threat 29 ♖a1 ♖xh3!! and if 30 gxh3, ... ♕g3+ 31 ♔f1 ♘e4 32 ♖d2 ♕xh3+ 33 ♔e1 (33 ♔g1 ♕e3+ and wins; 33 ♔e2 ♘xd2+ 34 ♔d1 ♕f3+ 35 ♔xd2 ♕e3+ 36 ♔d1 ♕e1 mate; 33 ♖g2 ♕h1+ 34 ♖g1 ♕f3+ 35 ♔e1 ♘c3+ 36 ♔d2 ♕e3 mate) ... ♘xd2+ 34 ♔d1 ♕f3+ 35 ♔xd2 ♕e3 mate. **29 ♚f2 ♞e4+ 30 ♚g1 ♞c5?!** Again Black misses a chance to decide the game immediately; 30 ... ♖xh3!! and a) 31 gxh3 ♕g3+ and mate next move; b) 31 ♗xa6 ♕c5+ forcing mate. **31 ♛d2 ♛xd2 32 ♜xd2 ♞e4 33 ♜d4** The only move that does not lose material. **... ♜e1+ 34 ♚h2 ♞c3** The misplacement of the White Rook at a2 now becomes painful. **35 ♜b2 ♜a8 36 ♝d3 a5** Finally PHILIDOR decides that it can afford to uncover b5, freeing its Rook from guard duty. Even better, though, was ... ♖a1 threatening ... ♘d1 winning the Exchange; after 37 ♗c4 ♘d1 White could safely resign.

PHILIDOR

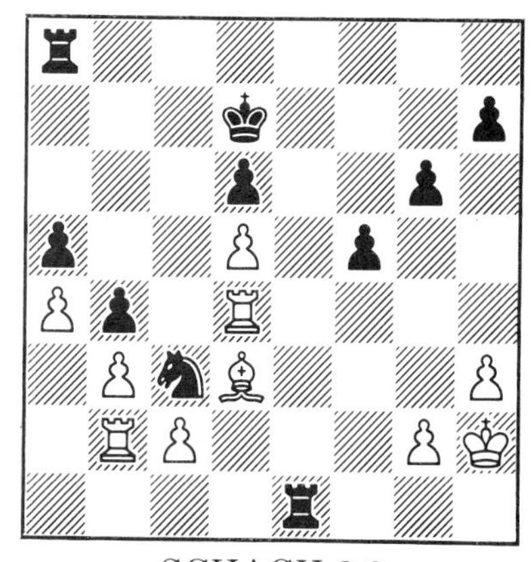

SCHACH 2.6

37 ♝b5+ SCHACH 2.6 is so delighted to get a breath of air that it jumps at this opportunity. **37 ... ♞xb5** This, however, is not best, even though it increases Black's advantage; simply moving the King and then playing ... ♖a1 as in the previous note would force resignation. **38 axb5 ♜b8 39 c4 bxc3 40 ♜c2 ♜e3!** Upsetting SCHACH 2.6's plans, and clearly demonstrating the inferiority of White's 37th move. **41 ♜c4 ♜xb5 42 ♜2xc3 ♜xc3 43 ♜xc3 ♜xd5** With an advantage of two Pawns, one would expect PHILIDOR to have an easy win in the endgame, but as noted before, easy wins for humans are not necessarily easy for computer programs. **44 ♚g3 ♜d4 45 ♚f2 ♜d2+** PHILIDOR is making things much too complicated. The simple continuation ... ♖e4, followed by the advance of the d-Pawn, wins easily. **46 ♚f3 h6 47 g4 fxg4+ 48 hxg4 ♚e6 49 ♚e3 ♜a2** This is still good enough to win, but ♖d1 was better. **50 ♚f3 ♚f6?!** PHILIDOR should get its Rook back into play by ... ♖a3! threatening ... a4. Black should be happy to give up its a-Pawn to exchange Rooks and reach a won King and Pawn ending. **51 ♜d3 ♚e5 52 ♜e3+ ♚d5 53 ♜d3+ ♚e6 54 ♜c3 d5?** After this, the win becomes problematic. **55 ♜c6+ ♚f7 56 ♜c7+ ♚f6 57 ♜c6+ ♚g7 58 ♚f4 ♜a1 59 ♚e5**

PHILIDOR

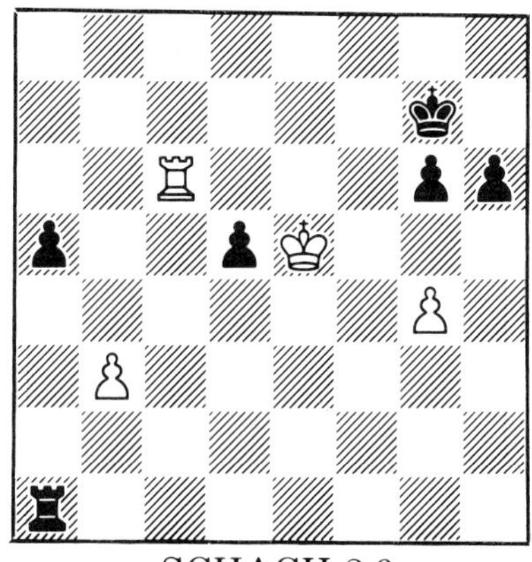

SCHACH 2.6

Here Tournament director Valvo was called upon to adjudicate the game, which had been delayed due to computer problems on the part of SCHACH 2.6. The position is extremely complicated, and to add spice the outcome of this game was highly significant for the last-round pairings — had PHILIDOR won, the pairings would literally have become an unholy mess. After prolonged analysis, even International Master David Levy was unable to produce a winning line for Black, and the game was adjudicated a draw. 1/2 - 1/2

SAVANT X - CHAOS
Sicilian(B22)

SAVANT gets an edge from the opening, but then is completely outplayed in the middlegame.
1 e4 c5 2 c3 ♞f6 3 e5 ♞d5 4 d4 cxd4 5 cxd4 d6 6 ♞f3 ♞c6 7 ♝c4 ♞b6 8 ♝b5 e6 9 ♝g5 ECO gives 9 0-0. **... ♝e7 10 ♝xe7 ♛xe7 11 ♞c3 ♝d7 12 0-0 0-0 13 ♜e1** An exchange on d6 would give White no more than an even game. **... a6 14 ♝d3 dxe5 15 dxe5 ♛c5** White now stands better, but the e-Pawn is likely in the long run to become a constant source of anxiety for a computer program. **16 ♛c2** Strong here is 16 ♘e4 ♕d5 17 ♘d6, and now Black cannot play ... ♘xe5, because 18 ♘xe5 ♕xd6 loses the Queen after 19 ♗xh7+, and 17 ... ♖b8 leads to a comfortable edge for White after 18 ♗e4 ♕xd1 19 ♖Raxd1. **... h6 7 a4?** After this, Black gets a definite edge. The obvious 17 a3 was better. **... ♞b4 18 ♛e2 ♞xd3 19 ♛xd3 ♜ac8** An inaccuracy; Black should play ... ♖fd8. **20 a5** Correct; now White regains the edge. **... ♞d5 21 ♜ec1?!** The best chances were afforded by 21 ♘xd5 exd5 (... ♕xd5 22 ♕xd5 exd5 23 ♖acl) 22 ♘d4. **... ♜fd8 22 h3 ♝c6 23 ♞xd5** Now the exchange has to be played anyway, in less favorable circumstances. **... ♛xd5 24 ♛xd5 ♜xd5** And now the e-Pawn is indeed a tangible weakness; Black stands better because of the Pawn weaknesses in White's game and the ineffectuality of the Knight. **25 ♜c3 ♜cd8 26 ♜c4?!** White is now in a bad way, but letting the Rook in at d3 just makes things worse. A possibility worth looking at is 26 ♖e3. **26 ... ♜d3.**

CHAOS

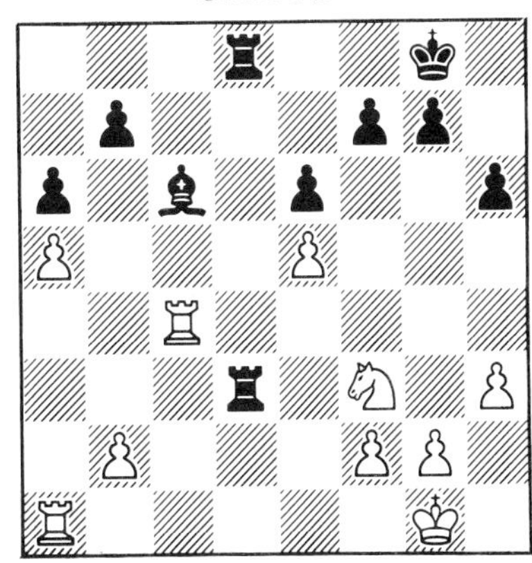

SAVANT X

27 ♞h2? This loses outright; SAVANT could try 27 ♖f4 or 27 ♖c3. **... ♜d1+ 28 ♜xd1 ♜xd1+ 29 ♞f1 ♝b5** Winning a piece and the game. **30 ♜c8+ ♚h7 31 ♚h2 ♜xf1 32 ♚g3 ♝c6 33 ♜c7♚g6 34 h4 ♜e1** After this, Black's Rook picks off the White Pawns, and there's not much interest in the rest of the game. **35 f4 ♜e2 36 b4 ♜xg2+ 37 ♚h3 ♜b2 38 h5+ ♚xh5 39 ♜xf7 ♜xb4 40 ♚g3 ♜b2 41 ♜e7 ♜g2+ 42 ♚h3 g5 43 fxg5 ♜xg5 44 ♜f7 ♜xe5 45 ♚g3 ♜xa5 46 ♚f4 ♜f5+ 47 ♚xf5+ exf5 48 ♚xf5 a5** 0-1

OSTRICH - SFINKS X
Sicilian(B40)

Monroe Newborn's OSTRICH is one of the grand old veterans of computer chess, having taken second place in the third U.S. Computer Chess Championship back in 1972, and remaining a feared competitor ever since. Since OSTRICH runs on a minicomputer (lately expanded into an array of minicomputers), its performance is processor-limited, and OSTRICH has not kept pace with other programs such as BELLE and CRAY BLITZ, running on more powerful machines, which it once surpassed — the program's rating seems to have stabilized at about 1600. Originally Monty named his program for its cowardly tendency to "bury its head" via the horizon effect, but lately the program has been playing enterprising chess, and its most distinguishing characteristic (well illustrated in this game) seems to be an uncanny ability to wriggle out of bad positions. When the author pointed out to Monty that his zoological analogy was obsolete, and that a more appropriate characterization would be that of a snake, he immediately thought of "Mr. Hiss" from the Disney animated epic "Robin Hood".

1 e4 c5 2 ♞f3 e6 3 c3 A variant on Alapin's system which is more commonly seen after 2 ... d6. **... d5 4 ♝b5+ ♝d7 5 ♝xd7+ ♞xd7?!** This falls right in with White's positional objective, which is to exchange on d5 and then play d4, so that Black will have an isolated d-Pawn. More thematic for Black is ... ♕xd7 as in Das - Justo, Malta 1980. **6 exd5 exd5 7 0-0 ♞gf6 8 d4 ♝e7 9 ♝f4** It would be slightly more accurate to play 9 ♗g5, applying pressure to d5. **... 0-0 10 dxc5 ♞xc5 11 ♛e2?!** This is not a good square for the Queen, which will soon have to move again. Better is 11 ♗g5 followed by ♘bd2. The program plays 11 ♕e2 because the natural developing move 11 ♘bd2 is refuted by ... ♘d3, which really shows that the Bishop doesn't belong on f4. **... ♛d7 12 ♞bd2 ♜fe8 13 b4?** Every now and then, computer programs seem to come up with a real positional atrocity, which this is a good example of. The weakness created along the c-file is glaring. **... ♝d6 14 ♝e3 ♞ce4 15 ♜ac1 ♞g4 16 ♛d3 ♞xe3 17 fxe3**

SFINKS X

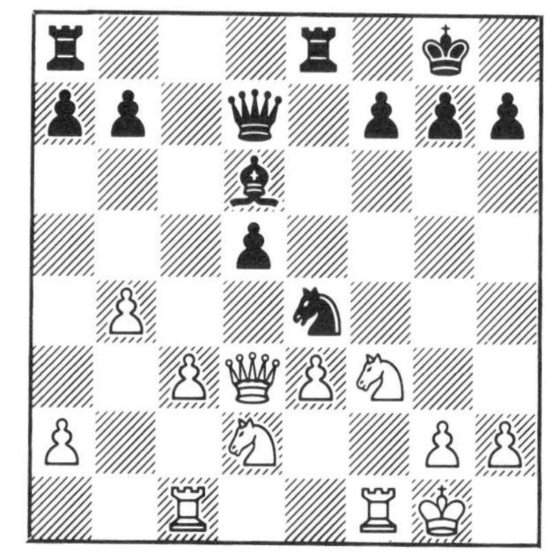

OSTRICH

SFINKS X now has an obvious positional advantage. **... ♞f6?!** This retreat is unnecessary, since the d-Pawn is not really threatened (18 ♕xd5?? ♗xh2+). SFINKS X should play ... ♖ac8, after which 18 c4? simply loses a Pawn. **18 ♜fe1 ♜ac8 19 ♛d4 ♛a4?!** This looks attractive to computer heuristics which value an attack on an undefended man highly, but now the Queen is out of play. Again, ... b5 was the move to play. **20 e4 dxe4 21 ♞xe4 ♞xe4 22 ♜xe4 ♜xe4 23 ♛xe4 ♝xb4?!** This looks clever but does not accomplish anything except to get SFINKS X in trouble. The simple continuation ... ♕c6 would pose some serious problems for White in the endgame. **24 ♛xb7 ♝c5+ 25 ♚h1 ♜d8 26 ♛b3** (See diagram next page)

26 ... ♛xb3? This makes it much more difficult for Black to hold the ending, although with proper play it still should be a draw. The protected passed Pawn is obviously a major asset for White; much better was ♕f4. **27 axb3 ♜d3** And here ... ♔f8, bringing the King toward the passed Pawn, is better. **28 ♞e1 ♜e3 29 b4 ♝e7 30 ♞f3 ♝f6?** SFINKS X clearly has no understanding of how to

Position after White's 26th move.
SFINKS X

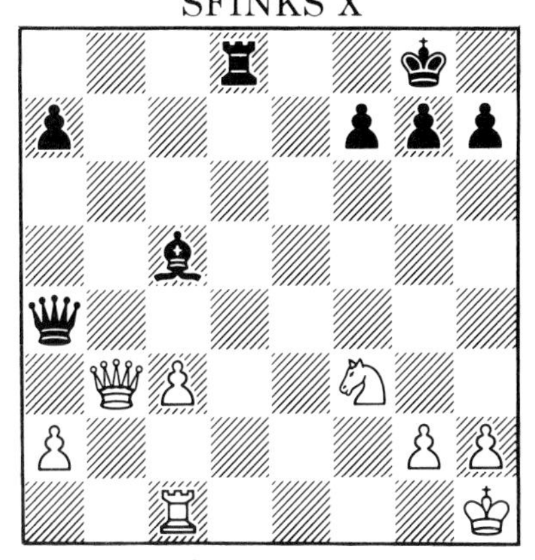

OSTRICH

go about restraining the advance of the White Pawns. 30 ... ♔f8 is still the move, but SFINKS X insists on ignoring the threat posed by the passed Pawn. The program plays the rest of the ending rather poorly. **31 c4 ♜b3 32 b5 ♜b2 33 h3 ♚f8** Finally! **34 h4 ♚e7?** The correct move is ... ♔e8, so that 35 ♖a1 can be answered by ... ♖xb5. After this fatal mistake, the a-Pawn goes. **35 ♜a1 ♜c2 36 ♜xa7+ ♚d6 37 ♜xf7?!** More accurate is 37 ♖a6+ ♔c5 38 ♖c6+ ♔b4 39 b6, maintaining connected passed Pawns. **... ♚c5?** A move with no relevance to the position. **38 ♜c7+ ♚b4??** ... and this is suicidal. After ... ♔b6 39 ♖c6+ ♔b7, Black can still hope for computer failure. **39 b6 ♝b2 40 b7 ♜c1+ 41 ♚h2 ♝f6 42 b8(♛)+** 1-0

CHATURANGA 2.0 - PION
Pirc(B09)

PION's quiet style allows CHATURANGA 2.0 to make its best showing of the tournament.

1 e4 d6 2 d4 ♞f6 3 ♞c3 g6 4 f4 ♝g7 5 ♞f3 0-0 6 ♝c4 6 ♗d3 is usual. **... ♞xe4 7 ♞xe4** The "book" line is 7 ♗xf7+ ♖xf7 8 ♘xe4. The text is also playable. **... d5 8 ♝xd5** This is not really a bad move, but it would be better to play 8 ♗d3 dxe4 9 ♗xe4. **... ♛xd5 9 ♞c5?!** This is premature. A sounder continuation was 9 ♘c3 with a slight advantage for Black. **9 ... ♞c6**

PION

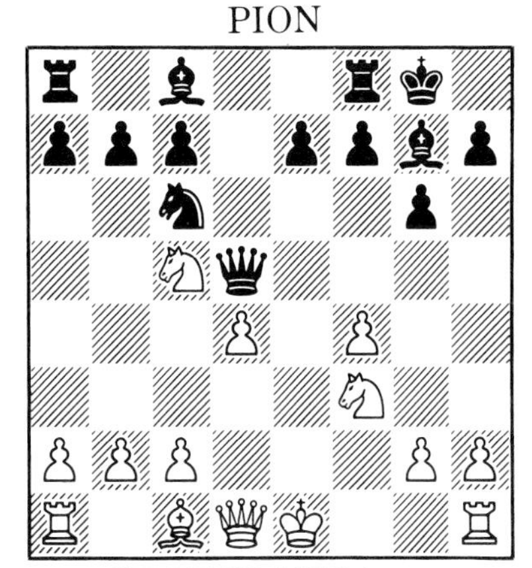

CHATURANGA 2.0

At this point, CHATURANGA 2.0 has a playable position, and could continue 10 ♘b3 with a reasonable game. Just when it seemed that John Poduska's program was finally playing chess, one of the program "bugs" that plagued CHATURANGA 2.0 throughout the tournament spoiled the game. **10 ♞h4??** CHATURANGA 2.0 still has problems in its evaluator function. **... ♛xd4 11 ♛xd4 ♞xd4 12 ♚d2?** White should castle and leave the c-Pawn to its fate. The program's King safety heuristic also seems to be deficient. **... ♜d8 13 ♞d3 ♝f6** Stronger is ... c5, since 14 ♘xc5? loses to either ... ♘f3+ or ... ♘b3+. **14 g3 ♝xh4 15 gxh4 ♝f5 16 ♜d1?! ♞f3+** Also winning another Pawn is ... ♘xc2+ 17 ♔xc2 ♖xd3 18 ♖xd3 ♖d8, and it will take more than Bishops of opposite colors to save White. **17 ♚e2 ♝g4 18 ♚f2 ♞d4 19 ♜d2 ♞xc2! 20 ♜xc2 ♜xd3 21 ♝e3?** Why not 21 ♖xc7? **... c6 22 ♜g1 ♝f5 23 ♜c5** Although White has a very bad game, CHATURANGA 2.0 still can hope for faint drawing chances, due to the presence of Bishops of opposite colors. **... ♚f8 24 ♜e5 b6 25 ♚e2 ♜ad8 26 ♜g5??** This blunder decides matters. The program has to play 26

♗c1, after which a long resistance is still possible. **... e6 27 ♜g3 f6** Trapping the Rook. **28 ♝xb6 axb6 29 ♜ee3 ♜d2+ 30 ♚f3 ♜xh2 31 ♜b3 ♜xh4** PION is not very efficient at winding things up; 31 ... ♖dd2! was crushing. **32 ♜xb6??** Suicide. **... ♜d3+ 33 ♚g2 ♝e4+ 34 ♚f2 ♜xf4+ 35 ♚e2 ♜xg3** In addition to being a Rook and Bishop down, CHATURANGA 2.0 is also in a mating net. **36 ♜b8+ ♚g7 37 ♜b7+ ♚h6 38 ♜f7 ♝d3+ 39 ♚d2 ♜f2+ 40 ♚c3 c5 41 ♜d7 ♝b5+ ♜d3 ♜xd3 mate** 0-1

ROUND 4

CRAY BLITZ - BELLE
Giuoco Piano(C50)

After transpositions, the opening of this game surprisingly turns out to be a Giuoco Pianissimo, but these tactically oriented programs find a wild variation which winds up clearly in BELLE's favor. After BELLE unwisely allows CRAY BLITZ to exchange Queens on c5, losing its advantage, the game evolves into an interesting Rook ending. BELLE passes up a safe draw for the advance of a threatening passed Pawn, and CRAY BLITZ still can do no better than a draw by repetition.

1 e4 e5 2 ♞c3 ♞f6 3 ♝c4 ♞c6 4 d3 ♝c5 5 ♞f3 d6 6 ♝g5 ♞a5 7 ♝xf6 ♛xf6 8 ♞d5 ♛d8 9 b4 ♞xc4 10 bxc5 It is wiser to play 10 dxc4, after which Black is slightly better. **... c6 11 dxc4 cxd5 12 cxd5 ♛a5+** One of the problems with setting up a computer

Fig. 9.7 CRAY BLITZ - BELLE: Left, Robert Hyatt; right, Ken Thompson

program's opening "book" from published material without critically editing it, is that many of the key lines given are bad for one side. Here both programs have followed a line from ECO (Blau-Euwe, - Lenzerheide 1956) which is known to give Black a clear advantage. **13 ♕d2 ♕xc5 14 0-0 0-0 15 ♜ab1 b6** In this position, Black has a clear advantage because its Pawn position is more compact, and its minor piece has better prospects. The Pawns at a2, c2, and e4 will require constant care and it is difficult for White to formulate a plan from a human perspective, let alone that of a computer program. An attacking player would be likely to try 16 ♖b3 followed by ♘h4 and a quick transfer of heavy pieces to the Kingside, forsaking the weak Pawns to their fate —and would probably go down in flames since there is no positional basis for such an attack. However, a quick incineration might be preferable to a more prolonged agony. **16 ♕b4?!**

BELLE

CRAY BLITZ

Fig. 9.8 BELLE captures CRAY BLITZ's Bishop in this complex opening.

In any case, White should not offer to exchange Queens, because the weaknesses in its position are more serious in an endgame. Computer programs have a tendency to exchange pieces in positions in which humans would not do so. In this particular case, CRAY BLITZ may have been motivated to trade Queens by the superior mobility of BELLE's Queen. **16 ... f5?** By allowing an exchange on c5, BELLE gives up most of its advantage. Why allow White to shield its weak c-Pawn by closing the c-file? The program should play ... ♕xb4 followed by ... ♗a6 and doubling Rooks on the c-file. **17 ♛xc5 bxc5 18 ♞d2 fxe4** The wisdom of this is doubtful, since it allows the White Knight to take up a strong post. BELLE could have continued ... ♗a6 followed by ... f4. **19 ♞xe4 ♝a6 20 ♜fc1 ♝c4!** One of BELLE's strongest assets is its tendency to play active moves. There's no future at all in trying to defend the d-Pawn. **21 ♞xd6 ♝xd5 22 c4 ♝c6 23 ♞b7 ♝xb7 24 ♜xb7 ♜f7 25 ♜b5** CRAY BLITZ has the initiative in the double-Rook ending. **... ♜c8 26 f3** More accurate is an immediate ♖d1. This Pawn later becomes a target. **... ♚f8 27 ♜e1 ♜e7 28 ♚f2 g6 29 ♜d1** To make any progress, CRAY BLITZ has to get this Rook into a more active role. But this gives BELLE an opportunity to liquidate its weak e-Pawn, and to exchange a pair of Rooks. **... e4! 30 ♜e1** Otherise it is BELLE's Rook which will become active. **... exf3 31 ♜xe7 ♚xe7 32 ♜b7+ ♚e6 33 gxf3** Almost any human player would prefer to keep the Pawns connected, and play ♔xf3. This, however, would allow ... ♖f8+ 34 ♔e3 ♖f7, with an even position. **... ♜d8!** BELLE keeps its Rook active, and goes after counterplay. The rest of the ending is generally well played and interesting. Both programs were searching to depths as great as 14 plies, and this tends to lead to accurate play even without knowledge of endgame principles. **34 ♜xa7 ♜d4 35 ♜xh7 ♜xc4 36 ♜c7**

BELLE

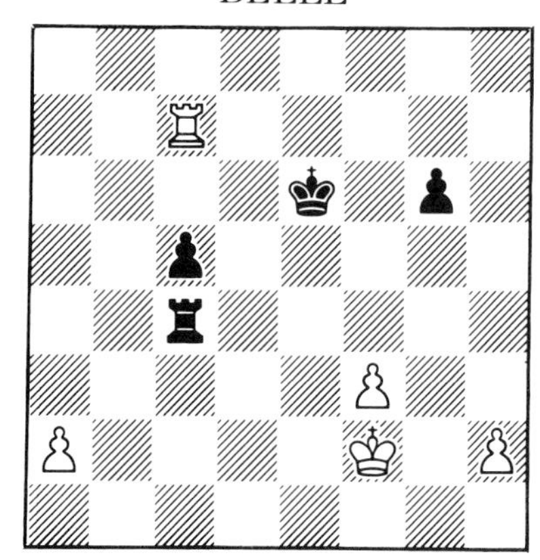

CRAY BLITZ

its g-Pawn. A human player would probably take an easy draw by ... ♖c2+ 37 ♔g3 ♖xa2 38 ♖xc5 ♔f7, where after a pair of Pawns are exchanged, the position is a book draw. **37 a3** More natural is 37 ♔g3. **... ♜c2+ 38 ♚g3 c4 39 ♜d7+ ♚e6 40 ♜g7 ♚f5 41 ♜c7 ♚e6 42 ♜c6+ ♚d5** BELLE burns its bridges. 42 ... ♔f5 holds the draw discussed above. **43 ♜xg6 c3 44 ♜g7 ♚c4 45 h4 ♜c1 46 ♜c7+ ♚b3 47 ♜b7+ ♚a2 48 ♚f4 c2 49 ♜c7 ♚b1 50 ♜b7+ ♚a2 51 ♜c7 ♚b1** At this point, it appeared that CRAY BLITZ might have been able to play for a win by sacrificing its Rook, e.g. 52 h5 ♖h1 53 ♔g5 c1(♕) 54 ♖xc1+ ♔xc1 55 f4, trying to take advantage of the poor position of the Black King. This, however, is a value judgment that no program can yet make, and had CRAY BLITZ done so, it would still not have won, e.g. 55 ... ♔d2 56 f5 ♔e3 57 f6 ♔e4 58 f7 ♖f1 59 ♔g6 ♔e5 60 ♔g7 ♖g1+ 61 ♔h8 ♖f1 62 ♔g8 ♖g1+ and the game would still end in a draw by repetition. **52 ♜b7+ ♚a2**
1/2 - 1/2

Fig. 9.9 ICCA President Ben Mittman (seated next to Ken Thompson) observes a tense moment in the exciting end game between CRAY BLITZ and BELLE.

NUCHESS - BEBE
Queen's Gambit Declined(D31)

BEBE was holding its own against top challenger NUCHESS in this long and difficult game, right up to the end. As the game was drifting into a draw by repetition (which would have left BELLE and CRAY BLITZ tied for first after both tiebreaks were computed, and given BEBE clear third), a "bug" in BEBE's repetition-detector caused the program to leave its Rook en prise — a tragedy that will long be remembered. **1 c3** The Saragossa opening, which in practice often transposes into the Exchange variation of the Queen's Gambit Declined. This is not a bad opening to play against a computer program, since White can often pick the moment for a favorable transposition. **... e5 2 d4 exd4 3 cxd4 d5 4 ♞c3 ♝e7 5 e3** This is passive, blocking the normal development of the Bishop at c1 to f4 or g5. It would be better to play 5 ♘f3 or even 5 ♗f4. **... ♞f6 6 ♝d3 0-0 7 ♞f3 ♞c6?!** It is normally considered unwise to block the advance of the c-Pawn in the Queen's Gambit, although this is not a normal position in the Exchange Variation because White's dark-square Bishop is locked in. Advancing the c-Pawn to c6 invites a minority attack via b4-b5. Probably the best move is ... ♗g4, postponing the decision on whether to place the c-Pawn at c6 or c5, until White's intentions are clear. **8 0-0 ♜e8 9 a3 ♝g4 10 h3 ♝xf3** It is better to play

... ♗h5, after which the Bishop can oppose its strong White counterpart on g6. **11 ♛xf3 ♜c8?!** This is carrying prophylaxis a bit far! Black should play ... a6 followed by ... ♗f8. **12 b4 a6 13 ♝d2 ♝f8 14 g4!?** NUCHESS pushes its Pawns eagerly, seeking to take advantage seeking to take advantage of the restricted position of the Black pieces and the insecurity of Black's d-Pawn. With the center closed there is some justification for this, though the plan is more successful than it deserves to be. **... h6 15 h4 ♞e4?** This leads to a terrible positional weakness. After 15 ... g6, Black has nothing in particular to fear from 16 g5 ♘h7, and much to hope for in the weakening of White's Kingside. **16 ♞xe4 dxe4 17 ♝xe4 ♛xh4 18 ♝xc6 bxc6** BEBE has maintained material equality for the time being, but the doubled isolated Pawn on the half-open c-file may be worse than the loss of a Pawn. It is very hard to find any plan or counterplay for Black, because of the static Pawn structure. **19 ♚g2 ♛g5 20 ♜ac1 ♛d5**

BEBE

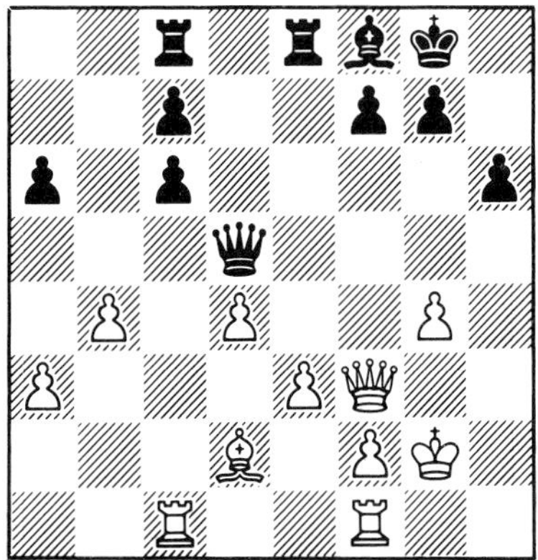

NUCHESS

21 ♛xd5?! This wins a Pawn, but much stronger was 21 ♖xc6!, a move which is difficult for a computer program to find, since the attack on c6 by the White Queen is indirect and does not appear in the program's attack bit boards. It is extremely difficult to play chess well without vision and spatial perception. **... cxd5 22 ♜c6 a5** 22 ... ♖e6 is met by 23 ♖fc1 and either the c-Pawn or the a-Pawn must fall. **23 bxa5 ♜e6** It would be a mistake for BEBE to take the a-Pawn: 23 ... ♗xa3 24 ♖a1 ♗d6 25 a6 and the a-Pawn becomes a terrible threat. But it is somewhat surprising that a normally materialistic computer program could forsee this. **24 ♜xe6 fxe6 25 ♝b4 ♜b8 26 ♜c1 ♝xb4?** This error makes things much easier for White. A sound continuation was ♖b7. **27 ♜b1!** Now NUCHESS gets its Pawns realigned, and the passed a-Pawn is protected. **... ♚f7 28 axb4 c6 29 a6?!** This makes it difficult again, tying the Rook down to the defense of the a-Pawn. The easy way is 29 f4, followed by ♔f2-e2-d3-c3-b3-a4, which would force the Black King to follow suit or the a-Pawn would become too dangerous. Then the White Rook could shift to the Kingside for an opportune break by g5, f5, or e4. **... ♜a8 30 ♜a1 ♜a7 31 ♚g3 ♚e7 32 e4 ♚d7 33 ♚f4 ♚d6 34 f3 ♜f7+ 36 ♚e3 ♜a7**

BEBE

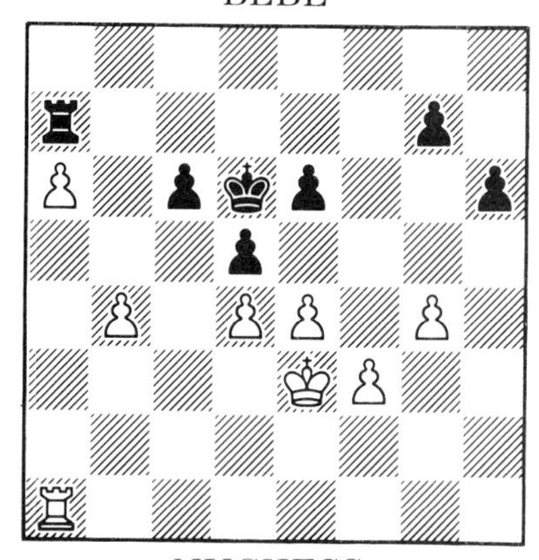

NUCHESS

36 exd5?! And this makes things very difficult indeed. Strong was 36 f4!, threatening 37 e5+ and 38 f5. **... exd5 37 ♚f4 ♚e6 38 ♚g3 ♚e7 39 ♚h4** NUCHESS doesn't know what to do. Since the program so cavalierly discarded the Pawn break in the center, the only way to try for a win is by playing b5. It takes NUCHESS quite a while to get the idea. **... g6 40 f4 ♔f7 41 ♖a2 ♔e6 42 ♖a3 ♔f6 43 ♔g3 ♔e6 44 ♖a1 ♔f6 45 ♖a2 ♔e6 46 ♖a3 ♔f6 47 ♔f3 ♔e6 48 ♖a2 ♔f6 49 ♖a4 ♔e6 50 ♖a5 ♔f6 51 ♔g3 ♔e6 52 ♔h4 ♔f6 53 b5** Finally NUCHESS sees that this is the only way to avoid a draw by repetition. **... cxb5 54 ♖xb5 ♖xa6 55 ♖xd5 ♖a3 56 ♖e5 ♖f3** With the White King cut off from the third rank, there is no way to make progress. **57 g5+ hxg5+ 58 fxg5+ ♔g7 59 d5 ♖d3** With the Rook behind White's passed Pawn, the draw is not difficult. As noted before, though, endings that would be simple for a human player can be difficult for computer programs. **60 ♔g4 ♔f8 61 ♔f4 ♖d4+ 62 ♔e3 ♖d1 63 ♔f3 ♖d4 64 ♔e2 ♔g8 65 ♔e3**

BEBE

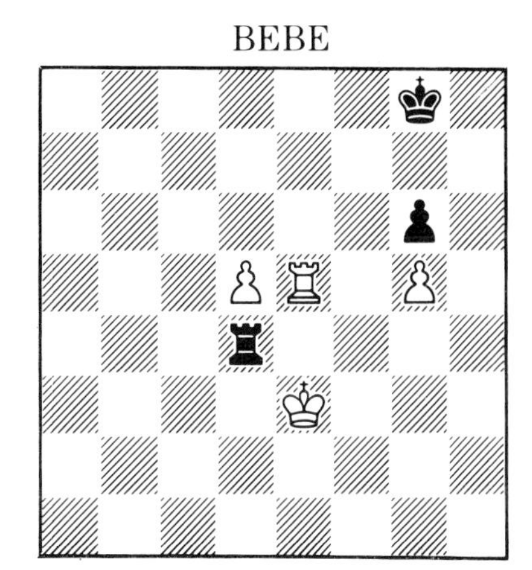

NUCHESS

Fig. 9.10 NUCHESS - BEBE: Left, Tony Scherzer; right, David Slate and William Blanchard.

65 ... ♚f8???? To detect draws by repetition involves some rather complex coding, and BEBE's repetition-detector has a "bug" in it! The program falsely concluded that ... ♔f8 created a threefold repetition, and claimed the "draw" by this move (much to programmer Tony Scherzer's horror), whereupon NUCHESS gleefully snatched the Rook and mated poor BEBE. **66 ♚xd4 ♚g7 67 d6 ♚h8 68 ♜e7 ♚g8 69 d7 ♚h8 70 d8(♛) mate** 1-0

CHAOS - OSTRICH
Nimzo-Indian(E32)

In this game, OSTRICH lives up to its name — burying itself! After the Canadian program commits positional suicide, CHAOS exploits its opportunity to force a win.

1 d4 ♞f6 2 c4 e6 3 ♞c3 ♝b4 4 ♛c2 0-0 5 a3 ♝xc3+ 6 ♛xc3 ♞c6? A theoretical novelty, which is not likely to be repeated. The "book" continuations are ... b6 and ... d6, preparing ... c5. **7 ♞f3 d6 8 ♝g5 h6 9 ♝h4 b6?** Now this move leads to an excruciating weakness at c6. **10 e3** Here it would be slightly more accurate to play an immediate 10 d5. **... ♝a6**

OSTRICH

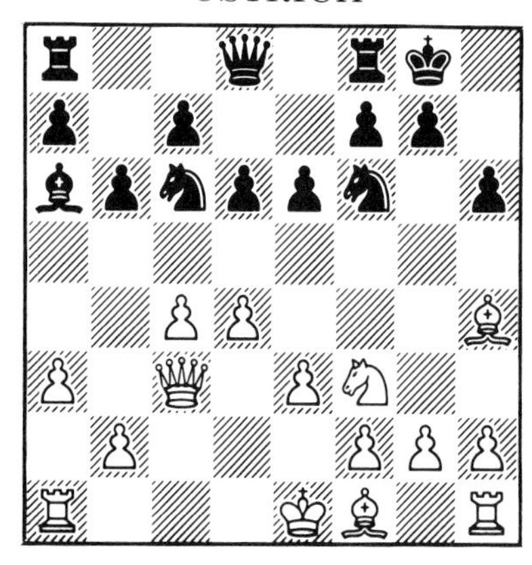

CHAOS

11 d5! The alert CHAOS capitalizes on the opportunity, although now this involves forfeiture of Kingside castling. **... exd5 12 cxd5 ♝xf1 13 ♜xf1 ♞b8?** This is hopeless, conceding White a dominating position with no possibility of counterplay. Although OSTRICH is in trouble whatever it plays, a more combative move is 13 ... ♘e5, e.g. 14 ♘xe5 dxe5 15 ♕xe5 g5 16 ♗g3 ♖e8 17 ♕d4 ♖e4 and Black, about to recapture the d-Pawn, is still in the game. The Knight retreat almost amounts to conceding the game. **14 ♝xf6!** Destroying the Black position by creating new weaknesses. **... ♛xf6** It's no better to keep the Queens by ... gxf6, since 15 ♘d4 followed by ♖c1 or 0-0-0 is very strong. Now, however, OSTRICH's Pawn structure is shattered and becomes completely immobile. **15 ♛xf6 gxf6 16 ♜c1** Positionally, the game is over. **... ♞a6 17 ♚e2!** Resolving the only doubt remaining in the game — whether CHAOS will get the King Rook into play. Programs have been known to leave a Rook sitting out of play in similar circumstances. **... h5 18 ♜c4 ♚g7 19 ♜fc1 ♞c5 20 b4** Chess is very simple, when you have that kind of a target to focus on. **... ♞a6 21 g3 ♜h8 22 ♜c6 ♜hc8 23 ♞d4 ♚f8 24 ♞b5** OSTRICH is completely helpless, without the slightest opportunity for counterplay. The incipient loss of the c-Pawn is only the beginning of the program's problems. **... ♜e8 25 ♞xc7 ♞xc7 26 ♜xc7 ♜e7** White threatens to double Rooks on the 7th rank after 26 ♖d7. **27 ♜xe7 ♚xe7 28 ♜c7+ ♚e8 29 ♚f3 a6** OSTRICH is in Zugzwang. **30 ♜c6 ♚d7 31 ♜xb6 ♚c7 32 ♜c6+ ♚d7 33 ♚f4 a5** Zugzwang again. OSTRICH could well resign here, but there's always the possibility of a computer failure, and against CHAOS, the added chance of a time forfeit. **34 b5 a4 35 ♜a6** This decides matters immediately; there is not the slightest chance that

Fig. 9.11 CHAOS - OSTRICH: Left, Fred Swartz; right, Monty Newborn.

Black can hold the King and Pawn ending. **... ♜xa6 36 bxa6 ♚c7 37 ♚f5 ♚b6 38 ♚xf6 ♚xa6 39 ♚e7 ♚a5 40 ♚xd6 ♚b5 41 ♚e7 f5** After ...♔c4 42 d6 ♔b3 43 d7 ♔xa3 48 d8(♕) ♔b2 49 ♕d4+ ♔b3 50 ♕a1, it's all over. **42 d6 ♚c4 43 d7 ♚b3 44 f4 ♚xa3 45 d8(♛) ♚b4 46 ♛d4+ ♚b5 47 ♛d3+ ♚b4 48 ♛xf5 a3 49 ♛xh5 a2 50 ♛h8** 1-0

ADVANCE 2.4 - SCHACH 2.6
Ruy Lopez(C90)

This game might well have been played by two human experts, and is destined to take a place in history as one of the best computer chess games. ADVANCE 2.4 gets a positional advantage out of the opening after SCHACH 2.6 recaptures the wrong way on its 15th move. This seems to have been the fatal error, for it is difficult to see how the defense could have been substantially improved afterward. ADVANCE 2.4 mercilessly piled on the pressure, with many fine tactical shots. Although the program appears to have missed the quickest win, it kept its advantage and wound up the game in nice style.

1 e4 e5 2 ♞f3 ♞c6 3 ♝b5 a6 4 ♝a4 ♞f6 5 0-0 ♝e7 6 ♜e1 b5 7 ♝b3 d6 8 c3 0-0 9 d3 ♞a5 10 ♝c2 c5 11 h3 This does not seem very exact, for if White does not play d4, the Black Bishop would be misplaced on g4. **... c4** An interesting continuation, in the best computer tradition of immediate direct action, but perhaps not so bad anyway. **12 dxc4** Somewhat stronger is 12 d4 with a typical Ruy Lopez center, but this is not bad. **... ♞xc4 13 a4 ♜d7 14 b3 ♞b6** Black now threatens ... bxa4. **15 axb5** Another slight inaccuracy, not that this is a mistake, but 15 a5 is even better.

SCHACH 2.6

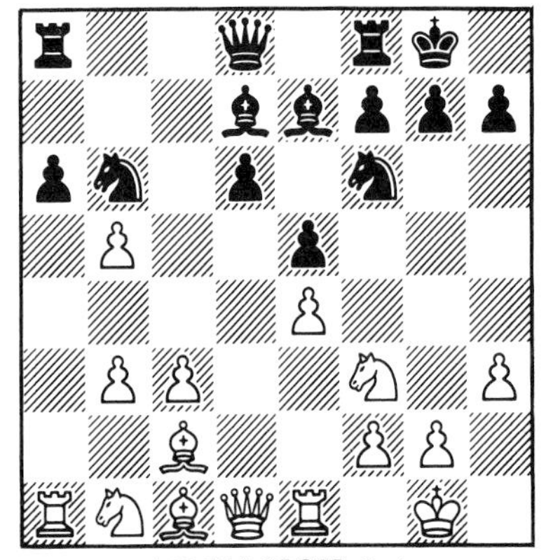

ADVANCE 2.4

15 ... ♝xb5? This, however, is a definite mistake. White now gets a powerful bind on the position; axb5 was necessary. **16 c4 ♝c6 17 ♞c3 h6 18 ♜e2 ♞bd7 19 ♝a3 ♛c7** On 19 ... ♘c5, White just plays b4. **20 ♞d5! ♞xd5** The Bishop at c6 seems to have inferior prospects for activity to the Knight, and so ... ♗xd5 would have been somewhat better — and would also have gained time to prevent White's 22nd move. The Black position, however, would still remain constricted and definitely inferior. **21 exd5** White is now in a position to force a passed Pawn. **... ♝b7 22 ♞d4!** ADVANCE 2.4 is playing this game in brilliant style **... ♞c5 23 ♞f5 ♝g5 24 b4 ♞d7 25 ♝b3 ♜fc8 26 ♝c1 ♝f6** SCHACH 2.6 does not want to exchange Bishops, bringing the Rook to c1, which clearly facilitates the planned breakthrough. But now White gets a new threat. **27 ♜e4!** Another example of using a Rook to good effect laterally. **... ♞f8**

SCHACH 2.6

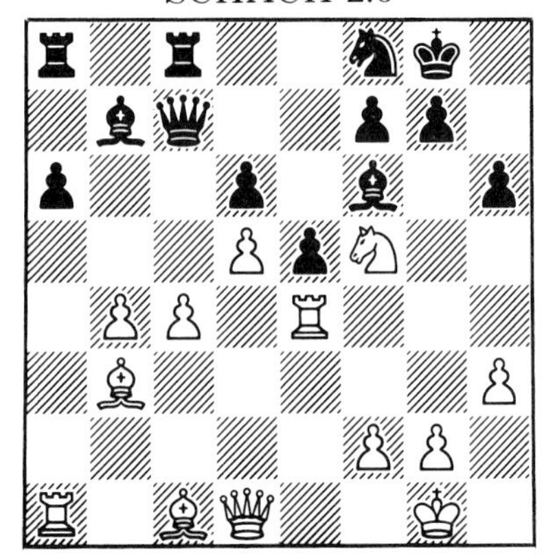

ADVANCE 2.4

28 ♜g4! ADVANCE 2.4 combines its Queenside threats with play on the Kingside; the Rook is powerfully placed on the fourth rank. In their excellent book "The Road to Chess Mastery", Euwe and Meiden comment that playing on more than one front to tie down the opponent's pieces is the final step in progressing from expert to master. Now a critical defender is lured away ... **... ♞g6** If Black plays ... ♔h7 or ... ,♔h8, White can force matters by 28 ♕d2. **29 c5!** ... and ADVANCE 2.4 breaks through. The pretty point behind this is that ... dxc5? loses immediately to 30 ♖xg6! **... h5** Another weakness, but SCHACH 2.6 has to do something about the threat to the Knight on g6. **30 ♜c4** Here the Exchange sacrifice 30 ♖xg6 fxg6 31 ♘xd6 is sound, but would not increase White's advantage over the move played. **... dxc5 31 bxc5 ♛d7 32 ♞d6** This move cannot be criticized, for it wins. But 32 ♘e3! would be even stronger, since the advance of the united Pawns will soon win a piece. **... ♜xc5!** Beleaguered SCHACH 2.6 buys itself a little time with this Exchange sacrifice, but the game is beyond redemption. **33 ♜xc5 ♛xd6 34 ♜ca5 e4 35 ♜1a2 ♜c8** Now nothing can prevent ADVANCE 2.4 from mobilizing its

Pawn by ♗a3, after which Black's game will soon collapse. The program, however, gets sidetracked and as a result the game lasts longer than it should have. **36 ♜a4 ♝e5 37 ♜xe4 ♝h2+ 38 ♚h1 h4 39 ♝g5** This is not bad, but 39 ♗a3 is much better. **... ♝f4**

SCHACH 2.6

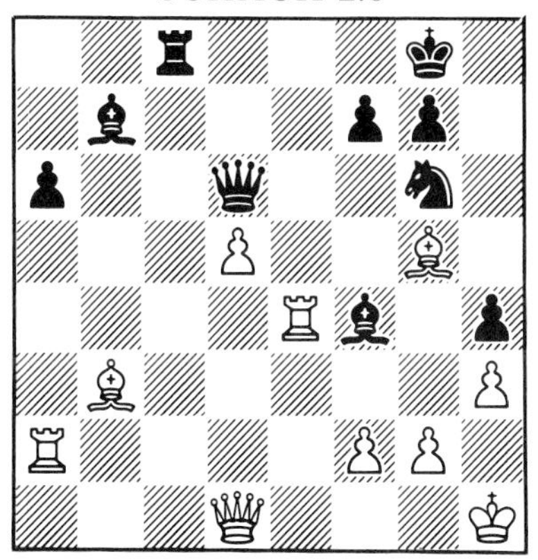

ADVANCE 2.4

40 ♜c2! Another interesting tactical point: if ... ♖xc2, then 41 ♗xf4! ♘xf4 42 ♗xc2 threatening ♖e8+ winning the Queen; or 40 ... ♗xg5 41 ♖xc8+ ♗xc8 42 ♖e8+ regaining the piece; in either case increasing White's advantage. **... ♜b8 41 ♝xf4 ♞xf4 42 ♛g4 ♞xd5 43 ♛h5 g6** The only move. **44 ♛xh4 ♝c6 45 ♜ec4 ♞e7 46 ♝a2** All of this is good for ADVANCE 2.4, and Black is under enormous pressure, but there doesn't seem to be a forced mate, and meanwhile SCHACH 2.6 hangs on and keeps the game alive. **... ♛d1+ 47 ♚h2 ♛d6+ 48 ♛f4 ♜d8 49 ♜b4** ADVANCE 2.4 could accomplish its goal of exchanging Queens by simply playing ♕xd6, but it is more advantageous to force SCHACH 2.6 to make the trade, since then the f-Pawn is en prise and has to be defended. After the exchange of its Queen, by far its best defensive piece, SCHACH 2.6 can't last much longer. **... ♛xf4+ 50 ♜xf4 ♜f8 51 ♜c5 ♚g7 52 ♝c4 f5 53 ♜e5** ADVANCE 2.4 uses its Rooks to maximum effect; this is much stronger than taking the a-Pawn, which will still be there after this maneuver. **... ♜e8 54 ♜d4** Threatening ♖d6. **... ♚f6 55 ♜c5 ♚g5** 55 ... ♔g7 is no better.

SCHACH 2.6

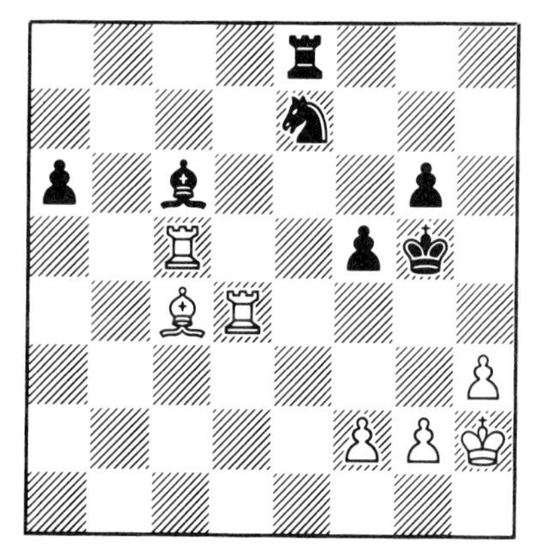

ADVANCE 2.4

56 ♜d6 Finally ADVANCE 2.4 has the position it wants, and moves in for the kill — rather late and not quite as clean as it should have been, but still an impressive triumph with a nice finish. **... ♝b5 57 ♝xb5 axb5 58 ♜e5!** Deadly. The threat of ♖de6 forces Black's reply. **... ♞c8 59 ♜xg6+! ♚xg6 60 ♜xe8 ♞a7** There's no salvation for the Knight which can't avoid being pinned or won by a check. **61 ♜a8 ♞c6 62 ♜a6** 1-0

Fig. 9.12 ADVANCE 2.4 (left), developed by Dave Wilson and Mike Johnson, plays its fine game against SCHACH 2.6 (right), developed by Matthias Engelbach.

PHILIDOR - PRESTIGE X
Sicilian

PHILIDOR goes badly wrong in the opening, and gets positionally strangled.

1 e4 c5 2 ♞f3 ♞c6 3 ♝b5 e6 4 ♞c3 a6 5 ♝e2?! 5 ♗xc6 is almost compulsory; this loses the initiative. **... d5 6 0-0?** After this, White becomes severely cramped. It was necessary to play 6 exd5 exd5 7 d4. **... d4 7 ♞b1 ♞f6 8 d3 ♝d6 9 ♝g5 0-0 10 ♞a3 h6 11 ♝d2 e5** Good, but slightly more accurate was an immediate 11 ... b5. **12 ♞c4 ♝c7 13 a4 ♝e6 14 b3 b5!** After the only well-posted White piece is driven away, PHILIDOR is positionally crushed. **15 axb5?** Another positional mistake; White should avoid this exchange and leave it up to Black to open lines on the Queenside. **... axb5 16 ♜xa8 ♛xa8 17 ♞b2 ♝a5** PRESTIGE prepares to exploit the holes in PHILIDOR's Queenside. It is also an advantage to exchange Black's "bad" Bishop. **18 ♝xa5 ♛xa5 19 ♛a1 ♜a8 20 ♛xa5 ♜xa5**

PRESTIGE X

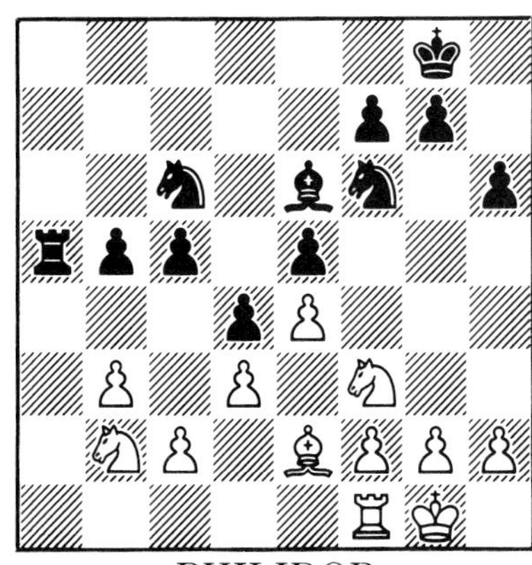

PHILIDOR

Although material is still exactly equal — both sides have the same pieces and all the Pawns are on the same files — PRESTIGE has many advantages. First, the program occupies or controls 37 squares compared to only 21 occupied or controlled by its opponent — a very great spatial advantage. Second, the program controls the only open file. Third, the White Queenside Pawns are very weak. Fourth, White's pieces are immobile — the Knights have no support points, and the Bishop is bad. Taken together, these advantages add up to a winning edge in practical play. **21 ♜c1 ♜a2 22 ♜b1 ♞d7** PRESTIGE prepares to open a second front on the Kingside. **23 ♞h4 ♞b4 24 ♝d1 g6 25 h3 ♚h7 26 ♞f3** PHILIDOR could delay Black's expansion by 26 g4, but then the Bishop is locked in forever. **... f5 27 exf5 ♝xf5** Here it would be more accurate for Black to recapture with the Pawn. **28 ♞d2 ♞d5** The Knight prepares to invade c3 with deadly effect, and there's nothing PHILIDOR can do to stop it. **29 g4 ♝e6 30 ♞e4 ♞c3 31 ♞xc3 dxc3**

PRESTIGE X

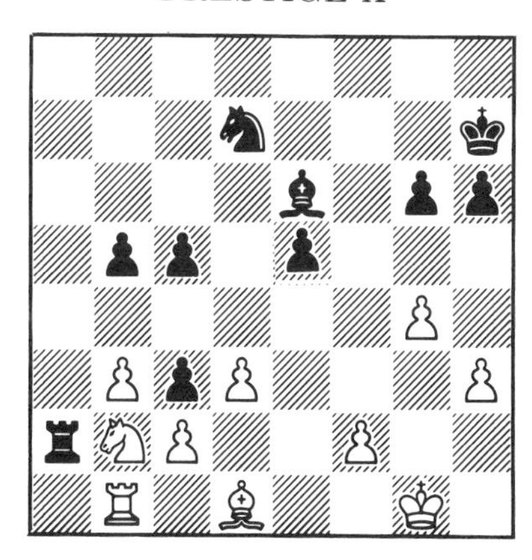

PHILIDOR

32 ♞c4 PHILIDOR has to give up its Knight for two Pawns, after which inexact play by PRESTIGE allows the British program to make a long, but hopeless, resistance. **... bxc4 33 bxc4 ♚g7** Strong for Black is ... e4, followed by ... ♘e5. PRESTIGE has played very well up to this point, with its moves conforming to the features of the position and forming an organic whole. But now, having won a piece, the program begins to shuffle its men about aimlessly, missing many opportunities to drive its advantage home. Technique just is not the computer program's strong point. **34 ♚g2 ♜b2** A false lead; the Rook stands better on a2. Still best was ... e4. **♜a1 ♚f6 36 ♜a3 ♚g5** PRESTIGE 's King placement heuristics drive the Black monarch to exploit the weak dark squares in the White position. **37 ♜xc3** PHILIDOR regains a Pawn which PRESTIGE needlessly left unguarded, but is still hopelessly lost. **... ♚h4?!** But this is a false lead; good was ... ♔f4. **38 ♜a3 h5 39 ♜a6 ♞f8 40 ♜a8 ♞h7 41 ♜h8** This maneuver would not have worked, with the Black King at f4. **... ♞f6 42 ♜f8 ♞d7 43 ♜e8 ♜b6** PRESTIGE realizes that it can't make progress until its own house is in order. **44 ♜h8 ♞f6 45 ♝f3 ♜b2 46 c3** The c-Pawn can't be held. **... ♜c2 47 ♜h6** 47 d4 loses quickly: ...cxd4 48 cxd4 exd4 and the passed Pawn wins. **... ♚g5 48 ♜h8 ♜xc3 49 gxh5 gxh5 50 ♜d8 ♝d7 51 ♝e2 ♚h4** Now this move is quickly decisive. **52 ♜f8 ♝xh3+ 53 ♚h2 ♜c2 54 ♜xf6 ♜xe2 55 ♚g1** Unfortunately for PHILIDOR, its Knight is caught in a mating net. **55 ... ♜e1+ 56 ♚h2 ♝f1 57 ♜d6 e4 58 d4 ♝e2 59 dxc5 ♝f3** 0-1

Fig. 9.13 PHILIDOR - PRESTIGE X: Left, David Levy; right, Dan and Kathe Spracklen.

PION - SAVANT X
King's Indian Attack(A07)

SAVANT X plays too aggressively against PION's quiet opening, and gets into difficulties (although PION does not find the strongest continuations). Then SAVANT X Castles "into it", and in the ensuing race to see who gets mated first, PION has a big lead. But Dave Kittinger's program emulates its author's coffeehouse style, sacrificing the Exchange "on spec" to denude the White King. PION doesn't bother to defend, and suddenly it's all over.

1 ♞f3 d5 2 g3 ♞f6 3 ♝g2 ♞c6 4 0-0 e5 Black has equalized, according to ECO. **5 d3 ♝g4 6 h3 ♝xf3** Here it is probably better to retreat the Bishop. **7 ♝xf3 e4?!** This is certainly an aggressive continuation — too aggressive, considering the state of development of the Black position. **8 ♝g2 ♝c5 9 ♞d2?!** Too quiet; PION continues according to its standard recipe for development, allowing Black to get a bind. **9 ... ♛e7** Here Black could play e3 immediately. **10 c4 e3! 11 fxe3 ♛xe3+?!** It's stronger to play 11 ... ♗xe3+. **12 ♚h2 ♛e6 13 ♞b3 ♝d4?!** SAVANT X has misplayed a promising position. Here ... ♗e3 is not possible due to 14 cxd5, but ... ♗e7 would have avoided the following strong line for White. **14 cxd5** Here PION could have embarrassed SAVANT X by playing 14 e3! ♗b6 (... ♗e5? 15 d4 ♗d6 16 cxd5 ♘xd5 17 e4 winning a piece with 18 d5, after the Knight moves) 15 c5! ♗a5 16 ♘xa5 ♘xa5 17 ♗d2 ♘c6 18 ♕f3, with a strong position for White, but the text may be even better. **... ♞xd5 15 ♞xd4 ♞xd4**

SAVANT X

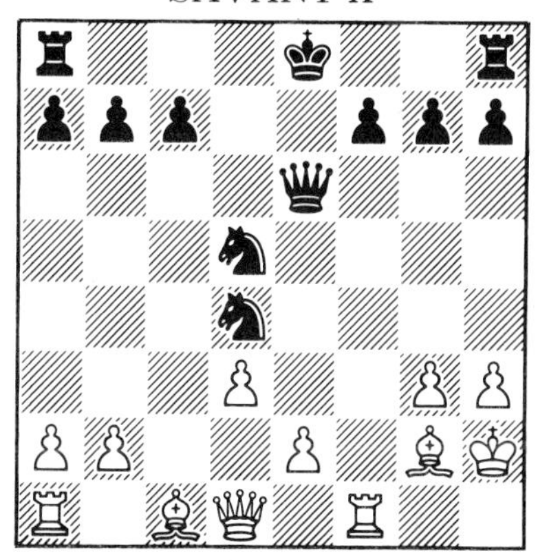

PION

16 e4? PION misses an opportunity. It's correct to play first 16 e3 ♘c6, then e4 ♘f6, and then d4 with a powerful position — the White center would be very strong, the Black Knights would have no good posts and the Bishops could easily become lethally effective. PION's move leaves a gaping hole at d4, and lets SAVANT X set up a blockade. **... ♞b6 17 ♝e3 0-0-0 18 h4** There's a subtle little threat here. **... ♚b8 19 ♝h3 ♛e7 20 a4 h6** As usual when the players have Castled on oppose wings, the game becomes a contest to see whose mating attack gets there first. **21 a5 ♞c8 22 ♛a4 ♞e6** The blockade on d4 can't be maintained. At this point, it seems certain that PION's attack will triumph. **23 ♜ad1?!** A nothing move, in a critical situation. The active 23 d4! would be strong. **... g5!** SAVANT X plays the correct continuation to open lines and get at the White King; computer programs usually have difficulty in playing such attacks. **24 ♝xe6?** And in defending against them! Why give up a strong Bishop, well placed to defend the King, for a not-too-well posted Knight, and bring the Black Queen onto a dangerous diagonal? Much better is 24 h5, followed if necessary by ♗g4. **... ♛xe6**

SAVANT X

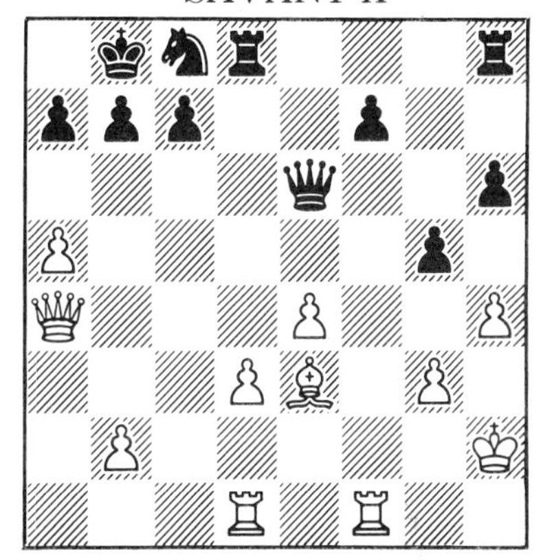

PION

25 ♝d4?! PION "thinks" Black has to move the Rook, after which it will play 26 ♗f6 and be well positioned to defend the Kingside. Unfortunately, the Rook moves which seem forced to PION aren't. The best continuation appears to be 25 ♕c4!, and if ... ♕g4, 26 ♖xf7. **25 ... gxh4!?** Another unusual move for a computer program, since chess programs usually hold on greedily to material. Evidently Dave Kittinger has managed to instill some attacking knowledge into his program — this is a good speculative sacrifice, at small cost; the White King is denuded of defenders, and in the absence of accurate defensive play, will probably not survive. **26 ♝xh8 hxg3+ 27 ♚xg3?** It is better to play 27 ♔g2, and after ... ♖xh8 then 28 ♖f3, after which Black might have some difficulty in proving that its sacrifice was correct. **... ♜xh8 28 ♛d4** PION still has no idea that it is in any particular danger. A move with defensive possibilities is 28 ♖f3. **... ♜g8+ 29 ♚h2??** Losing immediately. 29 ♔f2 still seems to hold the position. **... ♛g4** Now mate is forced. 0-1

Fig. 9.14 PION - SAVANT X: Left, PION's programmers; right, Dave and Glenda Kittinger.

SFINKS X - CHATURANGA 2.0
Queen's Gambit Declined(D10)

CHATURANGA 2.0 appears to play this game without being crippled by program "bugs", but now its limited search and the defects in its heuristics become apparent.

1 d4 d5 2 c4 c6 3 cxd5 ♛xd5? CHATURANGA 2.0 loves to bring its Queen out early, a problem characteristic of many of the first chess programs. **4♞c3 ♛c4?** It's relatively better to play ... ♕a5. Now White gains more time... **5 e4 ♛b4 6 a3 ♛a5** ... and still more time... **7 ♝d3 ♞f6 8 ♞f3 ♝g4 9 0-0 ♞bd7 10 b4** ... and, after completing its development, SFINKS X is ready to go on the attack. **... ♛h5?!** It seems better to play ... ♕c7, but that move also has its problems. **11 ♝e2 0-0-0?** Much too risky. CHATURANGA 2.0 should play ... e6, develop its Bishop, and Castle short. **12 ♝f4!** The Black King is now in a very dangerous situation, which of course CHATURANGA 2.0 doesn't know — it hasn't been told. **... ♞b6 13 h3**

CHATURANGA 2.0

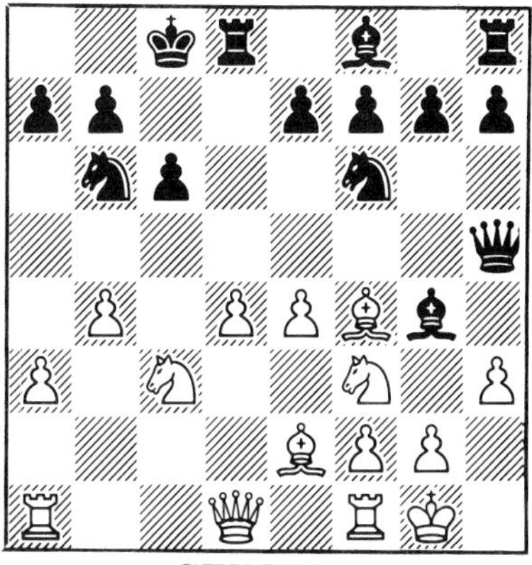

SFINKS X

13 ... ♗e6? Setting up a dangerous discovery; of course, ... ♗xf3 was necessary. **14 ♘g5 ♕h4?** The Queen must go to g6.This sets up yet another, decisive discovery on the Queen — clear evidence that CHATURANGA 2.0 is unable to evaluate pins and discoveries properly (a particularly difficult task for a program), perhaps because its search depth is too limited. **15 g3 ♕h6 16 ♘xe6 ♕xh3 17 ♘g5** SFINKS X is greedy, and wants to win a whole Rook. **... ♕h6 18 ♘xf7 ♕h3 19 ♘xh8 e5? 20 ♗xe5 ♗xb4 21 ♗xf6** With a threat that can't be parried except at ruinous cost, after which the rest will pass without comment. **... ♖xd4 22 ♗xd4 h5 23 axb4 c5 24 bxc5 ♘d7 25 ♖xa7 ♔b8 26 c6 ♕xf1+ 27 ♗xf1 ♘f8 28 ♖xb7+ ♔c8 29 ♗b6 ♘d7 30 ♕xd7 mate** 1-0

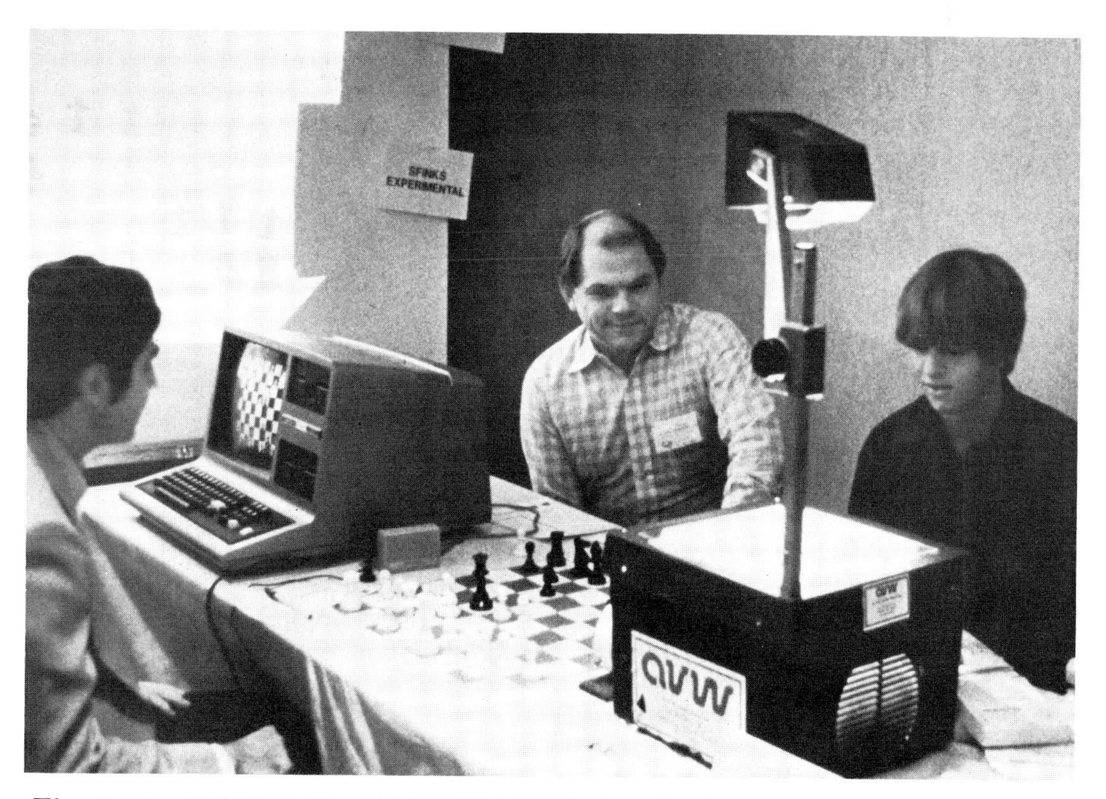

Fig. 9.15 SFINKS X - CHATURANGA 2.0: Right, John Poduska, teenage Chess programmer, and his proud father.

Fig. 9.16 The prizewinners. Left to right: Fred Swartz - CHAOS; David Slate - NUCHESS; Ken Thompson - BELLE; Robert Hyatt - CRAY BLITZ; William Blanchard - NUCHESS. In the rear, ICCA President Ben Mittman and Mike Valvo.

APPENDIX A

1982 USCF REGULATIONS FOR COMPUTER PARTICIPATION IN USCF EVENTS

During the USCF Convention, August 14-15, 1982, the USCF Board of Delegates adopted new regulations on computer participation in USCF events. These regulations are effective August 15, 1982 except where noted:

1. MEMBERSHIP
Computer programs may be registered by the originator or by the the legal owner of the program, as Computer Members of the USCF. The dues for Computer Members shall be the same as for regular adult members. The rights and privileges of Computer Members include and are limited to: the right to play in USCF tournaments subject to USCF regulations on computer participation; the right to acquire an official USCF rating; and a subscription to Chess Life magazine. Specific identification and registration procedures shall be determined administratively.

2. SALE OF MEMBERSHIP
Computer memberships may be sold only by the USCF office. (The address of the USCF Office is: 186 Route 9W, New Windsor, NY 12550. Inquiries should be sent to the attention of the Membership Director.) Owners may be required to sign a statement agreeing to specific rules.

3. PARTICIPATION IN TOURNAMENTS
For a period of one year, from Jan. 1, 1983 to Jan. 1, 1984, all tournaments advertised in Chess Life shall be designated as "C" (Computers allowed) or "NC" (No Computers), and the default shall be "C" if neither is specified by the organizer. Computer entries must be arranged in advance, and no director is obligated to accept the entry of any particular computer.

4. PAIRINGS
The director shall announce to the participants the presence of one or more computer entrants in a tournament. Within a reasonable time after this announcement, a player has the right to request the director not to pair him with a computer. The director should avoid such a pairing unless the pairing is forced.

5. ELIGIBILITY FOR PRIZES
Computers may win only prizes specifically designated for them. Other prizes shall be distributed as though computers were not entered.

6. RATINGS
In a tournament with human and computer participants, games between computers shall be rated. Directors should avoid pairing two computers when such pairing would result in a computer playing more than half its games against other computers. Events in which only computers participate will be rated at the USCF's discretion, except that matches involving computers will not be rated.

7. CONSULTATION
A player who consults a computer for advice about his game shall be subject to the same penalties that he would receive for asking advice from a friend.

OFFICIAL USCF RULES FOR PLAY INVOLVING COMPUTERS

During the USCF Convention, the Board of Delegates also adopted a set of official rules for play based on the ICCA rules as submitted by Ken Thompson. These new rules read as follows:

RULES FOR PLAY INVOLVING COMPUTERS

The following rules are for USCF-rated tournaments when one of the players (or both) is a computer. In matters not covered by these rules, play is governed by applicable human rules, as interpreted by the arbiter. In these rules, the term "computer" refers to a chess program running on a computer. The term "opponent" refers to the computer's opponent, human or computer. The term "operator" refers to the person running the computer. The following rules shall govern play:

1. PARAMETER SETTINGS
Before play begins, the operator shall do all initial setting up of the computer. At this time, the operator may freely specify any operational parameters, such as rate of play, suggested openings, value of a draw, etc. After play begins, the role of the operator is passive. As such, the operator is not allowed to alter any parameter settings during play that might alter the course of the game.

2. COMMUNICATION OF MOVES
During play, the operator is to communicate the opponent's moves to the computer.

3. EXECUTION OF MOVES
The operator is to execute the computer's specified move on the playing chessboard. "Touch" rules do not strictly apply to the operator, although blatant cases may be violations of other rules.

4. CLOCK
After the computer's move is executed, the operator is to start the opponent's clock.

5. RECONCILIATION OF POSITIONS
If, during play, different positions should arise on the playing chessboard and the computer's internal representation thereof, due to operator error, such differences shall be corrected with the assistance of the arbiter. The arbiter may choose either to accept the playing chessboard as official, or to retrace the moves to the point of departure. If the arbiter chooses to back up the game, then the arbiter shall readjust the clocks accordingly.

6. RESETTING THE COMPUTER
If, during play, the computer is unable to accept a legal move because of discrepancies, communication trouble, or computer trouble, then the operator may set up the current board position and status, along with clock times. Other parameters set must be the same as those in effect at the start of the game. The clocks are not stopped during the resetting of the computer.

7. CLOCK TIMES
The operator may communicate the clock times to the computer only if the computer initiates the request.

8. MEMORY UNIT EXCHANGE
The operator may change or insert memory units when the computer requests this and identifies the unit to be inserted, by description or by generating a coded signal or message with a single predetermined meaning. Diskettes, disk cartridges, tapes, ROM cartridges ("program modules" in commercial machines), and the like are all considered equivalent forms of memory units.

9. DRAW OFFERS AND RESIGNATION
The operator may offer a draw, accept a draw, or resign on behalf of the computer. This may be done with or without computer consultation.

10. TIME FORFEITS
The operator may claim the game in cases where the opponent has exceeded the time limit.

11. ADJOURNMENT
The operator shall carry out the necessary adjournment formalities.

12. SCORE
The operator and/or the computer must keep a score of the game.

APPENDIX B

THE USCF RATING SYSTEM

The United States Chess Federation originated and developed the system of classification now used worldwide and generally referred to as the Elo System. The system was originated by Kenneth Harkness, and was based on the premise that a rating of 2000 should be the dividing line beteen strong amateurs or club players, and players of unusual proficiency who deserve special recognition for their accomplishments. The USCF system, since its inception, has classified players into rating categories at intervals of 200 rating points. The categories, and their percentile rankings at the end of 1982, are as follows:

RATING RANGE	CATEGORY	PERCENTILE
Above 2400	Senior Master	99
2200-2400	Master	99
2000-2200	Candidate Master	95-98
1800-2000	Category I	86-91
1600-1800	Category II	69-78
1400-1600	Category III	47-58
1200-1400	Category IV	26-36
1000-1200	Category V	10-18
Under 1000	Category VI	6

The rating categories between 1000 and 2400 are each divided into 100 point intervals by the USCF for the purpose of percentile rankings. The first percentile rank given for these categories is that of the lower 100 point range; the second, that of the upper 100 point range.

The USCF system was originally organized without any special mathematical foundations, and by 1959 had begun to show serious statistical defects. In that year, the then President of the USCF, Jerry Spann, established a Ratings Committee which was chaired by Dr. Arpad E. Elo, a strong player (seven times Wisconsin State Champion) and a well-known chess organizer in the Midwest. Dr. Elo was formerly

President of the American Chess Federation, and helped to found the USCF in 1939. Dr. Elo — a mathematician and physicist — reorganized the USCF rating system along sound statistical lines, and since then the Elo System has been adopted by many other chess federations, most importantly the International Chess Federation, FIDE.

The USCF class intervals, statistically, are based on the standard deviation of the Elo system. The way in which this is calculated is interesting. It has been determined by observation that the standard deviation of players' scores in tournaments is about 13.7% — that is, 68.2 percent of the players will score between 63.7% and 36.3%, when the results of many tournaments are averaged. This is then defined as the standard deviation of the rating classification system by setting a performance differential of 13.7% equal to a rating differential of 100 points. Suppose that two players A and B play a rated match of 22 games, and A scores 14 — 8 for 63.6%. If A is unrated, and B has a rating of 1500, then A's performance rating for the match (and new USCF rating) would be 1600.

Using this measure of the standard deviation to construct a normal distribution, or Gaussian, probability curve leads to the following probability table which indicates the expected score for the stronger player in a match, or the odds that the stronger player will win any one game:

Rating Difference	Expected Score of Stronger Player
0	50%
100	64%
200	76%
300	85%
400	92%
500	96%
600	98%

The distribution of USCF ratings very nearly fits the Gaussian or normal distribution curve. The ratings of the 58,413 USCF-rated players as of November 1982 are graphed below by 50-point intervals:

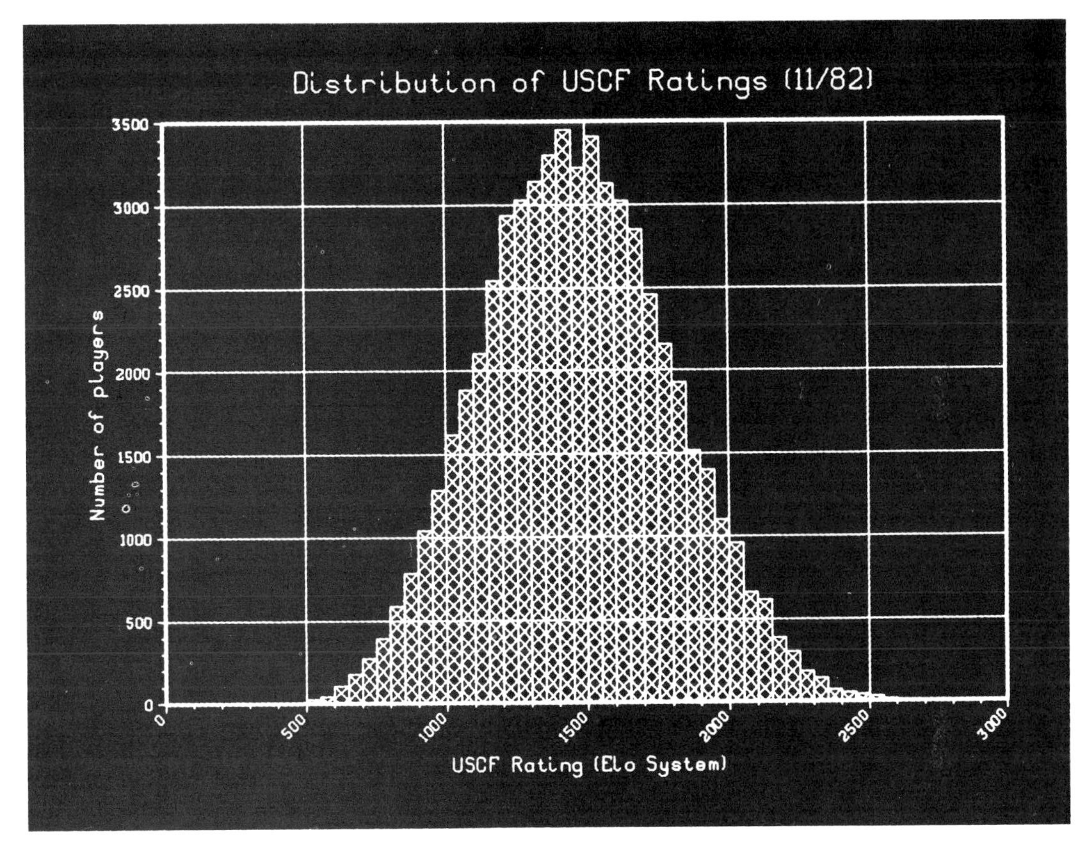

Fig. B.1 Ratings of all USCF members

Because stronger players are encouraged by their results to keep playing and to study chess, whereas weaker players tend to get discouraged and move on to other avocations, the actual distribution curve is slightly skewed. Ideally the average rating should be 1500; the actual average for this distribution is 1464. The statistician will recognize that this distribution approximates the Maxwell-Boltzman function, with a leading edge (at the right) longer than the trailing edge (at the left). For rating differentials of less than 400 points, the differences between the normal distribution function and special functions such as the Maxwell- Boltzman function and the Logistic distribution function are insignificant.

Because the stronger players are more active, the distribution of ratings in the 1982 USCF Annual Rating List, which includes only the 31,607 players who were active during 1982, is considerably different:

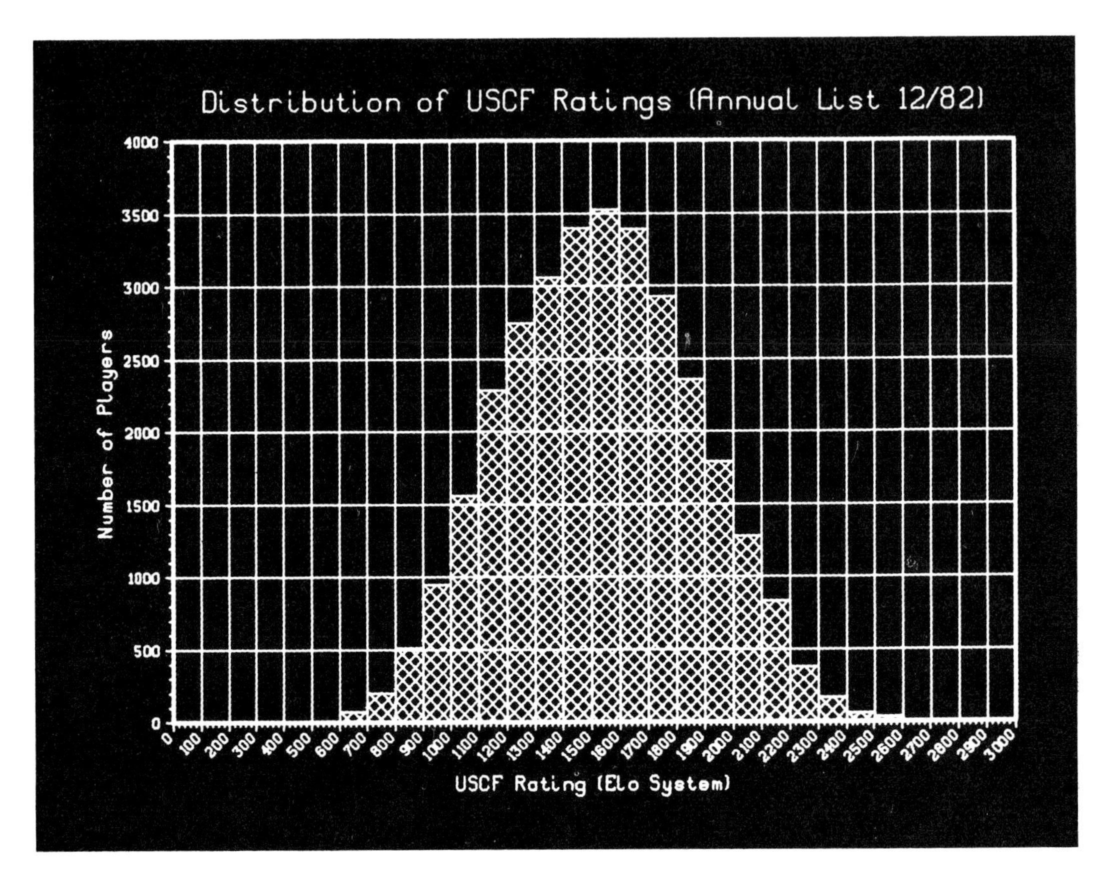

Fig. B.2 Ratings of active players.

The average rating for these players is 1530. In this graph the skewing of the curve is more marked, because the number of players in Categories V and VI is proportionately much lower than in Fig. B.1.

Both graphs indicate that the distribution of ratings is almost entirely confined to the range between 600 and 2600, and that the great majority of players are rated between 1000 and 2000. The average novice or "casual" player, who has not studied chess to any significant extent, tends to come into the system with an initial rating of around 1000 to 1200. The best "natural" players tend to have initial ratings of 1400 to 1800 before beginning a serious study of chess theory and eventually developing into masters and International titleholders.

One misleading thing about the Elo system is the use of a four-digit number to represent ratings. The last digit is meaningless. FIDE considers a player to have an established rating when 30 rated games have been played, but the probable error in a 30-game rating is still 35 Elo points. The probable error remains significant even after 100 rated games, as shown below:

Number of Games	Probable error in Elo points
10	60
20	42
30	35
40	30
50	27
100	19

One area in which Elo ratings have been misused is in advertisements for chess microcomputers. Aside from grossly inflated claims with no factual basis in rated games (once frequent but lately rare), manufacturers have obtained provisional USCF ratings based on as few as four rated games and (usually in good faith) advertised these as representing the true playing strength of the machine. An example of how misleading this can be is the following surprise which was experienced by Fidelity Electronics. Their former top-of-the-line model, the ELITE CHESS CHALLENGER, received a provisional USCF rating of 2032 based on 11 rated games. Its successor, the PRESTIGE CHESS CHALLENGER, which the Fidelity programmers knew to be a definite improvement, received a provisional rating of 1870 based on 17 rated games—how could that happen?

It's really rather simple: The rating for the ELITE was too high (probable error = 58 points; standard deviation = 85 points), and the rating for the PRESTIGE was too low (probable error = 45 points; standard deviation = 68 points). The difference between the two is slightly greater than the sum of the standard deviations, which indicates that Fidelity was rather unlucky in the way these ratings were obtained. The way in which these ratings overlap is shown in Fig. B-3; the "true" rating for both machines is probably in the 1900s, since the two curves intersect at about 1945. The shaded area represents the "true" ratings that might represent both the PRESTIGE and the ELITE; its area is 29% of the total area under both curves.

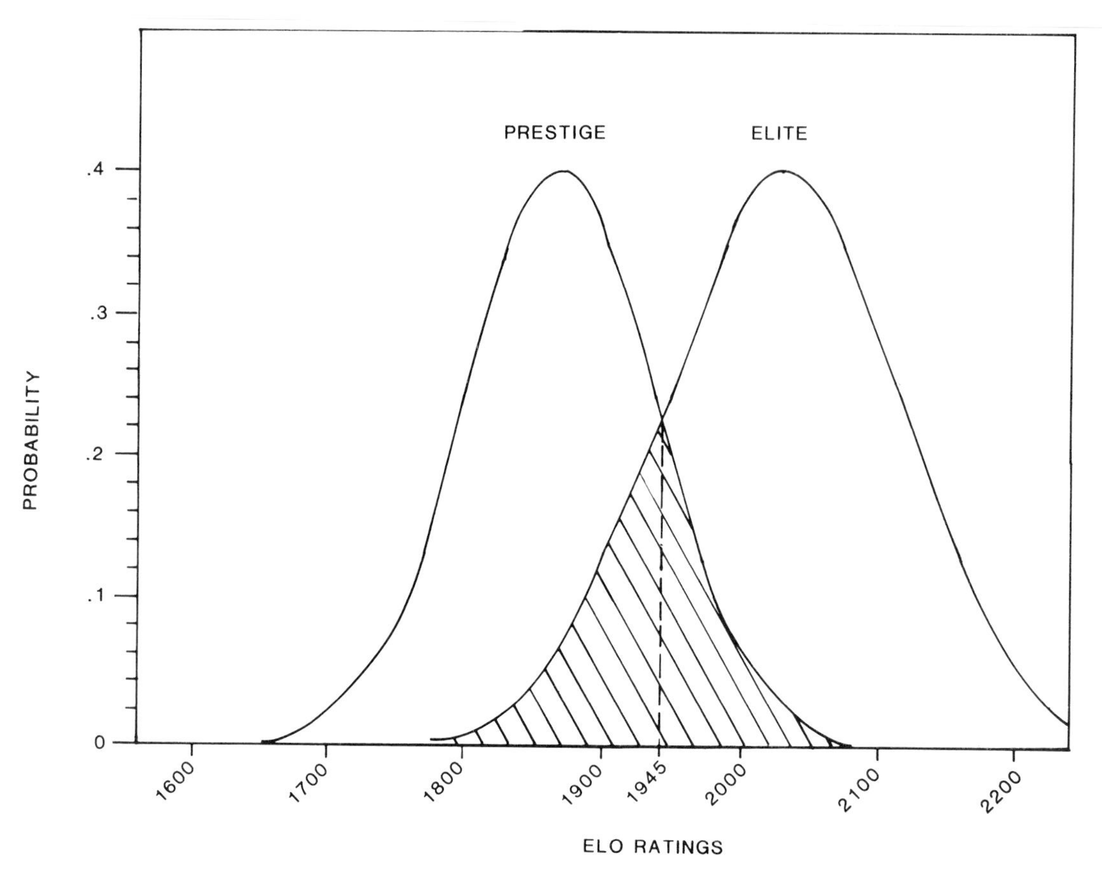

Fig. B.3 A practical example of rating variations.

From this example and the preceding table, the reader can easily see that ratings based on less than about 30 games are not to be trusted, and that in any case a rating difference of less than 50 Elo points is probably insignificant.

APPENDIX C

ACM TOURNAMENT GAMES 1970-1981

The following compilation of scores from the games of the twelve ACM tournaments which preceded the 1982 North American Computer Chess Championship was prepared by Ken Thompson of Bell Telephone Laboratories, and is reproduced by courtesy of the International Computer Chess Association.

ACM 1970 — New York

August 31 — September 2

	1	2	3	tot
1 CHESS 3.0	3+□	4+■	5+■	3
2 DALY	5+□	3−■	6+■	2
3 COKO 3	1−■	2+□	4=□	1½
4 J BIIT	6+■	1−□	3=■	1½
5 SCHACH	2−■	6+□	1−□	1
6 MARSLAND	4−□	5−■	2−□	0

Round 1

MARSLAND — J BIIT 1 c4 ♘f6 2 d4 e6 3 ♕d3 ♘c6 4 ♘f3 d5 5 ♘e5 d×c4 6 ♕×c4 ♗b4† 7 ♗d2 ♗×d2† 8 ♔×d2 ♘×e5 9 ♕c5 ♘e4† **0–1**

CHESS 3.0 — COKO 3 1 c4 e5 2 ♘c3 ♘c6 3 ♘f3 ♗c5 4 e3 d6 5 d4 ♗b4 6 ♗d2 ♘f6 7 ♘d5 ♗×d2† 8 ♕×d2 O-O 9 ♘×f6† ♕×f6 10 d×e5 d×e5 11 ♗d3 ♗g4 12 ♗e4 ♖ad8 13 ♕c2 h5 14 O-O ♗×f3 15 ♗×f3 h4 16 ♖ad1 ♘b4 17 ♕e4 ♘×a2 18 ♕×b7 ♖×d1 19 ♖×d1 ♕b6 20 ♖a1 ♕×b7 21 ♗×b7 ♖b8 22 ♖×a2 ♖×b7 23 f3 ♖b4 24 c5 c6 25 g3 h×g3 26 h×g3 ♖c4 27 ♖×a7 ♖c1† 28 ♔f2 ♖c2† 29 ♔e1 ♖×b2 30 ♖c7 ♖g2 31 g4 e4 32 f×e4 ♖×g4 33 ♖×c6 ♖×e4 34 ♔f2 ♔h8 35 ♖c8† ♔h7 36 c6 g5 37 ♔f3 f5 38 ♔f2 f4 39 c7 f×e3† 40 ♔e2 ♖e7 41 ♖h8† ♔×h8 42 c8♕† ♖e8 43 ♕×e8† ♔g7 44 ♕e6 **1–0**

DALY — SCHACH 1 e3 d5 2 ♕h5 ♘c6 3 ♗b5 g6 4 ♕e5 f6 5 ♕d4 e5 6 ♗×c6† ♗d7 7 ♗×d7† ♔e7 8 ♕×d5 ♕×d7 9 ♕×b7 ♕d8 10 ♕c6 ♗h6 11 d3 ♖b8 12 ♕c5† ♔e6 13 ♕×a7 ♖b6 14 ♕a4 c6 15 ♕c4† ♔e7 16 ♘c3 ♔e8 17 ♘a4 ♖b8 18 ♕×c6† ♕d7 19 ♕×d7† ♔×d7 20 ♘b6† ♔c6 21 ♘a4 **1–0**

Round 2

J BIIT — CHESS 3.0 1 d4 ♘f6 2 c4 e6 3 ♘c3 ♗b4 4 e3 ♗×c3† 5 b×c3 ♘c6 6 d5 ♘e7 7 d×e6 f×e6 8 ♖b1 ♘c6 9 ♗d3 ♕e7 10 ♘f3 e5 11 ♗f5 e4 12 ♘d4 ♕c5 13 ♖b5 ♕×c4 14 ♕b3 ♕×b3 15 a×b3 ♘×d4 16 e×d4 O-O 17 O-O a6 18 ♖c5 d6 19 ♗×c8 d×c5 20 ♗e6† ♔h8 21 d×c5 ♖ae8 22 ♗c4 ♘g4 23 ♗e2 ♘e5 24 ♗e3 g6 25 ♖d1 ♖f7 26 ♖d4 ♘c6 27 ♖d2 ♔g7 28 ♗c4 ♖ff8 29 ♖d7† ♖e7 30 ♖×e7† ♘×e7 31 ♗d4† ♔h6 32 ♗e5 ♖c8 33 h4 c6 34 ♗e6 ♖e8 35 ♗f7 ♖d8 36 ♗c4 ♖d1† 37 ♔h2 ♘d5 38 g4 g5 39 h×g5† ♔×g5 40 ♔h3 ♘f4† 41 ♗×f4† ♔×f4 42 ♗e2 ♖d2 43 ♗f1 ♖×f2 44 ♗c4 ♖f3† 45 ♔h4 ♖×c3 46 ♗g8 e3 47 ♗c4 ♖×c4 48 b×c4 e2 49 g5 e1♕† 50 ♔h5 ♕h1# **0–1**

COKO 3 — DALY 1 e4 e6 2 ♘c3 ♕g5 3 d4 ♕h4 4 ♘f3 ♕g4 5 h3 ♕h5 6 ♘b5 ♗b4† 7 c3 ♗a5 8 ♗f4 a6 9 ♘×c7† ♗×c7 10 ♗×c7 ♘c6 11 d5 e×d5 12 e×d5 ♘ce7 13 ♕d4 ♘×d5 14 g4 ♕g6 15 ♕×d5 ♕c2 16 ♗c4 ♘h6 17 ♕e5† ♔f8 18 ♗d6† **1–0**

SCHACH — MARSLAND 1 d4 e5 2 d×e5 **1–0**

Round 3

SCHACH — CHESS 3.0 1 d4 d5 2 c4 d×c4 3 ♘f3 ♘f6 4 e3 e6 5 ♗×c4 c5 6 O-O a6 7 ♕e2 ♘c6 8 ♘c3 c×d4 9 e×d4 ♘×d4 10 ♘×d4 ♕×d4 11 ♖d1 ♕h4 12 g3 ♕g4 13 f3 ♗c5† 14 ♔h1 ♕g6 15 ♗e3 ♗×e3 16 ♕×e3 O-O 17 ♕c5 ♗d7 18 a3 ♖fc8 19 ♕b4 ♗c6 20 ♖d3 b5 21 ♘×b5 a×b5 22 ♗×b5 ♗×b5 23 ♕×b5 ♖cb8 24 ♕c4 ♖×b2 25 ♖b3 ♖d2 26 ♕c6 ♖e8 27 ♖e1 ♖ed8 28 ♖b7 ♕d3 29 a4 ♖c2 30 ♕b6 ♕×f3† 31 ♔g1 ♕g2# **0–1**

COKO 3 — J BIIT 1 d4 d5 2 ♘c3 ♘c6 3 ♗f4 ♗f5 4 ♘b5 ♖c8 5 a4 e6 6 ♘f3 ♘f6 7 e3 ♘e4 8 ♗d3 ♗b4† 9 c3 ♗d6 10 ♗×e4 ♗×e4 11 ♗×d6 c×d6 12 O-O a6 13 ♘a3 O-O 14 b4 ♕f6 15 a5 ♘b8 16 ♖c1 ♘c6 17 ♕e2 ♕g6 18 ♕d1 ♗d3 19 ♖e1 ♖fd8 20 ♕d2 ♗e4 21 ♘h4 ♕f6 22 f3 ♕×h4 23 g3 ♕g5 24 f×e4 d×e4 25 ♖f1 f6 26 ♖f4 d5 27 ♖h4 ♖c7 28 ♖d1 ♖e7 29 ♖e1 e5 30 ♕d1 e×d4 31 e×d4 g6 32 ♘c2 e3 33 ♕f3 ♖e4 34 ♖×e4 d×e4 35 ♕×e4 f5 36 ♕e6† ♔g7 37 ♕×e3 ♕g4 38 ♕f4 ♕×f4 39 g×f4 h5 40 h4 ♔f6 41 ♘e3 ♖h8 42 d5 ♘a7 43 ♘c4 ♘b5 44 ♖e3 ♖c8 45 ♘b6 ♖×c3 46 ♖e6† ♔f7 47 ♘d7 ♘c7 48 ♘e5† ♔f8 49 ♖f6† ♔g7 50 ♖×g6† ♔h7 51 ♖g5 ♘×d5 52 ♖×h5† ♔g7 53 ♖×f5 ♖c1† 54 ♔h2 ♖c2† 55 ♔g1 ♖c1† 56 ♔f2 ♖c2† 57 ♔e1 ♖h2 58 ♖g5† ♔h7 59 ♖h5† ♔g8 60 ♖g5† ♔h7 61 ♘d3 ♘f6 62 ♖f5 ♔g6 63 ♖e5 ♖×h4 64 ♖c5 ♖h1† 65 ♔e2 ♖h2† 66 ♔e3 ♖a2 67 ♔f3 ♖a3 68 ♔e3 ♘g4† 69 ♔e4 ♘f6† 70 ♔e3 ♘g4† 71 ♔e2 ♔f6 72 ♖g5 ♖a2† 73 ♔f3 ♘h2† 74 ♔e4 ♖e2† 75 ♔d5 ♖d2 76 ♔e4 ♖e2† 77 ♔d5 ♖d2 78 ♔d4 ♘f3† 79 ♔e3 ♖×d3† 80 ♔×d3 ♘×g5 81 f×g5†

♔×g5 82 ♔e3 ♔f5 83 ♔f3 ♔e5 84 ♔e3 ♔d5 85 ♔d3 ♔e5 86 ♔e3 ♔d5 87 ♔d3 ♔e5 ½–½

MARSLAND — DALY 1 e3 e5 2 d4 ♕g5 3 h4 ♕f6 4 ♕f3 ♗b4† 5 ♘c3 ♕×f3 6 ♘×f3 ♗×c3† 7 ♗d2 ♗×b2 8 ♖b1 e4 9 ♘e5 ♗a3 10 ♗b4 ♗×b4† 11 c3 ♗×c3† 12 ♔d1 d6 13 ♗b5† ♔e7 14 ♔c2 d×e5 15 ♔×c3 ♗e6 16 d5 ♗×d5 17 ♗c4 ♗×c4 18 ♔×c4 b6 19 ♖bd1 ♘d7 20 f3 e×f3 21 ♖d2 ♔f6 **0–1**

ACM 1971 — Chicago

August 2 — August 4

		1	2	3	p	tot
1	CHESS 3.5	8+□	2+■	3+■		3
2	TECH	4+□	1−□	6+■	3+■	3
3	GENIE	7+□	6+■	1−□	2−□	2
4	DAVID	2−■	7+□	5=■		1½
5	CCCP	6−□	8+■	4=□		1½
6	COKO 3	5+■	3−□	2−□		1
7	SCHACH	3−■	4−■	8+□		1
8	MR. TURK	1−■	5−□	7−■		0

Round 1

CHESS 3.5 — MR. TURK 1 ♘f3 d5 2 ♘c3 ♘f6 3 d4 e6 4 ♗g5 ♘c6 5 ♗×f6 g×f6 6 e3 a5 7 ♗b5 f5 8 ♗×c6† b×c6 9 ♘e5 c5 10 ♕h5 **1–0**

CCCP — COKO 3 1 e4 e5 2 ♘f3 ♘f6 3 ♘×e5 ♕e7 4 d4 d6 5 ♗b5† c6 6 ♗×c6† ♘×c6 7 ♘×c6 ♕×e4† 8 ♗e3 ♕×g2 9 ♖f1 ♗h3 10 ♘d2 b×c6 11 ♕f3 ♕×f3 12 ♘×f3 ♗g2 13 ♘d2 ♗×f1 14 ♔×f1 d5 15 c4 d×c4 16 ♘×c4 ♘g4 17 h4 ♘×e3† 18 f×e3 f5 19 a4 ♗e7 20 h5 g6 21 h6 ♗g5 22 ♘d6† ♔e7 23 ♘c4 ♗×h6 24 b4 f4 25 e×f4 ♗×f4 26 ♖e1† ♔f6 27 b5 ♖ad8 28 b×c6 ♖×d4 29 ♘b2 ♖c8 30 a5 ♖×c6 31 ♔g1 ♗h2† 32 ♔×h2 ♖c2† 33 ♔h3 ♖c3† 34 ♔h2 ♖d2† 35 ♔g1 ♖g3† 36 ♔f1 ♖f3† 37 ♔g1 ♖g3† 38 ♔f1 ♖f3† 39 ♔g1 ♖×b2 40 a6 ♖a3 41 ♖f1† ♔g5 42 ♖f2 ♖×f2 43 ♔×f2 h6 44 ♔g2 ♔f4 45 ♔h1 ♔g3 46 ♔g1 ♖a1# **0–1**

GENIE — SCHACH 1 e4 e5 2 ♘f3 ♘c6 3 ♗b5 a6 4 ♗a4 ♘f6 5 O–O b5 6 ♗b3 ♘×e4 7 ♘a3 ♗×a3 8 b×a3 d5 9 ♖e1 ♗g4 10 ♖e3 ♗×f3 11 ♖×f3 O–O 12 ♖f5 g6 13 ♖f3 ♕d6 14 d3 ♘f6 15 ♗g5 ♘g4 16 ♖g3 ♘×f2 17 ♔×f2 ♕×a3 18 ♗c1 ♕c5† 19 ♔f3 e4† 20 d×e4 d×e4† 21 ♔e2 ♘d4† 22 ♔f1 ♔h8 23 ♖g5 ♘f5 24 ♕d7 ♕d6 25 ♕×f5 ♕d1† 26 ♔f2 e3† 27 ♗×e3 ♕×a1 28 ♕e5† ♕×e5 29 ♖×e5 ♖ad8 30 ♗c5 ♖g8 31 ♖d5 ♖ge8 32 ♖×d8 ♖×d8 33 ♗×f7 ♖d2† 34 ♔e3 ♖d7 35 ♗d4† ♖×d4 36 ♔×d4 c6 37 g4 g5 38 ♔c5 h6 39 ♔×c6 ♔h7 40 c4 **1–0**

TECH — DAVID 1 e4 e6 2 d4 ♕h4 3 ♘c3 ♘c6 4 ♘f3 ♕h5 5 ♗d3 ♕g4 6 O–O f6 7 ♗e3 a6 8 ♕e2 g5 9 d5 e×d5 10 e×d5 ♘d8 11 ♗f4† ♘e7 12 ♗×c7 f5 13 d6 ♘e6 14 d×e7 ♔×e7 15 ♘d5† ♔e8 16 ♘f6† ♔f7 17 ♘×g4 f×g4 18 ♕e5 g×f3 19 ♕×h8 ♘×c7 20 ♕×h7† ♗g7 21 ♕f5† ♗f6 22 g×f3 ♘e6 23 ♗c4 d5 24 ♗×d5 ♗d7 25 ♗×e6† ♗×e6 26 ♕e4 ♖b8 27 f4 g×f4 28 ♕×f4 ♖g8† 29 ♔h1 ♗d5† 30 f3 b5 31 ♖fd1 ♖d8 32 ♕f5 ♗e6 33 ♕×f6† ♔×f6 34 ♖×d8 ♔e7 35 ♖e1 ♔×d8 36 ♖×e6 a5 37 ♖e5 a4 38 ♖×b5 ♔c7 39 ♔g2 ♔c6 40 c4 ♔c7 41 f4 ♔c6 42 ♔f3 ♔c7 43 ♔e4 ♔c6 44 f5 ♔c7 45 ♔d5 ♔c8 46 f6 ♔d7 47 ♖b8 a3 48 f7 a×b2 49 f8♕ b1♕ 50 ♕g7# **1–0**

Round 2

TECH — CHESS 3.5 1 e4 c5 2 ♘f3 ♘c6 3 d4 c×d4 4 ♘×d4 ♘f6 5 ♘c3 d6 6 ♗c4 e6 7 O–O a6 8 ♗e3 ♘e5 9 ♕e2 ♕c7 10 ♗d3 ♘eg4 11 f4 e5 12 ♘f5 ♗e6 13 ♘d5 ♘×d5 14 e×d5 ♗×f5 15 ♗×f5 ♘h6 16 ♕d3 g6 17 ♗e4 f5 18 ♗f3 e4 19 ♕d4 ♗g7 20 ♕b4 e×f3 21 ♖×f3 ♕×c2 22 ♕×b7 O–O 23 ♖f2 ♕d3 24 ♖e1 ♘g4 25 ♖d2 ♕e4 26 ♖de2 ♖fb8 27 ♕d7 ♕×d5 28 b3 ♘×e3 29 ♖×e3 ♗d4 30 ♕c7 ♗×e3† 31 ♖×e3 ♖c8 32 ♕e7 ♕d1† 33 ♔f2 ♖c2† 34 ♖e2 ♕d4† 35 ♔f3 ♖c3† 36 ♖e3 ♕d1† 37 ♔f2 ♕d2† 38 ♖e2 ♕×f4† 39 ♔g1 ♖c1† 40 ♖e1 ♖×e1† 41 ♕×e1 ♕e4 42 ♕×e4 f×e4 43 ♔f2 ♔f7 44 ♔e3 d5 45 ♔f4 ♔e6 46 b4 ♖c8 47 h3 ♖c2 48 a4 ♖×g2 49 b5 a×b5 50 a×b5 g5† 51 ♔e3 ♔e5 52 b6 d4# **0–1**

COKO 3 — GENIE 1 d4 d5 2 ♘f3 ♘f6 3 ♗g5 ♗g4 4 ♘c3 ♘e4 5 ♘e5 ♗e6 6 ♘×e4 d×e4 7 c4 ♘d7 8 ♘×d7 ♗×d7 9 e3 f6 10 ♗f4 ♗e6 11 ♕h5† ♔d7 12 d5 ♗g8 13 ♕f5† e6 14 d×e6† ♗×e6 15 ♕×e4 c6 16 ♖d1† ♔e8 17 ♖×d8† ♔×d8 18 ♕×e6 ♗b4† 19 ♔e2 ♖e8 20 ♕g4 g6 21 ♕h4 g5 22 ♕×h7 ♗e7 23 ♕d3† ♔c8 24 ♗d6 ♔d7 25 ♗×e7† ♔×e7 26 ♕h7† ♔e6 27 ♕e4† ♔d6 28 c5† ♔×c5 29 ♕d4† ♔b5 30 ♔d1† ♔a5 31 b4† ♔a4 32 ♕c3 ♖ad8† 33 ♔c2 ♖d2† 34 ♔×d2 ♖d8† 35 ♔c2 ♖d2† 36 ♕×d2 ♔a3 37 ♕c3† ♔×a2 38 ♔c1 f5 39 ♔c2 f4 40 ♔c1 g4 41 ♔c2 f3 42 ♔c1 f×g2 43 ♔c2 g×h1♕ 44 ♔c1 ♕×f1† 45 ♔d2 ♕×f2† 46 ♔c1 ♕g1† 47 ♔c2 ♕×h2† 48 ♔c1 ♕h1† 49 ♔c2 ♕b1† 50 ♔d2 g3 51 ♕c4† ♕b3 52 ♕×b3† ♔×b3 53 e4 ♔×b4 54 e5 g2 **0–1**

DAVID — SCHACH 1 e4 e5 2 ♘c3 ♘f6 3 d4 d6 4 ♘f3 ♘g4 5 h3 ♘h6 6 d×e5 d×e5 7 ♕×d8† ♔×d8 8 ♗×h6 g×h6 9 ♖d1† ♗d6 10 ♘×e5 ♘d7 11 ♘×f7† ♔e7 12 ♘×h8 ♗e5 13 ♘d5† ♔f8 14 f4 ♗×h8 15 ♘×c7 ♗×b2 16 ♘×a8 ♗c3† 17 ♔f2 **1–0**

MR. TURK — CCCP 1 d4 d5 2 ♘f3 ♗g4 3 ♘a3 ♗×f3 4 e×f3 ♘c6 5 c3 ♕d6 6 ♘b5 ♕d8 7 a4 a6 8 c4 a×b5 9 c×d5 ♘a5 10 b4 ♘c4 11 h3 ♕d7 12 ♗d2 ♘b2 13 ♕e2 ♘×a4 14 ♖a2 ♕e6 15 ♕e3 ♕d7 16 ♗e2 f5 17 ♕f4 g5 18 ♕×g5 ♘f6 19 ♗d3 ♖g8 20 ♕×f5 ♕×f5 21 g4 ♕×d3 22 ♔d1 ♘c3† **0–1**

Round 3

GENIE — CHESS 3.5 1 e4 c5 2 ♘f3 ♘c6 3 d4 c×d4 4 ♘×d4 ♘f6 5 ♘c3 d6 6 ♘×c6 b×c6 7 ♗f4 e5 8 ♗e3 ♗e6 9 ♗g5 ♖b8 10 b3 ♗e7 11 ♗c4 ♗×c4 12 b×c4 ♕d7 13 ♖b1 ♖×b1 14 ♘×b1 ♘×e4 15 ♗c1 O–O 16 ♕h5 ♖b8 17 ♘d2 ♘×d2 18 ♗×d2 ♖b1† 19 ♕d1 ♖×d1† 20 ♔×d1 ♕g4† 21 f3 ♕×g2 22 ♖e1 ♕×f3† 23 ♔c1 f5 24 ♖e3 ♕f1† 25 ♗e1 ♗g5 26 c5 ♗×e3† 27 ♔b2 ♕×e1 28 c×d6 ♕b4† 29 ♔a1 ♗d4† 30 c3 ♗×c3# **0–1**

COKO 3 — TECH 1 e4 e5 2 ♘f3 ♘c6 3 ♗c4 ♘f6 4 d3 d5 5 ♗×d5 ♘×d5 6 e×d5 ♕×d5 7 ♘c3 ♗b4 8 O–O ♗×c3 9 b×c3 O–O 10 ♘g5 ♗f5 11 ♖b1 f6 12 c4

♕c5 13 ♘h3 ♗×h3 14 ♗e3 ♘d4 15 g×h3 ♕c6 16 c3 ♘f3† 17 ♔h1 ♘d2† 18 f3 ♘×f1 19 ♕×f1 f5 20 ♖b5 f4 21 ♖c5 ♕e6 22 ♗c1 c6 23 d4 ♖ae8 24 ♖×e5 ♕g6 25 ♖×e8 ♕×e8 26 ♕f2 ♕e6 27 ♕f1 ♖f5 28 h4 c5 29 d5 ♕d6 30 ♕h3 ♕e5 31 ♕f1 ♕×c3 32 d6 ♕d4 33 ♕e2 ♕×d6 34 ♕e8† ♖f8 35 ♕a4 ♖f5 36 ♕e8† ♖f8 37 ♕a4 ♕e6 38 ♕b3 ♕e2 39 h3 ♖d8 40 ♗×f4 ♖d1† **0–1**

CCCP — DAVID 1 e4 e6 2 d4 ♘c6 3 ♘c3 g5 4 ♗b5 a6 5 ♗×c6 d×c6 6 ♗e3 b5 7 ♕h5 b4 8 ♗×g5 ♘f6 9 ♗×f6 ♕×f6 10 e5 ♕g7 11 ♘e4 ♕×g2 12 ♕f3 ♕×f3 13 ♘×f3 ♗h6 14 ♘f6† ♔e7 15 a3 b×a3 16 ♖×a3 ♖b8 17 O-O ♖×b2 18 c4 a5 19 ♖×a5 ♖b3 20 ♔g2 ♖×f3 21 ♔×f3 ♗d2 22 ♖c5 ♗c3 23 ♖×c6 ♗b7 24 ♘d5† e×d5 25 ♖×c7† ♔e6 26 ♖×b7 d×c4 27 ♖b6† ♔f5 28 ♖f6† ♔g5 29 ♖g1† ♔h5 30 ♖f5† ♔h6 31 ♖f6† ♔h5 32 ♖f5† ♔h6 33 ♖f6† ♔h5 34 ♖f5† ½–½

SCHACH — MR. TURK 1 d4 d5 2 c4 d×c4 3 ♘f3 ♘h6 4 ♕a4† ♘c6 5 e4 **1–0**

Second Place Playoff

GENIE — TECH 1 e4 e5 2 ♘f3 ♘c6 3 ♗b5 ♘f6 4 O-O ♗c5 5 ♘c3 d6 6 d4 e×d4 7 ♘×d4 ♗d7 8 ♘f5 O-O 9 ♗g5 ♘e5 10 ♘a4 ♗×b5 11 ♘×c5 ♗×f1 12 ♘×b7 ♕b8 13 ♘e7† ♔h8 14 ♘×d6 c×d6 15 ♗×f6 g×f6 16 ♕×f1 ♕b4 17 ♘d5 ♕×e4 18 ♘×f6 ♕×c2 19 ♕c1 ♕×c1† 20 ♖×c1 ♔g7 21 ♘h5† ♔g6 22 ♘f4† ♔f5 23 ♘d5 ♖ad8 24 ♖e1 ♖b8 25 b4 ♘d3 26 ♖e2 ♘×b4 27 ♘c3 ♖fe8 28 a3 ♖×e2 29 ♘×e2 ♘d5 30 h4 ♔e4 31 h5 ♖d8 32 h6 ♖c8 33 g4 ♔f3 34 ♘g3 ♔×g4 35 a4 ♔f3 36 a5 ♖g8 37 a6 ♖×g3† 38 f×g3 ♔×g3 39 ♔f1 ♘b4 40 ♔e2 ♘×a6 41 ♔e3 ♘c5 42 ♔d4 ♔f4 43 ♔d5 ♘e4 44 ♔c6 ♔e5 45 ♔b7 a5 46 ♔c6 a4 47 ♔d7 a3 48 ♔e7 a2 49 ♔×f7 a1♕ 50 ♔e7 ♕c1 51 ♔d7 ♕×h6 52 ♔c6 ♕e3 53 ♔c7 d5 54 ♔c6 d4 55 ♔d7 d3 56 ♔c6 d2 57 ♔d7 d1♕† 58 ♔c6 ♕a7 59 ♔b5 ♕da4# **0–1**

ACM 1972 — Boston

August 13 — August 15

	1	2	3	p	p	tot
1 CHESS 3.6	2+□	4+■	3+□			3
2 OSTRICH	1−■	7+□	5+■	3+□	4+■	4
3 TECH	5+■	6+□	1−■	2−■	4+□	3
4 COKO 3	7+■	1−□	6+■	3−■	2−□	2
5 SCHACH	3−□	8+■	2−□			1
6 USC	8+□	3−■	4−□			1
7 MSU	4−□	2−■	8=□			½
8 LEVERETT	6−■	5−□	7=■			½

Round 1

CHESS 3.6 — OSTRICH 1 e4 c5 2 ♘f3 ♘c6 3 d4 c×d4 4 ♘×d4 e5 5 ♘f3 ♕b6 6 ♘c3 ♗c5 7 ♕d2 d6 8 ♘d5 ♕d8 9 b4 ♗d4 10 c3 ♗b6 11 ♘×b6 a×b6 12 ♗c4 ♗e6 13 ♗×e6 f×e6 14 ♘g5 ♕d7 15 O-O h6 16 ♘f3 O-O-O 17 ♖d1 ♘f6 18 ♕e2 ♕c7 19 ♗b2 ♘e7 20 ♘d2 d5 21 c4 d4 22 ♕d3 ♘g6 23 g3 ♕e7 24 ♗a3 ♔c7 25 ♖ab1 ♖h7 26 ♖e1 ♖d7 27 ♔g2 ♕d8 28 h3 ♘g8 29 ♖b3 ♕g5 30 ♔h2 ♖f7 31 ♕e2 ♘f6 32 ♖f3 h5 33 h4 ♘g4† 34 ♔h1 ♕e7 35 ♔g2 ♖×f3 36 ♘×f3 ♕f6 37 ♗c1 ♔d6 38 ♗g5 ♕f7 39 ♗d8 ♖h8 40 ♗×b6 ♔e7 41 ♘g5 ♕e8 42 b5 ♕c8 43 ♖b1 ♖f8 44 ♖f1 ♖e8 45 ♕f3 ♖f8 46 ♕a3† ♔d7 47 ♗c5 ♖h8 48 ♘f7 ♖h7 49 ♖c1 ♘h6 50 ♘d6 ♕c7 51 b6 ♕c6 52 ♖e1 ♖h8 53 ♔g1 ♘g4 54 ♖f1 ♖h6 55 ♘f7 ♕×e4 56 ♘×h6 ♘×h6 57 f3 ♕c6 58 ♔f2 ♔d8 59 ♖b1 ♕d7 60 ♔g2 ♘f5 61 ♔f2 ♕c8 62 ♖b5 ♔d7 63 ♖b2 ♔c6 64 ♕b4 ♔d7 65 ♕b5† ♕c6 66 ♖d2 ♕×b5 67 c×b5 ♔d8 68 ♖d3 ♘ge7 69 a4 g6 70 a5 ♔d7 71 a6 b×a6 72 b×a6 ♔c8 73 a7 ♔b7 74 ♖a3 ♔a8 75 b7† ♔×b7 76 a8♕† ♔c7 77 ♖a7# **1–0**

SCHACH — TECH 1 d4 d5 2 c4 d×c4 3 ♘f3 ♘f6 4 e4 b5 5 d5 ♘g4 6 ♗g5 ♘f6 7 ♗×f6 e×f6 8 ♗e2 ♗c5 9 ♘c3 ♗d7 10 O-O O-O 11 ♘h4 ♕e7 12 a3 ♘a6 13 ♘f5 ♕e5 14 ♘e3 c6 15 d×c6 ♗×c6 16 ♘×c4 b×c4 17 ♗×c4 ♘c7 18 ♕g4 ♗d4 19 ♖ac1 ♗×c3 20 ♖×c3 ♗×e4 21 ♖e1 ♗f3 22 ♖×e5 ♗×g4 23 ♖e7 ♘e6 24 ♗×e6 ♗×e6 25 g3 ♖fe8 26 ♖×e8† ♖×e8 27 ♖c7 ♗d5 28 f4 a6 29 ♖d7 ♗e4 30 ♔f2 ♔f8 31 b4 ♖e6 32 ♖d8† ♔e7 33 ♖d1 ♖d6 34 ♖e1 ♖d2† 35 ♔g1 f5 36 h4 ♖g2† 37 ♔f1 ♖×g3 38 a4 ♖b3 39 h5 ♖×b4 40 a5 ♖b1 41 ♔f2 ♖×e1 42 ♔×e1 ♗f3 43 h6 g×h6 44 ♔f2 ♗d5 45 ♔e3 ♔d6 46 ♔d4 ♗e6 47 ♔d3 ♗a2 48 ♔d4 ♗d5 49 ♔e3 ♔c6 50 ♔d4 h5 51 ♔e5 ♗e4 52 ♔d4 h4 53 ♔e5 h3 54 ♔d4 ♔b5 55 ♔e5 ♔×a5 56 ♔d4 h2 57 ♔e5 h1♕ 58 ♔d4 h6 59 ♔e5 ♕h4 60 ♔d6 ♕×f4† 61 ♔d7 ♔b6 62 ♔d8 h5 **0–1**

USC — LEVERETT 1 e4 ♘f6 2 e5 ♘e4 3 d3 ♘c5 4 ♘c3 ♘c6 5 ♘f3 d5 6 ♘e3 d4 7 ♘e4 ♘×e5 8 ♘×e5 ♘a4 9 ♘g5 ♘×b2 10 ♕f3 ♘×d3† 11 ♗×d3 ♗e6 12 ♘e×f7 ♕d5 13 ♘×h8 ♕×f3 14 g×f3 ♗×a2 15 ♗×d4 O-O-O 16 ♖×a2 ♖×d4 17 ♘e6 ♖d6 18 ♘×f8 ♖f6 19 ♘×h7 ♖×f3 20 ♖×a7 c5 21 ♘g6 ♖f7 22 ♗e4 e6 23 ♘g5 ♖f6 24 ♖×b7 ♖×g6 25 ♗×g6 ♔×b7 26 ♘×e6 c4 27 ♘×g7 ♔c6 28 ♗f7 ♔b5 29 ♖g1 ♔b4 30 ♖g4 ♔a3 31 ♗×c4 ♔b2 32 ♔d2 ♔a3 33 ♔c3 ♔a4 34 h3 ♔a5 35 ♖g5† ♔a4 36 ♗b3† ♔a3 37 ♖a5# **1–0**

MSU — COKO 3 1 e4 e5 2 ♗b5 c6 3 ♗c4 d5 4 e×d5 c×d5 5 ♗b5† ♗d7 6 a4 ♗c5 7 ♘f3 ♗×b5 8 a×b5 e4 9 d4 e×f3 10 O-O f×g2 11 ♔×g2 ♗d6 12 ♕g4 ♘d7 13 ♕×g7 ♕f6 14 ♖e1† ♘e7 15 ♗h6 ♕g6† 16 ♕×g6 h×g6 17 ♗g7 ♖×h2† 18 ♔g1 ♖h7 19 ♗f8 ♗h2† 20 ♔g2 ♘×f8 21 b6 a6 22 ♖a4 ♘e6 23 ♖×e6 f×e6 24 c4 d×c4 25 ♖×c4 ♘d5 26 ♘a3 ♘×b6 27 ♖b4 ♘d5 28 ♖c4 ♖h4 29 b4 b5 30 ♖c6 ♔d7 31 ♖c5 ♖g4† 32 ♔h3 ♖g5 33 ♖×d5† e×d5 34 ♔×h2 ♖h8# **0–1**

Round 2

COKO 3 — CHESS 3.6 1 d4 d5 2 ♘c3 ♘f6 3 ♘f3 ♗g4 4 ♕d3 ♘c6 5 ♘e5 ♗d7 6 ♗g5 ♘b4 7 ♕d1 ♗f5 8 ♘d3 h6 9 ♗×f6 e×f6 10 a3 ♘×d3† 11 c×d3 ♗e6 12 ♕b3 b6 13 e4 c6 14 ♕a4 ♕d7 15 e×d5 ♗×d5 16 ♘×d5 ♕×d5 17 ♖c1 ♔d7 18 ♕c4 ♗d6 19 ♕×d5 c×d5 20 ♗e2 ♖ae8 21 a4 f5 22 b3 ♗b4† 23 ♔d1 ♖c8 24 ♖×c8 ♖×c8 25 ♗f3 ♔d6 26 ♔e2 ♖e8† 27 ♔d1 ♗c3 28 g4 f×g4 29 ♗×g4 g6 30 f4 ♗×d4 31 b4 h5 32 ♗e2 ♖c8 33 ♖f1 ♗e3 34 ♔e1 ♖c2 35 f5 ♖a2 36 f×g6 f×g6 37 ♖f6† ♔e5 38 ♖×g6 ♔d4 39

♔d1 ♖×a4 40 b5 ♖a1† 41 ♔c2 ♖e1 42 ♗d1 ♖f1 43 h4 ♖f2† 44 ♔b3 ♖f4 45 ♗×h5 ♖×h4 46 ♗f3 ♔c5 47 ♖c6† ♔×b5 48 ♗×d5 ♖d4 49 ♗f3 ♖×d3† 50 ♖c3 ♖×c3† 51 ♔×c3 a5 52 ♗d5 a4 53 ♔d3 ♔c5 54 ♗e6 ♗d4 55 ♔c2 b5 56 ♔d2 ♔d6 57 ♗f7 ♔e5 58 ♔e1 ♔f6 59 ♗d5 b4 60 ♔e2 b3 61 ♔f3 b2 62 ♗e4 a3 63 ♗b1 ♔e5 64 ♗a2 ♗c3 65 ♗b1 ♗d2 66 ♗a2 ♗g5 67 ♗b1 ♔d5 68 ♗a2† ♔d4 69 ♗b1 ♔c3 70 ♔e2 ♔b3 71 ♔d1 a2 **0–1**

TECH — USC 1 e4 c5 2 ♘f3 ♘c6 3 d4 c×d4 4 ♘×d4 ♘f6 5 ♘c3 d6 6 ♗c4 e5 7 ♘f5 ♗e6 8 ♕d3 ♘b4 9 ♗b5† ♗d7 10 ♗×d7† ♕×d7 11 ♕e2 g6 12 ♗g5 ♘h5 13 a3 f6 14 a×b4 f×g5 15 ♘d5 ♕c6 16 O–O ♘f4 17 ♘×f4 g×f4 18 b5 ♕b6 19 ♘h4 ♗e7 20 ♘f3 a6 21 ♕c4 g5 22 ♖fd1 g4 23 ♘d2 h5 24 ♖a4 ♗g5 25 ♕e6† ♔d8 26 ♘c4 ♕×b5 27 ♕×d6† ♔c8 28 ♘b6† ♕×b6 29 ♕×b6 ♖h6 30 ♕c5† ♖c6 31 ♕f8† ♔c7 32 ♕×a8 ♖×c2 33 ♕g8 ♗h4 34 ♖c4† ♖×c4 35 ♕×c4† ♔b8 36 ♖d7 a5 37 ♕c7† ♔a7 38 ♕×b7# **1–0**

OSTRICH — MSU 1 c4 ♘c6 2 d4 ♘f6 3 d5 ♘b8 4 ♘f3 ♘a6 5 ♗g5 ♘e4 6 ♘bd2 ♘×g5 7 ♘×g5 f6 8 ♘ge4 f5 9 ♘g3 f4 10 ♘h5 ♘c5 11 b4 e5 12 b×c5 g6 13 e3 f×e3 14 f×e3 ♗×c5 15 ♕f3 ♕h4† 16 ♘g3 ♖f8 17 ♕e2 ♗b4 18 ♕d3 g5 19 O–O–O ♖f2 20 ♘f3 ♕g4 21 ♘×e5 ♕×d1† 22 ♔×d1 d6 23 ♘e4 ♖×f1† 24 ♖×f1 d×e5 25 ♘f6† ♔e7 26 ♕×h7† ♔d8 27 ♕h8† ♔e7 28 ♕e8† ♔d6 29 ♘e4# **1–0**

LEVERETT — SCHACH 1 ♘c3 d5 2 e4 d×e4 3 ♘×e4 e5 4 ♕h5 ♘c6 5 ♘f3 ♘f6 6 ♘×f6† g×f6 7 ♗c4 ♕d7 8 ♕×f7† ♕×f7 9 ♗×f7† ♔×f7 10 O–O ♖g8 11 d3 ♗c5 12 ♗e3 ♘d4 13 ♘×d4 e×d4 14 ♗f4 ♗d6 15 ♗g3 ♗e6 16 a4 ♖g5 17 h4 ♖g4 18 b4 ♗×g3 19 f×g3 ♖×g3 20 ♖f4 ♖d8 **0–1**

Round 3

CHESS 3.6 — TECH 1 e4 e5 2 ♘f3 ♘c6 3 ♗b5 ♘f6 4 O–O ♗c5 5 ♘c3 d6 6 ♗×c6† b×c6 7 d4 e×d4 8 ♘×d4 O–O 9 ♗g5 ♗g4 10 ♕d3 ♗×d4 11 ♕×d4 ♖b8 12 ♗×f6 ♕×f6 13 ♕×f6 g×f6 14 b3 ♖b4 15 h3 ♗e6 16 g4 ♖d4 17 ♖ad1 ♖×d1 18 ♘×d1 ♔g7 19 ♘e3 ♔g6 20 f4 ♔g7 21 ♔g2 ♖b8 22 ♔f3 ♖b5 23 c4 ♖a5 24 f5 ♗d7 25 ♖f2 ♖e5 26 ♖d2 a6 27 h4 c5 28 ♘d5 ♗c6 29 ♘×c7 ♗×e4† 30 ♔f4 h5 31 g×h5 a5 32 ♖×d6 ♗×f5 33 h6† ♔g6 34 h5† ♔×h5 35 ♖×f6 ♖e2 36 ♔×f5 ♖f2† 37 ♔e5 ♖h2 38 ♘d5 ♔g5 39 ♘c3 ♖h4 40 ♖×f7 ♔×h6 41 ♘e4 ♖h5† 42 ♔d6 ♔g6 43 ♖a7 a4 44 ♖×a4 ♔f7 45 ♖a7† ♔g6 46 a4 ♖f5 47 a5 ♖f3 48 ♖b7 ♔f5 49 ♘×c5 ♖c3 50 a6 ♖h3 51 a7 **1–0**

USC — COKO 3 1 e4 e5 2 ♘f3 d5 3 e×d5 ♕×d5 4 ♘c3 ♕a5 5 ♗b5† ♗d7 6 a4 ♗×b5 7 ♘×b5 ♘d7 8 c3 ♘gf6 9 b4 ♕b6 10 d4 c6 11 d×e5 c×b5 12 ♕d3 ♘g4 13 ♗e3 ♘×e3 14 f×e3 b×a4 15 ♖×a4 ♕e6 16 ♕b5 ♕b3 17 ♖f1 ♕×c3† 18 ♔e2 ♕c6 19 ♕a5 ♕c4† 20 ♔f2 b5 21 ♖aa1 ♗×b4 22 ♕a6 ♗c3 23 ♖fc1 O–O 24 ♖a3 ♘c5 25 ♖c2 ♘×a6 26 ♖c×c3 ♕e6 27 ♘d4 ♕×e5 28 ♖×a6 ♖fd8 29 g3 b4 30 ♖c4 ♖d6 31 ♖ac6 a5 32 ♖c8† ♖d8 33 ♖8c5 ♖d5 **0–1**

SCHACH — OSTRICH 1 d4 ♘f6 2 c4 e6 3 ♘c3 ♗b4 4 ♕c2 O–O 5 e3 ♘c6 6 ♗d2 a5 7 d5 e×d5 8 c×d5 ♗×c3 9 ♗×c3 ♘×d5 10 O–O–O ♘cb4 11 ♗×b4 ♘×b4 12 ♕c4 d5 13 ♕b3 ♗f5 14 a3 ♗c2 15 ♕c3 ♘a2† 16 ♔×c2 ♘×c3 17 b×c3 ♕g5 18 f4 ♕g6† 19 ♔b2 ♕b6† 20 ♔a2 a4 21 ♖d3 ♕b3† 22 ♔a1 ♕×a3† 23 ♔b1 ♖a5 24 ♘h3 ♖b5† 25 ♔c2 ♕a2† **0–1**

MSU — LEVERETT 1 d4 ♘f6 2 ♗g5 ♘e4 3 ♘f3 ♘c6 4 ♕d3 ♘×g5 5 ♘×g5 e6 6 ♘e4 ♗b4† 7 c3 f5 8 ♘c5 ♗×c5 9 d×c5 ♕e7 10 ♕b5 a6 11 ♕c4 O–O 12 e3 g5 13 ♗e2 f4 14 ♗h5 h6 15 e4 a5 16 ♔d2 ♔g7 17 a4 ♔h8 18 h3 ♖d8 19 ♖h2 ♖a7 20 f3 ♕f6 21 ♘a3 ♖a8 22 ♘b5 ♕e5 23 ♗g6 ♔g7 24 ♗h5 ♖h8 25 ♔d3 ♖f8 26 b3 ♘b4† 27 ♔d2 ♘c6 28 ♖a2 ♘e7 29 ♕d4 ♕×d4† 30 ♘×d4 e5 31 ♘b5 ♖a6 32 ♘×c7 ♖c6 33 ♘e8† ♖×e8 34 ♗×e8 ♖×c5 35 ♔d3 d5 36 ♖d2 ♗e6 37 ♖b2 b6 38 ♗h5 ♗d7 39 ♖f2 ♗c6 40 ♖d2 ♔h8 41 ♗f7 d×e4† 42 f×e4 b5 43 b4 a×b4 44 c×b4 ♖c1 45 ♗d5 b×a4 46 ♗×c6 ♘×c6 47 ♖b2 ♖g1 48 b5 ♖d1† 49 ♔e2 ♖d6 50 b×c6 h5 51 ♖b8† ♔h7 52 ♖e8 ♖×c6 53 ♖×e5 h4 54 ♔d3 a3 55 ♖e7† ♔g6 56 ♖a7 ♖d6† 57 ♔c2 ♖c6† 58 ♔d3 ♖d6† 59 ♔c4 ♖c6† 60 ♔d4 ♖d6† 61 ♔c3 ♖c6† 62 ♔d3 ♖d6† ½–½

Second Place Playoff

OSTRICH — TECH 1 c4 e5 2 ♘c3 ♘f6 3 e4 ♘c6 4 d3 ♗c5 5 ♗g5 O–O 6 ♘f3 d6 7 ♗e2 ♗e6 8 O–O ♘d4 9 ♘d5 c6 10 ♗×f6 ♘×f3† 11 ♗×f3 g×f6 12 ♘c3 ♗d4 13 ♕b3 ♕a5 14 ♘e2 ♖ab8 15 ♖ae1 b5 16 ♘×d4 e×d4 17 ♕a3 ♕×a3 18 b×a3 b×c4 19 ♖c1 ♖b5 20 d×c4 ♖c5 21 ♖fd1 ♗×c4 22 ♖×d4 ♗e6 23 ♖cd1 ♔g7 24 h4 ♖c8 25 ♖×d6 ♗×a2 26 h5 ♗e6 27 ♖1d3 ♖b8 28 ♗d1 ♖c8 29 f4 ♖e8 30 ♖g3† ♔f8 31 h6 ♔e7 32 ♖d2 ♖c8 33 f5 ♗c4 34 ♖g7 ♖e5 35 ♖×h7 ♖×e4 36 ♗c2 ♖h4 37 g3 ♖g8 38 ♖g2 ♖d4 39 ♔h2 **1–0**

TECH — COKO 3 1 e4 e5 2 ♘f3 ♘f6 3 d4 ♗b4† 4 ♗d2 ♗×d2† 5 ♘b×d2 e×d4 6 ♘×d4 O–O 7 ♗c4 ♘×e4 8 ♘×e4 d5 9 ♗×d5 ♕×d5 10 f3 ♘c6 11 c3 f5 12 ♘×c6 ♕×c6 13 ♘g5 ♖e8† 14 ♔f2 h6 15 ♕b3† ♗e6 16 ♘×e6 ♖×e6 17 ♖ad1 ♕b6† 18 ♖d4 c5 19 ♖d5 c4† 20 ♕×b6 a×b6 21 a4 ♖×a4 22 ♖×f5 g6 23 ♖d5 ♖a2 24 ♖b1 ♔f7 25 f4 ♖e4 26 ♔f3 ♖e7 27 f5 g×f5 28 ♖×f5† ♔e6 29 ♔e4 ♖a5 30 g4 h5 31 ♖×h5 ♖×h5 32 g×h5 ♔d6† 33 ♔d4 ♖h7 34 ♖d1 ♖×h5 35 ♔×c4† ♔c6 36 ♖d2 b5† 37 ♔d4 ♖d5† 38 ♔e3 ♖e5† 39 ♔d4 ♖d5† 40 ♔e3 ♖e5† 41 ♔f4 ♖h5 42 ♔e4 ♖h4† 43 ♔e5 ♖h5† 44 ♔e4 ♖h4† 45 ♔e5 ♖h5† 46 ♔e6 ♖h6† 47 ♔e7 ♖h7† 48 ♔e6 ♖h6† 49 ♔e7 ♖h7† 50 ♔f6 ♖h6† 51 ♔f5 ♔c5 52 ♔e5 ♖h5† 53 ♔e4 ♖h4† 54 ♔e5 ♖h5† 55 ♔e4 ♖h4† 56 ♔e3 b4 57 c×b4† ♖×b4 58 ♖c2† ♔d5 59 ♖d2† ♔e5 60 ♖c2 ♖b3† 61 ♔e2 ♖h3 62 ♔e1 ♔e4 63 ♖c4† ♔d5 64 ♖c7 b5 65 ♖d7† ♔e4 66 ♖e7† ♔d4 67 ♖d7† ♔e4 68 ♖e7† ♔d4 69 ♖e2 b4 70 ♔d2 ♖d3† 71 ♔c2 b3† 72 ♔c1 ♖h3 73 ♔d2 ♖d3† 74 ♔e1 ♖h3 75 ♔d2 ♖d3† 76 ♔e1 ♖h3 77 ♔d1 ♔d3 78 ♖f2 ♔d4 79 ♔d2 ♖d3† 80 ♔e2 ♖e3† 81 ♔d2 ♖d3† 82 ♔e2 ♖e3† 83 ♔d1 ♖h3 84 ♖f4† ♔e5 85 ♖b4 ♖d3† 86 ♔e2 ♖h3 87 ♔d2 ♖×h2† 88 ♔c3 ♖c2† 89 ♔×b3 ♖c6 90 ♖g4 ♖b6† 91 ♔c3 ♔f5 92 ♖d4 ♔e5 93 b4 ♖c6† 94 ♔d3 ♖b6 95 ♖e4† ♔d5 96 ♖f4 ♔e5 97 ♖e4† ♔d5 98 ♖f4 ♔e5 99 ♔e3 ♖b5 100 ♖c4 ♔e6

101 ♔e4 ♖e5† 102 ♔d4 ♖d5† 103 ♔e4 ♖e5† 104 ♔d4 ♖d5† 105 ♔e3 ♔d6 106 ♔e4 ♖e5† 107 ♔d4 ♖d5† 108 ♔e4 ♖e5† 109 ♔d4 ♖d5† 110 ♔e3 ♔e6 111 ♔f4 ♖f5† 112 ♔e3 ♖d5 113 ♔f4 ♖f5† 114 ♔g4 ♖d5 115 ♖c6† ♔e5 116 ♔f3 ♖d3† 117 ♔e2 ♖b3 118 ♖c4 ♖b2† 119 ♔e3 ♖b3† 120 ♔d2 ♔d5 121 ♖f4 ♔e5 122 ♖c4 ♔d5 123 ♖f4 ♔e5 124 ♖g4 ♖b2† 125 ♔e3 ♖b3† 126 ♔e2 ♖b2† 127 ♔d3 ♔f5 128 ♖e4 ♖b3† 129 ♔c2 ♔×e4 130 ♔×b3 ♔d4 131 b5 ♔c5 132 ♔a4 ♔b6 133 ♔b4 ♔c7 134 ♔c5 ♔c8 135 ♔c6 ♔d8 136 ♔b7 ♔d7 137 b6 ♔e7 138 ♔c7 ♔e8 139 b7 ♔f7 140 b8♕ ♔f6 141 ♔d6 ♔g6 142 ♔e6 ♔h6 143 ♔f6 ♔h7 144 ♕e8 ♔h6 145 ♕g6# **1–0**

COKO 3 — OSTRICH 1 d4 ♘f6 2 ♘f3 d5 3 ♘c3 ♘c6 4 ♘e5 e6 5 ♘×c6 b×c6 6 ♗g5 ♗b4 7 ♕d2 O–O 8 ♗×f6 g×f6 9 a3 ♗×c3 10 ♕×c3 ♕d6 11 ♕f3 e5 12 d×e5 f×e5 13 e4 f5 14 e×f5 ♗×f5 15 ♕g3† ♕g6 16 c4 ♖ab8 17 ♕×e5 ♖fe8 18 ♕×e8† ♕×e8† 19 ♗e2 ♖×b2 20 O–O ♕×e2 21 c×d5 c×d5 22 h4 c5 23 ♖ae1 ♕h5 24 ♖e3 ♕×h4 25 ♖e8† ♔f7 26 g3 ♕d4 27 ♖e3 c4 28 ♖f3 ♔g6 29 ♖c1 ♕d2 30 ♖a1 c3 31 ♖f4 c2 32 ♔g2 ♖b1 33 ♖a2 c1♕ 34 ♖h4 ♕g1† 35 ♔f3 ♖b3# **0–1**

ACM 1973 — Atlanta

August 26 — August 28

		1	2	3	4	p	p	tot
1	CHESS 4.0	7+□	5=■	8+□	3+■			3½
2	TECH 2	10−■	12+■	5+□	9+□	4+□	3+■	5
3	CHAOS	12+□	10+■	6+■	1−□	4+■	2−□	4
4	OSTRICH	8−■	11+■	10+□	6+□	3−□	2−■	3
5	DARTMOUTH	9+■	1=□	2−■	8=□			2
6	TECH	11+□	8+■	3−□	4−■			2
7	BELLE	1−■	9=□	12=□	10+□			2
8	COKO 4	4+□	6−□	1−■	5=■			1½
9	GA TECH	5−□	7=■	11+□	2−■			1½
10	THE FOX	2+□	3−□	4−■	7−■			1
11	USC	6−■	4−□	9−■	12+□			1
12	CHES	3−■	2−□	7=■	11−■			½

Round 1

CHESS 4.0 — BELLE 1 e4 e5 2 ♘f3 ♘c6 3 d4 e×d4 4 c3 d×c3 5 ♗c4 c×b2 6 ♗×b2 ♗b4† 7 ♘c3 d6 8 ♕b3 ♗×c3† 9 ♗×c3 ♕e7 10 ♗×g7 ♕×e4† 11 ♗e2 ♘d4 12 ♗×d4 f6 13 ♕b2 ♕f5 14 O–O h5 15 ♘h4 ♕g5 16 g3 ♖h7 17 f4 ♕d5 18 ♗f3 ♕c4 19 ♗×f6 ♘×f6 20 ♕×f6 ♕c5† 21 ♔h1 ♕c2 22 ♖fe1† ♗e6 23 ♕×e6† ♔f8 24 ♗×b7 d5 25 ♕f6† ♔g8 26 ♗×d5† ♖f7 27 ♕×f7† ♔h8 28 ♕f6† **1–0**

COKO 4 — OSTRICH 1 d4 ♘f6 2 c4 e6 3 ♘d2 ♗e7 4 e4 O–O 5 e5 ♘e8 6 ♘gf3 d6 7 ♗e2 d×e5 8 d×e5 ♘c6 9 O–O ♗c5 10 ♘b3 ♕×d1 11 ♖×d1 ♗b4 12 ♗e3 ♗e7 13 ♘c5 b6 14 ♘d7 ♗×d7 15 ♖×d7 ♖d8 16 ♖ad1 a5 17 a4 h5 18 ♘e1 ♖×d7 19 ♖×d7 h4 20 ♗f3 ♘×e5 21 ♖×e7 ♘×c4 22 ♗c6 ♘×e3 23 f×e3 ♘d6 24 ♖×c7 ♘c4 25 ♘f3 ♘×b2 26 ♘×h4 g5 27 ♘f3 f6 28 ♖b7 ♖c8 29 ♗d7 ♖c1† 30 ♔f2 ♘d3† 31 ♔g3 ♘c5 32 ♖b8† ♔f7 33 ♗e8† ♔e7 34 h4 ♘e4† 35 ♔h3 ♖h1† 36 ♔g4 f5† 37 ♔h5 g4 38 ♗c6 g×f3 39 g×f3 ♘f6† 40 ♔g5 ♖g1† 41 ♔h6 ♘g8† 42 ♔h7 ♘f6† 43 ♔h6 ♖b1 44 ♖b7† ♔d6 45 ♗b5 ♔c5 46 ♖c7† ♔b4 47 ♖c6 ♖e1 48 ♖×e6 ♘d5 49 e4 f×e4 50 ♖×e4† ♖×e4 51 f×e4 ♘c3 52 e5 ♘×b5 53 a×b5 ♔×b5 54 e6 ♔c6 55 ♔g6 ♔d6 56 ♔f7 a4 57 e7 ♔c5 58 ♔e6 ♔b4 59 e8♕ b5 60 ♕f8† ♔b3 61 h5 a3 62 ♕f3† ♔c4 63 ♕×a3 b4 64 ♕×b4† ♔×b4 65 h6 ♔c5 66 h7 ♔c4 67 h8♕ ♔d3 68 ♕e5 ♔c2 69 ♕e3 ♔b2 70 ♕d3 ♔a2 71 ♕c3 ♔b1 72 ♔d5 ♔a2 73 ♔c4 ♔b1 74 ♕d2 ♔a1 75 ♔b3 ♔b1 76 ♕b2# **1–0**

TECH — USC 1 e4 e5 2 ♘f3 ♘f6 3 d4 ♘×e4 4 ♗d3 d5 5 ♘×e5 f6 6 ♕h5† ♔e7 7 ♘g6† h×g6 8 ♕×h8 ♔f7 9 O–O c5 10 ♗×e4 d×e4 11 d×c5 ♘a6 12 ♗e3 b6 13 ♘c3 b×c5 14 ♘×e4 ♕b6 15 b3 ♗f5 16 f3 ♘b4 17 ♖f2 ♖e8 18 ♕h4 g5 19 ♕h5† ♗g6 20 ♕g4 ♔g8 21 ♕d7 a6 22 c4 ♖d8 23 ♕h3 ♘d3 24 ♖e2 ♖e8 25 ♕d7 ♘b4 26 ♖d1 ♘c6 27 ♖d5 ♘b8 28 ♕a4 ♖c8 29 ♔h1 ♗f7 30 ♖f5 ♗e6 31 ♗×c5 ♕c7 32 ♘×f6† g×f6 33 ♖×e6 ♗×c5 34 ♖f×f6 ♗e7 35 ♖f5 ♖d8 36 ♖d5 ♖f8 37 c5 ♔f7 38 ♕e4 ♖c8 39 ♖×e7† ♕×e7 40 ♖f5† ♔e8 41 ♖e5 ♔d8 42 ♖×e7 ♖×c5 43 ♕d4† ♔×e7 44 ♕×c5† ♔f6 45 ♕d6† ♔f7 46 ♕×b8 ♔e6 47 ♕b6† ♔d5 48 ♕×a6 ♔e5 49 h3 ♔f4 50 ♕f6† ♔g3 51 ♕×g5† ♔f2 52 b4 ♔f1 53 b5 ♔f2 54 b6 ♔f1 55 b7 ♔f2 56 b8♕ ♔e1 57 ♕e3† ♔f1 58 ♕b5# **1–0**

THE FOX — TECH 2 1 e4 e5 2 f4 e×f4 3 ♗c4 ♘f6 4 ♘c3 ♘c6 5 ♘f3 ♘×e4 6 O–O ♗c5† 7 d4 ♘×c3 8 b×c3 ♗d6 9 ♕e2† ♕e7 10 ♗d2 O–O 11 ♕×e7 ♘×e7 12 ♖fe1 ♘c6 13 ♗d3 f6 14 ♖ab1 ♖d8 15 ♖b5 g5 16 ♖f5 ♗e7 17 ♖b5 d5 18 ♖bb1 ♗d6 19 h3 ♔g7 20 ♖e2 ♖b8 21 ♔f2 g4 22 ♘g1 ♗d7 23 h×g4 ♗×g4 24 ♘f3 ♖d7 25 ♖h1 f5 26 ♖e6 **1–0**

CHAOS — CHES 1 d4 d5 2 c4 e6 3 ♘c3 d×c4 4 e4 ♘c6 5 ♘f3 ♘a5 6 ♗e3 b6 7 ♘e5 f6 8 ♕h5† ♔e7 9 ♕f7† **1–0**

GA TECH — DARTMOUTH 1 e4 c5 2 ♘f3 d6 3 d4 c×d4 4 ♘×d4 ♘f6 5 ♘c3 a6 6 ♗c4 e6 7 O–O b5 8 ♗d3 b4 9 ♘a4 ♕a5 10 c4 ♗d7 11 b3 ♗×a4 12 b×a4 ♘bd7 13 ♖e1 ♕e5 14 ♗e3 h5 15 ♕c2 ♘g4 16 f4 ♕c5 17 ♘×e6 ♘×e3 18 ♘×c5 ♘×c2 19 ♗×c2 d×c5 20 ♔f2 f6 21 e5 f×e5 22 f×e5 O–O–O 23 e6 ♘f6 24 e7 ♖d2† 25 ♖e2 ♖×e2† 26 ♔×e2 ♗×e7 27 a3 ♔c7 28 a×b4 c×b4 29 ♖b1 ♔c6 30 g3 ♔c5 31 ♗b3 ♖d8 32 ♖d1 ♖×d1 33 ♔×d1 ♗d6 34 ♔d2 ♘g4 35 h3 ♘f6 36 ♔e3 ♗×g3 37 ♔f3 ♗e5 38 a5 ♗c7 39 ♗a2 ♔d4 40 ♔e2 ♔c3 41 c5 ♘d7 42 c6 ♘b8 43 ♗d5 h4 44 ♔e3 ♗×a5 45 ♗e4 b3 46 ♗d5 ♔c2 47 ♗f3 ♗b6† 48 ♔f4 b2 49 ♗e4† ♔c1 50 ♔f3 ♘×c6 51 ♔e2 ♘e5 52 ♔e1 a5 53 ♔e2 a4 54 ♔e1 a3 55 ♔e2 a2 56 ♔e1 a1♕ 57 ♔e2 ♕a6† 58 ♔e1 ♕a5† 59 ♔f1 ♕b5† 60 ♔g2 ♕e2† 61 ♔h1 ♕×e4† 62 ♔h2 ♕e2† 63 ♔h1 ♕f1† 64 ♔h2 ♘f3# **0–1**

Round 2

DARTMOUTH — CHESS 4.0 1 e4 c5 2 ♘f3 ♘c6 3 d4 c×d4 4 ♘×d4 ♘f6 5 ♘c3 d6 6 ♗e3 ♘×d4 7 ♗×d4 e5 8 ♗e3 ♗e7 9 ♗b5† ♗d7 10 ♕d3 O–O 11 O–O–O ♘g4 12 ♗×d7 ♕×d7 13 ♘d5 ♗h4 14 f3 ♘f2 15 ♗×f2 ♗×f2 16 ♖d2 ♗c5 17 b4 ♗d4 18 c3 ♗b6 19 ♘×b6 a×b6 20 b5 ♔h8 21 ♕d5 ♖fc8 22 ♔b2 ♖c5 23 ♕×d6 ♖×b5† 24 ♔a1 ♕c8 25 ♕d3 ♖ba5 26 ♖b1 ♕c7 27 ♖b4 ♖a3 28 ♖c4 ♕e7 29 ♖b4 ♕f6 30 ♖b5

♖3a4 31 ♕d5 ♕h4 32 ♖×b6 ♖4a5 33 ♕d6 ♕e1† 34 ♖b1 ♕h4 35 ♕d7 b5 36 ♕×f7 ♕×h2 37 ♕d7 ♕f4 38 ♕d8† ♕f8 39 ♕×f8† ♖×f8 40 ♔b2 ♖fa8 41 ♖a1 ♖5a6 42 ♖d5 ♖g6 43 g4 ♖f6 44 ♖×b5 ♖×f3 45 ♖×e5 ♖b8† 46 ♔c2 ♖c8 47 ♔b3 ♖f×c3† 48 ♔b4 ♖c2 49 ♖e7 ♖b2† 50 ♔a3 ♖g2 51 e5 ♖×g4 52 e6 ♖g2 53 ♔a4 ♖b2 54 ♖a7 h5 55 a3 ♖c4† 56 ♔a5 ♖c5† 57 ♔a4 g5 58 e7 ♖c4† 59 ♔a5 ♖b8 60 ♖e1 ♖c5† 61 ♔a4 ♖cc8 62 ♖e5 ♖a8 63 ♖×a8 ♖×a8† 64 ♔b5 ♖e8 65 ♖×g5 ♖×e7 66 ♖×h5† ♔g7 67 ♔b6 ♖e6† 68 ♔b5 ♖e7 69 ♔b6 ♖e6† 70 ♔b5 ♖e7 71 ♔b6 ½–½

COKO 4 — TECH 1 d4 d5 2 ♘d2 ♘f6 3 c4 ♘c6 4 ♘gf3 ♗f5 5 c×d5 ♕×d5 6 e3 e5 7 ♘×e5 ♘×e5 8 d×e5 ♕×e5 9 ♕b3 ♗e4 10 ♗b5† c6 11 ♗c4 O-O-O 12 ♘×e4 ♕×e4 13 O-O ♘d5 14 f3 ♕e5 15 f4 ♕e4 16 ♗d3 ♕e6 17 f5 ♕e5 18 ♖f3 ♗c5 19 ♗d2 ♗×e3† 20 ♗×e3 ♘×e3 21 ♖e1 ♖×d3 22 ♕×d3 ♕×b2 23 ♖e2 ♕c1† 24 ♔f2 ♘g4† 25 ♔g3 ♖d8 26 ♕c2 ♕g5 27 h4 ♕h5 28 ♖e7 ♖d5 29 ♖f4 ♘h6 30 f6 g×f6 31 ♔h3 ♘f5 32 ♖e8† ♔c7 33 a4 h6 34 g3 c5 35 ♕c4 ♕d1 36 ♖f2 h5 37 ♕f4† ♔c6 38 ♕e4 ♔d7 39 ♖×f5 ♖×f5 40 ♖e7† ♔d6 41 ♖d7† ♔×d7 42 ♕×f5† ♔e7 43 ♕×c5† ♔e6 44 ♕e7† ♔×e7 **0–1**

THE FOX — CHAOS 1 e4 c5 2 ♘f3 ♘c6 3 ♗b5 ♘f6 4 O-O ♘×e4 5 ♘c3 ♘d6 6 d3 ♘×b5 7 ♘×b5 d6 8 ♕e2 ♗g4 9 ♗f4 e5 10 ♗g5 f6 11 ♗h4 ♗e7 12 ♘c3 O-O 13 ♘d5 ♘d4 14 ♕d1 ♘×f3† 15 g×f3 ♗e6 16 ♘×e7† ♕×e7 17 ♕e2 ♕f7 18 ♗g3 b6 19 ♕e3 ♗×a2 20 b3 ♗×b3 21 c×b3 ♕×b3 22 ♖a6 ♕b5 23 ♖a2 a5 24 ♕e4 ♕b3 25 ♖d2 ♖ae8 26 ♖c1 d5 27 ♕e3 a4 28 f4 e×f4 29 ♕×f4 d4 30 ♕d6 ♖e6 31 ♕d7 a3 32 ♕b7 ♖fe8 33 ♕d7 ♖e1† 34 ♖×e1 ♖×e1† 35 ♔g2 a2 36 ♗b8 a1♕ 37 ♗d6 ♕d5† 38 ♔h3 ♕e6† 39 ♕×e6† ♖×e6 40 ♗c7 ♕e1 41 ♖a2 ♕f1† 42 ♔g4 ♕×d3 43 ♖a8† ♔f7 44 ♖d8 f5† 45 ♔h4 ♕f3 46 ♖d7† ♔g6 **0–1**

USC — OSTRICH 1 e4 e5 2 d4 e×d4 3 ♕×d4 ♘c6 4 ♕d1 ♘f6 5 ♗g5 ♗e7 6 ♗×f6 ♗×f6 7 c3 O-O 8 ♗e2 d6 9 ♔f1 ♗e6 10 h3 d5 11 f3 d×e4 12 ♕×d8 ♖f×d8 13 f×e4 ♘e5 14 ♔f2 ♗h4† 15 g3 ♗e7 16 ♘f3 ♗c5† 17 ♔g2 ♘d3 18 b4 ♘f2 19 b×c5 ♘×h1 20 ♔×h1 ♗×h3 21 ♔h2 ♗g4 22 ♘d4 ♖×d4 23 ♗×g4 ♖c4 24 c6 ♖×c6 25 ♗f5 ♖c4 26 a3 g6 27 ♗h3 ♖×e4 28 ♖a2 ♖ae8 29 ♗d7 ♖d8 30 ♗h3 c6 31 ♖b2 b5 32 ♗g2 ♖e6 33 g4 f6 34 ♗f3 ♖d3 35 ♗h1 a5 36 ♗g2 ♖de3 37 ♗h1 ♔g7 38 ♔g2 ♖e1 39 ♔h2 ♖6e2† 40 ♖×e2 ♖×e2† 41 ♔g3 ♖e1 42 ♗×c6 ♖×b1 43 ♔f4 ♖b3 44 a4 b×a4 45 c4 a3 46 ♗e8 a2 47 ♗a4 ♖c3 48 ♗b5 a1♕ 49 ♗a6 ♕f1† 50 ♔e4 ♕d3† 51 ♔f4 ♕f3# **0–1**

CHES — TECH 2 1 e4 e5 2 ♘f3 ♘c6 3 ♗c4 ♘f6 4 d3 d5 5 e×d5 ♘×d5 6 ♕e2 ♗g4 7 ♗×d5 ♕×d5 8 c4 ♗b4† 9 ♔f1 ♕d6 10 ♘c3 O-O 11 ♕e4 f5 12 ♕e3 ♘d4 13 ♖b1 ♘×f3 14 g×f3 ♗h3† 15 ♔e2 ♗g2 16 ♖g1 ♕g6 17 ♘b5 f4 18 ♕e4 ♗×f3† 19 ♔×f3 ♕×g1 20 ♕d5† ♖f7 21 ♘×c7 ♕d1† 22 ♔g2 f3† 23 ♔g3 ♕g1† 24 ♔h4 ♗e7† 25 ♗g5 ♕×g5† **0–1**

BELLE — GA TECH 1 e4 e5 2 ♘c3 ♘f6 3 ♗c4 ♘c6 4 f4 ♘×e4 5 ♘f3 ♘×c3 6 d×c3 d6 7 O-O ♗e6 8 ♗×e6 f×e6 9 f×e5 ♘×e5 10 ♘×e5 d×e5 11 ♕h5† ♔d7 12 ♖d1† ♗d6 13 ♕×e5 ♕f8 14 ♗g5 h6 15 ♗h4 a5 16 ♖d3 a4 17 ♖f1 c5 18 ♖×f8 ♖h×f8 19 ♖×d6† ♔c8 20 ♕×c5† ♔b8 21 ♖×e6 ♖a6 22 ♗g3† ♔a8 23 ♕×f8† ♔a7 24 ♗b8† ♔a8 25 ♗c7† ♔a7 26 ♗b8† ½–½

Round 3

TECH — CHAOS 1 e4 c5 2 ♘f3 ♘c6 3 d4 c×d4 4 ♘×d4 ♘f6 5 ♘c3 e6 6 ♗c4 ♗b4 7 ♗g5 ♗×c3† 8 b×c3 O-O 9 O-O ♘e5 10 ♗×f6 ♕×f6 11 ♕e2 ♕f4 12 f3 ♘×c4 13 ♕×c4 ♕e3† 14 ♖f2 b6 15 ♖d1 a5 16 ♕b5 ♕×c3 17 ♕×b6 ♕c4 18 a3 ♗a6 19 ♕×a5 d5 20 ♕b4 d×e4 21 f×e4 e5 22 ♘f5 ♖fb8 23 ♘e7† ♔h8 24 ♕×c4 ♗×c4 25 ♘d5 f6 26 a4 ♖×a4 27 c3 ♖a2 28 ♖c1 ♖bb2 29 ♖×b2 ♖×b2 30 h3 ♗d3 31 c4 ♗×e4 32 g4 ♖g2† 33 ♔f1 ♖h2 34 ♖c3 ♖h1† 35 ♔f2 ♖h2† 36 ♔g3 ♖g2† 37 ♔h4 g5† 38 ♔h5 ♔g7 39 ♘e7 ♗g6† 40 ♘×g6 h×g6# **0–1**

CHESS 4.0 — COKO 4 1 e4 e5 2 ♘f3 ♘f6 3 d4 e×d4 4 e5 ♕e7 5 ♕×d4 ♘c6 6 ♕c3 ♘e4 7 ♕c4 ♘f6 8 ♕e2 ♘d5 9 ♗g5 ♕e6 10 c4 ♘b6 11 a4 ♗b4† 12 ♘bd2 O-O 13 g3 f6 14 e×f6 g×f6 15 ♗h6 ♖e8 16 ♕×e6† ♖×e6† 17 ♗e3 d5 18 c×d5 ♘×d5 19 ♗c4 ♖d6 20 O-O ♗e6 21 ♗h6 f5 22 ♖ae1 ♗f7 23 ♘g5 ♗h5 24 ♘e6 ♖c8 25 ♗b3 ♗f7 26 ♘g5 ♗×d2 27 ♘×f7 ♔×f7 28 ♗×d2 ♘d4 29 ♗d1 c5 30 ♗h5† ♔f8 31 ♗g5 h6 32 ♗h4 ♔g7 33 ♖e5 a6 34 ♖fe1 b5 35 a5 f4 36 ♗e7 ♘×e7 37 ♖×e7† ♔h8 38 ♖e8† ♖×e8 39 ♖×e8† ♔g7 40 g×f4 ♘c6 41 ♖c8 ♔f6 42 ♗f3 ♘×a5 43 ♖×c5 ♖d3 44 ♗g4 ♘b7 45 ♖c6† ♖d6 46 ♖c7 ♘a5 47 ♔g2 ♘c4 48 b4 **1–0**

TECH 2 — DARTMOUTH 1 e4 c5 2 ♘f3 d6 3 ♘c3 e6 4 d4 ♗d7 5 d×c5 d×c5 6 ♘e5 ♕h4 7 ♗e3 ♘f6 8 ♘b5 ♘a6 9 ♘×d7 ♘×d7 10 ♕f3 ♘e5 11 ♕f4 ♕×f4 12 ♗×f4 ♘g4 13 ♘d6† ♗×d6 14 ♗×d6 ♘b4 15 ♗b5† ♔d8 16 O-O ♘×c2 17 ♖ad1 ♘d4 18 ♗×c5 e5 19 ♖d3 a6 20 ♗c4 ♖c8 21 ♗×d4 ♖×c4 22 ♗×e5† ♔c8 23 ♗×g7 ♖g8 24 ♗d4 ♖a4 25 ♖c1† ♔b8 26 h3 ♖d8 27 ♗e5† ♘×e5 28 ♖×d8† ♔a7 29 ♖c3 ♖×a2 30 f4 ♘c6 31 ♖d7 ♔b6 32 ♖b3† ♔c5 33 ♖b×b7 ♖a1† 34 ♔f2 f6 35 ♖d5† ♔c4 36 b3† ♔c3 37 ♖c5† ♔d3 38 ♖×c6 ♖a5 39 ♖c4 ♖a1 40 ♖d7# **1–0**

OSTRICH — THE FOX 1 ♘f3 ♘f6 2 ♘c3 d5 3 d4 ♘c6 4 ♗f4 ♗f5 5 ♘b5 ♖c8 6 ♘×c7† ♖×c7 7 ♗×c7 ♕×c7 8 e3 ♕d6 9 ♗d3 ♕b4† 10 c3 ♕×b2 11 ♗×f5 ♕×c3† 12 ♘d2 e6 13 ♗c2 ♗a3 14 O-O O-O 15 ♖b1 ♗b2 16 a4 ♕a3 17 ♗b3 ♗c3 18 ♕c2 ♗a5 19 ♖a1 ♕d6 20 f3 ♗b4 21 ♖a2 ♘a5 22 ♖f2 ♖e8 23 ♖b2 ♘×b3 24 ♕×b3 ♗×d2 25 ♖f×d2 ♕c7 26 ♖dc2 ♕d7 27 ♕×b7 ♕×b7 28 ♖×b7 ♖a8 29 ♖×a7 ♖×a7 30 ♖c8† ♘e8 31 ♖×e8# **1–0**

BELLE — CHES 1 e4 e5 2 ♘c3 ♕h4 3 ♘f3 ♕h5 4 g4 ♕×g4 5 ♘×e5 ♕×d1† 6 ♘×d1 ♘f6 7 ♗c4 d5 8 ♗×d5 ♘×d5 9 e×d5 ♗c5 10 O-O ♗h3 11 ♖e1 ♘a6 12 ♘g6† ♔d7 13 ♘×h8 ♘b4 14 ♘×f7 ♘×c2 15 b4 ♗×b4 16 ♖e3 ♘×e3 17 ♘×e3 ♖f8 18 ♘g5 ♗f5 19 a3 ♗d6 20 ♗b2 h6 21 ♗×g7 ♖e8 22 ♘×f5 ♖e1† 23 ♖×e1 h×g5 24 ♘×d6 ♔×d6 25 ♖e5 g4 26 d4 c6 27 ♗f8† ♔d7 28 ♖e7† ♔d6 29 ♖e5† ♔d7 30 ♖e7† ♔d6 31 ♖e5† ½–½

GA TECH — USC 1 e4 e5 2 ♘f3 ♘f6 3 d4 ♘×e4 4

d×e5 ♗c5 5 ♗e3 ♗×e3 6 f×e3 ♘c6 7 ♘bd2 ♘×d2 8 ♕×d2 ♘×e5 9 ♘×e5 d6 10 ♘f3 O-O 11 O-O-O ♖e8 12 ♗c4 ♗g4 13 h3 ♗d7 14 ♕d5 ♖b8 15 ♕×f7† ♔h8 16 ♖he1 a6 17 e4 ♖f8 18 ♕h5 b5 19 ♗d5 ♕e7 20 e5 ♖f5 21 ♕g4 d×e5 22 ♕e4 ♕d6 23 ♗b3 ♕h6† 24 ♔b1 ♗c6 25 ♕×f5 ♗×f3 26 ♕×f3 ♕g5 27 ♕c6 a5 28 ♖d7 b4 29 ♕d5 ♖e8 30 ♗c4 a4 31 ♕b5 c6 32 ♕×c6 a3 33 ♖b7 ♖f8 34 ♕d5 ♖d8 35 ♕e4 ♕d2 36 ♗d3 ♕×e1† 37 ♕×e1 ♖e8 38 ♕e4 g6 39 ♕c6 **1–0**

Round 4

CHAOS — CHESS 4.0 1 d4 d5 2 c4 d×c4 3 ♘f3 ♘f6 4 e3 e6 5 ♗×c4 c5 6 O-O a6 7 ♕e2 b5 8 ♗b3 ♗b7 9 ♘c3 ♘bd7 10 ♗d2 ♗d6 11 ♖fe1 c×d4 12 e×d4 O-O 13 ♗g5 ♕b6 14 ♗c2 ♗×f3 15 ♕×f3 ♕×d4 16 ♖ad1 ♕b4 17 g3 ♕×b2 18 ♖e2 ♕a3 19 ♕c6 ♗b4 20 ♖×d7 ♖ac8 21 ♖c7 ♖×c7 22 ♕×c7 ♕×c3 23 ♕b7 ♕c4 24 ♗d1 ♖d8 25 ♖e5 ♖×d1† 26 ♔g2 ♕f1† 27 ♔f3 ♕h1† 28 ♔e2 ♖e1† 29 ♔d3 ♕f1† 30 ♔d4 ♕c4# **0–1**

OSTRICH — TECH 1 e4 e5 2 ♘f3 ♘c6 3 ♗b5 ♘f6 4 O-O ♘×e4 5 d3 ♘c5 6 ♗×c6 b×c6 7 ♘×e5 ♗e7 8 ♗e3 O-O 9 ♗×c5 ♗×c5 10 d4 ♕f6 11 a3 d5 12 ♖e1 ♖e8 13 ♘×c6 ♖×e1† 14 ♕×e1 ♗f5 15 ♕c3 ♖e8 16 g4 ♗d7 17 d×c5 ♕×c3 18 ♘×c3 ♗×c6 19 a4 d4 20 ♘b5 ♖e5 21 ♘×d4 ♖×c5 22 b4 ♖c4 23 ♘×c6 ♖×c6 24 ♖d1 ♖d6 25 ♖×d6 c×d6 26 h4 d5 27 c3 g6 28 a5 ♔g7 29 f4 ♔f6 30 ♔f2 a6 31 ♔e3 ♔e6 32 h5 f6 33 ♔d4 ♔d6 34 h6 g5 35 ♔e3 ♔e6 36 f5† ♔d6 37 ♔f3 d4 38 c4 ♔e5 39 b5 a×b5 40 c×b5 d3 41 a6 d2 42 ♔e2 d1♕† 43 ♔×d1 ♔e4 44 a7 ♔d5 45 a8♕† ♔c5 46 ♕c6† ♔d4 47 b6 ♔e5 48 b7 ♔f4 49 b8♕† ♔×g4 50 ♕e4† ♔h3 51 ♕f3† ♔h4 52 ♕bg3# **1–0**

TECH 2 — GA TECH 1 e4 e5 2 ♘f3 ♘c6 3 ♘c3 ♗c5 4 ♘×e5 ♗×f2† 5 ♔×f2 ♘×e5 6 d4 ♘c6 7 ♗c4 ♕f6† 8 ♔e3 ♕g5† 9 ♔f3 ♕h5† 10 ♔f2 ♘f6 11 ♕×h5 ♘×h5 12 ♘b5 ♔d8 13 ♗×f7 ♘f6 14 ♗f4 ♘×e4† 15 ♔e3 ♘d6 16 ♘×d6 c×d6 17 ♗×d6 b6 18 ♖hf1 g5 19 ♖f6 ♗a6 20 ♖d1 g4 21 c4 ♔c8 22 ♗d5 ♔b7 23 ♗e5 ♖hf8 24 ♖d6 ♖ad8 25 ♖h6 b5 26 c×b5 ♗×b5 27 ♖×h7 ♔b6 28 ♗d6 ♖f5 29 ♗c5† ♔b7 30 ♗e6 ♖g5 31 ♗×d7 g3 32 h4 ♖×c5 33 d×c5 ♖f8 34 ♖d6 ♖f1 35 ♗×c6† ♔a6 36 a4 ♗×c6 37 b4 ♖e1† 38 ♔f4 ♖e4† 39 ♔×g3 ♖e3† 40 ♔f2 ♖e6 41 b5† ♔a5 42 ♖×e6 ♗d5 43 ♖×a7† ♔b4 44 b6 ♗×e6 45 b7 ♔×c5 46 b8♕ ♔d5 47 ♔e3 **1–0**

DARTMOUTH — COKO 4 1 e4 e5 2 f4 e×f4 3 ♗c4 ♘c6 4 ♕h5 ♘h6 5 ♘f3 g6 6 ♕b5 a6 7 ♕b3 ♗c5 8 d3 g5 9 ♗d5 ♗e3 10 ♗×c6 ♗×c1 11 ♗d5 c6 12 ♗c4 g4 13 ♕c3 O-O 14 ♘bd2 g×f3 15 g×f3 ♗×d2† 16 ♔×d2 d6 17 ♖ag1† ♘g4 18 f×g4 ♗e6 19 g5 d5 20 e×d5 ♗×d5 21 ♗×d5 ♕×d5 22 a3 f3 23 ♔e3 ♖ae8† 24 ♔f4 f2 25 ♖c1 f5 26 ♔g3 ♖e2 27 ♕c4 ♕f7 28 ♕f4 ♖d8 29 ♖hf1 ♕h5 30 h4 b5 31 ♖×f2 ♖×f2 32 ♔×f2 ♕g4 33 ♕×g4 f×g4 34 ♔g3 ♖d4 35 b4 ♔g7 36 ♖f1 a5 37 b×a5 ♖a4 38 ♖f6 ♖×a5 39 ♖×c6 ♖×a3 40 ♔×g4 ♖a4† 41 ♔h5 ♖d4 42 ♖c7† ♔g8 43 ♖c8† ♔f7 44 ♖c7† ♔g8 45 ♖c8† ♔f7 46 ♖c7† **½–½**

BELLE — THE FOX 1 e4 e5 2 ♘c3 ♘f6 3 ♗c4 ♘×e4 4 ♕h5 ♘d6 5 ♗b3 ♘c6 6 d4 e×d4 7 ♘d5 a6 8 ♘f3 ♘e4 9 O-O g6 10 ♕g4 ♘c5 11 ♖e1† ♘e6 12 ♗f4 h5 13 ♕h3 ♗d6 14 ♗g5 ♗e7 15 ♗×e7 ♘×e7 16 ♘×d4 ♘×d5 17 ♗×d5 c6 18 ♗×e6 d×e6 19 ♕d3 ♕d5 20 c4 ♕d6 21 ♖ad1 O-O 22 ♖e3 ♗d7 23 ♕c2 ♕f4 24 ♘b5 ♗e8 25 ♘d6 ♖b8 26 ♕c3 ♗d7 27 a4 h4 28 ♘f5 ♕×f5 29 ♖×d7 **1–0**

USC — CHES 1 e4 e5 2 d4 ♗b4† 3 c3 ♗d6 4 d×e5 ♗×e5 5 f4 ♗d6 6 ♗c4 ♕h4† 7 ♔f1 ♗×f4 8 ♘f3 ♕g4 9 h3 ♕g3 10 ♗×f4 ♕×f4 11 ♕d4 ♘f6 12 e5 ♕c1† 13 ♘e1 ♕×b2 14 e×f6 ♘c6 15 ♕e3† ♔f8 16 f×g7† ♔×g7 17 ♕g5† ♔f8 18 ♕c5† d6 19 ♕f2 ♕×f2† 20 ♔×f2 ♗f5 21 g4 ♗e4 22 ♖f1 ♔e7 23 ♔e3 d5 24 ♗b3 ♔e6 25 ♗c2 ♗×c2 26 ♘×c2 ♘e5 27 ♘ba3 ♘c4† 28 ♘×c4 d×c4 29 ♔d4 b5 30 ♔c5 a6 31 a4 b×a4 32 ♔×c4 c5 33 ♔×c5 ♖hc8† 34 ♔d4 ♖d8† 35 ♔e3 ♖dc8 36 ♔d2 ♖d8† 37 ♘d4† ♖×d4† 38 c×d4 ♖d8 39 ♖×a4 ♖d6 40 ♔c3 ♖c6† 41 ♔d3 f6 42 ♖aa1 ♔d5 43 ♖f5† ♔d6 44 ♖×f6† ♔d5 45 ♖a5† **1–0**

Second Place Playoff

OSTRICH — CHAOS 1 d4 ♘f6 2 ♘f3 e6 3 e3 d5 4 ♘c3 ♗b4 5 a3 ♗×c3† 6 b×c3 ♘e4 7 ♗d2 O-O 8 h4 ♘c6 9 c4 ♗d7 10 ♗b4 ♘×b4 11 a×b4 ♕e7 12 c5 ♖fe8 13 c4 ♗c6 14 b5 ♗d7 15 ♕a4 c6 16 b×c6 ♗×c6 17 ♕c2 b6 18 c×d5 ♗×d5 19 c×b6 ♕b4† 20 ♘d2 ♖ec8 21 ♕d3 ♘×d2 22 ♕×d2 ♕×b6 23 h5 a5 24 h6 ♕b4 25 ♕×b4 a×b4 26 ♖b1 ♗e4 27 ♖d1 b3 28 h×g7 b2 29 f3 ♗c2 30 ♔f2 ♗×d1 31 ♗d3 ♗c2 32 ♖b1 ♗×b1 **0–1**

TECH 2 — OSTRICH 1 e4 e5 2 ♘f3 ♘c6 3 ♘c3 ♗b4 4 d4 e×d4 5 ♘×d4 ♕h4 6 ♕d3 ♘e5 7 ♕e3 ♘g4 8 ♕g3 ♕×g3 9 h×g3 ♗×c3† 10 b×c3 ♘8f6 11 ♗f4 ♘×e4 12 f3 c5 13 ♘b5 ♘e3 14 ♘c7† ♔d8 15 ♗×e3 ♔×c7 16 f×e4 d6 17 ♗b5 a6 18 ♗c4 ♗e6 19 ♗×e6 f×e6 20 ♔e2 ♔c6 21 ♔d3 e5 22 ♔c4 b5† 23 ♔b3 c4† 24 ♔b4 a5† 25 ♔a3 h5 26 ♖ad1 a4 27 ♖d5 ♖ad8 28 ♔b4 ♖b8 29 ♗g5 ♖he8 30 ♖×h5 ♖b7 31 ♗e3 ♖a8 32 a3 g6 33 ♖h1 ♖d8 34 ♖f1 g5 35 ♗×g5 ♖g8 36 ♖f5 ♖g6 37 g4 ♖g8 38 g3 ♖gg7 39 ♗e3 ♖×g4 40 ♖f6 ♔c7 41 ♖d×d6 ♔c8 42 ♔c5 ♖×e4 43 ♖f8† ♔c7 44 ♗g5 ♖e2 45 ♖c6† ♔d7 46 ♖d8# **1–0**

CHAOS — TECH 2 1 d4 d5 2 c4 d×c4 3 ♘f3 ♘c6 4 ♘c3 ♗d7 5 e4 ♘a5 6 ♘e5 b5 7 ♘×d7 ♕×d7 8 ♕h5 c6 9 ♗e3 ♘f6 10 ♕d1 O-O-O 11 b4 ♘b7 12 a4 e5 13 d×e5 ♗×b4 14 ♕×d7† ♖×d7 15 ♗d2 ♖×d2 16 ♔×d2 ♘×e4† 17 ♔e3 ♗×c3 18 ♖d1 ♘bc5 19 f4 b×a4 20 ♗×c4 ♖f8 21 ♔e2 a3 22 g3 ♔c7 23 ♖hf1 ♖b8 24 ♗×f7 ♖b2† 25 ♔e3 a2 26 ♖a1 ♖×h2 27 ♖×a2 ♖×a2 28 ♗×a2 ♘×g3 29 ♖c1 ♘ge4 30 ♖h1 h6 31 e6 ♔d6 32 f5 ♔e5 33 e7 ♘d6 34 ♔e2 ♘ce4 35 ♖g1 ♗d4 36 ♖×g7 ♘c3† 37 ♔d2 ♘×a2 38 ♖g6 ♘c3 39 ♖×h6 ♘ce4† 40 ♔d3 ♘f6 41 ♖h8 c5 42 ♖a8 c4† 43 ♔c2 ♔×f5 44 ♖h8 ♔e6 45 ♖h4 ♘f5 46 ♖f4 a5 47 ♔b1 ♔e5 48 ♖g4 c3 49 ♖g2 ♘×e7 50 ♔c2 a4 51 ♖e2† ♔d6 52 ♔d3 ♘c6 53 ♔c4 ♘d5 54 ♔b5 a3 55 ♔a4 ♗c5 56 ♖h2 c2 57 ♖×c2 ♘b6† 58 ♔b3 ♘d4† 59 ♔c3 ♘a4† 60 ♔c4 ♘×c2 61 ♔b3 ♘d4† 62 ♔c4 a2 63 ♔d3 a1♕ 64 ♔e4 ♕f1 65 ♔e3 ♘b3† 66 ♔e4 ♘d2# **0–1**

ACM 1974 — San Diego

November 10 — November 12

	1	2	3	4	tot
1 RIBBIT	10+□	7+■	8+■	2+□	4
2 CHESS 4.0	6+■	5+■	3+□	1−■	3
3 CHAOS	4+■	9+□	2−■	6+□	3
4 BELLE	3−□	10+■	11+□	5+■	3
5 DUCHESS	8+■	2−□	9+■	4−□	2
6 DART 4.1	2−□	11+■	7+□	3−■	2
7 OSTRICH	12+■	1−□	6−■	9+□	2
8 TECH 2	5−□	12+■	1−□	+	2
9 CHUTE 1	11+□	3−■	5−□	7−■	1
10 TYRO	1−■	4−□			0
11 XENARBOR	9−■	6−□	4−■		0
12 KCHES6	7−□	8−□			0

Round 1

DART 4.1 — CHESS 4.0 1 e4 e5 2 f4 e×f4 3 ♘f3 g5 4 ♘c3 g4 5 ♘e5 ♕h4† 6 g3 f×g3 7 ♕×g4 g2† 8 ♕×h4 g×h1♕ 9 ♕h5 ♗b4 10 ♘×f7 ♘f6 11 ♘d6† ♔d8 12 ♘f7† ♔e7 13 ♘d5† ♘×d5 14 ♘×h8 ♕×e4† 15 ♗e2 ♘f4 16 ♕g5† ♔f8 17 ♕g4 ♗d6 18 ♕f3 ♕×e2† 19 ♕×e2 ♘×e2 20 ♔×e2 ♗×h2 21 d3 ♗e5 22 ♗h6† ♔e7 23 ♗g5† ♔e6 24 ♖f1 ♗×h8 25 ♖f8 ♗×b2 26 ♖×c8 ♗e5 27 ♖e8† ♔d6 28 ♖f8 h5 29 c4 c6 30 a4 b6 31 ♖f7 ♘a6 32 ♔e3 ♘c5 33 a5 ♖g8 34 ♗h4 b×a5 35 ♔d2 ♖g2† 36 ♔e3 ♗d4† 37 ♔×d4 ♖g4† 38 ♔c3 ♖×h4 39 ♖f6† ♔e5 40 ♖f3 a4 41 ♖e3† ♔d6 42 ♔d2 a3 43 ♖g3 a2 44 ♖g1 a1♕ 45 ♖×a1 ♘b3† 46 ♔c3 ♘×a1 47 ♔b2 ♖h1 48 ♔c3 ♔e5 49 c5 ♖h2 50 ♔c4 a5 51 d4† ♔e4 52 ♔c3 ♖c2# **0–1**

RIBBIT — TYRO 1 e4 e5 2 ♘f3 ♘c6 3 ♗b5 a6 4 ♗a4 ♘f6 5 O-O ♗e7 6 ♕e2 b5 7 ♗b3 O-O 8 c3 ♗c5 9 d3 d6 10 h4 h6 11 ♘a3 ♗g4 12 ♗e3 ♖b8 13 ♗×c5 d×c5 14 ♕e3 ♕d6 15 ♔h2 ♖fd8 16 ♖fd1 ♕e7 17 ♔g3 b4 18 ♘c4 b×c3 19 b×c3 ♗×f3 20 ♕×f3 ♖b7 21 ♖ab1 ♖bb8 22 ♗a4 ♖×b1 23 ♖×b1 ♘b8 24 ♔h2 ♕e6 25 a3 ♘g4† 26 ♔h1 c6 27 ♕f5 ♔f8 28 f3 ♘f6 29 ♕×e5 ♘bd7 30 ♕×e6 f×e6 31 g4 g5 32 h×g5 h×g5 33 ♔g2 ♔e7 34 ♖b7 ♖f8 35 ♘e5 ♔d6 36 ♘×d7 ♘×d7 37 d4 c×d4 38 c×d4 e5 39 d×e5† **1–0**

BELLE — CHAOS 1 e4 c5 2 ♘f3 ♘c6 3 d4 c×d4 4 ♘×d4 ♘f6 5 ♘c3 e6 6 ♘×c6 b×c6 7 ♗f4 ♗b4 8 ♗d3 ♗b7 9 O-O O-O 10 ♕f3 ♕a5 11 e5 ♗×c3 12 b×c3 ♘d5 13 ♗d2 ♕c5 14 ♖fe1 f5 15 e×f6 ♖×f6 16 ♕g3 ♖af8 17 ♗e3 ♘×e3 18 ♕×e3 ♕×e3 19 f×e3 e5 20 ♖f1 d5 21 ♖×f6 ♖×f6 22 ♖f1 ♖×f1† 23 ♔×f1 ♗c8 24 ♔f2 g6 25 h4 ♔f7 26 h5 g×h5 27 ♗×h7 e4 28 g4 ♗×g4 29 ♔g3 ♔g7 30 ♗×e4 d×e4 31 ♔f4 ♗f3 32 ♔e5 h4 33 ♔d6 h3 34 ♔c5 h2 35 ♔×c6 ♔f6 36 c4 ♗g4 37 ♔b7 a5 38 c5 a4 39 c6 ♗e6 40 c7 h1♕ 41 a3 ♕c1 42 c8♕ ♗×c8† 43 ♔×c8 ♕×e3 44 ♔d7 ♕×a3 45 ♔c7 ♕c5† 46 ♔b7 ♕×c2 47 ♔b6 a3 48 ♔b7 ♕c5 49 ♔a6 a2 50 ♔b7 a1♕ 51 ♔b8 ♕aa7# **0–1**

TECH 2 — DUCHESS 1 e4 e5 2 ♘f3 ♘f6 3 ♘c3 ♘c6 4 d4 e×d4 5 ♘×d4 ♗b4 6 ♗g5 ♗×c3† 7 b×c3 O-O 8 ♗d3 ♕e7 9 ♕d2 d5 10 f3 ♗d7 11 O-O-O d×e4 12 f×e4 ♕a3† 13 ♔b1 ♕d6 14 ♕f4 ♖fe8 15 ♕×d6 c×d6 16 ♖he1 ♗g4 17 ♖d2 ♖e5 18 ♗f4 ♖a5 19 ♗×d6 ♖e8 20 ♖e3 ♗d7 21 ♖f2 ♖a4 22 ♘×c6 ♗×c6 23 ♖fe2 b5 24 ♖f3 ♖e6 25 ♗c5 a6 26 ♖f5 g6 27 ♖f1 ♘×e4 28 ♗×e4 ♗×e4 29 ♖d2 ♗f5 30 ♔b2 h6 31 ♖d4 ♖e2 32 ♖×a4 ♖×c2† 33 ♔b3 b×a4† 34 ♔c4 ♗e6† 35 ♔b4 ♖×a2 36 ♖f4 ♖×g2 37 ♖h4 ♖b2† 38 ♔×a4 ♔g7 39 c4 ♖c2 40 ♔b3 ♖g2 41 ♗d4† f6 42 ♖e4 ♔f7 43 h4 f5 44 ♖f4 ♔e8 45 ♔b4 g5 46 h×g5 h×g5 47 ♖f3 ♖g4 48 ♔c5 ♔e7 49 ♖c3 ♖e4 50 ♖b3 g4 51 ♖c3 f4 52 ♖b3 g3 53 ♖c3 g2 54 ♖c1 ♗d7 55 ♔d5 ♖e6 56 c5 ♗c6† 57 ♔c4 ♖e4 58 ♖b1 ♔e6 59 ♖c1 ♗b5† **0–1**

KCHES6 — OSTRICH 1 e4 d5 2 e×d5 ♕×d5 3 c4 ♕e4† 4 ♘e2 ♕×c4 5 b3 ♕d3 6 ♘ec3 ♕d8 7 ♗b5† ♗d7 8 ♕f3 ♗c6 9 ♕g3 e6 10 f3 ♘h6 11 ♗c4 ♘f5 12 ♕g4 h5 13 ♕h3 ♘d4 14 ♗d3 ♘×f3† 15 ♔f2 ♗c5† 16 ♔e2 ♘g1† 17 ♖×g1 ♗×g1 18 ♗e4 ♗×e4 19 ♘×e4 O-O 20 ♗a3 ♗d4 21 ♗×f8 ♗×a1 22 ♗b4 ♕d4 23 ♘c5 ♕×b4 24 ♕×h5 b6 25 ♘a4 ♕e4† 26 ♔f2 ♗d4† 27 ♔g3 ♕×b1 28 ♕f3 f6 29 ♕g4 ♗e5† 30 ♔f2 ♕×a2 31 ♕h5 ♗d4† 32 ♔e1 ♕×b3 33 ♕h4 ♕×a4 34 ♕f4 a5 35 g3 b5 36 h4 f5 37 ♔e2 ♕c4† 38 ♔e1 b4 39 ♔d1 b3 40 ♔e1 b2 41 ♔d1 b1♕# **0–1**

CHUTE 1 — XENARBOR 1 e4 c5 2 c4 ♘c6 3 ♘f3 e5 4 d3 ♘f6 5 ♗e2 ♗e7 6 O-O O-O 7 b3 d6 8 ♗b2 ♗e6 9 ♘g5 ♗d7 10 ♘d2 h6 11 ♘gf3 ♗e6 12 ♗c3 ♕b6 13 ♖b1 ♕a6 14 a4 ♖ac8 15 ♖a1 b6 16 ♕e1 ♖fd8 17 ♕d1 ♖f8 18 ♖b1 ♖fd8 19 ♖e1 ♖f8 20 ♔f1 ♖fd8 21 b4 ♕b7 22 b×c5 d×c5 23 ♗×e5 ♘d7 24 ♗c3 ♕a6 25 ♗b2 ♖f8 26 ♗c3 ♖fd8 27 e5 ♖f8 28 ♘e4 ♖cd8 29 ♖c1 ♖a8 30 ♕c2 ♖ad8 31 ♗d1 ♖a8 32 ♖e2 ♖ad8 33 ♕d2 ♖a8 34 ♔e1 ♖ad8 35 ♕e3 ♕c8 36 ♘d6 ♕a8 37 ♔d2 a5 38 ♕e4 g6 39 ♖e3 ♔g7 40 ♗b2 f5 41 e×f6† ♗×f6 42 d4 ♗g8 43 ♗c2 ♘db8 44 ♕×g6† ♔h8 45 ♕×h6† ♗h7 46 ♕×h7# **1–0**

Round 2

DUCHESS — CHESS 4.0 1 e4 e5 2 ♘f3 ♘f6 3 d4 ♘×e4 4 ♗d3 d5 5 ♘×e5 ♗d6 6 O-O O-O 7 c4 ♗×e5 8 d×e5 ♘c6 9 f4 ♘b4 10 c×d5 ♕×d5 11 ♗×e4 ♕×e4 12 ♘c3 ♕g6 13 ♘d5 ♘×d5 14 ♕×d5 ♕b6† 15 ♔h1 ♗e6 16 ♕f3 ♕a6 17 b3 ♗d5 18 ♕f2 ♗×b3 19 ♗a3 ♕×a3 20 a×b3 ♕×b3 21 ♖×a7 ♖×a7 22 ♕×a7 ♕c4 23 ♖d1 ♕×f4 24 ♕×b7 ♕×e5 25 ♕c6 f5 26 ♕a4 ♕c3 27 ♕a7 c5 28 ♖f1 c4 **0–1**

OSTRICH — RIBBIT 1 d4 ♘f6 2 ♗g5 e6 3 ♘c3 ♗d6 4 e4 h6 5 ♗×f6 g×f6 6 ♘f3 b6 7 e5 f×e5 8 d×e5 ♗b4 9 a3 ♗×c3† 10 b×c3 ♖g8 11 ♕d2 ♖h8 12 ♗b5 ♗a6 13 ♗×a6 ♘×a6 14 O-O ♕e7 15 ♕d3 ♘c5 16 ♕d4 ♖g8 17 c4 O-O-O 18 ♖fd1 d6 19 h4 ♖g6 20 h5 ♖gg8 21 g3 a5 22 ♔g2 ♔b7 23 ♖ab1 d×e5 24 ♕×e5 ♖×d1 25 ♖×d1 ♖g4 26 ♖d4 ♘d7 27 ♕e3 ♖×d4 28 ♘×d4 ♕c5 29 ♕f3† c6 30 c3 ♘e5 31 ♕f6 ♕d6 32 f4 ♘×c4 33 ♕×f7† ♔a6 34 ♕×e6 ♕×e6 35 ♘×e6 ♘×a3 36 ♘d8 ♔b5 37 ♘f7 a4 38 ♔f2 ♔c4 39 f5 ♘b5 40 ♔e3 a3 41 ♔d2 a2 42 ♘e5† ♔b3 43 ♘×c6 a1♕ 44 c4 ♔×c4 45 g4 ♕c3† 46 ♔e2 ♕d3† 47 ♔f2 ♕d6 48 ♘b8 ♕×b8 49 ♔g2 ♕f4 **0–1**

CHAOS — CHUTE 1 1 d4 d5 2 c4 e6 3 ♘c3 ♗b4 4 ♘f3 ♗×c3† 5 b×c3 ♘e7 6 c×d5 ♕×d5 7 ♗f4 ♘a6 8 e3 c6 9 ♗×a6 b×a6 10 O-O O-O 11 ♕c2 ♖d8 12 c4 ♕h5 13 ♗c7 ♖d7 14 ♗f4 f6 15 ♕e4 ♖b7 16 ♖ab1 ♖×b1 17 ♖×b1 f5 18 ♕e5 ♔h8 19 ♕d6 ♕e8 20 ♗g5 ♘g6 21 ♕d8 ♕×d8 22 ♗×d8 h5 23 ♗c7 ♗d7 24 ♖b8† ♖×b8 25 ♗×b8 ♘e7 26 ♗×a7 ♘c8 27 ♗b8 ♔h7 28 ♗c7 g6 29 ♘e5 ♗e8 30 ♘f3 ♗d7 31 ♘e5 ♗e8 32 f3 g5 33 ♘d3 ♔h6 34 ♘c5 ♗f7 35 ♘×a6 e5 36 ♗×e5 ♗×c4 37 ♘b4 ♘a7 38 a4 h4 39 a5 g4 40 ♗b8 ♘c8 41 a6 g×f3 42 g×f3 ♗d5 43 ♘×d5 c×d5 44 ♔f2 ♔g6 45 ♔e2 ♘b6 46 h3 ♘c8 47 ♔d3 ♔f7 48 a7 ♘×a7 49 ♗×a7 ♔g8 50 ♗b6 ♔h7 51 ♗d8 ♔g6 52 ♗×h4 ♔h6 53 ♗d8 ♔h7 54 f4 ♔g6 55 h4 ♔h5 56 ♗g5 ♔g6 57 ♔c3 ♔h5 58 ♔b4 ♔g4 59 ♔c5 ♔f3 60 h5 ♔e4 61 h6 ♔f3 **1–0**

KCHES6 — TECH 2 1 e4 e5 2 ♘f3 ♘c6 3 ♗c4 ♘f6 4 ♘g5 d5 5 e×d5 ♘×d5 6 d4 e×d4 7 ♕f3 ♗e6 8 ♘×e6 f×e6 9 ♕e4 ♗b4† 10 c3 d×c3 11 b×c3 ♘×c3 12 ♕g4 ♘×b1† 13 ♔e2 ♘d4† 14 ♔e3 ♘c2† 15 ♔e2 ♘c3† 16 ♔f3 ♘×a1 17 ♗g5 O-O† 18 ♔g3 ♘e4† 19 ♕×e4 ♕×g5† 20 ♔h3 ♕h5† 21 ♔g3 ♗d6† 22 f4 ♕g5† 23 ♔h3 ♕h6† 24 ♔g4 ♖×f4† **0–1**

XENARBOR — DART 4.1 1 d4 d5 2 c4 e6 3 ♘c3 ♘f6 4 ♗g5 ♘bd7 5 e3 c6 6 ♘f3 ♕a5 7 ♘d2 ♗b4 8 ♕c2 O-O 9 ♘b3 ♗×c3† 10 b×c3 ♕b6 11 c5 ♕c7 12 ♗×f6 ♘×f6 13 O-O-O ♗d7 14 ♗d3 b6 15 ♔b2 a5 16 ♗e2 b5 17 ♘c1 e5 18 f3 ♖fe8 19 ♘d3 e×d4 20 c×d4 ♖×e3 21 ♗f1 ♖ae8 22 ♘c1 ♔f8 23 h4 h6 24 ♔b1 ♗c8 25 ♔b2 ♕d8 26 ♔b1 ♕e7 27 ♕d2 ♗f5† 28 ♔b2 a4 29 h5 ♗h7 30 ♔a1 a3 31 f4 ♕e4 32 ♘b3 ♕×f4 33 ♕c1 ♕g4 34 ♖h2 ♕×d1 35 ♕×d1 ♖e1 36 ♕c1 ♖×c1† 37 ♘×c1 ♖e1 38 g4 ♖×c1# **0–1**

TYRO — BELLE 1 e4 e5 2 ♘f3 ♘c6 3 ♗b5 a6 4 ♗a4 ♘f6 5 O-O ♗e7 6 ♖e1 b5 7 ♗b3 O-O 8 d3 ♗b7 9 a3 ♗c5 10 c3 ♕e7 11 d4 e×d4 12 c×d4 ♗b6 13 e5 ♘g4 14 ♕d3 ♘a5 15 ♘g5 g6 16 ♗d1 h6 17 ♗×g4 h×g5 18 b4 ♘c4 19 f4 g×f4 20 ♖a2 ♘×e5 21 ♕d1 ♕d6 22 ♔h1 ♕×d4 23 ♖d2 ♗×g2† 24 ♔×g2 ♕a1 25 ♗b2 ♕a2 26 ♗×e5 ♕c4 27 ♗×d7 ♗e3 28 ♖d5 c6 29 ♖d3 ♕e4† 30 ♔h3 ♕×e5 31 ♗×c6 ♕e6† 32 ♕g4 ♕×c6 33 ♕d7 ♕f3† 34 ♔h4 ♕h5# **0–1**

Round 3

CHESS 4.0 — CHAOS 1 e4 c5 2 ♘f3 ♘c6 3 d4 c×d4 4 ♘×d4 ♘f6 5 ♘c3 e6 6 ♘×c6 b×c6 7 e5 ♘d5 8 ♘×d5 c×d5 9 ♗d3 g6 10 O-O ♗g7 11 ♗f4 O-O 12 ♕f3 ♕b6 13 c4 ♕d4 14 c×d5 ♗b7 15 ♕g3 ♗×d5 16 b3 ♖ac8 17 ♖ad1 ♕b4 18 ♖c1 ♖fd8 19 ♗e3 ♗e4 20 ♕h4 d5 21 e×d6 f5 22 ♖×c8 ♖f8 23 d7 ♕b7 24 ♖×f8† ♗×f8 25 d8♕ ♗×g2 26 ♕hf6 ♕b4 27 ♕e8 ♕e7 28 ♕f×e7 h5 29 ♕8×f8# **1–0**

TECH 2 — RIBBIT 1 e4 c5 2 ♘f3 d6 3 ♘c3 ♘c6 4 d4 ♘f6 5 ♗c4 c×d4 6 ♘×d4 ♘×d4 7 ♕×d4 e5 8 ♕d3 ♗d7 9 O-O ♗e7 10 ♗g5 ♕b6 11 ♗×f6 ♗×f6 12 ♘d5 ♕c5 13 ♘×f6† g×f6 14 ♗d5 ♗c8 15 ♖fe1 O-O 16 ♖e3 a5 17 ♖ae1 h5 18 ♖g3† ♔h7 19 ♕f3 ♗g4 20 ♕×f6 ♕b4 21 ♖c3 ♕×b2 22 ♗×f7 d5 **0–1**

DART 4.1 — OSTRICH 1 e4 d5 2 ♘c3 d×e4 3 ♘×e4 ♘d7 4 ♘f3 e6 5 ♗e2 ♘h6 6 O-O ♗e7 7 d4 O-O 8 ♗×h6 g×h6 9 c4 ♘b6 10 ♕c1 f5 11 ♘c3 ♗g5 12 ♕c2 a5 13 ♖fe1 ♗f6 14 ♖ad1 ♗d7 15 c5 ♘c8 16 ♗c4 ♕e8 17 ♕b3 ♔g7 18 ♕×b7 ♖a7 19 ♕b3 ♔f7 20 ♗×e6† ♗×e6 21 d5 ♖a6 22 d×e6† ♔g6 23 ♕c4 ♖c6 24 ♘e5† ♗×e5 25 ♖×e5 ♘b6 26 ♕d4 ♘c8 27 ♖de1 ♘e7 28 ♕a4 ♖f6 29 f4 ♕a8 30 ♕d4 ♕b7 31 ♘d5 ♖c×e6 32 ♖×e6 ♘×d5 33 ♖×f6† ♘×f6 34 ♖e6 ♕e4 35 ♕×f6† ♔h5 36 ♖×e4 ♔g4 37 ♕g7† **1–0**

CHUTE 1 — DUCHESS 1 e4 e5 2 ♘f3 ♘c6 3 ♗b5 a6 4 ♗×c6 d×c6 5 ♘×e5 ♕d4 6 ♘f3 ♕×e4† 7 ♔f1 ♗e6 8 d3 ♕b4 9 a3 ♕b6 10 b3 O-O-O 11 ♗e3 ♗c5 12 d4 ♗×d4 13 ♗×d4 c5 14 ♔e2 ♕b5† 15 c4 ♕e8 16 ♔f1 c×d4 17 ♕d3 ♗g4 18 ♘bd2 ♕d7 19 ♘e5 ♕e6 20 ♖e1 ♗h5 21 ♘ef3 ♕f6 22 ♘e4 ♕f4 23 ♘×d4 ♗g6 24 ♕e3 ♕×e3 25 ♖×e3 ♖×d4 26 ♘c5 ♘f6 27 ♖e7 ♘e4 28 ♖e5 ♖d1† 29 ♔e2 ♘c3† 30 ♔f3 ♖×h1 31 h3 ♖f8 32 ♔g3 ♖d8 33 ♖e7 ♖g8 34 h4 ♖d1 35 ♖e3 ♖c1 36 ♔h2 ♘b1 **0–1**

BELLE — XENARBOR 1 e4 c5 2 ♘f3 d6 3 d4 c×d4 4 ♘×d4 ♘f6 5 ♘c3 a6 6 h3 e5 7 ♘de2 ♗e6 8 g4 ♘fd7 9 ♗e3 ♕h4 10 ♗g2 ♘c6 11 O-O ♗e7 12 ♘d5 ♗d8 13 c4 ♖b8 14 ♘ec3 ♘a5 15 b3 ♘c6 16 ♕d2 O-O 17 ♖fe1 h5 18 f3 h×g4 19 h×g4 ♕h7 20 a3 ♗h4 21 ♗f2 ♗d8 22 ♖ad1 ♘a5 23 ♖b1 ♘c6 24 ♖b2 a5 25 ♘b5 ♗e7 26 ♘×e7† ♘×e7 27 ♘×d6 ♘c6 28 ♖d1 b6 29 ♘f5 ♘f6 30 a4 ♖fd8 31 ♘d6 ♘e8 32 c5 b×c5 33 ♗×c5 ♗×b3 34 ♖a1 ♘×d6 35 ♗×d6 ♖×d6 36 ♕×d6 ♖d8 37 ♕×c6 ♖d1† 38 ♖×d1 ♕g6 39 ♕×g6 f×g6 40 ♖×b3 **1–0**

Round 4

RIBBIT — CHESS 4.0 1 e4 c5 2 c3 d5 3 e×d5 ♕×d5 4 d4 c×d4 5 c×d4 ♘c6 6 ♘f3 ♗g4 7 ♘c3 ♕d6 8 d5 ♘b4 9 ♗b5† ♗d7 10 ♗×d7† ♔×d7 11 ♗e3 ♕a6 12 ♘e5† ♔e8 13 a3 ♕d6 14 ♕a4† ♘c6 15 d×c6 b×c6 16 ♘×c6 e5 17 ♘×a7† ♕d7 18 ♕×d7† ♔×d7 19 ♖d1† ♔e6 20 O-O ♘f6 21 b4 ♗e7 22 h3 h5 23 ♖fe1 h4 24 ♖d3 e4 25 ♗d4 ♖he8 26 ♗×f6 ♗×f6 27 ♖×e4† ♔f5 28 ♖×e8 ♖×e8 29 g4† h×g3 30 f×g3 ♖e1† 31 ♔f2 ♖c1 32 g4† ♔g6 33 ♘e4 ♗e5 34 b5 ♖c2† 35 ♔f3 ♖h2 36 ♘f2 ♗f6 37 ♖d6 ♔h7 38 ♖d5 ♗b2 39 ♔g3 ♖×f2 40 ♔×f2 ♗×a3 41 b6 ♗c1 42 b7 ♗f4 43 ♘c6 ♗c7 44 ♖d7 ♗f4 45 ♖×f7 ♗d6 46 b8♕ ♗×b8 47 ♘×b8 ♔g6 48 ♖f5 ♔h6 49 ♘d7 g6 50 ♖f6 ♔g5 51 ♔g3 ♔h6 52 ♘e5 ♔g7 53 g5 ♔g8 54 ♘×g6 ♔h7 55 h4 ♔g8 56 h5 ♔g7 57 h6† ♔h7 58 ♘e5 ♔h8 59 g6 ♔g8 60 ♔g4 ♔h8 61 ♖f8# **1–0**

CHAOS — DART 4.1 1 d4 d5 2 c4 e6 3 ♘c3 ♘f6 4 ♗g5 ♘bd7 5 e3 c6 6 c×d5 e×d5 7 ♗d3 ♗b4 8 ♘f3 ♗×c3† 9 b×c3 O-O 10 O-O ♖e8 11 ♕c2 ♘f8 12 ♖ab1 ♗g4 13 ♘e5 ♗c8 14 f3 c5 15 ♗b5 ♗d7 16 ♗×f6 g×f6 17 ♘×d7 ♘×d7 18 ♕f5 ♖e7 19 ♗d3 ♔f8 20 ♕×h7 ♖e6 21 ♖×b7 c×d4 22 ♗f5 ♖d6 23 ♕h8† ♔e7 24 ♕×d8† ♖×d8 25 e×d4 a5 26 a4 ♖c6 27 ♖e1† ♔d6 28 ♖e3 ♖b6 29 ♖a7 ♖b2 30 ♖e1 ♔c6 31 ♖×a5 ♖g8 32 ♗×d7† ♔×d7 33 ♖×d5† ♔c6 34 ♖c5† ♔d6 35 g4 ♖g5 36 ♖f5 ♖×f5 37 g×f5 ♖a2 38 h4 ♖×a4 39 h5 ♖c4 40 ♖c1 ♔e7 41 ♔h2 ♔f8 42 ♔g3 ♔g8 43 ♔f2 ♔g7 44 ♔g3 ♔h6 45 ♔h4 ♔g7 46 ♖c2 ♔h6 47 f4 ♔h7 48 ♔g4 ♔g7 49 d5 ♔f8 50 h6 ♖e4 51 d6 ♖e1 52 h7 ♔g7 53 ♖h2 ♖g1† **1–0**

DUCHESS — BELLE 1 e4 e5 2 ♘f3 ♘c6 3 ♗c4 ♗c5

4 c3 ♘f6 5 d4 e×d4 6 c×d4 ♗b4† 7 ♗d2 ♗×d2† 8 ♘b×d2 d5 9 e×d5 ♘×d5 10 ♕b3 ♘ce7 11 O–O O–O 12 ♖fe1 c6 13 a4 ♕b6 14 ♕×b6 a×b6 15 ♖e5 ♗d7 16 ♗d3 c5 17 b3 b5 18 d×c5 b×a4 19 ♖ae1 a×b3 20 ♘×b3 ♖fe8 21 ♘bd4 f6 22 ♖5e4 ♘c6 23 ♗c4 ♘cb4 24 ♖e7 ♖×e7 25 ♖×e7 ♖a1† 26 ♘e1 h5 27 ♘b3 ♔f8 28 ♖e2 ♖a8 29 ♘c2 h4 30 ♖d2 ♘×c2 31 ♗×d5 ♖e8 32 g3 h3 33 ♖d1 ♗c6 34 ♗×c6 b×c6 35 ♘a5 ♘d4 36 ♔f1 ♘f3 37 ♘×c6 ♔g8 38 ♖d8 ♖×d8 39 ♘×d8 ♔f8 40 ♘e6† ♔f7 41 ♘f4 ♔e7 42 ♔e2 ♘×h2 43 ♘×h3 ♔d7 44 ♘f4 ♘g4 45 ♘d3 ♔c6 46 f3 ♘e5 47 ♘×e5† f×e5 48 ♔e3 ♔×c5 49 ♔e4 ♔d6 50 ♔f5 ♔d7 51 ♔×e5 ♔c6 52 ♔f5 ♔b7 53 ♔g6 ♔b6 54 ♔×g7 ♔b7 55 ♔f6 ♔b6 56 f4 ♔b7 57 f5 ♔b6 58 ♔e5 ♔b7 59 f6 ♔b6 **0–1**

OSTRICH — CHUTE 1 1 d4 d5 2 e3 ♘f6 3 ♘f3 ♗g4 4 ♘c3 e6 5 ♗d2 ♗d6 6 ♗d3 O–O 7 O–O ♘c6 8 ♘b5 a6 9 ♘×d6 ♕b8 10 ♘×b7 ♕×b7 11 ♗c3 ♖ab8 12 ♕e2 ♖a8 13 h3 ♗h5 14 g4 ♗g6 15 ♗×g6 f×g6 16 ♘e5 ♘×e5 17 d×e5 ♘e4 18 ♕d3 ♖f3 19 b4 ♖af8 20 ♗e1 ♖×h3 21 c4 ♕c6 22 c×d5 ♕×d5 23 ♕×d5 e×d5 24 ♖d1 c6 25 ♖c1 ♘g5 26 f4 ♘f3† 27 ♔g2 ♖h2† 28 ♔×f3 ♖c8 29 e6 ♖×a2 30 e7 ♖a3 31 ♖×c6 ♖e8 32 ♗h4 d4 33 ♖e6 ♔f7 34 ♖e4 d3 35 f5 g×f5 36 g×f5 ♖a2 37 ♖d1 ♖a3 38 ♖d4 ♖b8 39 ♖d8 ♖×d8 40 e×d8♕ **1–0**

ACM 1975 — Minneapolis

October 19 — October 21

	1	2	3	4	tot
1 CHESS 4.4	12+■	3+□	4+■	2+□	4
2 TREEFROG	7+□	5+■	8+□	1−■	3
3 ETAOIN SHRDLU	8+□	1−■	5+□	9+■	3
4 CHAOS	9+□	10+■	1−□	6+□	3
5 CHUTE 1.2	11+■	2−□	3−■	10+□	2
6 DUCHESS	10−□	11+□	7+■	4−■	2
7 TYRO	2−■	9+□	6−□	12+■	2
8 OSTRICH	3−■	12+□	2−■	11=□	1½
9 WITA	4−■	7−■	10+□	3−□	1
10 BLACK KNIGHT	6+■	4−□	9−■	5−■	1
11 IRON FISH	5−□	6−■	12=□	8=■	1
12 SORTIE	1−□	8−■	11=■	7−□	½

Round 1

SORTIE — CHESS 4.4 1 ♘c3 e5 2 d4 d6 3 d×e5 d×e5 4 ♕×d8† ♔×d8 5 ♗e3 ♘f6 6 O–O–O† ♗d7 7 ♘d5 ♘g4 8 f3 ♘×e3 9 ♘×e3 ♔c8 10 ♘c4 ♘c6 11 ♔b1 b5 12 ♘e3 ♗c5 13 ♘d5 ♖d8 14 e3 ♘a5 15 ♗d3 c6 16 ♘c3 ♗×e3 17 ♖e1 ♗d4 18 ♗×h7 ♗×c3 19 b×c3 g6 20 ♖×e5 ♖h8 21 ♗×g6 f×g6 22 ♘e2 ♔c7 23 ♘f4 ♖h6 24 ♔a1 ♖ah8 25 h4 ♗f5 26 ♔b1 ♖×h4 27 ♖×h4 ♖×h4 28 g4 ♖h1† 29 ♔b2 ♘c4† 30 ♔b3 ♖b1# **0–1**

TREEFROG — TYRO 1 e4 e5 2 ♘f3 ♘c6 3 ♗b5 a6 4 ♗a4 ♘f6 5 O–O ♗e7 6 ♕e2 b5 7 ♗b3 O–O 8 c3 d6 9 d3 ♕e8 10 ♘a3 ♗d8 11 h3 ♖b8 12 ♘g5 h6 13 ♘f3 ♘h5 14 ♗e3 b4 15 c×b4 ♖×b4 16 ♖fc1 ♗e6 17 ♗×e6 f×e6 18 ♕c2 ♘d4 19 ♘×d4 e×d4 20 ♗d2 ♖b7 21 g4 ♘f4 22 ♗×f4 ♖×f4 23 ♘c4 ♗h4 24 ♖f1 ♖f7 25 a3 ♕c6 26 ♖ac1 d5 27 ♘e5 ♕×c2 28 ♖×c2 ♖f6 29 ♖d1 c5 30 e×d5 e×d5 31 ♖e1 ♖b5 32 ♘d7 ♖c6 33 ♖e5 c4 34 a4 ♖b3 35 ♖×d5 c3 36 b×c3 ♖b1† 37 ♔g2 ♖×c3 38 ♖×c3 d×c3 39 ♖c5 ♖c1 40 ♖c8† ♔f7 41 ♘e5† ♔e7 42 ♘g6† ♔d7 43 ♖a8 ♗f6 44 ♖a7† ♔c8 45 ♖×a6 ♖d1 46 ♘f4 ♗e5 47 ♘g6 ♗c7 48 ♖c6 ♖×d3 49 ♘f4 ♖d7 50 ♖×c3 ♔b8 51 ♘e6 ♗a5 52 ♖c5 ♗d2 53 g5 ♖f7 54 g×h6 ♗×h6 55 a5 g6 56 a6 ♖f6 57 ♖b5† ♔c8 58 a7 ♖×e6 59 a8♕† **1–0**

CHAOS — WITA 1 d4 ♘f6 2 c4 b6 3 f3 ♘c6 4 ♘c3 ♗a6 5 e4 e5 6 ♗e3 e×d4 7 ♗×d4 ♘×d4 8 ♕×d4 ♗d6 9 ♘ge2 O–O 10 e5 ♗c5 11 ♕h4 ♘e8 12 ♕e4 f5 13 ♕d5† ♖f7 14 f4 ♗b4 15 O–O–O c6 16 ♕d3 ♕h4 17 g3 ♕h6 18 a3 ♗c5 19 b4 ♗e7 20 ♗g2 ♖d8 21 ♘d4 g6 22 ♖d2 c5 23 ♗d5 c×d4 24 ♗×f7† ♔f8 25 ♘d5 ♔×f7 26 ♘×e7 ♔×e7 27 ♕×d4 ♗b7 28 ♖hd1 ♕h5 29 c5 ♕f3 30 ♕d3 ♕×d3 31 ♖×d3 ♗e4 32 ♖d4 b×c5 33 b×c5 **1–0**

IRON FISH — CHUTE 1.2 1 e4 c5 2 ♗c4 ♘f6 3 e5 ♘g8 4 d4 c×d4 5 ♕×d4 ♘c6 6 ♕c5 e6 7 ♕e3 ♕b6 8 ♘d2 ♕×e3† 9 f×e3 ♘×e5 10 ♘gf3 ♘×c4 11 ♘×c4 d5 12 ♘ce5 f6 13 ♘d3 e5 14 c3 e4 15 ♘f4 e×f3 16 g×f3 ♘e7 17 e4 d×e4 18 f×e4 ♗d7 19 ♗e3 ♗c6 20 ♔e2 ♗×e4 21 ♖hd1 ♘f5 22 ♔f2 ♗d6 23 c4 ♘×e3 24 ♔×e3 ♗×f4† 25 ♔×f4 ♗c6 26 ♖d3 O–O 27 ♖e1 ♖ae8 28 ♖ee3 ♖×e3 29 ♖×e3 g5† 30 ♔g4 ♗d7† 31 ♔f3 f5 32 ♖e7 ♗c6† 33 ♔e2 f4 34 ♔e1 f3 35 ♖e5 f2† 36 ♔f1 ♗g2† 37 ♔e2 f1♕† 38 ♔d2 ♕f4† 39 ♖e3 ♖d8† 40 ♔c2 ♕×e3 41 b4 ♖d2† 42 ♔c1 ♗e4 43 b5 ♖×a2† 44 ♔d1 ♖×h2 45 c5 ♕×c5 46 b6 a×b6 47 ♔e1 ♗d3 48 ♔d1 g4 49 ♔e1 g3 50 ♔d1 ♕f2 51 ♔c1 g2 52 ♔d1 g1♕# **0–1**

ETAOIN SHRDLU — OSTRICH 1 e4 e5 2 ♗c4 ♘f6 3 ♘f3 ♘×e4 4 ♘×e5 d5 5 ♗e2 f6 6 ♗b5† ♔e7 7 ♘f3 c6 8 ♗e2 ♗g4 9 O–O ♔f7 10 d4 ♗e7 11 ♘bd2 ♗×f3 12 ♘×f3 ♕d6 13 ♘h4 g5 14 ♘f5 ♕e6 15 ♗g4 ♔f8 16 ♘×e7 ♕×e7 17 f4 h6 18 f×g5 h×g5 19 ♖e1 ♖h4 20 g3 ♖h6 21 ♗d2 c5 22 d×c5 ♕×c5† 23 ♗e3 ♕b5 24 ♖c1 ♕×b2 25 ♕×d5 ♘×g3 26 ♗c5† ♔g7 27 h×g3 ♘a6 28 ♖b1 ♕×c2 29 ♕×b7† ♔g6 30 ♕×a8 ♕×c5† 31 ♔g2 ♖h7 32 ♕g8† ♖g7 33 ♕e8† ♖f7 34 ♗h5† ♔×h5 35 ♕×f7† ♔g4 36 ♕e6† ♔h5 37 g4† ♔h6 38 ♕×f6† ♔h7 39 ♖h1† ♔g8 40 ♖h8# **1–0**

DUCHESS — BLACK KNIGHT 0–1

Round 2

OSTRICH — SORTIE 1 e4 d5 2 e×d5 ♕×d5 3 ♘c3 ♕e6† 4 ♘ge2 ♗d7 5 d4 ♘f6 6 ♗f4 ♘a6 7 b3 O–O–O 8 d5 ♕g4 9 ♗e5 ♘b4 10 a3 ♘a6 11 ♘f4 g5 12 ♗×a6 b×a6 13 ♕d4 g×f4 14 ♕×a7 ♕×g2 15 ♕a8# **1–0**

TYRO — WITA 1 d4 ♘f6 2 c4 g6 3 ♘c3 ♗g7 4 e4 e6 5 ♗g5 h6 6 ♗×f6 ♗×f6 7 ♘f3 ♘c6 8 ♗e2 b6 9 O–O O–O 10 ♕d2 h5 11 ♖ae1 ♕e7 12 ♕e3 ♕b4 13 ♖b1 ♗a6 14 a3 ♕b3 15 e5 ♗e7 16 ♘d2 ♗g5 17 f4 ♗×f4 18 ♖×f4 ♕c2 19 ♗d3 ♕×b1† 20 ♗×b1 ♖ab8 21 d5 ♘d8 22 ♖f1 e×d5 23 ♘×d5 ♘e6 24 ♕h6 c6 25 ♘f6# **1–0**

DUCHESS — IRON FISH 1 e4 d6 2 d4 ♘f6 3 ♘c3

♗g4 4 ♘f3 ♗×f3 5 ♕×f3 ♘c6 6 ♗b5 ♕d7 7 O-O ♕g4 8 ♕×g4 ♘×g4 9 d5 a6 10 d×c6 a×b5 11 c×b7 ♖b8 12 f3 ♘e5 13 f4 ♘g4 14 h3 ♘f6 15 e5 ♘d7 16 e×d6 ♖×b7 17 d×c7 ♖×c7 18 ♘×b5 ♖×c2 19 ♖e1 e6 20 b3 ♗c5† 21 ♗e3 ♗×e3† 22 ♖×e3 ♖c5 23 ♘d6† ♔e7 24 ♖d1 ♖a8 25 b4 ♖c6 26 ♘f5† ♔d8 27 b5 ♖c5 28 ♘d6 ♔e7 29 a3 ♖a4 30 f5 g6 31 f×e6 f×e6 32 g4 ♖f4 33 ♔h1 ♖c2 34 ♔g1 e5 35 ♔h1 h6 36 ♘e4 ♖c4 37 ♘c3 ♔e6 38 a4 ♖f2 39 a5 ♔e7 40 ♔g1 ♖f8 41 b6 ♖c5 42 ♘d5† ♔d8 43 b7 ♖×a5 44 ♘b6 **1–0**

CHUTE 1.2 — TREEFROG 1 e4 d5 2 e×d5 ♘f6 3 ♗b5† ♗d7 4 ♗×d7† ♕×d7 5 c4 c6 6 d×c6 ♘×c6 7 ♘c3 ♘e5 8 ♕e2 ♘d3† 9 ♔f1 O-O-O 10 ♘b5 a6 11 ♘a7† ♔b8 12 ♕e3 ♘g4 13 ♕b6 ♘g×f2 14 ♘c6† ♕×c6 15 ♕×d8† ♕c8 16 ♕×c8† ♔×c8 17 ♔e2 ♘×h1 18 ♔×d3 e6 19 ♘f3 ♗d6 20 b3 ♘f2† 21 ♔e2 ♘g4 22 h3 ♘f6 23 ♗b2 ♖e8 24 ♖f1 e5 25 a3 h6 26 ♔d1 ♘e4 27 ♖e1 ♘f2† 28 ♔c2 e4 29 ♘g1 ♘d3 30 ♖f1 ♘×b2 31 ♔×b2 ♗e5† 32 ♔a2 ♖d8 33 ♖f2 ♗h2 34 ♘f3 e×f3 35 g×f3 ♗f4 36 ♖g2 ♖×d2† 37 ♖×d2 ♗×d2 38 ♔b2 a5 39 ♔c2 ♗e3 40 ♔d3 ♗c5 41 a4 f5 42 h4 **0–1**

BLACK KNIGHT — CHAOS 1 e4 c5 2 ♘f3 ♘c6 3 d4 c×d4 4 ♘×d4 ♘f6 5 ♘c3 e6 6 ♘f3 ♗b4 7 ♔e2 ♗×c3 8 b×c3 ♘×e4 9 ♕d3 d5 10 ♕e3 ♕b6 11 ♔d1 ♘×f2† 12 ♔e2 ♕×e3† 13 ♗×e3 ♘×h1 14 ♔d2 e5 15 ♗b5 e4 16 ♘d4 ♗d7 17 ♘b3 ♘e5 18 ♗×d7† ♔×d7 19 ♗g1 ♘c4† 20 ♔e2 e3 21 ♗×e3 ♖he8 22 ♔f1 ♘×e3† 23 ♔g1 ♘×c2 24 ♖d1 ♖e1† 25 ♖×e1 ♘×e1 26 ♘d4 ♖e8 27 ♘f5 ♘d3 28 g3 ♘hf2 29 a4 g5 30 h4 ♖e1† 31 ♔g2 ♖e7 32 ♘d4 g4 33 h5 ♖e5 34 ♘c2 ♘e1† 35 ♘×e1 ♖×e1 36 ♔×f2 ♖e7 37 a5 ♖e5 38 h6 a6 39 ♔g2 ♖e6 40 ♔f2 ♔c6 41 ♔g2 ♖×h6 42 ♔f2 ♖e6 43 ♔g1 ♔b5 44 ♔f2 ♔×a5 45 ♔g1 ♖e3 46 ♔g2 ♖×c3 47 ♔f2 h5 48 ♔g2 d4 49 ♔h2 d3 50 ♔h1 d2 51 ♔g2 d1♕ 52 ♔f2 ♔b6 53 ♔g2 ♖c2# **0–1**

CHESS 4.4 — ETAOIN SHRDLU 1 f4 d5 2 ♘f3 ♘c6 3 e3 ♗f5 4 ♗b5 ♘f6 5 ♘e5 ♕d6 6 O-O a6 7 ♗×c6† b×c6 8 g4 ♗d7 9 g5 ♘e4 10 ♘×d7 ♕×d7 11 d3 ♘d6 12 ♘d2 g6 13 ♕f3 ♗g7 14 c4 ♖b8 15 ♘b3 O-O 16 c×d5 c×d5 17 ♕×d5 c6 18 ♕g2 ♖b5 19 d4 ♖d8 20 ♘c5 ♕c8 21 a4 ♖b4 22 ♕e2 a5 23 b3 ♘f5 24 ♗b2 ♕c7 25 ♘a6 ♕d6 26 ♘×b4 ♕×b4 27 ♕d3 c5 28 ♗a3 ♕b6 29 ♖ac1 c×d4 30 e4 ♘d6 31 ♗c5 ♕b8 32 f5 g×f5 33 e×f5 h5 34 ♖cd1 ♗e5 35 ♕h3 ♘e4 36 ♗×e7 ♖d7 37 f6 ♖d5 38 ♔h1 ♘c3 39 ♖d3 ♕×b3 40 g6 ♕b7 41 ♕×h5 ♖d8† 42 ♖df3 ♕×f3† 43 ♖×f3 f×g6 44 ♕×g6† ♔h8 45 ♖h3# **1–0**

Round 3

IRON FISH — SORTIE 1 e4 d5 2 e×d5 ♕×d5 3 d4 e5 4 d×e5 ♕×e5† 5 ♕e2 ♕×e2† 6 ♗×e2 ♗f5 7 ♗b5† ♘c6 8 ♗×c6† b×c6 9 ♘a3 O-O-O 10 ♗e3 ♗×a3 11 b×a3 ♗×c2 12 ♗×a7 ♖d3 13 ♗c5 ♘f6 14 ♖c1 ♖e8† 15 ♘e2 ♗a4 16 f4 ♘e4 17 ♔f1 ♖e6 18 ♘c3 ♘×c3 19 ♖e1 ♖×e1† 20 ♔×e1 ♔b8 21 g3 ♖d1† 22 ♔f2 ♖×h1 23 ♔g2 ♖d1 24 f5 ♗c2 25 g4 ♔a8 26 h4 ♘×a2 27 ♗e3 ♘c3 28 ♔f3 ♘b5 29 ♗c5 ♖a1 30 h5 ♗d3 31 ♔e3 ♗c4 32 a4 ♖×a4 33 ♗d4 ♘×d4 34 ♔×d4 ♗b5† 35 ♔e5 ♖×g4 36 h6 g×h6 37 ♔f6 ♗c4 38 ♔e7 ♔b7 39 ♔f6 ♗d5 40 ♔e5 ♖e4† 41 ♔f6 ♖e3 42 ♔g7 h5 43 ♔×h7 ♖f3 44 ♔h8 ♖×f5 45 ♔h7 ♖f6 46 ♔g8 ♖g6† 47 ♔f8 ♗e6 48 ♔e8 ♖g8† 49 ♔e7 ♗d5 50 ♔f6 ♖g4 51 ♔e5 ♗e6 52 ♔f6 ♖g6† 53 ♔e7 ♖g5 54 ♔e8 ♔b6 55 ♔f8 ♖g4 56 ♔e8 ♖g8† 57 ♔e7 ♗d5 58 ♔d7 ♗c4 59 ♔e7 ♖g6 60 ♔f8 ♖g5 61 ♔e8 ♔b7 62 ♔f8 ♖g6 63 ♔e8 ♖g8† 64 ♔e7 ♖g3 65 ♔d8 ♖g5 66 ♔e8 ♗e6 67 ♔e7 ♖a5 68 ♔e8 ♖a8† 69 ♔e7 ♖g8 70 ♔f6 ♔b6 71 ♔e7 ♔c5 72 ♔f6 ♔d5 73 ♔e7 ♔e4 74 ♔f6 ♔d5 75 ♔e7 ♔e4 76 ♔f6 ♔f4 77 ♔e7 ♔e4 78 ♔f6 ♔f4 79 ♔e7 ♖b8 80 ♔f6 ♖g8 81 ♔e7 ♖c8 82 ♔f6 ♖g8 83 ♔e7 ♖c8 84 ♔f6 ♖g8 ½–½

WITA — BLACK KNIGHT 1 e4 e6 2 d4 d5 3 ♘c3 ♘c6 4 e5 f5 5 ♗b5 ♔f7 6 ♘f3 h6 7 ♗f4 ♗e7 8 h3 ♗b4 9 O-O ♗×c3 10 b×c3 g5 11 ♗c1 ♔f8 12 ♗×c6 b×c6 13 ♗a3† ♘e7 14 ♕d3 a5 15 ♖fb1 ♔f7 16 ♗c5 a4 17 ♖b4 ♘g6 18 ♖e1 ♘e7 19 g4 ♖f8 20 ♘d2 ♕d7 21 a3 ♔g7 22 ♕f3 ♖a5 23 ♖b8 ♖a6 24 ♕d3 ♖f7 25 ♖eb1 f4 26 ♔g2 ♖f8 27 ♖×c8 ♕×c8 28 ♗×e7 f3† 29 ♘×f3 ♖f4 30 ♗f6† ♔f8 31 ♖b8 ♖a8 32 ♖×c8† ♖×c8 33 ♕h7 ♖e4 34 ♗e7† ♔e8 35 ♗c5 ♖e2 36 ♕e7# **1–0**

TREEFROG — OSTRICH 1 e4 e5 2 ♘f3 ♘f6 3 ♘×e5 d6 4 ♘f3 ♘×e4 5 ♘c3 d5 6 ♕e2 ♗e7 7 ♘×e4 d×e4 8 ♕×e4 ♘d7 9 ♗c4 ♘f6 10 ♕e5 ♔f8 11 ♘g5 ♗d6 12 ♘×f7 ♗×e5 13 ♘×d8 ♗h3 14 ♘f7 ♗×g2 15 ♖g1 ♖e8 16 ♖×g2 ♗×b2† 17 ♔d1 ♗×a1 18 ♗a3† ♖e7 19 ♘×h8 ♘g8 20 ♗×g8 ♔×g8 21 ♗×e7 ♔×h8 22 f4 c6 23 ♔e2 g6 24 ♔e3 ♔g7 25 ♖g1 ♗f6 26 ♗×f6† ♔×f6 27 c4 h6 28 c5 b5 29 c×b6 a×b6 30 ♖c1 c5 31 ♖b1 g5 32 ♖×b6† ♔f5 33 f×g5 h×g5 34 ♖b5 ♔e6 35 ♖×c5 ♔f6 36 a4 ♔e6 37 ♖×g5 ♔e7 38 h4 ♔d7 39 a5 ♔c7 40 h5 ♔d6 41 h6 ♔e7 42 h7 ♔f7 43 h8♕ **1–0**

CHAOS — CHESS 4.4 1 d4 ♘f6 2 c4 c5 3 d5 e6 4 ♘c3 e×d5 5 c×d5 d6 6 e4 g6 7 ♗e2 ♗g7 8 ♘f3 O-O 9 O-O ♖e8 10 ♘d2 ♘a6 11 f3 ♘c7 12 a4 b6 13 ♘c4 ♗a6 14 ♗g5 h6 15 ♗h4 g5 16 ♗f2 ♘h5 17 a5 ♘f4 18 a×b6 a×b6 19 ♗e3 ♗×c3 20 b×c3 ♗×c4 21 ♗×c4 ♖×a1 22 ♕×a1 ♘c×d5 23 ♗×d5 ♘×d5 24 ♗×c5 ♘×c3 25 ♗b4 ♘e2† 26 ♔h1 ♘f4 27 ♖d1 ♕a8 28 ♗×d6 ♕×a1 29 ♖×a1 ♘e2 30 ♖b1 ♖c8 31 h3 ♖c6 32 ♗e5 ♔h7 33 ♖e1 ♖c2 34 ♔h2 b5 35 ♖b1 ♖c5 36 ♗d6 ♖c6 37 ♗f8 ♖c2 38 ♖a1 ♘f4 39 ♖g1 ♔g6 40 ♗b4 f5 41 e×f5† ♔×f5 42 ♗d6 ♖b2 43 ♔h1 ♔f6 44 ♗×f4 g×f4 45 ♔h2 b4 46 ♖c1 b3 47 ♖c6† ♔g5 48 ♖c5† ♔g6 49 ♖c6† ♔h5 50 ♖c5† ♔g6 51 ♖c6† ♔g5 52 ♖c5† ♔f6 53 ♖b5 ♔g6 54 ♔g1 ♖b1† 55 ♔h2 ♔g7 56 ♖b4 b2 57 ♖b6 ♔f7 58 h4 ♔g7 59 h5 ♔f7 60 ♖b8 ♔e6 61 ♖b7 ♔f5 62 ♖b5† ♔f6 63 g3 f×g3† 64 ♔g2 ♔e6 65 ♖b3 ♔f5 66 ♖b6 ♔g5 67 ♖b5† ♔h4 68 ♖b8 ♔×h5 69 ♖b5† ♔g6 70 ♖b6† ♔f5 71 ♖b5† ♔e6 72 ♖b6† ♔d5 73 ♖b5† ♔c6 74 ♖b3 h5 75 f4 h4 76 ♖b8 ♔d5 77 ♖b5† ♔e4 78 ♖b6 ♔f5 79 ♖b5† ♔g4 80 ♖g5† ♔×f4 81 ♖g4† ♔e3 82 ♖b4 ♔d3 83 ♖b5 ♔c3 84 ♖c5† ♔b4 85 ♖c6 ♖g1† 86 ♔h3 ♖h1† 87 ♔g2 ♔a5 88 ♖c5† ♔a6 89 ♖c6† ♔b7 90 ♖e6 b1♕ 91 ♖e7† ♔c6 92 ♔f3 ♕f5† 93 ♔e2 **0–1**

TYRO — DUCHESS 1 d4 d5 2 c4 e6 3 g3 ♘f6 4 ♘f3 ♗e7 5 ♗g2 O-O 6 O-O d×c4 7 ♕c2 a6 8 ♕×c4 b5 9 ♕c2 ♗b7 10 ♗f4 ♗d6 11 ♘e5 ♗×g2 12 ♔×g2 ♗×e5 13 ♗×e5 ♘d5 14 ♖c1 f6 15 ♗×c7 ♘×c7 16 ♕×c7 ♕×d4 17 ♖c2 ♕d5† 18 f3 b4 19 ♖d2 ♕b5 20 ♔h1 e5 21 a4 b×a3 22 ♘×a3 ♕c6 23 ♕a5 ♖a7 24 ♕d5† ♔h8 25 ♘c4 ♖c8 26 ♘d6 ♕×d5 27 ♖×d5 ♖c2 28 e4 ♘c6 29 ♘f5 g6 30 ♘h4 g5 31 ♘f5 a5 32 ♖b5 ♖d7 33 b3 ♖dd2 34 h3 ♖h2† 35 ♔g1 ♖cg2† 36 ♔f1 ♖f2† 37 ♔e1 ♖b2 38 ♖b8† ♘×b8 39 h4 ♖h1# **0–1**

ETAOIN SHRDLU — CHUTE 1.2 1 e4 c5 2 ♗c4 ♘f6 3 e5 ♘g8 4 ♘f3 e6 5 ♘c3 ♘c6 6 O-O ♘d4 7 ♘×d4 c×d4 8 ♘b5 ♕b6 9 ♕g4 ♘h6 10 ♕×d4 ♕×d4 11 ♘×d4 ♗e7 12 d3 ♘g4 13 ♖e1 ♗c5 14 c3 f6 15 e×f6 ♗×d4 16 c×d4 ♘×f6 17 d5 ♔f7 18 d×e6† d×e6 19 ♗f4 ♘d5 20 ♗e5 ♘b6 21 ♖e4 ♘×c4 22 ♖×c4 ♖d8 23 ♖c7† ♖d7 24 ♖ac1 ♖×c7 25 ♖×c7† ♔e8 26 ♖×g7 h6 27 ♖h7 ♔f8 28 g4 ♔g8 29 ♖×h6 ♔f8 30 h4 b6 31 ♖f6† ♔e7 32 ♖h6 ♗d7 33 ♖h7† ♔d8 34 ♗f6† ♔c7 35 ♗e5† ♔c6 36 g5 ♖g8 37 f4 a6 38 h5 ♖d8 39 ♗f6 ♖f8 40 d4 ♗e8 41 h6 ♗g6 42 ♖a7 ♗d3 43 h7 ♔b5 44 ♖f7 ♖a8 45 h8♕ ♖×h8 46 ♗×h8 ♗b1 47 ♗f6 ♗×a2 48 ♖h7 ♗b1 49 ♖h6 ♗e4 50 ♔f2 **1–0**

Round 4

SORTIE — TYRO 1 ♘f3 d5 2 d4 ♘f6 3 ♗f4 c5 4 d×c5 ♕a5† 5 ♘c3 e6 6 ♗×b8 ♖×b8 7 ♕d4 ♗×c5 8 ♕f4 ♖a8 9 e3 ♗b4 10 ♗b5† ♕×b5 11 O-O-O ♗×c3 12 b×c3 ♕c4 13 ♕×c4 d×c4 14 ♘e5 ♘e4 15 ♖d4 ♘×c3 16 ♖×c4 ♘d5 17 e4 ♘b6 18 ♖c5 ♘a4 19 ♖c4 b5 20 ♖b4 ♖b8 21 c4 ♘c3 22 ♖e1 ♘×a2† 23 ♔b1 ♘×b4 24 f4 f6 25 ♘g4 b×c4 26 ♖c1 h5 27 ♘×f6† g×f6 28 ♖×c4 a5 29 g3 ♖h7 30 h3 ♖d7 31 ♖c3 ♖d3 32 ♖×d3 ♘×d3† 33 ♔a2 ♔d7 34 ♔a1 ♘f2 35 ♔a2 ♘×e4 36 g4 h×g4 37 h×g4 ♗a6 38 ♔a1 ♘c3 39 g5 ♖b1# **0–1**

OSTRICH — IRON FISH 1 e4 d5 2 e×d5 ♕×d5 3 ♘c3 ♕e5† 4 ♘ge2 ♘f6 5 d4 ♕a5 6 ♗e3 ♗f5 7 ♘g3 ♗g4 8 ♗e2 ♗×e2 9 ♕×e2 ♘bd7 10 O-O ♕b4 11 ♕b5 ♕×b5 12 ♘×b5 O-O-O 13 ♘×a7† ♔b8 14 ♘b5 e5 15 d×e5 ♘×e5 16 ♗g5 ♗b4 17 ♗×f6 g×f6 18 c3 ♖d5 19 ♘×c7 ♖d2 20 c×b4 ♔×c7 21 b3 ♔c6 22 ♘e4 ♖e2 23 ♖fe1 ♖×e1† 24 ♖×e1 f5 25 ♘g3 ♘d3 26 ♖e7 f4 27 ♘h5 f5 28 a3 ♖a8 29 a4 b5 30 ♖×h7 b×a4 31 ♖h6† ♔c7 32 ♖h7† ♔c6 33 ♖h6† ♔c7 34 b×a4 ♖×a4 35 ♖h7† ♔d6 36 ♖h6† ♔e5 37 ♔f1 ♖a1† 38 ♔e2 ♘×b4 39 h4 ♖c1 40 ♖b6 ♘d5 41 ♖h6 ♖c2† 42 ♔f3 ♖c3† 43 ♔e2 ♖c2† 44 ♔f1 ♖c1† 45 ♔e2 ♖c2† ½–½

CHAOS — DUCHESS 1 d4 d5 2 c4 e6 3 ♘c3 ♘f6 4 ♗g5 ♗e7 5 e3 O-O 6 ♘f3 h6 7 ♗h4 ♘e4 8 ♗×e7 ♕×e7 9 c×d5 ♘×c3 10 b×c3 e×d5 11 ♕b3 ♕d6 12 ♗d3 ♘a6 13 O-O ♖e8 14 ♘e5 c5 15 ♕b1 ♖e7 16 ♗h7† ♔h8 17 ♗d3 b6 18 f3 h5 19 a4 ♗b7 20 ♕c2 c×d4 21 e×d4 ♖c8 22 ♖fe1 ♘b4 23 ♕d2 ♘×d3 24 ♕×d3 ♕h6 25 a5 b×a5 26 ♖×a5 ♕b6 27 ♖aa1 ♕c7 28 ♖×a7 ♕b6 29 ♖a2 ♕c7 30 ♖c1 ♕b6 31 ♕f5 ♖×c3 32 ♕×h5† ♔g8 33 ♖d1 ♖b3 34 ♖c2 ♖b1 35 ♖cd2 ♕b3 36 ♖×b1 ♕×b1† 37 ♔f2 ♗a6 38 ♔g3 ♕c1 39 ♖a2 ♕e1† 40 ♖f2 ♕c3 41 ♕g4 ♗b5 42 h4 ♗e8 43 ♔h2 f6 44 ♘g6 ♖e1 45 ♖a2 ♕c4 46 ♖a7 f5 47 ♕h5 ♖h1† 48 ♔×h1 ♕c1† 49 ♔h2 ♗×g6 50 ♕×g6 ♕f4† 51 ♔h3 ♕g4† 52 f×g4 f×g4† 53 ♔×g4 ♔f8 54 ♕f7# **1–0**

WITA — ETAOIN SHRDLU 1 c4 e5 2 ♘f3 ♘c6 3 d4 e×d4 4 ♘×d4 ♗c5 5 ♘f5 g6 6 ♘g3 ♘f6 7 ♗g5 ♗×f2† 8 ♔×f2 ♘g4† 9 ♔f3 ♕×g5 10 h4 ♕e3† 11 ♔×g4 d5† 12 ♘f5 ♗×f5# **0–1**

CHESS 4.4 — TREEFROG 1 e4 d5 2 e×d5 ♘f6 3 d4 ♘×d5 4 ♘f3 ♗g4 5 ♗e2 e6 6 O-O ♘c6 7 c4 ♘f6 8 ♘c3 ♗b4 9 d5 ♗×c3 10 d×c6 ♕×d1 11 ♖×d1 ♗b4 12 c×b7 ♖b8 13 h3 ♗f5 14 a3 ♗c5 15 g4 ♗c2 16 ♖d2 ♗b3 17 ♘d4 ♗×d4 18 ♖×d4 e5 19 ♖d2 ♖×b7 20 g5 ♘e4 21 ♖d5 f6 22 ♗h5† ♔e7 23 ♗f3 c6 24 ♖a5 ♗c2 25 b4 ♖hb8 26 ♗e3 ♘×g5 27 ♗×g5 f×g5 28 ♖×e5† ♔d6 29 ♖ae1 ♖f7 30 ♖e6† ♔c7 31 ♖×c6† ♔d8 32 ♖ce6 ♖b6 33 ♖e8† ♔d7 34 ♗d5 ♖f5 35 ♖1e7† ♔d6 36 ♗e6 ♖c6 37 ♗×f5 ♗×f5 38 c5† **1–0**

CHUTE 1.2 — BLACK KNIGHT 1 e4 e6 2 ♘c3 d5 3 e×d5 e×d5 4 ♘f3 ♗e6 5 ♘d4 ♕f6 6 ♘×e6 ♕×e6† 7 ♗e2 d4 8 ♘b1 ♘c6 9 O-O ♘f6 10 b3 ♗c5 11 ♗c4 ♕d7 12 ♖e1† ♔d8 13 d3 ♗f8 14 ♗d2 a6 15 a4 ♖a7 16 ♕f3 ♘b4 17 ♘a3 c5 18 ♗g5 ♖g8 19 ♕f4 ♔c8 20 ♗×f6 ♘d5 21 ♗×d5 b5 22 ♗e4 ♗d6 23 ♗e5 b4 24 ♘c4 g5 25 ♘×d6† ♔b8 26 ♕f6 ♖g6 27 ♘c4† ♔c8 28 ♘b6# **1–0**

ACM 1976 — Houston

October 19 — October 21

		1	2	3	4	tot
1	CHESS 4.5	6+■	5+□	3+■	2+□	4
2	CHAOS	8+□	7+■	5+□	1−■	3
3	BLACK KNIGHT	9+□	10+■	1−□	7+■	3
4	BLITZ 4	5−■	+	9+□	6+□	3
5	DUCHESS	4+□	1−■	2−■	11+□	2
6	WITA	1−□	9+■	8+□	4−■	2
7	CHUTE 1.2	11+■	2−□	10+■	3−□	2
8	L'EXCENTRIQUE	2−■	11+□	6−■	10+□	2
9	ETAOIN SHRDLU	3−■	6−□	4−■	+	1
10	CHESSTAR	+	3−□	7−□	8−■	1
11	XENARBOR 4	7−□	8−■	+	5−■	1

Round 1

WITA — CHESS 4.5 1 d4 ♘f6 2 g3 e6 3 ♗g2 ♘c6 4 ♘h3 ♗b4† 5 c3 ♗e7 6 O-O O-O 7 ♗f4 d6 8 ♘a3 e5 9 d×e5 d×e5 10 ♗e3 ♘g4 11 ♕×d8 ♖×d8 12 ♘b5 ♘×e3 13 f×e3 ♗×h3 14 ♗×h3 ♖d2 15 ♗g4 ♖×b2 16 ♘×c7 ♖d8 17 ♖fb1 ♖dd2 18 ♗f3 ♗c5 19 ♔f2 ♘a5 20 ♖×b2 ♖×b2 21 ♗d5 ♖d2 22 ♖b1 ♗b6 23 ♔e1 ♗×e3 24 a3 b6 25 g4 ♗f4 26 ♖b4 ♖c2 27 ♗e4 ♖c1† 28 ♔f2 ♗×h2 29 ♔g2 ♗g1 30 ♗d5 ♗c5 31 ♖e4 ♗d6 32 ♘b5 ♗b8 33 ♖a4 a6 34 ♘d4 e×d4 35 c×d4 ♖c3 36 ♔f1 ♗d6 37 g5 ♖×a3 38 ♖×a3 ♗×a3 39 ♔f2 ♗e7 40 ♔g3 ♗×g5 41 ♔g4 ♗e3 42 ♔f3 **0–1**

CHAOS — L'EXCENTRIQUE 1 d4 e6 2 c4 d5 3 ♘c3 d×c4 4 e4 e5 5 d5 b5 6 ♘×b5 ♗b4† 7 ♗d2 ♗×d2† 8 ♕×d2 a6 9 ♘c3 f5 10 ♘f3 f×e4 11 ♘×e5 ♕d6 12 ♕g5 ♕f6 13 ♘×e4 ♕×g5 14 ♘×g5 h6 15 ♘ef7 h×g5 16 ♘×h8 ♘e7 17 ♗×c4 ♘d7 18 O-O-O

♘e5 19 ♗e2 ♗f5 20 d6 c×d6 21 ♖×d6 ♖c8† 22 ♔d2 ♖c2† 23 ♔d1 ♖×b2 24 ♖f1 ♖×a2 25 ♖×a6 ♖×a6 26 ♗×a6 ♔f8 27 ♖e1 ♘g4 28 f3 ♘×h2 29 ♖h1 ♘×f3 30 g×f3 g4 31 f×g4 ♗×g4† 32 ♔d2 ♗f5 33 ♗d3 ♗×d3 34 ♔×d3 g5 35 ♖h5 ♔g7 36 ♖×g5† ♔×h8 37 ♔e4 ♔h7 38 ♔e5 ♘c6† 39 ♔f6 ♔h6 40 ♖d5 ♘b4 41 ♖d4 ♘c6 42 ♖h4# **1–0**

BLACK KNIGHT — ETAOIN SHRDLU 1 e4 d5 2 e×d5 ♕×d5 3 ♘c3 ♕d6 4 ♗b5† ♘c6 5 ♘ge2 ♗f5 6 ♘g3 ♕e5† 7 ♔f1 ♗d7 8 ♕h5 ♘f6 9 ♕×e5 ♘×e5 10 d4 ♘eg4 11 ♗×d7† ♘×d7 12 ♘b5 ♔d8 13 ♗g5 a6 14 ♘c3 f6 15 ♗f4 e5 16 d×e5 f×e5 17 ♗g5† ♘gf6 18 ♗×f6† g×f6 19 ♖d1 ♗c5 20 ♘f5 h5 21 ♔e2 ♖g8 22 ♘e4 ♗e7 23 h3 ♖×g2 24 ♘fg3 f5 25 ♔f1 ♖×g3 26 ♘×g3 e4 27 ♖g1 ♗f6 28 ♘×h5 ♗e7 29 ♖g8† ♗f8 30 ♖×f8† ♔e7 31 ♖×a8 e3 32 ♖g8 ♘f6 33 ♖g7† ♔f8 34 ♖d8† ♘e8 35 ♖×c7 f4 36 ♘g7 **1–0**

DUCHESS — BLITZ 4 1 e4 e5 2 ♘f3 ♘c6 3 ♗c4 ♗c5 4 c3 ♘f6 5 d4 e×d4 6 c×d4 ♗b4† 7 ♗d2 ♗×d2† 8 ♘b×d2 d5 9 e×d5 ♘×d5 10 ♕b3 ♕e7† 11 ♔f1 ♘f4 12 ♖e1 ♘e6 13 d5 ♕d6 14 d×e6 f×e6 15 ♗×e6 ♘e7 16 ♗×c8 ♕a6† 17 ♔g1 ♖×c8 18 ♕b4 c5 19 ♕g4 ♔f8 20 ♕e4 ♖e8 21 ♕f4† ♔g8 22 ♖×e7 ♖×e7 23 ♕b8† ♔f7 24 ♕×h8 ♕×a2 25 b3 h6 26 ♕d8 ♕a1† 27 ♘f1 ♕c3 28 ♕c8 g5 29 h4 ♔g6 30 h×g5 h×g5 31 ♕g8† ♕g7 32 ♕d5 g4 33 ♘h4† ♔h6 34 ♘f5† ♔g6 35 ♕d6† ♕f6 36 ♘×e7† ♔g7 37 ♖h7† ♔×h7 38 ♕×f6 b6 39 ♕g6† ♔h8 40 ♕g8# **1–0**

XENARBOR 4 — CHUTE 1.2 1 d4 d5 2 c4 e6 3 ♘c3 ♗b4 4 c×d5 ♕×d5 5 ♕d2 ♕a5 6 ♕c2 e5 7 d5 ♕×d5 8 e4 ♕c5 9 ♗e3 ♗×c3† 10 b×c3 ♕a5 11 ♗d3 ♘c6 12 ♘f3 ♘f6 13 O–O ♖b8 14 a4 ♘g4 15 ♗c1 O–O 16 h3 ♘f6 17 ♘d2 ♗e6 18 ♗a3 ♖fe8 19 ♘c4 ♗×c4 20 ♗×c4 a6 21 ♕b3 ♘d8 22 ♖fe1 b5 23 ♗f1 ♕b6 24 a×b5 a×b5 25 ♗b2 ♘e6 26 ♕c2 ♖a8 27 ♖×a8 ♖×a8 28 ♖e3 ♕c5 29 ♕c1 c6 30 g3 ♖a4 31 ♗g2 ♘g5 32 f3 ♘h5 33 h4 ♘e6 34 ♔f2 ♘f6 35 ♗h3 ♕a7 36 ♗×e6 f×e6 37 ♕d2 ♕c5 38 ♕d8† ♔f7 39 ♔e2 ♖a2 40 ♕d2 ♕c4† 41 ♖d3 ♘h5 42 ♕c2 ♘×g3† 43 ♔d2 c5 44 ♖d7† ♔f6 45 ♔c1 b4 46 c×b4 ♘e2† 47 ♔b1 ♕×c2† 48 ♔×c2 c4 49 ♔b1 ♖a4 50 ♖b7 c3 51 h5 c×b2 52 ♔×b2 ♘f4 53 ♔b3 ♖a1 54 h6 g×h6 55 ♖×h7 ♖b1† 56 ♔c2 ♖h1 57 ♖d7 ♖f1 58 ♖d2 ♖×f3 59 ♖h2 h5 60 b5 ♖e3 61 b6 ♖×e4 62 ♖d2 ♖b4 63 ♖d6 ♔e7 64 ♖c6 ♘d5 65 ♔c1 ♔d7 66 ♖c5 e4 67 ♖a5 ♖c4† 68 ♔d2 e3† 69 ♔e2 ♖c2† 70 ♔d1 ♖d2† 71 ♔e1 ♔c6 72 ♖a1 ♘c3 73 ♖c1 ♖d3 74 ♖×c3† ♖×c3 75 ♔e2 ♖b3 **0–1**

Round 2

CHUTE 1.2 — CHAOS 1 e4 c5 2 c4 e6 3 ♘c3 ♘c6 4 ♘f3 ♘f6 5 d3 ♗d6 6 ♗e2 O–O 7 O–O b6 8 ♘b5 ♗b8 9 ♘c3 ♗b7 10 ♗g5 h6 11 ♗×f6 ♕×f6 12 ♕a4 ♖c8 13 ♕b5 ♗c7 14 ♘a4 ♘d4 15 ♘×d4 ♕×d4 16 ♖ac1 ♗c6 17 ♕a6 f5 18 e×f5 ♕e5 19 g3 ♕×e2 20 f×e6 ♕f3 21 ♕×c8† ♖×c8 22 e×d7 ♕g2# **0–1**

ETAOIN SHRDLU — WITA 1 e4 c5 2 ♗c4 e6 3 ♘c3 d6 4 ♘f3 ♘f6 5 O–O ♗e7 6 d4 O–O 7 d5 e×d5 8 e×d5 ♗g4 9 ♖e1 ♖e8 10 ♗d3 ♕a5 11 ♗e3 ♘bd7 12 h3 ♗×f3 13 ♕×f3 ♘e5 14 ♕e2 ♕b4 15 ♗b5 ♕×b2 16 ♘a4 ♕b4 17 ♖ab1 ♕a3 18 ♗×c5 d×c5 19 ♕×e5 ♗f8 20 ♗×e8 ♖×e8 21 ♕f4 ♕×a2 22 d6 ♖×e1† 23 ♖×e1 ♕×c2 24 ♖c1 ♕e2 25 ♘×c5 ♘h5 26 ♕g4 ♕×g4 27 h×g4 ♘f4 28 ♖e1 b6 29 d7 b×c5 30 d8♕ c4 31 ♖e4 ♘e6 32 ♕d5 c3 33 ♖c4 c2 34 ♖×c2 g5 35 ♔h2 h6 36 ♔g1 ♔g7 **0–1**

CHESSTAR — BLACK KNIGHT 1 d4 d5 2 h4 e6 3 e4 d×e4 4 ♗g5 f6 5 ♗e3 e5 6 d×e5 ♕×d1† 7 ♔×d1 f×e5 8 ♘c3 ♘f6 9 ♗c4 ♗g4† 10 ♔c1 ♘c6 11 a3 O–O–O 12 b4 ♗d7 13 ♔b2 ♗e7 14 ♖b1 a5 15 ♘d5 ♘×d5 16 ♗×d5 a×b4 17 ♗×e4 b×a3† 18 ♔a1 ♗g4 **0–1**

CHESS 4.5 — DUCHESS 1 e4 e5 2 ♘f3 ♘c6 3 d4 e×d4 4 c3 d5 5 e×d5 ♕×d5 6 c×d4 ♗g4 7 ♗e2 O–O–O 8 ♗e3 ♗b4† 9 ♘c3 ♘ge7 10 O–O ♕d7 11 ♖c1 ♘d5 12 h3 ♗×f3 13 ♗×f3 ♗×c3 14 b×c3 ♘×e3 15 f×e3 ♕e7 16 ♗×c6 ♕×e3† 17 ♔h1 b×c6 18 ♕g4† ♕e6 19 ♕×g7 ♖hf8 20 ♕×h7 ♕g6 21 ♕h4 f5 22 ♖b1 ♕e6 23 ♕f2 ♕e4 24 ♖fe1 ♕d5 25 ♖e5 ♕d6 26 ♖×f5 ♕g6 27 ♖f1 ♖×f5 28 ♕×f5† ♕×f5 29 ♖×f5 ♖e8 30 ♖f2 ♖e1† 31 ♔h2 ♖c1 32 ♖f3 ♖a1 33 ♖f8† ♔d7 34 ♖f7† ♔d6 35 ♖f6† ♔d7 36 ♖f2 c5 37 g4 c×d4 38 c×d4 ♔d6 39 g5 c5 40 g6 c×d4 41 g7 ♖e1 42 g8♕ **1–0**

L'EXCENTRIQUE — XENARBOR 4 1 e3 ♘f6 2 ♗c4 e6 3 ♕f3 ♗e7 4 d4 d5 5 ♗d3 ♘c6 6 ♗b5 ♗d7 7 ♗d2 ♘e4 8 ♗×c6 ♗×c6 9 ♘c3 ♘×d2 10 ♔×d2 O–O 11 ♔d3 ♕d6 12 h4 ♗d7 13 a3 ♕a6† 14 ♔d2 c5 15 h5 c×d4 16 e×d4 ♗g5† 17 ♔e1 ♗h6 18 ♕d3 ♕×d3 19 c×d3 ♖ac8 20 ♘f3 f6 21 ♔e2 ♗f4 22 a4 a6 23 a5 ♔h8 24 g3 ♗h6 25 ♘h2 f5 26 f4 ♗e8 27 ♘f3 ♗d7 28 ♘e5 ♗e8 29 ♔f2 ♔g8 30 ♔g2 ♖c7 31 ♔f2 ♖f6 32 ♖ac1 ♖f8 33 ♘×d5 ♖×c1 34 ♘e7† ♔h8 35 ♖×c1 ♗×h5 36 ♔g2 g6 37 ♔f2 ♔g7 38 ♖c7 ♔h8 39 ♖×b7 g5 40 f×g5 ♗g7 41 ♔e3 ♖e8 42 ♘7c6 ♖c8 43 ♘c4 ♖f8 44 ♔f2 f4 45 g×f4 ♖×f4† 46 ♔e3 ♖f3† 47 ♔e4 ♖f8 48 ♘6e5 ♗e8 49 ♘e3 ♗h5 50 b4 ♗e8 51 ♖e7 ♗b5 52 ♖×e6 ♖f2 53 ♘f3 ♗f8 54 ♖b6 ♗×b4 55 ♖b8† ♔g7 56 ♖b7† ♔g8 57 d5 ♗×a5 58 ♘d4 ♗e8 59 ♖b8 ♖f8 60 ♘df5 ♗c3 61 ♘h6† ♔h8 62 ♘hf5 a5 63 ♘c4 ♔g8 64 ♘h6† ♔h8 65 ♔e3 ♗e1 66 ♘d6 ♗f2† 67 ♔d2 ♗h4 68 ♘hf7† ♗×f7 69 ♖×f8† ♗g8 70 ♘e4 ♔g7 71 ♖d8 h6 72 g×h6† ♔h7 73 ♖d6 ♗f7 74 ♖d7 ♔g8 75 h7† ♔×h7 76 ♖×f7† ♔g6 77 ♖b7 ♔f5 78 d6 ♔f4 79 ♖b8 ♔e5 80 d7 ♔e6 81 ♘c5† ♔d6 82 d4 ♗g5† 83 ♔e2 ♔c7 84 ♖a8 ♔b6 85 ♔d3 ♗e7 86 ♖e8 ♗g5 87 ♔c2 ♔c7 88 ♖a8 ♔b6 89 ♖g8 ♗e7 90 ♖b8† ♔c6 91 d8♕ ♗×d8 92 ♖×d8 ♔c7 93 ♖a8 ♔c6 94 ♖g8 ♔b5 95 ♔b3 ♔c6 96 ♔c4 ♔c7 97 ♔b5 ♔d6 98 ♖g7 a4 99 ♖d7# **1–0**

Round 3

BLITZ 4 — ETAOIN SHRDLU 1 e4 e5 2 ♘f3 ♘c6 3 ♗b5 ♘f6 4 O–O ♘×e4 5 d4 e×d4 6 ♖e1 d5 7 ♘bd2 ♗g4 8 ♘×e4 d×e4 9 ♖×e4† ♗e6 10 ♘×d4 ♕d5 11 ♗×c6† b×c6 12 ♕e2 ♖d8 13 ♘×e6 f×e6 14 ♖×e6† ♔f7 15 ♖e3 ♕d1† 16 ♕e1 ♕×c2 17 ♖f3† ♔g6 18 ♕e6† ♔h5 19 ♖h3# **1–0**

CHESSTAR — CHUTE 1.2 1 d4 d5 2 h4 ♘f6 3 ♕d3 e6 4 ♗g5 ♗e7 5 ♘d2 ♘c6 6 a3 h6 7 ♗f4 ♘h5 8 e3 ♗×h4 9 ♗h2 a5 10 ♗e2 g6 11 ♖d1 ♘g7 12

♘gf3 ♘f5 13 ♘×h4 ♘×h4 14 ♗f4 ♘×g2† 15 ♔f1 ♘×f4 16 e×f4 ♕f6 17 ♘e4 d×e4 18 ♕×e4 h5 19 c4 O-O 20 b3 h4 21 d5 ♘e7 22 d6 c×d6 23 ♕d4 ♕×d4 24 ♖×d4 ♘f5 25 ♖d3 ♖e8 26 ♖hh3 a4 27 b4 e5 28 f×e5 ♖×e5 29 ♗f3 ♘g3† 30 ♔g2 ♗×h3† 31 ♔×h3 ♘e4 32 ♗×e4 ♖×e4 33 f3 ♖×c4 **0–1**

CHAOS — DUCHESS 1 d4 d5 2 c4 e6 3 ♘c3 ♘f6 4 ♗g5 ♗e7 5 e3 O-O 6 ♘f3 h6 7 ♗h4 ♘e4 8 ♗×e7 ♕×e7 9 c×d5 ♘×c3 10 b×c3 e×d5 11 ♕b3 ♕d6 12 c4 d×c4 13 ♗×c4 ♘c6 14 ♖c1 ♘a5 15 ♕c2 ♘×c4 16 ♕×c4 ♗g4 17 h3 ♗×f3 18 g×f3 ♖fc8 19 ♖g1 c6 20 f4 ♖e8 21 ♔d2 a6 22 a4 a5 23 ♖b1 ♖e7 24 h4 ♖c8 25 ♕c3 ♕d5 26 ♕b3 ♕×b3 27 ♖×b3 ♖d8 28 ♔c2 f5 29 h5 ♔h8 30 ♖gb1 ♖dd7 31 ♖g1 ♖d5 32 ♖g6 b5 33 ♖×c6 b4 34 ♖c4 ♖b7 35 ♔c1 ♖e7 36 ♖c8† ♔h7 37 ♖c6 ♔g8 38 ♖c8† ♔f7 39 ♖b2 ♖e8 40 ♖×e8 ♔×e8 41 ♖c2 ♔d7 42 ♔b2 ♔d6 43 ♔b3 ♔d7 44 ♖c1 ♔e8 45 ♖c6 ♔f7 46 ♖a6 ♔g8 47 ♔c4 b3 48 ♔×b3 ♔f7 49 ♔c4 ♖d8 50 ♖×a5 ♔f6 51 ♖a6† ♔f7 52 ♔b5 ♔g8 53 a5 ♔h8 54 ♖b6 ♖d5† 55 ♔b4 ♖d7 56 ♖b5 ♖f7 57 a6 ♖a7 58 ♔a5 ♖f7 59 ♖b7 ♖f8 60 a7 ♔h7 61 ♖b8 ♖f7 62 a8♕ ♖a7† 63 ♔b6 ♖×a8 64 ♖×a8 g6 65 ♖a7† ♔g8 66 h×g6 h5 67 ♖f7 h4 68 d5 h3 69 d6 h2 70 d7 h1♕ 71 d8♕# **1–0**

BLACK KNIGHT — CHESS 4.5 1 e4 c5 2 ♘f3 ♘c6 3 d4 c×d4 4 ♘×d4 ♘f6 5 ♘c3 d6 6 ♗g5 e6 7 ♕d2 ♗e7 8 O-O-O O-O 9 f4 ♘×d4 10 ♕×d4 h6 11 ♗h4 ♕a5 12 ♗c4 ♖d8 13 e5 d×e5 14 ♕×e5 ♕b4 15 ♗b3 ♗d7 16 ♖d4 ♕b6 17 h3 ♗c6 18 ♖×d8† ♖×d8 19 ♕e2 ♕d4 20 ♖f1 ♗b4 21 ♗e1 ♗c5 22 f5 ♕e3† 23 ♗d2 ♕×e2 24 ♘×e2 ♗×g2 25 ♖f4 ♗×h3 26 f×e6 ♗×e6 27 ♘c3 ♗×b3 28 a×b3 ♘d5 29 ♖g4 f5 30 ♖a4 ♘e3 31 ♖f4 g5 32 ♖a4 ♘f1 33 ♗e1 ♖e8 34 ♗d2 ♘×d2 35 ♔×d2 g4 36 ♔d1 g3 37 ♔d2 g2 38 ♘e2 ♖×e2† 39 ♔×e2 g1♕ 40 ♖c4 b6 41 ♔d2 b5 42 ♖×c5 ♕×c5 43 c3 ♕e5 44 ♔c2 f4 45 ♔b1 f3 46 b4 f2 47 ♔c1 f1♕† 48 ♔c2 ♕d5 49 b3 ♕dg2# **0–1**

WITA — L'EXCENTRIQUE 1 ♘f3 b6 2 d3 d5 3 ♗f4 e6 4 g3 ♕f6 5 ♗e5 ♕f5 6 ♗×c7 a5 7 ♗×b6 e5 8 ♗c7 ♘c6 9 ♘c3 ♗b4 10 ♘d2 ♕d7 11 ♗b6 ♖b8 12 ♘a4 ♕g4 13 c3 ♗e7 14 ♗g2 ♘f6 15 O-O O-O 16 f4 e4 17 d×e4 d×e4 18 ♘×e4 ♘×e4 19 ♗×e4 ♖×b6 20 ♘×b6 ♗c5† 21 ♔h1 ♗×b6 22 ♗×c6 ♕e6 23 ♗d5 ♕h3 24 ♕b3 ♗e6 25 ♗×e6 ♕×e6 26 ♕×e6 f×e6 27 ♔g2 a4 28 c4 ♖c8 29 b3 a3 30 ♖ad1 ♗e3 31 ♖d3 ♗c5 32 ♖d7 ♖f8 33 h3 g5 34 f×g5 ♖e8 35 e4 e5 36 ♖b7 ♖d8 37 b4 ♗e3 38 ♖ff7 ♖d2† 39 ♔f1 ♖×a2 40 ♖g7† ♔f8 41 ♖bf7† ♔e8 42 c5 ♗×g5 43 c6 ♖c2 44 c7 ♖c1† 45 ♔g2 a2 46 c8♕† ♖×c8 47 ♖a7 ♖c2† 48 ♔f3 ♖c3† 49 ♔g4 h5† 50 ♔×h5 ♗h6 51 ♖a8† ♖c8 52 ♖×c8# **1–0**

Round 4

L'EXCENTRIQUE — CHESSTAR 1 d4 e5 2 d×e5 ♘c6 3 e4 a5 4 ♕d5 h6 5 a4 ♕e7 6 h4 ♕b4† 7 c3 ♕b6 8 ♗c4 ♗c5 9 ♕×f7† ♔d8 10 ♕×g7 d6 11 ♕f8† **1–0**

BLITZ 4 — WITA 1 e4 c5 2 ♘f3 d6 3 d4 c×d4 4 ♘×d4 ♘f6 5 ♘c3 a6 6 ♗g5 e6 7 ♗c4 ♗e7 8 O-O ♕a5 9 ♘f3 ♕c5 10 ♕d4 ♘c6 11 ♕×c5 d×c5 12 e5 ♘g4 13 ♗×e7 ♔×e7 14 ♖ae1 ♖d8 15 h3 ♘h6 16 ♘g5 ♖d2 17 ♗d3 ♘b4 18 ♖d1 ♖×d1 19 ♖×d1 ♗d7 20 ♗e4 ♗c6 21 ♗×h7 ♖c8 22 ♖d6 ♘f5 23 ♖d2 f6 24 ♗×f5 e×f5 25 e×f6† g×f6 26 ♖e2† ♔f8 27 ♘e6† ♔f7 28 ♘×c5 ♖g8 29 a3 ♗×g2 30 a×b4 b6 31 ♔h2 ♗f3 32 ♖e3 ♗h5 33 ♘×a6 f4 34 ♖e1 ♗f3 35 ♖g1 ♖×g1 36 ♔×g1 ♔g7 37 ♘c7 f5 38 ♘7d5 ♗×d5 39 ♘×d5 f3 40 ♘×b6 ♔g6 41 ♘d7 ♔g5 42 c4 ♔h4 43 ♔h2 ♔g5 44 ♔g3 f4† 45 ♔×f3 ♔f5 46 ♘c5 ♔g5 **1–0**

DUCHESS — XENARBOR 4 1 e4 c5 2 d4 c×d4 3 c3 d×c3 4 ♘×c3 ♘c6 5 ♘f3 d6 6 ♗c4 e6 7 O-O ♘f6 8 ♕e2 ♗e7 9 ♖d1 e5 10 ♗e3 ♘g4 11 ♗c5 h5 12 ♘b5 ♘d4 13 ♘b×d4 d×c5 14 ♘f5 ♕c7 15 ♘×g7† ♔f8 16 ♘f5 ♗×f5 17 e×f5 ♖d8 18 ♖×d8† ♗×d8 19 ♖d1 ♗f6 20 h3 ♘h6 21 ♖d5 ♘×f5 22 ♘×e5 ♘d4 23 ♕e3 ♕e7 24 ♘d7† ♔g7 25 ♘×f6 ♕×f6 26 ♖d7 ♘f5 27 ♕×c5 ♔g6 28 ♖×b7 ♘d6 29 ♗d3† ♔g7 30 ♖×a7 ♖h6 31 ♖d7 h4 32 b4 ♕a1† 33 ♔h2 ♕f6 34 a4 ♔g8 35 b5 ♕f4† 36 ♔g1 ♕f6 37 b6 ♕a1† 38 ♗f1 ♕×a4 39 ♖×d6 ♖×d6 40 b7 ♖e6 41 b8♕† ♕e8 42 ♕g5† ♔f8 43 ♕b4† ♖d6 44 ♕×d6† ♕e7 45 ♕d×e7# **1–0**

CHESS 4.5 — CHAOS 1 e4 c5 2 ♘f3 ♘c6 3 d4 c×d4 4 ♘×d4 ♘f6 5 ♘c3 e6 6 ♘×c6 b×c6 7 e5 ♘d5 8 ♘×d5 c×d5 9 ♗d3 g6 10 O-O ♗g7 11 ♕e2 ♗b7 12 b3 ♕e7 13 a4 ♕b4 14 ♗a3 ♕c3 15 f4 f6 16 ♗d6 f5 17 a5 ♔f7 18 ♕f2 ♗f8 19 ♗×f8 ♖h×f8 20 ♕h4 ♕c5† 21 ♔h1 ♔g7 22 b4 ♕×b4 23 ♖ab1 ♕×a5 24 ♖×b7 ♕a4 25 ♗b5 **1–0**

CHUTE 1.2 — BLACK KNIGHT 1 e4 e5 2 ♘f3 f5 3 e×f5 e4 4 ♘d4 ♕f6 5 ♘b5 ♘a6 6 ♕h5† ♔d8 7 ♘5c3 g6 8 f×g6 ♘b4 9 ♘a3 h×g6 10 ♕e2 d5 11 h3 ♗d6 12 ♘cb5 ♗f4 13 g3 ♗e5 14 ♘c3 ♘e7 15 ♕b5 ♕d6 16 d3 ♗d7 17 ♕×b7 ♗c6 18 ♕×a8† ♗×a8 19 d×e4 ♗×c3† 20 b×c3 ♕e6 21 c×b4 ♕×e4† 22 ♗e3 ♕×h1 23 h4 ♘f5 24 ♗g5† ♔d7 25 ♔d2 ♕f3 26 ♗e3 d4 27 ♗b5† c6 28 ♗×d4 ♘×d4 29 ♗d3 ♘b3† 30 a×b3 ♕×f2† 31 ♔c1 ♕×g3 32 ♘c4 ♔d8 33 ♔b2 ♕×h4 34 ♖d1 ♕d4† 35 ♔a3 ♔e7 36 ♖e1† ♔f6 37 ♘e5 c5 38 b×c5 ♕×c5† 39 ♔b2 ♕d4† 40 c3 ♖h2† 41 ♔b1 ♕×c3 42 ♘g4† ♔g5 43 ♘×h2 ♕×e1† 44 ♔c2 ♕f2† 45 ♔b1 ♕d2 46 ♗×g6 ♔×g6 47 ♘f1 ♗e4† 48 ♔a1 ♕c1† 49 ♔a2 ♗b1† 50 ♔a1 ♕c2 51 b4 ♕a2# **0–1**

ACM 1977 — Seattle

October 15 — October 17

		1	2	3	4	tot
1	CHESS 4.6	8+□	4+■	3+□	2=■	3½
2	DUCHESS	5+■	6+□	7+■	1=□	3½
3	CHAOS	10+□	9+■	1−■	5+□	3
4	XENARBOR	11+□	1−□	6+■	8=■	2½
5	BLITZ 5	2−□	8+■	9+□	3−■	2
6	BLACK KNIGHT	12+□	2−■	4−□	11+■	2
7	OSTRICH	9−■	12+□	2−□	10+■	2
8	CHUTE 1.2	1−■	5−□	10+■	4=□	1½
9	8080 CHESS	7+□	3−□	5−■	12−■	1
10	TYRO	3−■	11+■	8−□	7−□	1
11	WITA	4−■	10−□	12+■	6−□	1
12	BRUTE FORCE	6−■	7−■	11−□	9+□	1

Round 1

CHAOS — TYRO 1 d4 d5 2 c4 e6 3 ♘c3 ♘f6 4 ♗g5 h6 5 ♗×f6 g×f6 6 c×d5 e×d5 7 ♘f3 ♗b4 8 g3 O-O 9 ♗g2 ♗×c3† 10 b×c3 ♖e8 11 ♕d2 ♔g7 12 O-O ♗f5 13 ♕b2 b6 14 ♘h4 ♕d7 15 ♘×f5† ♕×f5 16 c4 c6 17 c×d5 c×d5 18 ♕b5 ♖d8 19 e4 ♕d7 20 ♕×d5 ♘c6 21 ♕×d7 ♖×d7 22 e5 ♖c8 23 ♗h3 ♖cc7 24 e×f6† ♔×f6 25 ♗×d7 ♖×d7 26 ♖ac1 ♘×d4 27 ♔g2 ♘e2 28 ♖fd1 ♘×c1 29 ♖×d7 ♘×a2 30 ♖×a7 ♘b4 31 ♔f3 ♘d5 32 ♔e2 b5 33 ♔d3 ♘e7 34 ♖b7 ♘g6 35 ♖×b5 ♘e5† 36 ♔e4 ♘g4 37 f3 ♘×h2 38 ♖b1 ♔e6 39 ♖h1 f5† 40 ♔f4 ♘×f3 41 ♖×h6† ♔f7 42 ♔×f3 ♔g7 43 ♖b6 ♔f7 44 ♔f4 ♔e7 45 ♔×f5 ♔d7 46 ♔f6 ♔c7 47 ♖e6 ♔d7 48 g4 ♔c7 49 g5 ♔d7 50 g6 ♔c7 51 g7 ♔d7 52 g8♕ ♔c7 53 ♕f7† ♔d8 54 ♖e8# **1–0**

BLACK KNIGHT — BRUTE FORCE 1 e4 d5 2 e×d5 ♕×d5 3 ♘c3 ♕e6† 4 ♘ge2 ♗d7 5 d4 ♘a6 6 ♗g5 h6 7 ♗e3 ♕b6 8 ♕b1 g5 9 h4 g×h4 10 d5 ♕b4 11 ♗d4 e5 12 d×e6 f6 13 a3 ♕e7 14 e×d7† ♔d8 15 ♕a2 c5 16 O-O-O c×d4 17 ♘×d4 ♘c5 18 ♗c4 ♕g7 19 ♘e4 ♕×g2 20 ♘×c5 ♕g5† 21 ♖d2 ♕×d2† 22 ♔×d2 ♗×c5 23 ♘e6† ♔×d7 24 ♘×c5† ♔c7 25 ♗d5 ♘e7 26 ♗×b7 ♖ad8† 27 ♔c3 ♖b8 28 ♕e6 ♘g8 29 ♕c6† ♔d8 30 ♕d7# **1–0**

XENARBOR — WITA 1 d4 ♘f6 2 c4 g6 3 ♘c3 ♗g7 4 e4 e6 5 ♘f3 d6 6 g3 ♘c6 7 ♗g2 h6 8 O-O O-O 9 d5 e×d5 10 c×d5 ♘b8 11 ♗e3 ♖e8 12 ♕c2 ♕e7 13 ♖fd1 ♘×e4 14 ♘×e4 ♕×e4 15 ♕×c7 ♗×b2 16 ♖ab1 ♘a6 17 ♕×d6 ♗g7 18 ♘d4 ♗e5 19 ♗×e4 ♗×d6 20 ♗g2 ♗f8 21 ♖dc1 ♗c5 22 a4 f6 23 a5 ♖b8 24 ♖×c5 ♘×c5 25 ♘c6 ♗f5 26 ♖b5 a6 27 ♖b6 b×c6 28 d×c6 ♖×b6 29 a×b6 ♖e5 30 c7 h5 31 h4 a5 32 ♗f1 a4 33 ♗d4 a3 34 ♗×e5 f×e5 35 ♗c4† ♔f8 36 ♔h2 ♔e7 37 f3 ♗c8 38 f4 e×f4 39 g×f4 ♘d7 40 ♗b3 ♗b7 41 ♗a2 ♔f6 42 ♗b3 ♔g7 43 f5 g×f5 44 ♗d5 ♗c8 45 b7 a2 46 b×c8♕ ♘f6 47 ♗×a2 f4 48 ♕f5 f3 49 ♕g5† **1–0**

8080 CHESS — OSTRICH 1 e4 e5 2 d4 ♘f6 3 d×e5 ♘×e4 4 ♘f3 ♗c5 5 ♘d4 ♘c6 6 ♘×c6 ♗×f2† 7 ♔e2 d×c6 8 ♕×d8† ♔×d8 9 ♗f4 ♗d4 10 c3 ♗g4† 11 ♔d3 ♘f2† 12 ♔×d4 ♘×h1 13 ♗c4 ♗e6 14 ♗d3 ♔c8 15 ♘d2 ♖d8† 16 ♔e3 ♘f2 17 ♗×h7 ♘g4† 18 ♔e2 ♖h8 19 ♗e4 ♘×h2 20 b4 ♖h4 21 g3 ♖h5 22 a4 ♗d5 23 ♗d3 ♘g4 24 c4 ♗g2 25 ♖g1 ♗h3 26 ♘f3 a5 27 b×a5 ♖×a5 28 ♘d4 ♘×e5 29 ♗×e5 ♖h×e5† 30 ♔f3 c5 31 ♘e2 ♖×a4 32 ♘f4 ♗e6 33 ♖c1 g5 34 ♘e2 ♖a2 35 ♖c3 ♗f5 36 ♘c1 ♖d2 37 ♗e2 ♖e4 38 ♗d3 **1–0**

CHESS 4.6 — CHUTE 1.2 1 e4 e5 2 ♘f3 ♘c6 3 ♗b5 ♘ge7 4 d4 e×d4 5 ♘×d4 ♘×d4 6 ♕×d4 a6 7 ♗e2 ♘c6 8 ♕c4 ♗d6 9 ♗e3 O-O 10 ♘c3 b5 11 ♕d5 ♗b7 12 O-O ♕e8 13 a3 ♕e6 14 f4 ♖ae8 15 ♕×e6 f×e6 16 ♖ad1 e5 17 f5 ♘e7 18 b3 ♖f6 19 b4 ♖a8 20 ♗g5 ♖f7 21 ♗h5 g6 22 ♗×e7 ♗×e7 23 f×g6 ♖×f1† 24 ♔×f1 ♖f8† 25 ♔e1 ♗h4† 26 g3 ♗×g3† 27 h×g3 h×g6 28 ♗×g6 ♖f3 29 ♖d3 ♖×d3 30 c×d3 ♔g7 31 ♗f5 d6 32 ♘d5 c6 33 ♘b6 ♔h8 34 ♘c8 d5 35 ♘d6 ♗a8 36 e×d5 c×d5 37 ♗c8 e4 38 ♗×a6 ♗c6 39 ♗×b5 ♗×b5 40 ♘×b5 e×d3 41 a4 ♔g7 42 a5 ♔h6 43 a6 ♔h5 44 a7 d2† 45 ♔×d2 ♔g4 46 a8♕ ♔×g3 47 ♘a3 d4 48 b5 ♔f2 49 b6 ♔g3 50 ♕e4 ♔f2 51 b7 ♔g1 52 b8♕ ♔f2 53 ♕e1† ♔g2 54 ♕bg3# **1–0**

BLITZ 5 — DUCHESS 1 e4 e5 2 ♘f3 ♘c6 3 ♗b5 a6 4 ♗×c6 d×c6 5 d4 e×d4 6 ♕×d4 ♕×d4 7 ♘×d4 ♗d7 8 ♗e3 O-O-O 9 ♘c3 ♗d6 10 O-O-O ♘f6 11 ♖d3 ♘g4 12 g3 ♘×e3 13 ♖×e3 ♗c5 14 ♖d3 ♗g4 15 f3 ♗h5 16 ♘ce2 ♗×d4 17 ♘×d4 c5 18 ♘f5 ♖×d3 19 c×d3 ♗×f3 20 ♖f1 ♗e2 21 ♘e7† ♔d8 22 ♖×f7 ♗×d3 23 ♘d5 ♗×e4 24 ♘×c7 ♖g8 25 ♘e6† ♔e8 26 ♖×g7 ♖×g7 27 ♘×g7† ♔e7 28 ♘h5 ♔d6 29 ♘f4 c4 30 ♔d2 ♗b1 31 a3 b5 32 g4 ♔e5 33 ♘e2 ♗d3 34 h4 ♗×e2 35 ♔×e2 ♔f4 36 g5 ♔g4 37 ♔e3 ♔×h4 38 ♔f4 a5 39 ♔f5 b4 40 a×b4 a×b4 41 g6 h×g6† 42 ♔e4 g5 43 ♔d4 g4 44 ♔×c4 g3 45 ♔×b4 ♔g5 46 ♔a5 g2 47 b4 g1♕ 48 b5 ♕a7† 49 ♔b4 ♔f5 50 ♔c4 ♔e5 51 ♔b4 **0–1**

Round 2

8080 CHESS — CHAOS 1 e4 c5 2 d4 c×d4 3 ♕×d4 ♘c6 4 ♕d5 ♘f6 5 ♕d3 e5 6 ♘f3 ♗c5 7 ♗g5 ♕b6 8 ♗×f6 ♗×f2† 9 ♔d2 ♕×b2 10 ♗×g7 ♖g8 11 ♕c3 ♕×c3† 12 ♔×c3 ♖×g7 13 ♘bd2 d6 14 ♘c4 ♗c5 15 h4 ♗e6 16 ♘b2 ♖g4 **0–1**

WITA — TYRO 1 d4 d5 2 c4 e6 3 e4 d×e4 4 ♘c3 ♗b4 5 a3 ♗×c3† 6 b×c3 ♘f6 7 ♖b1 O-O 8 ♗e2 b6 9 ♗f4 c6 10 ♘h3 ♕e7 11 ♕a4 ♘fd7 12 O-O ♗a6 13 ♗×b8 ♘×b8 14 ♖fd1 f5 15 ♔h1 e5 16 d×e5 ♕×e5 17 ♕b3 ♔h8 18 ♘g5 ♕f6 19 ♘h3 ♖d8 20 ♖×d8† ♕×d8 21 ♘f4 ♕h4 22 g3 ♕f6 23 ♖d1 ♗c8 24 ♘h5 ♕e7 25 h3 g6 26 c5 g×h5 27 c×b6 a×b6 28 f4 b5 29 ♗×h5 ♗e6 30 ♕b4 ♕×b4 31 c×b4 ♗d5 32 g4 f×g4 33 ♔h2 g×h3 34 f5 ♖×a3 35 ♗g4 ♖a2† 36 ♔×h3 ♘d7 37 ♗h5 ♘f6 38 ♔h4 ♖h2† 39 ♔g5 ♘×h5 40 f6 ♔g8 41 ♖g1 ♔f7 42 ♖a1 ♘×f6 43 ♔f5 ♖f2† 44 ♔g5 h5 45 ♔h6 ♖g2 46 ♖a7† ♔e6 47 ♖a1 e3 48 ♖a6 ♔f5 49 ♖a2 ♖g6# **0–1**

CHUTE 1.2 — BLITZ 5 1 e4 e5 2 ♘f3 ♘f6 3 ♘×e5 d6 4 ♘f3 ♘×e4 5 ♕e2 ♕e7 6 d3 ♘f6 7 ♗g5 ♘bd7 8 ♕×e7† ♗×e7 9 ♗e2 O-O 10 O-O h6 11 ♗d2 ♘b6 12 ♗a5 ♗e6 13 ♘c3 ♖fe8 14 ♗×b6 a×b6 15 ♘d4 ♗d5 16 ♘×d5 ♘×d5 17 ♗f3 c6 18 ♗×d5 c×d5 19 ♘f5 ♖ac8 20 ♖ae1 ♗f8 21 ♖×e8 ♖×e8 22 d4 ♖e2 23 ♘e3 ♖d2 24 ♘×d5 ♖×c2 25 ♖b1 ♖d2 26 ♘×b6 ♖×d4 27

♘d7 ♖d2 28 ♔f1 d5 29 ♔e1 ♖c2 30 ♘×f8 ♔×f8 31 ♖d1 ♖×b2 32 a4 ♖a2 33 ♖×d5 ♖×a4 34 ♖d8† ♔e7 35 ♖d3 b5 36 ♖e3† ♔d6 37 ♖d3† ♔c6 38 ♖c3† ♔b6 39 ♖c1 ♖e4† 40 ♔d2 b4 41 f3 ♖e5 42 ♖c4 ♖b5 43 g3 b3 44 ♖c8 ♔b7 45 ♖f8 b2 46 ♖×f7† ♔b6 47 ♖×g7 b1♕ 48 ♖d7 ♕a2† 49 ♔d3 **0–1**

DUCHESS — BLACK KNIGHT 1 e4 c5 2 d4 c×d4 3 c3 d×c3 4 ♘×c3 ♘c6 5 ♘f3 d6 6 ♗c4 e6 7 O-O ♘f6 8 ♕e2 ♗e7 9 ♖d1 e5 10 ♗e3 ♘g4 11 ♗d2 ♗h4 12 ♗e1 ♗e7 13 ♗d2 ♗e6 14 ♗×e6 f×e6 15 ♘g5 ♗×g5 16 ♕×g4 ♗×d2 17 ♕×g7 ♖f8 18 ♕×b7 ♕b6 19 ♕×a8† ♔e7 20 ♕×f8† ♔×f8 21 ♖×d2 ♕c7 22 ♖ad1 ♘d4 23 f4 ♕g7 24 ♖d3 h5 25 ♔h1 a6 26 f×e5 d×e5 27 ♖f1† ♔e8 28 ♖g3 ♕e7 29 ♖g8† ♔d7 30 ♖a8 ♔c6 31 ♖×a6† ♔b7 32 ♖a4 ♔c6 33 ♖a5 ♕b4 34 ♖×e5 ♕×b2 35 ♖c5† ♔d6 36 e5† ♔e7 37 ♖b1 ♕f2 38 ♖c7† ♔d8 39 ♖h7 ♘c6 40 ♖h8† ♔c7 41 ♘b5† ♔d7 42 ♖h7† ♔d8 43 ♘d6 ♕f8 44 ♔g1 h4 45 ♖bb7 ♘e7 46 ♖b8† ♔c7 47 ♖×f8 h3 48 ♖×e7† ♔c6 49 g×h3 ♔d5 50 ♘f7 ♔d4 51 ♖×e6 ♔d5 52 ♖d6† ♔e4 53 ♖c8 ♔f3 54 ♖c4 ♔e2 55 ♖e4† ♔f3 56 ♘g5# **1–0**

OSTRICH — BRUTE FORCE 1 e4 d5 2 e×d5 ♕×d5 3 ♘c3 ♕e5† 4 ♘ge2 a5 5 d4 ♕f5 6 ♗e3 g5 7 ♘g3 ♕g6 8 ♗d3 f5 9 O-O ♘f6 10 ♘b5 ♔d8 11 d5 g4 12 ♗d4 e6 13 d×e6 ♗b4 14 ♗×f5 ♔e7 15 ♗×g6 h×g6 16 ♗×f6† ♔×f6 17 ♕d4† ♔e7 18 ♕g7† ♔×e6 19 ♘×c7† ♔d6 20 ♘×a8 ♖e8 21 ♕c7† ♔e6 22 ♖fe1† ♗×e1 23 ♖×e1† ♔f6 24 ♖×e8 ♗d7 25 ♕e5† ♔f7 26 ♕e7# **1–0**

XENARBOR — CHESS 4.6 1 d4 ♘f6 2 c4 c5 3 d5 e6 4 ♘f3 e×d5 5 c×d5 d6 6 e3 ♗f5 7 ♘c3 ♘bd7 8 g3 ♘e5 9 ♘×e5 d×e5 10 ♕b3 ♕b6 11 ♕×b6 a×b6 12 ♗g2 ♗d3 13 e4 ♗d6 14 ♗e3 O-O 15 O-O-O ♗c4 16 b3 ♗a6 17 ♘a4 ♗b5 18 ♘×b6 ♖a6 19 a4 ♗e2 20 ♖d2 ♖×b6 21 ♖×e2 ♖×b3 22 ♖c2 ♖c8 23 ♗h3 ♖a8 24 ♖c4 b5 25 ♖c2 ♖×a4 26 ♗g2 c4 27 h4 c3 28 ♖e2 ♘×e4 29 ♗×e4 ♖×e4 30 ♖a2 ♖a3 31 ♖×a3 ♗×a3† 32 ♔c2 ♗b4 33 ♖a1 f5 34 ♖a8† ♔f7 35 ♖b8 f4 36 ♔d3 f×e3 37 f×e3 ♖c4 38 ♖×b5 c2 39 ♔×c4 ♗e7 40 e4 c1♕† 41 ♔d3 ♕f1† 42 ♔e3 ♕×b5 43 g4 ♗×h4 44 ♔d2 ♕c4 45 d6 ♕×e4 46 g5 ♗×g5† 47 ♔c3 h5 48 ♔b3 h4 49 ♔a2 ♕b4 50 ♔a1 ♗c1 51 ♔a2 ♕b2# **0–1**

Round 3

CHESS 4.6 — CHAOS 1 e4 c5 2 ♘f3 ♘c6 3 ♗b5 ♘f6 4 e5 ♘d5 5 O-O e6 6 ♗×c6 d×c6 7 d3 ♗e7 8 ♘a3 O-O 9 ♗d2 ♗d7 10 ♕e2 ♕b6 11 ♘c4 ♕d8 12 ♘d6 ♕b6 13 c4 ♕×b2 14 c×d5 c×d5 15 ♖fb1 ♕a3 16 ♖×b7 ♕a4 17 ♖c1 ♖ab8 18 ♖c7 ♖b2 19 ♖7×c5 ♖fb8 20 ♕e3 ♕×a2 21 ♖c7 ♗×d6 22 ♖×d7 ♗a3 23 ♕f4 f5 24 e×f6 ♗f8 25 f×g7 ♗e7 26 ♖×e7 h6 27 ♕f7† ♔h7 28 g8♕# **1–0**

TYRO — CHUTE 1.2 1 d4 d5 2 c4 e6 3 g3 d×c4 4 ♘f3 ♘c6 5 a3 ♘f6 6 ♘c3 a6 7 e4 b5 8 ♗f4 ♘h5 9 ♗h3 ♘×f4 10 g×f4 ♕f6 11 ♕d2 ♕h6 12 ♘g5 ♘d8 13 d5 ♗e7 14 ♗g4 f5 15 e×f5 e×f5 16 ♗f3 ♗b7 17 O-O ♕b6 18 ♖ae1 h6 19 ♕e3 ♕f6 20 ♘e6 ♖c8 21 ♘×d8 ♔×d8 22 ♗h5 g5 23 ♔h1 g×f4 24 ♕×f4 ♗d6 25 ♕f3 ♖g8 26 ♖g1 ♖×g1† 27 ♖×g1 ♕e5 28 ♕g2 ♔d7 29 ♖d1 ♗c5 30 ♖d2 ♕e1† 31 ♕g1 ♕×d2 32 ♕g7† ♗e7 33 ♕e5 ♕×f2 34 ♕e6† ♔d8 35 ♕×h6 ♕f1# **0–1**

BLACK KNIGHT — XENARBOR 1 e4 c5 2 ♘f3 ♘c6 3 ♘c3 d6 4 d4 c×d4 5 ♘×d4 ♘×d4 6 ♕×d4 ♘f6 7 e5 d×e5 8 ♕×e5 a6 9 ♗e2 ♕d6 10 ♕×d6 e×d6 11 ♗g5 ♗e6 12 ♗×f6 g×f6 13 ♗f3 O-O-O 14 O-O-O ♗h6† 15 ♔b1 ♗g7 16 ♖d3 f5 17 ♖hd1 ♗e5 18 ♗d5 ♗×d5 19 ♘×d5 ♗×h2 20 ♖h3 ♗e5 21 f4 h5 22 f×e5 d×e5 23 ♖f3 f4 24 g3 f×g3 25 ♖×g3 h4 26 ♖g7 f5 27 ♘b6† ♔b8 28 ♖dd7 ♖×d7 29 ♘×d7† ♔a7 30 ♘×e5 ♖e8 31 ♘c6† ♔a8 32 ♘e7 f4 33 ♖g8 ♖×g8 34 c4 ♖g1† 35 ♔c2 f3 36 ♘c8 ♔b8 37 ♘b6 f2 38 ♘d7† ♔a7 39 ♘e5 f1♕ 40 ♔c3 h3 41 c5 h2 42 a4 h1♕ 43 b4 ♕a1† 44 ♔d3 ♕×e5 45 a5 ♕he4† 46 ♔d2 ♕5d4# **0–1**

BLITZ 5 — 8080 CHESS 1 e4 e5 2 ♘f3 d5 3 ♘×e5 d×e4 4 ♗c4 ♘h6 5 O-O ♘c6 6 ♘×c6 b×c6 7 ♕e2 ♗f5 8 d3 ♗c5 9 ♗×h6 g×h6 10 ♕h5 ♕f6 11 d×e4 ♕×b2 12 ♕×f7† ♔d8 13 ♕×f5 ♗×f2† 14 ♕×f2 ♕×a1 15 ♕h4† ♔d7 16 ♖d1† ♔e8 17 ♕h5† **1–0**

OSTRICH — DUCHESS 1 e4 e5 2 ♘f3 ♘f6 3 ♗c4 ♘×e4 4 ♕e2 d5 5 ♘×e5 ♗e6 6 O-O ♗d6 7 ♘f3 O-O 8 d3 d×c4 9 d×e4 ♘c6 10 ♘g5 ♘d4 11 ♕h5 h6 12 ♘×e6 f×e6 13 ♕d1 c5 14 c3 ♘c6 15 ♘a3 ♕b8 16 h4 ♘e5 17 ♗e3 ♗e7 18 f4 ♘d3 19 ♘×c4 ♘×f4 20 g3 ♘g6 21 ♕g4 ♔h7 22 h5 ♘e5 23 ♖×f8 ♘×g4 24 ♖×b8 ♖×b8 25 ♗f4 ♖d8 26 ♘e5 ♘×e5 27 ♗×e5 ♗f6 28 ♗×f6 g×f6 29 ♖f1 ♔g7 30 ♔g2 ♔f7 31 ♔f3 ♖d3† 32 ♔g4 ♖d2 33 ♖b1 ♖f2 34 a4 ♔e7 35 b4 c4 36 ♖e1 ♖c2 37 ♖e3 b6 38 a5 b×a5 39 b×a5 ♔d6 40 ♔f4 ♖a2 41 ♖f3 ♖×a5 42 ♔e3 ♔e5 43 ♖f2 ♖a1 44 ♖c2 ♖e1† 45 ♔d2 ♖×e4 46 ♖c1 ♖g4 47 ♖e1† ♔d5 **0–1**

BRUTE FORCE — WITA 1 d4 ♘f6 2 ♘c3 ♘c6 3 d5 ♘×d5 4 ♕×d5 d6 5 a3 e6 6 ♕d2 ♗e7 7 b4 ♗f6 8 b5 ♘e5 9 f4 ♘g4 10 ♘f3 c6 11 b×c6 b×c6 12 h3 ♗h4† 13 ♔d1 ♘f2† 14 ♔e1 ♘×h1† 15 g3 ♘×g3 16 ♕d3 ♕f6 17 ♘×h4 ♕×h4 18 ♕f3 d5 19 ♕g4 ♕×g4 20 h×g4 ♘×f1 21 ♔×f1 a6 22 ♗e3 e5 23 f×e5 ♗×g4 24 a4 h5 25 a5 h4 26 ♖a4 ♗e6 27 ♗f2 h3 28 e3 h2 29 ♗g3 h1♕† 30 ♔e2 ♕c1 31 ♔d3 ♖b8 32 e4 ♖b2 33 ♖a3 ♖×c2 34 ♘a2 ♕d2# **0–1**

Round 4

DUCHESS — CHESS 4.6 1 e4 c5 2 d4 c×d4 3 c3 d×c3 4 ♘×c3 ♘c6 5 ♘f3 d6 6 ♗c4 e6 7 O-O ♘f6 8 ♕e2 ♗e7 9 ♖d1 e5 10 ♗e3 ♘g4 11 ♗d2 ♘d4 12 ♘×d4 e×d4 13 ♘b5 ♕b6 14 ♗f4 ♘e5 15 ♘×d4 ♘×c4 16 ♕×c4 ♗g4 17 ♕a4† ♗d7 18 ♕b3 O-O 19 ♕×b6 a×b6 20 a3 ♖fc8 21 ♖ac1 ♖×c1 22 ♖×c1 ♖a4 23 ♗e3 ♗d8 24 f3 ♖a5 25 ♖d1 ♗f6 26 ♖d2 ♖c5 27 ♘e2 ♖c6 28 a4 ♗e6 29 ♘d4 ♖c1† 30 ♔f2 ♗d7 31 ♘b5 ♗×b5 32 a×b5 ♖b1 33 ♗×b6 ♖×b2 34 ♖×b2 ♗×b2 35 ♔e3 ♔f8 36 ♗d4 ♗×d4† 37 ♔×d4 ♔e8 38 ♔d5 ♔d7 39 b6 g6 40 f4 ♔e7 41 h3 f6 42 h4 ♔d7 43 g4 h6 44 h5 g×h5 45 g×h5 ♔e7 46 ♔d4 ♔e6 47 ♔c4 ♔e7 48 f5 ♔d8 49 ♔b4 ♔d7 50 ♔b5 ♔e8 51 ♔a4 ♔e7 52 ♔b4 ♔d8 53 ♔c4 ♔e8 54 ♔d4 ♔d7 55

♔d5 ♔e7 56 ♔d4 ♔e8 57 ♔c4 ♔f7 58 ♔d3 ½–½

CHAOS — BLITZ 5 1 d4 d5 2 c4 e6 3 ♘c3 ♘f6 4 ♗g5 ♗e7 5 e3 O-O 6 ♘f3 h6 7 ♗h4 ♘e4 8 ♗×e7 ♕×e7 9 c×d5 ♘×c3 10 b×c3 e×d5 11 ♕b3 ♖d8 12 ♗d3 ♘c6 13 O-O ♖d6 14 ♖fc1 b6 15 c4 d×c4 16 ♕×c4 ♗g4 17 ♘d2 ♖ad8 18 ♗e4 ♗d7 19 ♖ab1 a5 20 ♗d5 ♘b4 21 ♗×f7† ♕×f7 22 ♕×c7 ♗e6 23 a3 ♕×c7 24 ♖×c7 ♘d5 25 ♖cc1 ♖c8 26 ♖×c8† ♗×c8 27 ♖c1 ♗b7 28 g3 b5 29 ♘b3 a4 30 ♘c5 ♗c6 31 e4 ♘b6 32 d5 ♗e8 33 ♘b7 ♖d7 34 ♘c5 ♖c7 35 ♖c3 ♗g6 36 f4 ♘c4 37 ♘a6 ♖e7 38 e5 ♗e4 39 d6 ♖f7 40 ♘c7 ♗c6 41 e6 ♖f8 42 e7 ♖c8 43 ♖d3 ♗d7 44 ♘a6 ♔f7 45 ♔f2 ♔e8 46 ♘c7† ♖×c7 47 d×c7 ♔×e7 48 ♔f3 ♗f5 49 ♖d5 ♗g4† 50 ♔×g4 ♘d6 51 ♖×d6 **1–0**

CHUTE 1.2 — XENARBOR 1 e4 c5 2 c4 ♘c6 3 ♘f3 e5 4 ♘c3 ♘f6 5 ♗e2 d6 6 O-O g6 7 d3 ♗g7 8 ♗g5 ♘d4 9 ♘×d4 c×d4 10 ♘d5 h6 11 ♘×f6† ♗×f6 12 ♗×f6 ♕×f6 13 ♕a4† ♗d7 14 ♕a5 b6 15 ♕d5 ♖b8 16 ♖ac1 a5 17 b3 h5 18 ♗f3 h4 19 a4 h3 20 ♖fe1 ♖c8 21 ♕b7 ♕d8 22 ♕a7 ♗c6 23 g×h3 ♖a8 24 ♕×a8 ♕×a8 25 ♗g4 g5 26 ♖c2 ♕d8 27 ♖ce2 ♕e7 28 f3 ♕f6 29 ♔g2 ♕f4 30 ♗f5 O-O 31 ♗g4 f6 32 ♗e6† ♔h8 33 ♗f5 ♖g8 34 ♗g4 ♖e8 35 ♗h5 ♖g8 36 ♗g4 ♖g7 37 ♗c8 ♖h7 38 ♗f5 ♖h4 39 ♗g4 ♖h7 40 ♗f5 ♖h6 41 ♗g4 ♖h4 42 ♗f5 ♖h5 43 ♗g4 ♖h6 44 ♗e6 ♖h7 45 ♗f5 ♖g7 46 ♗g4 ½–½

TYRO — OSTRICH 1 d4 d5 2 c4 d×c4 3 e4 ♘c6 4 d5 ♘e5 5 f4 ♗g4 6 ♘f3 ♗×f3 7 g×f3 ♘d3† 8 ♗×d3 c×d3 9 ♕×d3 c6 10 ♔e2 ♕d7 11 d×c6 ♕×d3† 12 ♔×d3 O-O-O† 13 ♔e2 b×c6 14 ♖d1 ♖d6 15 ♗e3 ♖h6 16 ♗×a7 ♖×h2† 17 ♗f2 h5 18 b3 ♖h6 19 a4 ♖f6 20 ♔e3 ♖h3 21 b4 e5 22 f×e5 ♖f×f3† 23 ♔e2 ♗×b4 24 ♗b6 ♘e7 25 ♖d4 ♖e3† 26 ♔f2 ♗e1† 27 ♔f1 ♖hf3† 28 ♔g1 ♖e2 29 ♖d8† ♔b7 30 ♗d4 ♖×e4 31 ♖d7† ♔c8 32 ♖×e7 ♖g4† 33 ♔h2 ♖×d4 34 ♔g2 ♖f2† 35 ♔g3 ♖d3† 36 ♔h4 ♖f5# **0–1**

WITA — BLACK KNIGHT 1 e4 c5 2 ♘f3 ♘c6 3 d4 c×d4 4 ♘×d4 ♘f6 5 ♘c3 d6 6 h3 a6 7 g4 ♘×d4 8 ♕×d4 e5 9 ♕d3 ♗e6 10 ♗g2 ♗e7 11 ♗e3 ♖c8 12 ♕d2 h5 13 g5 ♘d7 14 ♘d5 ♗×d5 15 e×d5 ♖c4 16 ♕e2 b5 17 b3 ♖h4 18 f4 O-O 19 O-O e×f4 20 ♗f2 f3 21 ♕×f3 ♗×g5 22 ♗×h4 ♗×h4 23 ♕×h5 ♗f6 24 ♖ae1 ♗c3 25 a3 ♕b6† 26 ♔h2 ♘f6 27 ♕d1 ♗×e1 28 ♖×e1 ♖c8 29 ♖e2 ♖c3 30 ♕d2 ♕a5 31 ♖e3 ♖×b3 32 ♕×a5 ♖×e3 33 a4 ♖e2 34 ♕×a6 ♖×c2 35 ♕a8† ♔h7 36 a×b5 ♖b2 37 ♕c6 ♘e4 38 ♕e8 ♘g5 39 ♕e7 ♔h6 40 b6 f5 41 ♕e3 ♔g6 42 h4 ♘e4 43 ♔g1 ♖b1† 44 ♕e1 ♖×e1† 45 ♔h2 ♖b1 46 ♗f1 ♖×f1 47 b7 ♖b1 48 b8♕ ♖×b8 49 ♔g1 ♘c3 50 h5† ♔×h5 51 ♔h2 g5 52 ♔g3 g4 53 ♔g2 f4 54 ♔f2 ♖b1 55 ♔g2 ♘e4 56 ♔h2 ♔h4 57 ♔g2 f3† 58 ♔h2 g3# **0–1**

BRUTE FORCE — 8080 CHESS 1 d4 d5 2 ♘c3 ♘c6 3 ♗f4 ♘f6 4 ♘b5 e5 5 ♗×e5 ♗b4† 6 c3 ♘×e5 7 d×e5 ♗×c3† 8 ♘×c3 ♘e4 9 ♘×e4 d×e4 10 ♕a4† ♗d7 11 ♕×e4 b5 12 g4 O-O 13 ♗g2 c6 14 h4 a5 15 O-O-O ♖a6 16 ♕d4 f5 17 ♕×d7 ♕×d7 18 ♖×d7 f×g4 19 ♖d6 ♖×f2 20 ♗×c6 ♖f5 21 ♗d5† ♔f8 22 ♖×a6 ♖×e5 23 e4 a4 24 ♖b6 g5 25 h×g5 ♔g7 26 ♖b7† ♔g6 27 ♖h×h7 ♔×g5 28 ♖×b5 ♔f4 29 ♖a5 a3 30 ♖f7† ♔e3 31 ♖×a3† ♔d4 32 ♖g7 ♔c5 33 ♖×g4 ♔d6 34 ♖a6† ♔c5 35 ♘f3 ♖e7 36 ♖c6† ♔b4 37 e5† ♔b5 38 ♘d4† ♔a5 39 ♘b3† **1–0**

ACM 1978 — Washington D.C.

December 3 — December 5

	1	2	3	4	tot
1 BELLE	8+■	2+□	3+■	4+■	4
2 CHESS 4.7	9+□	1−■	6+□	7+■	3
3 CHAOS	5+□	7+■	1−□	6=■	2½
4 BLITZ 6.5	10+□	6=■	11+■	1−□	2½
5 SARGON 2	3−■	12+□	8=■	11+□	2½
6 DUCHESS	11+■	4=□	2−■	3=□	2
7 OSTRICH 4	12+■	3−□	9+■	2−□	2
8 MIKE	1−□	9=■	5=□	10=■	1½
9 BLACK KNIGHT	2−■	8=□	7−□	12+■	1½
10 BS6676	4−■	11−□	12+■	8=□	1½
11 AWIT	6−□	10+■	4−□	5−■	1
12 BRUTE FORCE	7−□	5−■	10−□	9−□	0

Round 1

BRUTE FORCE — OSTRICH 4 1 e4 c6 2 ♘f3 d5 3 ♘c3 d×e4 4 ♘×e4 e6 5 ♗c4 b5 6 ♗e2 ♗e7 7 O-O ♗a6 8 d4 ♘f6 9 ♘×f6† ♗×f6 10 ♘e5 O-O 11 ♗e3 ♕c7 12 f4 h6 13 ♕d3 c5 14 ♗f3 b4 15 c4 b×c3 **0–1**

CHAOS — SARGON 2 1 d4 d5 2 c4 ♘c6 3 ♘c3 d×c4 4 ♘f3 ♗g4 5 d5 ♗×f3 6 e×f3 ♘e5 7 ♗f4 ♘d3† 8 ♗×d3 c×d3 9 O-O ♘f6 10 ♕b3 c6 11 ♕×b7 c×d5 12 ♕c6† ♘d7 13 ♘×d5 ♖c8 14 ♘c7† ♖×c7 15 ♗×c7 ♕c8 16 ♖fd1 g5 17 ♖×d3 e6 18 ♖ad1 ♗g7 19 ♖×d7 O-O 20 ♖d8 ♗×b2 21 ♖×c8 ♖×c8 22 ♕b7 ♖×c7 23 ♕×c7 ♗g7 24 ♖d8† ♗f8 25 ♕e7 h5 26 ♖×f8† ♔g7 27 ♖×f7† ♔g6 28 ♕×e6# **1–0**

CHESS 4.7 — BLACK KNIGHT 1 e4 c5 2 ♘f3 ♘c6 3 ♗b5 g6 4 O-O ♗g7 5 c3 a6 6 ♗×c6 d×c6 7 d4 c×d4 8 ♘×d4 e5 9 ♘f3 ♗e6 10 ♘a3 ♕×d1 11 ♖×d1 ♖b8 12 ♘g5 ♖d8 13 ♖×d8† ♔×d8 14 ♘×e6† f×e6 15 ♗e3 ♘f6 16 f3 b5 17 ♖d1† ♔c7 18 ♘c2 a5 19 c4 b×c4 20 ♘a3 c3 21 b×c3 ♗f8 22 ♘c4 ♘d7 23 ♘×a5 ♗e7 24 ♘c4 ♖b8 25 ♗a7 ♖f8 26 a4 c5 27 a5 ♖g8 28 a6 ♖h8 29 ♖b1 ♗g5 30 ♖b7† ♔c6 31 ♘a5† ♔d6 32 ♗b8† ♖×b8 33 ♖×b8 ♗e3† 34 ♔h1 ♗d2 35 a7 ♗×c3 36 ♖b7 ♗a1 37 a8♕ ♔e7 38 ♕c8 ♔f6 39 ♕d8† ♔g7 40 ♖×d7† ♔h6 41 ♕h4# **1–0**

BLITZ 6.5 — BS6676 1 e4 e5 2 ♘f3 ♘c6 3 ♗b5 a6 4 ♗a4 ♘f6 5 d3 ♗b4† 6 c3 O-O 7 c×b4 ♕e7 8 ♗×c6 d×c6 9 O-O ♗g4 10 a3 ♖fd8 11 h3 ♗×f3 12 ♕×f3 ♕d6 13 ♖d1 c5 14 b×c5 ♕×c5 15 ♗g5 ♕c2 16 ♗×f6 g×f6 17 ♖d2 ♕c5 18 ♕×f6 ♖d6 19 ♕f5 ♕c1† 20 ♔h2 ♖f8 21 ♕×e5 ♖c6 22 f3 ♖c5 23 ♕d4 b5 24 ♕g1 ♖e8 25 d4 ♖c2 26 ♕×c1 ♖×c1 27 ♔g3 ♖e6 28 ♔f4 h6 29 d5 ♖f6† 30 ♔e3 ♖g6 31 e5 ♖e1† 32 ♔f4 c5 33 h4 c4 34 d6 f6 35 d7 f×e5† 36 ♔f5 ♔f7 37 d8♕ **1–0**

MIKE — BELLE 1 e4 e5 2 d4 e×d4 3 ♕×d4 ♘c6 4 ♕a4 ♘f6 5 ♗b5 ♗c5 6 ♘e2 ♘g4 7 f3 ♘f2 8 O-O ♘g4† 9 ♔h1 ♘×h2 10 ♕c4 ♕h4 11 g3 ♕h3 12 ♘f4 ♕×f1† 13 ♕×f1 ♘×f1 14 ♗×f1 ♘d4 15 ♘d5 ♗d6 16

♗f4 ♘×c2 17 ♗×d6 c×d6 18 ♗d3 ♘×a1 19 ♘c7† ♔d8 20 ♘×a8 b5 21 ♘c3 ♗b7 22 ♘×b5 ♗×a8 23 ♘×d6 ♔e7 24 ♘f5† ♔f6 25 b4 ♖c8 26 ♘d6 ♖c1† 27 ♔h2 ♖d1 28 e5† ♔×e5 29 ♗e4 ♖×d6 30 ♗×a8 ♖d2† 31 ♔h3 ♖×a2 32 f4† ♔d4 33 ♗f3 d5 34 b5 ♖b2 35 ♗h5 g6 36 ♗d1 ♘c2 37 ♗×c2 ♖×c2 38 ♔h4 f6 39 ♔h3 ♔e4 40 ♔g4 ♖h2 41 f5 g×f5# **0–1**

AWIT — DUCHESS 1 b3 d5 2 ♗b2 c5 3 e3 ♘f6 4 ♘f3 ♘c6 5 ♗b5 ♕b6 6 ♘a3 ♗f5 7 ♘h4 ♗g4 8 f3 ♗d7 9 g3 a6 10 ♗×c6 ♕×c6 11 O–O b5 12 c4 d×c4 13 b×c4 g5 14 ♘g2 ♗g7 15 ♗×f6 ♗×f6 16 ♖b1 b4 17 ♘c2 ♕a4 18 a3 b×a3 19 ♖b7 a2 20 d4 ♕×c4 21 ♕d2 ♗f5 22 ♘a1 c×d4 23 e4 ♗e6 24 ♖c1 ♕a4 25 f4 g×f4 26 ♘×f4 ♗g5 27 h4 ♗×f4 28 ♕×f4 ♖d8 29 ♕g5 ♕a3 30 ♖c6 f6 31 ♕h5† ♗f7 32 ♕g4 ♖g8 33 ♕f4 ♕×g3† 34 ♕×g3 ♖×g3† 35 ♔f2 ♖e3 36 ♖cc7 ♖×e4 37 ♖c1 ♖×h4 38 ♖a7 ♖h3 39 ♖e1 e5 40 ♖×a6 ♔e7 41 ♔g2 ♖e3 42 ♖×e3 d×e3 43 ♔f3 e2 44 ♘c2 ♗c4 45 ♖a4 ♖d2 46 ♘e1 ♖d1 47 ♖a7† ♔e6 **0–1**

Round 2

BELLE — CHESS 4.7 1 e4 ♘c6 2 d4 d5 3 ♘c3 e6 4 ♘f3 ♗b4 5 e5 ♘ge7 6 ♗d2 ♘f5 7 ♘e2 ♗e7 8 c3 O–O 9 ♘f4 f6 10 ♗d3 f×e5 11 d×e5 g5 12 g4 ♘g7 13 ♘g2 b6 14 ♕e2 ♗b7 15 ♖g1 a5 16 a4 ♔h8 17 h3 ♔g8 18 ♖h1 h6 19 h4 d4 20 h×g5 ♘b4 21 g×h6 ♘×d3† 22 ♕×d3 d×c3 23 ♕g6 c×d2† 24 ♘×d2 ♖f7 25 h×g7 ♖×g7 26 ♕×e6† ♖f7 27 ♕h6 ♖g7 28 ♕h8† ♔f7 29 e6† ♔×e6 30 ♕×g7 ♗×g2 31 ♖h6† ♔d7 32 O–O–O ♗d5 33 ♘e4 ♔c8 34 ♖h8 ♗×e4 35 ♖d×d8† ♗×d8 36 ♕e7 ♔b7 37 ♕×e4† ♔a7 38 ♖g8 ♖b8 39 g5 ♗e7 40 ♖×b8 ♗×g5† 41 f4 ♗×f4† 42 ♕×f4 ♔×b8 43 ♔d2 ♔b7 44 ♔d3 ♔c8 45 b4 a×b4 46 ♕×b4 ♔d7 47 ♕b5† ♔d8 48 ♔e4 **1–0**

DUCHESS — BLITZ 6.5 1 e4 e5 2 ♘f3 ♘c6 3 ♗b5 a6 4 ♗a4 ♘f6 5 O–O ♗e7 6 ♕e2 b5 7 ♗b3 O–O 8 c3 d5 9 d3 d×e4 10 d×e4 ♗b7 11 ♖d1 ♕e8 12 a4 ♘a5 13 ♗c2 ♗d6 14 b4 ♘c4 15 ♘a3 ♘×a3 16 ♖×a3 ♕c6 17 ♘g5 h6 18 ♘f3 ♘×e4 19 a×b5 ♕×b5 20 c4 ♕c6 21 c5 ♘×c5 22 ♖c3 e4 23 ♘d2 ♕b5 24 ♕×b5 a×b5 25 b×c5 ♗e5 26 ♖b3 c6 27 ♘×e4 ♖a2 28 ♗b1 ♖aa8 29 f4 ♗b8 30 ♘d6 ♖d8 31 ♖bd3 ♗a6 32 ♗a2 b4 33 ♖d4 ♗a7 34 ♘×f7 ♖×d4 35 ♖×d4 ♗×c5 36 ♘e5† ♔h8 37 ♗b2 ♗×d4† 38 ♗×d4 ♗b7 39 ♗e6 ♔h7 40 ♗c5 ♖a4 41 ♘d3 ♔g6 42 ♗×b4 ♗a6 43 f5† ♔h7 44 ♘c5 ♖×b4 45 ♘×a6 ♖b2 46 ♘c5 ♖d2 47 ♘d7 ♖d4 48 ♘e5 c5 49 ♘d7 ♖d1† 50 ♔f2 ♖d2† 51 ♔f3 ♖c2 52 ♘f8† ♔h8 53 ♘g6† ♔h7 54 ♘e5 ♖c3† 55 ♔g4 ♖c2 56 ♔g3 ♖e2 57 ♘d7 ♖e3† 58 ♔f4 ♖e2 59 ♘f8† ♔h8 60 ♘g6† ♔h7 61 ♗d5 ♖f2† 62 ♔e5 ♖e2† 63 ♗e4 c4 64 ♘f4 ♖e1 65 ♔d4 ♔h8 66 ♗d5 ♖h1 67 h3 ♖f1 68 g3 c3 69 ♔×c3 ♖g1 70 g4 ♖a1 71 ♔d4 ♔h7 72 ♔e3 ♖a4 73 ♔f3 ♖a3† 74 ♔g2 ♖c3 75 ♗e6 ♖a3 76 ♘g6 ♖c3 77 ♘f8† ♔h8 78 ♗f7 ♖c2† 79 ♔g3 ♖c7 80 ♘g6† ♔h7 81 ♗d5 ♖c3† 82 ♔h4 ♖c8 83 ♔h5 ♖b8 84 ♘f4 ♖b5 85 ♗f7 ♖b7 86 ♗a2 ♖b2 87 ♗e6 ♖b1 88 ♔h4 ♖a1 89 ♘g6 ♖a8 90 ♗b3 ♖b8 91 ♗f7 ♖c8 92 ♗d5 ♖c5 93 ♗a2 ♖c8 94 ♘f4 ♖a8 ½–½

BLACK KNIGHT — MIKE 1 e4 e5 2 ♘f3 d5 3 e×d5 ♕×d5 4 ♘c3 ♕a5 5 ♗b5† ♗d7 6 ♘×e5 ♗×b5 7 ♕f3 f6 8 ♕×b7 ♗a6 9 ♕f3 ♕×e5† 10 ♔d1 ♗e2† 11 ♘×e2 c6 12 d4 ♕c7 13 ♗f4 ♗d6 14 ♕b3 ♗×f4 15 ♘×f4 ♕×f4 16 ♕b7 ♕×d4† 17 ♔c1 ♕×f2 18 ♕×g7 h6 19 ♖d1 ♕f4† 20 ♔b1 ♕×h2 21 ♖e1† ♔d8 22 g4 ♕d2 23 ♖h1 ♕d5 24 ♖f1 ♕c4 25 ♖d1† ♔c8 26 a4 ♖h7 27 ♕×h7 ♕×g4 28 ♖e1 ♘d7 29 ♖e8† ♔b7 30 ♖e4 ♕d1† 31 ♔a2 ♕d6 32 ♖g1 ♖d8 33 ♖×g8 ♕d5† 34 b3 ♖×g8 35 ♔b1 ♖g1† 36 ♔b2 ♕d2 37 ♖e7 ♖d1 38 ♕f5 ♔b6 39 ♖e4 a5 40 ♕f4 ♘e5 41 ♕×d2 ♖×d2 42 ♖h4 ♘f7 43 ♖f4 ♖d6 44 ♖f1 ♘e5 45 c4 c5 46 ♔c2 ♔c6 47 ♖h1 f5 48 ♖f1 ♖f6 49 ♔c3 h5 50 ♖h1 ♖h6 51 ♖f1 ♖f6 52 ♖h1 ♖h6 53 ♖f1 ♖f6 54 ♖h1 ½–½

SARGON 2 — BRUTE FORCE 1 e4 e5 2 ♘f3 ♘c6 3 ♘c3 ♘f6 4 d4 ♘×d4 5 ♘×d4 e×d4 6 ♕×d4 ♗e7 7 ♗f4 O–O 8 ♘b5 c5 9 ♕a4 a6 10 ♘d6 ♘g4 11 ♗e2 h5 12 ♗×g4 h×g4 13 O–O–O ♕c7 14 ♕c4 g5 15 ♗e5 ♕c6 16 ♕e2 ♗×d6 17 ♖×d6 ♕a4 18 ♕×g4 ♖e8 19 ♕×g5† ♔f8 20 ♖h6 ♕×c2† 21 ♔×c2 f6 22 ♕×f6† ♔g8 23 ♕g7# **1–0**

BS6676 — AWIT 1 d4 ♘f6 2 ♗f4 d6 3 ♘c3 ♘c6 4 ♘f3 g6 5 e4 ♗g7 6 ♗b5 ♘h5 7 ♗e3 ♗d7 8 a4 O–O 9 a5 e6 10 ♕e2 a6 11 ♗d3 b6 12 ♗×a6 b×a5 13 ♗b5 ♘b4 14 ♗c4 c6 15 ♗c1 ♕c7 16 g4 ♘f6 17 g5 ♘h5 18 ♖f1 ♖fb8 19 ♗b3 c5 20 ♕c4 ♖a7 21 d×c5 a4 22 ♘e2 d×c5 23 c3 ♗b5 24 ♗f4 ♘×f4 25 ♕×b5 ♖×b5 26 ♘×f4 ♕×f4 27 ♖×a4 ♖×a4 28 ♔e2 ♕×e4† 29 ♔d2 ♕d3† 30 ♔e1 ♗×c3† 31 b×c3 ♘c2† 32 ♗×c2 ♖e4# **0–1**

OSTRICH 4 — CHAOS 1 e4 c5 2 ♘f3 ♘c6 3 ♗b5 ♘f6 4 e5 ♘d5 5 O–O ♘c7 6 ♘c3 ♘×b5 7 ♘×b5 h6 8 c3 d5 9 e×d6 e×d6 10 ♕e2† ♗e6 11 d4 ♗e7 12 ♗e3 O–O 13 ♖fd1 c×d4 14 c×d4 ♘b4 15 a3 ♘d5 16 ♘c3 ♕b6 17 ♔h1 ♕b3 18 ♘×d5 ♕×d5 19 h3 ♖fe8 20 b4 ♖ac8 21 ♖dc1 ♕e4 22 ♖×c8 ♖×c8 23 ♘d2 ♕c6 24 b5 ♕c2 25 ♖b1 d5 26 ♖b3 ♗×a3 27 b6 a5 28 ♔g1 ♗b4 29 ♕d3 ♕×d3 30 ♖×d3 ♖c6 31 ♘b3 ♗f5 32 ♖d2 ♗×d2 33 ♗×d2 a4 34 ♘c5 a3 35 g4 ♗c2 36 ♗c1 a2 37 ♗b2 ♖×b6 38 ♗a1 ♖b1† **0–1**

Round 3

CHESS 4.7 — DUCHESS 1 e4 e5 2 ♘f3 ♘f6 3 d4 e×d4 4 e5 ♘e4 5 ♕×d4 d5 6 e×d6 ♘×d6 7 ♗d3 ♘c6 8 ♕f4 g6 9 O–O ♗g7 10 ♗d2 ♕f6 11 ♕×f6 ♗×f6 12 ♘c3 ♗e6 13 ♘g5 ♗c4 14 ♘ge4 ♘×e4 15 ♘×e4 ♗×b2 16 ♗×c4 ♗×a1 17 ♖×a1 ♖d8 18 ♖e1 O–O 19 ♗h6 b6 20 ♘f6† ♔h8 21 ♗×f8 ♖×f8 22 ♗b3 ♘d4 23 ♘d7 ♖d8 24 ♘e5 ♖f8 25 ♘×f7† ♔g7 26 ♘g5 ♔h6 27 ♘e6 ♖e8 28 ♔f1 ♘×e6 29 ♖×e6 ♖d8 30 ♖e7 c6 31 ♖×a7 ♖d1† 32 ♔e2 ♖d8 33 ♖c7 c5 34 f4 ♖d4 35 ♔f3 g5 36 g3 g×f4 37 g×f4 ♔g6 38 ♖c6† ♔f5 39 ♗e6† ♔f6 40 ♖×b6 ♔e7 41 ♗f5 ♖a4 42 ♗×h7 ♖a3† 43 ♔g4 ♖×a2 44 f5 ♔d7 45 f6 ♖a4† 46 ♔g5 ♖a1 47 f7 ♖a8 48 ♔f6 c4 49 ♗f5† ♔c7 50 ♖c6† ♔b7 51 ♔e7 ♖h8 52 ♖×c4 ♖×h2 53 f8♕ ♖e2† 54 ♔f7 ♖e5 55 ♕c8† ♔b6 56 ♕c7† ♔a6 57 ♖a4† ♔b5 58 ♗d7# **1–0**

AWIT — BLITZ 6.5 1 b3 ♘f6 2 ♗b2 ♘c6 3 e3 e6 4 ♘f3 ♗c5 5 ♗b5 O–O 6 a3 a6 7 ♗d3 d5 8 O–O h6 9 b4 ♗b6 10 c4 ♗a7 11 ♕c2 ♗d7 12 ♘c3 a5 13 b5 ♘e7 14 ♖fb1 c5 15 ♘a4 d×c4 16 ♕×c4 b6 17 ♗×f6 g×f6 18 ♕g4† ♔h8 19 ♕h3 ♔g7 20 ♗e4 ♖c8 21 ♕h4 ♖g8 22 ♕g3† ♘g6 23 ♘c3 ♕e7 24 a4 ♖cd8 25 d4 ♗b8 26 ♕h3 c4 27 ♕h5 ♔h7 28 g3 f5 29 ♗c2 ♖c8 30 ♘d2 ♕g5 31 ♗d1 ♕×h5 32 ♗×h5 ♖c7 33 ♖c1 ♖gc8 34 ♖ab1 ♔g7 35 f3 ♔h7 36 e4 f×e4 37 ♘c×e4 c3 38 ♘f6† ♔g7 39 ♘de4 ♘f8 40 ♘×d7 ♖×d7 41 ♖×c3 ♖×c3 42 ♘×c3 ♖×d4 43 ♖c1 ♘d7 44 ♖d1 ♖×d1† 45 ♘×d1 ♘c5 46 ♘c3 ♗e5 47 ♘e2 ♘×a4 48 ♘c1 ♘c3 49 f4 ♗d4† 50 ♔g2 a4 51 ♔f3 a3 52 ♔g2 a2 53 ♘b3 ♘×b5 54 ♗e2 ♘d6 55 h4 ♘e4 56 ♗f3 ♘d2 57 ♘×d2 a1♕ 58 ♔h3 ♕c3 59 ♔g4 ♕×d2 60 ♔h3 b5 61 ♗c6 f5 62 ♗×b5 ♗g1 63 ♗c4 ♕h2# **0–1**

BRUTE FORCE — BS6676 1 e4 d5 2 e×d5 e5 3 ♘c3 f5 4 ♘f3 e4 5 ♘e5 ♗b4 6 ♗c4 ♘e7 7 ♕h5† g6 8 ♕d1 ♘d7 9 ♘×d7 ♗×d7 10 O–O c6 11 d×c6 ♗×c6 12 ♗e6 ♕d6 13 ♗c4 ♕d4 14 ♗e6 ♕e5 15 ♗c4 O–O–O 16 ♖e1 h5 17 ♖e3 b5 18 ♗f7 h4 19 ♕e2 ♖h7 20 ♗b3 ♗c5 21 ♖h3 ♖dh8 22 d4 ♗×d4 23 ♔f1 ♔b8 24 ♗g5 b4 25 f4 e×f3 **0–1**

BLACK KNIGHT — OSTRICH 4 1 e4 c6 2 d4 d5 3 e×d5 ♕×d5 4 ♘c3 ♕a5 5 ♘f3 e6 6 a3 ♗d6 7 ♗d2 ♕d8 8 ♘e4 ♗e7 9 ♗d3 f5 10 ♘c3 ♘f6 11 O–O O–O 12 ♖e1 c5 13 ♗e3 c×d4 14 ♗×d4 ♘c6 15 ♗b5 ♕c7 16 ♗c4 ♖e8 17 ♖×e6 ♗×e6 18 ♗×e6† ♔h8 19 ♘g5 ♘×d4 20 ♕×d4 ♗c5 21 ♕h4 ♕b6 22 ♘a4 ♕c7 23 ♕c4 ♗×f2† 24 ♔f1 ♕×c4† 25 ♗×c4 ♖ec8 26 ♗b3 ♗h4 27 ♘f3 b5 28 ♘c3 b4 29 a×b4 ♖cb8 30 ♘×h4 ♖×b4 31 ♖a4 ♖×a4 32 ♗×a4 ♖b8 33 ♗b3 ♘e4 34 ♘×e4 f×e4 35 ♘f5 ♖f8 36 ♗e6 g6 37 g4 g×f5 38 ♔e1 f×g4 39 ♗×g4 e3 40 ♔d1 ♖f1† 41 ♔e2 ♖f2† 42 ♔d3 ♖d2† 43 ♔c3 ♖×h2 44 ♗f5 ♖f2 45 ♗e4 ♖f4 46 ♗d3 ♖f2 47 b4 ♖h2 48 b5 ♔g7 49 ♗e4 ♖d2 50 ♗f3 h6 51 ♗g4 ♔g6 52 ♗f3 ♖f2 53 ♗b7 ♖d2 54 ♗e4† ♔f6 55 ♗f3 ♖f2 56 ♗c6 ♖d2 57 ♗f3 ♖f2 58 ♗e4 ♖f4 59 ♗d5 e2 60 ♔d2 ♖d4† 61 ♔×e2 ♖×d5 62 c4 ♖d4 63 c5 ♖b4 64 ♔d3 h5 65 c6 ♔e6 66 ♔c3 ♖b1 67 ♔d4 ♔d6 68 c7 ♔×c7 69 ♔c5 h4 70 ♔c4 h3 71 ♔c5 h2 72 ♔c4 h1♕ 73 ♔d3 ♔d6 74 ♔e3 ♖×b5 75 ♔d4 ♖b3 76 ♔c4 ♕d5# **0–1**

MIKE — SARGON 2 1 e4 e5 2 d4 ♘c6 3 d5 ♘b4 4 c3 ♘a6 5 f4 ♘c5 6 f×e5 ♕h4† 7 ♔d2 ♘×e4† 8 ♔c2 ♘f2 9 ♕e1 ♗c5 10 ♘f3 ♕h5 11 ♖g1 ♘e7 12 ♗e3 ♕g6† 13 ♔c1 ♗×e3† 14 ♕×e3 ♘g4 15 ♕d2 d6 16 ♗d3 ♕h5 17 ♗b5† ♗d7 18 ♗×d7† ♔×d7 19 e×d6 c×d6 20 h3 ♘f6 21 ♕g5 ♕×g5† 22 ♘×g5 ♖hf8 23 c4 ♖ac8 24 ♘d2 ♘e×d5 25 ♔b1 ♘e3 26 ♘ge4 ♘×e4 27 ♘×e4 ♖×c4 28 ♘c3 f5 29 a4 d5 30 g3 ♖f6 31 ♖e1 d4 32 ♘b5 a6 33 ♘×d4 f4 34 g×f4 ♖×d4 35 ♖×e3 ♖f×f4 36 a5 ♖d1† 37 ♔a2 ♖a4† 38 ♖a3 ♖×a3† 39 b×a3 ♖d2† 40 ♔b3 ♖d3† 41 ♔c4 ♖×h3 42 ♖d1† ♔c6 43 a4 ♖h5 44 ♔b4 ♖h4† 45 ♔b3 ♖h3† 46 ♔c4 ♖h5 47 ♔b4 ♖h4† 48 ♔b3 ♖h3† 49 ♔c4 ♖h5 50 ♔b4 ♖h4† ½–½

CHAOS — BELLE 1 d4 d5 2 c4 d×c4 3 ♘f3 ♘f6 4 e3 e6 5 ♗×c4 c5 6 ♕e2 a6 7 O–O b5 8 ♗b3 ♘c6 9 ♘c3 ♗e7 10 ♖d1 c4 11 ♗c2 ♘b4 12 e4 ♘×c2 13 ♕×c2 ♗b7 14 ♗f4 b4 15 e5 ♘h5 16 ♘e2 ♘×f4 17 ♘×f4 g5 18 ♘h5 ♗×f3 19 g×f3 ♕d5 20 ♕e4 c3 21 ♕×d5 e×d5 22 ♖db1 c2 23 ♖e1 ♖c8 24 ♖ac1 ♖c4 25 ♖e2 ♖×d4 26 ♘f6† ♗×f6 27 e×f6† ♔d7 28 ♖e×c2 ♖f8 29 ♖c7† ♔e6 30 ♖1c6† ♔f5 31 ♖×a6 ♖d3 32 ♖b7 ♖×f3 33 ♖×b4 ♔e5 34 ♖g4 ♖g8 35 ♖g3 g4 36 ♔g2 ♖×f6 37 ♖a7 d4 38 ♔f1 ♖h6 39 ♖e7† ♔f6 40 ♖e4 ♖×h2 41 ♖×d4 h5 42 ♖f4† ♔g6 43 ♖c3 ♖h1† 44 ♔g2 ♖b1 45 ♖b4 ♖a8 46 ♖b6† ♔g7 47 a3 ♖a7 48 ♖cb3 ♖a4 49 ♖3b5 h4 50 ♖b7 ♖d4 51 ♖c7 ♔g6 52 ♖bb7 ♖dd1 53 ♖c8 ♖g1† 54 ♔h2 ♖h1† 55 ♔g2 ♖bg1# **0–1**

Round 4

BLITZ 6.5 — BELLE 1 e4 e5 2 ♘f3 ♘c6 3 ♘c3 ♘f6 4 ♗b5 ♘d4 5 ♗c4 ♗c5 6 ♘×e5 ♕e7 7 ♗×f7† ♔f8 8 ♘g6† h×g6 9 ♗c4 ♘×e4 10 O–O ♖×h2 11 ♔×h2 ♕h4† 12 ♔g1 ♘g3 13 ♕h5 g×h5 14 f×g3† ♘f3# **0–1**

OSTRICH 4 — CHESS 4.7 1 e4 e5 2 ♘f3 ♘f6 3 ♘×e5 d6 4 ♘f3 ♘×e4 5 ♕e2 ♕e7 6 d3 ♘f6 7 ♗g5 ♘bd7 8 ♘c3 ♕×e2† 9 ♔×e2 h6 10 ♗e3 b6 11 ♘b5 ♘d5 12 c4 a6 13 ♘×d6† ♗×d6 14 c×d5 ♗b7 15 ♘d4 ♗×d5 16 ♔e1 ♗e5 17 f4 ♗f6 18 ♔d2 c5 19 ♘c2 ♗×b2 20 ♖b1 ♗f6 21 a3 O–O 22 ♔d1 ♗a2 23 ♗×c5 ♖fc8 24 ♖×b6 ♘×b6 25 d4 ♗b3 26 ♔e1 ♘a4 27 ♘b4 ♘×c5 28 d×c5 ♖×c5 29 ♖g1 ♖c1† 30 ♔d2 ♖d8† 31 ♔e2 ♗d4 32 ♖h1 ♖e8† 33 ♔f3 ♗d1† 34 ♔g3 ♖e3† 35 ♔f2 ♖d3† 36 ♔e1 ♗g4# **0–1**

DUCHESS — CHAOS 1 e4 c5 2 d4 c×d4 3 c3 ♘f6 4 e5 ♘d5 5 ♕×d4 e6 6 ♗c4 d6 7 ♘f3 ♘c6 8 ♗b5 ♗d7 9 ♗×c6 ♗×c6 10 O–O f6 11 e×f6 g×f6 12 ♖e1 ♘c7 13 ♕d3 ♕d7 14 ♘d4 ♖b8 15 ♘×c6 b×c6 16 ♕d4 ♘d5 17 c4 ♘c7 18 ♕×a7 ♕c8 19 b3 e5 20 ♘c3 ♗e7 21 ♗h6 ♖g8 22 ♕e3 ♖g6 23 ♖ad1 ♕g4 24 g3 c5 25 ♕d2 f5 26 ♗e3 f4 27 ♗×c5 ♕h3 28 ♘d5 ♘×d5 29 ♕×d5 ♕c8 30 ♗a7 ♖a8 31 ♗b6 f×g3 32 f×g3 ♖×a2 33 ♖f1 ♕h3 34 ♕c6† ♕d7 35 ♕e4 ♕c8 36 ♖d5 ♕h3 37 ♗f2 ♖h6 38 ♕g2 ♕d7 39 ♔h1 ♖f6 40 ♖b5 ♕c8 41 g4 ♖f7 42 ♖b6 ♗h4 43 ♖×d6 ♖f×f2 44 ♖×f2 ♖×f2 45 ♕e4 ♗e7 46 ♖d3 ♖f1† 47 ♔g2 ♖a1 48 ♔h3 ♖g1 49 ♖g3 ♖×g3† 50 h×g3 ♕b8 51 ♕×h7 ♕×b3 52 ♕h5† ♔d8 53 ♕×e5 ♕×c4 54 ♕h5 ♗f6 55 ♕g6 ♕f1† 56 ♔h2 ♕f3 57 ♕f7 ½–½

BRUTE FORCE — BLACK KNIGHT 1 e4 c5 2 ♘f3 ♘c6 3 d4 c×d4 4 ♘×d4 ♘f6 5 ♘c3 d6 6 ♗c4 ♗d7 7 ♘×c6 ♗×c6 8 ♕d4 e5 9 ♕e3 ♕b6 10 ♕×b6 a×b6 11 ♘d5 ♗×d5 12 ♗×d5 ♘×d5 13 e×d5 ♖a5 14 ♗e3 ♖×d5 15 c4 ♖a5 16 ♗×b6 ♖a6 17 ♗e3 ♖a4 18 b3 ♖a8 19 O–O ♗e7 20 ♖fd1 O–O 21 ♖d5 ♖a3 22 ♖b5 ♖b8 23 ♔f1 h6 24 ♔e2 ♖ba8 25 ♖×b7 ♗h4 26 ♖d1 ♖×a2† 27 ♔f3 ♖e8 28 ♖×d6 e4† 29 ♔g4 ♗×f2 30 ♗f4 ♗e1 31 ♔h3 g5 32 ♗e3 ♖e2 33 ♗d4 h5 34 g4 h×g4† 35 ♔×g4 ♗f2 36 ♔×g5 ♗×d4 37 ♖×d4 ♖g2† 38 ♔f4 ♖×h2 39 ♖bd7 e3 40 ♔f5 e2 41 ♖g4† ♔h7 42 ♖×f7† ♔h8 43 ♖e4 ♖×e4 44 ♖f8† ♔g7 45 ♖f6 ♖h5† 46 ♔×e4 e1♕† 47 ♔d4 ♕d2† 48 ♔e4 ♔×f6 49 b4 ♖f5 50 b5 ♖f4# **0–1**

SARGON 2 — AWIT 1 e4 c5 2 d4 c×d4 3 ♕×d4 ♘c6 4 ♕e3 ♘f6 5 ♘f3 e6 6 ♘c3 ♗b4 7 ♗b5 a6 8 ♗×c6 d×c6 9 ♗d2 ♘g4 10 ♕f4 ♘f6 11 O–O O–O 12 ♖ad1 b5 13 ♗e3 ♕a5 14 ♗d4 ♗×c3 15 ♗×c3 ♕×a2

16 ♗×f6 g×f6 17 ♕×f6 ♕c4 18 ♕g5† ♔h8 19 ♕f6† ♔g8 20 ♕g5† ♔h8 21 ♖d8 ♖×d8 22 ♕f6† ♔g8 23 ♕g5† ♔f8 24 ♕×d8† ♔g7 25 ♕g5† ♔f8 26 ♕d8† ♔g7 27 ♕d4† ♕×d4 28 ♘×d4 ♗b7 29 ♖e1 ♔g6 30 ♖e3 ♖d8 31 ♖d3 c5 32 ♘×e6 ♖×d3 33 ♘f4† ♔g5 34 ♘×d3 ♗×e4 35 ♘×c5 ♗×c2 36 ♘×a6 ♗b3 37 ♘c5 ♗d5 38 g3 ♗f3 39 ♘b3 b4 40 ♘d4 ♗e4 41 f3 ♗b7 42 ♔f2 h6 43 ♔e3 ♗d5 44 ♘c2 b3 45 ♘d4 ♔g6 46 ♔d3 ♔h7 47 f4 ♔g8 48 ♔c3 ♔g7 49 ♘×b3 ♗×b3 50 ♔×b3 ♔f6 51 ♔c4 ♔e7 52 b4 ♔d7 53 ♔d5 h5 54 b5 ♔c7 55 ♔c5 ♔b7 56 b6 ♔b8 57 ♔c6 ♔c8 58 b7† ♔b8 59 ♔b6 h4 60 g×h4 f6 61 h5 f5 62 ♔c6 ♔a7 63 ♔c7 ♔a6 64 b8♕ ♔a5 65 ♕b3 ♔a6 66 ♕a4# **1–0**

BS6676 — MIKE 1 d4 d5 2 c4 d×c4 3 ♘f3 ♗e6 4 ♘c3 ♘f6 5 e4 c6 6 ♗g5 a5 7 a3 b5 8 ♗e2 ♖g8 9 O–O h6 10 ♗×f6 e×f6 11 d5 c×d5 12 e×d5 ♗d7 13 ♕d4 ♗d6 14 ♖fe1 ♔f8 15 a4 b×a4 16 ♗×c4 ♗b4 17 ♗d3 ♕c8 18 ♕f4 a3 19 ♖eb1 a×b2 20 ♖×b2 ♗×c3 21 ♕d6† ♔e8 22 ♖e1† ♗×e1 23 ♖e2† ♔d8 24 ♕e7† ♔c7 25 ♖c2† ♔b7 26 ♖×c8 ♖×c8 27 ♕×e1 ♖e8 28 ♕c3 ♖c8 29 ♕b2† ♔c7 30 ♗c2 ♗g4 31 d6† ♔d8 32 ♕b6† ♔e8 33 ♕e3† ♔f8 34 ♕e7† ♔g8 35 ♕e4 ♖×c2 36 ♕×c2 ♘d7 37 ♕c3 g5 38 ♕c4 ♖b8 39 ♘d2 ♗e6 40 ♕d4 ♘e5 41 ♔f1 ♖b4 42 ♕a1 ♖b5 43 ♕c3 f5 44 ♕h3 ♔g7 45 ♕c3 f6 46 f3 ♖d5 47 ♕c7† ♔g6 48 ♔e2 h5 49 ♕e7 ♗d7 50 ♘b3 a4 51 ♘d2 a3 52 ♘b3 a2 53 h3 ♗a4 54 ♕f8 ♗×b3 55 ♕g8† ♔h6 56 ♕h8† ♔g6 57 ♕g8† ♔h6 **½–½**

ACM 1979 — Detroit

October 28 — October 30

		1	2	3	4	tot
1	CHESS 4.9	9+□	8+■	3+□	2=■	3½
2	BELLE	5+■	4=□	7+■	1=□	3
3	DUCHESS	10+■	7+□	1−■	4+□	3
4	CHAOS	12+□	2=■	8+□	3−■	2½
5	L'EXCENTRIQUE	2−□	12+■	9+□	6=■	2½
6	MYCHESS	7−■	10+□	11+■	5=□	2½
7	SARGON 3	6+□	3−■	2−□	8=■	1½
8	BLITZ 6.9	11+■	1−□	4−■	7=□	1½
9	OSTRICH 80	1−■	11+□	5−■	10=□	1½
10	AWIT	3−□	6−■	12+□	9=■	1½
11	BS6676	8−□	9−■	6−□	12+■	1
12	RUFUS	4−■	5−□	10−■	11−□	0

Round 1

L'EXCENTRIQUE — BELLE 1 e4 e5 2 ♘f3 ♘c6 3 ♗b5 a6 4 ♗a4 ♘f6 5 O–O ♘×e4 6 ♕e2 ♘c5 7 ♗×c6 d×c6 8 d4 ♘e6 9 d×e5 ♘d4 10 ♘×d4 ♕×d4 11 h3 ♗e7 12 ♖d1 ♕b6 13 b3 ♗f5 14 g4 ♗e6 15 a4 O–O 16 a5 ♕b5 17 ♘c3 ♕×e2 18 ♘×e2 ♖fd8 19 ♗e3 ♗d5 20 c4 ♗f3 21 ♖×d8† ♖×d8 22 ♘d4 ♗e4 23 f3 c5 24 f×e4 c×d4 25 ♗d2 d3 26 ♔g2 f6 27 e×f6 ♗×f6 28 ♖f1 c6 29 g5 ♗e5 30 c5 g6 31 h4 ♗d4 32 b4 ♖d7 33 ♖f3 ♗e5 34 ♖f1 ♖d8 35 ♖d1 ♔f7 36 ♖h1 ♔e6 37 h5 ♗g7 38 h6 ♗h8 39 ♖f1 ♔e7 40 ♔g3 ♗d4 41 ♔h3 ♗e5 42 ♔g4 ♖d4 43 ♔f3 ♔e6 44 ♖h1 ♗c7 45 ♖a1 ♗d8 46 ♖f1 ♖d7 47 ♔g3 ♗c7† 48 ♔g2 ♔e5 49 ♖f4 ♔d4 50 ♖f3 ♔×e4 51 ♖f1 ♔d4 52 ♖e1 ♖f7 53 ♖e3 ♗e5 54 ♖e1 ♖f5 55 ♗e3† ♔c3 56 b5 d2 57 ♖d1 ♔d3 58 ♗×d2 ♔e2 59 b×a6 ♔×d1 60 a7 ♖f8 61 ♗b4 ♗f4 62 ♗c3 ♗×g5 63 ♗e5 ♖a8 64 ♔f3 ♖×a7 65 ♗c7 ♗×h6 **0–1**

CHESS 4.9 — OSTRICH 80 1 e4 c6 2 c4 d5 3 e×d5 c×d5 4 d4 e6 5 c×d5 ♕×d5 6 ♘c3 ♕d8 7 ♘f3 ♘f6 8 ♗f4 ♘c6 9 ♗b5 ♗d7 10 O–O a6 11 ♗d3 ♕b6 12 ♕b3 ♕×b3 13 a×b3 ♗e7 14 ♘e4 O–O 15 ♘×f6† ♗×f6 16 ♗e4 h6 17 ♘e5 ♗×e5 18 d×e5 g5 19 ♗g3 b6 20 ♖fd1 ♖a7 21 ♖×d7 ♖×d7 22 ♗×c6 ♖d2 23 h4 ♖×b2 24 ♖×a6 ♖×b3 25 ♖a7 ♖c3 26 ♗f3 g×h4 27 ♗×h4 b5 28 ♖b7 ♖b3 29 ♔h2 ♖c8 30 ♗h5 ♖c6 31 ♖b8† ♔h7 32 ♗f6 ♖h3† 33 g×h3 ♖c8 34 ♖×c8 b4 35 ♖h8# **1–0**

AWIT — DUCHESS 1 c4 ♘f6 2 d4 e6 3 ♘f3 d5 4 ♗g5 h6 5 ♗d2 d×c4 6 ♘c3 c6 7 e3 b5 8 ♘e5 ♗d6 9 ♖c1 O–O 10 ♗e2 ♗×e5 11 d×e5 ♘fd7 12 f4 ♘c5 13 O–O ♘d3 14 ♖c2 ♘a6 15 a4 b4 16 ♘e4 b3 17 ♖×c4 ♘×b2 18 ♕×b3 ♖b8 19 ♕c2 ♘×c4 20 ♗×c4 ♕b6 21 a5 ♕c7 22 ♖b1 ♖×b1† 23 ♕×b1 ♖d8 24 ♘d6 ♘b8 25 ♗c3 ♗a6 26 g4 ♗×c4 27 ♘×c4 c5 28 ♔f2 ♕d7 29 h3 ♘c6 30 h4 ♕d3 31 ♕×d3 ♖×d3 32 ♗d2 ♔f8 33 ♗e1 ♔e7 34 ♔e2 ♖b3 35 g5 h×g5 36 h×g5 ♔d7 37 ♔d2 ♖b1 38 e4 ♖a1 39 ♔e2 ♘d4† 40 ♔f2 ♘f3 41 ♔×f3 ♖×e1 42 f5 g6 43 f×g6 f×g6 44 ♔f4 ♖a1 45 ♔g3 ♖a4 46 ♘d2 c4 47 ♘×c4 ♖×c4 48 ♔f4 a6 49 ♔e3 ♖c5 50 ♔f3 ♖×e5 **0–1**

CHAOS — RUFUS 1 d4 f5 2 c4 e6 3 ♘f3 ♘f6 4 e3 d5 5 ♗d3 ♘c6 6 ♘c3 ♗b4 7 O–O O–O 8 ♗d2 ♗d7 9 ♕b3 d×c4 10 ♗×c4 ♕e7 11 a3 ♗×c3 12 ♗×c3 b6 13 ♔h1 ♘e4 14 ♗b4 ♘×b4 15 a×b4 ♕d6 16 ♗d3 ♗c6 17 ♗×e4 ♗×e4 18 ♘e5 ♖fe8 19 ♕c3 a6 20 b3 b5 21 f3 ♗d5 22 ♘d3 ♖ab8 23 ♕c2 g6 24 ♘c5 ♖b6 25 e4 f×e4 26 f×e4 ♗b7 27 ♕f2 ♖c8 28 ♕f7† ♔h8 29 ♘d7 ♗×e4 30 ♘f6 ♗×g2† 31 ♔×g2 ♕d5† 32 ♘×d5 e×d5 33 ♖ae1 ♖c6 34 ♖e8† ♖×e8 35 ♕×e8† ♔g7 36 ♕f8# **1–0**

BS6676 — BLITZ 6.9 0–1

SARGON 3 — MYCHESS 1 d4 d5 2 ♘f3 ♘f6 3 e3 e6 4 ♗d3 ♘c6 5 O–O ♗d6 6 ♘c3 a6 7 ♗d2 b6 8 a3 ♗b7 9 ♖e1 a5 10 e4 d×e4 11 ♘×e4 ♗e7 12 c3 ♘×e4 13 ♗×e4 O–O 14 ♕b1 g6 15 ♘e5 ♘×e5 16 ♗×b7 ♖b8 17 ♗h6 ♖e8 18 ♗e4 ♘g4 19 ♗f4 ♗d6 20 ♗g3 c5 21 d×c5 ♗×g3 22 h×g3 ♕d2 23 ♕c2 ♕×c2 24 ♗×c2 b×c5 25 b3 e5 26 f3 ♘f6 27 ♖ad1 ♖b6 28 ♔f2 h5 29 ♔e3 g5 30 ♔d3 ♖d8† 31 ♔c4 ♖×d1 32 ♖×d1 ♖b8 33 ♖d6 ♔g7 34 ♖a6 ♖d8 35 ♖×a5 ♘d5 36 ♗e4 ♘e3† 37 ♔×c5 ♖b8 38 b4 ♖c8† 39 ♗c6 ♔f6 40 ♖a7 ♘×g2 41 ♖d7 ♘e3 42 b5 ♘c2 43 a4 h4 44 g×h4 g×h4 45 ♔d5 ♖b8 46 ♖d6† ♔f5 47 ♗d7† ♔g5 48 ♔×e5 ♖a8 49 f4† ♔h5 50 ♗c6 ♖g8 51 ♗f3† ♖g4 52 ♖d8 ♔h6 53 ♗×g4 ♔g7 54 ♖d7 ♘e3 55 ♗e6 ♔f8 56 ♖×f7† ♔g8 57 ♔f6 ♔h8 58 ♔g6 ♔g8 59 ♖f6† ♔h8 60 ♖f8# **1–0**

Round 2

BELLE — CHAOS 1 d4 ♘f6 2 c4 e6 3 ♘c3 ♗b4 4 e3 c5 5 ♗d3 O–O 6 a3 ♗×c3† 7 b×c3 ♘c6 8 ♘e2 d6 9 e4 e5 10 d5 ♘a5 11 O–O b6 12 f4 ♕e8 13 f×e5 d×e5 14 ♗g5 ♘h5 15 ♕c2 ♗a6 16 ♕a2 ♕a4 17 g4 ♘f4 18 ♘×f4 e×f4 19 ♗×f4 ♗×c4 20 ♗×c4 ♘×c4 21 ♔g2 ♘e5 22 ♕e2 ♖fe8 23 ♖fe1 ♘c4 24 ♕a2 ♘a5 25 ♔f3 f6 26 d6† ♔h8 27 ♕d5 ♕d7 28 ♕f5 ♖ad8 29 ♕×d7 ♖×d7 30 e5 f×e5 31 ♖×e5 ♖×e5 32 ♗×e5 ♘c4 33 ♗f4 b5 34 a4 g5 35 ♗×g5 b×a4 36 ♖×a4 ♘×d6 37 ♖a5 ♖f7† 38 ♗f4 c4 39 ♖c5 ♖f8 40 ♖c6 ♘f7 41 ♔g3 ♔g7 42 ♖×c4 a6 43 ♖c7 ♖a8 44 c4 a5 45 c5 a4 46 ♗e5† ♔f8 47 ♗a1 a3 48 c6 ♖a6 49 ♗f6 ♖a8 50 ♖b7 a2 51 c7 ♖c8 52 ♖b8 ♘d6 53 ♔f4 ♔e8 54 ♖×c8† ♘×c8 55 ♔g5 ♔d7 56 ♔h6 ♔×c7 57 ♔×h7 ♘d6 58 ♗e5 ♔d7 59 g5 ♘f7 60 ♗b2 ♘×g5† 61 ♔g6 ♘f3 62 ♔f5 ♘×h2 63 ♔e4 ♔c6 64 ♔d4 ♔b5 65 ♔c3 ♔a4 66 ♔c2 ♘f3 67 ♗f6 ♔a3 68 ♗e7† ♔a4 69 ♔b2 a1♕† 70 ♔×a1 ½–½

BLITZ 6.9 — CHESS 4.9 1 e4 ♘c6 2 d4 d5 3 e5 f6 4 f4 ♗f5 5 ♘e2 e6 6 ♘g3 f×e5 7 f×e5 ♕h4 8 ♗e3 ♘h6 9 ♘c3 ♘g4 10 ♗g1 ♗e7 11 ♘b5 ♖c8 12 c4 d×c4 13 ♗×c4 a6 14 ♘c3 ♘b4 15 ♔d2 ♕g5† 16 ♔e2 ♘×e5 17 ♗×e6 ♗×e6 18 ♕b1 ♗g4† 19 ♔f1 O–O† 20 ♗f2 ♖×f2† 21 ♔g1 ♕e3 22 ♘d5 ♘f3† 23 g×f3 ♖f1† 24 ♔×f1 ♗h3# **0–1**

DUCHESS — SARGON 3 1 e4 g6 2 d4 ♗g7 3 ♘f3 d6 4 ♘c3 ♘f6 5 ♗e2 O–O 6 O–O ♘bd7 7 e5 d×e5 8 ♘×e5 ♘×e5 9 d×e5 ♘d7 10 f4 g5 11 f5 ♗×e5 12 ♗×g5 ♘f6 13 ♔h1 ♕d7 14 ♕e1 ♖d8 15 ♖d1 ♕e8 16 ♗d3 ♘g4 17 h3 f6 18 h×g4 ♗×c3 19 ♕×c3 f×g5 20 ♗c4† e6 21 f×e6 ♗×e6 22 ♖de1 ♖d6 23 ♗×e6† ♕×e6 24 ♖×e6 ♖×e6 25 ♕b3 ♖ae8 26 ♖f6 c5 27 ♖×e6 ♖×e6 28 ♕×e6† ♔g7 29 ♕e7† ♔g6 30 ♕×b7 a5 31 ♕b6† ♔f7 32 ♕×c5 h6 33 ♕×a5 ♔e6 34 ♕a6† ♔e5 35 ♕×h6 ♔f4 36 ♕e6 ♔g3 37 ♕e3† ♔×g4 38 ♕f3† ♔h4 39 ♕h3# **1–0**

RUFUS — L'EXCENTRIQUE 1 c4 f5 2 ♘c3 ♘f6 3 ♘f3 a5 4 e3 e6 5 ♗e2 ♗e7 6 O–O O–O 7 d4 ♘e4 8 ♗d2 d5 9 c×d5 e×d5 10 ♕b3 ♘×c3 11 ♕×c3 ♗b4 12 ♕c2 ♕e7 13 ♘e5 ♗×d2 14 ♕×d2 a4 15 ♖ac1 g6 16 ♖fe1 ♔g7 17 ♗f3 c6 18 ♕d3 ♘d7 19 ♘×d7 ♗×d7 20 ♖c5 b6 21 ♖cc1 h5 22 g3 h4 23 b3 a3 24 h3 ♖h8 25 ♗g2 g5 26 g4 f×g4 27 h×g4 h3 28 ♗f3 ♕f6 29 ♕e2 ♖af8 30 ♗h1 h2† 31 ♔f1 ♗×g4 32 ♕c2 ♗h3† 33 ♔e2 ♕×f2† 34 ♔d3 ♗f5† 35 e4 ♖h3† 36 ♗f3 ♖×f3† 37 ♖e3 ♕×e3# **0–1**

OSTRICH 80 — BS6676 1 e4 c5 2 ♘f3 ♘c6 3 ♗b5 g6 4 O–O ♗g7 5 ♘c3 a6 6 ♗×c6 d×c6 7 h3 b6 8 e5 ♗b7 9 d3 **1–0**

MYCHESS — AWIT 1 e4 c5 2 ♘f3 d6 3 d4 c×d4 4 ♘×d4 ♘f6 5 ♘c3 a6 6 ♗e2 e5 7 ♘b3 ♗e7 8 ♗e3 O–O 9 a4 a5 10 f4 ♘c6 11 f5 ♘b4 12 O–O d5 13 e×d5 ♘f×d5 14 ♘×d5 ♘×d5 15 ♗c5 ♗×c5† 16 ♘×c5 ♘e3 17 ♕×d8 ♖×d8 18 ♖f2 b6 19 ♗f3 ♖a7 20 ♘d3 ♗×f5 21 ♘×e5 ♖e8 22 ♘c6 ♖d7 23 c3 ♗e4 24 ♗×e4 ♖×e4 25 ♘d4 g6 26 ♖e1 ♔g7 27 ♖fe2 ♘×g2 28 ♖×e4 ♘×e1 29 ♖×e1 ♖d6 30 ♔f2 f5 31 ♖e6 ♖×e6 32 ♘×e6† ♔h6 33 ♘f4 ♔g5 34 ♘d5 ♔h4 35 ♘×b6 ♔h3 36 ♔g1 f4 37 b3 f3 38 ♘c4 f2† 39 ♔×f2 ♔×h2 40 ♘×a5 g5 41 ♘c6 g4 42 a5 g3† 43 ♔e2 g2 44 ♘e5 g1♕ 45 ♘f3† ♔g2 46 ♘×g1 ♔h2 47 a6 ♔×g1 48 a7 h5 49 a8♕ h4 50 ♕g8† ♔h2 51 ♔f2 ♔h1 52 ♕g2# **1–0**

Round 3

CHESS 4.9 — DUCHESS 1 e4 d5 2 e×d5 ♕×d5 3 ♘c3 ♕d6 4 d4 ♗f5 5 ♘f3 ♘c6 6 ♘b5 ♕d7 7 ♗f4 ♖c8 8 ♘e5 ♘×e5 9 d×e5 ♕c6 10 ♕f3 ♕×f3 11 g×f3 a6 12 ♘d4 ♗d7 13 O–O–O g6 14 ♘b3 ♖d8 15 ♘a5 ♗c8 16 ♖×d8† ♔×d8 17 ♗c4 ♔e8 18 ♖d1 ♗h6 19 ♗d2 ♗g7 20 ♗c3 c6 21 e6 ♗h6† 22 ♔b1 f6 23 ♘×b7 ♗×b7 24 ♗a5 ♔f8 25 ♖d7 ♗f4 26 h3 ♗e5 27 ♖×b7 g5 28 ♗×a6 h5 29 a4 ♖h6 30 ♗c4 f5 31 ♗d2 ♖g6 32 a5 ♗d4 33 a6 ♗×f2 34 a7 ♗×a7 35 ♖×a7 g4 36 ♗c3 ♘f6 37 ♗b4 ♘g8 38 ♖a8† ♔g7 39 ♗c3† ♔h6 40 ♗d2† ♔g7 41 f×g4 h×g4 42 h×g4 ♖×g4 43 ♗d3 f4 44 ♗c3† ♔h6 45 ♖f8 c5 46 ♗e5 f3 47 ♖×f3 c4 48 ♖f4 ♖g1† 49 ♗f1 ♔g5 50 ♖f7 ♔h6 51 ♔a2 ♖h1 52 ♗×c4 ♖e1 53 ♗g7† ♔g5 54 ♗f8 ♖e4 55 ♖g7† ♔f6 56 ♗d3 ♖a4† 57 ♔b3 ♖a7 58 ♖×g8 ♔×e6 59 ♗c4† ♔e5 60 ♖g7 ♖b7† 61 ♔c3 **1–0**

SARGON 3 — BELLE 1 ♘c3 d5 2 e4 ♘f6 3 e×d5 ♘×d5 4 ♘×d5 ♕×d5 5 ♘e2 ♘c6 6 d3 e5 7 ♘c3 ♗b4 8 ♗d2 ♗×c3 9 b×c3 ♗f5 10 c4 ♕d4 11 ♗e3 ♕c3† 12 ♗d2 ♕a3 13 g4 ♗d7 14 ♗g2 O–O 15 O–O f5 16 ♕b1 ♖ab8 17 g×f5 ♗×f5 18 ♕b5 a6 19 ♕d5† ♖f7 20 ♖fb1 ♖d8 21 ♕f3 ♘d4 22 ♕d1 c6 23 ♗g5 ♖df8 24 ♗e3 ♕c3 25 ♖c1 ♕b2 26 a4 ♗g6 27 ♖ab1 ♕a3 28 ♖a1 ♕c3 29 ♗d2 ♕b2 30 ♖ab1 ♕a2 31 ♖a1 ♕b2 32 ♗e3 ♔h8 33 ♖ab1 ♕a3 34 ♖a1 ♕c3 35 ♗d2 ♕b2 36 ♖ab1 ♕a2 37 ♖a1 ♕b2 38 ♗e3 ♖e7 39 ♖ab1 ♕a3 40 ♖a1 ♕c3 41 ♗d2 ♕b2 42 ♖ab1 ♕a2 43 ♗b4 ♖ff7 44 ♖a1 ♕b2 45 ♖ab1 ♕a2 46 ♗×e7 ♖×e7 47 ♖a1 ♕b2 48 ♔f1 ♖f7 49 ♖ab1 ♕a2 50 ♕e1 ♘×c2 51 ♕×e5 ♗×d3† 52 ♔g1 ♕a3 53 ♕b8† ♖f8 54 ♕×b7 ♘d4 55 ♖a1 ♕c5 56 ♖d1 ♗×c4 57 ♔h1 ♗d5 58 ♗×d5 ♕×d5† 59 ♔g1 ♘e2† 60 ♔f1 ♕f3 61 ♔e1 ♕×f2† 62 ♔d2 ♖d8† 63 ♔c2 ♘d4† 64 ♔d3 ♘b5† 65 ♕d7 ♖×d7† 66 ♔c4 ♕c2† 67 ♔b4 ♕c3# **0–1**

CHAOS — BLITZ 6.9 1 d4 d5 2 c4 e6 3 ♘c3 ♘f6 4 ♗g5 ♗e7 5 e3 O–O 6 ♘f3 h6 7 ♗h4 b6 8 c×d5 ♘×d5 9 ♗×e7 ♕×e7 10 ♘×d5 e×d5 11 ♗d3 ♘c6 12 ♕c2 ♘b4 13 ♕c3 ♘×d3† 14 ♕×d3 ♕b4† 15 ♕d2 ♕b5 16 ♕c3 ♗a6 17 O–O–O ♕a4 18 ♔b1 ♗c4 19 b3 ♕b5 20 ♘e5 ♗e2 21 ♖de1 f6 22 a4 ♕a6 23 ♘c6 ♗d3† 24 ♔b2 ♕b7 25 ♘×a7 ♗h7 26 ♘c6 ♖fe8 27 ♔a1 ♕a6 28 f3 ♖e6 29 ♘b4 ♕a5 30 ♖c1 ♖ae8 31 ♖he1 ♔h8 32 ♖e2 f5 33 h3 f4 34 ♘a2 ♖×e3 35 ♖×e3 ♖×e3 36 ♕×a5 b×a5 37 ♖×c7 ♖×b3 38 ♘c3 ♖b4 39 ♖a7 ♖×d4 40 ♖×a5 ♗g8 41 ♔b2 ♖d2† 42 ♔c1 ♖×g2 43 ♘×d5 ♖g1† 44 ♔d2 ♗×d5 45 ♖×d5 ♖g3 46 ♖d3 ♖×h3 47 ♖a3 g5 48 a5 g4 49 a6 ♖h2† 50 ♔c3 ♖e2 51 a7 ♖e3† 52 ♔b4 ♖e8 53 a8♕ ♖×a8 54 ♖×a8† ♔g7 55 f×g4 f3 56 ♔c4 f2 57 ♖a1 ♔g6 58 ♔d3 ♔g5 59 ♔e2 ♔×g4 60 ♔×f2 h5 61 ♖a4† ♔f5 62 ♔g3 **1–0**

L'EXCENTRIQUE — OSTRICH 80 1 e4 c6 2 d4 d5 3 ♘c3 d×e4 4 ♘×e4 ♘d7 5 ♗c4 ♘gf6 6 ♘g5 ♘d5 7 ♕h5 g6 8 ♕e2 ♘7f6 9 c3 h6 10 ♘e4 e6 11 ♘×f6† ♘×f6 12 ♘f3 ♗e7 13 a4 ♕d6 14 ♕e5 ♕×e5† 15 d×e5 ♘d7 16 h4 ♘b6 17 ♗d3 ♗d7 18 a5 ♘d5 19 ♗d2 O–O–O 20 O–O c5 21 c4 ♘b4 22 ♗×b4 c×b4 23

♗e4 ♗c6 24 ♗×c6 b×c6 25 ♖fd1 ♖×d1† 26 ♖×d1 g5 27 h×g5 h×g5 28 a6 g4 29 ♘h2 ♖g8 30 b3 g3 31 f×g3 ♖×g3 32 ♘f3 ♖g4 33 ♔h2 ♖g6 34 g3 ♔c7 35 ♔h3 ♖g8 36 g4 ♔b6 37 ♖a1 ♖d8 38 ♔g3 ♖d3 39 ♖b1 ♔×a6 40 ♔f4 ♖d7 41 ♖h1 ♖d3 42 ♖b1 ♖d7 43 ♖h1 ♗c5 44 ♔e4 ♔b6 45 ♖h2 ♔c7 46 ♖h1 ♔b6 47 ♖h2 ♖d1 48 ♖h7 ♖b1 49 ♖×f7 ♖×b3 50 ♘d4 ♗×d4 51 ♔×d4 c5† 52 ♔e4 ♖c3 53 ♖f2 ♖×c4† 54 ♔f3 ♖c3† 55 ♔f4 a5 56 g5 ♖c4† 57 ♔f3 ♖c1 58 g6 ♖g1 59 ♖g2 ♖f1† 60 ♔g4 ♖f8 61 ♔g5 ♖f5† 62 ♔h6 ♖f8 63 g7 ♖b8 64 ♖f2 ♖g8 65 ♖f8 ♖×g7 66 ♔×g7 ♔c7 67 ♖a8 ♔b6 68 ♔f7 c4 69 ♔×e6 c3 70 ♖b8† ♔a7 71 ♖c8 ♔b7 72 ♖c4 ♔a7 73 ♔f7 ♔a6 74 e6 c2 75 e7 ♔a7 76 e8♕ c1♕ 77 ♖×c1 **1–0**

AWIT — RUFUS 1 c4 e5 2 ♘c3 ♘f6 3 g3 ♗b4 4 a3 ♗c5 5 ♗g2 ♘c6 6 d3 O-O 7 ♘f3 d6 8 b4 ♗b6 9 O-O ♗f5 10 ♘a4 ♕d7 11 ♘×b6 a×b6 12 ♗b2 ♖fe8 13 ♘d2 ♘g4 14 h3 ♘f6 15 g4 ♗g6 16 ♕b3 ♖ac8 17 b5 ♘a5 18 ♕b4 ♖b8 19 a4 c5 20 b×c6 b×c6 21 ♘b3 ♕c7 22 ♔h2 ♘×b3 23 ♕×b3 c5 24 ♕b5 ♖bc8 25 f4 e×f4 26 ♖f2 ♘d7 27 ♗h1 h5 28 ♗d5 h×g4 29 h×g4 ♘f6 30 ♗×f6 g×f6 31 ♖h1 ♖e5 32 ♔g1 ♔g7 33 ♔g2 ♖h8 34 ♖×h8 ♔×h8 35 ♕b2 ♕e7 36 ♔h2 ♕e8 37 d4 c×d4 38 ♕×d4 ♕×a4 39 ♕×f4 f5 40 ♕h6† ♔g8 41 ♕×g6† ♔h8 42 ♗×f7 d5 43 ♕g8# **1–0**

BS6676 — MYCHESS 1 d4 d5 2 ♗f4 ♘f6 3 e3 ♘c6 4 ♘d2 e6 5 ♗b5 ♗d7 6 ♘e2 a5 7 ♘b3 a4 8 ♘c5 ♗×c5 9 d×c5 a3 10 b3 ♖a5 11 ♗×c6 ♗×c6 12 ♕d4 ♕e7 13 b4 ♖a8 14 f3 ♗b5 15 ♘c3 ♗c4 16 e4 c6 17 O-O-O ♘h5 18 e×d5 c×d5 19 ♖he1 b6 20 ♗e5 b×c5 21 ♕g4 c×b4 22 ♕×h5 ♔f8 23 ♗×g7† ♔×g7 24 ♘×d5 ♗×d5 25 ♖×d5 b3 26 a×b3 a2 27 ♖g5† ♔f8 28 ♕h6† ♔e8 29 ♔d2 a1♗ 30 ♔d3 ♕d6† 31 ♔e2 ♖a2 32 ♖d1 ♖×c2† 33 ♔e1 ♗c3† **0–1**

Round 4

BELLE — CHESS 4.9 1 d4 ♘f6 2 c4 c5 3 d5 e6 4 ♘c3 e×d5 5 c×d5 d6 6 e4 g6 7 ♘f3 ♗g7 8 ♗e2 O-O 9 O-O ♖e8 10 ♘d2 ♘a6 11 f3 ♘c7 12 a4 b6 13 ♘c4 ♗a6 14 ♗g5 h6 15 ♗h4 g5 16 ♗f2 ♘h5 17 ♘e3 ♗c8 18 ♕c2 ♘f4 19 ♗c4 ♗d7 20 ♖fd1 ♕f6 21 ♗g3 ♘h5 22 ♗e1 ♘f4 23 ♔h1 a6 24 ♗g3 b5 25 a×b5 a×b5 26 ♖×a8 ♖×a8 27 ♗f1 b4 28 ♘e2 b3 29 ♕b1 ♘h5 30 ♗f2 ♘f4 31 ♘c4 ♘×e2 32 ♗×e2 ♗b5 33 ♗g3 ♖a4 34 ♕c1 ♗f8 35 ♖d2 ♕d8 36 ♕f1 h5 37 ♔g1 h4 38 ♗f2 ♗g7 39 ♘e3 ♗×e2 40 ♕×e2 ♖a1† 41 ♖d1 ♖a2 42 ♕d3 ♖×b2 43 ♘c4 ♖c2 44 e5 ♗×e5 45 ♘×e5 d×e5 46 ♕×b3 ♖e2 47 ♔f1 c4 48 ♕b7 ♖a2 49 ♗b6 h3 50 ♕×c7 ♕f6 51 ♕d8† ♕×d8 52 ♗×d8 ♖×g2 53 ♖e1 c3 54 ♖×e5 c2 55 ♖e8† ♔g7 56 ♗×g5 ♖×g5 57 ♖c8 ♖g2 58 d6 ♖×h2 59 d7 ♖d2 60 ♔g1 ♖×d7 61 ♖×c2 ♖d3 62 ♖f2 ♔f6 63 ♔h2 ½–½

DUCHESS — CHAOS 1 e4 c5 2 ♘c3 ♘c6 3 g3 e6 4 ♘f3 d5 5 e×d5 e×d5 6 d4 ♗g4 7 ♗e2 ♘f6 8 ♗g5 ♗×f3 9 ♗×f3 ♕e7† 10 ♔f1 c×d4 11 ♘×d5 ♕d8 12 ♕e2† ♔d7 13 ♕b5 ♖b8 14 ♘×f6† g×f6 15 ♕f5† ♔c7 16 ♗×f6 ♗e7 17 ♗×h8 ♕×h8 18 ♕×f7 ♕g8 19 ♕×g8 ♖×g8 20 ♗e4 ♖h8 21 f4 ♘a5 22 ♔e2 ♘c4 23 ♖hb1 ♗f6 24 ♔d3 ♘b6 25 ♖e1 ♔b8 26 ♖ab1 ♘a4 27 ♗f5 h5 28 ♗g6 ♘c5† 29 ♔c4 ♘d7 30 ♖e8† ♖×e8 31 ♗×e8 ♘b6† 32 ♔c5 h4 33 g×h4 ♔c8 34 h5 ♔d8 35 ♗b5 ♔c7 36 h6 a6 37 ♗d3 ♗h8 38 ♗f5 ♘a4† 39 ♔b4 b5 40 ♔a5 ♔b7 41 ♗e4† ♔a7 42 h7 ♘b6 43 h4 ♘c4† 44 ♔b4 ♔b6 45 c3 a5† 46 ♔b3 d×c3 47 ♖d1 ♘d2† 48 ♖×d2 c×d2 49 ♔c2 b4 50 h5 ♔c5 51 ♔×d2 ♗×b2 52 h6 ♗h8 53 ♔e3 ♔c4 54 ♗c2 ♔d5 55 ♗b3† ♔c5 56 ♔e4 ♔d6 57 ♔f5 ♔d7 58 ♔g6 ♔e7 59 f5 ♗e5 60 ♗c2 ♗f6 61 ♗e4 ♗h8 62 ♗f3 ♗e5 63 ♗c6 ♗f6 64 ♗e8 ♗e5 65 ♗b5 ♗h8 66 ♗c4 a4 67 ♗g8 ♗f6 68 ♗d5 ♗e5 69 ♔g5 ♗f6† 70 ♔f4 ♔f8 71 ♔e4 ♔e7 72 ♗e6 a3 73 ♔d3 ♗h8 74 ♔c4 ♗c3 75 ♔c5 ♔d8 76 ♔d6 ♔e8 77 ♗b3 ♗b2 78 ♔e6 ♗h8 79 ♗a4† ♔f8 80 ♗d1 ♔e8 81 f6 ♔f8 82 ♗b3 ♔e8 83 ♗a4† ♔f8 84 ♗d1 ♔e8 85 ♗b3 ♔f8 86 ♗c4 ♔e8 87 ♗b5† ♔f8 88 ♗a4 b3 89 ♗×b3 ♔e8 90 ♗c2 ♔f8 91 ♗d3 ♔e8 92 ♗b5† ♔f8 93 ♗a6 ♔e8 94 ♗d3 ♔f8 95 ♗e2 ♔e8 96 ♗h5† ♔f8 97 ♗g4 ♔e8 98 ♗f3 ♔f8 99 ♗e4 ♔e8 100 ♗g6† ♔f8 101 ♗f5 ♔e8 102 ♗e4 ♔f8 103 ♗b1 ♔e8 104 ♗f5 ♔f8 105 ♗c2 ♔e8 106 ♗a4† ♔f8 107 ♗d1 ♔e8 108 ♗e2 ♔f8 109 ♗f3 ♔e8 110 ♗c6† ♔f8 111 ♗d5 **1–0**

MYCHESS — L'EXCENTRIQUE 1 e4 e5 2 ♘f3 ♘f6 3 ♘×e5 d6 4 ♘f3 ♘×e4 5 d4 d5 6 ♗d3 ♘c6 7 O-O ♗e7 8 ♖e1 ♗g4 9 ♗×e4 d×e4 10 ♖×e4 ♗×f3 11 g×f3 O-O 12 d5 ♕d7 13 ♕e2 ♕×d5 14 ♘c3 ♕d6 15 ♗f4 ♕g6† 16 ♔h1 ♕f5 17 ♗×c7 ♕d7 18 ♖d1 ♕×c7 19 ♘d5 ♕a5 20 ♘×e7† ♘×e7 21 ♖×e7 ♕×a2 22 ♖×b7 ♕e6 23 ♕×e6 f×e6 24 ♖dd7 ♖×f3 25 ♖×g7† ♔f8 26 ♖×h7 ♔e8 27 ♖he7† ♔d8 28 ♔g2 ♖f6 29 ♖ed7† ♔e8 30 ♖e7† ♔f8 31 ♖×a7 ♖g6† 32 ♔f3 ♖×a7 33 ♖×a7 ♖h6 34 ♖a8† ♔e7 35 ♔g3 ♖g6† 36 ♔f3 ♖h6 37 ♔g3 ♖g6† 38 ♔f3 ♖h6 39 ♔g3 ♖g6† ½–½

OSTRICH 80 — AWIT 1 e4 c5 2 ♘f3 d6 3 ♗b5† ♘c6 4 O-O ♗d7 5 ♘c3 ♘f6 6 d4 a6 7 ♗×c6 ♗×c6 8 ♗e3 ♕b6 9 b3 ♘×e4 10 ♘×e4 ♗×e4 11 c3 ♕c6 12 ♕e2 O-O-O 13 ♘g5 ♗g6 14 ♘f3 ♗h5 15 ♗g5 ♔d7 16 ♖ad1 ♗×f3 17 g×f3 c×d4 18 c×d4 ♕d5 19 f4 h6 20 ♗h4 g5 21 f×g5 h×g5 22 ♗g3 ♖c8 23 ♖d3 ♗g7 24 ♖fd1 e6 25 ♕e3 b5 26 f4 f6 27 f×g5 ♖c2 28 ♖1d2 ♖c1† 29 ♗e1 ♕×g5† 30 ♕×g5 f×g5 31 ♖e3 ♔e7 32 ♔g2 g4 33 ♖ee2 ♗f6 34 ♗g3 ♗g5 35 ♖d3 d5 36 a4 b×a4 37 b×a4 ♖a1 38 ♗e5 ♖g8 39 ♔g3 ♗h6 40 ♔h4 ♖×a4 41 ♖g2 a5 42 ♖×g4 ♖f8 43 ♔h5 ♗c1 44 ♖g7† ♖f7 45 ♗d6† ♔×d6 46 ♖×f7 ♖c4 47 ♔g6 ♖c2 48 h4 a4 49 ♖ff3 a3 50 ♖b3 a2 51 ♖b6† ♔c7 52 ♖a6 ♔b7 53 ♖a4 ♔b6 54 ♖f6 ♔b5 55 ♖a8 ♗e3 56 ♖×e6 ♗×d4 57 ♖b8† ♔a5 58 ♖a8† ♔b5 59 ♖b8† ♔c4 60 ♖c6† ♔d3 61 ♖b3† ♗c3 62 ♖a6 ♖g2† 63 ♔h5 ♔c4 64 ♖ba3 a1♕ 65 ♖6a4† ♔d3 66 ♖×a1 ♗×a1 67 ♖×a1 ♖g8 68 ♖d1† ♔e4 69 ♖e1† ♔f5 70 ♖f1† ♔e4 71 ♖e1† ♔f4 72 ♖d1 ♔e5 73 ♖e1† ♔d6 74 ♖d1 ♔e5 75 ♖e1† ♔d6 76 ♖d1 ♔e5 ½–½

BLITZ 6.9 — SARGON 3 1 e4 g6 2 d4 ♗g7 3 ♘f3 d6 4 ♗c4 ♘f6 5 ♕e2 ♘c6 6 O-O ♗g4 7 c3 e5 8 d×e5 ♘×e5 9 ♘bd2 ♘×c4 10 ♘×c4 O-O 11 ♗g5 ♕e8 12 ♖fe1 ♕e6 13 h3 h6 14 ♗×f6 ♗×f3 15 ♕×f3 ♗×f6 16 ♘e3 ♗e5 17 ♘d5 ♖ac8 18 ♖ed1 ♖fe8 19 ♕e3 c6 20 ♘f4 ♕d7 21 ♖ac1 ♗g7 22 ♘d3 b6 23 ♕f4 ♕e6 24 ♖e1 g5 25 ♕g3 ♔h7 26 ♖cd1 c5 27 ♕h2 c4 28 ♘b4 ♗e5 29 ♕h1 ♕d7 30 ♘d5 ♕a4 31 a3 ♕c2 32 h4 g4 33 ♖b1 ♖c5 34 g3 ♗g7 35 ♕g2 ♔h8 36 f3 ♕×g2† 37 ♔×g2 g×f3† 38 ♔×f3 f5 39 ♖bd1 ♖e5 40 ♘f4 ♖×e4 41 ♖×e4 f×e4† 42 ♔×e4 ♖e5† 43 ♔f3 ♖b5 44 ♖d2 ♔h7 45 a4 ♖a5 46 ♖×d6 ♖×a4 47 ♖d7 ♔h8 48 ♘d5 ♖a2 49 g4 b5 50 g5 h×g5 51 h×g5 ♖×b2 52 ♖×a7 ♖d2 53 ♔e4 ♖e2† 54 ♔f4 ♔h7 55 ♖d7 ♖f2† 56 ♔g4 ♖g2† 57 ♔h4 ♖h2† 58 ♔g3 ♖a2 59 ♔f3 ♖a1 60 ♔e4 ♖f1 61 ♖d6 ♖e1† 62 ♔f5 ♖f1† 63 ♔g4 ♖c1 64 ♖d7 ♖e1 65 ♖b7 ♖g1† 66 ♔f5 ♖f1† 67 ♔e4 ♖e1† 68 ♔f4 ♖f1† 69 ♔g3 ♖f5 70 ♖×b5 ♖×g5† 71 ♔f4 ♖g1 72 ♖b4 ♖d1 73 ♔e4 ♖e1† 74 ♔f3 ♖f1† 75 ♔e2 ♖f5 76 ♘e3 ♖f4 77 ♔d2 ♖f2† 78 ♔d1 ♗×c3 79 ♖×c4 ♗g7 80 ♔e1 ½–½

RUFUS — BS6676 1 c4 ♘f6 2 ♘c3 d5 3 c×d5 ♘×d5 4 d4 e6 5 e4 ♘×c3 6 b×c3 b6 7 ♘f3 ♗e7 8 ♗c4 O–O 9 O–O c5 10 ♗f4 ♘c6 11 ♕d2 ♗b7 12 ♖fe1 c×d4 13 ♘×d4 ♘a5 14 ♗d3 ♖c8 15 ♗e5 ♖c5 16 ♘f3 ♘c6 17 ♗d4 ♖h5 18 ♖ab1 ♖a5 19 ♗c4 ♔h8 20 ♕c2 ♕c8 21 a4 ♖d8 22 ♗e3 ♘e5 23 ♘×e5 ♖×e5 24 ♗d3 ♖h5 25 ♗f4 e5 26 ♗e2 ♖h4 27 g3 ♖h3 28 ♗×e5 ♔g8 29 ♗f3 ♖h6 30 ♖ed1 ♖e8 31 ♗g2 g5 32 c4 ♕g4 33 a5 ♗c5 34 h3 ♕e6 35 a6 ♗×a6 36 ♖a1 ♗b7 37 ♖×a7 ♗c6 38 ♗c3 b5 39 ♖aa1 ♕×c4 **0–1**

ACM 1980 — Nashville

October 26 — October 28

	1	2	3	4	tot
1 BELLE	6+□	5+■	2+□	3+■	4
2 CHAOS	7+■	9+□	1−■	5+□	3
3 CHALLENGER	4=□	7+■	9+■	1−□	2½
4 BEBE	3=■	6+■	5−□	9+□	2½
5 CRAY BLITZ	8+□	1−□	4+■	2−■	2
6 MYCHESS	1−■	4−□	8+■	10+■	2
7 OSTRICH 81	2−□	3−□	10+■	8=□	1½
8 CUBE 2.0	5−■	10+□	6−□	7=■	1½
9 AWIT	10+□	2−■	3−□	4−■	1
10 CLASH	9−■	8−■	7−□	6−□	0

Round 1

AWIT — CLASH 1 b3 e5 2 ♗b2 ♘c6 3 e3 ♗c5 4 ♘f3 d6 5 ♗c4 ♘f6 6 d4 e×d4 7 e×d4 ♗b4† 8 c3 ♕e7† 9 ♗e2 ♗a5 10 O–O ♘d5 11 ♗c4 ♘f4 12 ♖e1 ♗e6 13 d5 ♔d7 14 d×c6† ♔×c6 15 ♘d4† ♔c5 16 b4† ♔×c4 17 ♘d2† ♔d5 18 c4# **1–0**

BELLE — MYCHESS 1 e4 e5 2 ♘f3 ♘f6 3 d4 e×d4 4 e5 ♘e4 5 ♕×d4 d5 6 e×d6 ♘×d6 7 ♘c3 ♘c6 8 ♕f4 ♗f5 9 ♗b5 ♕e7† 10 ♗e3 ♗×c2 11 ♗×c6† b×c6 12 ♘d4 ♗e4 13 O–O c5 14 ♘db5 ♘×b5 15 ♘×b5 g5 16 ♕g3 ♖c8 17 f3 c6 18 ♗×g5 f6 19 ♘×a7 ♖a8 20 ♖ae1 ♕×a7 21 ♗×f6 c4† 22 ♔h1 ♗g7 23 ♗×g7 ♖g8 24 ♖×e4† ♔f7 25 ♖fe1 ♖×g7 26 ♕f4† ♔g8 27 ♖e8† ♖×e8 28 ♖×e8# **1–0**

OSTRICH 81 — CHAOS 1 e4 c5 2 ♘f3 ♘c6 3 d4 c×d4 4 ♘×d4 ♘f6 5 ♘×c6 b×c6 6 ♘c3 e6 7 ♗e2 ♗b4 8 ♗d2 d5 9 f3 d×e4 10 ♘×e4 ♘×e4 11 f×e4 ♕h4† 12 ♔f1 ♕f6† 13 ♗f3 ♗a6† 14 ♔f2 ♗c5† 15 ♗e3 ♗×e3† 16 ♔×e3 ♖d8 17 ♕c1 ♕g5† 18 ♔f2 ♖d2† 19 ♕×d2 ♕×d2† 20 ♔g3 ♕×c2 21 b3 ♕d2 22 ♖he1 ♕g5† 23 ♔f2 ♔e7 **0–1**

CRAY BLITZ — CUBE 2.0 1 e4 e5 2 ♘f3 ♘c6 3 ♗c4 d6 4 ♘c3 ♘f6 5 ♘g5 d5 6 e×d5 ♘d4 7 d6 ♗e6 8 ♗×e6 f×e6 9 d×c7 ♕×c7 10 O–O **1–0**

CHALLENGER — BEBE 1 e4 c5 2 ♘f3 d6 3 d4 c×d4 4 ♘×d4 ♘f6 5 ♘c3 g6 6 f4 ♘bd7 7 ♗e2 ♗g7 8 O–O O–O 9 ♗e3 a6 10 ♖c1 e6 11 ♘f3 ♘g4 12 ♕d2 ♘×e3 13 ♕×e3 ♕c7 14 ♖cd1 b5 15 ♕d2 b4 16 ♘a4 ♖b8 17 b3 d5 18 e×d5 e×d5 19 ♕×d5 ♕×f4 20 ♗c4 ♘b6 21 ♘×b6 ♕e3† 22 ♔h1 ♕×b6 23 ♘g5 ♗b7 24 ♕d7 ♗c8 25 ♗×f7† ♔h8 26 ♕d6 ♗f5 27 ♗c4 ♕×d6 28 ♖×d6 ♗c3 29 ♗×a6 ♗×c2 30 ♖d7 ♖×f1† 31 ♗×f1 ♗g7 32 ♗c4 h6 33 ♘f7† ♔h7 34 ♘d8 ♗f5 35 ♘e6 ♗×e6 36 ♗×e6 ♖a8 37 ♖d2 ♖a6 38 ♗c4 ♖a7 39 ♔g1 h5 40 ♖e2 ♗d4† 41 ♔f1 ♔g7 42 ♖e4 ♗b2 43 ♗d3 ♗c3 44 ♖e2 ♖f7† 45 ♖f2 ♖d7 46 ♗b5 ♖d5 47 ♗c4 ♖a5 48 g3 ♗d4 49 ♖d2 ♗c3 50 ♖e2 g5 51 ♖f2 h4 52 g4 h3 53 ♖f5 ♖×f5† 54 g×f5 ♔f6 ½–½

Round 2

MYCHESS — BEBE 1 e4 c5 2 ♘f3 d6 3 d4 c×d4 4 ♘×d4 ♘f6 5 ♘c3 g6 6 ♗e3 ♗g7 7 ♗e2 O–O 8 ♕d2 ♘c6 9 O–O–O ♗d7 10 ♔b1 ♖e8 11 h4 ♖c8 12 h5 ♘×h5 13 ♗×h5 g×h5 14 ♘×c6 b×c6 15 ♗×a7 ♖a8 16 ♗d4 ♗×d4 17 ♕×d4 ♖a5 18 a4 ♖g5 19 f4 ♖×g2 20 ♖dg1 ♖×g1† 21 ♕×g1† ♔h8 22 ♕d4† f6 23 ♖×h5 ♖g8 24 b3 ♖g3 25 b4 e5 26 f×e5 d×e5 27 ♕c5 ♗h3 28 ♖h4 ♕b8 29 ♘e2 ♖f3 30 a5 ♗f1 31 ♘g1 ♖g3 32 ♕e7 ♖g7 33 ♕c5 ♖×g1 34 ♕×g1 ♕×b4† 35 ♔a2 ♗c4† 36 ♔a1 ♕a3† 37 ♔b1 ♗a2† 38 ♔a1 ♗b3† 39 ♔b1 ♕a2† 40 ♔c1 ♕×c2# **0–1**

CRAY BLITZ — BELLE 1 e4 e5 2 ♘f3 ♘c6 3 ♗c4 ♘f6 4 ♘g5 d5 5 e×d5 ♘a5 6 ♗b5† c6 7 d×c6 b×c6 8 ♗e2 h6 9 ♘f3 e4 10 ♘e5 ♗d6 11 f4 e×f3 12 ♘×f3 O–O 13 O–O ♕c7 14 d4 c5 15 ♘c3 a6 16 d×c5 ♗×c5† 17 ♔h1 ♗b7 18 ♕e1 ♖ae8 19 ♕h4 ♘e4 20 ♗f4 ♕c6 21 ♘×e4 ♕×e4 22 ♗d3 ♕e6 23 ♕h5 ♕b6 24 ♕f5 g6 25 ♕h3 h5 26 ♗h6 ♕×b2 27 ♗×f8 ♗×f8 28 ♕d7 ♖e7 29 ♕a4 ♕c3 30 ♕f4 ♗d5 31 ♗×a6 ♕×c2 32 ♖fc1 ♕b2 33 ♕d2 ♕×d2 34 ♘×d2 ♗g7 35 ♖ab1 ♗×a2 36 ♖b6 ♖e6 37 ♖b8† ♔h7 38 ♗f1 ♗h6 39 ♖b2 ♗×d2 40 ♖×d2 ♘b3 41 ♖×a2 ♘×c1 42 ♖d2 ♔g7 43 g3 ♘b3 44 ♖d5 ♖c6 45 ♔g2 ♖c2† 46 ♔h3 ♔f6 47 ♖d6† ♔e5 48 ♖d8 ♘d4 49 ♗d3 ♖f2 50 ♖c8 g5 51 ♖h8 ♘f3 52 ♖×h5 f5 53 ♗×f5 ♔×f5 54 g4† ♔f4 55 ♖h6 ♖×h2# **0–1**

CHAOS — AWIT 1 d4 ♘f6 2 c4 g6 3 ♘c3 d5 4 c×d5 ♘×d5 5 e4 ♘×c3 6 b×c3 ♗g7 7 ♗c4 c5 8 ♘e2 O–O 9 O–O ♘c6 10 ♗e3 c×d4 11 c×d4 ♗d7 12 ♖c1 ♖c8 13 f3 ♘a5 14 ♗d3 ♕b6 15 ♕d2 ♖×c1 16 ♖×c1 ♖b8 17 d5 ♕d8 18 ♗×a7 ♖c8 19 ♖×c8 ♗×c8 20 ♗c5 b6 21 ♗e3 ♗e5 22 ♕b4 ♗c7 23 ♕b2 ♕d6 24 ♗f4 ♕c5† 25 ♔h1 ♘c4 26 ♕c3 ♗×f4 27 ♘×f4 b5 28 ♗e2 ♕a3 29 ♕×a3 ♘×a3 30 ♔g1 g5 31 ♘d3 ♔g7 32 ♔f2 h6 33 ♘b4 h5 34 ♔e3 f5 35 ♔d4 g4 36 ♗d3 g×f3 37 g×f3 ♔f6 38 e5† ♔g6 39 ♘c6 ♔f7 40 ♘a7 ♗b7 41 ♗×f5 ♗a6 42 f4 ♘c4 43 ♗d3 h4 44 ♘×b5 ♗×b5 45 ♗×c4 ♗×c4 46 ♔×c4 ♔e8 47 d6 h3 48 ♔d5 e×d6 49 ♔×d6 ♔f7 50 e6† ♔g6 **1–0**

OSTRICH 81 — CHALLENGER 1 e4 e5 2 ♘f3 ♘c6 3 ♗b5 a6 4 ♗×c6 d×c6 5 d4 e×d4 6 ♕×d4 ♕×d4

7 ♘×d4 ♗d7 8 O-O ♗d6 9 ♗e3 ♘f6 10 ♘c3 ♘g4 11 ♘f3 ♘×e3 12 f×e3 ♗e6 13 ♖fd1 O-O-O 14 ♘d4 ♗e5 15 ♘×e6 f×e6 16 ♖×d8† ♔×d8 17 ♘d1 ♔c8 18 h3 ♖d8 19 ♔f1 ♖d2 20 c3 ♔d7 21 a4 ♔d6 22 ♖b1 ♗g3 23 c4 ♔c5 24 b3 ♔b4 25 a5 c5 26 e5 h5 27 e4 ♔×a5 28 ♖a1† ♔b4 29 ♖b1 ♗×e5 30 ♘e3 ♔c3 31 ♔e1 ♔d3 32 ♘d1 ♗d4 33 b4 ♖×g2 34 ♖b3† ♔×c4 35 ♘e3† ♗×e3 36 ♖×e3 **0–1**

CUBE 2.0 — CLASH 1 e4 e5 2 ♘f3 ♘c6 3 ♗b5 ♗c5 4 c3 ♕f6 5 b4 ♗b6 6 d3 ♘ge7 7 ♘a3 d5 8 ♗g5 ♕d6 9 e×d5 ♘×d5 10 ♘c4 ♕e6 11 ♗d2 e4 12 ♘g5 ♕f6 13 ♘×e4 ♕f5 14 ♘ed6† c×d6 15 ♘×d6† ♔e7 16 ♘×f5† ♗×f5 17 ♕f3 ♔e6 18 ♗×c6 b×c6 19 c4 ♘e7 20 c5 ♗c7 21 ♕e3† ♔d7 22 ♕d4† ♘d5 23 ♕×g7 ♔c8 24 O-O-O ♗g6 25 ♕f6 ♔b7 26 b5 ♗×h2 27 b×c6† ♔b8 28 ♖×h2 ♘c7 29 ♕×g6 h×g6 30 ♖×h8† ♘e8 31 ♗f4† ♔c8 32 ♖×e8# **1–0**

Round 3

CLASH — OSTRICH 81 1 e4 d5 2 ♘c3 ♘f6 3 ♘×d5 ♘×e4 4 ♘c3 ♘×c3 5 d×c3 ♕×d1† 6 ♔×d1 ♗f5 7 ♗d3 e6 8 ♗f4 ♗c5 9 ♔e2 ♗×d3† 10 c×d3 ♘a6 11 ♗e5 O-O 12 b4 f6 13 b×c5 f×e5 14 d4 e×d4 15 c×d4 e5 16 d×e5 ♘×c5 17 ♖d1 ♘e4 18 ♘f3 ♘c3† 19 ♔e3 ♘×d1† 20 ♖×d1 c5 21 ♖d7 b6 22 e6 ♖ae8 23 e7 ♖f7 24 ♖×a7 ♖e×e7† 25 ♖×e7 ♖×e7† 26 ♔d3 ♖a7 27 h3 ♖×a2 28 ♔e3 c4 29 g4 b5 30 ♘e5 ♖a3† 31 ♔e4 ♖×h3 32 f3 c3 33 ♔d4 c2 34 ♘d3 ♖×f3 35 ♘e1 ♖f4† 36 ♔e5 c1♕ 37 ♘d3 ♕e3† 38 ♔d6 ♕×d3† 39 ♔c6 ♖×g4 40 ♔c7 ♖g6 41 ♔b8 ♕d8† 42 ♔b7 ♖b6† 43 ♔a7 ♕b8# **0–1**

BELLE — CHAOS 1 e4 c5 2 c3 ♘f6 3 e5 ♘d5 4 d4 c×d4 5 c×d4 d6 6 ♘f3 ♘c6 7 ♗c4 ♘b6 8 ♗b5 e6 9 O-O ♗e7 10 e×d6 ♕×d6 11 ♘c3 O-O 12 ♖e1 ♗d7 13 ♗e3 ♘d5 14 ♗a4 ♘×e3 15 f×e3 ♖fc8 16 e4 a6 17 ♗×c6 ♖×c6 18 ♘e5 ♖c7 19 ♖e2 ♗e8 20 ♘f3 ♖ac8 21 e5 ♕b4 22 d5 ♕c5† 23 ♔h1 e×d5 24 ♘×d5 ♖d8 25 ♖d2 ♖cd7 26 b4 ♕×d5 27 ♖×d5 ♖×d5 28 ♕e1 ♗a4 29 ♕c3 ♗c6 30 a3 ♗g5 31 ♕c2 ♗f4 32 ♖e1 ♖d3 33 ♕c4 ♗h6 34 e6 ♖×a3 35 e×f7† ♔f8 36 ♕c5† ♔×f7 37 ♕e7† ♔g8 38 ♕×d8† **1–0**

AWIT — CHALLENGER 1 b3 d5 2 ♗b2 ♘f6 3 e3 e6 4 ♘f3 ♗d6 5 ♗e2 O-O 6 O-O ♗d7 7 ♘a3 ♘g4 8 h3 ♕e7 9 ♘b5 ♗×b5 10 ♗×b5 ♘f6 11 ♘e5 c6 12 ♗e2 ♘bd7 13 f4 ♘e4 14 ♘×d7 ♕×d7 15 ♕e1 ♕d8 16 d3 ♘f6 17 ♗f3 ♖c8 18 a4 ♖e8 19 ♕g3 ♗c5 20 ♖fe1 ♗b4 21 ♖e2 ♗e7 22 ♖ae1 ♖f8 23 ♔h2 ♗b4 24 c3 ♗d6 25 e4 d×e4 26 d×e4 ♗c5 27 b4 ♗e7 28 ♕f2 c5 29 ♖d2 ♕c7 30 e5 c×b4 31 e×f6 ♗×f6 32 c×b4 ♕×f4† 33 g3 ♕×b4 34 ♗×f6 g×f6 35 ♖b2 ♕×a4 36 ♗×b7 ♖c4 37 ♖a2 ♕b4 38 ♖×a7 f5 39 ♕e3 ♖c2† 40 ♔g1 ♖b8 41 ♗f3 f4 42 g×f4 ♖c3 43 ♕e5 ♖×f3 44 ♔g2 ♕×f4 45 ♕×f4 ♖×f4 46 ♔g3 ♖c4 47 ♖e7 ♖b3† 48 ♔h2 ♖c2† 49 ♔g1 ♖g3† 50 ♔f1 ♖f3† 51 ♔g1 ♖×h3 52 ♖f1 ♖g3† 53 ♔h1 ♖h3† 54 ♔g1 h5 55 ♖e×f7 ♖g3† 56 ♔h1 h4 57 ♖1f4 e5 58 ♖f8† ♔g7 59 ♖8f7† ♔g6 60 ♖4f6† ♔h5 61 ♖h7† ♔g5 62 ♖hh6 e4 63 ♖hg6† ♔h5 64 ♖h6† ♔g4 65 ♖c6 ♖×c6 66 ♖×c6 **0–1**

BEBE — CRAY BLITZ 1 e4 c5 2 ♘f3 e6 3 ♗e2 ♘c6 4 O-O ♘f6 5 ♘c3 ♗e7 6 d4 c×d4 7 ♘×d4 O-O 8 ♗f4 ♘×d4 9 ♕×d4 d6 10 e5 d×e5 11 ♕×e5 ♕b6 12 ♖ab1 ♗d7 13 ♖fd1 ♗c5 14 ♗g3 ♖ac8 15 a3 ♖fd8 16 b4 ♗e7 17 ♗f4 ♗e8 18 ♖×d8 ♗×d8 19 ♖b3 ♗c7 20 ♕g5 ♗×f4 21 ♕×f4 ♖d8 22 ♗f3 ♗c6 23 ♗×c6 ♕×c6 24 ♔f1 b6 25 a4 ♕e8 26 a5 e5 27 ♕c4 ♖d2 28 a×b6 a×b6 29 ♖b2 e4 30 ♖a2 h6 31 ♕c7 ♕e6 32 b5 ♘g4 33 ♔e1 ♖×f2 34 h3 ♖×g2 35 h×g4 ♖g1† 36 ♔f2 ♖×g4 37 ♖a8† ♔h7 38 ♔e3 f5 39 ♖b8 f4† 40 ♔d4 e3 41 ♕c8 f3† 42 ♔d3 **0–1**

CUBE 2.0 — MYCHESS 1 d4 ♘f6 2 c4 g6 3 ♘f3 e6 4 ♕a4 ♘c6 5 a3 a5 6 ♘c3 ♗g7 7 e4 ♘g4 8 h3 ♘h6 9 d5 ♘e7 10 d×e6 f×e6 11 ♗g5 ♘f7 12 ♗h4 O-O 13 ♖d1 ♘e5 14 ♘×e5 ♗×e5 15 ♗d3 d6 16 ♗c2 c5 17 ♕b3 ♕c7 18 ♘b5 ♕d7 19 ♕d3 ♖a6 20 b3 ♔g7 21 ♗g3 ♗×g3 22 f×g3 d5 23 e×d5 e×d5 24 c×d5 ♘×d5 25 ♘c3 ♖e6† 26 ♘e4 ♖e5 27 ♖f1 ♕e7 28 ♖×f8 ♕×f8 29 ♔d2 ♗f5 30 ♕f3 ♕e7 31 ♔c1 ♖×e4 32 g4 ♗×g4 33 h×g4 ♕g5† 34 ♔b1 ♖d4 35 ♖×d4 c×d4 36 ♗d3 h6 37 ♗c4 ♘c3† **0–1**

Round 4

CLASH — MYCHESS 1 e4 e5 2 ♗c4 ♘f6 3 ♘c3 ♘c6 4 d3 ♗c5 5 ♕f3 d6 6 ♗e3 ♗g4 7 ♕g3 ♗×e3 8 ♕×e3 ♘d4 9 ♖c1 O-O 10 ♘ce2 b5 11 ♗b3 ♘×b3 12 c×b3 c5 13 ♘f3 ♕a5† 14 ♘c3 b4 15 ♘d5 ♘×d5 16 e×d5 ♕×a2 17 ♖c4 f5 18 h3 ♗×f3 19 ♕×f3 a5 20 O-O ♕×b2 21 ♕d1 a4 22 b×a4 ♕a2 23 ♕f3 ♕×a4 24 g4 f×g4 25 ♕×g4 ♖f6 26 ♕e4 ♖f4 27 ♕e3 ♖×c4 28 d×c4 ♕a3 29 ♖e1 ♕×e3 30 ♖×e3 ♖a3 31 ♔g2 ♖×e3 32 f×e3 b3 33 ♔f3 b2 34 h4 b1♕ 35 e4 ♕d3† 36 ♔f2 ♕×e4 37 h5 ♕×c4 38 ♔g3 g6 39 h×g6 h×g6 40 ♔g2 e4 41 ♔g3 ♕×d5 42 ♔h4 e3 43 ♔g3 ♕f5 44 ♔h2 e2 45 ♔g3 c4 46 ♔g2 c3 47 ♔g3 c2 48 ♔g2 d5 49 ♔g3 d4 50 ♔g2 d3 51 ♔h2 d2 52 ♔g3 c1♖ 53 ♔g2 d1♖ 54 ♔g3 ♖g1† 55 ♔h4 ♕g4# **0–1**

CHALLENGER — BELLE 1 e4 e5 2 ♘f3 ♘c6 3 ♗b5 a6 4 ♗a4 ♘f6 5 O-O ♘×e4 6 d4 b5 7 ♗b3 d5 8 d×e5 ♗e6 9 c3 ♗c5 10 ♗e3 ♗×e3 11 f×e3 ♖b8 12 ♘bd2 ♘c5 13 ♕e1 ♘d3 14 ♕g3 O-O 15 ♖ab1 ♕e7 16 ♗c2 ♕c5 17 ♘g5 ♘c×e5 18 ♘×h7 ♖fd8 19 ♘f6† ♔f8 20 ♗×d3 ♘×d3 21 ♘h5 g6 22 ♘f6 ♗f5 23 ♕g5 b4 24 ♘h7† ♔e8 25 ♘f6† ♔f8 26 ♘b3 ♕c4 27 ♘h7† ♔e8 28 c×b4 ♖×b4 29 ♘f6† ♔f8 30 ♘g4 ♖d6 31 ♘h6 ♕e4 32 ♖×f5 g×f5 33 ♕g8† ♔e7 34 ♕×f7† ♔d8 35 ♘×f5 ♖c6 36 h4 ♖c2 37 ♕f8† ♔d7 38 ♕f7† ♔c8 39 ♕g6 ♔b7 40 ♘a5† ♔a8 41 ♕×a6† ♔b8 42 ♕g6 ♘e5 43 ♕g8† ♔a7 44 ♖f1 ♖b×b2 45 ♔h1 ♖×g2 46 ♘c6† ♘×c6 47 ♕a8† ♔×a8 48 a4 ♔b8 49 a5 ♔a8 50 a6 ♔a7 51 h5 ♔b6 52 a7 ♖g1† 53 ♔×g1 ♕g2# **0–1**

CHAOS — CRAY BLITZ 1 d4 d5 2 c4 e6 3 ♘c3 ♘f6 4 ♗g5 ♗e7 5 e3 O-O 6 ♘f3 h6 7 ♗h4 ♘e4 8 ♗×e7 ♕×e7 9 c×d5 ♘×c3 10 b×c3 e×d5 11 ♕b3 ♖d8 12 c4 d×c4 13 ♗×c4 ♘c6 14 ♗e2 ♖d6 15 O-O ♗e6 16 ♕c3 ♖ad8 17 ♖ab1 ♗×a2 18 ♖×b7 a5 19 ♗d3 ♗d5 20 ♖fb1 a4 21 ♕a1 ♖a8 22 ♘d2 ♖dd8 23 ♘c4 ♕e6 24 ♖×c7 ♕g4 25 ♗f1 ♘a5 26 ♘b6 ♘b3 27 ♕a2 ♗e4 28 ♘×a8 ♗×b1 29 ♕×b1 ♖×a8 30 ♗c4 ♘×d4 31 e×d4 ♕×d4 32 ♗×f7† ♔h8 33 g3 ♖f8 34

♕f5 ♕a1† 35 ♔g2 ♕b2 36 ♗g6 ♕b8 37 ♕d7 ♕a8† 38 ♔g1 ♖g8 39 ♖a7 ♕f3 40 ♖×a4 ♕c3 41 ♕d5 ♖f8 42 ♔g2 ♕b2 43 ♗f5 ♕b8 44 ♗d3 ♕b2 45 ♖f4 ♖g8 46 ♕e4 **1–0**

BEBE — AWIT 1 e4 c5 2 ♘f3 d6 3 d4 c×d4 4 ♘×d4 ♘f6 5 ♘c3 a6 6 ♗e2 e5 7 ♘f3 ♘c6 8 O–O ♗e7 9 ♗e3 ♗d7 10 ♘d5 O–O 11 ♗b6 ♕c8 12 ♘×f6† g×f6 13 c3 f5 14 ♗d3 ♗d8 15 ♗×d8 ♕×d8 16 e×f5 d5 17 ♗c2 ♕b6 18 f6 ♕b5 19 ♕d2 ♖fc8 20 ♕h6 **1–0**

OSTRICH 81 — CUBE 2.0 1 e4 c5 2 ♘f3 ♘f6 3 ♘c3 ♘c6 4 ♗e2 d6 5 O–O ♗g4 6 h3 ♗×f3 7 ♗×f3 g6 8 ♖e1 ♗h6 9 e5 ♘×e5 10 ♗×b7 ♖b8 11 ♗a6 ♕a5 12 ♗e2 O–O 13 d3 ♗×c1 14 ♕×c1 ♘c6 15 ♖b1 ♘d4 16 a4 ♕b4 17 ♔h1 a5 18 ♕d1 ♕b7 19 b3 ♕b4 20 ♘e4 ♘×e4 21 d×e4 ♘×e2 22 ♖×e2 c4 23 ♖e3 ♖fc8 24 ♕f3 ♖b6 25 ♕g4 ♖cb8 26 ♕h4 ♕d2 27 ♖be1 ♕×c2 28 ♖1e2 ♕d1† 29 ♖e1 ♕d4 30 b×c4 e5 31 ♖c1 ♖b4 32 ♖a3 ♖×c4 33 ♖×c4 ♕×c4 34 ♖a1 f5 35 f3 f×e4 36 f×e4 d5 37 ♕e1 ♕×e4 38 ♕×a5 ♖b1† 39 ♖×b1 ♕×b1† 40 ♔h2 ♕b7 41 ♕d8† ♔g7 42 a5 ♕f7 43 a6 ♕f4† 44 ♔h1 ♕f1† 45 ♔h2 ♕×a6 46 ♕e7† ♔h6 47 ♕×e5 ♕d3 48 ♕f4† ♔g7 49 ♕e5† ♔g8 50 ♕e8† ♔g7 51 ♕e7† ♔h6 52 ♕h4† ♔g7 **½–½**

ACM 1981 — Los Angeles

November 8 — November 10

	1	2	3	4	tot
1 BELLE	7+□	9+■	2=□	3+■	3½
2 NUCHESS	10+■	4+□	1=■	5=□	3
3 CRAY BLITZ	6+■	5+□	11+■	1−□	3
4 BEBE	12+□	2−■	14+■	7+■	3
5 DUCHESS	15+□	3−■	8+□	2=■	2½
6 PHILIDOR	3−□	15+■	9+□	8=■	2½
7 OSTRICH	1−■	16+□	12+■	4−□	2
8 CHALLENGER	14+■	11=□	5−■	6=□	2
9 L'EXCENTRIQUE	16+■	1−□	6−■	11+□	2
10 MYCHESS	2−□	12−■	15+□	14+□	2
11 CHAOS	13+□	8=■	3−□	9−■	1½
12 CUBE 2.1	4−■	10+□	7−□	13=■	1½
13 SCHACH 2.5	11−■	14−□	16+■	12=□	1½
14 CHATURANGA	8−□	13+■	4−□	10−■	1
15 AWIT	5−■	6−□	10−■	16+□	1
16 PRODIGY	9−□	7−■	13−□	15−■	0

Round 1

BELLE — OSTRICH 1 e4 d5 2 e×d5 ♘f6 3 d4 ♘×d5 4 c4 ♘b6 5 ♘f3 ♗g4 6 ♗e2 c6 7 ♘a3 e6 8 c5 ♘d5 9 ♗g5 f6 10 ♗d2 ♕e7 11 ♘c4 ♕d7 12 ♘h4 ♗f5 13 ♘×f5 e×f5 14 O–O ♗e7 15 ♗d3 O–O 16 ♘e3 ♘×e3 17 f×e3 g6 18 ♗c4† ♔h8 19 b4 b5 20 ♗b3 a6 21 a4 ♕b7 22 ♗c3 ♗d8 23 ♗e6 ♕e7 24 d5 b×a4 25 ♖e1 c×d5 26 ♗×d5 ♖a7 27 ♖×a4 ♕e8 28 ♗c4 h5 29 ♕a1 ♕c6 30 b5 ♕c8 31 b×a6 ♕c6 32 ♖d1 ♗e7 33 ♗d5 **1–0**

PHILIDOR — CRAY BLITZ 1 e4 e5 2 ♘f3 ♘c6 3 ♗c4 ♗c5 4 O–O ♘f6 5 d4 e×d4 6 c3 d×c3 7 e5 c×b2 8 ♗×b2 ♘g4 9 ♗×f7† ♔×f7 10 ♕d5† ♔g6 11 ♕×c5 d6 12 ♕b5 ♘c×e5 13 ♗×e5 ♘×e5 14 ♘×e5† d×e5 15 ♕×e5 c6 16 ♕e4† ♗f5 17 ♕e5 ♖e8 18 ♕g3† ♕g5 19 ♕d6† ♖e6 20 ♕a3 ♖d8 21 f3 ♗d3 22 f4 ♕f6 23 f5† ♗×f5 24 ♕g3† ♕g5 25 ♕f2 ♕e3 26 h3 ♕×f2† 27 ♔×f2 ♗d3 28 ♖c1 ♖e2† 29 ♔g1 ♗e4 30 g4 ♖g2† 31 ♔f1 ♖h2 32 ♘c3 ♖f8† 33 ♔e1 ♗d3 34 ♘d5 ♖e2† 35 ♔d1 ♖f1# **0–1**

CHAOS — SCHACH 2.5 1 d4 d5 2 c4 e6 3 ♘c3 ♘f6 4 ♗g5 ♗e7 5 e3 O–O 6 ♘f3 h6 7 ♗h4 b6 8 c×d5 ♘×d5 9 ♗×e7 ♕×e7 10 ♘×d5 e×d5 11 ♗d3 ♗e6 12 ♕c2 ♕b4† 13 ♕c3 ♕×c3† 14 b×c3 ♘d7 15 ♖b1 ♖ae8 16 O–O c5 17 d×c5 ♘×c5 18 ♗b5 ♗d7 19 ♗×d7 ♘×d7 20 ♖b5 ♘f6 21 ♖fb1 ♖e4 22 ♘d4 ♖c8 23 ♖5b3 ♔f8 24 ♘b5 ♖a4 25 ♖1b2 ♔e7 26 f3 ♖cc4 27 ♘d4 ♘d7 28 ♘f5† ♔f6 29 ♘d6 ♖c6 30 ♘b5 ♘c5 31 ♘d4 ♖c7 32 ♖b5 ♘d3 33 ♖c2 ♖e7 34 ♖e2 ♖e5 35 f4 ♖h5 36 g4 ♖h4 37 ♖g2 ♘c5 38 ♘f5 ♖h3 39 ♖d2 h5 40 ♖×d5 h×g4 41 ♖b2 ♘e4 42 ♘d4 ♖×e3 43 ♖f5† ♔g6 44 ♖e5 ♔f6 45 ♖f5† ♔e7 46 ♖e5† ♔f8 47 f5 **1–0**

MYCHESS — NUCHESS 1 e4 c5 2 ♘f3 ♘c6 3 d4 c×d4 4 ♘×d4 ♘f6 5 ♘c3 d6 6 ♗g5 e6 7 ♗e2 ♗e7 8 ♘db5 O–O 9 O–O a6 10 ♗×f6 g×f6 11 ♘d4 ♔h8 12 ♘×c6 b×c6 13 ♕d2 ♗d7 14 ♖ad1 ♕a5 15 b3 d5 16 e×d5 ♗b4 17 ♕e3 ♗×c3 18 d×e6 ♗×e6 19 ♖d3 ♗b2 20 ♗f3 ♗f5 21 ♖d6 ♖ae8 22 ♕d2 ♕×d2 23 ♖×d2 ♗c3 24 ♖d6 ♖e6 25 ♖dd1 ♖fe8 26 ♖c1 ♖d6 27 g4 ♖g8 28 h3 h5 29 ♗e2 h×g4 30 h×g4 ♗×g4 31 ♗×g4 ♖×g4† 32 ♔h2 f5 33 f3 ♖h6# **0–1**

DUCHESS — AWIT 1 e4 c5 2 d4 c×d4 3 c3 d×c3 4 ♘×c3 ♘c6 5 ♘f3 d6 6 ♗c4 e6 7 O–O ♘f6 8 ♕e2 ♗e7 9 ♖d1 O–O 10 e5 ♘e8 11 e×d6 ♘×d6 12 ♗f4 ♘b4 13 a3 ♘c6 14 ♗×d6 ♗×d6 15 ♘e4 ♗×h2† 16 ♘×h2 ♕e7 17 ♕h5 ♗d7 18 ♖ac1 ♖ad8 19 ♘d6 ♗e8 20 ♘×e8 ♖×d1† 21 ♖×d1 ♖×e8 22 ♘f3 ♕c7 23 ♕h4 h6 24 ♕h2 ♕×h2† 25 ♔×h2 ♖d8 26 ♖×d8† ♘×d8 27 ♔g3 g5 28 ♘d4 h5 29 ♔f3 ♔f8 30 ♔e4 g4 31 ♔f4 ♔g7 32 ♔g5 a6 33 ♔×h5 b5 34 ♗b3 e5 35 ♘f5† ♔f6 36 ♔×g4 ♘b7 37 ♘g3 ♘c5 38 ♗c2 ♔e7 39 ♔f5 ♘d7 40 b4 ♔d8 41 ♘e4 ♔e7 42 g4 ♔e8 43 ♘f6† ♔e7 44 ♘×d7 ♔×d7 45 ♔×e5 ♔e7 46 ♗e4 ♔e8 47 ♔f6 ♔f8 48 ♗b7 **1–0**

PRODIGY — L'EXCENTRIQUE 1 d4 f5 2 ♗g5 g6 3 e3 h6 4 ♗h4 ♘f6 5 ♘f3 g5 6 ♗g3 e6 7 ♘bd2 ♘e4 8 ♗e5 ♖h7 9 ♘×e4 f×e4 10 ♘d2 ♖f7 11 ♘×e4 ♘c6 12 f3 d5 13 ♘g3 ♗d7 14 ♗h8 ♖h7 15 ♗e5 ♘×e5 16 d×e5 ♕e7 17 ♗d3 ♖h8 18 ♗g6† ♔d8 19 ♕d4 c5 20 ♕c3 ♕g7 21 ♗h5 a5 22 O–O–O b5 23 f4 b4 24 ♕d3 g×f4 25 e×f4 c4 26 ♕d4 a4 27 ♕b6† ♔c8 28 c3 b3 29 a3 ♗e7 30 ♖d2 ♕f8 31 ♕f2 ♗c5 32 ♕f3 ♗c6 33 f5 e×f5 34 ♘×f5 ♔c7 35 ♘d4 ♕×f3 36 g×f3 ♗e8 37 ♗g4 ♔b7 38 ♔d1 h5 39 ♗e6 ♖d8 40 h4 ♖f8 41 ♘f5 ♗c6 42 ♖e1 ♔c7 43 ♖ee2 ♖de8 44 ♘g7 ♖e7 45 ♖g2 d4 46 ♖ge2 ♖×g7 47 ♔c1 d×c3 48 ♖d1 ♗×f3 49 ♗×c4 ♗×e2 50 ♗×b3 **0–1**

BEBE — CUBE 2.1 1 e4 c5 2 ♘f3 ♘f6 3 ♘c3 ♘c6 4 ♗b5 ♘d4 5 ♗a4 ♕a5 6 e5 ♘g8 7 O–O g6 8 ♖b1 ♗g7 9 ♖e1 b5 10 ♘×d4 b×a4 11 ♘db5 ♖b8 12 ♖e4 ♖×b5 13 ♖×a4 ♕b6 14 ♘×b5 ♕×b5 15 c4 ♕b6 16 ♕e2 ♘h6 17 d3 ♗b7 18 ♗×h6 ♗×h6 19 ♖a3 ♗f4 20 ♖b3 ♕c7 21 ♖e1 ♕c6 22 ♕e4 ♕×e4 23 ♖×e4

♗×h2† 24 ♔×h2 ♗c8 25 ♖b5 O-O 26 ♖×c5 **1–0**

CHATURANGA — CHALLENGER 1 e4 e5 2 ♘f3 ♘c6 3 ♗b5 a6 4 ♗a4 ♘f6 5 O-O ♗e7 6 ♘c3 b5 7 ♗b3 d6 8 ♖b1 ♗g4 9 g3 ♘d4 10 ♗d5 ♗×f3 11 ♗c6† ♔f8 12 ♕e1 ♘×c2 13 ♗×a8 ♘×e1 14 ♗b7 ♕d7 15 ♖×e1 ♕h3 16 ♘d5 ♕g2# **0–1**

Round 2

L'EXCENTRIQUE — BELLE 1 e4 e5 2 ♘f3 ♘c6 3 ♗b5 a6 4 ♗a4 ♘f6 5 O-O ♘×e4 6 ♕e2 ♘c5 7 ♗×c6 d×c6 8 d4 ♘e6 9 d×e5 ♘d4 10 ♘×d4 ♕×d4 11 h3 ♗e7 12 c3 ♕b6 13 ♖d1 ♗e6 14 b4 a5 15 ♗e3 ♕a6 16 ♕×a6 ♖×a6 17 ♗c5 a×b4 18 ♗×e7 ♔×e7 19 c×b4 ♖×a2 20 ♖×a2 ♗×a2 21 ♘c3 ♗b3 22 ♖d2 ♖f8 23 g4 f6 24 e×f6† ♖×f6 25 ♖b2 ♗c4 26 ♔g2 ♗d5† 27 ♘×d5† c×d5 28 ♖d2 ♔d6 29 f3 ♖f4 30 ♖b2 ♖c4 31 h4 d4 32 ♖b3 ♔c6 33 b5† ♔b6 34 ♔g3 ♖c5 35 ♖d3 ♖d5 36 h5 ♔×b5 37 ♖b3† ♔a6 38 ♖a3† ♖a5 39 ♖d3 c5 40 f4 ♖a1 41 g5 ♔b5 42 f5 ♖h1 43 f6 g×f6 44 g×f6 ♖g1† 45 ♔f4 ♖g8 46 ♔f5 ♔c4 47 ♖d1 ♖f8 48 ♔e6 ♔c3 49 f7 ♔c2 50 ♖a1 d3 51 ♔e7 ♖×f7† 52 ♔×f7 d2 53 ♔g7 c4 54 ♖a2† ♔d3 55 ♖a8 d1♕ 56 h6 c3 **0–1**

CRAY BLITZ — DUCHESS 1 e4 e5 2 ♘f3 ♘c6 3 ♗c4 ♗c5 4 c3 ♘f6 5 d4 e×d4 6 c×d4 ♗b4† 7 ♗d2 ♗×d2† 8 ♘b×d2 d5 9 e×d5 ♘×d5 10 ♕b3 ♘ce7 11 O-O O-O 12 ♖fe1 c6 13 ♖ac1 a5 14 ♘e4 a4 15 ♕a3 ♘f5 16 h3 ♘b6 17 ♕c5 ♘×c4 18 ♖×c4 ♗e6 19 ♖b4 ♕c7 20 g4 ♘h6 21 ♘d6 ♖fb8 22 ♘c4 ♖a6 23 ♕d6 ♕×d6 24 ♘×d6 b5 25 a3 ♖aa8 26 ♘g5 ♗d5 27 f4 ♖f8 28 f5 ♖fd8 29 ♘b7 ♖e8 30 ♖×e8† ♖×e8 31 ♘d6 ♖e7 32 ♘c8 ♖e1† 33 ♔f2 ♖e8 34 ♘b6 ♗b3 35 ♘f3 ♖e7 36 ♘e5 ♖b7 37 ♘×a4 ♗×a4 38 b3 ♖c7 39 b×a4 f6 40 ♘d3 b×a4 41 ♘f4 **1–0**

CHALLENGER — CHAOS 1 e4 ♘f6 2 e5 ♘d5 3 d4 d6 4 ♘f3 d×e5 5 ♘×e5 g6 6 g3 ♗g7 7 ♗c4 f6 8 ♘f3 ♘c6 9 O-O ♗h3 10 ♖e1 ♗g4 11 ♗b5 O-O 12 ♗×c6 b×c6 13 ♗d2 ♕b8 14 b3 f5 15 c3 f4 16 g×f4 ♘×f4 17 ♗×f4 ♖×f4 18 ♖e3 ♕b5 19 ♘bd2 ♖af8 20 h3 ♗×h3 21 ♘e5 ♗e6 22 c4 ♕b6 23 c5 ♕b5 24 a4 ♕b7 25 ♘df3 ♗×e5 26 ♘×e5 ♗d5 27 ♖a2 ♕b4 28 ♖d3 e6 29 f3 g5 30 ♖h2 a6 31 ♖h5 ♖8f5 32 ♖h3 a5 33 ♖h5 ♔g7 34 ♔h2 h6 35 ♔g1 ♖f8 36 ♖h2 ♔h7 37 ♕b1 ♔g7 38 ♕d1 ♔h7 39 ♕b1 ♔g7 40 ♕d1 **½–½**

NUCHESS — BEBE 1 f4 d5 2 ♘f3 ♘f6 3 e3 e6 4 b3 ♗d6 5 ♗e2 O-O 6 O-O ♘c6 7 ♗b2 a6 8 ♘e5 ♗×e5 9 f×e5 ♘d7 10 ♗a3 ♖e8 11 d4 ♕g5 12 ♕d3 b5 13 ♘d2 b4 14 ♗b2 a5 15 c4 a4 16 ♖ac1 ♗a6 17 e4 a3 18 ♗a1 ♘b6 19 e×d5 e×d5 20 ♖cd1 d×c4 21 ♘×c4 ♘×c4 22 b×c4 ♘a5 23 ♖c1 c6 24 ♕f3 ♖e7 25 ♕e4 ♖ae8 26 ♗d3 ♕h6 27 ♕e1 ♖b7 28 ♖b1 ♗×c4 29 ♗×c4 ♘×c4 30 ♖×b4 ♖×b4 31 ♕×b4 ♘e3 32 ♖f3 ♘g4 33 h3 ♕c1† 34 ♖f1 ♕e3† 35 ♔h1 ♘f2† 36 ♔h2 ♘e4 37 ♖f3 ♕c1 38 ♗c3 ♘g5 39 ♖f5 ♘e6 40 ♕b3 ♖d8 41 ♖f3 ♘g5 42 ♖f2 ♕e3 43 ♖f5 ♘e6 44 ♕b7 ♖f8 45 ♖f3 ♕c1 46 ♗b4 c5 47 d×c5 ♕b2 48 ♖e3 ♘×c5 49 ♕b5 ♘e6 50 ♖×a3 ♖c8 51 ♖c3 ♖a8 52 ♕c6 ♖d8 53 ♗e7 ♖b8 54 ♖c2 ♕b1 55 ♕c8† ♘f8 56 ♕c4 ♘e6 57 ♗d6 ♖d8 58 a4 ♕b6 59 ♗e7 ♖e8 60 ♕c8 ♕b8 61 ♕×b8 ♖×b8 62 a5 ♘d4 63 ♖c4 ♘f5 64 ♗b4 ♘e3 65 ♖c6 h5 66 a6 ♖a8 67 ♗c5 ♘c4 68 a7 ♔h7 **1–0**

OSTRICH — PRODIGY 1 e4 e6 2 d4 d5 3 e5 c5 4 ♘f3 ♘c6 5 ♗b5 c×d4 6 O-O ♗c5 7 ♗×c6† b×c6 8 a3 ♗a6 9 ♖e1 ♕a5 10 ♘bd2 d3 11 c×d3 ♕b6 12 d4 ♗×d4 13 ♘×d4 ♕×d4 14 g3 O-O-O 15 ♕c2 ♗b7 16 ♘f3 ♕g4 17 ♘g5 f6 18 ♘f7 ♘e7 19 ♕c5 ♘f5 20 ♘×h8 ♖×h8 21 e×f6 ♘d4 22 f×g7 ♘f3† 23 ♔h1 ♖d8 24 g8♕ ♖×g8 25 ♖g1 ♘×g1 26 ♔×g1 a6 27 ♗e3 e5 28 ♗d2 ♕d4 29 ♕e7 ♕×b2 30 ♕e6† ♔b8 31 ♕×g8† ♗c8 32 ♖d1 ♕c2 33 ♖a1 ♕×d2 34 ♕×h7 ♕c3 35 ♖b1† ♔a8 36 ♕c7 ♕e1† 37 ♖×e1 ♗f5 38 ♖×e5 d4 39 ♖e8† ♗c8 40 ♖×c8# **1–0**

AWIT — PHILIDOR 1 b3 e5 2 ♗b2 ♘c6 3 e3 ♘f6 4 ♗b5 d6 5 ♘e2 ♗g4 6 O-O ♗e7 7 h3 ♗h5 8 f4 ♗×e2 9 ♕×e2 e4 10 d3 O-O 11 d×e4 ♘×e4 12 ♖e1 ♗f6 13 ♗×f6 ♕×f6 14 ♘a3 ♘c3 15 ♕f3 d5 16 ♗d3 ♘b4 17 g4 ♘b×a2 18 g5 ♕e7 19 ♘b5 ♘×b5 20 ♗×b5 ♘b4 21 ♖ec1 a6 22 c3 a×b5 23 c×b4 c6 24 ♖×a8 ♖×a8 25 ♕f2 ♖e8 26 ♖c3 ♕×b4 27 ♕d2 ♕e4 28 ♖d3 ♕f3 29 ♕g2 ♕×g2† 30 ♔×g2 b4 31 h4 ♖e4 32 ♔f3 f5 33 g×f6 g×f6 34 ♖d2 ♔f7 35 ♖h2 c5 36 ♖d2 ♔e6 37 ♖a2 ♔f5 38 ♖c2 b6 39 ♖c1 d4 40 ♖g1 ♖×e3† 41 ♔f2 ♖h3 **0–1**

SCHACH 2.5 — CHATURANGA 1 e4 e5 2 ♘f3 ♘c6 3 ♗b5 a6 4 ♗×c6 d×c6 5 ♘c3 ♗g4 6 d3 ♗d6 7 h3 ♗×f3 8 ♕×f3 ♘e7 9 ♗e3 ♗b4 10 ♕g3 ♘g6 11 a3 ♗d6 12 ♗g5 f6 **0–1**

CUBE 2.1 — MYCHESS 1 e4 e5 2 ♘f3 ♘f6 3 ♘×e5 d6 4 ♘f3 ♘×e4 5 ♘c3 ♘×c3 6 d×c3 ♗e7 7 ♗f4 O-O 8 ♗c4 ♘c6 9 O-O ♗e6 10 ♗×e6 f×e6 11 ♗c1 d5 12 ♖e1 ♕d7 13 ♕e2 ♖f6 14 ♗g5 ♖g6 15 ♗×e7 ♕×e7 16 ♕b5 ♖b8 17 a4 ♕f6 18 ♔f1 ♖g4 19 ♖e3 ♕g6 20 a5 ♖×g2 21 a6 ♘d8 22 ♕d7 ♖g4 23 ♕×c7 ♘c6 24 a×b7 ♕e8 25 ♖ae1 ♖g6 26 b4 ♖d8 27 b5 ♘b8 28 ♘e5 ♖f6 29 ♖g3 g6 30 ♘g4 ♖f5 31 ♘h6† ♔f8 32 ♘×f5 ♕×b5† 33 ♔g2 ♕d7 34 ♕×d7 ♖×d7 35 ♘d4 ♖×b7 36 ♘×e6† ♔g8 37 ♖e5 ♖b2 38 ♖×d5 a6 39 ♖d8† ♔f7 40 ♘g5† ♔g7 41 c4 h6 42 ♖b3 ♖×b3 43 c×b3 ♘c6 44 ♖d7† ♔f6 45 ♖d6† **1–0**

Round 3

BELLE — NUCHESS 1 e4 e5 2 ♘f3 ♘f6 3 d4 ♘×e4 4 ♗d3 d5 5 ♘×e5 ♗d6 6 O-O O-O 7 c4 ♗×e5 8 d×e5 ♘c6 9 f4 ♘b4 10 c×d5 ♕×d5 11 ♗×e4 ♕×e4 12 ♘c3 ♕g6 13 ♗e3 ♗e6 14 ♕f3 ♘c2 15 ♖ac1 ♘×e3 16 ♕×e3 c6 17 ♖cd1 f6 18 ♖d6 f×e5 19 ♖f3 e4 20 ♘×e4 ♖ae8 21 ♕d4 ♕f5 22 a3 a5 23 ♖g3 ♖f7 24 ♖d8 ♖×d8 25 ♕×d8† ♖f8 26 ♕c7 g6 27 ♕e5 ♗c4 28 ♕×f5 ♖×f5 29 ♖c3 b5 30 g3 ♗d5 31 ♖e3 ♖f7 32 ♔f2 ♔g7 33 ♘c5 ♔f6 34 g4 ♔g7 35 ♔g3 ♔h6 36 ♘e6 b4 37 a4 ♖d7 38 f5 g×f5 39 g×f5 ♗h1 40 f6 ♗d5 41 ♔f4 ♗×e6 42 ♖×e6 ♖d2 43 b3 ♔g6 44 ♖×c6 ♖f2† 45 ♔e4 ♖b2 46 ♖c5 ♔×f6 47 ♖×a5 ♖×b3 48 ♖f5† ♔g6 49 ♖b5 ♖h3 50 ♔d5 ♖×h2 51 ♖×b4 ♖h5† 52 ♔c4 ♖f5 53 ♖b6† ♔f7 54 ♖b5 ♖f4† 55 ♔b3 ♖f3† 56 ♔c2 ♔g6 57 a5 h5 58 a6 ♖a3 59 ♖b6† ♔f5 60 ♔b2 ♖a5 61 ♔c3 h4 62 ♔b4 ♖a1 63 ♖b5† ♔f4 64 ♖a5 ♖b1† 65 ♔c5 **½–½**

CHAOS — CRAY BLITZ 1 d4 ♘f6 2 c4 c5 3 d5 e5 4 ♘c3 ♕a5 5 e3 d6 6 ♗d2 ♕b6 7 ♕c2 ♗e7 8 ♘f3 ♘a6 9 ♘a4 ♕d8 10 ♗d3 O-O 11 O-O h6 12 b3 ♗g4 13 h3 ♗×f3 14 g×f3 ♘b4 15 ♗×b4 c×b4 16 ♕d2 a5 17 ♔h1 ♔h8 18 ♖g1 ♖c8 19 h4 ♘h5 20 ♗f5 ♖c7 21 ♗g4 g6 22 ♗×h5 g×h5 23 e4 ♔h7 24 ♕e1 ♗×h4 25 ♕e3 ♕c8 26 ♖g2 ♗g5 27 ♕b6 ♕h3† 28 ♔g1 ♖g8 29 ♖g3 ♗f4 30 ♖×g8 ♔×g8 31 ♖e1 ♗h2† 32 ♔h1 f6 33 ♕c5 ♗f4† 34 ♔g1 ♖g7# **0–1**

DUCHESS — CHALLENGER 1 e4 e5 2 ♘f3 ♘c6 3 ♗c4 ♘f6 4 ♕e2 ♗c5 5 d3 O-O 6 O-O d6 7 c3 ♗g4 8 ♗g5 ♘a5 9 ♗b5 a6 10 ♗a4 b5 11 ♗c2 h6 12 ♗d2 ♘c6 13 b4 ♗b6 14 a4 ♗e6 15 ♗e3 ♗×e3 16 f×e3 ♘g4 17 ♘bd2 ♘e7 18 ♘h4 ♕d7 19 a×b5 a×b5 20 ♗b3 ♗×b3 21 ♘×b3 c6 22 ♘f5 h5 23 ♘a5 ♘×f5 24 ♖×f5 g6 25 ♖f3 d5 26 e×d5 c×d5 27 h3 ♘h6 28 e4 d×e4 29 ♕×e4 ♕c7 30 c4 ♘f5 31 ♔h2 b×c4 32 d×c4 ♖fe8 33 c5 ♘d4 34 ♖f6 ♕d8 35 ♖af1 ♕c7 36 ♘c4 ♘f5 37 ♖1×f5 g×f5 38 ♖×f5 ♖ad8 39 ♖×h5 f6 40 ♘d6 ♖e7 41 ♕g4† ♖g7 42 ♕e6† ♖f7 43 ♘×f7 ♕×f7 44 ♖h8† ♔×h8 45 ♕×f7 ♖g8 46 c6 f5 47 c7 ♖a8 48 b5 f4 49 b6 ♖g8 50 b7 ♖×g2† 51 ♔×g2 f3† 52 ♔f2 e4 53 c8♕# **1–0**

PHILIDOR — L'EXCENTRIQUE 1 e4 c6 2 d4 d5 3 e5 ♗f5 4 ♘e2 e6 5 ♘g3 ♗g6 6 ♗d3 h5 7 O-O h4 8 ♘e2 ♗×d3 9 ♕×d3 ♘d7 10 ♘d2 ♗e7 11 c3 ♕c7 12 ♘f3 O-O-O 13 ♗f4 b5 14 a4 ♕b7 15 b4 b×a4 16 ♖×a4 f5 17 ♗e3 ♘b6 18 ♖a2 ♘c4 19 ♗f4 ♔d7 20 ♖a4 a6 21 g3 h3 22 ♖a2 ♖h5 23 ♖e1 ♖f8 24 ♗c1 g5 25 ♘d2 ♘×d2 26 ♗×d2 ♖a8 27 ♖ea1 ♕b5 28 ♕×b5 c×b5 29 f4 g4 30 ♖×a6 ♖×a6 31 ♖×a6 ♗d8 32 ♖d6† ♔e7 33 ♗e1 ♗c7 34 ♖a6 ♘h6 35 ♗d2 ♘f7 36 ♖c6 ♔d7 37 ♖a6 ♘d8 38 ♘c1 ♖h7 39 ♘d3 ♔c8 40 ♘c5 ♗b8 41 ♘×e6 ♖h6 42 ♘c7 ♖×a6 43 ♘×a6 ♘e6 44 ♗e3 ♗c7 45 ♔f1 ♔d7 46 ♘×c7 ♘×c7 47 ♔e2 ♘a8 48 ♔d3 ♘b6 49 ♗d2 ♘c4 50 ♗c1 ♔e7 51 ♗d2 ♘×d2 52 ♔×d2 ♔f7 53 ♔e3 ♔e7 54 ♔f2 ♔d7 55 ♔e3 ♔c7 56 ♔d3 ♔d7 57 ♔d2 ♔e7 58 ♔e3 ♔d7 59 ♔d3 ♔e7 60 ♔d2 ♔d7 **1–0**

CUBE 2.1 — OSTRICH 1 e4 d5 2 e×d5 ♘f6 3 c4 c6 4 d4 c×d5 5 ♘c3 e6 6 ♘f3 ♗b4 7 ♕a4† ♘c6 8 ♗g5 O-O 9 c×d5 ♕×d5 10 ♗×f6 ♗×c3† 11 b×c3 ♕e4† 12 ♗e2 g×f6 13 ♕c4 ♕g4 14 h3 ♕f4 15 O-O ♗d7 16 ♖ab1 ♘d8 17 ♕b4 h6 18 ♕e7 ♗c6 19 ♕a3 b6 20 ♖fe1 h5 21 ♖b2 ♘b7 22 g3 ♕f5 23 ♔g2 e5 24 ♕b3 ♘a5 25 ♕b4 ♗e4 26 ♗d1 ♘c6 27 ♕c4 ♘a5 28 ♕b5 ♗c6 29 ♕b4 ♘b7 30 d×e5 f×e5 31 g4 h×g4 32 h×g4 ♕f6 33 ♔g3 a5 34 ♕×b6 ♕f4† 35 ♔h4 ♔g7 36 ♔h3 ♗×f3 37 ♗×f3 ♕×f3† 38 ♔h2 ♖h8† 39 ♔g1 ♕h1# **0–1**

PRODIGY — SCHACH 2.5 1 d4 d5 2 ♗g5 h6 3 ♗h4 ♘f6 4 e3 g5 5 ♗g3 ♘e4 6 c4 ♘×g3 7 f×g3 d×c4 8 ♗×c4 e6 9 ♘c3 c5 10 ♘f3 c×d4 11 e×d4 ♕b6 12 ♕d2 ♕b4 13 ♗b5† ♗d7 14 ♗×d7† ♘×d7 15 ♖c1 ♘b6 16 ♖c2 ♘c4 17 ♕c1 g4 18 ♘e5 ♗g7 19 ♘×g4 ♗×d4 20 ♖f1 ♘×b2 21 ♕d2 ♖d8 22 ♖×b2 ♗×c3 23 ♘f6† ♔e7 24 ♖×b4 ♗×d2† 25 ♔e2 ♗×b4 26 ♔e3 ♖d2 27 a3 ♗a5 28 ♘g4 ♖×g2 29 ♖b1 ♗b6† 30 ♔f3 ♖a2 31 ♖e1 ♖×a3† 32 ♔g2 h5 33 ♘f2 ♖a2 34 ♖f1 ♖h6 35 h3 a5 36 h4 ♖×f2† 37 ♖×f2 ♗×f2 38 ♔×f2 a4 39 ♔f3 a3 **0–1**

MYCHESS — AWIT 1 e4 c5 2 ♘f3 d6 3 d4 c×d4 4 ♘×d4 ♘f6 5 ♘c3 a6 6 ♗e2 e6 7 O-O ♗e7 8 ♗g5 ♗d7 9 ♘b3 ♗c6 10 ♗f3 O-O 11 a4 ♘bd7 12 ♘d4 ♕b6 13 ♘×c6 ♕×c6 14 e5 d5 15 e×f6 ♘×f6 16 ♖e1 ♕c5 17 ♕d2 ♖ac8 18 ♕d3 ♖fd8 19 ♕e2 ♕b4 20 ♖ab1 d4 21 ♗×f6 ♗×f6 22 ♘e4 ♗h4 23 b3 ♗e7 24 ♖bd1 g6 25 ♕d2 ♕×d2 26 ♘×d2 ♖×c2 27 ♗×b7 ♗b4 28 ♘f3 ♗×e1 29 ♖×e1 a5 30 ♔f1 ♖b2 31 ♖e5 ♖×b3 32 ♗e4 ♖a3 33 ♖×a5 ♖a2 34 ♘e5 ♖a1† 35 ♔e2 ♖a2† 36 ♔e1 ♔g7 37 ♖a7 ♖f8 38 ♘c6 ♖c8 39 ♗f3 ♔f6 40 a5 h5 41 ♖d7 ♖a1† 42 ♔d2 e5 43 ♖d6† ♔g7 44 ♖d7 ♔f6 45 ♗d5 ♔g5 46 ♖×f7 ♖g8 47 ♖e7 ♖a8 48 ♖×e5† ♔f6 49 f3 ♖8×a5 50 ♖e6† ♔g7 51 ♘×a5 ♖×a5 52 ♖d6 **1–0**

CHATURANGA — BEBE 1 e4 c5 2 ♘f3 d6 3 ♗d3 ♘f6 4 e5 d×e5 5 ♘×e5 ♕d5 6 ♘f3 ♗f5 7 ♘c3 ♕e6† 8 ♗e2 ♘c6 9 d3 ♘d4 10 ♘×d4 c×d4 11 ♘b5 ♕b6 12 c4 d×c3 13 ♘×c3 O-O-O 14 ♗e3 ♕×b2 15 ♘d5 ♘×d5 16 ♗d2 ♘c7 17 g4 ♗×d3 18 ♗×d3 ♖×d3 19 ♔e2 ♕d4 20 f4 ♕e4† 21 ♔f2 ♕d4† 22 ♔e2 ♕e4† 23 ♔f2 ♕d5 24 ♗e3 ♖×d1 25 ♖h×d1 ♕c4 26 ♗d4 e6 27 ♗e3 ♗c5 28 ♔f3 ♕c3 29 ♖e1 ♗×e3 30 ♔e4 ♗d2 31 ♖e2 ♘e8 32 ♖×d2 ♘f6# **0–1**

Round 4

CRAY BLITZ — BELLE 1 e4 e5 2 ♘f3 ♘c6 3 ♗c4 ♘f6 4 ♘g5 d5 5 e×d5 ♘a5 6 ♗b5† c6 7 d×c6 b×c6 8 ♕f3 ♖b8 9 ♗×c6† ♘×c6 10 ♕×c6† ♘d7 11 d3 ♗e7 12 ♘e4 ♗b7 13 ♕a4 ♕c7 14 ♘bc3 ♗c6 15 ♕c4 ♕c8 16 ♘d5 ♗×d5 17 ♕×d5 ♕×c2 18 O-O f6 19 f4 ♘b6 20 ♕a5 ♕×d3 21 ♕×a7 O-O 22 ♕×e7 ♕×e4 23 ♕e6† ♔h8 24 f×e5 f×e5 25 ♖×f8† ♖×f8 26 h3 ♕e1† 27 ♔h2 h6 28 ♕×b6 ♖f1 29 ♕d8† ♔h7 30 ♕d3† e4 31 ♕×f1 ♕×f1 32 a3 e3 33 ♗×e3 ♕×a1 34 ♗d4 h5 35 ♗c3 g5 36 ♗e5 ♕e1 37 ♗c3 ♕f2 38 ♔h1 g4 39 h×g4 h×g4 40 ♔h2 ♕h4† 41 ♔g1 g3 42 ♔f1 ♔g6 **0–1**

NUCHESS — DUCHESS 1 f4 ♘f6 2 e3 g6 3 b3 ♗g7 4 ♗b2 O-O 5 ♘f3 c5 6 ♗e2 b6 7 O-O ♗b7 8 ♕e1 e6 9 ♘c3 d5 10 ♕h4 ♘e4 11 ♘g5 h6 12 ♘f3 ♕×h4 13 ♘×h4 ♘×d2 14 ♖fd1 ♘e4 15 ♘a4 ♗×b2 16 ♘×b2 ♘c3 17 ♖e1 ♘×e2† 18 ♖×e2 d4 19 e×d4 g5 20 f×g5 h×g5 21 ♘f3 g4 22 ♘e5 c×d4 23 ♘×g4 ♔g7 24 ♖ae1 ♘c6 25 ♘d3 ♖h8 26 ♖f1 f5 27 ♘gf2 ♖ae8 28 g4 ♘d8 29 g×f5 e×f5 30 ♖×e8 ♖×e8 31 ♘h1 ♖e2 32 ♖f2 ♖×f2 33 ♘h×f2 ♘e6 34 ♔f1 ♔f6 35 ♘h3 ♗f3 36 ♔e1 ♗g2 37 ♘hf4 ♘×f4 38 ♘×f4 ♗f3 39 ♔d2 ♔e5 40 ♘d3† ♔e4 41 ♘f2† ♔d5 42 ♘d3 b5 43 h4 ♔e4 44 ♘c5† ♔f4 45 a4 b×a4 46 ♘×a4 ♔e5 47 ♘c5 f4 48 ♘d3† ♔f5 49 ♘b4 a5 50 ♘d3 ♗h5 51 ♔e1 ♗e8 52 ♘c5 ♗g6 53 ♘d3 ♗h5 54 ♘c5 ♗f7 55 ♔d2 ♗d5 56 ♘d3 ♗g8 57 ♘e1 ♔g4 58 ♔d3 f3 59 ♘×f3 ♔×f3 60 ♔×d4 ♔e2 61 ♔c5 ♔d2 62 ♔b5 ♔×c2 63 ♔×a5 ♔×b3 **½–½**

OSTRICH — BEBE 1 e4 c5 2 ♘f3 d6 3 d4 c×d4 4 ♘×d4 ♘f6 5 ♘c3 g6 6 ♗e2 ♗g7 7 O-O O-O 8 ♗e3 ♗d7 9 a4 ♘c6 10 ♘b3 ♘b4 11 f4 ♕c7 12 a5 ♘×e4 13 ♘×e4 ♕×c2 14 ♗f3 ♗×b2 15 ♖b1 ♕×d1 16 ♗×d1 ♗g7 17 ♗f3 ♗b5 18 ♖f2 ♗c6 19 ♘g5 ♗×f3 20 ♘×f3 ♘d5 21 ♗d2 ♖ac8 22 ♘c1 ♖c7 23 ♘d3 ♖fc8 24

♖b3 e6 25 ♗b4 ♖d7 26 ♗d2 ♖c2 27 ♘fe1 ♖a2 28 ♘c1 ♖a4 29 ♘e2 ♖a2 30 ♘c1 ♖a4 31 ♘e2 ♖e7 32 ♘c2 ♖a2 33 ♘ed4 ♖c7 34 g4 e5 35 f×e5 d×e5 36 ♘b4 ♘×b4 37 ♘b5 ♖cc2 38 ♖×b4 ♗f8 39 ♘a3 ♖×a3 40 ♖×b7 ♗c5 41 ♗e1 ♗×f2† 42 ♗×f2 ♖a1† **0–1**

CHALLENGER — PHILIDOR 1 e4 c5 2 c3 d5 3 e×d5 ♕×d5 4 d4 e6 5 ♘f3 ♘f6 6 ♗e3 ♘e4 7 c4 ♕d8 8 ♗d3 f5 9 ♗×e4 f×e4 10 ♘e5 c×d4 11 ♗×d4 ♕g5 12 O–O ♘d7 13 ♘×d7 ♗×d7 14 ♕e2 ♗c6 15 ♘c3 e5 16 ♗e3 ♕f5 17 ♖ad1 ♗e7 18 ♕d2 O–O 19 ♘d5 ♗d8 20 ♗c5 ♖f7 21 ♘e3 ♕g5 22 ♔h1 ♗b6 23 ♗×b6 a×b6 24 b3 ♖af8 25 ♔g1 b5 26 c5 ♖f3 27 h4 ♕×h4 28 g×f3 e×f3 29 ♕d6 ♕g5† 30 ♔h1 ♕h4† 31 ♔g1 ♕g5† 32 ♔h2 ♕h4† 33 ♔g1 ½–½

L'EXCENTRIQUE — CHAOS 1 e4 c5 2 ♘f3 ♘c6 3 d4 c×d4 4 ♘×d4 ♘f6 5 ♘c3 e6 6 ♘db5 ♗b4 7 a3 ♗×c3† 8 ♘×c3 d5 9 e×d5 e×d5 10 ♗d3 O–O 11 O–O h6 12 ♗f4 d4 13 ♘b5 ♘d5 14 ♗g3 ♗e6 15 ♖e1 ♕d7 16 h3 ♖ad8 17 ♕f3 ♘de7 18 a4 ♗f5 19 ♗d6 ♗×d3 20 c×d3 a6 21 ♗×e7 ♘×e7 22 ♘a3 ♖fe8 23 ♘c4 ♘d5 24 b3 ♖c8 25 ♖×e8† ♖×e8 26 a5 ♘c3 27 ♔f1 ♕e7 28 ♕g4 ♕e2† 29 ♕×e2 ♖×e2 30 ♘d6 ♖e7 31 ♘f5 ♖e2 32 ♘×d4 ♖d2 33 ♘f5 ♖×d3 34 f3 ♘d5 35 ♖a3 ♖c3 36 ♔f2 f6 37 g4 ♘f4 38 h4 ♘d3† 39 ♔g3 ♘e5 40 ♘d4 ♔f7 41 ♖a2 ♖d3 42 ♖a4 ♖d2 43 ♖b4 ♔g8 44 ♘f5 ♖d7 45 ♖b6 ♘c6 46 b4 g6 47 ♘×h6† ♔g7 48 g5 f5 49 f4 ♖d3† 50 ♔f2 ♖d2† 51 ♔e1 ♖d7 52 b5 a×b5 53 a6 b×a6 54 ♖×c6 ♖a7 **1–0**

SCHACH 2.5 — CUBE 2.1 1 e4 c5 2 ♘f3 ♘f6 3 e5 ♘d5 4 ♘c3 ♘c7 5 ♗d3 d6 6 e×d6 ♕×d6 7 ♘e4 ♕d5 8 O–O ♗g4 9 h3 ♗×f3 10 ♕×f3 ♘d7 11 c4 ♕d4 12 ♕e3 ♕×e3 13 d×e3 e6 14 ♗e2 f5 15 ♘g3 ♗e7 16 ♗d2 ♗f6 17 ♖ad1 O–O–O 18 ♖b1 ♘b8 19 ♖fd1 g6 20 b3 ♘c6 21 ♖bc1 ♖he8 22 ♗c3 ♖×d1† 23 ♗×d1 ♗×c3 24 ♖×c3 ♖d8 25 ♗e2 h5 26 a4 h4 27 ♘f1 e5 28 f3 ♘e6 29 ♔f2 f4 30 ♘h2 f×e3† 31 ♔×e3 ♘f4 32 ♗f1 ♖d1 33 ♔e4 ♖e1† 34 ♖e3 ♖c1 35 ♗d3 ♘×g2 36 ♖e2 ♘f4 37 ♖e3 ♖d1 38 ♘g4 ♘×h3 39 f4 ♘×f4 40 ♘×e5 ♘×e5 41 ♗c2 ♘×c4 42 ♗×d1 ♘×e3 43 ♔×e3 ♘d5† 44 ♔d3 ♘f6 45 ♔c4 b6 46 a5 b×a5 47 ♔×c5 h3 48 ♔b5 h2 49 ♗f3 ♘h5 50 ♔×a5 ♘g3 51 ♔b5 h1♕ 52 ♗×h1 ♘×h1 53 ♔c5 ♘f2 54 ♔d4 g5 55 ♔e5 ♔d7 56 ♔f5 a5 57 ♔×g5 ♘e4† 58 ♔f5 ♘c5 59 ♔e5 ♘×b3 60 ♔d5 a4 61 ♔c4 ♔d6 62 ♔b4 ♘c5 63 ♔a3 ♔c6 64 ♔b4 ♔d5 65 ♔a3 ♔c4 66 ♔b2 ♘d3† 67 ♔a3 ♔b5 68 ♔a2 ♔b4 69 ♔b1 ♔b3 70 ♔a1 a3 71 ♔b1 a2† 72 ♔a1 ♘b2 ½–½

AWIT — PRODIGY 1 b3 d5 2 ♗b2 ♗g4 3 ♘f3 c5 4 e3 e6 5 h3 ♗×f3 6 ♕×f3 ♘c6 7 ♘a3 e5 8 ♗b5 e4 9 ♕f5 ♘ge7 10 ♕g4 h5 11 ♕g5 f6 12 ♕f4 ♘g6 13 ♕g3 ♘ge5 14 ♗×e5 f×e5 15 ♕×e5† ♔f7 16 ♕f5† ♔g8 17 ♗×c6 b×c6 18 ♕e6† ♔h7 19 ♕×c6 ♖c8 20 ♕a6 ♕d7 21 c4 ♖c6 22 ♕a4 d4 23 O–O d×e3 24 d×e3 ♗d6 25 ♖ad1 h4 26 ♖d5 ♔h6 27 ♘b5 ♖b8 28 ♘×d6 ♕c7 29 ♘×e4 ♖b7 30 ♖fd1 ♖bb6 31 ♕a5 ♕f7 32 ♘×c5 ♖g6 33 ♘a4 ♕f3 34 g4 h×g3 35 ♖h5† ♕×h5 36 ♕×h5† ♔×h5 37 ♘×b6 g×f2† 38 ♔×f2 a×b6 39 ♖d4 ♖f6† 40 ♔g3 ♖c6 41 ♔f3 ♖h6 42 a4 ♔g5 43 h4† ♔h5 44 ♖e4 ♖f6† 45 ♔g3 ♖g6† 46 ♔h3 ♖d6 47 c5 b×c5 48 ♖e5† ♔h6 49 ♖×c5 ♖d3 50 ♖b5 ♖×e3† 51 ♔g4 ♖e4† 52 ♔g3 ♖e3† 53 ♔f4 ♖d3 54 b4 ♖d4† 55 ♔g3 ♖d3† 56 ♔g4 ♖d4† 57 ♔h3 ♖d3† 58 ♔h2 **1–0**

MYCHESS — CHATURANGA 1 e4 e5 2 ♘f3 ♘c6 3 ♗b5 a6 4 ♗a4 d6 5 c3 ♘f6 6 ♗×c6† b×c6 7 d4 e×d4 8 ♕×d4 c5 9 ♕d3 ♗e6 10 c4 ♗e7 11 ♘c3 ♕b8 12 O–O ♘g4 13 ♘d5 ♘e5 14 ♘×e5 d×e5 15 ♘×e7 ♔×e7 16 ♕c3 c6 17 ♗e3 ♕d6 18 ♖ad1 ♕c7 19 ♗×c5† ♔f6 20 ♗d6 ♕b6 21 ♗×e5† ♔e7 22 ♗×g7 ♖hc8 23 c5 ♕b5 24 ♕f6† ♔e8 25 ♕e5 ♕c4 26 ♕d6 ♕×f1† 27 ♔×f1 ♗c4† 28 ♔g1 ♗d5 29 e×d5 f5 30 ♕e6† ♔d8 31 d×c6† ♔c7 32 ♗e5# **1–0**

A GLOSSARY OF COMPUTER CHESS TERMINOLOGY

ACCUMULATOR - A register in the CPU of a computer, used for temporary storage of data, usually the results of the CPU's operations.

ADDRESS - A location in the computer's memory, defined by a binary number one word in length.

ALGORITHM - A method or procedure for solving a specific task. The same algorithm can be expressed or coded in many different detailed ways; the overall structure and effect of the method define the algorithm, rather than the details of its implementation.

ALPHA - A quantity used by a computer program to speed up the search of a game tree; the minimum value that the side to move can achieve, according to the variations already examined.

ALPHA-BETA ALGORITHM - The method of searching a game tree using two quantities, alpha and beta, as test values when examining a new branch of the tree. If efficiently executed, this method saves a tremendous amount of time, and allows the program to search several plies deeper than it could otherwise.

ARRAY - A group, or string, of things; here used to describe things stored in the memory of a computer, and the addresses at which they are located.

ARTIFICIAL INTELLIGENCE - The branch of computer science which attempts to enable computers to imitate intelligent human behavior.

ASCII - The American Standard Code for Information Interchange; a code for representing letters of the alphabet and other characters as binary numbers.

ASPIRATIVE SEARCH - A refinement to the alpha-beta algorithm. Assumptions are made about the values of alpha and beta, based on experience, to reduce the range or "window" of values and speed up the search.

ASSEMBLER - A program which translates a list of instructions written in human-readable mnemonics (assembly language) into binary machine language readable by a computer.

ATTACK - The ability of a piece to move to a given square; a piece which can do so is said to attack that square.

BACKED-UP - In searching a game tree, the scores of terminal positions are backed-up to represent the outcome of a given branch in the tree, when the program determines that the position represents the best play for both sides. The scores of other terminal positions are discarded.

BENCHMARK - A test by which the relative performance of a program may be measured.

BETA - The converse of alpha; the maximum value that the opponent of the side to move has to concede, according to the variations already examined.

BINARY NUMBER - A number to the base of two.

BIT - A digit of a binary number; 1 or 0.

BIT BOARD - An array of 64 bits, used to represent one characteristic of the position on the chessboard, such as all the squares attacked by a given piece, the squares on which White Knights are placed, etc.

BRUTE FORCE - Without any attempt at being clever or elegant; in computer chess, relying mainly on the speed and power of a large computer.

BUG - A problem in a computer program. In the early days of computers, when the machines were made up of vacuum tubes, they generated immense amounts of heat, and in the summer the operators would leave the windows of the computer rooms open (this being beyond the capacity of the air-conditioning of the times to handle). Insects attracted by the bright lights would fly in, and sometimes get into the wiring of the machines, where in the process of being electrocuted they would create a momentary unintended connection that would disturb the operation of the computer.

BYTE - An array of eight bits or binary digits; a binary number with eight digits.

CAPTURE SEARCH - An extension to the normal search process of the program, which examines only capture moves for each side.

CHESS PROCESSOR - A computer, or a section of a computer, specifically designed to run a chess program.

CODE - The statements of a program.

COMPILER - A program which translates the statements of a high- level language into binary machine language or an intermediate form.

COMPUTER - An electronic device constructed for the purpose of automatically carrying out computations.

CPU - The Central Processing Unit, the part of a computer in which the computations actually occur.

CRASH - A disaster to a computer program. The program becomes inoperative, perhaps because the computer has been turned off or has failed.

CUTOFF - The elimination of a branch of the game tree from further consideration, by the action of the alpha-beta algorithm.

DATA BASE - The sum of the data which defines the current position, and the relevant status of such things as the ability to Castle, previously repeated positions, etc. in a chess program.

DEBUGGING - The art of getting a computer program to work. Few do, when first written.

DIGITAL - Discretely-valued data; as opposed to analogue data, which varies smoothly and continuously rather than in discrete steps.

EVALUATOR FUNCTION - The part of a computer chess program which decides how favorable a position is for the program.

EXCHANGE RESOLVER - An algorithm for calculating the effects of a sequence of forced exchanges, without actually generating and searching a branch of the game tree.

FANOUT - The number of "plausible" moves generated at a given level in the game tree of a selective-search program.

FORWARD SEARCH - The process of looking at the possible moves for each side, to determine which move is the best in the initial position which is being searched.

FULL WIDTH SEARCH - A forward search in which all possible moves are considered.

FUNCTION - A part of a program which is repeatedly used by the main program.

GAME TREE - The array of possible positions which could result from all of the possible moves considered by the program in its forward search.

HARDWARE - The computer and any associated processor.

HEURISTIC - A rule of thumb or strategy used to improve the efficiency of a problem-solving algorithm. In a chess program, heuristics are the factors by which the program evaluates the merits of its decisions.

HEXADECIMAL - A number to the base 16. There are 16 values which each hexadecimal digit can have: 0, 1, 2, 3, 4, 5, 6, 7, 8, 9, A, B, C, D, E, F — the letters represent 10, 11, 12, 13, 14, 15 decimal.

HIGH-LEVEL LANGUAGE - A language that is more powerful and compact than assembler, usually at the cost of efficiency.

HORIZON EFFECT - A problem encountered in chess programs, in which the program makes incorrect and often ridiculous decisions because it is unable to consider anything which will happen even one ply beyond the depth of its forward search.

INSTRUCTION SET - The group of basic operations which a computer is capable of performing.

INTERFACE - The method of interconnection between two electronic devices.

ITERATIVE SEARCH - A search technique whereby the program searches to a depth of N ply, then uses the result to reorder its possible first moves in order of apparent merit, then searches to a depth of N + 1 ply, etc.

KEYBOARD - The peripheral attachment to a computer, on which a human can type instructions or data.

KILLER MOVE - A move particularly successful in causing alpha-beta cutoffs.

LOGICAL OPERATION - A type of basic operation in which binary digits have the values TRUE and FALSE. The logical operations are AND, OR, and NOT.

LOOKAHEAD - The operation of conducting a forward search.

MACHINE TIME - The use of a computer for a period of time; often expensive and hard to come by.

MAINFRAME - A large general-purpose computer, usually filling a good-sized room and costing millions of dollars.

MEMORY - The part of a computer in which information is stored.

MHZ - Megahertz; one million cycles per second.

MICROCOMPUTER - A computer whose CPU is a microprocessor.

MICROPROCESSOR - The CPU for a computer, packaged in a single integrated circuit or "chip". May contain some other parts of the computer as well.

MINICOMPUTER - A small general-purpose computer, larger than a microcomputer but smaller than a mainframe. Minicomputers range in size from a machine which can sit atop a desk, to one which would fill a small room.

MINIMAX ALGORITHM - The basic process used in conducting the search of a game tree. The minimax algorithm assumes that at each move, the player to move will make the decision which ultimately leads to the most favorable (or least unfavorable) position for that player.

MNEMONIC - A code used to represent a computer operation in a form more easily remembered by a human.

MOBILITY - A measure of the number of squares that each side can move to in a given position.

MODULE - A segment of a program.

MOVE GENERATOR - The module or subroutine which generates the moves to be considered by the program in each position searched in the game tree.

OPENING BOOK - A list of positions or moves used to enable the program to play the opening without having to calculate its moves.

OVERFLOW - A condition in which the capacity of a register is exceeded.

PATTERN RECOGNITION - The process of automatically classifying and recognizing patterns.

PLAUSIBLE MOVE - A move which a selective-search program considers worthy of examination.

PLY - A move by one side in a chess game. 1 e4 e5 is one move, but two plies.

POSITION SCORING - The process of assigning relative values to positions encountered during the forward search.

PRINTER - A peripheral attachment which the computer uses to print out data in a permanent form.

PROGRAM - A sequence of instructions to be automatically executed by a computer.

PRUNING - The process of eliminating moves and the branches in the game tree which descend from them, in conducting the forward search.

PSEUDOCODE - A statement of an algorithm in a form which resembles a computer program, and can be easily translated into one, but which does not conform to the syntax of any particular language.

QUIESCENCE - An attribute of a position which defines the position as "quiet" - no captures are possible, and neither King is in check.

RATING - The relative ranking of a chess player according to playing strength.

REFUTATION - A move which shows that the preceding move being examined would be bad.

REGISTER - A part of the CPU of a computer, into which data or instructions are loaded so that operations may be performed.

ROUTINE - A segment of a program.

SCRATCHPAD - A part of memory repetitively used to store the results of computations on a temporary basis.

SEARCH - The process of determining which is the best move for a chess program to make.

SEARCH DEPTH - The number of plies to which a program searches during its lookahead.

SELECTIVE SEARCH - A forward search in which only a limited number of moves at each turn are examined.

SENSORY BOARD - An attachment for a chessplaying computer, by which the moves can be sensed as they are made on a special board, and do not have to be typed in on a keyboard.

STACK - An area of memory used to store the results of calculations.

STATIC EVALUATOR - An evaluation function which assigns scores to positions, without considering whether they are "quiescent".

SUBROUTINE - A segment of a program, which can be repetitively executed.

TERMINAL POSITION - A position in the last or deepest ply of a program's forward search.

TRANSPOSITION TABLE - A table containing descriptions of chess positions and the position scores assigned to them. Used to speed up the forward search, since the same positions occur over and over in the search due to different move sequences.

WINDOW - The difference between alpha and beta. In aspirative searching, the window is set by the program, which assumes that the position score in the "best" position will not be very much different from that of the position being searched from. This speeds up the search by allowing most positions to be eliminated from consideration quickly, on the basis of material alone.

WORD - The length of the binary numbers which a computer uses. Varies from 8 to 64 bits.

BIBLIOGRAPHY

Although obviously all the references listed are worth reading, those which are especially recommended to the interested reader are indicated by an asterisk (*).

(1) Wiener, N. 1948. **Cybernetics.** New York : Wiley.

(2) Von Neumann, Jr., and O. Morgenstern 1944. **Theory of Games and Economic Behavior.** Princeton : Princeton.

(3) Shannon, C. 1950. Programming a digital computer for playing chess. **Phil. Mag**. 41 : 356.

(4) Bowden, B. V. 1953. **Faster Than Thought - A Symposium On Digital Computing Machines.** London : Pitman.

(5) Bell, A. 1978. **The Machine Plays Chess?** Oxford : Pergamon.

(6) Kister et al. 1957. Experiments in chess. **JACM 4** : 174.

(7) Bernstein et al. 1958. A chess playing program for the IBM 704. **Proc. Western Jt. Comp. Conf.** 13 : 157.

(8) Newell et al. 1958. Chess-playing programs and the problem of complexity. **IBM J. Res. Develop.** 2 : 320.

(9) Feigenbaum, E. and J. Feldman 1963. **Computers and Thought.** New York : McGraw-Hill.

(10) Edwards, D. J. and T. P. Hart 1963. The alpha-beta heuristic. **Art. Int. Memo No. 30 (Rev.).** Cambridge : MIT Res. Lab. of Elect. and Comp. Ctr.

(11) Nilsson, N. 1971. **Problem-Solving Methods in Artificial Intelligence.** New York : McGraw-Hill.

*(12) Newborn, M. 1975. **Computer Chess.** New York : Academic.

(13) Kotok, A. 1962. **A Chess Playing Proqram for IBM 7090.** B. Sc. Thesis. Cambridge : MIT.

*(14) Botvinnik, M. 1970. **Computers, Chess and Long-Range Planning**. Berlin : Springer-Verlag.

(15) 1967. **Chess Life Magazine** 12 (2) : 28.

(16) Greenblatt et al. 1967. The Greenblatt chess program. **Proc. Fall Jt. Comp. Conf.** 801.

(17) **ACM SIGART Newsletters.** No. 6(1967) : 8; No. 9(1967) : 9; No. 15(1969) : 8; No. 16(1969) : 9; No. 39(1973) : 23.

*(18) Martin, G. R. R. 1972. The computer was a fish. **Analog Magazine,** August : 61.

(19) **New York Times** September 2, 1970 : 39.

(20) Zobrist, A. and F. Carlson 1973. An advice-taking computer. **Scientific American,** June : 93.

*(21) Frey, P. 1977. **Chess Skill in Man and Machine.** Berlin : Springer-Verlag.

*(22) Clarke, M. R. B. 1982. **Advances in Computer Chess 3.** Oxford : Pergamon.

*(23) Levy, D. 1976. **Chess and Computers.** Woodland Hills : Computer Science.

(24) Levy, D. 1976. **1975 U.S. Computer Chess Championship.** Woodland Hills : Computer Science.

(25) Levy, D. 1977. **1976 U.S. Computer Chess Championship.** Woodland Hills : Computer Science.

*(26) Levy, D. and M. Newborn 1980. **More Chess and Computers.** Woodland Hills : Computer Science.

(27) Elo, A. 1978. **The Rating of Chessplayers Past and Present.** New York : Arco.

(28) Spracklen, D. and K. 1978. **SARGON - A Computer Chess Program.** Rochelle Park : Hayden.

(29) ELIZA. Artificial Intelligence Research Group, 921 N. La Jolla Ave., Los Angeles CA 90046 (available for several types of personal computers).

*(30) Kaplan, J. 1980. **How to Get the Most from Your Chess Computer.** Great Neck : RHM.

INDEX OF ANNOTATED GAMES

INDEX OF OPENINGS

INDEXED BY RABAR CLASSIFICATION NUMBER:

INDEXED BY NAME:

GENERAL INDEX